THE VATICAN AND THE
AMERICAN HIERARCHY
FROM 1870 TO 1965

THE VATICAN AND THE AMERICAN HIERARCHY FROM 1870 TO 1965

BY

GERALD P. FOGARTY, S.J.

A Michael Glazier Book
THE LITURGICAL PRESS
Collegeville, Minnesota

A Michael Glazier Book
published by
THE LITURGICAL PRESS

Library of Congress Cataloging-in-Publication Data

Fogarty, Gerald P.
    The Vatican and the American hierarchy from 1870 to 1965 / by
Gerald P. Fogarty.
    Reprint. Originally published: Stuttgart : Hiersemann, 1982.
    Includes bibliographical references.
    ISBN 0-8146-5533-5
    1. Catholic Church—United States—History. 2. Catholic Church—
United States—Bishops—History. 3. United States—Church history.
4. Catholic Church—Relations (diplomatic)—United States.
5. United States—Foreign relations—Catholic Church. I. Title
BX1407.B57F64   1990
282'.73—dc20   90-24730
                                                                CIP

FRATRIBUS MEIS
SOCIETATIS JESU

TABLE OF CONTENTS

FOREWORD

Congress will probably never send a minister to his Holiness, who can do them no service, upon condition of receiving a Catholic legate or nuncio in return; or, in other words, an ecclesiastical tyrant, which, it is to be hoped, the United States will be too wise ever to admit into their territories[1].

It was in a letter of August 4, 1779, to the President of the Continental Congress that John Adams thus expressed a commonly held American sentiment on relations with the Holy See a decade before the formal launching of the new Republic with George Washington as its first president. In spite of that rather grim warning, however, four months after Adams himself took office in March, 1797, as Washington's successor, John B. Sartori, a native of Rome, was commissioned as the first consul to represent the United States in the papal dominions. True, that did not constitute diplomatic relations with the Papal States, but it did indicate that the new nation was prepared to further its trading interests unimpeded by religious prejudice, and that at a time when its relations with much of western Europe were gravely threatened by revolutionary France.

If this is a far cry from the substance of Father Fogarty's thoroughly documented and detailed account of American-Vatican relations from 1870 to 1965, it affords a distant glimpse of the obstacles encountered in one of the central themes of this book, namely, the repeated efforts – and failures to 1984 – of the Holy See to win diplomatic recognition from the United States. Never before has any work set forth those efforts in such detail and with such solid documentary evidence. The reader who scans the list of archival depositories consulted by the author cannot but be impressed by the widespread coverage both in this country and in European archival centers. The Fogarty volume, incidentally, represents one of the first scholarly works to profit from the opening of the Vatican Archives for the reign of Pope Leo XIII (1878–1903), which was owed to Pope John Paul II's action in December, 1978.

At a time when the Catholic Church as an institution is no longer in fashion with many of her own members, the clear delineation in the author's preface of what kind of history he is writing – and what he is not writing – should be noted, lest certain readers feel disappointment on the score that this narrative does not embody a 'people's history'. It is not intended to do so, and it would be a mistake to anticipate such. History that encompasses the lower clergy, the laity and lay movements, minority groups, and popular social phenomena within the ecclesias-

---

[1] Charles Francis ADAMS (Ed.): *The Works of John Adams*, Boston 1852, VII, 109–110.

tical framework – all have their proper place in the American Catholic story, but they do not constitute the whole of that story. Similarly, bishops are not held in the awe and respect that was once true in the Catholic community. In that they share the fate that has befallen all who exercise authority in other walks of life, for ours is an age that prides itself on its individualism and on the right of every man and woman to make up his and her own mind on religious issues as well as on issues that touch the commonweal and public life. Yet to attempt to relate the significant events of the American Catholic bishops' relations with the Holy See, as well as with their own government, in terms of current historiographical concepts would be to violate one of history's unchanging principles, namely, that the past should be interpreted in terms of the time period being treated, not in terms that happen to enjoy current popularity. In a word, the relations of the American hierarchy to the Roman Curia form an important aspect of the Catholic history of the United States, and that is precisely what Father Fogarty has undertaken and achieved in a way to satisfy the most exacting canons of the historian's profession.

If the Master's reply to the question of the Pharisees and Herodians about paying taxes to Caesar, took the latter by surprise and caused them to depart more perplexed than when they came, the point at issue has not ceased to puzzle the authorities of Church and State to our own time. "Give back to Caesar what belongs to Caesar – and to God what belongs to God" (*Matthew*, 22:22) left ample room for maneuver and disagreement. The intervening centuries have written many a stormy chapter over the interpretation of the Church's role in the State's affairs and vice versa, and the United States has been no exception in that regard. In the working out of the problems between the two principals tempers have at times flared and led, in turn, to statements and actions which their authors may well have regretted in moments of calm and reflection. That this book should describe incidents of this kind will come as no surprise to sophisticated readers, for they will have accepted the fact of human frailty in churchmen as well as statesmen. Lacordaire once put the point in a forceful way when he wrote the Oratorian historian, l'abbé Henri Perreyve of the Sorbonne:

Ought history to hide the faults of men ...? It was not in this sense that Baronius understood his duty as an historian of the Church. It was not after this fashion that the Saints laid open the scandals of their times. Truth, when discreetly told, is an inestimable boon to mankind, and to suppress it, especially in history, is an act of cowardice unworthy of a Christian. ... God indeed has conferred upon His Church the prerogative of infallibility, but to none of her members has He granted immunity from sin. Peter was a sinner and a renegade, and God has been at pains to have the fact recorded in the Gospels[2].

---

[2] Lacordaire to Perreyve, April 2, 1855, Paul FOISSET: *Vie du R. P. Lacordaire*. Paris 1870, II, 532.

Here, then, the reader of the University of Virginia historian will find an authentic account of the many and varied problems that arose between Vatican Council I and the close of the last ecumenical council in 1965. That century witnessed the startling growth of the Catholic community — largely an immigrant community — in this country, a community whose very character as a poor, often illiterate, and multi-lingual and multi-ethnic religious body created grave problems of accommodation and adjustment to their new environment. Some features of that society have ceased to concern the bishops, for example, secret societies and the legitimacy of labor unions which worried episcopal gatherings in the 1880's, and that to such a degree that the bishops sought a solution by appeals to the Holy See. Other problems of the years after 1870 are still a source of anxiety such as the maintenance of the Church's commitment to its private religious schools. Nor were matters made easier for the American bishops when the suspicions of a few French conservative theologians cast a shadow of heresy over the Church of the United States and succeeded in eliciting from Leo XIII a letter warning against the dangers of what the Europeans called 'Americanism'.

It is with these and a score of other matters that Gerald Fogarty deals in this fascinating book, and with none in more detail than the final resolution of a problem that had worried American Catholics from the beginning of their national history, namely, the American constitutional principle of separation of Church and State *vis-à-vis* their own Church's official teaching of the need for a union between the two. It mattered not that one would look in vain for American Catholics who championed the union of Church and State; so long as Rome did so it remained a source of embarrassment and uneasiness. The solution began to evolve in the 1950's in a gradual – and sometimes painful – way with the efforts of John Courtney Murray, S.J., to find a theological accommodation, so to speak. Father Fogarty relates the story in full detail with the aid of documents hitherto unpublished, and that to its culmination with the promulgation by Pope Paul VI on December 7, 1965, of the Declaration on Religious Freedom of Vatican Council II.

Admittedly, the discipline of history – and that includes ecclesiastical history – has come upon days of doubt as to its future. It is a situation that is known to the educated public, one that is receiving increasing recognition. That recognition has seldom been expressed in more dramatic terms than those employed by Czeslaw Milosz in his Nobel Prize lecture of 1980. Noting the threat that this condition poses for a complete loss of a people's memory, Milosz asked if it did not constitute, "a danger more grave than genetic engineering or poisoning of the natural environment". He maintained that in the minds of some "modern illiterates" who know how to read and write, and who even teach in universities, "history is present but blurred, in a state of strange confusion. Molière becomes a contemporary of Napoleon, Voltaire a contemporary of Lenin". Milosz went on to say, "Those who are alive receive a mandate from those who are silent forever. They can fulfill their duties only by trying to reconstruct precisely things as they were and by wresting the past from fictions and legends"[3]. That is what Father Fogarty has attempted to do in this ambitious work, and he has achieved it with a very large measure of success. As I read his manuscript and noted the painstaking efforts to seek out the truth about the persons and events described, to exercise interpretative judgment in a fair and balanced fashion, and to present the tangled story of American bishops' relations to the Pope and to the Roman Curia in a manner that would invite acceptance and conviction, I was reminded of the praise once accorded to the English historians, H. Outram Evennett and David Knowles. The unnamed writer there spoke of

close research and wide survey together – the style being remarkable in its consistency and quietness, occasionally stirred into a musical ripple, or stroked by a gentle light, when a deep feeling has been aroused[4].

I have found something akin to that kind of history in Professor Fogarty's pages, and I would predict that readers with an interest in the way Catholicism evolved within the American framework will find the same.

John Tracy Ellis

Professorial Lecturer in
Church History
The Catholic University of America

---

[3] Czeslaw MILOSZ: *Nobel Lecture*. New York 1981, pp. 16, 22.
[4] "The Sense of the Past", *Times Literary Supplement*, August 17, 1956, p. x.

PREFACE

Writing a preface has always struck me as a pleasant literary exercise. Having completed a book, the author can at last slough off scholarly objectivity and address the reader in the first-person singular. In this case, I have several purposes in mind: to explain why I wrote this and not some other book, the methodology used, and the system for archival citations; and, finally, to make the acknowledgements which justice demands of me.

First of all, I am not writing about the Vatican's relations with the Catholic Church in the United States. Vatican II has too deeply impressed upon me the teaching that the Church is the People of God for me to believe that the portion of the Church, the hierarchy, treated here, can be equated with the Church. As I wrote this book, I came to the increasing realization that, while the bishops in this study were involved in frequently political and occasionally scandalous behavior, the people were believing, listening to the Gospel, receiving the sacraments, and building up one of the most vibrant churches in the contemporary world. Absent from treatment here are not only most of the bishops, clergy, and laity, but also those members of the American Church who probably had more direct pastoral influence than most bishops or even priests and who can take credit for inculcating religious values in the people – the thousands of religious women to whom was entrusted the task of education. In the twentieth century, I found only one archival reference to the Vatican's concern for religious women – Cardinal Francis Spellman's opposition to their holding a national congress. He expressed his annoyance that the Sacred Congregation of Religious had summoned the congress without consulting the bishops[1].

I am not apologizing for what I have done, but only reminding the reader that historians, at times, tend to present as typical what was actually unique. The stuff of history, like that of journalism, is what makes news. While Father Edward McGlynn, for instance, was in conflict with Archbishop Michael Corrigan, thousands of other priests were faithfully and uncontroversially nurturing the faith of their people. While Archbishop John Ireland was creating the impression that he was the Church, Bishop John Moore left his missionary diocese, risked his personal reputation, and flitted onto the stage of history to have McGlynn reconciled to the Church. Like many political historians, I can be accused of subscrib-

---

[1] AANY, Larraona to Spellman, Rome, Apr. 30, 1952; Spellman to Larraona, n.p. May 28, 1952 (draft).

ing to the "great man" theory of history, but only if greatness is construed as prominence and not necessarily as virtue or lovability.

Having explained something about the book I did not write, I would like to say something about the book I did write. My interest in the Vatican's relations with the American hierarchy grew out of my earlier study on the Vatican and the Americanist crisis. When I was approached to contribute a volume, originally entitled "The Vatican and the American Church after 1870", to the series *Paepste und Papsttum*, the topic seemed an apt continuation of my original area of interest. Little did I realize, however, that I was plunging into basically uncharted waters. Aside from the well-researched – and perhaps exhausted – liberal movement of the late nineteenth century, the topic had been barely touched in the secondary literature. I had to depend primarily on archives – all to which I could gain access – in the United States and Rome.

The method I followed was first to examine the ecclesiastical archival material and then check it against contemporary newspapers and journals and other manuscript depositories and archives to determine what was of public knowledge. Where there were published reports or information in secular archives, I used this to fill out what I had discovered in ecclesiastical archives. Where there was no corroborating evidence, e.g. for Spellman's meeting with George Marshall in 1948 about the United States policy toward the Italian election, I was compelled to rely solely upon the evidence from ecclesiastical archives. My conclusions in such cases are, therefore, necessarily tentative until the National Archives and other depositories are open to research. In using diocesan archives, moreover, I checked not only correspondence from Rome but also from other bishops, who might have mentioned issues of concern to the Vatican. This led to some further tentative conclusions. From the extant material, there was almost no correspondence in the twentieth century between bishops of the American east and those of the mid-west and west – regionalization and local autonomy seemed to be the order of the day.

Granted my methodology, there are obvious limitations. In some instances, either some bishops did not keep their correspondence or someone subsequently destroyed it. Such was the case in San Francisco, where there is almost no extant correspondence from the Vatican or other bishops to Archbishops Patrick Riordan, Edward J. Hanna, or John J. Mitty. I was also assured by Monsignor Bernard E. Granich of St. Louis that this was also true of Archbishops Peter R. Kenrick and John J. Kain and Cardinal John J. Glennon.

Still another problem arises – the accessibility of archives. Some are simply not open to research. Others are open only up to a given date. Those of the Archdiocese of Chicago, for example, are open only to 1926, so that the documents for the critical years of Cardinal George Mundelein's episcopate and for Cardinal

Samuel Stritch's entire tenure are unavailable. The archives of the Archdiocese of Detroit, at the time of the research for this book, had not been found. Some of Cardinal Edward Mooney's papers have since been discovered and should shed some light upon some of my conclusions, particularly in regard to his role in the National Catholic Welfare Conference and his support of John Courtney Murray, S.J., and religious liberty. I should mention in regard to Detroit that the file on Father Charles Coughlin is extant, but is not yet open to research.

The Vatican Archives and the Archives of the Sacred Congregation de Propaganda Fide present yet another difficulty. In the summer of 1976, the late Cardinal Sergio Pignedoli, President of the Secretariat for Non-Christians, tried unsuccessfully to gain me access to the Vatican and Propaganda archives for the pontificate of Leo XIII. Lacking this material, I proceeded to complete the first draft of this book, but then Pope John Paul II, late in 1978, announced the opening of the archives for this period. While my original draft had considerably condensed the treatment of the late nineteenth century, the newly available archives made an expansion necessary. Though this period of American Catholic history has now been well researched, there still remain some mysteries. While the available documents do elucidate the manner in which the Vatican and other authorities perceived the American Church, some crucial documents have not been discovered. Cardinal James Gibbons' response to the apostolic letter, *Testem Benevolentiae*, as I note in the text, cannot be located and is not even entered in the protocol book of the Secretariat of State. A search through the holdings of the Congregations of Latin Letters and of Letters to Princes also failed to disclose either Gibbons' response or other information pertaining to the commission which investigated Americanism.

The *spogli* or papers of Cardinals Mieceslaus Ledochowski and Camillo Mazzella, S.J., who were involved in the examination of Americanism, likewise, cannot be found. It was in an effort to locate Mazzella's papers that I examined the Archives of the Roman Curia of the Society of Jesus and those of the Pontifical German-Hungarian College, where Mazzella and his colleague, Cardinal Andreas Steinhuber, S.J., both lived.

Working within the method and limitations sketched above, I did discern four major themes in the relations between the Vatican and the American bishops. First, and probably foremost, the question of religious liberty remained critical right up to Vatican II. The answer given at the council, it seems to me, was not only due to the theoretical justification for it but was also a concrete example of the development of doctrine. To understand the latter, it is necessary to see theology, not as abstract ideas, but as the interface of ideas with historical and political realities. The United States with its peculiar religious situation simply could not be ignored in the 1950s and 1960s when it had emerged as the strongest western political and military bulwark against Communism. John Ireland, Denis O'Connell, and the other Americanists in 1898 spoke in behalf of the nation which represented to many Europeans the overthrow of the old political order. John Courtney Murray, S.J., as a theologian, and Cardinals Samuel Stritch and Francis Spellman, as practical churchmen, in the 1950s and 1960s defended the practice of the nation which had come to represent both vibrant Catholicism and defense of the Church and the world against the new threat of Communism. The words used in both periods may have been similar, but their content and context were different. I am, therefore, a firm believer that ideas have no independent existence, but they are thought and accepted by people in response to concrete historical circumstances which change over time.

A second theme which emerges from the documents is the success of the policy of Romanization of the hierarchy, which began before but was pursued with vigor after the debacle of Americanism. The strong sense of nineteenth-century collegiality gave way to a more vertical concept of authority with each bishop autonomous in his own diocese and not only dependent upon but directly responsible to the Holy See alone, or more specifically a Roman patron. This gave rise to a variety of local expressions of Catholicism, which had a pastoral effect. Thoroughly convinced that their diocese represented the only authentic expression of Catholicism, the faithful of each diocese were unaware that other dioceses represented different expressions and practices.

Yet a third theme arises. Immigration and with it ethnic diversity has contributed to the development and growth of the American Church. From ethnic pluralism has emerged and continues to emerge amalgamation into one Church – a process encouraged even in the Holy See's instructions to Archbishop Francesco Satolli. The point of this observation is that, while the history of the United States and the Church within its borders is brief, the histories of its people are considerably longer and embrace the traditions of Europe and all those other nations from which people have emigrated. The American Church during the period covered moved from being a patch-work quilt of various nationalities to being a composite of various ethnic and racial groups. The story of the gradual amalgamation of these groups – often with great pain and tension – also belongs to this study.

A fourth and final theme which emerges here is the acceptance of Catholics as first-class American citizens, a necessary condition for the Holy See's acceptance of American religious liberty. The American Catholic's spiritual loyalty to Rome was traditionally construed as an allegiance to foreign political leaders. The acceptance of Catholics as Americans came about partly because of the increased American fear of Communism, against which the Catholic Church was the strongest spiritual bulwark, and partly because the popes since John XXIII stressed greater openness to our "separated brethren" and thus attained greater spiritual authority than their predecessors had enjoyed. Yet, there remains a tension. Catholicism, with its loyalty which transcends national boundaries, will always be alien to those segments of the American population, which stress the individual or, at most, the nation as the sole source of authority.

Because of the concentration on the above themes, other themes, though important in themselves, have had to be relegated to more minor positions. One issue upon which I have only briefly touched is that of the settlement of Church claims and the regularization of the Church in the former Spanish territories after the Spanish-American War. The reasons for treating this so briefly are threefold. First, the situation in each of the conquered territories was such that either a passing reference had to suffice or a whole new book written. There is scattered material on the settlement of the war claims and on the Aglipayanos in various archives[2], but those stories are so complex that a competent account of them would distract from the main trends within continental Catholicism. Second, though some of the material in the Vatican archives was generated prior to the death of Leo XIII in 1903, it was not filed until later and is thus unavailable. The current secondary literature on the topic, therefore, had to serve for the present purposes. Finally, while some members of the American hierarchy opposed Philippine independence as late as the 1930s, the archival evidence does not point to any Vatican directive on the matter[3].

My method for citing archives needs explanation for those readers unfamiliar with the material. Let me begin with the Vatican and Propaganda archives. The documents of the Vatican Secretariat of State are first divided into rubrics or numbers assigned a nation, nations subject to a given congregation, or general topic. The rubrics are filed according to years and then broken down into fascicles. Rubric 280 designates the various churches which reported to Propaganda. To economize space, I have indicated after the appropriate abbreviation simply the rubric number, followed by the year, fascicle, folio, and pertinent description of the document. Thus, ASV, SS, 280 (1897), fasc. 1, 47^v–48^r means that the document is found in the Archivio Segreto Vaticano, Segreteria di Stato, Rubric 280, for the year 1897, the first fascicle, folios 47^v–48^r. The year for the rubric, I should mention, refers not to the date of the material contained in it but to the year in which the material was filed.

The archives of the Sacred Congregation of Propaganda are arranged differently. The *Acta* of the general and particular congregations are simply divided into volumes. The *Scritture originali riferite nelle congregazioni generali* (SOCG) con-

---

[2] See AANY, Agius to Farley, Manila, Nov. 3. 1905 and Jan. 19, 1906; Harty to Farley, Manila, Sept 10, 1907.

[3] See AANY, Dougherty to Hayes, Philadelphia, Jan. 1, 1932.

tain the original correspondence from which were drawn up the *ponenze* or formal presentations contained in the *Acta;* this source is again divided into volumes. The *Scritture riferite nei congressi, America Centrale* (SCAmerCent) contain the correspondence from the United States to the congregation, except for that culled out for the SOCG; this, too, has been divided into volumes. Finally, there are the *Lettere e Decreti*, which contain copies of all the letters sent by the prefect or secretary of the congregation. For all of these sources, I have designated the volume simply with arabic numbers followed by the year in parentheses.

In 1893, however, Propaganda changed its filing system for original documents sent to the congregation. This new system – Archives of Propaganda, New Style (APNS) – replaced both the SOCG and the SCAmerCent. All the material is first divided into a series of numerical rubrics, designating provenance, topics, or nations. These rubrics are filed in order and divided into volumes, but a given rubric may be split between two volumes for the same year. To avoid confusion from the proliferation of arabic numbers, I have placed the sign "Rub" before the rubric number, followed by the volume number. Thus, APNS, Rub 153, vol. 57 (1893) indicates the Archives of Propaganda, New Style, Rubric 153, volume 57 for the year 1893.

Although the archdiocesan archives of Baltimore and Boston are notable exceptions, most other American ecclesiastical archives are not well organized. It is, therefore, frequently necessary to use such generic designations as AANY to indicate that the document is in the Archives of the Archdiocese of New York, but is not filed in any consistent manner.

I now wish to acknowledge the numerous people who have helped me with my research and writing. In Rome, I would have been considerably delayed but for the guidance of Father Robert Wister, who provided invaluable aid in discovering the documents in the Vatican and Propaganda archives. At the Vatican, Monsignor Charles Burns took the time to lead me through the intricacies of the archival material, while answering all my questions with characteristic Scottish charm; Monsignor Herman Hoberg kindly granted me permission to consult the archives during extended hours; and Signor Nicola Raimondo generously assisted me in locating numerous documents which were improperly filed. At the Propaganda, I received the able assistance of Father Josef Metzler, O.M.I. Father Charles O'Neill, S.J., director of the Historical Institute of the Society of Jesus, not only placed at my disposal the resources of the institute, but also enlisted the assistance of Father Paolo Dezza, S.J., in an unsuccessful effort to locate the papers of Cardinal Mazzella. To Father Karlheinz Hoffmann, S.J., for seeking to obtain information for me from the Congregation for the Doctrine of the Faith; to Father Robert Lachenschmid, S.J., prefect of studies and librarian at the Pontifical German-Hungarian College, and Wolfgang Berta, its student archivist; and to Father

Edmond Lamalle, S.J., and Father József Fejér, S.J., of the Archives of the Roman Curia of the Society of Jesus, I am sincerely grateful. Finally, the community of the Collegio Bellarmino extended me fraternal hospitality for three months.

In the United States, I wish to thank the following for their encouragement and permission to use their respective archives: His Eminence, Lawrence Cardinal Shehan, former Archbishop of Baltimore, and his archivist, Father John Tierney; Archbishop Joseph L. Bernardin, formerly of Cincinnati and now of Chicago; Auxiliary Bishop Thomas Daily of Boston; Bishop John J. Russell of Richmond and his successor, Bishop Walter F. Sullivan; Thomas Kelly, O. P., former Secretary General of the United States Catholic Conference and now Archbishop of Louisville; Bishop James A. Hickey of Cleveland, now Archbishop of Washington; Monsignor George Tiffany of New York; Father Nelson Callahan of Cleveland; Father John B. DeMayo of Philadelphia; Monsignor Francis Weber of Los Angeles; Father Leonard Blair of Detroit; Father Menceslaus Madaj of Chicago; Father Robert McNamara of Rochester; and Mr. James Abajian of San Francisco. Although I must take sole responsibility for what is contained in this study, I am indebted to Monsignor John Tracy Ellis, Monsignor George Higgins, Father James Hennesey, S. J., and Father R. Emmett Curran, S. J., for their careful reading and helpful criticism of the manuscript. To Mrs. Kathy Squires for typing and preparing the manuscript and to Mary Ann Sastri for patient proofreading of the galleys, my sincere thanks. Finally, I wish to express my gratitude to the Jesuit Community at Georgetown University.

The research for this book would not have been possible without the financial assistance I have received. For summer research grants in 1976, 1977, and 1981, I want to thank the University of Virginia. I especially want to acknowledge the American Council of Learned Societies, which awarded me a fellowship for the academic year 1979–1980 and thus enabled me to undertake extensive research in Rome and to complete this book.

Charlottesville, Va.   Gerald P. Fogarty, S.J.

ABBREVIATIONS

AAB Archives of the Archdiocese of Baltimore

AABo Archives of Archdiocese of Boston

AAC Archives of the Archdiocese of Chicago

AACi Archives of the Archdiocese of Cincinnati

AAI Archives of the Archdiocese of Indianapolis

AANY Archives of the Archdiocese of New York

AAP Archives of the Archdiocese of Philadelphia

AASF Archives of the Archdiocese of San Francisco

AASP Archives of the Archdiocese of St. Paul

AASPOW Archives of the Abbey of St. Paul's Outside the Walls, Rome

ACC Archives of Civiltà Cattolica, Rome

ACSP Archives of the Congregation of St. Paul the Apostle

Acta et Decreta (official) = *Acta et Decreta Concilii Plenarii Baltimorensis Tertii.* Baltimore 1886.

Acta et Decreta (unofficial) = *Acta et Decreta Concilii Plenarii Baltimorensis Tertii in ecclesia Metropolitana Baltimorensi habita a die IX. Novembris usque ad diem VII. Decembris, A.D. MDCCCLXXXIV. Baltimore 1884.*

ACUA Archives of the Catholic University of America

ADC Archives of the Diocese of Cleveland

ADR Archives of the Diocese of Richmond

ADRo Archives of the Diocese of Rochester

ADSS *Actes et documents du Saint Siège relatifs à La Seconde Guerre Mondiale,* edited by Pierre BLET, Angelo MARTINI, Robert GRAHAM, and Burkhart SCHNEIDER, 8 vols. Vatican 1965–1980.

AGU Archives of Georgetown University

AMPSJ Archives of the Maryland Province of the Society of Jesus

ANCWC Archives of the National Catholic Welfare Conference

APF Archives of the Congregation de Propaganda Fide
Acta = Acta della Congregazione
APNS = Archives of Propaganda, New Style
Lettere = Lettere e Decreti
SCAmerCent = Scritture referite nei congressi, America Centrale
SOCG = Scritture originale referite nelle congregazioni generali

ARCSJ Archives of the Roman Curia of the Society of Jesus

ASMS Archives of St. Mary's Seminary, Baltimore

ASV Archivio Segreto Vaticano
SS = Segreteria di Stato
DAUS = Delegazione Apostolica degli Stati Uniti

AUND Archives of the University of Notre Dame

AWC Archives of Woodstock College

FDRL Franklin D. Roosevelt Library, Hyde Park, N.Y.
OF = Official File
PPF = President's Personal File
PSF = President's Secretary's File

FRUS *Foreign Relations of the United. States: Diplomatic Papers*

NA National Archives of the United States of America
DS = Decimal File, Department of State
RG = Record Group

CHAPTER I

FROM VATICAN I TO BALTIMORE III

A. The Bishops Return from the Council

"I have now no difficulty in accepting the dogma [of papal infallibility], although to the last I opposed it; because somehow or other it was in my head that the Bishops ought to be consulted".[1] The speaker was Bernard McQuaid, Bishop of Rochester, New York. His audience was the congregation which had assembled in his cathedral to hear him speak after returning from the First Vatican Council. At that council, he, together with several other Americans, had been a member of the minority, which opposed the definition. His viewpoint expressed the American tradition of episcopal collegiality.[2]

On the eve of the council, the American bishops had expressed this tradition in the Second Plenary Council of Baltimore: "Bishops, therefore, who are the successors of the Apostles, and whom the Holy Spirit has placed to rule the Church of God, which He acquired with His own blood, agreeing and judging together with its head on earth, the Roman Pontiff, whether they are gathered in general councils, or dispersed throughout the world, are inspired from on high with a gift of inerrancy, so that their body or college can never fail in faith nor define anything against doctrine revealed by God."[3]

The definition of the First Vatican Council, therefore, required considerable adjustment on the part of the Americans. McQuaid, for his part, was granted permission to return early from the council. His speech, quoted above, represent-

---

[1] Frederick, J. Zwierlein, *The Life and Letters of Bishop McQuaid*, 3 vols. Rochester, N. Y. 1926, II, 63.

[2] See James Hennesey: *Papacy and Episcopacy in Eighteenth and Nineteenth Century America*, in: Records of the American Catholic Historical Society of Philadelphia 77 (1966) 175–189 and *The First Council of the Vatican: The American Experience*, New York 1963. See also Gerald P. Fogarty: *Church Councils in the United States and American Legal Institutions*, in: Annuarium Historiae Conciliorum 4 (1972) 83–105.

[3] *Concilii Plenarii Baltimorensis II., in Ecclesia Metropolitana Baltimorensi, a die VII., ad diem XII. Octobris, A. D. MDCCCLXVI., habiti, et a Sede Apostolica recogniti, Decreta*, Baltimore 1866, p. 41, no. 50.

ed his submission to the dogma. But the submission of other bishops was more complicated.

Most of the bishops at the Vatican Council, who had opposed the definition, signed a protest against the dogma and then absented themselves from the solemn definition on July 18, 1870. Among these were Archbishops John Baptist Purcell of Cincinnati and Peter Richard Kenrick of St. Louis. Purcell, according to Martin John Spalding, Archbishop of Baltimore, had created "great scandal" in an interview he gave in the New York *Herald*, but "after speaking a lot of foolishness and imaginary things about the course of the council, finally gave his adhesion to the definition" after his return to his diocese.[4] Kenrick's submission was still more complicated because of the way in which the Vatican sought his formal acceptance.

At the council, Kenrick had delivered a speech against the proposed dogma in which he argued on the grounds that it was theological opinion only, which could not, therefore, become a doctrine of faith. He was attacked for his position by Archbishop Henry Edward Manning of Westminster, Cardinal Paul Cullen of Dublin, and Archbishop Martin Spalding. He prepared a second speech summarizing and defending his position when cloture was invoked cutting off debate. Since the Roman presses were forbidden to publish on the subject, he then had his speech, *Concio habenda at non habita*, printed at Naples and distributed to the bishops. In it, he restated his position that papal infallibility was a theological opinion and could not become doctrine even if defined by the council – a position he also maintained in regard to the definition of the Immaculate Conception.

After leaving the council, Kenrick travelled for some months in Europe. He was clearly a man in turmoil. Late in the fall, he met Lord Acton, who wrote Ignaz Döllinger that Kenrick "remained unchanged, and gave his consent to the reprinting of his writings with the avowal that he took back not a word of them." Having no definite plans on a course of action, he would "most probably keep silent, but will retract nothing, will not teach the dogma and will not believe it." According to Acton, he was even "prepared to be deposed, but says that this does not save him, since even as a layman he could not submit, and still less as a deposed archbishop".[5] Acton, of course, could have been placing his own interpretation on Kenrick's words, but the Vatican, too, was concerned.

On September 20, 1870, Rome had fallen to the forces of the Kingdom of Italy. Much of the attention of the Catholic world was, therefore, directed not only to the new definition, but also to the loss of papal temporal power. The Vatican's

---

[4] APF, SCAmerCent, 23 (1870), 519ʳ – 521ʳ, Spalding to Simeoni, Malines, Oct. 14, 1870 in HENNESEY: *First Council*, p. 279.

[5] Acton to Döllinger, Dec. 23, 1870, in HENNESEY: *First Council*, p. 317.

political isolation may very well have conditioned its ecclesiastical response to Kenrick. From Malines, on October 14, Spalding wrote Archbishop Giovanni Simeoni, Secretary of Propaganda, suggesting, among other things, that the future sessions of the council be transferred to Belgium. About Kenrick, he said he had heard nothing, but feared that he was disposed to stir up "trouble and give scandal." He was principally concerned with the *Concio,* which he thought "semi-heretical" and which was "already being spread throughout the United States with gravest scandal to the faithful." Spalding believed that a committee of the council had submitted a report "condemning the discourse throughout".[6]

Actually, Vatican officials were at that time taking action on Kenrick. But their mode of procedure only served to heighten the confusion. On October 15, Cardinal Filippo de Angelis, one of the presidents of the council, wrote Kenrick that the Congregation of the Index had condemned the *Concio* as containing grave errors, but would not publish the condemnation if the archbishop explicitly accepted the decrees of the council.[7] De Angelis, however, did not send the letter directly to Kenrick. Instead, he entrusted it to Cardinal Alessandro Barnabò, Prefect of Propaganda, who in turn, on November 9, enclosed it with one of his own and transmitted it, through Francis Silas Chatard, Rector of the American College, to John Joseph Hogan, Bishop of St. Joseph, Missouri, one of Kenrick's suffragans. Hogan was to hand the letter personally to Kenrick. Because the letter from de Angelis was sealed and Hogan was ignorant of the precise contents, another factor was added to the developing confusion.

Kenrick, in the meantime, had returned to the United States. On Christmas Day, in Philadelphia, he met Michael O'Connor, S.J., former Bishop of Pittsburgh. According to O'Connor, Kenrick "said the only way he could reconcile matters was by the development theory of Dr. Newman just as he was becoming a Catholic." O'Connor pleaded with him to submit and subsequently sent Kenrick a note on the subject, which is unfortunately now lost.[8] The next day, Kenrick assured O'Connor in writing that he would take the first opportunity after returning to his diocese to submit.[9] This intelligence, Father James O'Connor, the bishop's brother, immediately transmitted to Cardinal Barnabò,[10] who should therefore have been anticipating some action from Kenrick.

---

[6] APF, SCAmerCent, 23 (1870), 519–521, Spalding to Simeoni, Malines, Oct. 14, 1870.

[7] The contents of the letter are described in Kenrick to Acton, St. Louis, Mar. 29, 1871, given in HENNESEY: *First Council,* p. 315.

[8] AMPSJ, 228 S 4, O'Connor to Joseph Keller, S. J., Provincial of the Maryland Province, Philadelphia, Dec. 26, 1870.

[9] *Ibid.,* O'Connor to Keller, Philadelphia, Jan. 3, 1870.

[10] APF, SCAmerCent, 23 (1870), 605ʳ–606ᵛ, O'Connor to Barnabò, Philadelphia, Dec. 26, 1870.

Kenrick was true to his word. On January 2, 1871, he celebrated Mass in his cathedral as part of the formal reception welcoming him back to his diocese. After the Communion, Father Patrick J. Ryan, vicar general and administrator of the diocese during the archbishop's absence, gave an address mentioning Kenrick's pastoral work in the diocese and the submission already made by other members of the minority at the council. He concluded by saying: "No one can think that in having sacrificed personal interests, and, perhaps, somewhat pained life-long friends by your course, after a life too, of such unswerving adherence to principle, that now, in the evening of your days, you would belie the record of that life by submission from any other motive than the deep conviction that God speaks through his Church, and it is man's greatest glory to obey her Voice".[11]

Here was Kenrick's opportunity to make a face-saving submission. In reply to Ryan's address, he narrated the motives for his opposition to the definition and then said: "The motive of my submission is simply and singly the authority of the Catholic Church. That submission is a most reasonable obedience, because of the necessity of obeying an authority established by God; and having the guaranty of our Divine Saviour's perpetual assistance is in itself evidence, and cannot be gainsayed by any one who professes to recognize Jesus Christ as his Savior and his God. Simply and singly on that authority I yield obedience and full and unreserved submission to the definition the character of which there can be no doubt as emanating from the Council, and subsequently accepted by the greater part even of those who were in the minority on that occasion".[12] Kenrick's submission to the dogma contained no retraction of the arguments he had used against it. Rather he held that the authority of the Church, not only of the bishops who supported the definition but also of those who subsequently submitted, took precedence over theological opinion and personal belief. Like Archbishop Georges Darboy of Paris, he held that the affirmation in Rome of the majority of the episcopate and the later adhesion of the minority made up for any defect in the council.[13]

Kenrick's address in St. Louis should have ended the proceedings against him, but it did not. On January 10, 1871, Ryan sent Chatard the newspaper accounts of Kenrick's "clear and unreserved profession of faith in the Infallibility dogma".[14] Kenrick himself, on January 21, wrote Barnabò asking for certain faculties connected with his office and concluded by saying: "Having returned home at the end of the past year, I indicated in a public gathering that I adhere to those

---

[11] Given in J. J. O'SHEA: *The Two Archbishops Kenrick*, Philadelphia 1904, p. 332.
[12] *Ibid.*, pp. 333-334.
[13] Roger AUBERT: *Le pontificat de Pie IX (1846–1878)* Paris 1952, pp. 361–362.
[14] AAI, Ryan to Chatard, St. Louis, Jan. 10, 1871.

things which were passed in the fourth session of the Vatican Council".[15] In the meantime, Hogan visited Kenrick, but, in view of the archbishop's address, decided to withhold de Angelis' sealed letter.[16] Even Spalding wrote Simeoni that Kenrick "has submitted without reservation" and he was thankful "that we have not had a scandal".[17] Hogan, however, had complicated the matter still further by withholding de Angelis' letter.

Chatard, who acted as the agent for the American bishops with Vatican officials, wrote Hogan on January 27, before Barnabò would have received Kenrick's letter, that both the pope and cardinal prefect insisted on Kenrick's complete retraction of his writings and that, therefore, Hogan should deliver de Angelis' letter. Still Hogan procrastinated and instead merely wrote Kenrick telling him he was to write the pope and cardinal retracting his *Concio*. Kenrick replied that he had already written Barnabò, but had received no reply.[18] When Barnabò did reply, Kenrick was understandably angry. The cardinal said that he was pleased at Kenrick's submission, but urged him to write personally to the pope as other members of the minority had done. He added that he was still waiting for an answer to de Angelis' letter, which Chatard assured him had been delivered.[19] Barnabò, of course, was misinformed. It was only when Kenrick received Barnabò's letter that he learned that de Angelis had written him. Kenrick immediately wrote Hogan who finally forwarded the letter on March 25.[20] Although Hogan himself wrote Barnabò that he had withheld the letter until a "suitable day,"[21] the cardinal must have been confused.

Immediately upon receipt of de Angelis' letter, Kenrick replied:

St. Louis
March 28, 1871

Eminence:

Today there was handed to me the letter of Your Eminence, dated October 15 of last year, by which you exhort me openly to repudiate the speech which I published, by explicitly adhering to the decrees of the ecumenical Vatican Council. Two months ago I informed His Eminence the Cardinal Prefect of the S[acred] Cong[regation] de fide propaganda in a letter, that, immediately upon my return home, namely on January 2, I

---

15 ASV, Concilio Vaticano I: Adhaesiones.
16 AAI, Hogan to Chatard, St. Joseph, Mar. 29, 1871.
17 APF, SCAmerCent., 23 (1870–1871), 967ʳ, Spalding to Simeoni, Baltimore, Jan. 31, 1871.
18 AAI, Hogan to Chatard, St. Joseph, Mar. 29, 1871.
19 APF, Lettere, 366 (1871), 1319ᵛ–1322ᵛ, Simeoni to Holy Office, July 14, 1871.
20 AAI, Hogan to Chatard, St. Joseph, Mar. 29, 1871.
21 APF, SCAmerCent, 23 (1870–1871), 94ʳ, Hogan to Barnabò, St. Joseph, Mar. 29, 1871.

had declared in a public gathering, that I accepted the decrees passed in the fourth Session of the Vatican Council, and that I was led to that by the authority of the Catholic Church, which seemed to place that obligation upon me.

> I am Your Eminence's
> humble servant in the Lord
> Peter Richard Kenrick
> Archbishop of St. Louis

His Eminence and Most Rev.
P. Cardinal de Angelis[22]

Kenrick's letter essentially repeated his terse submission to Barnabò of January 21 and presented the main argument used in his response to Ryan's address: that he submitted on the basis of the authority of the Church. That submission, in his mind, implied a repudiation of the conclusions he had reached against the dogma in his *Concio*. But he did not retract the *Concio's* arguments themselves.

One day later, Kenrick recounted these events to Lord Acton, who had asked for information about the archbishop's address of January 2. He noted that both he and Purcell had been attacked in the Catholic press for their position at the council. He explained: "I could not defend the Council or its action; but I always professed that the acceptance of either by the Church would supply its deficiency." Acton would, he said, "perceive that I gave as the motive of my submission 'simply and singly' the authority of the Church, by which I was well understood to mean, that the act was one of pure obedience, and was not grounded on the removal of my motives of opposition to the decrees, as referred to in my reply and set forth in my pamphlets." Although Chatard had told him that the pope would insist on a retraction of the *Concio*, he refused to do so. Neither would he write a pastoral letter on infallibility, as he had been urged to do by Barnabò, Archbishop Joseph Alemany of San Francisco, and Hogan nor would he write personally to the pope, as Barnabò had urged. Neither had he taken part in the demonstrations in favor of papal temporal power nor had he signed the address of St. Louis Catholics to the pope sympathizing with him because of the fall of Rome. For Acton, he then outlined the process by which he came to make his submission: "I reconciled myself intellectually to submission by applying Father Newman's theory of development to the case in point. The Pontifical authority as at present exercised is so different from what it appears to have been in the early Church, that it can only be supposed identical in substance by allowing a process of doctrinal development. This principle removed Newman's great difficulty and convinced him that, notwithstanding the difference, he might and should become a Catholic. I thought it might justify me in remaining one". This was as far as Ken-

---

[22]ASV, Concilio Vaticano I: Adhaesiones. Given in MANSI, LIII, 955.

rick was prepared to go. He acknowledged the doctrine on the authority of the Church and admitted that he might not have recognized it as a doctrine accepted by the majority of the Church prior to its definition. But he would not deny the arguments used in his *Concio*, for, he believed, its condemnation by the Index would rule out "liberty in future sessions of the Council, with this example to warn Bishops that they must not handle roughly the delicate matters on which they have to decide".[23]

During the spring and early summer of 1871, the Vatican, however, still wanted a complete public retraction of the *Concio*, but it began to receive conflicting advice. On April 2, Ryan wrote Chatard arguing that Kenrick had already complied with de Angelis' command and urged "that the matter had better terminate here". He noted also that the archbishop's address "has satisfied the Jesuits here – the warmest friends of the definition, and has satisfied the entire country".[24] All of this information Chatard translated and submitted to Propaganda.[25] Hogan, on the other hand, thought a retraction was necessary. He had received no reply to his letter to Kenrick telling him that the Holy See demanded a retraction. He feared, if he went to see the archbishop personally, he would not be received. In the meanwhile, the *Concio* was being circulated in translation and "unless His Grace publicly retract the pamphlet and condemn it soon or immediately we can no longer remain spectators of the controversy with the Holy See. The Faith begins to be jeopardized, and the Little Ones of Christ whom we have instructed must be defended and saved".[26] Spalding, too, on June 8, noted that the Protestants had published the *Concio* "to the great scandal of the faithful. The archbishop is not going to respond to it – in fact he cannot, because he would be placed in contradiction with himself".[27] Still another voice urged moderation. Archbishop John Joseph Lynch of Toronto wrote Barnabò on June 8 that he had information from a "reliable source" that Kenrick had already "condemned everything which the pamphlet contained contrary to the dogma of Infallibility". But "if it were demanded of him to repudiate his pamphlet in its entirety, I fear, there would be a certain repugnance to do it".[28]

Although in the early summer of 1871 the Vatican still seemed intent on demanding Kenrick's retraction, by July the case was coming to a close. All the material was submitted to the Holy Office: Kenrick's address, a report from Arch-

---

[23] Kenrick to Acton, Mar. 29, 1871 in HENNESEY: *First Council*, pp. 321–324.

[24] AAI, Ryan to Chatard, St. Louis, Apr. 2, 1871.

[25] APF, SCAmerCent, 23 (1870–1871), 942ʳ–943ʳ, Chatard to Barnabò, Rome, Apr. 28, 1871.

[26] AAI, Hogan to Chatard, St. Joseph, June 7, 1871.

[27] APF, SCAmerCent, 23 (1870–1871), 1147ʳ, Spalding to Simeoni, Baltimore, June 8, 1871.

[28] *Ibid.,* 944ʳ–945ʳ, Lynch to Barnabò, Toronto, June 8, 1871.

bishop Giovanni Simeoni, Secretary of Propaganda, recounting the way in which de Angelis' letter was sent to Kenrick, and Kenrick's letter to Barnabò of January 21. On July 19, the Holy Office met. Its report noted the condemnation of the *Concio* and Kenrick's submission. Although the Holy Office had hoped Kenrick would follow the example of the other bishops who submitted their formal adherence to the pope, its report concluded that "the manner in which the Archbishop conducted himself on this point contented the faithful, and also the Jesuits" and therefore on July 19, 1871, "with all things considered their Eminences decreed: it should not be further insisted upon".[29]

The confusing aspects of the controversy could have been avoided, either if de Angelis' letter had been sent to Ryan for delivery to Kenrick on his return or if Hogan had not retained it. But the Vatican was ultimately satisfied to accept Kenrick's original submission to infallibility. It was led to this in great part through the influence of Ryan, who was already under consideration for appointment as Kenrick's coadjutor. Indeed, his support of Kenrick's character, though not his doctrine, was thought by some, notably Spalding, Lynch, and Henry Muehlsiepen, Ryan's fellow vicar general, to have delayed his appointment.[30] He was appointed Coadjutor Archbishop of St. Louis on February 15, 1872, whereupon Kenrick virtually retired for over a decade from public appearances. He had kept his earlier promise to Acton that he would remain silent.

Kenrick's situation was psychologically similar to that of Karl Josef von Hefele, the famous bishop-historian of Rottenburg. Both experienced deep personal crises. Von Hefele's submission took the form of a letter to his clergy on April 10, 1871, just at the time that Kenrick's letter was on its way to de Angelis. Hefele had written on the advice of Bishop Fessler, secretary of the council, and stated that the new dogma of papal infallibility should in no way be taught or preached to the neglect of the ancient doctrine of the infallibility of the Church. Kenrick would have been at home with that position, but he did not have the historical expertise to express it in his statements. He might have been more comfortable with the implications of the definition, had he realized that the Holy See accepted von Hefele's letter as a legitimate interpretation of what had been defined at Vatican I.[31]

---

[29] ASV, Concilio Vaticano I: Adhaesiones.

[30] Cf. S. J. MILLER: *Peter Richard Kenrick, Bishop and Archbishop of St. Louis: 1806–1896*, in: Records of the American Catholic Historical Society of Philadelphia, 84 (1973) 127; APF, SCAmer-Cent., 23 (1870–1871), 945ʳ, Lynch to Barnabò, Toronto, June 8, 1871; 1273ᵛ, Muehlsiepen to Barnabò, St. Louis, July 22, 1871.

[31] For the whole Kenrick episode, see Gerald P. FOGARTY: *Archbishop Peter Kenrick's Submission to Papal Infallibility*, in: Archivum Historiae Pontificiae 16 (1978) 205–222; for a comparision with von Hefele, see p. 220.

Kenrick was not the last American bishop formally to submit to the doctrine. Michael Domenec, C.M., Bishop of Pittsburgh, wrote Barnabò only on December 21, 1871. But this was due to a technicality. He had preached the doctrine publicly in his diocese and had subscribed his signature to an address to the pope, but was unaware of the demand that bishops of the minority write Barnabò until Spalding informed him of this late in 1871.[32] His was not as notorious a case as that of Kenrick.

American bishops had thus attracted attention to themselves at their first corporate contact with the European Church. They were noted for a sense of collegiality among themselves and of relative autonomy from a Roman central authority, which was far removed from the United States and its situation. The American Church was small, in European terms, but growing, principally through immigration. Its dioceses by 1853 had already spanned a continent. In 1870, American Catholics numbered 4,504,000 out of a total white population of 33,589,377. Jurisdictionally, the nation was divided into forty-six dioceses, including two erected while the First Vatican Council was in session, and seven archdioceses: Baltimore, St. Louis, Cincinnati, New York, New Orleans, Oregon City (later transferred to Portland, Oregon), and San Francisco. The still relatively young Church had brought itself forcibly to Rome's attention.

B. The First American Cardinal and New Metropolitan Sees

On March 15, 1875, Pius IX acknowledged the growing maturity of the American Church by naming as its first cardinal Archbishop John McCloskey of New York. The new cardinal received his red biretta on April 27, 1875, from Monsignor Cesare Roncetti. The reasons for selecting McCloskey for this honor were probably several. In terms of size, his see was the most important in the United States. It had, moreover, weathered the waves of immigrants flowing through its port and the storms of nativism occasioned by their arrival; it had created a parochial school system, second to none in the country, to preserve the faith of Catholic children; and, in general, the diocese was well administered.

McCloskey, however, was not personally an impressive man. Originally an inopportunist at the First Vatican Council, he had in the end voted with the majority.[33] He was a man of moderation, which, together with other qualities, singled him out from his fellow archbishops. The country's oldest see and first archdiocese, Baltimore, had not been allowed the title of primacy. Archbishop Spalding,

---

[32] HENNESEY: *First Council*, p. 313.
[33] *Ibid.*, pp. 101, 229, 281.

moreover, who had tried to play a mediating role at the Vatican Council, had died in February of 1872, and his successor James Roosevelt Bayley, only three years in office, was himself not well. Purcell and Kenrick were not apt candidates because of their strong stance against infallibility. The other three archdioceses were too small and their ordinaries not sufficiently known on the national level for them to be given the red hat. If the Holy See was to recognize the maturity of the American Church through the conferral of the cardinalate, McCloskey was the only logical choice for the honor.

McCloskey's elevation occurred simultaneously with the establishment of four new metropolitan provinces. At the Second Plenary Council of Baltimore in 1866, the bishops had requested Rome to create the new provinces of Milwaukee and Philadelphia.[34] Early in 1875 Propaganda decreed the erection of those two provinces and added Boston and Santa Fe.[35] Cesare Roncetti, the papal ablegate who brought the red biretta to McCloskey, attended the ceremonies of imposing the pallium on Archbishop John Williams of Boston on May 2, Archbishop John Martin Henni of Milwaukee on June 3, and Archbishop Frederick Wood of Philadelphia on June 17. He had thought of going to Santa Fe, but his report to Cardinal Alessandro Franchi, who had succeeded Cardinal Barnabò as Prefect of Propaganda, indicated how little the Roman understood the United States. His account struck a humorous chord: "Then in regard to Monsignor Lamy, Archbishop of Santa Fe, after I consulted with his Eminence Cardinal MacCloskey [sic] and other persons well informed about travel in North America, [I have decided to give up] such a trip, both because of the great distance of about three thousand miles, about as far as a journey from the United States to Europe, and also because of the difficulty of this travel of which more than [?] four hundred miles would have to be done in a coach or on horseback, and finally because of the danger of encountering the Indians, who entertain themselves by taking from the foreigners they encounter the hair on the top part of the cranium. ... Although because of my baldness I would not have to fear becoming the victim of this act, nevertheless I think it well not to venture on this journey, and therefore taking advantage of the happy occasion of the return of Monsignor Salpointe, Vicar Apostolic of Arizona, who was passing through New York, I have personally consigned to him the Brief and the Pallium".[36]

Roncetti's observations of the vast distance to Santa Fe and the danger of an Indian attack stood in contrast to his description of the conferring of the pallium on Williams in the still unfinished, Gothic-style cathedral of Boston, opened to

---

[34] Concilii Plenarii Baltimorensis II ... Decreta, p. 269.
[35] APF, Acta, 243, (1875), 1–12.
[36] APF, SCAmerCent, 26 (1875), 218ʳ–220ᵛ, Roncetti to Franchi, New York, May 22, 1875.

the public for the first time for the ceremony.[37] From Boston, Roncetti returned to New York and then set off for Milwaukee, with a detour that took him first to Washington, where Thomas Murphy, a prominent New York Catholic had arranged a meeting for him with President Ulysses S. Grant. On May 30, he wrote Cardinal Antonelli about relations between Catholics and the American government. From Washington, he went by train to Pittsburgh and Chicago and then to Milwaukee by steamboat. At the pallium ceremony for Archbishop Henni, he witnessed the heterogeneity of the American Catholic population as he listened to the apostolic brief read in Latin and then in both English and German. All the suffragans of the new province were present together with Archbishop Ryan, Coadjutor of St. Louis, of which Milwaukee had until now been a suffragan. Roncetti also undertook a special assignment in St. Louis, the nature of which is unfortunately undisclosed.[38] Then he travelled to Cincinnati and to Philadelphia for the imposition of the pallium on Archbishop Wood on June 17.[39] Early in July, he left New York to return to Rome. His had been one of the most extended tours of the United States made by a Roman official and his trip had made an obvious impression.

Even as Roncetti was making his tour of the eastern United States, the Vatican's attention was being drawn to a series of issues which would occupy it for the remainder of the century. The first was the increasing population which required the establishment of new dioceses; seven were established between 1872 and 1880. Another was the Church's existence in a pluralistic society. The two issues became intertwined as the bishops appointed to the new sees and to existing ones not only reshaped the composition of the American hierarchy but also took strong stances on the direction they believed the American Church should take. One new diocese was that of Peoria, whose separation from the territory of Chicago Propaganda had decided at the same time that it established the new provinces of Milwaukee and Santa Fe. The first priest chosen as bishop, however, refused the post and the bishops of the Province of St. Louis had to submit a second and then a third *terna* or list of three names. On this final list, they named in first place Father John Lancaster Spalding, a nephew of the deceased Archbishop of Baltimore. Born in Kentucky, educated at the American College in Louvain, and ordained for the Diocese of Louisville, he was in 1875 engaged in pastoral work in New York City. Then there arose a complication. Spalding's name had also been second on the list for the Diocese of Wheeling. Bishop Thomas Becker

---

[37] *Ibid.*, 216ʳ–217ᵛ, Roncetti to Franchi, New York, May 10, 1875.

[38] *Ibid.*, 223ʳ–227ʳ, Roncetti to Franchi, Chicago, June 8, 1875.

[39] *Ibid.*, 229ʳ–231ᵛ, Roncetti to Franchi, Cincinnati, June 15, 1875, 237ʳ–241ᵛ, Roncetti to Franchi, Philadelphia, June 21, 1875.

of Wilmington, who was the secretary for the bishops of the Province of Baltimore in drawing up that *terna*, added the warning that Spalding was thought to hold some philosophical propositions on ontologism recently condemned at the University of Louvain and to have had an unorthodox view of papal infallibility prior to its definition.[40]

The procedure followed in Rome was for one cardinal member of Propaganda to be designated the *ponente* to take the *ternae*, analyze the documents pertaining to each candidate, usually letters from bishops and priests giving their opinions of the candidates, and draw up a *ponenza* or position paper to be printed and distributed to all the other cardinals of the congregation. Usually a *sommario* or printed version of all the letters on the candidates accompanied the *ponenza*. Having first studied the *ponenza*, the cardinals then met in general session to select one name for submission for the pope's approval. The congregation followed the same procedure on questions other than selection of bishops.

In the case of Peoria, on January 24, 1876, Cardinal Franchi wrote McCloskey asking his opinion of Spalding's orthodoxy. McCloskey replied that he knew nothing unorthodox in Spalding's philosophical views and that, like his uncle, he had held the definition of papal infallibility to be inopportune prior to the council but had used every opportunity to defend it since.[41] Still Propaganda delayed and Franchi asked Archbishop Bayley for more precise information. Bayley turned over the investigation to Becker, who had made the original charges. On August 2, 1876, Becker wrote Franchi stating that he could find no substance to the charges which he had forwarded to Rome. Finally, on November 26, Propaganda met and recommended Spalding's appointment as Bishop of Peoria to Pius IX, who gave his approval on December 3.[42] In the years to come, Spalding would have a remarkable influence on the American Church, but his was always an independent mind, taking sides on issues rather than personalities.

Another new episcopal leader was John Ireland. Born in Ireland, raised in Minnesota, and educated at Meximieux and Montbel in France, he had served briefly as a chaplain in the Union Army during the Civil War and represented his bishop, Thomas Grace, at the First Vatican Council. He had been named in third place on the first *terna* for Peoria in 1875, but his name was withdrawn from later consideration because he was also nominated as Vicar Apostolic of the Ne-

---

[40] APF, Acta, 243 (1875), 1^r–12^r, Franchi Ponenza, Jan., 1875: 24^v–25^v, Sommario, Becker to Franchi, Wilmington, Sept. 14, 1874; David Francis SWEENEY: *The Life of John Lancaster Spalding: First Bishop of Peoria, 1840–1916*, New York 1965, pp. 100–104.

[41] AANY, Franchi to McCloskey, Rome, Mar. 29, 1876, duplicate of letter of Jan. 24, 1876; SWEENEY: *Spalding*, p. 104.

[42] SWEENEY: *Spalding*, pp. 105-106.

braska Territory on February 12, 1875.[43] In June, however, acting on the recommendation of Bishop Grace, Propaganda presented his name to Pius IX as Coadjutor of St. Paul.[44] He succeeded to the see on July 31, 1884. Ireland was to become the dominant, if most controversial, figure in the American Church, as he took the lead on some of the issues which were already surfacing in 1875.

Parochial schools and clerical discipline

One such issue was that of parochial schools. In 1872, Father Edward McGlynn, rector of St. Stephen's Church in New York City, spoke out in favor of public schools, whose non-sectarian character he thought presented no danger to the Catholic faith. For James A. McMaster, the convert editor of the New York *Freeman's Journal*, this was a position clearly listed as condemned in the Syllabus of Errors. For him there could be no toleration for any system of education not under Church supervision or for parents who sent their children to non-Catholic schools. Although he was opposed by many bishops in early 1874, McMaster succeeded in bringing his case to Rome, through Father Edmund De Pauw of Chateaugay, New York, and Ella B. Edes, a convert who did secretarial work for Propaganda. In his memorandum, McMaster condemned the moral standards of public schools, even where there were Catholic teachers, and questioned whether pastors could absolve parents who sent their children to public schools, when parochial ones were available. On the basis of this memorandum, Cardinal Franchi wrote the American bishops about the issue on April 10, 1874. This letter the archbishops discussed when they met in Cincinnati to plan the establishment of new metropolitan provinces. They answered the cardinal that the public schools, being non-sectarian, were not anti-Catholic, that denial of absolution to parents whose children attended public schools would cause more harm than good, and that the principal difficulty was to provide parochial schools of equal quality to public ones.[45]

Before the Holy See could reach a decision on the school question, Roncetti came to the United States. While he was in New York, the issue again came before the public. This time the occasion was an arrangement which Father Patrick McSweeny of Poughkeepsie, a town in the Archdiocese of New York, had made with the local school board. The parish leased its school building to the school board, conducted religious instruction outside of school hours, and used the same

---

[43] APF, Acta, 243 (1875), 5ᵛ, Franchi Ponenza, Jan. 1875.

[44] *Ibid.*, 283ʳ–285ᵛ.

[45] Thomas T. McAvoy: *Public Schools vs Catholic Schools and James McMaster*, in: Review of Politics 28 (1966) 22–36.

text books as the public schools. In return, the school board paid the teachers' salaries. On April 14, the *Buffalo Commercial Advertiser* published the account of a Protestant minister who had visited the school and who expressed the sole reservation that religious images remained in some of the classrooms. McSweeny's brother, Father Edward McSweeny, assured the minister how satisfied his brother and the majority of his congregation were with the arrangement. At this point McMaster was too busy describing the conferral of the red biretta on McCloskey to take note of the story. In early June, however, the *New York Tablet* favorably editorialized on the arrangement. This led McMaster to speak out. Among other things, he accused the McSweenys of violating their oaths as alumni of Propaganda by yielding to the state control over their schools and by removing religious images from the classrooms. Edward McSweeny replied in the *Tablet* that his brother would have preferred Catholic schools but could see no reason to decline the school board's offer to allow his congregation to share in the benefits from its tax money.[46] He then refused to engage any further in what was becoming a heated newspaper debate with McMaster and, on Roncetti's advice, wrote Propaganda explaining his and his brother's position.[47]

McMaster forwarded all the newspaper stories to Rome, where Ella B. Edes translated them into Italian for Propaganda. On November 24, 1875, the Holy Office, to which the issue had been referred, issued an instruction, which Propaganda did not publish until exactly a year later. It spoke of the dangers of public schools, much in the manner of McMaster. It then urged that schools be built where none existed and that existing ones be improved. Parents were to send their children to these schools, unless they provided sufficient reason to the bishop, such as the unavailability or unsuitability of a parochial school. Children in public schools should be given catechetical instruction. But Propaganda's instruction was vague in regard to denying absolution to parents who sent their children to public schools without showing cause to the bishop.[48] The American hierarchy virtually ignored this instruction until officials at Propaganda placed it on the agenda for the plenary council held in Baltimore in 1884. The issue of parochial schools would become a burning question in the 1890s, but it had already begun to surface as early as McCloskey's cardinalate.

Beneath the issue addressed by the Holy Office was how to provide Catholic education in a pluralistic society in which the Church had no relation with the State and where the State, unlike the European liberal State, usurped none of the Church's rights. It was still a new and strange experience for Vatican officials.

---

[46] *Ibid.*, pp. 38–40.
[47] APF, SCAmerCent, 26 (1875), 679ʳ–680ᵛ, McSweeny to Franchi, Poughkeepsie, June 18, 1875.
[48] McAvoy: *Public Schools*, pp. 40–42; text in *Acta et Decreta* (official), pp. 279–282.

Related to this was another issue. In an emerging nation, whose population was spreading across a continent, what form of clerical discipline best served the Church? There was an anomaly in the American Church, for there was a regularly established hierarchy of ordinary bishops, but there were no canonically established parishes with pastors enjoying the status and rights guaranteed them in canon law. As early as 1833, Bishop John England of Charleston had recognized the anomaly and had unsuccessfully recommended that some priests be constituted pastors.[49] But England's was a lone episcopal voice and as a result a bishop could transfer or remove a priest at will. In 1855, the First Provincial Council of St. Louis adopted a form of trial for clerical cases. If a priest protested his transfer or removal, the bishop or his vicar general was to appoint two of his diocesan consultors to hear the case. If the consultors went against the bishop, he was to appoint a third consultor. If the consultors still failed to uphold the bishop's decision, appeal was to be made to the metropolitan or, if the case originated in a metropolitan see, to the senior suffragan bishop. The decision of the metropolitan or senior suffragan was final, except for appeal by either the bishop or priest to the Holy See. The Second Plenary Council of Baltimore extended this form of trial to the entire American Church.[50]

The St. Louis form naturally favored the bishop. It met with protests from some vocal priests, notably Eugene O'Callaghan of the Diocese of Cleveland, who, in turn, gained the support of James McMaster. Writing under the pen-name *Jus* in the New York *Freeman's Journal*, O'Callaghan played on the word *"suspensus"* and stated that this was the only form of law in which a man was first hanged and then tried. He called for a change in the discipline and for increased rights to priests. Soon he had a clerical disciplinary problem of his own. Bishop Amadeus Rappe transferred him in 1869 from Youngstown to Lima, Ohio. O'Callaghan protested the decision and gained Rappe's permission to go to Rome to present his case. He arrived in January, 1870, and was therefore present during the Vatican Council. He was ultimately successful in pleading his cause, but his reputation remains besmirched for his part in gaining the removal of Bishop Rappe on false charges of solicitation in the confessional.[51] It was this

---

[49] Peter GUILDAY: *The Life and Times of John England, First Bishop of Charleston: 1786–1842*, 2 vols. New York 1927, II, 85.

[50] Col. Lac., III, 308, 311–312, 423.

[51] Robert TRISCO: *Bishops and Their Priests in the United States*, in: John Tracy ELLIS (ed.): The Catholic Priest in the United States: Historical Investigations, Collegeville, Minn. 1971, pp. 158–194; Nelson J. CALLAHAN: *A Case for Due Process in the Church: Father Eugene O'Callaghan, American Pioneer of Dissent*, Staten Island, N.Y. 1971, pp. 30–35; Henry B. LEONARD: *Ethnic Conflict and Episcopal Power: The Diocese of Cleveland, 1847–1870*, in: Catholic Historical Review 62 (1976) 388–407.

type of frequent appeal to Rome which concerned the Holy See. For this and other reasons, the Vatican dispatched a visitor to the American Church.

George Conroy, Bishop of Ardagh, Ireland, was sent as apostolic delegate to Canada in 1877. As winter approached, he applied for and received permission to go to the United States for reasons of health. Propaganda asked him to use the occasion of his visit to conduct an investigation of the American Church. Word of his coming for this purpose had already reached the United States by late November.[52] His visit coincided with a turning point in the history of both the American and the universal Church.

C. Gibbons' Appointment to Baltimore and Conroy's Visitation

In April, 1876, Archbishop Bayley of Baltimore requested of Rome the appointment of a coadjutor archbishop and especially recommended for the post James Gibbons, Bishop of Richmond and Vicar Apostolic of North Carolina. The bishops of the Province of Baltimore seconded this request and placed Gibbons first on their *terna*. Six of the other ten archbishops submitted their opinions and all favored Gibbons. Then Bishop Becker of Wilmington, whose name was third on the list and who may have ambitioned the post, wrote Propaganda that Gibbons was too young and not learned enough "to occupy the primatial See of North America" and that he had held unorthodox views both of the Syllabus of Errors and of papal infallibility at the First Vatican Council. Cardinal Alessandro Franchi, Prefect of Propaganda, drew up the *ponenza* for the congregation. In regard to Becker's accusations, he reminded the cardinals that the bishop had brought similar unsubstantiated charges against Spalding. An archival note on Gibbons' role at the council banished all fears of his orthodoxy, even if it did not heighten his reputation for theological acumen. "Monsig. Gibbons in 1870", it said, "was irreprehensible. He did not sign the postulate *against* [the definition of papal infallibility]: he was always favorable; he never spoke". Although other bishops expressed reservations about Gibbons, he was the preferred candidate of Bayley and had the support of most of the other archbishops, including McCloskey. Propaganda, therefore, nominated Gibbons as coadjutor on May 7, 1877, and Pius IX appointed him on May 25.[53]

---

[52] AAB 73 I 13, O'Connell to Gibbons, Rome, Nov. 26, 1877.

[53] APF, Acta, 245 (1877), 55ʳ–61ᵛ, Franchi Ponenza, Apr. 1877; John Tracy Ellis: *The Life of James Cardinal Gibbons: Archbishop of Baltimore, 1834–1921*, 2 vols. Milwaukee 1952, I, 152–159. For some of the letters which expressed reservations, see APF, SCAmerCent., 27 (1876–1877), 326ʳ–333ʳ.

Before Gibbons had even arrived in Baltimore, however, Bayley died on October 3 and Gibbons automatically succeeded to the see. To obtain his pallium and the apostolic briefs, he dispatched to Rome as his procurator Denis J. O'Connell, a Richmond priest who had just returned to the United States after his ordination in Rome earlier that year. Gibbons had planned his investiture for February 10, 1878, when he received word three days before that Pius IX had died. Though he considered postponing the ceremony, he followed the advice of Cardinal McCloskey and held the investiture as planned. Present for it were twelve other bishops, including Conroy, whom Gibbons invited at the suggestion of Michael Augustine Corrigan, Bishop of Newark.[54] Gibbons thus assumed the leadership of the nation's oldest see on the eve of the pontificate of Leo XIII. Both would greatly influence the American Church, a vignette of which Conroy's visitation provided at the dawn of this new epoch.

The American bishops were sensitive about Roman visitors, not only because of the nativist riots which had accompanied Archbishop Gaetano Bedini's visit in 1853,[55] but also because they cherished a relative degree of autonomy from Rome and deemed themselves competent to keep the Holy See faithfully informed of their own affairs. Perhaps to counter possible negative influences on Conroy, Gibbons had his young friend, O'Connell, accompany the bishop. Conroy set out in February, 1878, visited Cincinnati and St. Louis, made a rapid tour of the west and arrived in San Francisco on March 23. For the next month he remained in California, where he received additional, unspecified instructions from Propaganda. He ended his visitation in late April or early May.[56]

If Gibbons' intention in having O'Connell accompany Conroy was to prevent an unfavorable report from the bishop, his plan was only partially successful. Much of Conroy's report would have aroused the anger of the American bishops. He first noted, that, while the Church in the United States, had made remarkable progress, it was heavily in debt. This gave rise to four problems. First, the clergy were constantly asking the faithful for money. Second, "in the selection of bishops priority is given to financial, rather than pastoral, abilities ... Whenever there is a deliberation to choose a candidate for the episcopacy, the bishops of a province feel constrained to seek, at all costs, a man skilled in financial administration. Indeed, it has too often happened that the most valued gifts in a candidate proposed to the Holy See were properly those of a banker, and not of a Pas-

---

[54] Gerald P. FOGARTY: *The Vatican and the Americanist Crisis: Denis J. O'Connell, American Agent in Rome, 1885–1903*, Roma 1974, pp. 16–25; ELLIS: *Gibbons*, I, 173.

[55] Cf. James P. CONNELLY: *The Visit of Archbishop Gaetano Bedini to the United States of America (June, 1853–February, 1854)*, Roma 1960.

[56] FOGARTY: *Vatican*, p. 26.

tor of Souls." Third, bishops frequently used the same criterion for choosing priests for a given church. Fourth, one bishop, at least, established an ecclesiastical bank, from which he loaned out the deposits to churches of his diocese at rates of interest higher than he paid his depositors.

The feeling toward the Church was mixed. On the one hand, anti-Catholicism was on the wane with most citizens. "Protestantism," said Conroy, "as a doctrinal system in America is dead and buried". The American people were basically unreligious and spiritually starved. On the other hand, there was political tension. The Catholic Church was regarded as a political force in America. Americans tended to view Catholics as foreigners and "parasites in the glorious Republic, having come from Ireland, Germany, Italy, and other nations in order to fatten themselves from the riches of America". Furthermore, they were thought "blindly [to] submit themselves to the direction of the Church even in political matters, and that consequently they come to the ballot box not to promote the interests of the country, but to support the designs of the clergy ...". The previous January, Conroy had met with Charles W. Eliot, President of Harvard University, who spoke of the attempt to unite Protestant denominations by laying aside doctrinal differences and told the bishop that President Grant was engaged in "an attempt to unite the political factions in a social war against the Church to the profit of the Republican party".

Prudence was, therefore, necessary in the Church to prevent the outbreak of anti-Catholicism and Conroy thought the bishops had exercised this with "great dexterity". Yet there was a danger in this. "In order to demonstrate that Catholics are good Americans", he said, "some would shape the Church along American lines. The latter claim that the disciplinary customs of the Church in other countries and even the dispositions of canon law do not apply to them; and they affect a kind of ecclesiastical independence which, if the faith were to fail among the clergy or the people, would not be without damage to the very unity of the Church". This, indeed, would be the interpretation placed by the Holy See upon Americanism, the movement at the end of the century in which Gibbons, Ireland, and O'Connell played major roles.

Conroy had also received instructions to investigate the possibility of appointing an apostolic delegate to the hierarchy of the United States. In his report, he listed the nineteen archbishops and bishops he consulted and he noted that he had interviewed several priests. He concluded that, while only a few bishops thought the delegation was necessary, none would oppose it. But it was essential that the delegate appointed not be an Italian. If an American could not be appointed, it would be better if the delegation were not permanent.

The establishment of a delegation, said the bishop, would help alleviate one of the problems which had brought him to the United States – the strained relations between bishops and priests. Although he singularly praised Gibbons for the harmony which existed in the Archdiocese of Baltimore, he was critical of the situation elsewhere. He summed up the complaints of the clergy under two headings: first, the manner in which bishops were selected, and second, the failure of bishops to respect the provisions of canon law in regard to the rights of priests. According to the Second Plenary Council, bishops were to send to their metropolitan or archbishop as well as to Propaganda triennial *ternae* or lists of three names of those eligible for the episcopate; when a see was vacant, the bishops of the province in which the vacancy existed were to meet and decide on a *terna* to be sent to Rome.[57] The secrecy surrounding these proceedings, he reported, and the consultation of bishops only resulted in priests saying "it is enough ... to cast a glance at the American Episcopate! Of the total number of 68 Bishops, there are hardly ten distinguished in talent of any kind. The others hardly approach a decent mediocrity, and in theological knowledge they do not reach even mediocrity!" To remedy this in part, Conroy proposed giving pastors a consultative voice in the selection of a bishop.

Treating the complaint about the mode of procedure in disciplinary cases, Conroy asserted that neither bishops nor priests appealed to the legislation of the Second Plenary Council in its entirety, but only to those sections which supported their own cases. The priests did not argue against episcopal authority, but they did say that a bishop should not remove them from their missions without cause. Conroy, therefore, proposed that Propaganda devise some practical procedure for clerical discipline.[58]

Conroy's relation of his visit virtually provided the Holy See with its American agenda for the remainder of the century. It is doubtful, however, if his report actually influenced Propaganda's next step in regard to clerical discipline. In 1878, the congregation issued an *Instructio* on clerical trials. It decreed that every bishop was to appoint, preferably in a diocesan synod, an investigating commission of five or at least three priests, trained in canon law, to analyze all the evidence, collect testimony, examine witnesses, and help the bishop reach a decision. In order to remove a rector of a mission against his will, the bishop had to have the advice of at least three members of this commission. If an appeal was to be made, the metropolitan or senior suffragan was to proceed in the same manner, and his investigating commission was to have at hand the records of the trial in the first instance.[59]

---

[57] *Concilii Plenarii Baltimorensis II ... Decreta*, nos. 101–107, pp. 69–74.

[58] APF, SCAmerCent, 36 (1882), 194^r–217^r, [George Conroy], Relazione sullo stato presente della Chiesa Cattolica negli Stati Uniti dell' America.

[59] Acta Sanctae Sedis 12 (1879) 88–89.

The American bishops viewed this new system as undermining their authority. Bishop Bernard McQuaid, therefore, petitioned Propaganda to clarify whether a bishop needed to consult his investigating commission before removing a rector. The congregation replied that a bishop must always listen to his commission, but that its vote in such cases was only consultative while the definitive decision was reserved to the bishop alone.[60] For the time being, at least, the American bishops had preserved their authority.

The problem of clerical discipline was only one of those reported by Conroy and the *Instructio* of 1878 solved only part of it, for Rome continued to receive numerous appeals from priests. Yet it was a sign of things to come as American ecclesiastical law became increasingly Roman in origin. Many of the other issues Conroy discussed – financial difficulties, election of bishops, the appointment of an apostolic delegate – would contribute to the Holy See's decision to convoke a third plenary council of the Church in the United States. But the prelates who took a leading role at that council were a different group than those who had attended the Vatican Council.

Other New Leaders

When Gibbons was elevated to Baltimore, the See of Richmond became vacant. In December, 1877, Gibbons convened his suffragans. They recommended for Richmond John J. Keane, assistent rector of St. Patrick's Church in Washington, Monsignor Francis Silas Chatard, Rector of the American College, and Henry Northrop, a priest of Charleston. On the grounds that he preferred not to see Chatard removed from the American College, Gibbons strongly recommended Keane to Cardinal Franchi. Late in December, however, he received information from O'Connell, then in Rome, that Franchi favored Chatard. The death of Pius IX caused a further delay in making the appointment, and, in the sequel, Leo XIII appointed Chatard as Bishop of Vincennes. Finally, on April 13, 1878, Cardinal Giovanni Simeoni, who had succeeded Franchi as Prefect of Propaganda, informed Gibbons that the new pope had named Keane as Bishop of Richmond.[61] Born in Ireland, raised in the United States, and educated at the Sulpician seminary in Baltimore, Keane would later emerge as a national ecclesiastical leader,

---

[60] ZWIERLEIN: *McQuaid,*, II, 177; Gerald P. FOGARTY: *American Conciliar Legislation, Hierarchical Structure and Priest–Bishop Tension*, in: The Jurist 32 (1972) 403–405.

[61] Patrick H. AHERN: *The Life of John J. Keane, Educator and Archbishop*, Milwaukee 1955, pp. 30–32. See also FOGARTY: *Vatican*, pp. 30–31.

when he became the first Rector of the Catholic University of America. His close personal friendship with Gibbons further enhanced his importance.

Other shifts in the hierarchy were necessitated not only by replacement of aging or transferred prelates, but by particular problems of certain dioceses. In his report, Conroy had made an allusion to the financial crisis in Cincinnati, where Archbishop Purcell had established his own bank for the diocese. His brother Edward Purcell's management of the bank increased the diocesan debt to over $1,000,000. Early in 1879, Purcell asked to resign his see, giving as reasons his desire to rest and the financial situation of the diocese. On April 24, 1879, the bishops of the Province of Cincinnati submitted the *terna* of Bishops Edward Fitzgerald of Little Rock, one of the two bishops who in 1870 had voted *non placet* to the solemn definition of papal infallibility, McQuaid of Rochester and Chatard. When both Fitzgerald and McQuaid withdrew their names from consideration, Cardinal Franchi asked for a new list. Construing this letter as Propaganda's rejection of Chatard, the bishops drew up a new list of Bishops William H. Elder of Natchez, William G. McCloskey of Louisville, and Fitzgerald, even though the latter had withdrawn his name. Elder had actually already been named the Coadjutor Archbishop of San Francisco, but, after the apostolic briefs were sent, had declined the position; he, therefore, remained theoretically the administrator of Natchez, since the see was officially vacant. In the poll of the nation's archbishops about Cincinnati, however, all preferred Elder except Henni of Milwaukee who favored McCloskey. Despite the confusion on the *ternae*, Propaganda nominated Elder and on January 11, 1880, Leo XIII appointed him Archbishop of Cincinnati.[62] Elder would be a gentle neutral in the disputes which were to come. Moreover, with Purcell's passing from the ecclesiastical scene, only Kenrick remained as a link with the nascent days of the American collegial tradition, nurtured by Bishop John England and by Kenrick's brother, Francis, Archbishop of Baltimore.[63]

Elder's appointment was basically routine housekeeping, necessitated by Purcell's advanced age of seventy-nine and his financial mismanagement. It was the type of issue emphasized in Conroy's report and which Propaganda would use in convoking the Third Plenary Council. But there were more substantive issues. Conroy had mentioned the danger of the independent spirit of some American Catholics, but he said nothing about the specific disagreement among the bishops

---

[62] APF, Acta, 247 (1879), 541^r–545^r, Bartolini Ponenza, Dec., 1879; ELLIS: *Gibbons*, I, 190-191. On the failure of Purcell's bank, see M. Edmund HUSSEY: *The 1878 Financial Failure of Archbishop Purcell*, in: The Cincinnati Historical Society Bulletin 36 (1978) 7–41.

[63] Cf. Archives of the English College (UND microfilm), James Whitfield to Nicholas Wiseman, Baltimore, June 6, 1833; see also FOGARTY: *Church Councils*, pp. 91–92.

themselves on this very issue. Nor did he allude to the ethnic tension which was so much a part of American Catholic life. Between his visitation and the council, however, there began to appear many of the signs of the later division among the hierarchy: tensions between ethnic groups and conflicts of personalities.

The tension among ethnic groups would last well into the twentieth century, but an example of it occurred in 1878. At that time, Archbishop Henni of Milwaukee asked for a coadjutor. He submitted a *terna* consisting of Bishops Michael Heiss of LaCrosse, Joseph Dwenger, C.PP.S, of Fort Wayne, and Francis Xavier Krautbauer of Green Bay. He also distributed his *terna* to the other archbishops. In the meantime, the English-speaking priests of his archdiocese charged that he was attempting to perpetuate a German influence in the province. Gibbons, who received these complaints, made no comment on the *terna* until he consulted with some of the other archbishops, but he felt that Bishop Spalding of Peoria, might well be placed second or third on the *terna*, since he spoke fluent German. Propaganda, as it turned out, rejected Henni's nominations because he had failed to consult with his suffragans in accordance with the legislation of the Second Plenary Council.[64]

On September 4, 1878, Henni held a meeting of his suffragans. Bishop Thomas Grace of St. Paul later informed Gibbons that only with the greatest difficulty did he succeed in getting Spalding's name on the list, even though the Bishop of Peoria enjoyed the respect of both German and English-speaking Catholics. In the final vote, the bishops dropped Dwenger's name and submitted a *terna* of Heiss, Krautbauer, and Spalding. A group of Milwaukee priests then began urging the other archbishops to support Spalding's candidacy. Gibbons himself wrote Cardinal Simeoni, Prefect of Propaganda, urging the appointment. In May, 1879, Simeoni informed Henni that the cardinals of the congregation favored Spalding because he was young and American-born, but, in deference to Henni, had postponed a decision. If Henni found Spalding unacceptable, he was to submit another *terna*. In the meantime, both Spalding and Krautbauer removed themselves from consideration. In the fall, Henni submitted his third *terna*, consisting of Heiss, Kilian C. Flasch, Rector of the Milwaukee seminary, and Bishop James O'Connor, Vicar Apostolic of the Nebraska Territory. Grace, the senior suffragan, opposed Heiss for his poor knowledge of English and wanted to drop the whole *terna* in favor of another native American, Bishop Becker of Wilmington, a candidate also favored by Michael Augustine Corrigan, Bishop of Newark. Ultimately Propaganda selected Heiss as coadjutor,[65] but it is important to note that

---

[64] SWEENEY: *Spalding*, p. 114.
[65] APF, Acta, 248 (1880), 105ʳ–108ʳ, Franzelin Ponenza, Feb. 1880; SWEENEY: *Spalding*, pp. 115–117; ELLIS: *Gibbons*, I, 339.

at this point the congregation, or at least Cardinal Simeoni, would have preferred to appoint a native-born American. But the question was: what was an American?

Ethnic tension was not the only problem complicating an answer to the question. The American-born and English-speaking prelates and people disagreed among themselves as to how American the Church should be, as Conroy had already indicated in his report. A prime example of this disagreement was the appointment in 1880 of a coadjutor to Cardinal McCloskey. As early as 1874, before becoming a cardinal, McCloskey had obtained permission from Pius IX to nominate a coadjutor, but he had deferred action. In 1876, he spoke openly of it and at that time Bishop Corrigan of Newark was mentioned as a candidate. Only on April 7, 1880, however, did McCloskey finally assemble his suffragans to nominate a successor. According to the notes of Corrigan, the secretary at the meeting, the criteria for a coadjutor were sound doctrine, integrity, a "knowledge of languages, and experience and familiarity with the style of dealing with the Roman Curia".[66]

The terna listed in order the names of Bishops Patrick Lynch of Charleston, John Loughlin of Brooklyn, and Corrigan. McCloskey personally favored Lynch and indicated his preference to the other archbishops. In his letter to Propaganda accompanying the list, he drew attention to Lynch's skill in restoring the churches and other property in his diocese after the Civil War. But then he added a confidential postcript saying that "if the Holy Father, either for reason of age, or for the needs of the diocese, or for any other motive, did not believe Monsignor Lynch, the first candidate, was suitable for the post", he preferred Corrigan. In response, Simeoni queried McCloskey whether "any other motive" referred to Lynch's role during the Civil War in defending slavery and in attempting to gain Vatican recognition of the Confederacy. The prefect was concerned that the choice of Lynch might alienate the people of the North and the government.[67]

McCloskey assured Simeoni that there was nothing to fear in Lynch's appointment because the spirit of antagonism between North and South had long since disappeared. Lynch also received the firm support of Kenrick and Purcell, which may not have helped his cause in Rome. But he also met opposition from the United States. Archbishop Alemany of San Francisco opposed him both because of his age and because of the fear that his creditors in Charleston might go to civil court against him. Propaganda also heard that Lynch was not too popular with his clergy and it was of the opinion that most of McCloskey's suffragans op-

---

[66] Quoted in Robert Emmett CURRAN: *Michael Augustine Corrigan and the Shaping of Conservative Catholicism in America, 1878–1902*, New York 1978, p. 56.

[67] AANY, Simeoni to McCloskey, Rome, June 23, 1880.

posed the choice but did not have the courage to speak out openly. Lynch, for his part, was eager for the appointment for it would give him a chance to satisfy his creditors from the funds he could collect in New York. With this information before it, the congregation turned to Loughlin, about whom none of the archbishops had said anything except Alemany who thought that at sixty-two he was too old. The congregation was then left with the third name on the list, Michael Augustine Corrigan. The only oppostion to him, said Cardinal Enea Sbarretti, who drew up the *ponenza,* came from those who thought him "troppo Romano".

In his comments on the candidates, McCloskey had cited Corrigan for his "spirito Romano" and for "a certain familiarity with the Roman manner of conducting affairs, which would be of no small usefulness in my coadjutor". Here was the ideal candidate for Propaganda and one who possessed the quality it had sought in favoring Spalding for the coadjutorship of Milwaukee. Corrigan was born in 1839 in Newark of Irish immigrant parents and had been in the first class to live at the American College in Rome. On September 21, the congregation met and nominated Corrigan as Coadjutor of New York and on September 26, Leo XIII appointed him.[68] Four days later, Simeoni wrote McCloskey informing him of the choice of Corrigan "according to your desires".[69]

In retrospect, it is difficult to determine if Simeoni's reference to McCloskey's "desires" indicated that the American cardinal had shifted his support from Lynch to Corrigan. Ella B. Edes, whose information on this and other occasions proved to be surprisingly accurate, wrote Corrigan on September 28 saying nothing about McCloskey's having ceased to support Lynch and stating that Propaganda had rejected him because of his age, health, poor administration of his diocese, and especially his role during the war. Moreover, she reported, many bishops had written in support of Corrigan over Lynch.[70] The appointment of Corrigan brought into a prominent position an American-born, English-speaking bishop whose Roman leanings ran contrary to the Americanizing tendencies of bishops such as Gibbons and Ireland. The face of the American hierarchy had changed drastically since the close of the Vatican Council and it would change yet more in the few years remaining before the calling of the Baltimore Council, with the elevation of Chicago to an archdiocese, the appointment of a Coadjutor Archbishop of San Francisco, and, as will be seen, the appointment of a new Archbishop of Philadelphia.

Chicago presented a complicated situation. In 1867, Bishop James Duggan began manifesting erratic behavior and a faction of priests grew up in opposition to

---

[68] APF, Acta 248 (1880), Ponenza on New York Coadjutorship, 330H^r–330L^v, 331^r.
[69] AANY, Simeoni to McCloskey, Rome, Sept. 3, 1880.
[70] AANY, Edes to Corrigan, Rome, Sept. 28, 1880, in CURRAN: *Corrigan*, p. 58.

him. In 1869, he went hopelessly insane and was placed by Kenrick in an asylum near St. Louis. To administer the diocese, Thomas Foley, a priest of Baltimore, was appointed coadjutor. His death on January 11, 1879, revived some of the old factional disputes, which had arisen in part from a desire to be independent of the domination of St. Louis, of which Chicago was a suffragan.[71] On April 16, 1879, the bishops of the Province of St. Louis met to petition the Holy See to make Chicago an archdiocese and to name Duggan to a titular see with a pension provided from Chicago. They also submitted a *terna* consisting of Bishops Patrick Feehan of Nashville, James O'Connor, Vicar Apostolic of Nebraska, and Spalding. Gibbons agreed with this order of names, but expressed curious reservations about Spalding. Whereas he had urged his appointment for Milwaukee earlier that same year, now he believed the Bishop of Peoria lacked the maturity and experience for Chicago. But Spalding, in any case, had withdrawn his name from consideration. Propaganda, therefore, decided on August 16, 1880, to accept the petition of the bishops of the Province of St. Louis by making Duggan a titular bishop, elevating Chicago to an archdiocese, and naming Feehan the first archbishop.[72] The elevation of Chicago, only ninety miles south of Milwaukee, indicated the growing importance of the Church in the mid-west and brought the total number of metropolitan provinces to twelve.

The appointment of a coadjutor to aging Archbishop Joseph Sadoc Alemany of San Francisco presented different complications. Elder, as was seen, was originally chosen coadjutor in 1879, but declined the appointment to the sprawling archdiocese, almost half the size of France. Alemany again summoned his two suffragans, the Bishops of Monterey-Los Angeles and Grass Valley (title later changed to Sacramento) to draw up a *terna*, this time consisting of Bishops Chatard of Vincennes and Spalding and of Father Patrick W. Riordan of Chicago. On January 15, 1883, however, Propaganda delayed action in order to obtain more information from Alemany about Chatard and Riordan. Alemany replied that he felt Chatard was not suitable for the position and he preferred Riordan. Spalding, in the meantime, had withdrawn his name and supported the nomination of Riordan, a contemporary of his at Louvain. Propaganda's only reservation about Riordan was his involvement in the opposition of Chicago priests

---

[71] James P. GAFFEY: *Patterns of Ecclesiastical Authority: The Problem of the Chicago Succession, 1865–1881*, in: Church History 42 (1973) 257–270; see also GAFFEY: *Citizen of No Mean City: Archbishop Patrick Riordan of San Francisco (1841–1914)*, Wilmington 1976, pp. 24–39.

[72] APF, Acta, 248 (1880), 254ʳ-257ᵛ, 265ʳ-266ʳ, Teodolfo Mertel Ponenza, Aug. 1880. Gibbons also had reservations about making Chicago an archdiocese since it would have only two suffragans, Peoria and Alton. Mertel pointed out, however, that San Francisco had only two and that Santa Fe had none, since the vicariates apostolic of Arizona and Colorado were not, properly speaking, dioceses. See also GAFFEY: *Riordan*, pp. 51–55.

to Bishop Duggan, but his role was so minor, it decided, that he could not be considered a leader of a faction. In June, the congregation, therefore, named Riordan Coadjutor of San Francisco.[73] Riordan would later be a minor figure in the already emerging liberal party and would become involved in a painful episode regarding his friend and promoter, John Lancaster Spalding. But his appointment to San Francisco was of further significance and illustrated the heterogeneity of the American Church. Spanish in origin, the area was now English-speaking. It was not the locus for the ethnic tensions which characterized the appointment of a coadjutor to Milwaukee in 1880 and again in 1890. San Francisco was then the only major city in what was to become in the twentieth century the nation's most populous state.

The fourteen years between the First Vatican Council and the Third Plenary Council of Baltimore were years of dramatic growth in the Church and change in the hierarchy. Of the seven archdioceses existing in 1870, six had either new ordinaries or coadjutors by 1884, although, as will be seen, Kenrick would come out of retirement after Ryan was named Archbishop of Philadelphia. Of the four archdioceses established in 1875, Milwaukee and Philadelphia had new ordinaries and Santa Fe had a coadjutor by 1884. Of the ten men elevated to archiepiscopal rank since 1870, four had not been bishops at the time of the Vatican Council: Corrigan of New York, Ryan of St. Louis and later of Philadelphia, Riordan of San Francisco, and Charles Seghers of Oregon City. Of the three principal new bishops, Ireland, Spalding, and Keane, only the first attended the Council, as the procurator for his bishop. A new generation was, therefore, taking over the leadership of the American Church.

Behind these routine changes, however, a pattern was beginning to emerge, which became more evident during the next twenty years. First, Propaganda seems at this time to have been oblivious of the ethnic diversity of the United States or at least to have preferred appointing native-American candidates to sees which experienced a conflict of nationalities. On this point it would change in the coming years. Second, in the case of Corrigan at least, the congregation saw Roman training and orientation as desirable qualities in an episcopal candidate. This too would become a growing trend, as Roman education was seen as guaranteeing loyalty to Rome. Finally, related to the desire to appoint Roman-trained candidates was the trend for Roman officials to take a more active role in the American Church, through issuing legislation, of which the instructions on parochial schools and on clerical discipline were but the beginning. These and other problems, which the Holy See recognized as existing in the American Church, precipitated its call for the bishops to gather in the Third Plenary Council.

---

[73] APF, Acta, 252 (1883), 503^r–505^v, Relazione; GAFFEY: *Riordan*, pp. 55–56.

CHAPTER II

THE THIRD PLENARY COUNCIL AND THE DIVISION OF
THE HIERARCHY

A. THE THIRD PLENARY COUNCIL (1884)

The First Vatican Council had seemed to sound the death knell for the American tradition of collegiality. Although the American hierarchy had gathered at its own initiative in nine national councils between 1829 and 1866, after 1870 it made no plans to hold another one. But a series of factors led the Holy See, for the first time, to take the initiative and convoke the American bishops in the Third Plenary Council of Baltimore in 1884. First, there was the continued growth of the Church through immigration. By 1880, Catholics in the United States numbered 6,259,000 out of a total white population of 43, 402, 970. During the decade of the 1880s, moreover, immigration increased still more, with immigrants from German-speaking nations for the first time outnumbering the Irish.[1] Second, there was the problem of religious pluralism, which the Holy See was slow to understand. Since many American Catholics belonged to the working class, they banded together with members of other faiths to join the Knights of Labor, a forerunner of contemporary labor unions, and other secret societies. Furthermore, to educate and preserve the faith of Catholic children, Rome, prompted by suggestions from the United States, remained sceptical of public schools and saw parochial schools as a practical necessity, as it had already indicated in its *Instructio* of 1876.

A third factor was the perennial problem of priest-bishop tension, as the Holy See continued to be plagued by appeals from American priests against their bishops. Despite the Vatican's legislation on clerical discipline in 1878, the bishops were adamant in maintaining their rights over priests. Early in 1882, Gibbons advised Archbishop Elder, who was about to convoke the Fourth Provincial Council of Cincinnati, to "assert the broad principle that priests, even Rectors may be removed without trial by Bishops from one place to another whenever in his judgement the interests of religion call for such a removal.... We cannot too

---

[1] Gerald SHAUGHNESSY: *Has the Immigrant Kept the Faith?: A Study of Immigration and Catholic Growth in the United States, 1790–1920*, New York 1925, pp. 149–165.

much insist on the rights of Bishops on this point, as they are so often called in question, & the exercise of this right is essential to the discipline of the Church".[2]

A fourth reason may have been Rome's recognition that the bishops themselves were divided on the issue of holding a council. In 1880, Propaganda consulted Gibbons about holding a council, but he, like most of the eastern bishops, believed a decision should be postponed for some years. In August, 1881, however, Heiss wrote him that "as far as I know the Western Bishops, I think there will be scarcely one opposed to it".[3] But a fifth factor may well have been determinative in Rome's decision to convoke a council – it wished to test the loyalty of the American bishops, since many had opposed the definition of papal infallibility. This it would do by bringing the American Church more directly under Roman supervision.

For some time Rome had been making overtures to American bishops about a council. On March 26, 1883, Bishop Richard Gilmour of Cleveland wrote Gibbons that during a recent visit to Rome, he was questioned about "our difficulties in the church and our position in the civil relations of Catholics". He was "also consulted and asked to write out views on the questions of a Legate and a Plenary Council ...". Gilmour replied that an agent in Rome, preferably a bishop well-versed in American affairs, be appointed instead of a legate who would live in the United States. He felt that a council, though necessary, could not be held for at least three years. But he warned Gibbons that the American hierarchy had to take immediate action, for Propaganda was "determined to send here a Legate 'to see with their own eyes'. This may be delayed until an agent would be tried from here there, if proper remonstrance be made; if neglected then he will come".[14] Gilmour perfectly expressed the tradition of the American bishops, which included not only independence of the lower clergy but also relative autonomy from Rome. A papal legate could destroy this tradition.

By June, 1883, however, Propaganda summoned the American archbishops to Rome for meetings in November to discuss the agenda for a forthcoming council. Bishop Keane of Richmond, who was then in Rome, assured Gibbons that the call was "issued in a spirit of the most entire friendship towards the American hierarchy, and through the desire to have all their relations with their priests and with the Holy See placed on the footing that will be the most advantageous & agreeable to our Hierarchy". Keane, too, had discussed the issue of appointing an

---

[2] AACi, Gibbons to Elder, Baltimore, Feb. 1, 1882.

[3] Heiss to Gibbons, Milwaukee, Aug. 26, 1881, in ELLIS: *Gibbons*, I, 204–205.

[4] AAB 77 E 7, Gilmour to Gibbons, Cleveland, Mar. 26; 1883. For the Roman motivations for calling a council, see Thomas T. MCAVOY: *The Great Crisis in American Catholic History: 1895–1900*, Chicago 1957, pp. 10–11.

American agent in Rome, but reported that "they never will recognize it when it is advanced as a substitute for the appointment of a Papal Delegate".[5]

Before the archbishops arrived, the cardinals of Propaganda held their own meetings on October 1, 6, and 8, 1883. For their discussions, they had at hand Conroy's report on his visit, the instructions on clerical discipline and parochial schools, and other material relating to these. They also had the *ponenza*, which Cardinal Johann Baptist Franzelin, S. J., had prepared. It was sprinkled with references to increasing the Romanization of the American Church. In regard to seminaries, for instance, Franzelin praised those in Baltimore, Philadelphia, Troy, New York, and Milwaukee, but singled out the Philadelphia seminary as "preferable for Roman instruction". While many of the priests were poorly educated, he continued, some in Baltimore, Boston, New York, Philadelphia, and Cincinnati were distinguished for their learning and piety, but those of the last two sees were outstanding because among them "graduates of Rome are in good number ...". Some American bishops, however, complained that alumni of the American College in Rome ambitioned the best assignments, were disloyal to the Holy See, and frequently caused difficulty by recounting "scandals and stories to the discredit of the Roman Curia". On the subject of episcopal support of the college, the cardinal noted that, while the Archdiocese of Baltimore had two burses for students, Gibbons preferred to send his students to St. Mary's Seminary in Baltimore, operated by the Sulpicians.[6]

Turning to other matters, Franzelin reported that the instruction on clerical discipline "was received with joy by the priests and was greeted by the more advanced as a magna charta which put an end to their slavery".[7] He also brought up the issues of parochial schools, the conversion of the Negroes, and the problem of Italian immigration. Then he broached the topic which Propaganda officials had already discussed with Gilmour and Keane, namely the establishment of an apostolic delegation. For Franzelin, this was not only useful but necessary if the Holy See was to have precise information on episcopal candidates, to know better both the secular and religious clergy, to be informed on the relations between priests and bishops, and to encourage bishops to proceed according to canon law and thus give priests less cause to complain. Gilmour's suggestion that Rome accept an American agent could not be seriously considered, the cardinal thought, for it implied that information from a delegate in the United States would take more time to reach Rome than information from the United States to an agent in Rome.

---

[5] AAB 77 H 8, Keane to Gibbons, Rome, June 25, 1883.

[6] APF, Acta, 252 (1883), 1088^r–1089^v, Franzelin Ponenza, Oct., 1883; for Conroy's report and other material, see *ibid.*, 1132^r–1197^v.

[7] *Ibid.*, 1092^v.

Furthermore, in what was a surprising revelation in light of later developments, Spalding was reported to favor a delegate and had said there would be little opposition to the appointment. Franzelin concluded by saying that the coming plenary council provided an opportunity for appointing a delegate and that an American bishop, favorable to Rome, could be appointed.[8]

Franzelin's excursus on establishing an apostolic delegation has to be distinguished from appointing a delegate to preside over the council. On August 26, 1883, Leo XIII had already confirmed Bishop Luigi Sepiacci, an Augustinian consultor to Propaganda, as apostolic delegate for the council and to enhance his authority he was to be elevated to the rank of archbishop.[9] When the Americans learned of this, as will be seen, they protested and the appointment was withdrawn. But in the matter of a permanent delegation, the congregation decided not to follow Franzelin's recommendation and not even to allow the archbishops officially to know that the matter had been discussed. On other issues Propaganda drew up a list of chapters for presentation to the archbishops.[10]

On November 13, 1883, the archbishops began their meetings with the officials of Propaganda. All the metropolitan provinces of the United States, except San Francisco, were represented. Gibbons had with him as an adviser Denis O'Connell. The Americans were confronted with a series of proposals distinctly Roman in origin,[11] but succeeded in recasting these in an American vein. Where the cardinals spoke of cathedral chapters in American dioceses with irremovable members whose consent would be necessary for temporal affairs, the archbishops successfully substituted diocesan consultors removable by the bishops. In this draft proposal, however, the bishop needed to have his consultors' consent in financial matters – a point to be controverted at the council. The Americans also agreed to accept the appointment of a certain number of irremovable rectors as had been done in England. They likewise accepted the proposal that each diocese

---

[8] *Ibid.*, 1106ʳ–1108ᵛ.

[9] *Ibid.*, 1080ʳ, Audience, Aug. 26, 1883.

[10] *Ibid.*, 1109ʳ–1112ᵛ, General Congregation, Oct. 1, 6, 8, 1883.

[11] The document presented to the American archbishops was *Capita praecipua quae Emi Cardinales S.C. de Propaganda Fide censuerunt a Rmis. Archiepiscopis et Episcopis Foederatorum Statuum A.S. Romae congregatis praeparanda esse pro futuro Concilio.* After the meetings, a revised version was printed: *Capita proposita et examinata in collationibus, quas coram nonnullis Emis. Cardinalibus Sacrae Congregationis de Propaganda Fide ad praeparandum futurum Concilium plenarium habuerunt Rmi. Archiepiscopi et Episcopi foederatorum Statuum Americae Septemtrionalis Romae congregati.* The Minutes of these meetings were printed as *Relatio Collationum quas Romae coram S.C. de P.F. Praefecto habuerunt Archiepiscopi pluresque Episcopi Statuum Foederatorum Americae, 1883.* An English translation is given in *Minutes of Roman Meetings Preparatory to the III Plenary Council of Baltimore,* in: The Jurist 11 (1951) 121–133, 302–312, 417–424, 538–546.

establish a curia or court, which essentially developed out of the *Instructio* of 1878.

Propaganda also presented a chapter containing a blanket condemnation of secret societies. Gibbons and the majority of the Americans, however, had this redrafted to allow each bishop, with competent theological advice, first to examine suspect societies and, in doubtful cases, appeal to the Holy See. The Americans offered no disagreement to the schema on parochial schools, which essentially embodied the instruction of 1876. Some of Propaganda's proposals, however, illustrated the European rather than American concern of the Church. The Roman origin of these schemata, for instance, is indicated by the chapter *De Colonis in Americam immigrantibus* in which the congregation referred only to the care of Italians. The Americans quietly assented to the proposal and extended it to all ethnic groups.[12]

Propaganda's intention was to use the council to further Romanizing the American Church. One sign of the divergent views of the Holy See and the American hierarchy was Sepiacci's appointment as delegate. Had Baltimore enjoyed the title of primary, its archbishops would have had the canonical right to preside over a plenary council. At the previous two plenary councils, Archbishops Francis P. Kenrick and Martin J. Spalding had been respectively appointed as delegates.[13] Keane and Gilmour had earlier warned Gibbons that Propaganda seemed intent on appointing an Italian delegate. As was seen, the pope had actually appointed Sepiacci as delegate in August. Sepiacci had been present for the archbishops' meetings, but at their conclusion, his American secretary, Father Patrick A. Stanton, O.S.A., informed Gibbons of his superior's appointment. When the Americans protested the selection of an Italian, Leo XIII conceded by appointing Gibbons as delegate to preside over the council.[14]

Gibbons' appointment brought into the open some of the tension seething beneath the superficial unity of the hierarchy. Ella B. Edes wrote Corrigan, who had represented Cardinal McCloskey at the meetings, giving her reactions. She charged that Gibbons had waited until Corrigan had left Rome before representing McCloskey as unwilling to be delegate because of his ill health. Furthermore, she had met "His Grace [Gibbons] and Denis [O'Connell] marching along the Piazza di Spagna", outside the headquarters of Propaganda, and then went herself to the congregation, where she learned that Gibbons was not named "Apostolic Delegate", as he claimed, but was merely delegated to preside over the coun-

---

[12] FOGARTY: *Vatican*, pp. 40–41.
[13] FOGARTY: *Church Councils*, pp. 93–94.
[14] The letter of appointment, dated Jan. 4, 1884, is given in *Acta et Decreta* (official), pp. xx–xxii; see ELLIS: *Gibbons*, I, 217.

cil. Later, she continued, "Denis arrived on one of his exploring expeditions" and she confronted him with an Italian newspaper story about Sepiacci's rejection and Gibbons' appointment. To O'Connell's surprise that the story was public, she replied "that the Sulpitians [sic] ... had the name in Rome of being tremendous gossips". Lecturing O'Connell that she had discovered Gibbons' plot to capture the appointment after Corrigan's departure, she concluded: "I then told Denis that it was very silly of his Archbishop to go around talking in that style the more so that it was not true he knew very well he had not discovered it [Propaganda's appointment of Sepiacci] and that he had not checked it".[15] This was but the first in a series of Miss Edes' colorful comments on "His Little Grace" and "Denis". But her disclosure at this time revealed that behind the tension between Gibbons and Corrigan was a conflict between Americanization and Romanization, with the Sulpicians seen as decided opponents of the latter. Franzelin had already made a veiled allusion to this in his *ponenza* before the archbishops' meeting. It would become one of the minor themes in the developing division of the hierarchy.

That Gibbons did not enjoy the Holy See's full confidence and that there was already tension between him and Corrigan might also be indicated in the appointment of a new Archbishop of Philadelphia. In June 1883, Archbishop Wood had died. The suffragans of the province, however, failed to reach a clear consensus on any candidate on their *terna*. They nevertheless submitted their list to Propaganda which delayed any nomination in order to get the opinions of the archbishops.[16] The latter showed no enthusiasm for any of the three candidates proposed by the suffragans and, instead, mentioned three additional names: Chatard of Vincennes, Ryan of St. Louis, and Spalding of Peoria. As he had done earlier, Gibbons spoke of Spalding as a man of zeal and piety, well known in America, who "intimately understands the public spirit of the Republic". He ranked Chatard behind Spalding and said nothing of Ryan. Williams likewise, without giving his reasons, preferred Spalding to Chatard. McCloskey, however, felt neither Spalding nor Chatard had the administrative experience necessary for governing a large diocese and feared Spalding would "dominate the clergy". He therefore preferred the transfer of Ryan from the coadjutorship of St. Louis to the archbishopric of Philadelphia. Corrigan then privately wrote Propaganda saying that Kenrick would be willing to let Ryan go if he were elected to Philadelphia. The congregation met on May 27, 1884, and elected to transfer Ryan to Philadelphia.[17] Though Gibbons had been only recently appointed delegate to the

[15] AANY (UND photostat), Edes to Corrigan, Rome, Jan. 8, 1884.

[16] APF, Acta, 253 (1884), 15^r–16^r; 17^r, Pitra Ponenza, Jan., 1884.

[17] *Ibid.*, 300^r–303^r, Pitra Ponenza, May, 1884.

council, Propaganda had disregarded his preference for the Philadelphia succession. Ryan would seldom play a major role in the disputes which later divided the Church, but, when he did, he was on Corrigan's side.

In preparation for the council, Gibbons divided the schemata emanating from the Roman meetings into chapters and submitted one or more to each of the twelve metropolitan provinces for reaction. When the *relationes* or reports from the provinces were received, the schemata were then redrafted into the form in which they were discussed at the council. On November 8, 1884, 14 archbishops and coadjutor archbishops, 57 bishops, 7 abbots, and 31 superiors of religious orders processed into the Cathedral of the Assumption in Baltimore for the solemn opening of the council. Holding their private congregations or meetings at St. Mary's Seminary, about half a mile away, they remained in session until December 7. It was up to that time the largest assembly of the hierarchy the American Church had witnessed. As secretaries to the council, Gibbons appointed Denis O'Connell, Sebastian Messmer, and Henry Gabriels.

At the council, the bishops strengthened their authority beyond what was contained in the Roman schemata and, in addition, introduced new legislation. They modified still further what had originally been Propaganda's proposal of cathedral chapters and decreed that a bishop needed to seek the advice of his consultors before he could buy or sell property, disband or erect a parish, but did not need their consent.[18] When they discussed the proposal of irremovable rectors, John Ireland asked the opinion of Gibbons, who replied that the Holy See was so intent on having them that, if the council failed to legislate for them, Rome would intervene with some embarrassment to the bishops.[19] Treating clerical discipline, they wished to retain the St. Louis form, applied to the whole Church in the Second Plenary Council. But if this proved impossible, they petitioned that it be retained in those dioceses which found it difficult to implement the instruction of 1878.[20] The final aspect of priests' rights with which they dealt was episcopal elections. The council decreed that when a diocese was vacant, the consultors and irremovable rectors of the diocese should meet and draw up a *terna*. The bishops of the province were then to meet and draw up their own *terna*, after commenting on the priests' list. In the case of a metropolitan see, the two lists were still to be distributed for comment to the other archbishops.[21]

The bishops also tried to add another note to the sense of their authority – control over religious orders. Spalding, Gilmour, and Ireland proposed and succeed-

---

[18] *Acta et Decreta* (unofficial), pp. xxxiii–xxxiv, no. 20, pp. 7–8.
[19] *Ibid.*, pp. xl–xlii, xlvii–xlix, nos. 31–39, pp. 10–13.
[20] *Ibid.*, pp. lxxxviii, xci, xcviii, nos. 301, 302, pp. 100–101.
[21] *Acta et Decreta* (official), no. 15, pp. 12–13.

ed in having adopted a decree making it obligatory for religious who purchased property or erected buildings with funds raised from the faithful to vest title to the property in the name of the bishop. This decree, however, was later rejected by Rome, particularly through the influence of Cardinal Franzelin.[22]

Finally, in a series of actions designed to keep control over the domestic affairs of the Church, they modified some of Propaganda's proposals. They decreed that those cases dealing with secret societies should be submitted to a plenum of the archbishops. If the metropolitans failed to reach unanimity, the case was to be referred to Rome.[23] As will be seen shortly, this had a two-fold effect. First, unanimous consent was virtually impossible to achieve and cases still had to go to Rome. Second, the referral of such cases to the metropolitans as well as their right to comment on candidates for vacant archiepiscopal sees led them to hold annual meetings, an adaptation of the earlier collegial tradition. In regard to parochial schools, the bishops attempted to specify and limit the original Roman schema. They decreed that every parish should erect a school within two years of the council, "unless in the judgement of the bishop the building or maintenance of a school is impossible".[24] This too would prove to be a controversial point.

Finally, the bishops also introduced new legislation on topics not discussed at the Roman meetings. Their most prominent innovation was the establishment of the Catholic University of America, a project long advocated by John Lancaster Spalding. The university was originally intended as a *"seminarium principale"*, a graduate school in theology for the diocesan clergy.[25]

After the council, the decrees had to receive papal approval. To gain this, Gibbons appointed Denis O'Connell and Bishops John Moore of St. Augustine and Joseph Dwenger, C.PP.S., of Fort Wayne to see the legislation through Propaganda. They arrived in Rome in March, 1885, and were shortly after joined by Bishop Richard Gilmour of Cleveland. There were a number of controverted points, among them: the advice or consent of diocesan consultors in financial matters, the erection of parochial schools, and the role of religious. As Bishop Moore told Leo XIII on July 3, the "Bishops of America feared that too big a dose of cannon [sic] law might be given them all at once …".[26] Ultimately, the legislation on the role of diocesan consultors was allowed to stand for ten years, but in serious matters, the bishop was to consult Propaganda, while, in other cases, he had to take

---

[22] *Acta et Decreta* (unofficial), pp. xciii, xcvi, xcviii–xcix, no. 90, p. 27 and no. 271, p. 90. On this issue, see Gerald P. FOGARTY: *The Bishops versus Religious Orders: The Suppressed Decrees of the Third Plenary Council of Baltimore*, in: The Jurist 33 (1973) 384–398.

[23] *Acta et Decreta*, (unofficial), no. 259, p. 84.

[24] *Ibid.*, no. 203, p. 60.

[25] *Ibid.*, nos. 186–187, pp. 54–55.

[26] AAB 79 O 5, Moore to Gibbons, Rome, July 6, 1885.

advice of his consultors. Propaganda also refused to allow the continuation of the St. Louis form of clerical discipline.[27] Although O'Connell had urged Bishop Sepiacci, Propaganda's consultor on the decrees, not to allow the question of parochial schools to go beyond the instruction of 1875,[28] the decree adopted by the bishops was modified to allow the bishop to grant only an extension of time within which a school was to be built.[29] Finally, the decree on religious owning property was suspended until the next plenary council.

The legislation of the Third Plenary Council has governed the American Church, except as modified by the Code of Canon Law of 1918 and by developments after the Second Vatican Council, up to the present. The council seemed to express the harmony which Rome desired of the American episcopate. Yet, at best, even after passing through the grist mill of the American bishops, the decrees were American formulations of basically Roman documents. They indicated more Rome's concerns about the American Church than the issues which were actually present or developing in the American Catholic community. They did not settle the issue of priests' rights or secret societies or Catholic education. Their inefficacy was shown by the burning questions which arose within a year of the council and which began to divide the hierarchy. Even before the council, as was seen, there was tension between Gibbons and Corrigan. After the council, while the decrees were being examined Bishops Gilmour and Dwenger manifested the growing tension between the Germans and the English-speaking prelates. These two tensions, Gibbons-Corrigan and German-English-speaking would be exacerbated within a year of the council through both a conscious formation of what can be described as the liberal party, with Gibbons as the titular head, and the stand this party took on the German question, parochial schools, and the social question.

B. The Formation of the Liberal Party

The formation of the liberal party involved a series of events. These were in chronological order: the appointment of Denis O'Connell as Rector of the American College in Rome, the elevation of Gibbons to the cardinalate, the official approval of the Catholic University of America and its establishment under

---

[27] AAB 79 R 10, O'Connell to Gibbons, Rome, Sept. 11, 1885.
[28] AAB 79 I 13, O'Connell to Gibbons, Rome, April 12, 1885.
[29] APF, Acta, 254 (1885), 350ᵛ, minutes of Propaganda meeting; *Acta et Decreta* (official), no. 199, p. 104.

the rectorship of John J. Keane, and the erection of the Archdiocese of St. Paul, which brought John Ireland into the ranks of the archbishops.

The Rector of the American College held a strategic post. He frequently acted as the Roman agent for the American hierarchy, as was seen in the case of Chatard. While the archbishops were in Rome for their meetings with Propaganda in the fall of 1884, Monsignor Louis Hostlot, the rector, died. During the vacancy, Father Augustine Schulte, the young vice-rector from Philadelphia, acted as pro-rector. But immediately rumors began that Gibbons would nominate Denis O'Connell for the position. He desired formally to make the new rector the official Roman agent of the bishops, the solution which many of the American bishops preferred to an apostolic delegate. Ella B. Edes had her ear tuned to such rumors and poured out her venomous comments to Corrigan. "I hope 'our Primate' will not be allowed his choice", she wrote; "perhaps he would send O'Connell fancy! a protege of his harried old Sulpitians [sic]".[30] A week later, she was still hoping that Gibbons "is not going to be suffered to interject at will and have all the say. He is an intriguer and an ambizioso of *the first water* for all his pretended sanctity, though he and his Father Achates O'Connell were so clumsy that they were easily detected though, no doubt assisted by French Sulpitian [sic] cunning, he has succeeded pretty generally in serving his own ends". Gibbons, she thought, was being duped by "would be adulators and friends", especially "Denis O'Connell, the Sulpitians [sic], and that ass [George T.] Montgomery [later Bishop of Monterey-Los Angeles]".[31]

The rumors Miss Edes had heard were true. Immediately after returning to the United States, Gibbons attended a meeting of the executive board of the college, which submitted a *terna* to Propaganda with O'Connell's name in third place. In forwarding the list to Rome, however, Gibbons gave O'Connell his strong endorsement.[32] But in the spring, Propaganda decided to postpone a decision and left Father Schulte as pro-rector.

In the meantime, two events occurred which heightened the importance of the college and its rector. The first was the attempted confiscation of the college by the Italian government. This had occurred because at the time of the college's opening in 1859, the American bishops had not raised enough money to purchase the property outright, so that title to it was formally held by Propaganda. Early in 1884, the Italian courts ruled that all property still in Propaganda's possession was to be considered like any other part of the papal patrimony and therefore subject to confiscation. Only the mediation of the United States government pre-

---

[30] AANY (UND photostat), Edes to Corrigan, Rome, Feb. 12, 1884.
[31] *Ibid.*, Edes to Corrigan, Rome, Feb. 20, 1884.
[32] ELLIS: *Gibbons*, I, 220, 264; FOGARTY: *Vatican*, p. 45.

vented the take over of the college, although Propaganda continued to hold the title.

The second event was the formal canonical establishment of the college as a pontifical institution, delayed until this time because of lack of proper endowment. As long as the institution did not have full canonical status, the Secretary of Propaganda was juridically the rector. Although both Cardinal Simeoni, the Prefect of Propaganda, and Archbishop Domenico Jacobini, the Secretary, opposed the Americans' desire to obtain the college's canonical establishment, on October 25, 1884, Leo XIII issued the apostolic brief, *Ubi Primum*, handing over the entire administration of the college to the American bishops.[33] The bishops then discussed this at the council and published it among their decrees.[34]

With the canonical status of the college thus elevated, the post of rector became yet more important. Gibbons, previously lukewarm in regard to the college, seems to have undergone a change of mind. He instructed Dwenger to add the charge of winning the appointment of O'Connell as rector to his task of gaining Roman approval of the conciliar legislation. Immediately after his arrival in Rome, Dwenger began working on the appointment and by March had already spoken to Simeoni.[35] Only on May 7, however, did the executive board of the college meet to draw up a new *terna*. This time O'Connell's name was in first place and had the recommendation of Gibbons, Williams, Ryan, Corrigan, Spalding, and Ireland.[36] Simeoni himself drew up the *ponenza* for the rectorship. He noted that both Dwenger and Moore reported that the bishops wanted a priest as rector who was conversant with "the state and needs of the American Church" in order to prepare the students for their future ministry. O'Connell, they said, possessed the qualities necessary and, furthermore, as secretary of the council had become known to and appreciated by all the bishops. Gibbons' own letter in O'Connell's favor indicated the extent of his change of mind over the previous year. Whereas in 1884 he had mentioned O'Connell as preferable to the other candidates, in 1885 he wrote of O'Connell alone. He recalled O'Connell's distinguished career as a student in Rome, noted his work on the Third Plenary Council, where he was regarded by the theologians as their leader, though he was younger than they, and recorded his extensive knowledge of the country gained not only in pastoral work but also as the secretary to Bishop Conroy. Simeoni was deeply concerned with the attitude of the bishops toward the college. They

---

[33] Robert F. MCNAMARA: *The American College in Rome, 1855–1955*, Rochester 1956, pp. 278–285.
[34] *Acta et Decreta* (official), pp. 193–196.
[35] AAB 79 G 9, Dwenger to Gibbons, Rome, Mar. 19, 1885.
[36] AAB, Gibbons Diary, May 8, 1885.

greeted the brief canonically establishing it, he said, "with great coldness if not indifference". It was, therefore, necessary to have as rector a man of proven ability and prudence who well understood the Church in America and who could win the esteem of the bishops. This was all the more important, he concluded, because the bishops wished the new rector to represent them in Rome as their procurator. The congregation may have also recalled Gibbons' reputation 'for not sending students to the college and may now have thought that, by accepting his candidate, they would increase his support for the college. In any case, on June 8, 1885, the cardinals nominated O'Connell for papal approval.[37]

At this juncture, Simeoni seems to have acquiesced in the desire of at least some of the American bishops to have the rector act as a resident agent for the American Church. He also seems to have believed that O'Connell's appointment would win Gibbons' support for the college and would thus aid in the Romanization of the American Church. But O'Connell regarded himself at times more as agent than as rector and increasingly used his office to promote the Americanizing programs of Gibbons and Ireland, the opposite of what Simeoni had hoped. O'Connell's influence in Rome was enhanced through his known friendship with Gibbons who, in 1886, became the second American to be elevated to the cardinalate.

Cardinal McCloskey had died on October 10, 1885, just as the approval of the Third Plenary Council was being given. Within a few days rumors made the rounds of Vatican circles that Gibbons would soon be named a cardinal.[38] In February, 1886, American newspapers prematurely announced that Gibbons had been given the honor. Gibbons ordered a disclaimer, but confided to O'Connell that Archbishop Williams had requested the Holy See to confer the red hat on him. He also wrote Corrigan about the newspaper stories and suggested that the archbishop write both Cardinal Lodovico Jacobini, the Secretary of State, and Cardinal Simeoni, explaining that Gibbons had not been responsible for the stories and had ordered a correction. On May 5, however, O'Connell cabled Gibbons that the appointment was official, but he should remain silent until he received the *biglietto*.[39]

On June 7, Gibbons was officially proclaimed Cardinal Priest with the title of Santa Maria in Trastevere. The imposition of the red biretta was to take place on June 30. Monsignor Germano Straniero, secretary to the nunciature in Vienna,

---

[37] APF, Acta, 254 (1885), 219^r–221^v, Simeoni Ponenza, June 1885.

[38] AAB 79 T 12, O'Connell to Gibbons, Rome, Oct. 13, 1885; AAB 79 T 19, O'Connell to Gibbons, Rome, Oct. 22, 1885.

[39] AANY, Gibbons to Corrigan, Baltimore, Feb. 24, 1886; AAB 80 U 10, O'Connell to Gibbons, Rome, May 5, 1886; cf. 80 U 13, same to same, Rome, May 7, 1886.

was appointed the papal ablegate to bring the biretta to Baltimore. Archbishop Kenrick of St. Louis, as the oldest metropolitan, was to confer it.[40] The growing attitude of the liberal party toward Roman officials was already indicated in O'Connell's remarks about Straniero. O'Connell advised Gibbons to telegraph Kenrick, as soon as possible, to come to Baltimore and to send messengers to New York to meet Straniero "in order to relieve him (the Mgre) of the necessity of 'making a little trip to St. Louis, to deliver to Mgre Kendrick [sic] the brief of the Holy See'". O'Connell also warned Gibbons to have Father John Foley of Baltimore read over Straniero's speech, for "he was saying at one time 'that tho' the liberty which prevailed in America was not good in itself, still the church knew how to make use of it, and to draw from it the benefits which she diffused through the middle ages'. I told him, better not go to America, at all, than go there and say that. When that was eliminated, he put in its stead that America was a country distinguished for her 'inventions'. I said if that were the only point he could mention with praise, better omit it, and speak in generalities. We then put 'Alma Americana respublica, quae ubique terrarum summis laudibus cele-bratur'. If he has not changed it, that will not hurt".[41]

Had O'Connell and his friends been able to read Straniero's report to the Holy See, however, they would have had no fears, for it was a lengthy paean to American religious liberty. In the United States, he wrote, "liberty" was "not just a sound, but a fact" and the Church was "perfectly free" to "carry out its good works and exercise its power without obstacles of any sort".[42] He carefully distinguished the European from the American meaning of a "free church in a free state" by showing that in the United States both Church and State were distinct societies, each independent of the other in its proper order. For Straniero, American religious liberty was a product of its history because in the United States, "the Church was born and remained separate from the State. It was born free and such it has always remained. In Europe, on the other hand, both Church and State, in a manner of speaking, were born together from the ruins of Paganism".[43] Only in regard to the refusal of state governments to support Catholic schools did Straniero find grounds for criticizing the relationship between Church and State in America.[44] While he included in his summary a strong argument for having an apostolic delegate,[45] Straniero's report probably shocked his Roman readers.

---

[40] AAB, 80 W 12, Y 16, Y 17, O'Connell to Gibbons, Rome, May 24, 29, 1886 (cables).
[41] AAB 81 B 5, O'Connell to Gibbons, Rome, June 2, 4, 1886.
[42] ASV, SS, 280 (1902), fasc. 10, Straniero, Report on conditions of the Church in the United States, June–Nov. 1886, 5ᵛ.
[43] Ibid., 26ʳ.
[44] Ibid., 58ʳ–60ʳ.
[45] Ibid., 83ʳ–87ᵛ.

The imposition of the biretta on Gibbons was a symbolic event. Not only was the United States given the only cardinal it would have until 1911, but it also linked the older tradition of collegiality, exemplified by Kenrick, with the emergence of a new group of prelates convinced that America was different from Rome. It was also symbolic for it brought together in celebration and harmony men who would be opposed to one another within a few years. Assisting Straniero, in addition to Father Foley, was Salvatore Brandi, S. J., professor of theology at Woodstock College in Maryland.[46] Subsequently the editor of *La Civiltà Cattolica*, Brandi became an ardent partisan of Corrigan and opponent of Gibbons, Ireland, and the liberals. He was but one representative of the Jesuits, who, in general, sided with the conservatives. Moreover, at the same time that Gibbons was elevated, the Jesuits became more influential in Rome as Camillo Mazzella, S. J., a former professor and dean of Woodstock College and then professor of theology at the Gregorian University, was also given the red hat. On July 4, American Independence Day, O'Connell hosted this future enemy of the liberals.[47]

The consistory at which Gibbons and the other new cardinals would receive the red hat was held on March 17, 1887. Gibbons arrived in Rome on February 13. Already present were Bishops Ireland and Keane. The apparent harmony of the Third Plenary Council had already broken down and Gibbons threw his influence behind the two bishops, who had originally come to Rome to gain approval of the statutes for the Catholic University. But to their agenda, as will be seen, they had added the issue of the Knights of Labor and related social problems, and the burgeoning tension with the Germans as Father Peter Abbelen of Milwaukee brought a petition to Propaganda asking for a stronger voice for German-American Catholics. Gibbons, the two bishops, and O'Connell, discussed all these problems with Propaganda in the month preceding the consistory. On March 25, the feast of the Annunciation which was also celebrated in his see as Maryland Day, he took possession of his titular Church of Santa Maria in Trastevere.

Through O'Connell's influence, he altered his original brief remarks and delivered an address, which, in retrospect, encapsulated the Americanist movement. His boldness in 1887 contrasted sharply with Cardinal Samuel Stritch's timidity in 1953, when the latter offered a short toast on American liberty at the dedication of the new North American College. Gibbons began by attributing the progress of the American Church, "under God and the fostering vigilance of the Holy See, to the civil liberty we enjoy in our enlightened republic". Citing Leo XIII's

---

[46] Baltimore *Sun*, July 1, 1886.
[47] AAB 81 K 12, O'Connell to Gibbons, Rome, July 4, 1886.

encyclical *Immortale Dei*, he declared that "the Church is not committed to any form of civil government. She adapts herself to all. She leavens all with the sacred leaven of the Gospel". To those countries where governments hampered the Church's divine mission he contrasted the United States "where the civil government holds over us the aegis of its protection, without interfering with us in the legitimate exercise of our sublime mission as ministers of the Gospel of Christ. Our country has liberty without license, and authority without despotism". Finally, in the name of American Catholics and "of our separated brethren", he thanked the pope for bestowing the high honor on him.[48] Here was the gauntlet of the benefit of American religious liberty thrown down by the new world to the old, which could not understand it until the Second Vatican Council.

Gibbons was considered by many of his fellow bishops to be "slippery" and difficult to make take a stand. But in the final analysis, he was always to be found on the side of his friends, O'Connell, Ireland, and Keane, although it was difficult, if not impossible at times, to determine who led and who followed. One of the first issues in which he became involved through the influence of his friends was the establishment of the Catholic University, a move which catapulted John Keane, who had succeeded Gibbons as Bishop of Richmond, into national prominence.

Gibbons had been lukewarm about the university and its proposed location in Washington, D. C., the site favored by Bishop Spalding and Miss Mary Gwendoline Caldwell, a young New York heiress, who provided the first endowment of $300,000. The site placed the university in Gibbons' archdiocese and was opposed by Archbishops Ryan of Philadelphia and Corrigan of New York.[49] Although the bishops in council had approved the establishment of the university, the project was from the beginning controversial. The bishops had appointed an episcopal university committee to which they named Archbishop Heiss to give it a German representative. In the summer of 1886, however, he resigned, which, O'Connell reported, "was made to look ominous" in Rome.[50]

In the meantime, however, on May 12, 1886, the committee delegated Gibbons, Ryan, Corrigan, and Williams to select a rector. They first chose Spalding, the guiding light of the project, who, for unexplained reasons, refused.[51] Next, they turned to Keane, who was to accompany Bishop Ireland making his *ad limina* visit to Rome, to gain official approval of the university and rector chosen by the committee. The personal delegation to Rome was necessary, Keane confided to O'Connell, because of Corrigan's rising opposition. At its meeting, the

[48] ELLIS: *Gibbons*, I, 308–309.
[49] AAB 79 N 13, O'Connell to Gibbons, Rome, June 28, 1885.
[50] AAB 81 R 10, O'Connell to Gibbons, Rome, Aug. 14, 1886.
[51] SWEENEY: *Spalding*, pp. 179–180.

committee voted to petition the Holy See not to allow the establishment of any other Catholic university for twenty-five years. Corrigan, who, unknown to Gibbons, was hoping to establish such an institution in New York under Jesuit auspices, moved that the time be limited until the next plenary council. He also claimed to know that the Holy See opposed the project. When confronted with a letter from Pope Leo XIII favorable to it, however, he admitted that the opposition came from Propaganda.[52]

On O'Connell's advice to Keane, the committee drew up letters to both the pope and Cardinal Simeoni. These letters were signed at the meeting by Gibbons, Williams, Corrigan, and Ryan and subsequently by Archbishops Kenrick of St. Louis, Francis J. Leray of New Orleans, Elder of Cincinnati, Feehan of Chicago, and John Baptist Salpointe of Santa Fe who were summoned to Baltimore to discuss suspect secret societies. Only three archbishops did not sign: Patrick Riordan of San Francisco, William H. Gross, C.Ss.R., of Oregon City, and Michael Heiss of Milwaukee. Armed with these letters, Keane and Ireland set out for Rome.[53]

Once in Rome, Ireland and Keane learned that there was indeed serious opposition to the university and that the letters from the archbishops were given little credence.[54] On December 14, 1886, they, therefore, wrote all the archbishops asking them to send personal declarations in favor of the university.[55] They were also informed by Archbishop Jacobini, Secretary of Propaganda, that the university matter would be deferred until Gibbons arrived to receive his red hat and then postponed indefinitely. They then spoke to the pope, who stated he had not formed his opinion and asked them to remain in Rome until Gibbons' arrival.[56]

When Gibbons arrived in Rome, he learned officially what he had previously heard only informally, that Corrigan was opposed to the university. He was prepared to give up the project, but Ireland prevailed on him to ask the pope's approval. On April 10, 1887, Leo XIII approved the establishment of the university, but left its site to the further determination of the bishops. By the time Gibbons left Rome, the bishops were already drafting their opinions on the location. Although some, like Bernard McQuaid, wrote that "they seem bent on placing the university near Washington City to make the inevitable failure a monumental one",[57] when, on September 7, Gibbons convened a meeting of the university committee, he was able to report that a majority of the bishops favored the Wash-

---

[52] ADR, Keane to O'Connell, Richmond, May 20, 1886.
[53] ELLIS: *Gibbons*, I, 400–401.
[54] AAB 82 G 9, O'Connell to Gibbons, Rome, Dec. 10, 1886.
[55] AAB 82 H 3, Keane and Ireland to "Monseigneur," Rome, Dec. 14, 1886.
[56] ELLIS: *Gibbons*, I, 402.
[57] ADR, McQuaid to O'Connell, Rochester, June 28, 1887.

ington site. The committee ratified this choice and also formally announced the selection of Keane as rector. Again Corrigan had said nothing openly against the site or the rector of the university, but shortly thereafter he resigned from the committee.[58]

There was manifold opposition to the university. The Jesuits opposed it, not only because it would conflict with their own college of Georgetown in Washington, but because it would counter Corrigan's plan for establishing a university in New York under their direction.[59] Nevertheless, on March 7, 1889, Leo XIII approved the university statutes. Keane immediately set about to gather a faculty for the new institution, which would reflect the finest in European and American scholarship.[60] The inauguration of the university was scheduled to coincide with the centennial of the American hierarchy. At the dual celebration, Leo XIII was represented by Archbishop Francesco Satolli, former professor of dogma at the Urban College and then President of the Pontifical Academy of Noble Ecclesiastics, the papal diplomatic school. Four years later, he returned as the the first Apostolic Delegate.

The centennial of the establishment of the hierarchy was commemorated with a solemn pontifical Mass at the Cathedral of the Assumption in Baltimore on November 10, 1889. The next two days were devoted to a Catholic Congress, at which Charles Bonaparte read a paper on papal independence prepared by Father Thomas O'Gorman, recently appointed professor of Church history at the new university. The paper was the substitute which Gibbons and others had arranged for "spontaneous" mass demonstrations against the loss of papal temporal power, which the Vatican had requested.[61] On November 13, Gibbons accompanied O'Connell and Satolli, the pope's official representative, to Washington for the opening of the Catholic University.[62] Satolli and O'Connell then remained in the United States for some months sounding out the American bishops on establishing an apostolic delegation.

Despite the opposition to it, the university had finally opened. Corrigan had even been persuaded by Father John Farley of New York to return to the university committee in the summer of 1888. Because of its location in the Archdiocese of Baltimore, Gibbons was the Chancellor. With Keane as rector, the university became a bastion of the liberals with the ardent support of John Ireland.

---

[58] ELLIS: *Gibbons*, I, 408; CURRAN: *Corrigan*, pp. 166–167.

[59] ADR, Moore to O'Connell, St. Augustine, Feb. 22, 1888; E. J. BURRUS: *Father Joseph Havens Richards' Notes on Georgetown and the Catholic University*, in: Woodstock Letters 83 (1954) 83.

[60] Patrick H. AHERN: *The Catholic University of America, 1887–1896: The Rectorship of John J. Keane*, Washington 1948, pp. 5–33.

[61] FOGARTY: *Vatican*, pp. 116, 118; ELLIS: *Gibbons*, II, 342–345.

[62] AAB, Gibbons Diary, Nov. 10, 1889; ELLIS: *Gibbons*, I, 419.

Ireland had emerged as a powerful leader at the Third Plenary Council. At that time his Diocese of St. Paul was a suffragan of Milwaukee, a German stronghold. In October, 1886, Heiss reported that Ireland desired the erection of the new province of St. Paul but noted that he and the majority of the other suffragan bishops opposed it. In December, Ireland was in Rome for his *ad limina* visit and to gain approval for the Catholic University. At that time, in his name and in that of Martin Marty, Vicar Apostolic of the Dakota Territory, he requested that the Holy See erect the new province. His argument was that Milwaukee had little in common with Minnesota, where his diocese was located, and with the adjacent Dakota Territory and that Heiss had refused to hold a provincial council until May, 1886. While discussing the university and other issues, early in 1887 Ireland rehearsed his plans for the new archdiocese, but he left the final negotiations in O'Connell's hands. In June, Donato Sbarretti, the *minutante* at Propaganda who handled American affairs, informed O'Connell that Heiss wished the decrees of the Milwaukee provincial council approved before establishing the new archdiocese so that the legislation would bind the new province, the approval of which Sbarretti thought was imminent.[63]

Cardinal Simeoni, in the meantime, requested Heiss to summon his suffragans to a meeting to discuss the division. They met on August 4 and unanimously agreed on the division of the province, but Heiss added the negative comment in his report of the meeting that "I could not persuade myself that a division of this Province is necessary now or useful, but I gave my consent, in order that the peace might not be disturbed and that nationalism, from which beyond doubt this motion has arisen, might not be more exacerbated".[64] Despite Heiss' animadversions, Propaganda met on February 21, 1888, and voted to erect the new Province of St. Paul with John Ireland as archbishop.[65] His reception of the pallium was virtually a meeting of the liberal party. O'Connell had originally intended to bring it personally to Ireland, but then consigned it to an American College student returning to New York. In August, Keane brought it to the University of Notre Dame, where Gibbons presented it to Ireland. On September 27, 1888, Gibbons formally invested the new archbishop with the symbol of his metropolitan authority.[66]

By the time of the opening of the Catholic University of America in 1889,

---

[63] AASP, O'Connell to Ireland, Rome, June 24, 1887; AANY, Ireland to Corrigan, July 11, 1887.

[64] APF, Acta, 258 (1888), Sommario, 79ʳ, Heiss to Simeoni, Milwaukee, Aug. 17, 1888; 72ʳ–75ʳ, Mazzella Ponenza, Feb. 1888; AASP, O'Connell to Ireland, Rome, March 15, 1888.

[65] *Ibid.*, 78ʳ⁻ᵛ.

[66] AASP, O'Connell to Ireland, Rome, Sept. 4, 1887 and June 15, 1888; ADR, Ireland to O'Connell, St. Paul, Aug. 18, 1888; James MOYNIHAN: *The Life of Archbishop John Ireland*, New York 1953, pp. 15–16; ELLIS: *Gibbons*, II, 327n.

therefore, the major members of the liberal party were already in place. There were similarities which all had in common. All were of Irish birth or Irish descent, but this was not enough to distinguish them from their conservative counterparts. Gibbons and Keane had both studied at St. Mary's Seminary in Baltimore under the Sulpicians; Ireland had studied in France. Of the group, only O'Connell was Roman-trained, but even he was regarded, at least by Miss Edes, as a protege of the Sulpicians. Except for O'Connell's, their letters to the Vatican and Propaganda stand out, for they were consistently written in French rather than Italian. But most of all, they were bound together by a common optimistic vision of making the American Church an integral part of American society. They came to the fore when anti-Catholicism in the United States again began to rise, notably in the American Protective Association (APA), founded in 1887. To overcome anti-Catholic prejudice, they wished to slough off unessential Roman traditions and to rid the Church of its foreign taint by rapidly Americanizing the immigrants. In this, they were all influenced by and enamored of the ideas of Father Isaac Hecker, the founder of the Paulist Fathers. Their program brought them into conflict with the conservatives, led by Corrigan, McQuaid, and the German bishops.

C. THE EMERGENCE OF THE CONSERVATIVES

Nationalities in Conflict

a. The German Question

The evolution of the conservative party as a cohesive force was gradual, but it began with the liberal stance on the role of German-American Catholics in the American Church and on the issues of parochial schools and social teaching. Corrigan initially sided with the liberals on the German question, but he turned against them as other issues, notably the school question, became involved. The conflict between the liberals and German-Americans went through three phases: Father Peter Abbelen's memorial to Propaganda in 1886, the succession to Archbishop Heiss in 1890, and the proposals for immigrant care presented by Peter Paul Cahensly and the St. Raphaels-Verein in 1891–1892.

Late in 1886, Abbelen, a priest of the Archdiocese of Milwaukee, arrived in Rome. His mission manifested the growing friction between German and English-speaking immigrants. Immediately prior to the Third Plenary Council, Henry Muehlsiepen, vicar general of the Archdiocese of St. Louis and formerly a strong supporter of his archbishop, protested to Rome about Kenrick's policies. In 1845, Kenrick had issued a pastoral letter in which he ruled that only one church or quasi-parish could be constituted in a given territory; other churches established for various nationalities were only "ecclesiae succursales," or "chapels of ease". As time went on, however, these national churches obtained the same rights as territorial ones. But when one priest raised the question of the canonical status of these national churches, Kenrick replied that his directive in the 1845 pastoral remained in effect. This, said Muehlsiepen, dealt a severe blow to all who did not speak English.[67] Propaganda consulted Archbishop Ryan, Kenrick's former coadjutor. Since the disciplinary decrees of the Council of Trent had been fully promulgated in St. Louis, explained Ryan, Kenrick had believed that only one parish could be established within a given territory but in practice had given full equality to the national parishes and in general there had been few occasions of English-speaking rectors administering the sacraments to German speakers.[68]

At the Third Plenary Council, the bishops had discussed quasi-parishes, whose rectors would be irremovable, but they had not treated the specific question of national parishes. Prior to Roman approval of the council, Bishop Kilian Flasch of La Crosse, Wisconsin, queried Rome on two points: first, whether there could be more than one parish in a given territory; and second, whether children born to parents of a given national origin should be obliged to attend national parishes as long as they remained under the jurisdiction of their parents.[69] Simeoni forwarded these queries to the American bishops in whose dioceses there were German populations. Early in 1886, the bishops had unanimously responded in favor of establishing national as well as territorial parishes, and on the second point they wished only to preserve the right of parents to send their children to the school of another parish and the right of grown children to choose to attend the territorial parish.[70]

The question of the relationship between English and non-English speaking churches was therefore settled when Abbelen arrived in Rome. He bore a petition in the name of several German priests of Milwaukee, Cincinnati, and St. Louis, which had the explicit approval of Archbishop Heiss. Before leaving the United States, he had also obtained a letter of introduction to Simeoni from Gibbons, who thought the petition concerned only Milwaukee. Gibbons' introduction, in retrospect, was made to appear an endorsement of Abbelen's proposals. In addition to Flasch's original two questions, Abbelen called for the appointment of a German-speaking vicar general in those dioceses where there was a large German

---

[67] APF, SOCG, 1026 (1887), 1028ʳ–1030ʳ, Muehlsiepen to Simeoni, St. Louis, July 31, 1884.

[68] *Ibid.*, 1031ʳ⁻ᵛ, Ryan to Simeoni, Philadelphia, Oct. 12, 1884.

[69] *Ibid.*, 943ʳ–944ʳ, Flasch to Simeoni, La Crosse, April 7, 1885.

[70] *Ibid.*, 884ʳ–902ᵛ, 1003ʳ–1024ᵛ, responses of Gibbons, Corrigan, Heiss, Gilmour, Hennessy, Dwenger, Elder, Gross, Riordan, Keane, Williams, and Feehan.

population and where neither the bishop nor the vicar general spoke German, and for the requirement that formal consent of the pastor of a national church be obtained before children of immigrants could join a territorial one. He argued that German Catholics frequently settled among fellow Germans, who were non-believers and who ridiculed the Catholics for being second-class citizens in relation to the "Irish", the term Abbelen used to designate all English speakers.[71]

Keane and Ireland, then in Rome, obtained a copy of the memorial, had it printed, and, with Propaganda's authorization, distributed it to the American hierarchy. Of it Keane said to Gibbons: "A more villainous tissue of misstatements I have seldom read"; Abbelen he described as "a secret emissary of a clique of German Bishops among us".[72] While waiting for the reaction of the other bishops, Keane and Ireland submitted their own lengthy response to the congregation.[73] Alerted to the pending crisis, Corrigan wrote Gibbons asking him to meet with him and Archbishop Williams.[74] Instead, Gibbons summoned a meeting of the eastern archbishops in Philadelphia on December 16, 1886. Ryan, Corrigan, and Williams met with him. Elder of Cincinnati had been invited, but was unable to attend and sent his opinions in writing. Corrigan summarized their positions taken at the meeting and sent them to Rome on December 17.[75]

In the meanwhile, Gibbons collected the opinions of other bishops and forwarded them to Rome. Ireland and Keane then presented this information to Propaganda in time for its meeting originally scheduled for January, 1887, to decide on the questions raised by Flasch. Of particular importance in their presentation were letters from non-American-born bishops. Camillus Maes, the Belgian-born Bishop of Covington, Kentucky, wrote Archbishop Elder that the petition sent to Rome by "German prelates" was "nothing less than an insult to the hierarchy of the United States". Bishops Joseph Rademacher of Nashville, Tennessee, and Henry J. Richter of Grand Rapids, Michigan, both German-born, repudiated Abbelen's memorial and Heiss' signature of approval.[76] In view of continued protests from both sides, Propaganda decided to postpone its meeting.

Both sides had indeed manifested increased sensitivity to precisely what it meant to be American. Swiss-born Bishop Martin Marty, Vicar Apostolic of the Dakota Territory, told O'Connell that Abbelen's mission was "a secret for the German Bishops and Clergy" and that his expenses were paid by St. Louis priests

---

[71] Ibid., 927ʳ–942ʳ; given in Colman J. BARRY: The Catholic Church and German-Americans, Milwaukee 1953, pp. 289–296; see also pp. 62–64.

[72] AAB 82 G 4, Keane to Gibbons, Rome, Dec. 4, 1886.

[73] APF, SOCG, 1026 (1887), 1109ʳ–1143ʳ; given in BARRY: German-Americans, pp. 296–312.

[74] AAB 82 H 1, Corrigan to Gibbons, New London, Dec. 11, 1886.

[75] APF, SOCG, 1026 (1887), 945ʳ–948ᵛ, Corrigan to Simeoni, New York, Dec. 17, 1886.

[76] Ibid., 1068ʳ–1081ʳ, Ireland and Keane, "La question allemande ..."

who wished to be named irremovable rectors. Marty's own opinion was that Abbelen, who had been a theologian at the plenary council, could have voiced his grievances at that time; and for Propaganda now to issue a new decree would be an insult to the American bishops so soon after the council had been held.[77] Wherever Marty gained his information on the lack of support of the German bishops for Abbelen, he was certainly ignorant of the strong letter Bishop Frederick Katzer of Green Bay had written to Simeoni saying not only that he had read and fully approved Abbelen's petition but also that Propaganda should accept all its propositions. "This whole question", he stated, "is particularly between the congregations and priests of the Irish, whether native-born or immigrant, on the one hand and the congregations and priests of other nations on the other". All who were not Irish, he concluded, were reduced to second-class citizenship in the American Church.[78]

The fears and suspicions which divided English and German-speaking bishops were widespread also among priests. Augustine Zeininger, Rector of St. Francis Seminary in Milwaukee, had heard rumors that Propaganda would forbid that national churches have the same canonical rights as territorial ones.[79] James J. Keogh, rector of the Milwaukee cathedral, wrote Keane, enclosing a clipping from the diocesan paper which contained Heiss' instructions for the congregations at Fond du Lac. No pastor, said the archbishop, could admit to his congregation a parishioner from a national parish without the knowledge or consent of the previous pastor. This, of course, was one of Abbelen's proposals. Keogh, however, thought Heiss had no intention of making such a practice universal and had issued such instructions only when requested by German pastors. But his fear was for what would happen under Heiss' successor. "If Bp. Ireland leaves us", he continued, "we shall be given over body and soul to the Germans and the whole province will be Germanized", something he argued that German people themselves opposed.[80]

With all the pertinent information then at hand, Cardinal Mazzella was designated to draw up the *ponenza* on both Flasch's original questions and on Abbelen's memorial. Noting that the congregation had been ready to decide on Flasch's two questions, when Abbelen arrived, Mazzella summarized the material received after that time.[81] On April 11, the cardinals held their meeting postponed since January. At the same time Gibbons was named a cardinal, he was also appointed to the Congregation of Propaganda. He too was in attendance and

---

[77] *Ibid.*, 1103ʳ–1104ᵛ, Marty to O'Connell, St. Francis, Wisc., Feb. 16, 1887.

[78] *Ibid.*, 1085ʳ-1086ʳ, Katzer to Simeoni, Green Bay, Jan. 3, 1887.

[79] *Ibid.*, 1083ʳ–1084ʳ, Zeininger to Simeoni, Milwaukee, Jan. 1887.

[80] *Ibid.*, 1108ʳ⁻ᵛ, Keogh to Keane, Milwaukee, Mar. 3, 1887.

[81] *Ibid.*, Acta, 257 (1887), 187ʳ–196ʳ, Mazzella Ponenza, Apr., 1887.

submitted his own personal views. The congregation decided only on the questions raised by Flasch: that parishes for different nationalities could exist within the same territory; that they could have irremovable rectors; and that children should remain in the parish of their parents until reaching their majority. The congregation did not consider the other questions raised by Abbelen, such as a German-speaking vicar general and the requirement that the pastor of a national parish give his formal consent before a parishioner could join a territorial church. Instead the congregation then voted that Simeoni write Gibbons to communicate its response to the other archbishops "so that every hope will be taken away of accepting in the future in any way the petitions of Father Abbelen".[82] Only on June 8, however, after Gibbons' departure, did Simeoni write him the official letter communicating the congregation's decision.[83]

From every aspect, Abbelen's mission was unfortunate. Before his arrival, Propaganda had already decided on the essential points raised by his later memorial and it had done so with the consent of the American bishops it had consulted. Whether he represented more than a small group of German-American priests, who indeed had legitimate complaints, is even now difficult to determine. What is certain is that his mission, far from settling the issues, intensified animosity on both sides. From the English-speaking or "Irish" side, this animosity was frequently small-minded.

In July, 1888, as German-American Catholics prepared to hold their second *Katholikentag*, for example, Ireland informed O'Connell that "the German question is reviving in view of the approaching convention in Cincinnati – but reviving with the cough of death in its throat".[84] For this celebration German Catholics had requested a papal blessing, which Propaganda had already dispatched, when O'Connell succeeded in having it recalled.[85] Ireland and the liberals may have been successful but they won the enmity of Cardinal Paul Melchers, former Archbishop of Cologne, with whom German-American Catholics had been in correspondence for some time.[86] The conferral of a papal blessing was a relatively minor issue. But the liberals soon took on a major one.

Although the Archdioceses of Cincinnati, St. Louis, and Milwaukee were principal centers for German-American Catholics, only Milwaukee had a German archbishop. In March, 1890, Archbishop Heiss died. The liberals, led by Ireland,

---

[82] *Ibid.*, 198ʳ, General Congregation, Apr. 11, 1887.

[83] AAB, 88 S 5, Simeoni to Gibbons, Rome, June 8, 1887, quoted in BARRY: *German-Americans*, pp. 72–73.

[84] ADR, Ireland to O'Connell, St. Paul, July 11, 1888.

[85] AASP, O'Connell to Ireland, Grottaferrata, Sept. 17, 1888.

[86] AAB, 83 D 12, O'Connell to Gibbons, Grottaferrata, July 31, 1887; AASP, O'Connell to Ireland, Grottaferrata, Oct. 8, 1888.

immediately began a campaign to wrest control of this stronghold from German domination. On April 15, the consultors of the archdiocese, three German and two English speakers, met; included in their number was Abbelen. Their *terna* reflected the ethnic division. With three out of five votes, they placed Bishops Frederick Katzer of Green Bay first and Kilian Flasch of La Crosse second; with two votes they named Bishop Henry Richter of Grand Rapids third. The next day, the suffragans of Milwaukee, all German-born, ratified the priests' list. There was intrigue on all sides, Father L. Batz, former vicar general of Milwaukee, later told Gibbons, with nationalism rather than the religious needs of the archdiocese being the prevailing motivation. Batz himself, claiming to speak for the older priests of Milwaukee, looked to the archbishops for a solution and personally favored the appointment of an American-born prelate.[87]

Katzer was "a man thoroughly unfit to be an archbishop", Ireland wrote Gibbons, asking his "enlightened cooperation in solving" the question.[88] Gibbons was equally opposed to Katzer and received Propaganda's permission to consult the other archbishops before the congregation would act.[89] By the end of May, Ireland had his candidate for the post. "John Lancaster Spalding is the only man for Milwaukee", he wrote O'Connell. "We may as well decide that at once & work up to it. Bp. [John] Vertin of Marquette, the Senior of the Province, will favor him".[90] On July 23, 1890, the archbishops gathered in Boston for the first of their annual meetings. All were present except Gross of Portland and Corrigan, who was then in Rome. Voting secretly, they unanimously decided to set Katzer's name aside. By a vote of five to four, with Gibbons abstaining, they likewise set Flasch aside. Out of deference to the bishops of the Milwaukee Province, they retained Richter's name and constructed a new *terna* around him. The new *terna* had Spalding in first place, Martin Marty, Bishop of Sioux Falls, second, and Richter third.[91] They then sent this new list to Archbishop Jacobini, together with a covering letter from Gibbons to Simeoni, which made it clear that Spalding had been placed first because he was an American. Katzer, said Gibbons, had been rejected because he was too German and his appointment would cause further dissension.[92] But there may well have been other motives behind the archbishops' *terna*. The liberals knew that in 1886 Richter had opposed Abbelen's petition and Katzer had favored it.

---

[87] APF, SOCG, 1037 (1890), 490^r–491^r, Batz to Gibbons, Milwaukee, Nov. 18, 1890.

[88] AAB 87 J 5, Ireland to Gibbons, St. Paul, Apr. 21, 1890.

[89] APF, SOCG, 1037 (1890), 428^r, Gibbons to Simeoni, Baltimore, May 13, 1890; AAB 87 M 8, John Farrelly to Gibbons, Rome, May 19, 1890.

[90] ADR, Ireland to O'Connell, St. Paul, May 28, 1890.

[91] AAB 87 R 4, Report of the Meeting of the Archbishops in Boston, July 23 & 24, 1890.

[92] APF, Acta, 260 (1890), 383^r–384^r, Gibbons to Simeoni, July 25, 1890.

In Rome, O'Connell was to handle the process, but, unfortunately for the liberals, he had been in the United States from November, 1889 to July, 1890. During his absence, Corrigan had visited Rome and on May 9 had submitted a letter to Propaganda supporting Katzer.[93] Nevertheless, in early August, O'Connell wrote Gibbons that Jacobini opposed Katzer and was happy the question had been submitted to the archbishops.[94] Shortly later, he told Ireland that Propaganda would reject Spalding, because he was not trusted, and Katzer, because he was "the recognized head of a party". By elimination, the congregation would probably choose Richter, because he was on all three lists.[95] For the next few months, O'Connell kept warning Ireland to gain support for Spalding or else Richter would be appointed.[96] As late as November 15, he thought he had convinced Jacobini to support Spalding and to win over Simeoni. To do this he represented Spalding as a "neutral man & a good German scholar".[97]

But even as O'Connell was writing to Ireland, the forces against Spalding were building up. First, both Archbishop Ryan of Philadelphia and Bishop Vertin of Marquette supported Marty. Then, Archbishop Elder of Cincinnati told Propaganda that he suspected, without giving his reasons, that the congregation had already formed its judgment against Spalding and that he had information that neither Marty nor Richter would be acceptable to the clergy of Milwaukee. Finally, both Katzer and Flasch protested against Ireland's influence on the archbishops in having them reject their names. All of this information Mazzella placed in his *ponenza* for the congregation. He first of all questioned whether the archbishops' right to be consulted on metropolitan sees gave them the right to draw up a new *terna*. He then recognized that the issue was essentially a "battle" between Germans, who wanted a German, and non-Germans, who wanted an American.[98] On December 15, Propaganda met and elected Katzer as Archbishop of Milwaukee.[99] That Katzer was trained by the Jesuits in Linz, a fact Mazzella mentioned in his *ponenza*, may have influenced the cardinal to promote the bishop's cause. The appointment was a blow to the liberal party. Gibbons called it "a great surprise to us all. We must accept it for the best".[100] Ireland thought

---

[93] *Ibid.*, 372^v–373^r, Mazzella Ponenza, Dec., 1890.

[94] AAB 87 S 5, O'Connell to Gibbons, Rome, Aug. 4, 1890.

[95] AASP, O'Connell to Ireland, Aug. 18, 1890; cf. AAB 87 U 1, O'Connell to Gibbons, Grottaferrata, Aug. 20, 1890.

[96] AASP, O'Connell to Ireland, Rome, Sept. 21 and Oct. 1, 1890.

[97] AASP, O'Connell to Ireland, Rome, Nov. 15, 1890.

[98] APF, Acta, 260 (1890), 372^r–380^r, Mazzella Ponenza, Dec., 1890.

[99] *Ibid.*, 381^r.

[100] ADR, Gibbons to O'Connell, Baltimore, Dec. 30, 1890.

that "what is most galling in the whole affair is the slight put upon the arch-bishops by Rome".[101]

The reasons for the Katzer appointment were varied. The issue of the Mil-waukee succession and of the entire German question, as will be seen, had be-come intertwined during the summer of 1890 with Ireland's position in favor of public schools. On the school question, O'Connell wrote Gibbons on November 21, 1890, when he was still promoting Spalding, that "complaints are coming in from those Germans and they are saying Ireland cares nothing about Rome and wants no Roman interference and they write as if there were no reliable Catholics in America, but themselves".[102] Rome thus saw the Milwaukee succession less as a German-Irish feud than as a dispute between the liberals and conservatives, among whom the Germans were but one faction. This vision of the American Church represented a shift in Propaganda's thinking. In 1880, the congregation had seemed to favor the American-born Spalding as Coadjutor of Milwaukee, but in 1890, it rejected him in favor of Katzer. Rome was now suspicious of Spalding's orthodoxy; included in Propaganda's file on the Milwaukee succession was a letter from Corrigan to Simeoni, enclosing a theological critique of Spald-ing's address at the laying of the cornerstone of the Catholic University.[103] Moreover, the operative motive for Mazzella, in addition to the technical ques-tion of whether the archbishops had the right to submit their own *terna*, seems to have been fear of growing American independence from Rome.

After the Katzer appointment, O'Connell narrated for Ireland what he could find out about Propaganda's motives. "Now about Milwaukee, I enquired how it was done in spite of the letter of the Archbishops. The answer was: 'the Arch-bishops have a right if they wish to send us their views on the candidates; they have no right to send us another list'. That recalled to me what Card. Mazzella, the ponente, had said to me a short time previous: 'For me there are only two lists' i.e. of the consultors & of the suffragans. This is founded on a deeper deter-mination on the part of the Cardinals to put the American Bps. a little more in their place. On my way over here, [Herbert] Vaughan told me in Manchester that he noticed a growing disposition on our part to get away from the Holy See. I re-ally believe they fear it here.... I went to see Mazzella a few days ago about the nomination of [Placide] Chapelle [as coadjutor of Santa Fe].... I never knew the Card. could wax so warm: 'Do you wish to know my real sentiments, I say mine, not of the congregation; that, for me, would be an argument against him. If they are going to make their Bps over there by themselves, why send the names over

---

[101] AAB 88 G 1, Ireland to Gibbons, St. Paul, Jan. 2, 1891.

[102] AAB 88 D 6, O'Connell to Gibbons, Rome, Nov. 21, 1890.

[103] APF, SOCG, 1037 (1890), 383r–405r, Corrigan to Simeoni, New York, May 16, 1889.

here at all?' He it was who only saw 'Two lists'. This sounds strange in view of the fact, that in Europe every power except Italy names its own Bps". The appointment of Chapelle had been first postponed in September, 1890, and represented a turning point in Mazzella's relationship with the liberals. In the meantime, however, O'Connell had learned still more disturbing information about Jacobini from Monsignor Eugene Boeglin, the editor of the *Moniteur de Rome*, whom Ireland and O'Connell had arranged to be appointed as the Associated Press correspondent at the Vatican. Jacobini told Boeglin that "there are eight archbishops in the United States all liberals with Ireland at their head, and that there were three very obedient to the Holy See as we call them, intransigenti".[104]

For the next few months, O'Connell sought to recoup the liberals' losses with Propaganda. On March 10, 1891, he reported to Ireland that Katzer's appointment "was intended as a snub and was to mark the beginning of a new departure for America – to check the Liberals and to patronize the Conservatives". On his own, he went to see the pope. With the aid of Jacobini, who apparently had been restored to confidence, he succeeded in having the pope call for all the documents on the Milwaukee succession and issue a reprimand to Propaganda. Jacobini had said that the cardinals of the congregation "went with breakneck speed" in appointing Katzer, but O'Connell suspected the real villain was Mazzella.[105]

Ireland was still angry at Katzer's appointment and waxed sarcastic about O'Connell's account of Jacobini, who, he said, "while he was talking so strangely of me to Boeglin, ... was thanking me for my checque of $200". But, he continued, "the traitor is Mazzella. How has he turned against us? Through what influence?"[106] The influence would have been readily discernible to both Ireland and O'Connell, could they have read a letter the cardinal received the previous November from Corrigan, saying "a party of advanced views ... is now seeking to rule the church in this country. The most prominent members are Archbishops Ireland and Riordan, Bishops Keane, [John] Foley [of Detroit] and Spalding, acting with and under His Eminence of Baltimore. The meeting of the Archbishops recently held in Boston (July 23) affords proof of the disposition of these gentlemen to take the practical administration of affairs into their own hands, E.G. the nomination of the Archbishop of Milwaukee. To promote the same general plan of ruling the Church here, and controlling the authorities abroad, the proposition was made to have Msgr. O'Connell made a titular Bishop. We will make him a Bishop first said Dr. Ireland, then push him into the S. College. His Eminence of

---

[104] AASP, O'Connell to Ireland, Rome, Dec. 31, 1890.
[105] AASP, O'Connell to Ireland, Rome, Mar. 10, 1891.
[106] ADR, Ireland to O'Connell, St. Paul, Mar. 8, 1891.

Baltimore, who had already solicited Episcopal [dignity?] for his instrument, was deputed to take the necessary steps to carry out this plan".[107]

The division in the American hierarchy, which Corrigan described, had its counterpart in the Roman Curia. The first documentary evidence for personality clashes within Propaganda in regard to American affairs occurred with the nomination of Placide Chapelle as coadjutor of Santa Fe. Chapelle, then the rector of St. Matthew's Church in Washington, was placed first on the consultors' and suffragans' list for Santa Fe and then received the unanimous endorsement of the archbishops at their annual meeting in 1890. Cardinal Serafino Vannutelli drew up the *ponenza*, but in September the cardinals voted to delay a decision to obtain more information on Chapelle.[108]

In the meantime, Propaganda received word from an unnamed priest, then in Rome, that Chapelle was not exact in his theology, that he had officiated at the marriage of a Protestant senator, who had been married before, and that he was arrogant toward the assistants in his parish. The congregation, therefore, sought the opinion of Corrigan, who was then in Rome. Corrigan acknowledged that the accusations against Chapelle were true, but said that the senator had lied about his previous marriage. Despite some additional personal reservations, Corrigan still believed that Chapelle possessed the necessary qualities to be named coadjutor. On February 23, 1891, Propaganda met a second time on Santa Fe and again Serafino Vannutelli prepared the *ponenza*.[109] This time the cardinals voted to ask for a new *terna*. Vannutelli, however, asked that his personal vote in favor of Chapelle be recorded. Mazzella abstained from voting, but requested that his reasons be recorded: first, because he was not satisfied with the *ponenza*; second, because during the nomination of Katzer he came to be regarded as "an enemy of the Americans"; and finally, because the secretariat of Propaganda was not observing "the secrecy and necessary independence, especially regarding the affairs of the United States of America".[110] Only through the intervention of Gibbons and Archbishop Salpointe did the pope in August revoke Propaganda's decision asking for a new *terna* and name Chapelle coadjutor.[111]

Mazzella's remark about Propaganda not preserving secrecy would have ironic implications within a year when he himself may have been responsible for obtaining a secret memorial of Ireland and passing it on to Salvatore Brandi. But in early 1891, the tension between Vannutelli, later an Ireland supporter, and Mazzella, a

---

[107] AUND, Soderini Ms., Corrigan to Mazzella, New York, Nov. 9, 1890.
[108] APF, Acta, 260 (1890), 274ʳ–278ᵛ, S. Vannutelli Ponenza, Sept., 1890.
[109] *Ibid.*, 261 (1891), 35ʳ–36ᵛ, S. Vannutelli Ponenza, Feb. 1891.
[110] *Ibid.*, 37ʳ⁻ᵛ, General Congregation, Feb. 23, 1891.
[111] *Ibid.*, 411ᵛ–412ʳ, Audience of Aug. 2, 1891.

Corrigan supporter, was already apparent; Propaganda was reflecting the growing division in the American hierarchy. Ireland's surprise at Mazzella's hostility probably derived from his imagining the cardinal to be a friend since he had written the *ponenza* establishing the Archdiocese of St. Paul.

But for Ireland to think Mazzella was sympathetic with his Americanizing program was simply naive. Mazzella had come to the United States as an exile from Italy during the *Risorgimento*; he was incapable of understanding that the American concept of "a free church in a free state" meant something different from Cavour's. Himself a Jesuit, he was further alienated by the liberals' attitude toward religious orders and, as will be seen, their position on parochial schools. He would seem, moreover, to have resented the notion, as he told O'Connell in December, that the archbishops had met as a body not only to reject the nomination of Katzer but also to promote the nomination of Chapelle. Such a vestige of collegiality ran counter to the growing centralization in Rome of which Mazzella was an advocate. Finally, his antagonism for Vannutelli may have stemmed from the latter's conciliatory stance toward the Kingdom of Italy in order to end the Roman Question, with which the American liberals unwittingly became involved. By late 1890, therefore, the conservatives both in the United States and in Rome were, like the liberals, becoming a cohesive force. The German-Americans were brought still closer to the conservative party through the liberals' xenophobia made manifest in the final phase of the German question – Cahenslyism.

Peter Paul Cahensly, a devout Catholic merchant of Limburg an der Lahn and member of the Center Party, had founded the *St. Raphaels-Verein* to care for German immigrants to the new world. The organization soon spread to other countries from which emigrants went to America – Austria, Belgium, and Italy. In 1883, Cahensly himself founded a branch in New York. He and his society became controversial when the boards of directors of the various branches, unfortunately excluding the American one, held a meeting in Lucerne, Switzerland, on December 9 and 10, 1890. At this meeting, the Marchese Volpe-Landi of the Italian *Società San Raffaele* submitted a draft of a memorial. Its recommendations resurrected some of the demands already made in the Abbelen petition. It called for national parishes; priests who would teach catechism in the native tongue of immigrants where their number was too small to warrant establishing a separate parish for them; national parishes with parochial schools where the native language would be taught; immigrant priests sharing equal rights with the native clergy; the formation of Catholic mutual aid societies to offset secret societies; and the Holy See's sponsorship of seminaries to train missionary priests for the United States. But a final recommendation especially provoked the Americanizers: "It seems very desirable that the Catholics of each nationality, wherever it is deemed possible, have in the episcopate of the country where they immigrate, several bishops who are of the same origin. It seems that in this way the organization of the Church would be perfect, for in the assemblies of the bishops, every immigrant race would be represented, and its interests would be protected".[112] Volpe-Landi's memorial was adopted at the meeting and later on signed by the directors of all the branches of the society.[113]

Volpe-Landi and Cahensly were delegated to present the memorial to the pope. They arrived in Rome in April, 1891, but just before they were to present the document, Volpe-Landi was called away. It was therefore Cahensly alone who presented it to Leo XIII on April 16. This was reported in the press on May 4 by way of a telegram from the Wolff Continental Telegraph Bureau in Rome. The text itself was published on May 8 in Boeglin's *Moniteur de Rome*. Next there appeared three cable dispatches from the Associated Press on May 8, 26, and 27, respectively datelined Rome, Brussels, and Berlin, dispatches which had been arranged by O'Connell through Boeglin.

The first two dispatches, which provoked editorials in American Catholic newspapers, claimed that Cahensly alone was responsible for the memorial and charged him with advocating bishops, clergy, and schools for each nationality and with having consulted both Cardinal Mariano Rampolla, the papal Secretary of State, and Simeoni. Finally, they reported that Ernst Leiber, a leader of the German Center Party, had made two visits to the United States precisely to build up support for the project and that the whole plan had actually originated with a group of German priests and laymen in the United States. The third dispatch stated that Cahensly had "put himself in communication not only with the Propaganda and the Vatican, but also Cardinals Mazella [*sic*], Ledochowski, and Melchers, who approved of the project and the memorial submitted to the Holy See", and that he had also invoked the influence of Kurd von Schlözer, the Prussian minister to the Holy See. Von Schlözer was, moreover, quoted as saying that Katzer's appointment was "an important act that will interest all Prussia, whether Catholic or Lutheran". The Austro-Hungarian ambassador to the Holy See was also said to have offered his government's support.[114]

The reaction in the United States was strong. Ireland gave an interview to the Associated Press expressing his indignation that foreigners should deign to interfere in the American Church with the collaboration of a small clique in America.[115] Despite Ireland's accusations against certain German-Americans, Katzer disclaimed any knowledge of the memorial or even of Cahensly, until the news

---

[112] Given in BARRY: *German-Americans*, p. 136; text is given on pp. 313–315.
[113] *Ibid.*, pp. 131–136.
[114] Quoted *ibid.*, pp. 138–139.
[115] New York *Herald,* May 31, 1891, quoted in *ibid.,* pp. 140–141.

accounts.[116] Corrigan was among the few American bishops who knew Cahensly personally, since he had helped found the branch of the *St. Raphaels-Verein* in New York. Asked for comment by newspapers, Corrigan wrote Simeoni for instructions on May 25. Cahensly, the archbishop stated, was not well informed on all American matters and his proposal would increase the "opposition of nationalities".[117] Corrigan subsequently wrote directly to Cahensly criticizing him for having played to American prejudice and advising him to consult with the American bishops about any future plans for the American Church.[118] In the meantime, if O'Connell's narration to Ireland was accurate, the Vatican seems to have been initially sympathetic with the memorial's proposals. On June 11, he reported: "When I spoke to Card. Rampolla of the indignation the Amer. Bps. would feel, if the Cahensly plan were approved, it made no impression on him. They were Irish, they were interested and their opposition & indignation were only a matter of course. But when I said that the American government would settle the matter for itself without Cahensly, the Cardinal changed his manner. It was an idea they never contemplated, and I said a Culturkampf [*sic*] was as possible in America as in Germany". If "English speaking Catholics" were to "stand shoulder to shoulder with their fellow citizens" in ridding the Church of the taint of foreignism, he advised Ireland, "the apprehension of the American government must be your protection".[119]

As American protests against the Lucerne memorial continued to reach Propaganda, Cahensly touched off another round of dispute. When he was in Rome to present the memorial, Rampolla suggested he draw up more specific recommendations. Cahensly complied and together with Volpe-Landi drew up a new memorial for Rampolla. This one claimed that sixteen million immigrants and their descendants had been lost to the American Church. Among the causes alleged were lack of Catholic organizations to protect the workingmen and the existence of public schools, both issues dear to the liberals.[120] O'Connell obtained a copy of the new document and sent it to Ireland for release to the press.[121]

Even as O'Connell was writing Ireland, however, Rome was formulating its response. On June 15, Rampolla sent Simeoni an account written by the American Church historian, John Gilmary Shea, in the New York *Catholic News* for May 13, 1891. Shea denied that there had been a disproportionate number of Irish ap-

---

[116] CURRAN: *Corrigan*, p. 324.
[117] APF, SCAmerCent, 58 (1892), 1056[r–v], Corrigan to Simeoni, New York, May 25, 1891.
[118] AANY, Corrigan to Cahensly, New York, July 22, 1891 (copy), in CURRAN: *Corrigan*, pp. 324–325.
[119] AASP, O'Connell to Ireland, Rome, June 11, 1891.
[120] Given in BARRY: *German-Americans*, p. 316.
[121] AASP, O'Connell to Ireland, Rome, June 13, 1891; cf. BARRY: *German-Americans*, p. 148.

pointed to the hierarchy and saw the danger of foreign interference to Catholic liberty in the United States.[122] Informed of the American reaction to the first memorial, the pope reserved the decision to himself. On June 28, Rampolla communicated this decision to Gibbons. "The Apostolic See", he wrote, "after careful examination, finds that plan neither opportune nor necessary". The Holy Father, concluded Rampolla, had instructed him: "to address Your Eminence not only to dissuade you from encouraging or assisting this movement, caused by unfounded fear, but also to beg you to labor, in union with your brother bishops, for the restoration of peace, being assured that the Sovereign Head of the Church is not inclined to accept any of the proposals which could provoke even the slightest misgivings, while the pastoral care of the Catholic immigrants from different countries may be entrusted to national parish priests as is already the customary practice".[123]

On June 27, Simeoni told Corrigan that he had conferred with Cahensly and clearly rejected "his proposals on an international episcopate in the United States".[124] Corrigan was gratified to find that Propaganda shared his idea, which, he said, "is simply the idea of Catholics of America".[125] On the issue of foreign interference in the American Church, Corrigan was at one with Gibbons and Ireland.

The controversy would have ended there, had the liberals not decided to push their advantage with Rome. Earlier in the controversy, O'Connell had advised Ireland to obtain a formal protest against the Lucerne memorial from James G. Blaine, the American Secretary of State. Although O'Connell, like Ireland and Gibbons, was a strong advocate of the American form of the separation of Church and State, he feared that on this issue the Vatican might succumb to European political pressures. "In America", he wrote, "religion is always free, but in Europe it is bound up with the State, and the State with it".[126] The desired protest from the United States government, however, was actually a statement of concern and came about from an accidental meeting Gibbons had with President Benjamin Harrison. The cardinal had just received Rampolla's letter and informed the president of the decision. Harrison told Gibbons that he had "fol-

---

[122] APF, SCAmerCent, 58 (1892), 1070ʳ–1071ʳ, Rampolla to Simeoni, Vatican, June 15, 1891, with enclosure.

[123] Rampolla to Gibbons, Rome, June 28, 1891, in BARRY: *German-Americans*, p. 155. APF, SCAmerCent, 58 (1892), 1074ʳ & 1075ʳ⁻ᵛ, Rampolla to Simeoni, Vatican, July 4, 1891, enclosing a copy of his letter to Gibbons.

[124] APF, Lettere, 387 (1891), 481ᵛ, Simeoni to Corrigan, Rome, June 27, 1891 (copy).

[125] APF, SCAmerCent, 58 (1892), 1078ʳ⁻ᵛ, Corrigan to Simeoni, New York, July 14, 1891.

[126] AASP, O'Connell to Ireland, Rome, June 27, 1891.

lowed the questions with profound interest, and I regard it as a subject of deep importance to our country at large, one in which the American people are much concerned", because "foreign and unauthorized interference with American affairs cannot be viewed with indifference". The president praised Gibbons' public statements on the question and had considered writing him, but "refrained from doing so lest I should be interfering with church matters".[127]

O'Connell made copies of Gibbons' account and presented them to Simeoni and Rampolla. To the latter he complained that the letter to Gibbons had not dealt properly with the issue but had spoken almost as if the bishops were responsible. Rampolla defended the letter, for "the Holy Father had to reply in general terms without alluding to anyone". According to O'Connell, Rampolla justified listening to Cahensly, Volpe-Landi, and even von Schlözer, "when these men come to us and request us to look after the interests of their *Connazionali* that they say are losing their faith in America". Rampolla's attitude reinforced the belief of O'Connell and the liberals that many immigrants in the United States continued to regard themselves as subjects of foreign governments; and that the Vatican was seeking to placate the Central Powers by giving a friendly hearing to the proposals of Cahensly and Volpe-Landi. As O'Connell told Gibbons, "I am convinced that this question which is a purely spiritual one for us is a political one for them and that it forms part of their policy in dealing with the Central powers. Nothing will ever restrain them in America, but the voice of the civil power. It is a question of dealing with England about Ireland over again, and the language to the Episcopate is identical. The only mistake is that the Irish in America have a government behind them and that the American government has no regard for Germany. The voice of the Bps is not much in such matters".[128]

O'Connell and Ireland had of course vastly exaggerated the crisis. It seems highly unlikely, for example, that Cahensly, a member of the Center Party, would have made personal contact with von Schlözer, the Prussian minister. On the other hand, von Schlözer counted among his closest Roman friends, Archbishop Jacobini, the Secretary of Propaganda, who quite likely may have consulted the minister. Moreover, two leading German newspapers, the *National-Zeitung* and the *Magdeburger-Zeitung*, both stated that Rampolla's letter to Gibbons indicated the opposition of Leo XIII to Germany and the Triple Alliance.[129]

---

[127] AAB 88 U 2, Gibbons to O'Connell, Cape May, N.J., July 12, 1891 (copy).
[128] AAB 88 U 2, O'Connell to Gibbons, Rome, Aug. 3, 1891.
[129] See Leopold VON SCHLÖZER: *Kurd von Schlözer letzte römische Briefe: 1892–1894,* Stuttgart–Berlin–Leipzig 1924, pp. 107, 167; BARRY: *German-Americans,* pp. 158–159; see *ibid.,* p. 181 for the Holy See's policy toward Germany and the unlikelihood of Cahensly's making any direct contact with von Schlözer.

Despite the liberals' exaggeration, in other words, they may have correctly assessed that the Vatican would heed European governments in regard to American ecclesiastical affairs. Yet their exaggeration, carried to the extreme of implicating German-Americans in the foreign plot, was totally without substance. They had exacerbated the already strained relations between German-Americans and their English-speaking fellow citizens. Moreover, the two memorials and the reactions to them occurred on the eve of Katzer's installation as Archbishop of Milwaukee. He had asked Cardinal Gibbons to impose the pallium on him and to preach at the ceremony on August 20, 1891. Gibbons used the occasion to preach against discord and against the tendency of some immigrants to regard their birth-place as their real country. "God and our country!" he said, "this our watchword. Loyalty to God's Church and to our country! – this our religious and political faith".[130] The cardinal seemed to believe that Katzer and other German-Americans needed the object lesson in citizenship, for he later regarded his sermon as "one of the most audacious things I ever did".[131]

Although Ireland had been urging Gibbons to summon the archbishops to meet earlier, they did not hold their second annual meeting until November, 1891. There all the prelates, including Katzer, condemned the exaggerations contained in the memorials about losses to the Church and protested against a foreigner's interference in American Church affairs.[132] The final episode in the Cahensly issue came with Ireland's securing a government protest against the memorials. On April 22, 1892, Senator Cushman Kellogg Davis of Minnesota managed to work mention of Cahensly into his address on the Chinese Exclusion Act. The memorials, the senator declared, had attempted "to prostitute religious power to political purposes". Relying on the cable dispatches, he repeated the misrepresentations of Cahensly's consultation with European political powers. But the pope, he said, had responded to the loyal protests of the American bishops and had prevented the adoption of any of the proposals of the memorials. "Leo XIII", he declared, was "the greatest statesman since Ganganelli who has sat in the Chair of St. Peter".[133] This allusion must have been suggested by O'Connell's information to Ireland that it was the Jesuits whose influence in Rome was working against the liberals; for one of the statesmanly acts for which Lorenzo Ganganelli, when Pope Clement XIV, was remembered was the suppression of the Jesuits in 1773.

What melded the Jesuits, the Germans, and the Irish conservatives into a cohe-

---

[130] In James Cardinal GIBBONS: *A Retrospect of Fifty Years*, 2 vols., Baltimore 1916, II, 148–155.

[131] Quoted in Allen Sinclair WILLS: *Life of Cardinal Gibbons, Archbishop of Baltimore*, New York 1922, II, 530.

[132] AAB, 89 D 5, Minutes of the Meeting of Archbishops, St. Louis, Nov. 1891; ELLIS: *Gibbons*, I, 378–379.

[133] Quoted in BARRY: *German-Americans*, pp. 202–203.

sive group, as will be seen shortly, was not the nationality question, but the issue of parochial schools and of state supervision of education in a pluralistic society. Simultaneously with the interrelated problems of German-Americans and schools, however, occurred a tragic and neglected episode — the attitude of the American hierarchy toward the new immigrants of the Byzantine Rite from eastern Europe. Again the episcopal leader in the controversy was John Ireland, but this time he had the consistent support of Michael A. Corrigan.

b. Oriental Catholics

In the late 1880s and 1890s a relatively small but significant number of Carpatho-Russian and Galician Uniate Catholics settled in the coal mining regions of Pennsylvania and in Minnesota. They presented a new phenomenon for both American culture and Catholicism. Unlike the earlier immigrants from Germany and Ireland, these did not speak a western European language nor did they follow the Latin Rite, uniformly practiced by Catholics throughout the United States up to that time. One of their most obvious and controversial departures from the uniformity of American Catholicism was their introduction of a married clergy. They wished, moreover, to remain separate from American culture and resisted being either Americanized or Latinized. But it was the issue of celibacy which brought them into conflict with Ireland.

In 1889, Ruthenian Catholics had established a congregation in Minneapolis and brought over Father Alexis Toth, who had the recommendation of his bishop in Eperjes. After several months ministering to his congregation, Toth presented himself to Archbishop Ireland. It was an unfortunate confrontation. Toth argued that he did not need the authorization to function from a Latin Rite bishop. But, in addition, he had been married, though he was then a widower. Ireland had him ejected from his residence and Toth and his congregation were subsequently received into the Russian Orthodox Church. Toth then became a leading figure in the conversion of other Uniates to the Orthodox Church.[134]

Ireland introduced the issue of Oriental Rite Catholics at the first meeting of the archbishops in 1890. The prelates unanimously requested that Gibbons write Propaganda in their names "praying that all Priests of the Greek Rite in America derive their jurisdiction entirely and exclusively from the Ordinaries in this country; and that none others but celibate Priests be allowed to come hither".[135] Propaganda made no formal reply to Gibbons' request, but, instead, in October wrote Ireland and Bishop Tobias Mullen of Erie, supporting their actions toward

---

[134] Keith S. RUSSIN: *Father Alexis G. Toth and the Wilkes-Barre Litigations*, in: St. Vladimir's Theological Quarterly 16 (1972) 132–135.

[135] AAB 87 R 4, Minutes of the Meeting of Archbishops, Boston, July 23–24, 1890.

Oriental Rite Catholics and decreeing that priests of that rite who went to the United States permanently were to be celibate. Many Oriental Rite priests, however, claimed that this letter was not applicable outside the Archdiocese of St. Paul and the Diocese of Erie. At their second meeting in 1891, therefore, the archbishops, principally preoccupied with Cahenslyism, requested that Gibbons formally promulgate Propaganda's letter to the entire hierarchy.[136]

In the meantime, the Oriental Rite Catholics found one friendly voice among the Latin Rite bishops, John Lancaster Spalding. Spalding sponsored an appearance before the archbishops in 1892 of Father Nicephorus Chenith, pastor of St. Michael's Greek Catholic Church in Passaic, New Jersey. Chenith and two other Oriental Rite priests made up the Priests' Committee which sought to provide priests for congregations of their rite, guarantee them a proper salary, and represent the needs of their rite before both the Latin bishops and Rome. At their meeting in 1892, the archbishops were principally concerned with discussing a series of proposals on public and parochial schools, presented by Archbishop Francesco Satolli. They took time, however, to listen to Chenith's plea that married priests be allowed to function among Oriental Rite Catholics in the United States, that an Oriental priest, under the jurisdiction of Latin ordinaries, be appointed as superior of Oriental Catholics, and that the legal customs of the rite be preserved. In response, the archbishops delegated Corrigan to present their views to Propaganda that the congregation should enforce its earlier ruling on both jurisdiction and on celibacy and that Basilian monks be induced to take over the spiritual care of eastern Catholics in the United States.[137]

Propaganda replied that for the time being married priests could exercise the ministry, but that monks should be used as much as possible. This to the archbishops was totally unacceptable. "The presence of married priests of the Greek rite in our midst is a constant menace to the chastity of our unmarried clergy" and "a source of scandal to the laity", they resolved at their meeting in 1893; "the sooner this point of discipline is abolished ..., the better for religion, because the possible loss of a few souls of the Greek rite bears no proportion to the blessings resulting from uniformity of discipline".[138]

The prelates, so seriously divided among themselves on other issues, were yet united in excluding a married eastern clergy. In their efforts both to preserve their jurisdiction over Oriental Rite Catholics and to guarantee a celibate clergy, they were successful. On April 12, 1894, Propaganda issued a circular letter to all bishops of the Latin Rite. Oriental prelates, it said, were ordered not to send a

---

[136] AAB 89 D 5, Minutes of the Meeting of Archbishops, St. Louis, Nov. 27, 1891.
[137] AAB 90 Q 3, Minutes of the Meeting of Archbishops, New York, Nov. 16–19, 1892; 91 B 8, Corrigan to Ledochowski, New York, Jan. 18, 1893 (copy).
[138] AAB 91 V 1/1, Minutes of the Meeting of Archbishops, Chicago, Sept. 12–13, 1893.

priest to the United States or other Latin Rite territories, unless he was celibate or widowed, had obtained the permission of the bishop of the place to which he was going, the written authorization of Propaganda, and the proper faculties of his own bishop.[139] Such a complicated procedure did little to obviate the difficulties.

Chenith again appeared before the archbishops in 1894. This time he asked for the appointment of an Oriental vicar general and for the temporary granting of faculties to married priests, as Propaganda had earlier suggested. Ireland and Feehan both strongly objected to these proposals and, together with Corrigan and Ryan, were appointed a committee to examine the problem. They adopted a proposal, originally made by Archbishop Williams, that an Oriental priest "enjoying the confidence of his Ecclesiastical Superior, should be recommended to other Bishops in whose Dioceses the Greek faithful are found", so that he could provide information on the clergy and laity of that rite. Without any jurisdiction, "he should receive in each Diocese such powers, only, as the Ordinary might see proper to confer". The committee unanimously rejected "the project of the appointment of a Vicar Apostolic for the Greek faithful, or even of a Vicar General, whose powers over the Greeks should extend throughout various Dioceses, or even over the whole country". Finally, it requested that Gibbons "inquire in Rome, if the Latin rite exclusively could be observed in the United States".[140] As the committee saw the issue, then, it was not merely a question of celibacy but of having an independent ecclesiastical jurisdiction within the territorial limits of a diocese. Such a situation was a step beyond what the Lucerne memorial had proposed in suggesting representation of each nationality in the hierarchy.

Propaganda did not accede to the wishes of the archbishops, if they were ever proposed formally to it. Instead, on May 1, 1897, the congregation decreed that, while the earlier prescriptions remained in force, an Oriental Catholic, temporarily resident in North America, could conform to the Latin rite, until he returned to his own country; an Oriental, permanently resident in North America, was not to transfer to the Latin rite, without the Holy See's permission; and finally, each archbishop, after consulting his suffragans, was "to depute a Ruthenian priest commendable for his celibacy and capability" or "a Priest of the Latin rite acceptable to the Ruthenians, who should exercise vigilance and direction over the people and clergy of the aforesaid rite, with, however, entire dependence on the Ordinary of the place, who in accordance with his judgment should give him the faculties which he judges in the Lord to be necessary".[141] Propaganda thus

---

[139] Circular letter of Propaganda, Apr. 12, 1894, included in AAB, Fumasoni-Biondi to Curley, Washington, Nov. 19, 1931.

[140] AAB 93 L 5, Minutes of the Meeting of Archbishops, Philadelphia, Oct. 11, 1894.

[141] Acta Sanctae Sedis 30 (1897–1898) 635–636.

guaranteed the continuation of the Oriental rites in the United States, while not yet making provision for the appointment of a national vicar general or bishop. That would have to wait until the early twentieth century.

A year after Propaganda's decree, Archbishop Sebastian Martinelli, the apostolic delegate, circularized the archbishops for an evaluation of the new regulations. Ryan wrote: "I know no good *unmarried* Greek priest. The one I know is intemperate". He had therefore appointed a married priest as his vicar, but he strongly recommended that a visitor be sent by the Holy See.[142] In the metropolitan Province of San Francisco, Riordan wrote, there were "twenty families of Syrians and a few wandering Armenians". He had therefore not appointed a vicar.[143] Ireland said the decree had little application in his province, because there were so few Oriental Catholics. He noted that there had been a small community of perhaps thirty families in Minneapolis, whose "Pastor sold himself out for Russian gold, and since then these people, or the larger number of them, are under the jurisdiction of the Greek Schismatic Bishop of San Francisco". Some of these people had since returned, he continued, and "have united with Polish parishes of the Latin rite and are perfectly satisfied". As far as Ireland was concerned, these people were now members of the Latin rite and he urged that where Oriental Catholics were "scattered in small number, all facilities should be allowed them to join the Latin rite".[144] Ireland was by that time deeply enmeshed in the controversy of Americanism, in the aftermath of which he accepted what he had previously opposed in Cahenslyism — the influence of a foreign government in American ecclesiastical affairs. But the stance which he and the other archbishops, liberal and conservative, had taken in the 1890s resulted in the loss of over 225,000 Carpatho-Russian and Galician Uniates to the Orthodox Church.[145]

The establishment of a separate jurisdiction for Oriental rite Catholics occurred only after the liberal-conservative controversy was ended. While it played no major role in that controversy, it did manifest the mindset of the late nineteenth-century bishops, all of whom were eager not to upset the delicate balance with the American cultural majority by introducing a tradition, so foreign to American Catholicism, as a married clergy. But the bishops were far from agreement on other areas of rapproachment with American society and no issue was more controversial than that of parochial schools.

---

[142] ASV, DAUS, "Stati Uniti," 28, Ryan to Martinelli, Philadelphia, Mar. 24, 1898.

[143] *Ibid.*, Riordan to Martinelli, San Francisco, Mar. 26, 1898.

[144] *Ibid.*, Ireland to Martinelli, St. Paul, Mar. 24, 1898.

[145] For a fuller treatment of this topic, see Gerald P. FOGARTY: *The American Hierarchy and Oriental Rite Catholics, 1890–1907*, in: Records of the American Catholic Historical Society of Philadelphia 85 (Mar., June, 1974) 17–28.

CHAPTER III

THE SCHOOL CONTROVERSY: WAR OF THE PRELATES

A. IRELAND'S SCHOOL ADDRESS

The Third Plenary Council, as was seen, legislated that every parish was to have a school within two years of the end of the council, an ideal which was impossible to realize. For the Germans, the parochial school was a choice means of preserving their culture in a foreign land. For the Irish conservatives, praise of the public school was tantamount to promoting religious indifference. For European conservative Catholics, public education was inextricably linked with the liberal State's exclusive demand of the right to educate with the consequent denial of that right to the Church. From the American liberals, praise of the public schools was soon forthcoming. Addressing the American Education Association in 1890, John Ireland spoke of the public school as "our pride and glory. The Republic of the United States has solemnly affirmed its resolve that within its borders no clouds of ignorance shall settle upon the minds of the children of its people. In furnishing the means to accomplish this result its generosity knows no limit. The free school of America! Withered be the hand raised in sign of its destruction".[1]

Ireland's only complaint against the public schools was that they excluded from their curriculum the religion which civilized the western world and safeguarded the family and society. To alleviate this situation, he made two proposals. The first was to adopt the system operative in England where the state paid for all or part of the secular education given in denominational schools. The second was to imitate the practice of Poughkeepsie, New York, where the Church built the schools, but the school board rented them during class hours, paid teachers' salaries, and examined both teachers and students. Religious instruction was conducted only outside of class hours.[2]

Ireland gave his speech just as he and the other liberals were working to promote Spalding to Milwaukee. The school and German issues soon became intertwined and gave rise to what one historian has aptly described as "The War of the

---

[1] John IRELAND: *The Church and Modern Society*, St. Paul 1905, I, 220.
[2] Cf. *ibid.*, pp. 217–232.

Prelates".[3] For his stance on public schools Ireland now found himself delated to Rome. Among his accusers was Cardinal Paul Melchers, former Archbishop of Cologne, who wrote to Simeoni on August 19. Enclosing a copy of Ireland's address from a Milwaukee German Catholic newspaper and noting that he was in correspondence with many priests and laymen in the United States, he asserted that many aspects of the address could not be reconciled with Catholic teaching. The Holy See would have to intervene, he said, or else Ireland's speech could endanger the very existence of parochial schools, which were already the objects of contention with both "the government of the republic and the sects".[4] O'Connell soon got word of this intervention. He notified Ireland and alerted Gibbons to write in Ireland's defense.[5] Gibbons' response was an accolade of the archbishop, whose detractors, he said, "are narrow and contracted & who do not understand the country in which they live".[6] O'Connell retained Gibbons' letter for future presentation to Propaganda. He was well aware of the growing American opposition to Ireland, for according to Ella B. Edes, she had told him that "Ireland was the stuff of which heretics were made".[7]

Ireland's speech helped the Germans and English-speaking conservatives coalesce into a single party. They were in correspondence not only with Melchers, but, O'Connell reported, also with Mazzella.[8] The reason for German opposition to Ireland on the school question was not hard to discover. His speech came just at the time that the German-American bishops were mounting a campaign against the Bennett Law introduced in the Wisconsin legislature. The law would require that English be the language of instruction in all schools. It was aimed at German schools, both Catholic and Lutheran, where English was not used. In March, 1890, Archbishop Michael Heiss of Milwaukee and his suffragans, Frederick Katzer and Kilian Flasch, published a protest against it in Wisconsin. Ireland's speech seemed to give public support to the proposed legislation,[9] although he himself denied it.

In the meantime, Ireland had become the darling of liberal journalists in Europe and America whose reporting further complicated his situation. William

[3] CURRAN: Corrigan, p. 316.
[4] APF, SCAmerCent, 53 (July–Oct. 1890), 288^r–290^r, Melchers to Simeoni, Frascati, Aug. 19, 1890.
[5] AASP, O'Connell to Ireland, Rome, Sept. 12, 1890; AAB 87 V 4, O'Connell to Gibbons, Grottaferrata, Sept. 6, 1890.
[6] AAB 87 V 5, Gibbons to O'Connell, Baltimore, Sept. 10, 1890 (copy).
[7] AASPOW (CUA microfilm), Edes to Smith, Rome, Sept. 22, 1890.
[8] AASP, O'Connell to Ireland, Rome, Nov. 15, 1890.
[9] AASP, Correspondence Copy Book, p. 23, Nov. 1, 1890, cited in MOYNIHAN: Ireland, p. 82. For another view, cf. BARRY: German-Americans, pp. 184–185.

T. Stead reported on Ireland's address at the centenary celebration of the American hierarchy in 1889, which was published in the Milan *Corriere della Sera*. Stead interpolated in Ireland's address the words: "If he were Pope he would not wring his hands in anguish over the dead and buried temporal power. Neither would he root about in the scholastic tomes of Thomas Aquinas or rely upon stimulating devotion by the granting of Indulgences". O'Connell received confidential information from Archbishop Jacobini, that this statement added to the complaints against Ireland and that the cardinals of the congregation might make their decision on the school question based on his faulty information.

Arming himself with the Peter's Pence collection from three dioceses, a copy of the newspaper article, and Gibbons' letter defending Ireland, O'Connell went to Leo XIII. Having explained the *Corriere* article, he then described the financial burden on the American Church in maintaining parochial schools without any State aid. Ireland's address, he said simply stated that the Church was not opposed to public education. The Germans, he continued, blamed Ireland for the Holy See's response to Abbelen's memorial and were intent on maintaining the German language in their schools. Ireland, on the other hand, thought that education was so important that, if parents neglected to provide it, the State could act in *loco parentis*. This provoked the Germans into writing against Ireland to Rome. O'Connell then read Gibbons' defense of Ireland to the pope who asked that it be left with him. Leo had already requested Cardinal Rampolla to write Gibbons on the school question and promised O'Connell that he would not permit the cardinals of Propaganda to reach a decision until Gibbons had replied. To assist Gibbons in answering, O'Connell forwarded this and additional information about the arrangements made for Catholic education in Germany, Italy, France, England, Ireland, and Austria.[10]

Gibbons, in consultation with Ireland, drafted a reply to Rampolla on December 30, 1890. He defended Ireland's address and then turned to the reasons against any condemnation. First, he said, a rebuke to Ireland would substantiate the Protestants' charge "that in the Catholic Church there can be neither liberty nor broadness". Second, he cited Ireland's pastoral and educational work not only in his own diocese but throughout the country.

Finally, the cardinal of Baltimore said: "There are facts which give evidence that in this campaign conducted against the Archbishop of St. Paul it is not the disinterested love of truth nor the pure zeal of sound doctrine which has alone set minds in motion. His enemies have gone so far as to attribute to him sentiments and works which are no less contrary to all his thoughts and his entire conduct

---

[10] AAB 88 D 6, O'Connell to Gibbons, Rome, Nov. 24, 1890, also in Daniel F. REILLY: *The School Controversy, 1891–1893*, Washington 1943, pp. 233–236.

than to the respect and submission that every Catholic owes to the Holy See. These calumnious accusations have found an echo in certain Italian papers and it is sad to think that they have been able to make their way even to Rome, but I have the consolation, Most Holy Father, to know that it is Your Holiness himself who will judge this question with the wisdom and goodness which characterizes all your acts and I am confident that Mgr. Ireland will be all the stronger for it to continue and extend the good that he is doing". In conclusion, Gibbons enclosed a copy of Ireland's address and said that the archbishop was willing to make any changes the pope found necessary.[11]

O'Connell presented Gibbons' letter to Leo XIII. In a subsequent audience, the pope expressed his pleasure with Gibbons' support of Ireland and with the archbishop's willingness to change anything objectionable. O'Connell took the opportunity to mention that the attacks on Ireland and the appointment of Katzer, however, had created a "painful impression".[12] During the next three months there was silence and Ireland grew apprehensive. O'Connell again saw the pope, complained of the appointment of Katzer, and linked it with the indictment of Ireland. Later he learned that the pope was displeased at Propaganda for "their recent treatment of the Amer. Bps". He then began to urge Ireland to come to Rome to discuss the school address with the pope and to "roll back this reactionism forever into its grave".[13]

Other events caused O'Connell to alter the scenario which he had planned for his friend in St. Paul. In April, Cahensly presented his memorial to Propaganda and in May, the cables about the memorial appeared in the press. They linked the memorial with the school question. By June, O'Connell was urging Ireland to obtain government support for their views. He wrote: "It is likely that to settle the school question, yourself, Katzer and some other leaders from each side will be invited to Rome to give your views. If the element of apprehension on the part of the Amer. government is left out, you cannot have a chance here against Katzer. You will talk against prejudice, he will talk to them. You will stand alone, he will have Prussia behind him. I do not think it would be a bad thing to have all schools, public & private, placed under government inspection. It would improve the schools, and make some persons more cautious, nor would the government overstep its powers. It inspects the Cath. schools of England, Ireland & Canada. If they are so anxious for parochial schools, why not establish them in Italy where

---

[11] Gibbons to Leo XIII, Baltimore, Dec. 30, 1890, in REILLY: *School Controversy*, pp. 242–247.

[12] AAB 88 H 7, O'Connell to Gibbons, Rome, Jan. 25, 1891; cf. AASP, Gibbons to Ireland, Baltimore, Feb. 3, 1891.

[13] AASP, O'Connell to Ireland, Rome, Mar. 10, 1891; see also ARD, Ireland to O'Connell, St. Paul, Mar. 8, 1891.

unemployed priests have become so numerous as to constitute a pest? But here there is no national division to be kept up. In Germany the Poles are not allowed even by the Bps. to use their own tongue even for cathechism. If this evil is torn out now root & branch, the 'Liberal' Bps of America must again be taken into favor. You cannot imagine the deep secrecy & cunning with which this last movement was carried on".[14] The suggestion of a meeting in Rome with Katzer evoked an ironic response from Ireland. "Imagine the insult to myself and to the Republic", he wrote Gibbons, "to be brought to argue with Katzer, a man who knows as little of America as a Huron. Such a question must be referred to the archbishops of America, from which a joint paper should go to Rome".[15]

B. Faribault-Stillwater Plan

Ireland might never have had to discuss his educational theories in Rome if he had not put them into practice. Between August and October, 1891, the pastors of Faribault and Stillwater in his archdiocese concluded arrangements with the local school boards according to which the boards rented the parochial schools during class hours; nuns taught in the schools but were certified and had their salaries paid by the boards; and religious instructions were conducted outside class hours. Ireland now found himself attacked by Protestants who thought the State had granted too much to the Church and by Catholic opponents who thought the Church had conceded too much to the State.[16] At the forthcoming archbishops' meeting, Ireland would have not only to explain his address on schools, but also to defend the cooperative venture he had undertaken.

Just prior to the meeting, however, a pamphlet war broke out on the school question. Thomas Bouquillon, professor of moral theology at the Catholic University of America, published *Education: To Whom Does It Belong?* Originally planned as an article, it was published as a pamphlet at the suggestion of Gibbons. In it Bouquillon argued that the right of education belonged to the individual, the family, the State and the Church. If parents failed in their obligation either at home or in a school of their choice, he concluded, the State had the right to "provide by compulsory education for the future of the rising generation and for the conservation of the social body".[17] At Corrigan's request, Renè Holaind, S. J., professor of moral theology at Woodstock College, replied with *The Parent*

---

[14] AASP, O'Connell to Ireland, Rome, June 11, 1891.
[15] AAB 88 S 2, Ireland to Gibbons, St. Paul, July 2, 1891.
[16] Reilly: *School Controversy,* pp. 75–86.
[17] *Ibid.,* p. 111.

First.[18] In it the Jesuit denied the rights which Bouquillon attributed to the State and argued that the United States was a non-Christian State and had no such rights over education. The State in any case, he concluded, could provide schools only when they were absolutely necessary and not when they were merely useful.[19]

At the meeting of the archbishops held in St. Louis on November 29, 1891, there was no discussion of the pamphlets, but after the meeting Ireland was asked to explain his Faribault-Stillwater arrangements. Several archbishops explicitly agreed with the plan. The rest remained silent.[20] Though the pamphlets had not been discussed at the meeting, they made good copy for newspapers. A few weeks after the meeting, Ireland was in New York and gave an interview to the New York *Herald*. The difference between Bouquillon and Holaind, he said, was the difference between progress and reaction. "The world moves. Father Holaind remains stationary. That's the whole question as between the Jesuit Father and the Professor of the Catholic University".[21] Following this, there appeared a cable dispatch from the Associated Press in Berlin, published on December 23, 1891, in the Baltimore *Sun*. Prepared by Boeglin and O'Connell, it reported the arrangements made by the Church for education in Prussia, Austria, France, Belgium, and Italy. It concluded: "*First*, that the Catholic church does not practically contest the right of the state over primary schools, and that this implied recognition is especially admitted in German-speaking countries; *Second*, that the Church everywhere strives to have religious instructions given in the public schools by adapting itself to existing laws; *Third*, that the church never condemns to deprivation of the sacraments those who send their children to public schools in which there is no immediate danger to faith and morals; *Fourth*, that the State schools in which religious instruction is given seem to be the practical ideal of the Catholic parties of the continent".[22] The story, in other words, stated that in Europe the Church did precisely what Ireland was urging in the United States. What the liberals failed to note, however, was the difference between the Church accommodating itself to a liberal government in Europe and the Church through its leaders voluntarily surrendering its rights to the government. This was the issue which divided the liberals and the conservatives and carried the school question across the Atlantic.

Late in December, 1891, and again early in January, 1892, Katzer had written

---

[18] ARCSI, Maryl. 11–I, 36, Campbell to Anderledy, Washington, Dec. 17, 1891.

[19] REILLY: *School Controversy*, pp. 112–113; CURRAN: *Corrigan*, p. 341.

[20] Gibbons to O'Connell, Dec. 18, 1891, in: Civiltà Cattolica, an. 43 ser. 15, I (1892) 756–757.

[21] Quoted in REILLY: *School Controversy*, pp. 94–99.

[22] Quoted in *ibid.*, p. 103.

Propaganda against Ireland's school plan, which, he said, would allow the school
board to transfer students and teachers from one school to another. Corrigan too
had informed Propaganda that Ireland forced upon American Catholics a "new
and foreign theory: that state schools best suited the needs of our times".[23] These
letters helped create the atmosphere in Rome for Brandi then to write an unfavorable review of Bouquillon's pamphlet.[24] At this point, Ireland decided to go
to Rome personally to present his case.

He was entering a potentially explosive situation. Brandi explained to Gibbons
that there was some Roman mistrust and opposition to the American Church because of the activities of a small minority of the American Catholics. Ireland's interview with the *Herald* was an example. Some cardinals, he said, accepted these
statements as fact and would judge accordingly. "They have an innate hatred of
Liberalism", he said, "which here is always taken as meaning 'rebellion', 'dis-
order', 'denial of the rights of the church' etc. Unhappily they have generally understood the reports referred to as expressions of *Liberalism*, and consequently
look on their authors with suspicion. I may add that this suspicion is strengthened
by those who, going to the other extreme, wish to appear more Roman than the
Romans, and speak and write of their opponents as 'liberals', 'revolutionary men'
etc."[25] The term "Liberalism" had a frightening ring in the Rome of the 1890s
and only a few months before Brandi had assured Holaind "(confidentially) that
Archbishop Ireland is now well known in Rome as a liberal and revolutionary
bishop. I have had occasion to speak of him to Cardinals Rampolla [Raffaele]
Monaco (the Vicar of Rome) and Mazzella".[26] Father Thomas Campbell, Jesuit
Provincial of the Maryland-New York Province, had already written to Anthony
Anderledy, the Jesuit General, that Ireland had "denounced Father Holaind in the
public press, especially because he does not agree, as he is accustomed to say,
with American ideas". Campbell concluded with the ominous warning that "that
Archbishop is a quasi tribune of the plebes, and, even though he is himself an
Irishman, he continuously appeals to the prejudices of the nation".[27]

Ireland arrived in Rome early in February, 1892. There he found friends as well
as enemies. Cardinal Miecislaus Ledochowski, who became Prefect of Propaganda after Simeoni's death in January, seemed favorably disposed to the school
plan.[28] Archbishop Francesco Satolli, who had been reported in the St. Louis

---

[23] APF, Acta, 262 (1892), Sommario, 197^r–202^v, Corrigan to Simeoni, Jan. 1, 1892; Katzer to Simeoni, Dec. 19, 1891 and to Ledochowski, Jan. 23, 1892; CURRAN: *Corrigan*, pp. 343–344.
[24] Civiltà Cattolica, an. 43, ser. 15, I (1892) 82–92.
[25] AAB 89 K 1, Brandi to Gibbons, Rome, Jan. 18, 1892.
[26] AGU, Brandi to Holaind, Rome, Oct. 16, 1891.
[27] ARCSI, Maryl. 11–I, 36, Campbell to Anderledy, Washington, Dec. 17, 1891.
[28] AASP, Gibbons to Ireland, Baltimore, Feb. 26, 1892.

Amerika as stating that Ireland had been ordered to come to Rome, not only denied the report but praised Ireland's "practical wisdom", his "untiring zeal", and his "veneration and submission to the Holy See" by his voluntarily coming to Rome.[29] On March 1, O'Connell cabled Gibbons the news: "Tide turned. Papa, Rampolla espouse Ireland's cause". On the same day, Gibbons wrote the pope defending the Faribault-Stillwater plan and confided to O'Connell: "It is not the Faribault school that is on trial, but the question to be decided is whether the Church is to be governed by men or by children, – by justice and truth, or by diplomacy and intrigue, whether the church is to be honored as a bulwark of liberty and order, or to be despised and suspected as an enemy of our Institutions". Gibbons, then, shared Ireland's notions about "American ideas". He closed his letter to O'Connell by saying that he had asked the pope to "write something in commendation of Abp. Ireland. This would put a stop to the barking".[30]

Gibbons' letter to the pope was "magnificent and Abp. Ireland is delighted", O'Connell reported to Alphonse Magnien, S.S., Gibbons' theological adviser. The only open question, he continued, was a papal letter vindicating Ireland, but on the basic school issue "all Rome has gone over to Ireland and the Pope". Cardinals Lucido Parocchi and Serafino Vannutelli praised Ireland's school plan. Moreover, O'Connell continued: "Rampolla expressed his regret for the articles in the 'Civiltà'. Parocchi says these are most imprudent and dangerous in America. 'It does not do', he says, 'to argue to the American people with a drawn sword'."[31]

The *Civiltà* and the Jesuits had been the principal Roman opponents to the liberals and Ireland now took the offensive against them. On March 7, he wrote to Rampolla complaining bitterly of the attacks from *Civiltà* and noting that Ledochowski had enjoined him to silence while Propaganda was considering the case.[32] He did not point out that the day before he had written to Brandi demanding that he publish Gibbons' letter of December 18, 1891, to O'Connell, reporting the action of the archbishops' meeting. Brandi complied by publishing both Ireland's letter to him and Gibbons' letter. One paragraph in the latter soon created turmoil: "The Archbishop expressed a willingness to discontinue this system [at Faribault and Stillwater], if his colleagues should so advise him. But he received no such advice, because the advantage was totally on his side. The Archbishop answered several questions asked by his colleagues and the result was a triumphant vindication". Brandi however, added the note that the *Civiltà* at-

---

[29] ADR, Satolli to Ireland, Rome, Mar. 18, 1892.
[30] ADR, Gibbons to O'Connell, Baltimore, Mar. 1, 1892.
[31] ASMS, O'Connell to Magnien, Rome, Mar. 15, 1892.
[32] ASV, SS, 280 (1897), fasc. 6, 51ʳ–52ᵛ, Ireland to Rampolla, Rome, Mar. 7, 1892.

tacked not Ireland's school plan, but only Bouquillon's attributing the right of education to the State. Furthermore, he noted that Gibbon's letter was three months old and contained his private opinion expressed to D'Connell. Prefacing the letter was the statement that Ireland had to take sole responsibility for the publication.[33]

The conservative reaction to Gibbons' letter was disingenuous at best. On March 15, O'Connell informed Corrigan that "Abp. Ireland's case is progressing favorably"[34] to which Corrigan replied: "If not indiscreet, I would like to know what it is, and how it is progressing".[35] On March 28, Corrigan wrote Gibbons about the last paragraph in the cardinal's letter to O'Connell, "from which, at least on the principle that 'silence gives consent', one might infer that all the Archbishops of the United States sanctioned the Faribault. No reference to such approval is found, as far as I know, in the official Record of the meeting drawn up by Mgr. Ireland Himself". All Corrigan could recall was that an explanation was given but no opinions asked.[36] He was of course directly challenging Gibbons' veracity, but the cardinal stood behind his letter and replied: "As none of the Prelates advised him [Ireland] to give up his plan, though this seemed to be the time and place to do so, if that plan had been considered to be truly objectionable, and as the archbishop's statements and answers to difficulties were such as to elicit an expression of dissent, I could not help believing and stating that his explanations were regarded as a triumphant vindication of his cause".[37]

But Corrigan was hard at work devising a plot against Ireland behind Gibbons' back. He secretly circulated a letter among the archbishops stating that at their meeting Ireland had explained the arrangements he had made with the school boards; that some archbishops raised some objections to this "secularization"; but that they were not expected to render judgment on the plan. The letter, addressed to *Civiltà* and Cardinal Ledochowski, was signed by Corrigan, Patrick Feehan of Chicago, William Henry Elder of Cincinnati, Patrick John Ryan of Philadelphia, William Gross of Oregon City, Francis Janssens of New Orleans, and Frederick Katzer of Milwaukee.[38] Williams of Boston and Kenrick of St. Louis declined to take part in discussion of the matter and Salpointe of Santa Fe

---

[33] Civiltà Cattolica, an. 43, ser. 15, I (1892) 755–761; the originals of the letters are in ACC. See also AAB 89 R 6, Brandi to Gibbons, Rome, Mar. 11, 1892.

[34] AANY, O'Connell to Corrigan, Rome, Mar. 15, 1892.

[35] ADR, Corrigan to O'Connell, New York, Mar. 27, 1892.

[36] AAB 89 S 6, Corrigan to Gibbons, New York, Mar. 28, 1892.

[37] AANY, Gibbons to Corrigan, Baltimore, Mar. 29, 1892; copy in AAB 89 S 8, quoted in ELLIS: *Gibbons*, I, 678.

[38] ACC, Corrigan *et al.* to Brandi, New York, Apr. 16, 1892.

had not replied.[39] Ireland was furious at the letter and thought the seven signers were "men not having the courage of their convictions when they should speak — and intriguers when they think they are not to be found out".[40] For a while Ireland turned his ire on Patrick Riordan, Archbishop of San Francisco, who he suspected had broken the liberal line. Riordan's reply to Corrigan's circular was that at the meeting the archbishops were not a judicial body but had been asked to listen to Ireland's report without passing judgment.[41]

The publication of Gibbons' letter about the archbishops' meeting had caused a stir in Rome. Rumors made the rounds that Bouquillon's pamphlet would be condemned and that Ireland's position on the "secularization" of the Faribault and Stillwater schools as well as on papal temporal power would be investigated. Cardinal Camillo Mazzella, who was supposed to have been deputed to make a judgment on Ireland, was carefully informed of the conservative stance.[42] Cardinal Rampolla, also reputed to have been appointed to judge the case, was informed by a cable from Corrigan that the letter of the seven archbishops had been sent.[43]

In the meantime, however, sometime late in March or early in April, Ireland presented to Propaganda Gibbons' letter of March 1 and his own memorial on the school question. He moved beyond a defense of the Faribault-Stillwater plan to concern for the religious education of children attending public schools. He pointed out that while he had diligently worked to implement the decrees of the Third Plenary Council, they placed an unrealistic financial burden on the American Catholic people. Finally, he argued that the public schools provided for the financial improvement of poorer Catholics and that therefore bishops should not compel parents to send their children to parochial schools.[44]

Propaganda's 'tolerari potest.'

Before the letter from the seven archbishops could have reached Rome, the school question was referred to a special commission of Propaganda and Cardi-

---

[39] AANY, Corrigan to Rt. Rev. dear Friend (Healy?), Apr. 20, 1892.

[40] AAB 89 W 8, Ireland to Gibbons, Genoa, June 5, 1892.

[41] AANY, Corrigan to Rt. Rev. dear Friend, Apr. 20, 1892; ACC, Russo to Brandi, New York, Apr. 19, 1892; AAB 89 W 4, Riordan to Gibbons, San Francisco, May 29, 1892; cf. AAB 89 U 9, Riordan to Magnien, San Francisco, Apr. 23, 1892.

[42] AANY, Katzer to Corrigan, Milwaukee, Apr. 18, 1892; ACC, Russo to Brandi, New York, n.d. (Apr. 8, 1892).

[43] AANY, Corrigan to Katzer, New York, Apr. 20, 1892 (copy); CURRAN: Corrigan, p. 347.

[44] Ireland to Ledochowski, Rome, n.d., quoted in REILLY: School Controversy, pp. 250–266.

nal Serafino Vannutelli was delegated to draw up the *ponenza*. He outlined Ireland's arrangement with the school boards in Faribault and Stillwater and noted that this, when followed by Bouquillon's pamphlet, had revived the polemic against Ireland's speech in 1890. He reported the responses of the bishops polled by Simeoni and quoted a letter from Bishop John Kain of Wheeling stating that the "reason for opposition to Monsig. Ireland is the *question of nationality*". Holaind's attack on Bouquillon, according to Kain, was part of the general lack of Jesuit sympathy for the Catholic University. Vannutelli then listed the canonical legislation in the United States regulating education and said that Ireland had been given the arguments against his arrangement, but not the names of the bishops opposed, so that he could draw up his defense. It was now up to the cardinals to judge whether his defense was adequate and in accord with the existing legislation.[45]

On April 21, the special congregation of Cardinals Parocchi, Ledochowski, Zigliara, Vannutelli, and Rampolla, met. Noticeably missing was Mazzella, who had earlier been reported as having been deputed to investigate Bouquillon's pamphlet and who would have been expected to side with his fellow Jesuits against Ireland. On the other hand, as will be seen, the actions of Brandi during the investigation may have antagonized the members of the commission. All the members, moreover, except Zigliara, had already been reported as favoring Ireland's plan. The commission's judgment was an overwhelming vindication of Ireland. Not only did it state that in view of the circumstances cited by Ireland his plan could be "tolerated" *(tolerari potest)*, but, as Gibbons had hoped, it also directed the prefect in the name of the pope to write Ireland saying his explanation had fully satisfied Propaganda and assuring "him that he enjoys the confidence of the Holy See". Papal approval for the decision was given the same day,[46] but it was not communicated to Ireland until April 30.[47]

The liberals were elated. Gibbons congratulated Ireland, but warned him to "do nothing to wound or irritate. Your victory is sufficient ground for the humiliation of others".[48] Keane thought the decision was "a triumph which marks an epoch".[49] Bishop John Foley of Detroit added the humorous remark to O'Connell, who had engineered the Roman phase of the liberal victory, that Corrigan's "head may be sore, I do not think it will ever be *red*".[50]

---

[45] APF, Acta, 262 (1892), 150ʳ–154ʳ, S. Vannutelli Ponenza, Apr., 1892.

[46] *Ibid.*, 155ʳ⁻ᵛ.

[47] Ledochowski to Ireland, Rome, Apr. 30, 1892, in REILLY: *School Controversy*, pp. 160–162.

[48] AASP, Gibbons to Ireland, Baltimore, Apr. 28, 1892.

[49] ADR, Keane to Ireland, Washington, Apr. 29, 1892.

[50] ADR, Foley to O'Connell, Detroit, June 20, 1892.

Foley's remark about Corrigan's not getting a red hat came at a time of serious effort to get one for Ireland. The initiative for the cardinalate for Ireland came from two lay friends, Austin Ford of the New York *Freeman's Journal*, and Richard C. Kerens, Republican national committeeman from Missouri and a friend of President Benjamin Harrison. Kerens obtained from Harrison a statement that the government would be pleased if Ireland were named a cardinal. He then had James Blaine, the Secretary of State, write in favor of the proposal to Cardinal Rampolla through Cardinal Gibbons. Gibbons himself wrote Rampolla on April 17 urging the honor for Ireland. At a suitable opportunity, O'Connell presented the letters and for a while the reaction was encouraging. Rampolla and Ledochowski personally hinted to Ireland that he would soon receive the red hat.[51] Rampolla implied to Gibbons that it was simply a matter of waiting until the next consistory.[52] But Ireland was not to get a red hat and one reason was that the *tolerari potest*, far from silencing opposition, had increased it. Trouble was brewing on both sides of the Atlantic.

In Rome, Brandi had hatched a plot against Ireland so surreptitiously that the archbishop insisted on blaming Ella B. Edes.[53] On April 7, possibly through Mazzella, he managed to get a copy of Ireland's supposedly confidential memorial to Propaganda. He then wrote a detailed rebuttal of all the charges Ireland made against *Civiltà* and submitted it to Propaganda, but it is uncertain whether he did this before or after the commission met.[54] To Campbell he confided that he had "secured" the document "with no little diplomacy for His Grace of New York".[55] He had also obtained a copy of Gibbons' letter of March 1 defending Ireland. Making excerpts of both documents, he passed them on to Campbell who transcribed them for Corrigan.[56] Corrigan's possession of these documents caused another controversy.

In his letter to Leo XIII, Gibbons had stated that if the Holy See maintained its silence on the school question, the American public would view it as a condemnation of Ireland. If this attitude grew, the cardinal feared "that national sentiment would be excited and measures obnoxious to Catholics, would be proposed in school matters".[57] Gibbons here merely expressed his moderate stance of doing

---

[51] AAB 89 W 8, Ireland to Gibbons, Genoa, June 5, 1892.

[52] ADR, Ireland to O'Connell, Washington, July 11, 1892.

[53] AAB 89 W 8, Ireland to Gibbons, Genoa, June 5, 1892; ADR, Ireland to O'Connell, St. Paul, Aug. 10, 1892.

[54] APF, Acta, 262 (1892), 175^r–180^v.

[55] AMPSJ, Brandi to Campbell, Rome, June 11, 1892.

[56] AMPSJ, Brandi to Campbell, Rome, Apr. 8, 1892; AANY, Campbell to Corrigan, New York, Apr. 24, 1892 with enclosure.

[57] Quoted in REILLY: *School Controversy*, p. 178.

nothing to arouse the anti-Catholic bias which the American Protective Association was then trying to stir up.

Ireland's approach was different. He appealed to the sensitivities of Roman cardinals in words reminiscent of O'Connell's expression on Cahensly's proposals. With the publicity given to the question, the archbishop said: "public opinion considers me as the representative of the Church party in the United States in favor of the government and considers my opponents as a foreign party to the United States and a great danger to the Republic. In case of an adverse decision, I have serious reason to be alarmed. We Catholics are only one in eight in the United States, without wealth and influence, and a much larger proportion of Catholics than this, both in point of wealth and influence, did not prevent the Kulturkampf in Germany".[58]

Corrigan's attention focused on the two passages quoted above. On April 25, four days after Propaganda had reached its decision on the school question, he discussed Ireland and Gibbons' letters with his suffragans who were gathered for the consecration of Bishop Charles McDonnell of Brooklyn. The New York bishops petitioned the pope not to be swayed by any threats of persecution in rendering his decision.[59] On May 23, Leo coldly responded that he had reached his decision based, not on false rumors of persecution, but on the premise that, while the legislation of the Third Plenary Council was to be upheld, exceptional cases could be tolerated. He concluded by calling on all the bishops to be united "by the most perfect bonds of charity to the other venerable brethren" in the United States.[60] Like the earlier petition of the seven archbishops, the protest of the New York bishops "fell flat", said Ireland. Leo had told him of the protest and read "to me his reply, which was a lesson to Corrigan a justification of myself".[61]

Corrigan had, indeed, overstepped himself and he succeeded in antagonizing the pope yet further. On May 3, Ledochowski wrote the American hierarchy officially confirming the Faribault-Stillwater decision and asking them to discuss the religious education of children in public schools at the next archbishops' meeting. At this time also, Ireland and O'Connell probably discussed not only the sending of Satolli to attend the meeting but also his becoming a permanent apostolic delegate. On May 5, at a dinner following the consecration of Bishop Henry Gabriels of Ogdensburg, Corrigan announced that he had received a cable from Rome

---

[58] Quoted in *ibid.*, p. 179.

[59] ASV, SS, 280 (1897), fasc. 1, 63ʳ, Corrigan to Rampolla, New York, Apr. 25, 1892; CURRAN: *Corrigan*, pp. 353–354.

[60] ASV, SS, 280 (1897), fasc. 1, 66ʳ–71ᵛ and 72ʳ–76ᵛ (two separate drafts); the final version is given in ZWIERLEIN: *McQuaid*, III, 170–174.

[61] AAB 89 W 8, Ireland to Gibbons, Genoa, June 5, 1892; cf. ADR, Ireland to O'Connell, Meci Merite, May 10, 1892.

stating that the Faribault system was condemned, but that the special case only was tolerated. The *Civiltà Cattolica*, silent on the issue since publishing Gibbons' letter, returned to the fray on May 18 with an article supporting the conservatives' view that Ireland's plan was actually condemned and was to be tolerated only in Faribault and Stillwater. Ireland protested to Rampolla on May 22. He specifically mentioned that Corrigan and Father Joseph Jerge, S. J., assistant provincial of the Maryland-New York Jesuit Province, spoke of *Civiltà*'s articles having "extraordinary authority from the fact that they are read and approved in the Vatican before being printed".[62] At Ireland's request, Rampolla assured him that there had been no correspondence between the Vatican and *Civiltà* on the school question and that the pope had ordered the journal not to publish any articles on the matter while it was being discussed.[63]

Rampolla's letter did little to silence Ireland's critics in Rome. Brandi went to see the pope who, the Jesuit said in a letter published in *Civiltà*, promised to have Rampolla "repair the evil done".[64] Ruggiero Freddi, S. J., the director of the journal, complained to Rampolla that, since the cardinal's letter to Ireland, English and American journals attacked *Civiltà*.[65] Brandi also denied the truth of Rampolla's letter and stated that he himself had been ordered by the pope to write on the doctrinal aspects of the school question; he had actually submitted one manuscript to the pontiff before publication, he told Campbell. Moreover, the letter recounting his audience would explain the true position of *Civiltà*. This he would publish in European papers while he left it to Campbell to do the same in the United States. "This publication", he said, "will cool down the Arch. of St. Paul, who has repeatedly declared in Rome that *he would crush the Jesuits and the Civiltà*. In this he will shamefully fail".

"In Rome", Brandi continued, "with the exception of Card. Ledochowski and Seraphinus Vannutelli, the majority of the Cardinals are utterly disgusted at the manner the affair has been treated". The other bishops, he said, should use the same tactics as Ireland. If they insisted "on their right to give freely their opinion on a matter which affects the welfare of their Church", and if they addressed "themselves directly to the Holy Father, the case of Arch. Ireland is certainly lost", for so far "his official informations have come from Card. Gibbons, Arch. Ireland and the Catholic University". Brandi was so livid with anger that it is difficult to determine whether the cause was the rejection of his ideas or the insult to

---

[62] ASV, SS, 280 (1897), fasc. 1, 77^r–78^r, Ireland to Rampolla, Rome, May 22, 1892; copy in ADR.

[63] ASV, SS, 280 (1897), fasc. 1, 79^{r-v}, Rampolla to Ireland, Vatican, May 23, 1892 (draft); copy in ADR, given in REILLY: *School Controversy*, pp. 175–176.

[64] Brandi to Ruggiero Freddi, S. J., in Civiltà Cattolica (June 18, 1892), quoted in REILLY: *School Controversy*, p. 177.

[65] ASV, SS, 280 (1897), fasc. 1, 81^{r-v}, Freddi to Rampolla, Rome, June 8, 1892.

his order. "I have been informed on very good authority", he continued, "that Arch. Ireland has spent enough in Rome to support the Faribault and Stillwater schools for at least ten years. ... He is far from being satisfied, and has every reason to fear that *the Jesuits* will finally succeed in upsetting all his plans. As far as the *Civiltà* is concerned, we are full of courage and activity. As we have fought for the last 43 years, so, with God's help, we shall continue to fight in this case. The Archbishop will have reason to regret during his whole life, to have slandered the Civiltà. On this point the whole staff is agreed". In Rome, he concluded, "our greatest enemy ... is Monsignor O'Connell", who used "dinners and presents" to secure "the services of several Monsignors belonging to the Curia ...".[66] Brandi's self-righteous defense and accusation of the liberals were dishonest at best, for only a few weeks before he had stolen Ireland's memorial and passed it on to Corrigan. He had, however, pointed out O'Connell, the most vulnerable of the liberals, who, for the moment, were all riding in the wake of Ireland's triumph.

But Ireland entertained no false hopes for the future. He urged Bishop Keane, then in France, to go to Rome to consolidate the liberal victory; he added the remark: "I forgive the Germans – they are blinded by a false patriotism. But the Jesuits & Corrigan, and other bishops of America! Sad the revelations made to me!"[67] Upon his return to the United States, Ireland followed the advice of O'Connell and Gibbons to maintain silence. But this was not easy because Corrigan and McQuaid continued to state publicly that Ledochowski's *tolerari potest* and Rampolla's statement that *Civiltà* did not represent the mind of the Holy See were only private communications. The only communication which they considered official was Ledochowski's request that the archbishops discuss the school question at their next meeting.[68]

In the meantime, Corrigan made a blunder. He made copies of Leo's letter to the New York bishops and of Ireland's memorial and sent them to several Roman cardinals. Learning of this, O'Connell prepared a cable story for the Associated Press laying Corrigan open to the charge of impugning the pope's veracity. Newspapers immediately demanded interviews with Corrigan. As Ireland reported: "The papers throughout the country have taken my side – berating Corrigan for having stolen goods, for correcting the Pope, and for refusing to accept his version of the memorial".[69] The pope was so angry at Corrigan's distributing the documents among the cardinals that Jacobini ordered the archbishop to make an apology. He only intended to defend the actions of his suffragans, a humiliated

---

[66] AMPSJ, Brandi to Campbell, Rome, June 11, 1892.

[67] ADR, Ireland to Keane, on the ocean, July 3, 1892.

[68] ADR, Ireland to O'Connell, July 7 and July 9, 1892.

[69] ADR, Ireland to O'Connell, St. Paul, Aug. 10, 1892. The cable appeared in the New York *Sun*, Aug. 4, 1892, cited in REILLY: *School Controversy*, p. 185.

Corrigan wrote Leo, and in no way to oppose the decisions of the pope. He was all the more pained because "my American enemies always accuse me of being too devoted to the Holy See".[70]

C. SATOLLI'S SPECIAL MISSION

Into this charged atmosphere O'Connell escorted Francesco Satolli on October 12, Columbus Day, 1892. Publicly, Satolli came to represent the pope at the opening of the Columbian Exposition in Chicago, but this was a cover story for his becoming the first apostolic delegate. O'Connell, as his interpreter, carefully contrived to prevent Corrigan from greeting him upon his arrival and guided the ablegate to his liberal friends in preparation for the archbishops' meeting which began on November 16.

At the meeting Satolli said he bore the pope's commission to speak to them on the school question and proceeded to lay before them fourteen propositions which O'Connell had carefully prepared for him in Rome.[71] Several of the propositions interpreted, in a liberal sense, the existing legislation of the Third Plenary Council. One restored the council decree to its original form, before it was altered by Propaganda by leaving it to the bishops' judgment whether parochial schools should be built in certain places, but it laid heavy emphasis on the religious education of children in public schools. The rest of the propositions explicitly emphasized Ireland's school plan and recognized the right of the State to educate; one went so far as to say that "the Holy See ... desires ... that, by joint action of civil and ecclesiastical authorities, there should be public schools in every state".[72]

When the archbishops were asked to sign the propositions, all but Ireland refused, so Satolli agreed to the formation of a committee of archbishops to draw up resolutions. At the closing session of the meeting on November 19, Satolli was present. He had made no substantial alterations in his document, but promised not to publish it until the archbishops could send their opinions to Rome. When Corrigan brought up several objections to the propositions, Satolli left the room in a rage. Despite Ireland's intercession, he refused to return to the meeting, but agreed not to insist that the archbishops either sign or state their consent to the

---

[70] ASV, SS, 280 (1897), fasc. 1, 90^r–91^r, Corrigan to Leo XIII, New York, Aug. 22, 1892; see CURRAN: *Corrigan*, pp. 355–356.

[71] Soderini Ms. UND.

[72] Given in REILLY: *School Controversy*, pp.271–276.

propositions. Instead he would add the clause: "all these were read and considered at the archbishops' meeting, the difficulties answered, and the requisite alterations made, November 17, 1892".[73] What the archbishops did resolve, however, was first to promote the building of parochial schools and second to provide for the religious instructions of students not in Catholic schools, preferably several times each week, and to encourage parents to instruct their children at home.[74]

Satolli's fourteen points, far from settling the dispute, had increased disagreement among the hierarchy. On November 18, while the meeting was still in session, Satolli wrote Rampolla that the archbishops had reached "unanimity in approving" his proposals. In the same letter, drafted in O'Connell's hand, he said that he had undertaken "the delicate task", entrusted to him by the pope, of "investigating what would be the impression and effects if he elevated Mons. Ireland to the cardinalate". After careful investigation, and recognizing that no one enjoyed more esteem among the lower clergy, most of the hierarchy, and the civil authorities, than Ireland, he nevertheless concluded that "it is not expedient that for the time being the Holy Father procede to create Mons. Ireland a cardinal".[75] Satolli was clearly trying to cover up the dissension which existed among the archbishops. On November 21, after the meeting, O'Connell wrote Rampolla enclosing the fourteen points and saying that Satolli asked that they be given pontifical approval. The controversy had ended, he concluded, and once passions had died down, peace would be restored.[76] What the liberals now tried to do was to make it appear that opposition to Satolli's proposals was opposition to the pope.

Shortly after the archbishops' meeting, Archbishop Elder sought to mediate between Corrigan and Satolli and to have the legate modify his proposals. He paid his respects to Satolli at the Catholic University in Washington, but did not directly discuss the issue. "It seems to me", Elder wrote Corrigan, "that Mgr. O'Connell is beginning to appreciate the force of our difficulties; and that if you could have a good conversation with him, you would get him to see them clearly".[77] No suggestion could have been more naive, but at this point Elder and other bishops were not yet as aware as Corrigan of how partisan O'Connell was. A few weeks later, Brandi wrote Corrigan that all Rome knew of the "fiasco and

---

[73] AMPSJ, James Conway, "The School Question in America," New York, Sept. 21, 1900. Cf. ELLIS: *Gibbons*, I, 695–696.

[74] AAB, 90 Q 3, Minutes of the Meeting of Archbishops, New York, Nov. 16–19, 1892.

[75] ASV, SS, 241, "Missioni Straordinarie," Busta, Sept. 92, Satolli to Rampolla, New York, Nov. 18, 1892.

[76] ASV, SS, 280 (1897), fasc. 1, 103ʳ, O'Connell to Rampolla, Baltimore, Nov. 21, 1892.

[77] AANY (Photostat, UND), Elder to Corrigan, Cincinnati, Nov. 25, 1892; see FOGARTY: *Vatican*, pp. 216–217.

blunder of Mgr. Satolli". Nevertheless, he hesitated to write an article on the doctrinal side of the school question "for fear of giving personal offence to Mgr.
Satolli". He had communicated Corrigan's views to Cardinal Mazzella, but he
urged the archbishop to have his colleagues "without delay, send an official account of the fact to Cardinal Rampolla, so as to have it made known *officially*,
before others may misrepresent the case to him".[78] Brandi here proposed the tactic, later used by Propaganda, of supporting Satolli without canonizing his school
proposals – a tactic which would subsequently undermine the liberals.

In the meantime, American newspapers continued to carry stories of the controversy. "It is manifestly war, and a war to the death", Ireland wrote Rampolla
in January, 1893. The journalistic attacks on Satolli's propositions, he continued,
were really attacks on himself and the Holy See and "the author of this criminal
act perpetrated against the archbishop of St. Paul, Mgr. Satolli, and the Holy
Father himself, the chief who directs all the operations of the war, is Monsignor
Corrigan of New York".[79] Corrigan was now on the defensive and was further
alienated from Satolli by the reconciliation of Father Edward McGlynn. Satolli
was for the time totally on Ireland's side. He had received from Elder, he told
Rampolla, several exceptions to his school proposals, "but those exceptions are
clearly false, futile and absurd in respect to the Council of Baltimore". Corrigan
was behind a conspiracy and inspired newspapers in Chicago, New York, and
elsewhere to diminish Ireland's influence and "to *constrain* the Pope to withdraw
his Delegate from America". In view of the evidence against the Archbishop of
New York, Satolli concluded: "I have to repeat, that I think it indispensable to
call Archbishop Corrigan immediately to Rome".[80]

Corrigan, on the defensive since his reprimand of the previous summer, attempted to counter newspaper stories that "I will be denounced to the Holy See
as rebellious with the effect of being removed from the see of New York". He
therefore asked Rampolla to prevent his being summoned to Washington to meet
with Satolli and in a letter enclosed for the pope pledged his "sincere fidelity and
obedience".[81] In a second, personal letter to Rampolla, Corrigan described the
conspiracy of Ireland and O'Connell against him which had made it impossible
for him to greet Satolli when the delegate first arrived in the United States. He had
collected documentation to substantiate his case, but so far had not received any
reply to his letters to Satolli.[82] At no point in the history of the controversy were

---

[78] AANY, Brandi to Corrigan, Rome, Dec. 12, 1892.
[79] ASV, SS, 280 (1897), fasc. 1, 117^r–122^v, Ireland to Rampolla, St. Paul, Jan. 10, 1893.
[80] *Ibid.*, 115^r–116^v, Satolli to Rampolla, Washington, Jan. 13, 1893.
[81] *Ibid.*, fasc. 2, 28^{r-v}, Corrigan to Rampolla, New York, Jan. 13, 1893.
[82] *Ibid.*, 29^r--30^v, Corrigan to Rampolla, New York, Jan. 13, 1893; see CURRAN: *Corrigan*,
pp. 380–383, 397–398.

the liberals more successful. Corrigan was fearful of being deposed and Brandi was hesitant to write against Satolli's propositions. Further to enhance the liberal position, on January 23, 1893, Satolli was appointed the first Apostolic Delegate to the United States. The liberals appeared to dominate the American Church.

The liberal domination, however, was only an appearance. When the hierarchy was polled for its opinion on the fourteen points, only seventeen were in favor, of whom six had reservations. Fifty-three were opposed and fourteen gave no response. The opposition to the schema crossed party lines. Riordan wrote Leo XIII arguing for the absolute necessity of parochial schools.[83] Elder, after addressing the pope, wrote also to Mazzella.[84] The Italian cardinal had had a first-hand experience of the American situation, Elder reminded him. Those who argued for cooperation between the Church and State in providing education did so on the grounds that America was religious. But religion in America, he said, meant that it excluded no error. One had only look to the trial of Professor Charles Augustus Briggs at Union Theological Seminary in New York and the turmoil it created in the Presbyterian Church to see that Americans disliked "heresy hunters".[85] Corrigan, as could have been expected, argued to the pope that Satolli's plan seemed to encourage children to attend public schools.[86]

But one of the most devastating critiques of Ireland and Satolli came from John Lancaster Spalding. Since Satolli spoke no English, French, or German, Spalding told Leo, he was seen as the tool of a "clique" opposed to Corrigan and Mc-Quaid. Ireland, he continued, "has tried to excite hatred against German Catholics in the United States; he has proclaimed that the Jesuits are his enemies; he has criminally attempted a *coup d'état* against our religious instruction, and now he publicly announces that one of his confreres is a conspirator against the authority of the pope. He has made the Catholic University a center of agitation for his ideas, a fact which threatens the total ruin of this institution: and in whatever he does he represents himself as the special friend and authorized agent of Your Holiness. The danger is great, and it has become extremely urgent to put an end to the notion which the clique spreads throughout the country, that Your Holiness approves of everything which the prelate of St. Paul does. I am American, he is Irish, and I am convinced that I know the American character as well as he ...".[87] Spalding had again raised the question of what it meant to be an Ameri-

---

[83] GAFFEY: *Riordan*, p. 208.

[84] APF, APNS, Rub. 153, vol. 74 (1895), 121^r–126^r, Elder to Leo XIII, Cincinnati, Jan. 19, 1893.

[85] *Ibid.*, 119^r–120^r, Elder to Mazzella, Cincinnati, Feb. 14, 1893.

[86] *Ibid.*, 246^r–256^r, Corrigan to Leo XIII, New York, Jan. 16, 1893.

[87] *Ibid.*, 278^r–282^r, Spalding to Leo XIII, Peoria, Jan. 11, 1893; given in GAFFEY: *Riordan*, pp. 208–209. See also SWEENEY: *Spalding*, pp. 210–216.

can and, in his mind, Ireland clearly did not have the answer. The Vatican was now all the more confused on the nature of American Catholicism.

On May 15, 1893, the cardinals of Propaganda met on Satolli's proposals. The cardinals decided that the pope should issue a letter upholding the congregation's instruction of 1876 and the legislation of the council. At the same time, the letter was to make no statement which would diminish Satolli's authority.[88] On May 31, 1893, Leo XIII wrote Gibbons that Satolli's propositions in no way had abrogated the existing legislation on parochial schools.[89] Regarding the decision as a personal victory, Ireland urged Gibbons to have the letter translated and published, lest Corrigan twist its meaning.[90] From a conservative perspective, Ryan saw the decision as the vindication of the entire parochial school system. In retrospect, the New York *World's* assessment was probably more accurate in judging that the letter had created a stalemate in the controversy.[91] By October, Gibbons reported to O'Connell that "we are now I think in our ante-bellum condition".[92]

Gibbons' evaluation was too optimistic. By the time he wrote, any victory for Ireland on Faribault and Stillwater was theoretical, for both school boards had abrogated their agreements. More importantly, not only did the division within the hierarchy, engendered by the controversy, remain, but Ireland had also succeeded in alienating the majority of the bishops with his school plan and Satolli's fourteen points. Though Corrigan declined in favor among Roman officials, opposition to the liberals increased both in Rome and in the United States. The liberal approach to what it meant to be an American had transcended the ethnicity of the German-Irish tension and the questions of ecclesiastical jurisdiction and of clerical celibacy in regard to Oriental Rite Catholics. The liberals also argued that the American was so different from the European State, that a relationship of Church-State cooperation was possible in the United States. In allowing the American State the right to educate, they fed the fears of European conservatives who were trying to defend the Church from the encroachments of the European liberal State precisely in the area of education.

The liberals' view of American culture, however, went beyond the intertwined German and school questions. They further antagonized the conservative opposition through their stance on the rights of labor, secret societies, and priests who

[88] APF, Acta, 263 (1893), 222^r–235^v, Persico Ponenza, May, 1893.

[89] ASV, SS, 280 (1897), fasc. 2, 15^r–20^v, Leo XIII to Gibbons, Vatican, May 31, 1893 (draft), given in REILLY: *School Controversy,* pp. 226–230.

[90] AAB 91 M 4, Ireland to Gibbons, St. Paul, June 13, 1893.

[91] CURRAN: *Corrigan,* pp. 418–419.

[92] ADR, Gibbons to O'Connell, Baltimore, Oct. 6, 1893.

appealed to Rome against their bishops. For the Vatican, the American Church was in chaos and to bring some order to it the Holy See decided to appoint an apostolic delegate. Such an official the American bishops had always consistently opposed, but the liberals, at least Ireland and O'Connell, agreed to the appointment in order to gain victory for their view of American Catholicism. Their agreement was paradoxical, for the appointment of the apostolic delegate continued the Romanization of the American Church, the very antithesis of what their overall vision demanded.

CHAPTER IV

ALLIANCE OF THE CHURCH WITH THE PEOPLE:
SOCIAL ISSUES AND EDWARD MCGLYNN

The liberals and conservatives had violently disagreed on the rapid Americanization of Catholic immigrants, the nature of the American State, and the possibility of cooperation with it in the realm of education. This disagreement increased as, under the guidance of the liberals, the Church became identified with the rights of workers, particularly as manifested in the Knights of Labor. Having won Vatican toleration for the Knights, the liberals turned to the defense of other secret societies, some 490 of which blossomed in the United States during the last two decades of the nineteenth century claiming a membership of 6,000,000.[1]

More directly related to the issue of labor was the case of Father Edward McGlynn of New York, who supported the Knights, advocated the social reform theories of Henry George, and was excommunicated by Rome in 1887. The liberals' support of the rights of labor and their later initiative in gaining the reconciliation of McGlynn led them to argue that what was condemned in Europe need not be dangerous in the United States, that with the American separation of Church and State the Church should be allied with the people, that, in order further to liberalize the Church, priests should have rights against their bishops. These issues, occuring simultaneously with those seen in the previous chapter, led the Holy See in turn to appoint the first permanent apostolic delegate.

Until the 1880s, most American Catholic leaders were hesitant to recognize as legitimate certain tactics of organized labor, such as the right to strike, which became accepted by the end of the century. They also failed to see as valid the criticism of social structures and concentrated instead on the need for individual reform.[2] After the Third Plenary Council, however, the bishops were forced to confront the issue when they had to examine the Knights of Labor, many of whose members were Catholic. It was the first test case of the council's decree that a suspect secret society should be referred to a plenum of the archbishops to determine if it fell under the papal condemnation of Freemasonry; and, if this body

---

[1] ELLIS: *Gibbons,* I, 439.

[2] Cf. Aaron I. ABELL: *American Catholicism and Social Action,* Notre Dame, Ind. 1963, pp. 27–53.

failed unanimously to agree on a given society, the case was then to be referred to Rome.[3]

A. THE KNIGHTS OF LABOR

The Knights had been founded in 1869 and used Masonic ritual. They took a pledge of secrecy in part to keep their affairs secret from employers. Working-class Catholics joined the organization and some soon reached prominence in it. One of these was Terence V. Powderly, who was elected mayor of Scranton, Pennsylvania, in 1878 and became Grand Master Workman of the Knights in 1879. In 1884, on the eve of the Third Plenary Council, however, Archbishop Eleazar Taschereau of Quebec obtained from the Holy Office a condemnation of the Knights as a forbidden secret society. This condemnation was then published in the neighboring Diocese of Portland, Maine, by Bishop James A. Healy, who declared that Catholic members would be excluded from the sacraments.[4] The Canadian condemnation now became a concern for the American bishops.

Gibbons, recently named a cardinal, needed little urging to defend the labor organization. He first consulted Father Aloysius Sabetti, S. J., professor of moral theology at Woodstock College, who assisted him in drafting a letter to Simeoni deprecating a condemnation. This the cardinal sent on September 3, 1886, in care of O'Connell.[5] Next, he procured a copy of the Knights' constitution, which Powderly had been revising, and decided to discuss the matter with the bishops of the Catholic University committee who were to meet in Baltimore on October 27. Because Bishops Ireland and Keane would be present and were to go to Rome to win approval for the university, Gibbons thought they could also be entrusted with the defense of the Knights.[6]

In the meanwhile, some bishops had been writing to Rome asking that the Holy Office condemn the Knights. This O'Connell sought to prevent. On September 8, he reported to Gibbons that Mazzella had assured him that Cardinal Raffaele Monaco, Sub-Secretary of the Holy Office, would postpone proceedings against the Knights. Simeoni, however, "did not at all seem well pleased with the state of things in America" and wished Gibbons to submit his own opinion together with translations of the old and new constitutions of the Knights with the

---

[3] *Acta et Decreta* (official), pp. 143 f.

[4] Henry J. BROWNE: *The Catholic Church and the Knights of Labor,* Washington 1949, pp. 34–37, 96–108, 129 f. ELLIS: *Gibbons,* I, 489–491.

[5] AAB, Gibbons Diary, Sept. 3, 1886. A copy of this letter is in AWC. See also ELLIS: *Gibbons,* I, 498 and BROWNE: *Knights,* pp. 192 f.

[6] ELLIS: *Gibbons,* I, 497.

passages marked which had been altered. Most of all, O'Connell was intent upon following the procedure legislated by the council for secret societies and he seems to have converted Simeoni and Mazzella to this view.[7]

A few weeks later, O'Connell sent the alarming news to Gibbons that he suspected Corrigan was calling for a condemnation, because "the Catholic papers in New York are inspired carefully what to say and McM[aster, editor of the *Freeman's Journal*] lately has turned against them. Then Miss Ed[es]. has nothing to say in their favor and states that you are entirely on their side". On the other hand, he found that Archbishop Domenico Jacobini, Secretary of Propaganda, thought "the American Bishops took too much alarm at the condemnation in Canada" and urged the application of the council's decree. Jacobini was further "of the opinion that the Holy Office will recommend it [the council's decree] in the case of the Knights as it was done in case of the Grand Army [of the Republic]", an organization of Union Army veterans. In view of Gibbons' decision to summon a meeting of the archbishops, O'Connell had decided to withhold his letter to Simeoni of September 3.[8]

Gibbons first learned from Corrigan of Simeoni's request that the archbishops meet on the Grand Army. He enlarged the agenda to include both the Knights of Labor and the Ancient Order of Hibernians, and on September 17 invited all the archbishops either to come personally or submit written opinions for a meeting on October 28, the day after the university committee would meet.[9] At the meeting, nine of the metropolitans were present. Of the three who were absent Riordan and Heiss wrote Gibbons opposing a condemnation of any of the societies, and Gross said he would go along with Gibbons' views. The archbishops unanimously agreed that the Grand Army and the Hibernians should not be condemned. On the Knights of Labor, however, they did not agree. John Baptist Salpointe of Santa Fe and Peter R. Kenrick of St. Louis, in both of whose dioceses there had been violent labor strikes, voted for condemnation. Corrigan, as O'Connell had earlier suspected, expressed reservations about the organization, which was then supporting Father Edward McGlynn.[10] In its first major test, the council decree was found wanting. It was designed to keep such decisions in the hands of the American hierarchy; now the case had to be referred to Rome.

Ireland and Keane were now instructed to add the cause of the Knights of Labor to their charge of gaining approval for the university. By the middle of November they were in Rome where they joined O'Connell, as was seen, in re-

---

[7] AAB 81 U 7, O'Connell to Gibbons, Rome, Sept. 8, 1886.
[8] AAB 81 W 1, O'Connell to Gibbons, Grottaferrata, Sept. 25, 1886.
[9] BROWNE: *Knights,* pp. 188, 198.
[10] ELLIS: *Gibbons,* I, 453 f., 501–503.

pudiating the Abbelen memorial. By December, the three had provided Propaganda with authentic copies of the constitutions of the Knights with translations in Latin, Italian, or French. At the same time, they won for the liberal party an important source of support. The *Moniteur de Rome,* a semi-official Vatican organ, had published an article unfavorable to the Irish-Americans and the Knights of Labor. After Ireland and Keane registered a strong protest to the editor, Monsignor Eugene Boeglin, he promised, said Keane, "to publish anything we would send them".[11] This was the beginning of the close relationship between O'Connell and Boeglin which resulted in the cable stories on the German and school questions.

The mood in Rome seemed in favor of condemning the Knights because, as will be seen, the issue was so closely connected with the suspension from priestly functions of McGlynn, who, with Terence Powderly, supported Henry George's single-tax theory as well as his candidacy for Mayor of New York. Ireland, Keane, and O'Connell sought to separate these issues and with this in mind, Keane wrote Cardinal Henry Edward Manning requesting a letter against a condemnation of the Knights.[12] In the meantime, Gibbons had consulted with Corrigan on the labor question before leaving New York for Rome to receive the red hat. He sailed on the same ship with Taschereau, who had obtained the condemnation of the Knights for Quebec and who, like himself, had just been named a cardinal. After his arrival in Rome, he joined his three American friends in trying to convince each member of the Holy Office not to allow the Knights to be condemned in the United States.[13]

On February 20, 1887, Gibbons presented Propaganda with a memorial in their favor. The approach he took was similar to that he later took on the school question. He argued that not only were the Knights of Labor not subject to the proscriptions against secret societies, but also a condemnation of them would be seen in the United States as a Roman intrusion, would alienate the working people from the Church, and would diminish financial contributions, including the Peter's Pence. Apropos of this, he added an argument which was destined to increase his difficulties with Corrigan. If the condemnation of one priest, who was considered to be a friend of the people, created "sad and threatening confusion," he said, how much greater would be the reaction to the condemnation of the people themselves.[14]

---

[11] AAB 82 G 4, Keane to Gibbons, Rome, Dec. 4, 1886; see also 82 G 9, O'Connell to Gibbons, Dec. 10, 1886.

[12] Shane LESLIE: *Henry Edward Manning: His Life and Letters,* London 1921, p. 360.

[13] WILL: *Gibbons,* I, 332.

[14] In BROWNE: *Knights,* pp. 239–242.

The memorial was intended to be a private communication to Propaganda, but Charles Henry Meltzer, an American journalist, procured a copy of it and had it published in the New York *Herald* on March 3. This version contained the allusion to McGlynn, which was construed as meaning that Gibbons sided with him in his dispute with Corrigan. Gibbons' initial apprehension at the publication, however, gave way to encouragement as the general American reaction supported the arguments he had made with Propaganda. Moreover, through Keane, he received Manning's endorsement of his views. Encouraged by the favorable reception of his memorial, he had it published, minus the allusions to McGlynn, in the *Moniteur de Rome* on March 28.[15]

Gibbons left Rome late in April, but Keane and O'Connell kept him informed of developments in Rome. Keane sent the Holy Office French translations of the letters supporting Gibbons' memorial and also the proceedings of the Richmond meeting of the Knights in 1886 together with their new constitution.[16] O'Connell was optimistic that the Holy Office "came so very near creating great trouble in this instance, that it will learn caution in the future". More importantly for the emerging Americanist platform, he remarked: "The authorities of the Church have been drawn nearer the people by the publication of that document, and the people to the Church. All counter-representations amount to little since Cardinal Manning has spoken so bravely".[17]

The Holy Office apparently found itself so bogged down with documentation on the Knights of Labor that it did not reach a decision until the summer of 1888. In June, O'Connell informed Gibbons and Ireland that the congregation had decided the organization could be "tolerated".[18] Two months went by, however, and Gibbons grew apprehensive at not having received official confirmation of the decision. On August 14, O'Connell wrote to assure Gibbons, but noted that in view of the Holy Office's previous decision about the Knights in Canada, "they do not care about publishing their own contradiction". In his own opinion, Gibbons "never did anything that so added to your prestige in Rome as that action of yours in regards to the Knights of Labor". Furthermore, he continued, Satolli, a member of the Holy Office, had said his congregation "wished to condemn the Knights of Labor, and the American Bishops opposed it, and Cardinal Gibbons, 'great statesman as he is' laid the matter before the Holy See, and showed that in

---

[15] *Ibid.*, pp. 244–257.

[16] AAB 82 Q 1, Keane to Gibbons, Rome, May 14, 1887.

[17] AAB 82 Q 10, O'Connell to Gibbons, Rome, May 18, 1887.

[18] AAB 84 P 7, O'Connell to Gibbons, Rome, June 17, 1888; AASP, O'Connell to Ireland, Rome, June 15, 1888.

Canada the Knights had been condemned for an accidentality, and thus saved the commission of a great mistake".[19]

O'Connell's information was proof of his resourcefulness, for only on August 16 did the Holy Office formally meet on the question. On August 29, Simeoni forwarded the decision to Gibbons. His letter stated that the "Knights of Labor may be allowed for the time being", provided that whatever was offensive in the organization's constitutions be corrected. In particular, said the prefect, whatever "words which seem to savor of socialism and communism must be emended in such a way as to make clear that the soil was granted by God to man, or rather the human race, that each one might have the right to acquire some portion of it, by use however of lawful means and without violation of the right of private property".[20]

Gibbons was convinced, he told O'Connell, that conditions were attached to the toleration only "to save the Holy Office from a charge of inconsistency, and to get out of the difficulty as quietly as they can". As soon as he received Simeoni's letter, he asked Powderly to meet with him. In the meantime, he "did not wish to give publicity to the letter even to the Bishops till I had taken the little sting out of the Decree — by being able to produce together with the letter Mr. Powderly's entire willingness to make the corrections which I have no doubt he will do".[21] On September 24, Powderly met with Gibbons and agreed to all the requested changes. This information together with Simeoni's letter Gibbons then communicated to the rest of the hierarchy.[22]

Not all the bishops were pleased with the decision to allow Catholic membership in the Knights of Labor, and, as a consequence, Corrigan became increasingly cold toward Gibbons.[23] In Rome, O'Connell reported that "Miss Edes did not take the decree about the Knights so well. Everybody else seemed glad".[24] Thomas Preston, the convert vicar-general of New York, played on the Vatican's fears, expressed in Simeoni's letter. "Socialism dominates the Card. [Gibbons]", he wrote Abbot Bernard Smith, O. S. B., a consultor of Propaganda.[25] Fear of socialism remained a concern for the Vatican, but the Knights of Labor ceased to be an issue. No sooner had the decree of toleration been issued than they suffered a drastic decline in membership as other labor organizations came into being. Gibbons himself wrote Simeoni recalling that one argument he had used in his

---

[19] AAB 84 V 5, O'Connell to Gibbons, Rome, Aug. 14, 1888.

[20] Quoted in BROWNE: *Knights,* p. 324.

[21] ADR, Gibbons to O'Connell, Baltimore, Sept. 20, 1888.

[22] BROWNE: *Knights,* pp. 327 f.

[23] *Ibid.,* pp. 328 f.

[24] AAB 85 F 4, O'Connell to Gibbons, Grottaferrata, Oct. 8, 1888.

[25] AASPOW, Smith Papers, Preston to Smith, New York, Dec. 18, 1888.

memorial was the foolishness of condemning a society which would soon die out.[26] Short-lived though the Knights of Labor may have been, it had taken courage for Gibbons to defend them in the face of European prejudice. His support of them and his related attitude against a condemnation of Henry George were stepping stones toward *Rerum Novarum,* which placed the Church firmly on the side of labor.

The liberals' position on the Knights of Labor and other secret societies was one among several in which they held that the United States was different than Europe. In a moment of pique with the Roman Curia, O'Connell let out his frustration to Ireland. "We would have very few condemnations of secret societies had there been no temporal power and no prohibition to citizens or subjects to agitate their grievances publicly".[27] His *obiter dictum* may have summed up the liberals' situation in regard to Rome better than any of them realized. They looked at America where the Church existed in harmonious separation from the State and where secret societies offered no threat to either. Leo XIII saw only Europe pervaded by Freemasonry, which, in his eyes, generated communism, socialism, and naturalism and which took over the State and deprived the Church, especially in Italy and France, of her traditional rights in the temporal order.[28] The liberals had to have known Leo's thought on Freemasonry, especially as he expressed it his encyclical *Humanum Genus* in 1884. That they chose to ignore it can only be explained by their optimistic belief, as O'Connell summed it up, that the more hopeless the Church found her situation in Europe, the more she would "desire to live on good terms with America".[29]

The liberals may well not have encountered Leo's attitude toward Freemasonry first hand, were it not for the inadequate American legislation on secret societies and the deep division among the bishops. In 1893, after a year's examination of two secret societies, the archbishops again failed to reach an unanimous agreement and again the case was referred to Rome. But, as will be seen, this time there was a new factor in their now complex equation, the apostolic delegate, Francesco Satolli. The support of the liberals, particularly of Gibbons, for secret societies was the decisive turning point in Satolli's movement toward the conservative camp. It was an irony, for the liberals had engineered his arrival not only to speak on the school question but also to reconcile McGlynn to the Church.

---

[26] BROWNE: *Knights,* pp. 328, 376; FOGARTY: *Vatican,* pp. 163–164.

[27] AASP, O'Connell to Ireland, Rome, Sept. 21, 1890.

[28] John Courtney MURRAY: *Leo XIII on Church and State: The General Structure of the Controversy,* in: Theological Studies 14 (1953) 3–9. See also Lillian Parker WALLACE: *Leo XIII and the Rise of Socialism,* Durham, N.C. 1966, pp. 218–220.

[29] AAB 88 D 9, O'Connell to Gibbons, Rome, Nov. 29, 1890.

B. THE MCGLYNN CASE AND HENRY GEORGE

1. McGlynn's Excommunication

Edward McGlynn was the charismatic rector of St. Stephen's Church in New York. In 1859, after three years of theology at the Urban College of Propaganda, he was appointed the first prefect of the newly opened American College in Rome; among the in-coming students that year was Michael Corrigan. Ordained in Rome, McGlynn arrived back in New York, where he soon became a principal in a group of priests, mainly fellow graduates of the Urban College, known in chancery circles as "The Accademia." Besides him, the group included Richard Burtsell, rector of Epiphany Church and a leading canonist, and Edward McSweeny, who had defended his brother Patrick's arrangement with the Poughkeepsie school board in 1875. Politically, they urged radical reconstruction in the South after the Civil War. Ecclesiastically, they discussed limitations on papal infallibility, clerical celibacy, the vernacular liturgy, and the need to update Catholic theology. But of the group, McGlynn was the social activist. By 1865, he was the rector of St. Stephen's which he turned into a model "institutional church", that is, a church which met needs other than the strictly religious, the type of church characteristic of the later Protestant social gospel. Among other operations, he ran a parish home for over 500 children. On the other hand, he refused to build a parochial school. He held that the right to educate belonged to the State and that the Church should be more concerned with reaching adults than with building parochial schools.[30] Here was an ideal member of the liberal party, but such he was not to be for a long while, for his stance on ecclesiastical discipline initially antagonized Ireland and the others who held to their concept of a strong episcopacy.

By the early 1880s, McGlynn became enamoured of the social theories of Henry George. In *Progress and Poverty,* George had proposed a single tax on the unearned increment of the value of land as the panacea for the problems of poverty. McGlynn's espousal of Georgism, however, immediately placed him in the midst of an international controversy, for at the same time Michael Davitt, collaborator with Charles Stewart Parnell and founder of the Irish Land League, had also adopted George's solutions. Although many Irish and American bishops had initially supported the aims of the League, after Davitt and Parnell issued their "No Rent Manifesto", this episcopal support was withdrawn. Davitt, nevertheless, continued his campaign to win converts to George's theories. On a visit to New York in June, 1882, he began to waver, but was buoyed up by McGlynn's

---

[30] CURRAN: *Corrigan,* pp. 168–176.

public encouragement. McGlynn's speech was published in the *Irish World*, translations of which, probably made by Miss Edes, were given to Simeoni. Then in Cleveland on August 15, McGlynn addressed the Parnell Branch of the Land League. Its women members had the distinction of first being told by Bishop Richard Gilmour that women did not belong in politics and of then being excommunicated for saying they rejected "Scotch dictation by Bishop Gilmour".[31]

McGlynn's defiance of episcopal authority by speaking to an excommunicated group on what was in itself a controversial topic aroused Archbishop Elder of Cincinnati to demand that Cardinal McCloskey discipline his priest and Bishop Chatard of Vincennes to protest to Rome. In response to Elder's complaint, McCloskey spoke with McGlynn who promised to make no more political speeches. In the meantime, Simeoni addressed two letters to McCloskey about McGlynn. The first was a reaction to McGlynn's speech in New York which the cardinal prefect believed expressed views incompatible with the Church's social teaching. The second was in response to Chatard's report on McGlynn's Cleveland speech and stated that he was to be suspended unless he changed his attitude. In view of McGlynn's promise to make no more political speeches, McCloskey took no further disciplinary action.

Nonetheless, McGlynn continued to speak and attract Roman attention. On May 10, 1883, Simeoni wrote McCloskey complaining of a speech McGlynn had given on St. Patrick's Day and forbidding him to make any further inflammatory statements. McCloskey gave McGlynn the letter and suggested that he go personally to Propaganda to explain his views. This McGlynn refused to do on the grounds that his speech was typical of St. Patrick's Day orations and that absence from his parish would prevent him from paying off its debt. Corrigan, then the coadjutor, was not satisfied with McGlynn's explanations and discussed the matter with Simeoni during the archbishops' meeting in Rome prior to the plenary council. For almost three more years, however, the hierarchy was too distracted with the council and other matters to pay much attention to the radical priest in New York.[32]

What again drew the attention of the American bishops and Rome to McGlynn was the nomination by the United Labor Party of Henry George for Mayor of New York in 1886. By that time, McCloskey had died and Corrigan was the archbishop. George had the support of McGlynn and the Knights of Labor. McGlynn had arranged for a fruitless interview between Corrigan and George in order for the latter to explain his positions. He had also agreed to give a speech in George's favor on October 1. This Corrigan forbade, but McGlynn argued that

---

[31] *Ibid.,* pp. 179–184.
[32] *Ibid.,* pp. 184–189.

he would have to fulfill his commitment, after which he would take no further part in the campaign. For this act of disobedience, Corrigan invoked Propaganda's earlier prohibition against McGlynn's political addresses and suspended him from the priestly ministry for two weeks. The priest gave no more campaign speeches, but on November 2, election day, he rode through the streets in an open carriage with George and Powderly. Later that month, Corrigan held the Fifth Diocesan Synod of New York at the conclusion of which he issued a pastoral letter. In one passage he strongly supported the right to private ownership as well as use of property. It was his public rebuke to McGlynn and to George, whose theories he now sought to have Rome condemn.[33]

The pastoral received wide publicity. George called it Corrigan's "private opinion", but most of the bishops hailed it as a needed exposition of Catholic teaching. On November 24, Charles McDonnell, Corrigan's secretary, wrote O'Connell of the events up to that point, that McGlynn's suspension was based on Propaganda's instructions to McCloskey in 1882, that Corrigan had written the congregation for further direction, and that one bishop, probably McQuaid, had suggested McGlynn's removal from his parish to one in the country. Then he added, "as Henry George's 'Progress & Poverty' has been sent to Propaganda for examination, it is to be hoped, that if the doctrine of Henry George is found worthy of condemnation, that the decree of the Holy Office will come in good time to complete the effect of the Abp's Pastoral". In the meantime, O'Connell was to keep Corrigan informed of Propaganda's actions.[34]

Even as McDonnell was writing O'Connell, however, McGlynn gave an interview to the New York *Tribune*, in which he was reported to have made disparaging remarks about papal social teaching. Without verifying the accuracy of the report, Corrigan again suspended him, this time until the end of the year. Furthermore, he again cabled for instructions from Propaganda, which responded on December 4 summoning McGlynn to Rome. Denying he had said anything contrary to Catholic teaching, however, McGlynn refused to proceed to Rome. As his reasons he gave poor health, lack of financial resources, and the need to care for his recently deceased sister's children. Moreover, he said, he did not know and could only surmise the charges against him. Confronted with this refusal, Corrigan then removed McGlynn as rector of St. Stephen's. The case was fraught with further confusion by the suspicion that at least some of the cables bearing Simeoni's signature were forged.[35]

---

[33] *Ibid.*, pp. 193–205.

[34] ADR, McDonnell to O'Connell, New York, Nov. 24, 1886.

[35] CURRAN: *Corrigan*, pp. 208–218. Corrigan forwarded a copy of this letter to Simeoni; see APF, SOCG, 1028 (1888), 128ʳ–129ʳ, McGlynn to Corrigan, New York, Dec. 20, 1886 (copy).

On December 23, Corrigan had outlined his case against McGlynn. In addition to the priest's theories on the private ownership of land, said the archbishop, he went to extremes on other topics. Theologically, for example, he so praised the Eucharist that he encouraged its daily reception. Politically, he asserted the proposition that "Independence of the Church from the state is good: therefore it should be complete and absolute, and never a union". McGlynn had indeed made similar statements in a strictly American context, but Corrigan's formulation made it appear that the priest specifically upheld a proposition condemned in the Syllabus of Errors.[36]

The liberals initially supported Corrigan's action toward McGlynn on the grounds of upholding episcopal authority, but they disagreed with him on asking for a condemnation of George. On his way to Rome in mid-January to receive the red hat, Gibbons stopped for a few days in New York. While there, he received a visit from Father Richard Burtsell, rector of the Church of the Epiphany and McGlynn's canonical adviser. The cardinal urged Burtsell to have McGlynn comply with the summons to Rome and, according to Burtsell, promised to speak to Roman officials on the matter.[37]

Gibbons did speak about McGlynn with both Simeoni and the pope and discovered their annoyance at McGlynn's refusal to come to Rome. At Leo's request, he wrote McGlynn, in care of Burtsell, urging him to answer the summons. He also informed Corrigan of his action and assured him that there was no fear that McGlynn would have to be restored to St. Stephen's. But Gibbons and the other liberals distinguished between the issues of disciplining McGlynn and of condemning George. On February 25, 1887, the same day he wrote Propaganda in favor of the Knights of Labor, Gibbons submitted another memorial against the condemnation of the works of George. This may have succeeded in stopping the process against George for the next year. But his letter to McGlynn and the publication of his memorial on the Knights of Labor, with the reference to the New York situation, drew comments in American papers and he found himself considered a McGlynn sympathizer. O'Connell in response to a letter no longer extant wrote McDonnell that he could not "imagine how anyone could think of Dr. McG.'s return to St. Stephen's, and from the way things look now, I do not clearly see how he will even find his way back to any church at all". He then explained Gibbons' actions about which Corrigan had been informed, but when the

---

[36] APF, SOCG, 1028 (1888), 133ʳ–141ᵛ, Corrigan to Simeoni, New York, Dec. 23, 1886. For the context of some of McGlynn's remarks about the separation of Church and State and for Preston's opinion of his view on the Eucharist, see CURRAN: *Corrigan*, pp. 176, 212.

[37] ELLIS, *Gibbons*, I, 553 f.

cardinal "saw the construction put upon his action, he determined to do nothing more".[38] The heart of the issue was upholding episcopal authority. Elder, who was in close correspondence with Corrigan, cabled Gibbons in Rome: "Speedy & decisive support of authority of New York needed for whole country. Scandal grievous and growing".[39] This message O'Connell forwarded to Gibbons, who was then in Florence, and received the reply that the Holy See should again summon McGlynn to Rome.[40] Although Gibbons at this time still defended the rights of bishops over priests, his minor role in the McGlynn affair only served to increase the friction between him and Corrigan.

Back in New York Corrigan was busy trying to muster his clergy's support for his actions. During April, apparently at the instigation of McQuaid, all the priests of the archdiocese were asked to sign a pledge supporting the archbishop. Among the first to sign were the German clergy – a fact which may have contributed to Corrigan's alliance with the German conservatives. There was a virtual witch-hunt to coerce all the clergy into signing the statement. Among the last to do so was John Farley, one of Corrigan's consultors.[41]

On May 19, Corrigan received the Roman support for which he had been hoping. In a letter dated May 4, Simeoni gave McGlynn forty days after receipt of the letter to appear in Rome or be excommunicated. Keane, still in Rome working on the university's approval, may have best expressed the liberals' reaction. He endorsed the excommunication, he told Gibbons, "provided the question be limited to the disciplinary case, and not permitted to drag us into a doctrinal & political question". But he resented the reports he heard that Father Thomas Lynch, one of the leaders of the movement to gain clerical support for Corrigan, said "the address of loyalty to him 'was intended to be used in Rome, to counteract the efforts of Cardinal Gibbons and Bp. Keane'". Keane had accordingly written Corrigan a firm but fraternal letter protesting these reports.[42]

When Gibbons returned to the United States, he resisted being drawn further into the McGlynn controversy. Bishop John Moore of St. Augustine, a classmate and close friend of McGlynn's, had begun his long campaign to gain McGlynn's reinstatement. At this point, acting as an intermediary for Burtsell, he sought to have Gibbons intervene to prevent the excommunication.[43] Although Gibbons would not endorse a cable from Moore to Simeoni seeking suspension of the ex-

---

[38] AANY, O'Connell to McDonnell, Rome, Apr. 14, 1887.
[39] AANY, Elder to Corrigan, Cincinnati, Apr. 11, 1887, in CURRAN: *Corrigan*, p. 232.
[40] ADR, Gibbons to O'Connell, Florence, Apr. 22, 1887; ELLIS: *Gibbons*, I, 554–565.
[41] CURRAN: *Corrigan*, pp. 237–241.
[42] AAB 82 Q 1, Keane to Gibbons, Rome, May 14, 1887.
[43] AAB 82 V 5, Burtsell to Moore, New York, June 25, 1887.

communication, he seems to have made a last-minute effort through Archbishop Elder to have Corrigan abstain from applying it.[44]

In the meantime, McGlynn had escalated his activities. Not only did he remain adamant in refusing to go to Rome, but he also was one of the founders of the Anti-Poverty Society to promulgate his notions on property and social reform. At last, on July 1, Propaganda cabled Corrigan that he was to excommunicate McGlynn. Two days later the archbishop wrote McGlynn of the penalty he had incurred. Here seemed to be a prime example of the Church's authoritarianism violating the freedom of speech of a priest who was an American citizen, a theme voiced by George and McGlynn's other followers as well as the secular press.[45]

The public reaction to the disciplining of McGlynn may have conditioned Gibbons' own ambiguous response. On the one hand he wrote to O'Connell, perhaps for Roman consumption: "I hope I am mistaken, but my impression is that it will lead to the loss of many souls, & to a weakening in some places of the reverence due to the Holy See. It was prudent not to require the reading of the excommunication in the churches".[46] On the other hand he seems still to have wanted to maintain episcopal authority, even when misused. Recognizing Rome's attitude on the case, he told Moore not to write any further letters to the Holy See on McGlynn's behalf.[47]

Moore, however, was not to be put off. McGlynn had never been presented with the formal charges against him nor had he been given a trial. After his excommunication Moore and Burtsell met with him following a dinner in Burtsell's honor. For this both Moore and Burtsell received a reprimand from Corrigan. But at the meeting the bishop had won from McGlynn the promise that he would proceed to Rome, if his excommunication were lifted, a condition he would maintain for the next four years. This information Moore sent to Propaganda, which the pope ordered to meet on the case in a general congregation, a plenary session of all the members. At this point, further confusion developed. In preparation for the congregation's examination, Archbishop Jacobini requested that the Secretariat of State send him two documents, the one a letter from the pope to Corrigan about McGlynn and the other the declaration that McGlynn would be excommunicated if he failed to obey the pope. But the documents could no longer be found, Jacobini was informed, and since they were sent out during

---

[44] ELLIS: *Gibbons*, I, 570.
[45] CURRAN: *Corrigan*, pp. 250–252.
[46] ADR, Gibbons to O'Connell, Baltimore, July 15, 1887.
[47] AANY, Burtsell Diary, Sept. 19, 1887. Moore attributed Gibbons' action to O'Connell's advice. In September, McGlynn stated in an interview that Burtsell had sent Propaganda a defense through Gibbons, but that O'Connell said it was probably thrown away; cf. ELLIS: *Gibbons*, I, 572.

the final days of Cardinal Lodovico Jacobini as Secretary of State, they were perhaps lost.[48]

In January, Mazzella was delegated to present the material on the McGlynn case to the other cardinals. He rehearsed McGlynn's involvement in the social question and the Irish Land League and narrated Corrigan's charges against him, particularly as outlined in his letter of December 23, 1886. The cardinal concluded his presentation by mentioning the dinner to which Burtsell had invited McGlynn to meet Moore and the reprimand which Corrigan had issued. On January 23, the congregation rejected Moore's petition that McGlynn be given a hearing and upheld the excommunication on doctrinal and disciplinary grounds.[49] But the facts that the pope, who supposedly ordered McGlynn's excommunication, had asked that the congregation hear the case and that the critical documents could not be found in the Secretariat of State lend credence to the charges that Corrigan had acted toward McGlynn without proper authorization.

2. The Condemnation of Henry George

After Propaganda's decision in January, 1888, not to reopen the McGlynn case, the Holy See took no more official action on it for almost five years. But the doctrinal issue of Henry George remained alive and prompted Gibbons to take action which ultimately contributed to the promulgation of *Rerum Novarum*. In February, 1888, the New York *Herald* somehow procured and published a copy of Gibbons' memorial against condemning George. Simultaneously there was a renewed effort to place George's works on the Index. Alarmed by the possible damage to Gibbons' reputation if George were to be condemned, O'Connell won the assurance of an official of the Congregation of the Index that proceedings would be delayed until he could write privately for the bishops' opinions. In light of Propaganda's recent decision on McGlynn, he made a curious remark which indicated the Vatican attitude was changing. "All are sad about the McGlynn affair", he told Gibbons, "and wish it were otherwise".[50]

---

[48] ASV, SS, 280 (1897), fasc. 6, 116^r, Jacobini to Mocenni, Rome, Nov. 16, 1887; 117^{r-v}, Mocenni to Jacobini, Vatican, Nov. 19, 1887 (draft).

[49] APF, Acta, 258 (1888), 1^r–27^v, Mazzella Ponenza, Jan., 1888; 28^r–29^v, General Congregation, Jan. 23, 1888. Curiously, only three days before, Mazzella seems to have leaned toward the position that, while the Holy See had acted prudently in excommunicating McGlynn, Corrigan should be given the faculties to absolve him as soon as he embarked for Rome; *ibid.*, SOCG, 1028 (1888), 29^r, Mazzella, Consulta, Jan. 20, 1888.

[50] AAB 84 D 4, O'Connell to Gibbons, Rome, Feb. 25, 1888; cf. also AASP, O'Connell to Ireland, Rome, Feb. 23, 1888. See ELLIS: *Gibbons*, I, 575.

In response to O'Connell, Gibbons remarked that the publication of his memorial had had the good effect of winning the approval of the secular press and of showing that a condemnation "would probably have been the occasion of much injury to the peace of the Church in this country". Meanwhile, *Progress and Poverty* had been virtually forgotten. George had not only ceased to be a candidate for political office but was actually supporting the reelection of President Cleveland. A condemnation would only reawaken interest in his single-tax theory and make it appear that the Church "is the enemy of liberty, that she is opposed to the legitimate exercise of reason and is unwarrantably interfering with the social & political affairs of the country". The peace and toleration which the Church enjoyed in the United States, he concluded, were due to the "prudence and discretion of the Bishops of the country", who, if consulted, would certainly oppose any condemnation.[51]

Gibbons immediately set about consulting the other bishops. To Ireland and Elder he suggested that they make no mention of knowing that George's works were being re-examined by the Index but use the occasion of his memorial's publication to report the favorable American reaction to it.[52] Ireland complied on March 24 and he had Bishops John Lancaster Spalding and Martin Marty do likewise. These letters were sent to O'Connell who received similar ones from Archbishop Williams and Bishops Keane and O'Connor.[53]

The liberals were by no means enamoured of George's social theories, but they feared the repercussions of a condemnation which seemed imminent. In early April, O'Connell cabled Gibbons to have more bishops write Rome. In the middle of the month, he brought the cardinal abreast of the Roman situation. Hearing the rumor – false as it turned out – that the Province of Cincinnati had petitioned for the condemnation, O'Connell sounded out the opinion of Roman officials. Abbot Bernard Smith felt that Gibbons should write the pope directly, but Cardinal Simeoni believed that the Holy Office was compelled to condemn such "pernicious doctrines, just like Rosminianism which should have been condemned long ago".[54]

O'Connell himself submitted a memorial to Propaganda requesting that a condemnation would impugn the reputations of both Gibbons and Manning. He urged Gibbons to write the pope that it would be better not to condemn George especially with the forthcoming presidential election and to treat the social ques-

---

[51] ADR, Gibbons to O'Connell, Baltimore, Mar. 19, 1888; a copy is also in AAB 84 E 7.

[52] AASP, Gibbons to Ireland, Baltimore, Mar. 19, 1888; AACi, Gibbons to Elder, Baltimore, Mar. 20, 1888.

[53] ADR, Ireland to O'Connell, St. Paul, Mar. 24, 1888; AAB 84 I 12, O'Connell to Gibbons, Rome, Apr. 17, 1888, no. 1; AAB 84 F 11, Ireland to Gibbons, St. Paul, Mar. 26, 1888.

[54] AAB 84 I 5, O'Connell to Gibbons, Rome, Apr. 14, 1888.

tion afterwards. But the issue had clearly become partisan. O'Connell approached Archbishop Ryan of Philadelphia, then in Rome, about petitioning either against a condemnation or for awaiting the opinions of Gibbons and Manning. The archbishop, a friend of Corrigan's, refused.[55]

Meanwhile, Elder's position in regard to a condemnation of George was cleared up. In response to Gibbons' original request in March, he had written Rome against a condemnation, but his letter never arrived. Informed by Gibbons of the rumor that his province called for a condemnation, he cabled O'Connell of his opposition and followed it with a letter. Probably influenced by information received from Gibbons that the pope might issue an encyclical, he suggested that means as an answer to the social question without any specific mention of George. While both capital and labor had been partially at fault, he said, the unrest of the laboring class was partly due to the "unchristian spirit of the rich".[56] As on a number of issues, Elder displayed his independence of mind. Although he had been one of Corrigan's most ardent supporters in disciplining McGlynn and, as was seen, in the school question, he would disagree with his New York friend in calling for George's condemnation. Gilmour of Cleveland, though still chafing from McGlynn's insult to him, likewise opposed a condemnation.[57]

On May 3, Gibbons, acting on O'Connell's advice again wrote the pope deploring a condemnation, but this time he added a plea for an encyclical on the social question.[58] For reasons not altogether clear O'Connell did not present this letter to the pope. From the tone of O'Connell's explanation of his action, the cardinal's letter, now lost, seemed to have called for an encyclical on George rather than a condemnation. But the danger of a condemnation had now passed, said O'Connell, and "if it were undignified or unnecessary for the Holy Office to note George, as is agreed in all the letters I have rec'd, it would I think be more undignified on the part of the Holy Father to encounter him". All the letters he had received, except one, counselled a policy of "absolute silence & ignoring of George" and there was a danger that an encyclical "might awake him". He suggested that Gibbons' letter agree with those of the other bishops who said

---

[55] AAB 84 I 12, O'Connell to Gibbons, Rome, Apr. 17, 1888, no. 1.

[56] ADR, Elder to O'Connell, Hot Springs, N.C., Apr. 26, 1888; cf. AACi, Gibbons to Elder, Baltimore, Mar. 26, Apr. 15, and Apr. 28, 1888; O'Connell to Elder, Rome, Apr. 19, 1888.

[57] ADR, Gilmour to Gibbons, Cleveland, Apr. 16, 1888. In addition to letters addressed directly to O'Connell, Gibbons forwarded to him those which he had received; see ADR, Kain to O'Connell, Wheeling, Apr. 23, 1888; Janssens to O'Connell, Richmond, Apr. 20, 1888; Haid to Gibbons, Belmont, N.C., Apr. 20, 1888; O'Connor to Gibbons, Omaha, Apr. 24, 1888; and Northrop to Gibbons, Charleston, May 11, 1888. See ELLIS: Gibbons, I, 580.

[58] AAB, Gibbons Diary, May 3, 1888.

"George is dead and leave him alone". Only Elder had called for an encyclical and his letter met "difficulties from itself and from the letters of his suffragans".[59]

It is difficult to assess the Roman attitude toward George during the summer of 1888. O'Connell may well have believed that, seeing the opinions of so many bishops and the carefully prepared articles appearing in Boeglin's *Moniteur de Rome,* the Congregation of the Index might not even consider the case. In addition, Donato Sbarretti, who had prepared the case for Propaganda against George, had said that he thought the question was at rest. Moreover, there was a change in the administration of the Index during the spring. Cardinal Placido Schiaffino had just been named Prefect. Ireland hastened to congratulate him and, in passing, urge him not to condemn George. Finally, the Holy Office's favorable decision on the Knights of Labor during the same summer may well have lulled O'Connell into a false optimism that the George question was closed.[60]

Whatever may have been the motivation for O'Connell's not presenting Gibbons' letter, he reverted to his original position and on July 30, 1888, at his suggestion, Gibbons sent the pope a second letter arguing against placing George on the Index and requesting an encyclical on the social question.[61] "Your letter on the George question is masterly", said O'Connell, but instead of giving it directly to the pope he entrusted it to Simeoni, for "it will not hurt him to know its contents".[62]

Still the Vatican delayed reaching a decision on George. Late in November the proponents for his condemnation received a boost with the arrival late in November of Bishop McQuaid of Rochester. He had continued to advise Corrigan on the McGlynn case and had suggested that he forbid Catholics to attend meetings of the Anti-Poverty Society. This stance caused the liberals some apprehension and ultimately led them to work for the reconciliation of McGlynn. McQuaid reported this attitude on O'Connell's part to Corrigan in January, 1889. O'Connell, he wrote, "here thinks you should have allowed the McGlynn business die out of itself. I told him that I had advised you to adopt the present course inasmuch as waiting for a natural death had proved useless, and only enabled disaffected priests to absolve habitual and persistent sinners, and Burtsell to claim that McGlynn had done no wrong in going to these meetings, and they had not been forbidden. I cannot make out just how the rector stands toward you. He has great influence at the Propaganda, and a little word from him tells. Miss

[59] AAB 84 L 11, O'Connell to Gibbons, Rome, May 17, 1888.

[60] AAB 84 R 11, O'Connell to Gibbons, Rome, July 8, 1888; AAB 84 K 4, Ireland to Gibbons, St. Paul, May 7, 1888; cf. AASP, O'Connell to Ireland, Rome, June 15, 1888.

[61] ELLIS: *Gibbons,* I, 581 f.

[62] AAB 84 V 6, O'Connell to Gibbons, Rome, Aug. 14, 1888.

E[des] thinks that his affection for Gibbons and Keane is weakening. I am not sure that she is right".[63]

McQuaid was wide of the mark in assessing O'Connell's affection for Gibbons and the liberals. Shortly after his departure from Rome, O'Connell remarked to Ireland: "the N.Y. trouble is beginning to nauseate & dissatisfy".[64] But this remark came shortly after the Holy Office reached a compromise on George on February 6, 1889. George's works were placed on the Index, but the condemnation did not have to be published. It was a "brutum fulmen", O'Connell said, and it proved the necessity of the counter-representations from the bishops a year earlier. McQuaid's exasperation crackled beneath O'Connell's matter-of-fact account: "Bp. McQuaid said it came too late, and 'what's the use of it, if you can't publish it'".[65]

3. McGlynn's Reconciliation

The unpublicized condemnation of George was a minor victory for the liberals in their growing battle with the conservatives, but with the decision they gradually shifted toward settlement of the McGlynn case. This shift, according to O'Connell, reflected a shift in Roman attitudes. "The management of the McGlynn case was considered bad", O'Connell told Ireland, "and Abp. Corrigan's strongest point is the great service he renders Rome, particularly in investing money for them". "Gibbons", on the other hand, "commands the influence. His wavering is his greatest enemy". In regard to ecclesiastical discipline, he continued, Corrigan, McQuaid, and Gilmour represented one approach, "that here is held to be excessive".

Behind this new Roman attitude toward ecclesiastical discipline, however, lay, in O'Connell's analysis, a more important and fundamental stance toward the modern world: "Another thing, at the Vatican and elsewhere, it is clearly felt that the Pope's policy miscarried, and that after his death a new policy must be pursued. They feel that princes in whom they trusted have failed them and that in the future they must turn to the people. The force of events is teaching them truths they would not have listened to from anyone else. So the trump men of the future will be the men of the people. Still Abp. Corrigan will always stand well with individuals over here, for his sweet compliance and his gentle obedience and great

---

[63]AANY, McQuaid to Corrigan, Rome, Jan. 22, 1889 (photostat, UND). ZWIERLEIN: *McQuaid*, III, 62 f.

[64] AANY, O'Connell to Ireland, Rome, Feb. 24, 1889.

[65] AASP, O'Connell to Ireland, Rome, June 14, 1889; cf. ELLIS: *Gibbons*, I, 583 f.

devotion to the Holy See. ... Insinuations came from N.Y. against Fath. Hecker's orthodoxy, and in the same place suspicions were cast on Bp. Keane".[66] Here O'Connell had virtually outlined the program of the liberals for the next decade as they increasingly identified with democracy and the American people on the issues which they gradually formulated into Americanism. On the issue of McGlynn, they may very well have acted out of pragmatic concern to end a pastoral embarrassment.

During the fall of 1889 and spring of 1890, O'Connell was on an extended tour of the United States, partly to attend the ceremonies for the centennial of the American hierarchy and the opening of the Catholic University and partly to sound out American churchmen on other issues. Among these was the McGlynn case. He was present in the country when in December Corrigan removed Burtsell from Epiphany Church and transferred him to Rondout in upstate New York. The reasons for his transferral were the alleged disaffection of his parishioners, declining parish revenues, and his having administered the sacraments to and said a funeral Mass for a known member of McGlynn's forbidden Anti-Poverty Society.[67] Burtsell decided as an alumnus of the Propaganda College to appeal to the congregation. O'Connell became involved with the case toward the end of his American tour. Meeting Father Daniel Burke, a friend of Burtsell's, he asked whether people still attended Burtsell's church knowing his association with McGlynn. Assured that they did, he repeated much of the information which he had previously given to Ireland, that Corrigan was declining in Roman favor but kept "a hold on the Roman authorities" through his investing Propaganda's funds. He concluded by asking Burke to tell Burtsell "that he had taken no part in the McGlynn affair that Miss Edes was the responsible party, but he felt that Abp. Corrigan was now so involved in ... [Burtsell's] case as to be likely to proceed to the bitter end".[68]

During the summer Burtsell used O'Connell's statement in his protest to Propaganda against his transferral.[69] Yet O'Connell's comments on Burtsell, McGlynn, and Corrigan at that time were curiously ambiguous. To Gibbons he said: "Dr. Burtsell hung himself in his defenses: 'My only crime was to defend McGlynn, and that was no crime, because he was unjustly dealt with by the Propaganda and the Pope'".[70] To Ireland he wrote: "Burtsell wrote the Prop 'una bellissima lettera e repudia tutte le dottrine di McGlynn'. Abp. Corrigan, in many things, is af-

[66] AASP, O'Connell to Ireland, Grottaferrata, July 23, 1889.
[67] CURRAN: Corrigan, pp. 304–307.
[68] AANY, Burtsell Diary, June 20, 1890.
[69] Ibid., July 1, 1890.
[70] AAB 87 S 5, O'Connell to Gibbons, Rome, Aug. 4, 1890.

ter their own heart".[71] Was he trying to plant the seed in Gibbon's mind that McGlynn had been mistreated or did he find that Corrigan still wielded more power in Rome than he had previously thought?

Whatever O'Connell's evaluations were of the Roman mood in the summer of 1890, by the late fall, at Ireland's instigation, he began sounding out Roman officials on what would be required for McGlynn's reconciliation. Without mentioning Ireland's name, O'Connell spoke to Archbishop Jacobini, who agreed that McGlynn need not cite George by name, but had "simply to say he accepted all the church accepted and condemned all the church condemned …". The problem of making specific reference to Corrigan, Jacobini thought, could be disposed of by using the general phrases "lawful authority" of "my lawful superiors". O'Connell broke off the conference then until he could learn more of McGlynn's terms.[72]

This first overture of the liberals toward settling the McGlynn case occurred just at the time that they were working unsuccessfully against the appointment of Katzer to Milwaukee. After that appointment, O'Connell reported to Ireland that he had spoken to Simeoni who complained for the third time of the "apathy of the American episcopate that did not assemble to defend the Holy See against the aspersions of McGlynn". Propaganda's attitude toward McGlynn was similar, O'Connell thought, to the one it had taken on the German question. In turn, he felt that general policy was destroying the Church in Italy "and in spite of this sad experience and experiment, they will apply the same disastrous methods to America" by following "the narrow policy of the 'three intransigenti' bps", Corrigan, Ryan, and Katzer.[73] In the coming years the liberals increasingly saw the relationship between the Roman Question and the Vatican's stance on the separation of Church and State and on the Church having some type of privileged position within a nation. On the McGlynn question, however, Bishop Moore continued to petition Propaganda for a solution, but Simeoni remained adamant.[74] Nevertheless, by March, 1891, the liberals were actively working for a reconciliation. Ireland, who probably received his information from Burtsell, reported that "McGlynn is patient and hopeful".[75]

For the next year, little was said of McGlynn, but the way for his reconciliation was paved with Leo XIII's encyclical *Rerum Novarum*, on May 15, 1891. While

---

[71] AASP, O'Connell to Ireland, Grottaferrata, Aug. 18, 1890.
[72] AASP, O'Connell to Ireland, Rome, Nov. 15, 1890.
[73] AASP, O'Connell to Ireland, Rome, Dec. 31, 1890.
[74] AAB 89 H 2, O'Connell to Gibbons, Rome, Jan. 19, 1891.
[75] ADR, Ireland to O'Connell, St. Paul, Mar. 8, 1891. A month later, Ireland dined in New York with Burtsell and discussed the McGlynn case; AANY, Burtsell Diary, Apr. 13–14, 1891.

the pope condemned socialism, he also declared that ownership of property was the natural right of all and the just reward for the laborer's work. Opposing class war, he delineated the mutual rights and obligations of both employers and employees. Every man, he said, should receive a wage sufficient not only to support himself and his family but also to save for the future in order to purchase some property. To insure these advantages the worker had the right to form and join labor unions.[76] In many ways, the encyclical was not new for the American Church, where there was already in practice what now became official Catholic teaching. Gibbons hastened to congratulate the pope and tell him how pleasing the encyclical would be to the American workingmen. But he apparently also made an allusion to George. O'Connell, therefore, decided not to make the letter public, for, he said, "the George question is a thing of the past".[77]

By the spring of 1892, the stage was being set for McGlynn's reconciliation. On January 22, Moore wrote Rampolla, the Secretary of State, that a year and a half before at the cardinal's request he had sent material on McGlynn to the Vatican, but he had received no reply. Now Corrigan had published Propaganda's letter to him in 1887 ordering McGlynn's excommunication. Rampolla promised Moore that he would discuss the matter with Ireland who was then coming to Rome on the school question.[78] Moore then corresponded directly with Ireland. McGlynn, he said, would be willing to go to Rome, if both the papal excommunication and Corrigan's suspension were removed.[79] As Moore confided to O'Connell, this would be his last effort in McGlynn's behalf, but he was optimistic that Ledochowski, newly appointed Prefect of Propaganda, would not be committed to past decisions of the congregation.[80] On April 3, Moore wrote both Ledochowski and Rampolla, enclosing to the latter a letter for the pope.[81] Ledochowski, with whom Rampolla was in communication, praised Moore's zeal in trying to win McGlynn back. Since the priest had been excommunicated by name for "irreverence toward the supreme authority of the church", it was first necessary that he make a "humble submission" to the Holy See. After that, he should come to Rome where his case could be examined and a decision rendered "with all charity and prudence in regard to him and to the censures with

[76] Given in Etienne GILSON (ed.): *The Church Speaks to the Modern World: Social Teachings of Leo XIII*, New York 1954, pp. 204–244.

[77] AAB 88 U 2, O'Connell to Gibbons, Rome, Aug. 3, 1891; ELLIS: *Gibbons*, I, 530.

[78] ASV, SS, 280 (1897), fasc. 1, 47^{r-v}, Moore to Rampolla, St. Augustine, Jan. 22, 1892; 48^{r}, Rampolla to Moore, Feb. 8, 1892 (draft).

[79] AASP, Moore to Ireland, St. Augustine, Mar. 31, 1892, quoted in MOYNIHAN: *Ireland*, p. 232.

[80] ADR, Moore to O'Connell, St. Augustine, Mar. 31, 1892.

[81] ASV, SS, 280 (1897), fasc. 6, 119^{r}, Moore to Rampolla, St. Augustine, Apr. 3, 1892.

which he is burdened". Moore was instructed to continue his contact with McGlynn to effect a reconciliation.[82]

In late May, Moore saw McGlynn in New York and convinced him to write Ledochowski. The priest's letter, reported Moore, expressed "his great desire to be reconciled with the Holy See, his regret for any faults he may have committed; his willingness to go to Rome if relieved from censures and invited to do so". The bishop thought "part of the letter was not as submissive in tone as I would have wished", so he asked O'Connell's assistance with the case.[83] Ledochowski's response to McGlynn was encouraging but firm. After telling of his gratitude for McGlynn's letter, the prefect said: "I therefore exhort you not to defer returning to the paternal heart of the Holy Father with an act of filial and complete submission humbly begging pardon for all you have done, which in the judgment of the Vicar of God on earth has merited you the terrible full declaration of a personal excommunication, and declaring yourself ready to adhere fully to his commands and to his instructions for obtaining the grace of being readmitted to the communion of the faithful. God will bless this act of rightful submission, which I hope you will have the courage to make and in my sincere interest in your welfare I offer to do what I can to facilitate your reconciliation to the Church of J.C."[84] Ledochowski had said nothing either to McGlynn or to Moore about removing the censures against the priest before he went to Rome.

McGlynn's was by far the most notorious case of a priest making an appeal to Rome against his bishop, but there were others. To end these and, as was seen, to discuss the school question, Leo XIII decided to send Archbishop Satolli on a special mission to the American Church – a mission which O'Connell and Ireland knew might turn into a permanent delegation. As O'Connell remained in Rome to finalize the arrangements, Ireland returned to the United States. Already Corrigan had been placed on the defensive with the papal reprimand for his stance on the school question. During a brief stay in New York, Ireland studiously avoided seeing the archbishop, but he did receive a visit from McGlynn at his hotel. "I had either to refuse him – & embitter him – or see him – & expose myself to publicity", he wrote O'Connell. "I thought it best to see him. I am now glad that Ledochowski took the matter well. McGlynn is rather well-disposed".[85] Subse-

---

[82] APF, Lettere, 388 (1892), 276^r−v, Ledochowski to Moore, Rome, May 6, 1892 (copy). Curiously, there is no record that Ledochowski informed Corrigan of these renewed negotiations, even though the prefect wrote him a short time later upholding the reasons for Corrigan's transfer of Burtsell; see *ibid.*, 309^v−310^r, Ledochowski to Corrigan, Rome, May 24, 1892 (copy).

[83] ADR, Moore to O'Connell, St. Louis, June 7, 1892.

[84] APF, Lettere, 388 (1892), 415^r−v, Ledochowski to McGlynn, Rome, July 5, 1892 (copy).

[85] ADR, Ireland to O'Connell, St. Paul, Aug. 3, 1892.

quently Ireland convinced McGlynn to cease his speeches to the Anti-Poverty Society.[86]

The first formal step in McGlynn's reconciliation was his retraction of any heresy and the removal of his excommunication. This whole episode even now remains confusing and may very well have been an indication of friction between the Secretariat of State and Propaganda. Satolli's instructions from Propaganda spoke of the frequent appeals of American priests to Rome because of a lack of proper juridical procedure and "too absolute a spirit of some Bishops". But the instructions did not give him any specific faculties for hearing such appeals or ending disputes.[87] On November 14, however, Ledochowski instructed Satolli to take advantage of his "temporary presence in the United States". Enclosing a copy of the letter which he had written to McGlynn the previous July, the prefect asked Satolli "to procure the return of McGlynn to his duty and to the Church".[88] Satolli was to act in accord with faculties, issued by Propaganda with the pope's approval, "to hear and settle well known controversies" after every appeal had been properly made.[89] The faculties were sufficiently vague as to have caused Satolli some confusion.

Meanwhile, on November 16, the day the archbishops began meeting on the school question in New York, Burtsell arranged for Satolli to meet with McGlynn.[90] Two days later, while the archbishops were still assembled, Satolli requested of Rampolla "the faculty of absolving him from the censures on two conditions, the first is to clarify those teachings on public economy which led to his disgrace, and [to make] a formal declaration to accept the truth and the teachings of the Catholic church, by taking an oath according to the customary formula; the second is that, once absolved from the censures, he immediately go to Rome and place himself at the disposal of the H. Father. If His Holiness agrees, I can first of all now invite Dr. McGlynn to explain his opinions to me and in that way form a criterion for myself. That was certainly a disgrace and every mode of prudence and charity should have been adopted to avoid it. Dr. McGlynn has never ceased to enjoy the good opinion and affection of almost all the clergy of this archdiocese, as well as the Catholic laity and also the religious. It is the universal desire that this scandal be removed from the diocese of New York and that McGlynn, in the best way possible, be rehabilitated. He could leave this diocese

---

[86] ADR, Ireland to O'Connell, St. Paul, Aug. 10, 1892.

[87] ASV, DAUS, "Delegazione Apostolica", doss. 3 a. Persico to Satolli.

[88] APF, Lettere, 388 (1892), 641^r and 641^v, Ledochowski to Satolli, Rome, Nov. 14, 1892, 2 letters (copies).

[89] Ibid., 686^r. The pope had given his approval on Oct. 30, 1892.

[90] AANY, Burtsell Diary, Nov. 16, 1892.

to go to another where he would be benevolently received".[91] It was a strong letter and made it appear that the scandal, at least in part, was Corrigan's doing and that McGlynn was regarded in Catholic circles as a martyr. Satolli had indeed signed the letter, but it was written for him by O'Connell.

When Satolli dispatched his letter to Rampolla, he could not yet have received the faculties issued to him by Propaganda on November 14. Rampolla responded on November 30. The pope, he said, granted Satolli approval to "adopt the conditions you indicated to lead the aforesaid priest back to the right path".[92] Armed with this authorization, Satolli asked McGlynn to submit a written statement of his opinions to a committee of theologians at the Catholic University. McGlynn distinguished in his statement between the "exclusive private possession" of land, which was necessary if an individual was to enjoy the fruits of his labor, and the "dominion" of the "organized community, through civil government", over the land, in order to assure all men "their equal right of access directly or indirectly" to land.[93]

On December 21, Thomas O'Gorman, Charles P. Grannan, and Edward A. Pace, professors at the Catholic University of America, examined the statement and declared "we judge that nothing can be found in the aforesaid exposition which is contrary to Catholic teaching".[94] On December 23, McGlynn acknowledged the judgment of the theologians and said to Satolli that "I assure you that I have never consciously said, nor will I say, a word contrary to the teachings of the Church and of the Apostolic See, to which teachings and especially to those contained in the encyclical *Rerum Novarum,* I give and have always given full adherence". Likewise, if he had ever let slip a word which seemed irreverent toward the Holy See, "I will be the first to regret it and retract it". Finally, he originally promised to go to Rome in May of 1893, but crossed this out to read that he would go within three or four months.[95] On the basis of this statement Satolli removed the excommunication and suspension from McGlynn.

The conservatives were astonished. Corrigan learned of McGlynn's reconciliation only from reading the newspapers on Christmas Eve. Commenting on McGlynn's appearance before a tumultuous group of his followers, the New York *Tribune* remarked: "The McGlynn incident...means that American

---

[91] ASV, SS, 241, "Missioni straordinarie", Busta, Sept. '92, Protocol no. 9462, Satolli to Rampolla, New York, Nov. 18, 1892.

[92] *Ibid.,* Rampolla to Satolli, Vatican, Nov. 30, 1892 (draft); also in AUND, Soderini Ms.

[93] Given in ZWIERLEIN: *McQuaid,* III, 75–79; see CURRAN: *Corrigan,* p. 390.

[94] ASV, SS, 241, "Missioni straordinarie", Busta, Sept. '92, no protocol no., statement signed by O'Gorman, Grannan, and Pace, Washington, Dec. 21, 1892.

[95] *Ibid.,* McGlynn to Satolli, n.p., Dec. 23, 1892. There is an original in McGlynn's hand and a copy. In the original, the reference to *Rerum Novarum* was inserted.

Catholicism is adjusting itself to the free institutions of the country. There is no doubt that the mission of Monsignor Satolli is to hasten this process".[96] Only on December 26 did Satolli, returning Corrigan's Christmas greetings, inform the archbishop of the matter-of-fact way in which he had reconciled McGlynn.[97] It reached an angry Corrigan on December 28. To McQuaid he immediately stated: "Our people are terribly worked up, particularly the better classes". Richard Croker, the leader of Tammany Hall, the New York City Democratic party machine, stated to him that it was "the greatest blow the Church in this country ever received".[98] He had already complained bitterly to Ledochowski about Satolli's ignoring him in restoring McGlynn and now wrote in the same vein directly to the archbishop protesting that McGlynn had not made a public retraction or done penance.[99] Satolli gave the cold reply that since Corrigan himself had said the case was in the hands of Rome and since McGlynn had never had a formal trial, Corrigan had no grounds to complain of a usurpation of power.[100]

Corrigan, in the meantime, had forwarded to Ledochowski copies of Satolli's official notification of McGlynn's reconciliation and of his letter to the delegate.[101] His protests were not in vain and may have fed the tensions between the congregation and the Secretariat of State. On January 20, 1893, Ledochowski sent Satolli a reprimand. He was happy to learn of McGlynn's restoration, which was in accord with the desires he expressed in his letter of November 14, 1892, but he presumed that, before McGlynn was relieved of his censures and reconciled to the Church, he had made a retraction and a profession of faith. Furthermore, the pope in no way thought the matter closed and insisted on McGlynn's coming to Rome as soon as possible.[102] When Ledochowski communicated to Satolli his faculties as permanent apostolic delegate in February, he found it necessary to add in regard to conflicts between priests and their bishops that "I believe it opportune that generally they not be used except in the second or third instance", after the procedures outlined in instructions of the congregation and in the plenary councils had been followed.[103] As a final reminder, Ledochowski warned Satolli in March that he was not to interpret his faculties regarding such

---

[96] New York *Tribune,* Dec. 25, 1892 in CURRAN: *Corrigan,* p. 391.

[97] ASV, SS, 280 (1897), fasc. 6, 121^r, Satolli to Corrigan, Washington, Dec. 26, 1892 (copy).

[98] ADRo, Corrigan to McQuaid, N.Y., Dec. 28, 1892, in CURRAN: *Corrigan,* p. 392.

[99] ASV, SS, 280 (1897), fasc. 6, 127^r–129^r, Corrigan to Satolli, New York, Dec. 29, 1892 (copy); 120^r, Corrigan to Ledochowski, New York, Dec. 29, 1892.

[100] CURRAN: *Corrigan,* p. 393.

[101] ASV, SS, 280 (1897), fasc. 6, 120^r, Corrigan to Ledochowski, New York, Dec. 29, 1892.

[102] *Ibid.,* fasc. 1, 156^{r-v}, Ledochowski to Satolli, Jan. 20, 1893 (copy). Cf. also 159^{r-v}, Ciasca to Corrigan, Rome, Jan. 19, 1893 (draft).

[103] ASV, DAUS, "Delegazione Apostolica", doss. 3 a., Ledochowski to Satolli, Rome, Feb. 6, 1893.

cases too broadly and was not to use them when priests had gone against the "decrees or resolutions of their ordinaries".[104]

Satolli had been duped by the liberals into seeing the McGlynn case as simply a facet of Corrigan's intractableness. He was now in trouble with his superiors at Propaganda. Yet his restoration of McGlynn was understandable in view of the conflicting instructions he had received from Ledochowski and Rampolla. The reconciliation of McGlynn had done as much as the liberals' stance on the school question to drive a wedge between them and the conservatives. But it had also further alienated them from Propaganda from which, as will be seen, they had hoped to have the American Church withdrawn if they agreed to the delegation.

In the meantime, McGlynn continued to act strangely. During Lent of 1893, he went to Florida to work in Moore's diocese. But still he delayed going to Rome. On May 2, several days past the four months deadline he had placed on his departure for Rome, he wrote Rampolla from Brooklyn asking if he could be excused from going. As his reasons he gave his poor health and the need to care for his nieces – the same reasons he had given in 1887. Moreover, he said, he wanted no post in New York or another diocese and was content to celebrate Mass privately.[105] It was again Moore who played the role of intermediary. Writing from New York on May 6, he assured Satolli that McGlynn would go to Rome and that he himself would remain with the priest until his departure.[106]

McGlynn may have had excellent reason for not going to Rome. In addition to the charges of heresy and disobedience, there were on file, at least in the New York chancery, accusations that he had solicited several women in the confessional and had fathered at least one illegitimate child. The last charge was made by his former housekeeper at St. Stephen's who had been a strong McGlynn supporter at the time of his dismissal and had now become his most bitter accuser. In April, McGlynn had received assurance from Satolli that no one in Rome would raise the question of an illegitimate child.[107] Since such accusations are handled by the Holy Office, whose archives are closed, it is impossible to determine how seriously the Holy See regarded these charges.

Whatever may have been McGlynn's real reasons for not wanting to go to Rome, under Moore's prodding he made the trip. Satolli had helped prepare his way. Writing Rampolla on May 8, he expressed the fear that McGlynn's letter to the cardinal would not "make a good impression". But he hastened to assure Rampolla "that Dr. McGlynn from the day of his absolution has conducted him-

---

[104] *Ibid.*, doss. 4, Ledochowski to Satolli, Rome, Mar. 6, 1893.
[105] ASV, SS, 280 (1897), fasc. 6, 137^r–138^r, McGlynn to Rampolla, Brooklyn, May 2, 1893.
[106] *Ibid.*, 139^{r-v}, Moore to Satolli, New York, May 6, 1893.
[107] CURRAN: *Corrigan*, pp. 276–285.

self irreprehensibly". He noted the charges of immorality against the priest, which, he said, were all too easily brought against priests and even bishops. In McGlynn's case, he thought the charges were fabricated by his opponents in order to disgrace him. Reporting that he had assured McGlynn that the topic of his moral conduct would not be broached in Rome, he asked Rampolla that the priest be treated with "the most extraordinary charity, so that the H. Father in the fullness of his power not allow any severity against him, nor any new procedure". Should McGlynn leave Rome in any type of disgrace, Satolli warned, it would produce "the greatest evil for the Catholic Church in this country", where the priest enjoyed the esteem of public opinion, and "I will be in the most critical condition". On the other hand, the delegate concluded, "if he, as I firmly hope, finds in Rome paternal good will and merciful charity", there would then result "the greatest advantage to the interests of the Catholic Church in the United States".[108] Satolli's reference to the possibility of finding himself "in the most critical condition" makes it difficult to determine whether he was more concerned with the real issues in the McGlynn case than with upholding his own authority.

By June 9, McGlynn, staying in a hotel and using the name "Mr. Edward", had had an interview with Rampolla. The cardinal listened to the priest with the charity he deserved, Rampolla told Ledochowski, asking him to use the same approach in dealing with McGlynn.[109] McGlynn had hoped to leave Rome as soon as possible, but Corrigan caused him to delay. Hearing that McGlynn might speak against the New York chancery, the archbishop dispatched his Italian secretary, Father Gherardo Ferrante, to Rome to present his side of the case. His plan fitted in with Propaganda's desire to control the delegation, engineered, without its knowledge, by the Secretariat of State. Ledochowski, in particular, was angry at having been misled by Ireland on the school question. In Rome, Ferrante presented a letter from Corrigan asking that McGlynn be transferred to another diocese to avoid scandal. The archbishop agreed to retain the priest in New York only on the conditions that McGlynn retract the theories which he continued to teach and which had been condemned by the Church, that he do public penance, and that he be entirely at Corrigan's disposal.[110]

---

[108] ASV, SS, 280 (1897), fasc. 6, 133^r–135^r, Satolli to Rampolla, Washington, May 8, 1893. McGlynn's letter had, indeed, created a bad impression in Rome, but Rampolla said Satolli's letter had dispelled it; 140^{r-v}, Rampolla to Satolli, Vatican, May 25, 1893 (draft).

[109] Ibid., 141^{r-v}, Rampolla to Ledochowski, Vatican, June 9, 1893 (draft).

[110] Ibid., 145^r–146^v, Ledochowski to Rampolla, Rome, June 27, 1893. In response, Rampolla asked that Ledochowski entrust the case to Archbishop Agostino Ciasca, the secretary of the congregation; 147^{r-v}, Rampolla to Ledochowski, Vatican, June 29, 1893 (draft).

It is evident that at this time there was not only tension but failure of communication between the Vatican and Propaganda. On June 14, Rampolla warned Satolli not to antagonize Corrigan too much. The pope was worried, he said, that the archbishop still had many friends both in the United States and in Rome who could make difficulties for Satolli.[111] After hearing from Ledochowski about Ferrante's mission, Rampolla requested that Satolli send him the statement McGlynn had submitted to the Catholic University professors. He received the reply that the statement had already been sent to Propaganda on June 16.[112] On July 2, Ferrante reported to Corrigan that the pope informed McGlynn that he wished to re-examine the statement he had made.[113] The pope's desire to see the statement probably was the reason for Rampolla's requesting it from Satolli. In any event, the secretary of state seemed unaware that Propaganda was independently examining the case.

Where Leo XIII stood in the controversy is likewise difficult to determine. The pope was a close friend of Satolli's, as Ferrante was quick to find out in his efforts to resurrect all the charges against McGlynn, including the moral one, and to undermine the delegate's authority.[114] But Leo also sought to reconcile Satolli with Corrigan, as will be seen. On the eve of that reconciliation, the pope wrote Satolli that McGlynn had still not made sufficient satisfaction for the scandal he had given. For him the issue was the authority of the pope and archbishop and the publicity. Reparation to Corrigan in a "formal and public retraction" was an indispensable condition for the absolution from his censures.[115] The public reconciliation between Corrigan and Satolli took place as scheduled, but McGlynn's "formal and public retraction" did not. Instead, he waited almost another year and a half before speaking with Satolli about obtaining a parish in the Archdiocese of New York. Satolli agreed that he was entitled to a post. McGlynn then made an appointment with Corrigan for December 21, 1894, almost two years to the day after his reconciliation. In preparation for this, he sent the archbishop a copy of Satolli's letter informing him of his right to a post, but, querelous to the end, he also sent a translation, since he was not sure if Corrigan understood Italian.[116]

The role of the liberals in McGlynn's restoration had done as much as their position on the school question to widen the gap between them and the conserva-

---

[111] *Ibid.*, fasc. 2, 25^r–26^r, Rampolla to Satolli, Vatican, June 14, 1893 (draft).

[112] *Ibid.*, fasc. 6, 143^r, Rampolla to Satolli, Vatican, June 28, 1893; 142^r, Sbaretti to Rampolla, Washington, July 11, 1893.

[113] CURRAN: *Corrigan,* p. 424.

[114] *Ibid.*, pp. 425–426.

[115] ASV, DAUS, Leo XIII to Satolli, Vatican, Aug. 14, 1893.

[116] AANY, McGlynn to Corrigan, Brooklyn, Dec. 20, 1894.

tives. But it had also further alienated them from Propaganda, as their hopes were dashed of having the American Church declared no longer a missionary territory and removed from the congregation's control. But why had they taken such a major role in the reconciliation? They could have begun to realize that priests' rights were not only dictated by canon law but were consonant with their growing conviction that the American Church should be united with the people, not the State, and governed by an ecclesiastical legal system which was in harmony with the liberty guaranteed by the Constitution of the United States. Ireland, at least, seemed to realize this. After Burtsell returned from making an unsuccessful plea in Rome against his removal from Epiphany Church, Ireland wrote him. "At the Council of Baltimore, I did not favor the establishment of irremovable rectors", he stated, "I was young, and did not understand bishops and priests the way I know them now."[117] On the other hand, none of the liberals ever personally befriended McGlynn. When he came to Rome in June of 1893, O'Connell, who was well aware of the liberals' difficulties with Propaganda, "had an opportunity of going to Norway and I went".[118] In his absence, McGlynn borrowed a cassock for his papal audience from Frederick Z. Rooker, then vice-rector of the American College and later Satolli's secretary and Bishop of Jaro in the Philippine Islands. For this relatively minor act of charity, Bishop McDonnell of Brooklyn, Corrigan's former secretary, refused to send any more students to the American College.[119]

The liberals, joined by the English-speaking conservatives, had been successful in defeating Cahenslyism. They had defended the rights of labor. They had won, however, only a Pyrrhic victory in the school question and in McGlynn's reconciliation, for to gain this they paid the price of the establishment of the apostolic delegation. They thus began to undermine their own program of Americanization. They were innocents abroad when it came to explaining their program in the complicated European situation, the context within which they were operating.

---

[117] ASV, SS, 280 (1897), fasc. 2, 131^r–132^r, Ireland to Burtsell, St. Paul, Jan. 10, 1893 (copy).
[118] AAB 91 R 1, O'Connell to Gibbons, Rome, Aug. 1, 1893.
[119] AANY, Burtsell Diary, Dec. 2, 1893.

CHAPTER V

THE APOSTOLIC DELEGATION

A. The Liberals Promote the Delegation

From its inception in 1789, the American hierarchy had been jealous of its relative degree of autonomy from Rome. There had never been diplomatic relations between the Holy See and the United States involving the appointment of a nuncio; nor had there been an apostolic delegate appointed to the hierarchy. Instead of a permanent delegate, the Archbishops of Baltimore through the time of Gibbons had fulfilled many of the functions of a resident representative of the Holy See. Rome, on the other hand, was eager to bring the American Church into conformity with European practice. In 1853, Archbishop Gaetano Bedini, nuncio to Brazil, visited the United States. In his report to the Holy See, he commended the denial of the title of primate to the Archbishop of Baltimore and, instead, suggested the appointment of a nuncio as a means of uniting the American episcopate and of cementing its loyalty to Rome.[1] Again in 1878, as was seen, Bishop George Conroy recommended a delegation, but thought that either an American bishop should be appointed or the delegation not be permanent.

The Vatican next made overtures directly to some bishops about establishing a delegation immediately before and after the plenary council. Propaganda's principal concern at the time was the number of appeals of priests against their bishops. For the time being, the hierarchy convinced the congregation to accept O'Connell as the American agent in Rome. The intention of the bishops was to have their agent perform the same function in Rome as Cardinal Edward Howard performed for the English hierarchy. But there was a vast difference between having the brother of the Duke of Norfolk as the recognized agent for the English bishops and a man who had no ties with the American government. In 1886, the Vatican dispatched Monsignor Paolo Mori to the United States to sound out the government on establishing diplomatic relations. In this he received the assistance of Bishop Joseph Dwenger, who claimed to have influence with President Grover

---

[1] CONNELLY: *Bedini*, pp. 275–277. The best study on the delegation is Robert James WISTER: *The Establishment of the Apostolic Delegation in the United States of America: The Satolli Mission, 1892–1896*, unpublished D.E.H. dissertation, Rome: Università Gregoriana 1980.

Cleveland and who may have himself wished the post of delegate or nuncio. Such Roman overtures on establishing diplomatic relations provoked Bishop Moore into a typically American remark. The Church in America, he said, was free from government interference, but Rome was showing "a constantly ruining disposition to ask it to interfere".[2]

Rumors of these overtures persisted as Gibbons set out to receive his red hat and, as was seen, Straniero had indeed suggested the appointment of a nuncio. Upon Gibbons' return to the United States, he gave an interview to the New York *Herald* denying that the Vatican intended to appoint a nuncio. His statement was immediately challenged in the *Herald* by McGlynn who asserted that not only did the Holy See desire the appointment but also Gibbons knew it.[3] McGlynn, of course, had his own personal reasons for wanting such a Roman representative. It was the frequent appeals of priests to Rome against their bishops which Gibbons feared would offer the Holy See the pretext of sending a representative and of thus diminishing episcopal authority.[4]

Gibbons was accurate in his assessment of Roman intentions. In November, 1889, Satolli came to the United States to represent the pope at the hierarchy's centennial and the opening of the Catholic University. Upon his return to Rome, he submitted a report to Rampolla, the contents of which he revealed to Father John Farrelly, O'Connell's secretary, with the request that he transmit them to Gibbons. Satolli believed "that more direct means of communication between the Holy See and the American Church were desirable, and that his views and reasons were favorably received by both". Rampolla wanted to discuss this personally with Gibbons who could perhaps bring with him two "of the most prominent and prudent archbishops ...". Above all, Satolli advised that Gibbons give no intimations of the plan to Propaganda.[5] Which bishops Satolli had consulted is unknown.

In the meantime, O'Connell had also used his American tour to sound out a number of the bishops about establishing an ecclesiastical tribunal possibly to be headed by Archbishop Williams of Boston. When the archbishops gathered for their first annual meeting in July, they made no allusions to the establishment of any type of delegation or tribunal. They did, however, vote to have Gibbons request that O'Connell be made a titular bishop to enhance his prestige as the agent for the hierarchy.[6] As was seen above, Corrigan was absent from that meeting,

---

[2] AAB 81 S 2, Moore to Gibbons, St. Augustine, Aug. 20, 1886; see FOGARTY: *Vatican,* pp. 219–222.

[3] ELLIS: *Gibbons,* I, 616–617.

[4] AACi, Gibbons to Elder, Baltimore, Mar. 21, 1889.

[5] AAB 81 A 1, Farrelly to Gibbons, Rome, Jan. 1, 1890.

[6] AAB 87 R 4, Minutes of meeting of archbishops, 1890.

but that proposal, among others, prompted him to write his angry diatribe to Mazzella about the liberals. He could not reveal his sentiments to Propaganda directly, he said, because Jacobini would leak them to O'Connell.[7]

Early in 1891, Jacobini did broach the subject of a delegation with O'Connell. One reason for Katzer's appointment, he said, was that on the one hand, the cardinals responsible thought the American bishops too independent and, on the other, the bishops felt misunderstood in Rome. Unlike many of the cardinals, he liked the Americans' frankness and openness, but still felt "they seem to be jealous of us. See for instance, they never wanted a Delegate there". This provoked O'Connell's response that, if the congregation did not think the bishops had confidence in it, the reason was it had "not treated them with sufficient confidence". As evidence for this, he cited the visit of Bedini, the attempted appointment of Sepiacci as delegate for the council, and the secret missions of Dwenger, Mori, and Straniero, all of which occurred without consultation of the bishops. Jacobini recommended that O'Connell discuss this directly with the pope.[8]

O'Connell did not see the pope until June when he took the opportunity of presenting Gibbons' Peters' Pence collection to register a protest against the Lucerne Memorial and the question of appointing German bishops to American sees. The pope, however, turned to what he felt was the real problem. In O'Connell's account of their conversation, the pontiff said: "'The whole evil is in this: that they do not want to have a representative of me there. If they had one of my representatives there now, that could speak to them the sentiments of the Pope, this trouble would never have happened. But for some reason of jealousy among themselves, they don't want to have my representative there tho' I would only name some one acceptable to them all. Why don't they want the Pope there? If Christ were to return again to earth, you would all rejoice to give him a welcome. Why not then receive his Vicar. No, if I had my Nunzio there, all would go better and you would be rendered independent of the Propaganda and made [to] depend immediately on the department of State'. I said it was believed the presence of a nunzio w'd curtail the dignity of each individual Bp. 'On the contrary', he said. 'However' he said 'I respect their sentiments in the matter, and I don't love them the less for it. Let us talk of something else'. There was no tone of bitterness or of reproach in all this, it was the tone rather of sorrowful regret and of surprise".[9] The suggestion of independence from Propaganda may have been a sop offered to the Americans to accept a delegation if one were established. At any rate, it was

---

[7] AANY, Corrigan to Mazzella, New York, Nov. 30, 1890 (draft). This English version differs slightly from the Italian given in AUND, Soderini Ms. See above, pp. 53–54.

[8] AAB 89 H 2, O'Connell to Gibbons, Rome, Jan. 19, 1891.

[9] AAB 88 S 1, O'Connell to Gibbons, Rome, July 1, 1891.

becoming obvious to the liberals that the pope would seize the first opportunity to appoint a delegate. The most they could do was turn the appointment to their advantage.

The pope's opportunity came early in 1892 when Ireland came to Rome to discuss his school plan. Most likely, it was around the time that Propaganda issued its *tolerari potest* of the Minnesota school plan that Rampolla broached the subject of a delegate with O'Connell and Ireland, for later on Ireland referred to their "night's deliberation" about it.[10]

But what had provoked Ireland and O'Connell not only to accept but even welcome a delegate? Their action has to be seen in the context of late nineteenth-century Vatican diplomacy. On February 16, 1892, shortly after Ireland's arrival in Rome, Leo XIII issued his *Au milieu des sollicitudes* calling for the *ralliement* of French Catholics to the Third Republic. The following day he was quoted in a newspaper as citing the United States as a republic where Church and State lived in harmony and concluding: "What is fitting for the United States with all the more reason is fitting for republican France".[11] Thus the pope adopted the pro-French policy of Rampolla, who had become Secretary of State in 1888. But the Vatican's pro-French policy was intended both to provide a counter-balance to the Triple Alliance of Italy, Germany, and Austria and also to enlist French assistance for the restoration of papal temporal power or at least the settlement of the Roman Question.[12]

In view of the pope's own words and of his earlier promise of independence from Propaganda, O'Connell and Ireland had good reason for seeing the papal action as rapprochement between the Vatican and republican government, whether French or American. But the curia was not united on this policy. Cardinal Miecislaus Ledochowski, who became Prefect of Propaganda in January, 1892, began to move toward Germany.[13] Cardinal Serafino Vannutelli, a member of the congregation, favored Austria and the settlement of the Roman

---

[10] ADR, Ireland to O'Connell, St. Paul, Oct. 4, 1893.

[11] *Petit Journal*, Feb. 17, 1892, quoted in Edouard LECANUET: *Les premières années du pontificat de Léon XIII, 1878–1894*, Paris 1931, pp. 506–507.

[12] D.W. BROGAN: *The Development of Modern France: 1870–1939*, New York 1966, I, 257–267; J. SCHMIDLIN: *Papstgeschichte der Neuesten Zeit*, Vol. II.: *Papsttum und Päpste gegenüber den modernen Strömungen: Pius IX, und Leo XIII (1846–1903)*, Munich 1934, p. 435.

[13] Miecislaus Ledochowski (1822–1902) became Archbishop of Gniesen and Posen in 1865. In 1870 Pius IX asked him to go to Versailles and use his known friendship with the Prussian government to convince Bismarck to restore the Papal States. Imprisoned in 1874, during the *Kulturkampf*, he was made a cardinal in 1875 and released from prison the following year. In 1886 he resigned his see as part of the understanding ending the *Kulturkampf*. In January, 1892, he was appointed Prefect of Propaganda.

Question.[14] This division in the Curia helps explain why the pope in establishing the apostolic delegation at Washington did so without consulting Propaganda.

Ireland and O'Connell failed to grasp all these intricacies of diplomacy. Enamoured of Leo's apparent pro-republican policy and already a Francophile, Ireland left Rome after receiving the *tolerari potest* on his school plan and undertook a three-week visit to France, where, he told Rampolla, he thought he "could be, in an indirect manner, a means for explaining and recommending those just and wise ideas of the Holy Father in regard to" that nation. There were still many monarchists, but the pope had forever destroyed "the notion that one cannot be a good Catholic and at the same time recognize the republic".

During the course of many speeches and discussions, the Archbishop of St. Paul had met with Sadi Carnot, the President, and other political leaders, including the anticlerical Jules Ferry; all spoke to him "in terms of admiration and affection for the Holy Father". If the Church continued this new policy, thought Ireland, it would undermine the anticlerical radicals and "many who are now with the persecutors of the Church will ally themselves with those who offer her liberty". The attitude of the bishops in not speaking in favor of the republic, however, he found "troublesome", for they were more skilled in "the use of vinegar than of honey". As an example of what a bishop could do in France, he had only to point to the friendly response of the Parisian press to one of his addresses, which showed "that a bishop will be well received by the French if he moves their hearts and excites their patriotism".[15] Ireland was therefore urging that bishops in France do what he was doing in the United States. In retrospect he was mistaken about both, but at the time he was convinced that his vision of the American Church would be upheld by the delegate who would articulate Leo's policy.

The first apostolic delegate to the American hierarchy was Archbishop Francesco Satolli. He had taught Thomism in the seminary in Perugia under the direction of Cardinal Gioacchino Pecci and, when the latter was elected pope, was brought to Rome to implement Thomism in the Urban College. He had already visited the United States in 1889 and was at that time President of the Pontifical Academy of Noble Ecclesiastics. The question for the liberals now was how to smuggle him into the country without the conservatives knowing the true nature

---

[14] Serafino Vannutelli (1834–1915) had been nuncio to Brussels from 1875 until 1880 when he was transferred to Vienna. There he continued the policy of his predecessor, Ludovico Jacobini, who had become Secretary of State and brought an end to the *Kulturkampf*. Vannutelli favored continuing the rapprochement with Germany. Created a cardinal in 1887, he was a member of the Congregation of Propaganda. His brother, Vincenzo (1836–1930), became a cardinal in 1891 and gradually worked for the solution of the Roman Question.

[15] ASV, SS, 248 (1900), fasc. 6, 54^r–57^v, Ireland to Rampolla, Paris, June 27, 1892. For Rampolla's response, see *ibid.*, 58^{r-v}, Rampolla to Ireland, Vatican, Aug. 8, 1892 (draft).

of his office. They found their answer in the Columbian Exposition to be opened in Chicago in October, 1892. Ireland, at first, ran into difficulties obtaining an invitation for the pope to be an exhibiter at the exposition because its commissioners feared arousing anti-Catholic sentiment in an election year. Gibbons, therefore, met with John W. Foster, the American Secretary of State, who had been minister to Spain when Rampolla was nuncio there. At the eleventh hour, as Satolli was about to depart from Rome, Foster wrote Rampolla in the name of the government inviting the pope to send some mosaics and fifteenth-century maps from the Vatican library to the exposition. These might be sent, wrote Foster, either through an agent of the American government "or should His Holiness see fit to entrust them in the care of a personal representative who will bring them to the United States, I am authorized by the President to assure His Holiness that such representative shall receive all possible courtesy upon his arrival and during his sojourn in this country".[16] Thus Ireland and O'Connell, with Gibbons' assistance, had engineered a complex arrangement or, some might say, a conspiracy.

But how much they actually told Gibbons about the possibility of a permanent delegation remains unclear. On June 5, Ireland wrote the cardinal stating only that the pope had taken the occasion of the school controversy "to revive the talk of a delegate".[17] Upon his arrival back in the United States, Ireland reported that he met with Gibbons and "at last I spoke of the delegate – telling that the delegate would be confided to him, that Leo was determined that we must stand by Leo. He was delighted, and asked at once how we could get the delegate to Washington – away from New York. So all is settled – and all is right".[18] But in view of Gibbons' later opposition to the appointment of a permanent delegation, it does not appear that O'Connell and Ireland told him Satolli might possibly be a permanent delegate.

On August 3, O'Connell unfolded for Ireland his complicated plans for Satolli's arrival. His tone implies that he and Ireland knew at this point that the delegation might be permanent, or at least of some duration.

"Well, my dear Friend, I have just had a long talk with the Pope, and it is all arranged. Only the forms are wanting. Satolli & I are to leave here about the middle of September to assist at the dedication services of Chicago Oct. 12. Then after a little tour, he returns to Washington to remain in the University at least the first year. There were but two occasions possible, since he must go un-

---

[16] Foster to Rampolla, Washington, Sept. 15, 1892, quoted in WILLS: *Gibbons,* I, 464–465. While this letter is listed in ASV with the Protocol No. 8639, it cannot be located with the other papers pertaining to Satolli's mission.

[17] AAB 89 W 8, Ireland to Gibbons, Genoa, June 5, 1892.

[18] ADR, Ireland to O'Connell, Washington, July 11, 1892.

der cover of the Exposition, either the dedication or the opening next May. That would be too late. Who knows what turn things may take before then or what reaction set in. Moreover his instructions must be made out just now under the influence of the favorable sentiments that are dominant at present. Then those instructions and those influences will shape all the future. Then too the mission of the delegation from New York & Zardetti [Otto Zardetti, Bishop of St. Cloud] will end in smoke. I know about the presidential elections, but the apprehension is not real enough to make us lose our opportunity. I have an invitation to the dedication services. You must secure one for Satolli. Now I count on you to carry these plans out firmly, and to have us met down the Bay [in the New York harbor]. I shall write the Cardinal to send a car to meet us at N. Y. I told the Pope you would meet us at Balto, and take us to Chicago. Then I saw Satolli. He puts himself entirely in my hands. 'In manu tua', he said, 'vita mea'. And in everything, he will be guided by me. That means the perpetuation of your victory, and nothing he could do it [sic]. Now please, without hesitation, carry out this plan.

Then the meeting of the abps. Oct. 12 must be deferred. The necessity of holding services in every cathedral furnishes a pretext. I shall write the Cardinal to that effect. But you must be in Chicago Oct. 12, and introduce us.

I said many other things to the Pope I cannot write here, and that some parties would not like to hear, but that you would not be displeased with.

Your interview made a bad impression here. You will compromise yourself if you continue. That's why I cabled you. Let the fight stay now between them and the Pope, and do nothing to put the delegate into other hands. After October, you may talk as much as you please.

Au revoir

Yours as ever
D. J. O'Connell

P. S. Please don't mention anything of this except to the Cardinal. If the enemy know it, they will try to alter everything.

I shall write Abp. Corrigan on the eve of our departure".[19]

As Satolli was about to leave Rome, he was handed two letters from Rampolla, the one for Gibbons and the other for Ireland, entrusting him to their care.[20] "Satolli has not the official title of delegate", O'Connell wrote Ireland. "His let-

---

[19] AASP, O'Connell to Ireland, Rome, Aug. 3, 1892; emphasis mine.

[20] ASV, SS, 241, "Missioni straordinarie", Busta, Sept. '92; Protocol no. 8359, Rampolla to Gibbons, Vatican, Sept. 12, 1892; Protocol no. 8406, Rampolla to Ireland, Vatican, Sept. 12, 1892.

ters state that he goes on a temporary mission. He is commended especially to your care...". It is therefore possible that the Vatican had at this point not made up its mind to appoint a permanent delegate and that O'Connell and Ireland had not actually deceived Gibbons. But even though Satolli was not yet a delegate, properly speaking, O'Connell was elated at this coming. He had just seen the pope, who said: "Satolli metterà Corrigan al muro". O'Connell assured Ireland, "this mission perpetuates your victory, and gives you more independence".[21]

O'Connell, who was officially appointed on September 23 to accompany Satolli,[22] now contrived a plot which presented many aspects of a comic opera, at least as far as the role he wrote for Corrigan, as villain, to play. On October 5, O'Connell notified Gibbons by cable and Corrigan by letter that he and Satolli were sailing that day on the *Majestic*. In the meantime, Ireland, who had been previously informed of the travel arrangements, sought to give Satolli's mission proper publicity. Praising the pope's decision to send a "delegate", he urged Austin Ford, the editor of the New York *Freeman's Journal*, to gain an interview with O'Connell. The interview, he said, could be arranged through Thomas O'Gorman, professor of Church history at the Catholic University, who "will be in New York to welcome the delegate in my name". As for Satolli, "the policy to be followed out by the delegate will be fully along the lines of Americanism".[23]

Corrigan had gotten wind of some of these arrangements.[24] His first inkling of Satolli's date of arrival came from a chance conversation with John Keiley, a friend of Gibbons. On October 3 or 4, Keiley mentioned the plans O'Connell and Ireland had worked out with the government and Gibbons for the proper reception of Satolli. Then on October 11, the day before the *Majestic* was scheduled to arrive, Ford informed Corrigan that since Satolli came as the guest of the government, a government cutter, the *General Grant*, would meet the *Majestic*, take O'Connell and Satolli on board, and convey them the rest of the way to the shore, where Alphonse Magnien and O'Gorman would meet him.[25] Corrigan vainly sought to learn where the government cutter would bring Satolli.[26] He knew he

---

[21] AASP, O'Connell to Ireland, Rome, Sept. 16, 1892.

[22] ASV, SS, 241, "Missioni straordinarie", Busta, Sept. '92, Protocol no. 8522, Rampolla to O'Connell, Vatican, Sept. 23, 1892.

[23] AUND, Austin Ford Papers, Ireland to Ford, St. Paul, Sept. 23, 1892.

[24] John Farley, on his way to Rome, met Satolli in Paris. Satolli confided that he was to get the archbishops to sign an "Act" of adherence to the pope's decision on the school question, work for the restoration of McGlynn, and sound out the episcopate on making Ireland a cardinal. With all these intenations Farley was in accord, but to Corrigan he stated only that he had met Satolli who was happy to be returning to the United States. See CURRAN: *Corrigan*, pp. 361–364.

[25] AAB J 7, Ford to Corrigan, New York, Oct. 11, 1892 (copy), quoted in ELLIS: *Gibbons*, I, 624 n.

[26] CURRAN: *Corrigan*, p. 368.

had been duped and was helpless to do anything about it. As the *Majestic* sailed into New York harbor on October 12, it was met, according to schedule, by the *General Grant*. On board were Magnien and O'Gorman representing Gibbons and Ireland. Corrigan's absence from the deck of the cutter and from the place where it docked was publicly construed as displaying his hostility for the papal representative.[27]

The liberals escorted Satolli to Corrigan's residence for a chilly dinner and an overnight stay. The next day, they spirited him away to Baltimore in a special car provided by the president of the Baltimore and Ohio Railroad at Gibbons' request. O'Connell was careful to report all the courtesies shown Satolli from the delegations of Gibbons, Ireland, and the government on board the cutter to Satolli's blessing a statue of Columbus ending a three-day civic festival commemorating the fourth centenary of the discovery of America. He was equally careful to avoid mentioning Corrigan at all.[28] On October 14, Satolli met Secretary of State Foster, acting as the representative of President Harrison, who was attending his dying wife. Praising the friendly relations between the Holy See and the United States government, O'Connell reported, Satolli assured Foster that the pope was so much in tune with American ideals that the government "would never have to fear that Catholicism and hierarchical authority" would ever do anything prejudicial "to those liberties established by the Constitution, but, on the contrary, the liberty of the Catholic Church in these states ought to be the greatest guarantee of civil liberties and of every other good". While in Washington, Satolli stayed at the Catholic University where he was warmly received by Keane and Bouquillon. On October 16, Satolli attended the Columbian quadro-centennial observances in Baltimore.[29] On October 18, Ireland joined Satolli's party to begin the liberals' triumphant trip to Chicago.

At the Columbian Exposition, Ireland delivered a speech and Gibbons gave the invocation for the dedication of the buildings. On the evening of October 20, Satolli attended a huge banquet, at which were also present Levi P. Morton, Vice President of the United States, and numerous other dignitaries. The liberals had shown Satolli the prestige they enjoyed in the United States and O'Connell again skillfully narrated the events for Rampolla. But Satolli wished to notify the cardinal that the occasion had been marred by a New York Catholic newspaper using language hostile to the government. Such comments were "highly injurious to the interests of the Church and restrains the good trend in its relation with the State

---

[27] New York *Herald,* Oct. 13, 1892, in ELLIS: *Gibbons,* I, 624.

[28] ASV, SS, 241, "Missioni straordinarie," Busta, Sept. '92, Protocol no. 9275, O'Connell to Rampolla, Baltimore, Oct. 13, 1892.

[29] *Ibid.,* Protocol no. 9224, O'Connell to Rampolla, Baltimore, Oct. 16, 1892.

and principally in regard to schools". If an end could be put to such "ill-omened imprudences, ... Mons. Satolli will make it possible to recommend the matter to the archbishops and bishops of all the states".[30] With the New York Catholic newspaper attacks on the school plan, the liberals were beginning to reap the first harvest of their planned isolation of Corrigan from Satolli. Their next step was to introduce Satolli to the other archbishops assembled for their meeting in New York. In preparation for this, Satolli left Chicago to spend several days in St. Paul under Ireland's tutelage.

On November 16, as was seen, Satolli presented his fourteen points on the school question and then met with Burtsell in preparation for McGlynn's reconciliation. The next day, he asked the archbishops for their opinions on the pope's desire to appoint, with their concurrence, a permanent apostolic delegate. Soon after Satolli's arrival, he had discussed the matter with Gibbons who recommended that he place it before the metropolitans.[31] Gibbons, at least, even if Ireland and O'Connell had kept him ignorant of the full extent of their Roman discussions, should not have been surprised at Satolli's introducing the topic. When the prelates were polled, however, all, except Ireland, said they would have to consult with their suffragans. Such reluctance Satolli found incomprehensible, he told Rampolla, but he was convinced that a permanent delegation would meet with no difficulty from the government and would be advantageous to the Church. "Therefore," he concluded, "I must affirm that sooner or later it will be necessary that the Holy See establish this delegation on its own impulse and there will not be anything to fear, even from the reluctant archbishops, and no difficulty, but they will never ask for it themselves...".[32] Satolli had offered the archbishops the opportunity to initiate the request for the delegation. Once they proved reluctant, he recommended that the Holy See simply establish it.

The archbishops were more than reluctant. At the conclusion of their meeting, they instructed Gibbons to thank Satolli for the able manner in which he had conducted his "special mission". Corrigan, who had already antagonized Satolli on the school question, was then deputed to draft a report of the metropolitans' actions on a permanent delegation. "The country is not yet in a position to profit by the establishment" of it, Corrigan wrote Gibbons.[33]

Corrigan by this time was being caught in the trap so carefully set for him by O'Connell and Ireland. His opposition to Satolli's fourteen points would be construed as opposition to a delegate. As was seen, he had sought to untangle himself

---

[30] *Ibid.*, Protocol no. 9224, O'Connell to Rampolla, Chicago, Oct. 22, 1892.

[31] *Ibid.*, Protocol No. 9275, O'Connell to Rampolla, Baltimore, Oct. 13, 1892.

[32] *Ibid.*, Protocol no. 9462, Satolli to Rampolla, New York, Nov. 18, 1892.

[33] AAB 90 S 5, Corrigan to Gibbons, New York, Nov. 30, 1892.

from the web through Elder's mediation with O'Connell. On November 22, the latter wrote him patronizingly that "things all around are cooling down and that, as you say, it was only an incidente accidentale". Some archbishops had personally called on Satolli and others had written him, and this displayed "a disposition to give him proof of respect". Satolli "was awfully angry the morning he left New York", O'Connell concluded, "but let us hope that everything will end in peace".[34]

O'Connell at this time was trying to promote everything but peace between Corrigan and Satolli. On the day before he wrote Corrigan, he had written Rampolla urging that the pope give his full approval to Satolli's fourteen points.[35] On December 4, he informed his secretary, John Farrelly, that there was organized opposition to Satolli and that Gibbons remained silent only out of fear. It was therefore imperative for the pope to support all of Satolli's actions and perhaps address an apostolic letter to the American Church embodying all of Satolli's opinions. Only Satolli's program could "make possible some type of accord with the State, and ... present some type of practical means which would put an end to the murmuring always rising from the priests and faithful".[36]

Farrelly forwarded a copy of O'Connell's letter to Rampolla together with additional observations. The opposition to Satolli, he said, was due to the old alliance between Corrigan and the Germans. This attempt to "abort" Satolli's mission was in turn a reflection of the opposition to the papal policy in France and explained "the concentration of many European Catholics with the party opposed to Mons. Ireland in America, with the 'scholastic question' being nothing more than a pretext for ruining the policy of His Eminence Cardinal Gibbons, Monsignor Ireland, and the Supreme Pontiff himself".[37] Farrely's account, resonating the ideas of O'Connell and Ireland, was geared to strike a sensitive nerve with Rampolla. The cardinal secretary was asked to see the American dispute in the context of the opposition to his own pro-French policy.

For a while the liberal strategy of making opposition to Satolli's school proposition appear to be opposition to a delegation was successful. Several months went by, as was seen, before the Holy See realized that the overwhelming majority of the bishops opposed Ireland's position on education so carefully written

---

[34] AANY, O'Connell to Corrigan, Baltimore, Nov. 22, 1892.
[35] ASV, SS, 280 (1897), fasc. 1, 103ʳ, O'Connell to Rampolla, Baltimore, Nov. 21, 1892, given also in AUND, Soderini Ms.
[36] *Ibid.*, 127ʳ⁻ᵛ, O'Connell to Farrelly, n.p., Dec. 4, 1892 (copy).
[37] *Ibid.*, 125ʳ–126ʳ, Account of Secretary of American College, n.p., n.d., but probably around Dec. 20, 1892. See also AUND, Soderini Ms., O'Connell to Rampolla, Washington, Dec. 4, 1892. This letter could not be found in ASV, but contained information similar to Farrelly's account to Rampolla.

into Satolli's proposal by O'Connell. But it was Ireland who was most positive in wanting a permanent delegation. The other archbishops opposed it, he told Rampolla, because some imagined it would diminish episcopal authority. Such a mentality, he thought, proved the necessity of having a delegate and when Satolli returned to Rome another delegate could be sent in his place.[38] From the available evidence, it seems that it was at this juncture that the Secretariat of State made its final decision to make the delegation permanent. Corrigan had been protesting to Ledochowski about Satolli's school propositions. The prefect then forwarded the archbishop's letter to Rampolla, who replied that he had shown it to the pope and that Ledochowski should notify the American bishops that Leo had decided to "entrust to Monsigr. Satolli an extraordinary delegation," which would last for the duration of the pope's will.[39]

In the meanwhile, American newspapers picked up the controversy. Some reported that Corrigan was about to be deposed; others denied Satolli's authority to speak for the pope. Corrigan was behind the opposition to the delegate, Ireland wrote Rampolla, and had inspired many of the hostile articles which were written anonymously.[40] Satolli himself told Rampolla that Corrigan was the center of opposition both to the solution to the school question and to the establishment of a delegation and that he should therefore be summoned to Rome.[41] Corrigan was also worried about his reputation in Rome. On January 13, 1893, he wrote two letters to Rampolla, one official and the other unofficial. In the first he noted that the newspapers were reporting that he would be deposed for his rebellion to the Holy See. He asked Rampolla to stop these rumors, which were being encouraged by his "enemies" and professed his loyalty to the pope.[42] In the second, unofficial letter, he recounted why he had not met Satolli at the port. Two other dignitaries, he wrote without giving names, had so arranged it that "I could not meddle without inconvenience and perhaps with something of a scene". He knew that his absence had been made to appear as "coldness" and hostility to the delegate, but in fact he had been "excluded from taking part". Clearly he intended Ireland and O'Connell and sent documentation to show how they had plotted against him and were responsible for hostile articles in a New York newspaper.[43] The liberals had again succeeded in placing Corrigan on the defensive with the Vatican.

---

[38] Ibid., 166ʳ–169ʳ, Ireland to Rampolla, St. Paul, Dec. 15, 1892.

[39] Ibid., 141ʳ⁻ᵛ, Rampolla to Ledochowski, Dec. 28, 1892 (draft); cf. also 140ʳ, Ciasca to Rampolla, Rome, Dec. 26, 1892.

[40] Ibid., 117ʳ–122ᵛ, Ireland to Rampolla, St. Paul, Jan. 10, 1893.

[41] Ibid., 115ʳ–116ᵛ, Satolli to Rampolla, Washington, Jan. 13, 1893.

[42] Ibid., 28ʳ⁻ᵛ, Corrigan to Rampolla, New York, Jan. 13, 1893.

[43] Ibid., 29ʳ–30ᵛ, Corrigan to Rampolla, New York, Jan. 13, 1893; copies also in AANY.

O'Connell, who had returned to Rome, now sought to capitalize on Corrigan's difficulties with Rome. On January 3, 1893, Gibbons wrote Leo XIII saying that all the archbishops, except one, did not think a permanent delegation would serve the best interests of the Church in the United States.[44] Even before this letter reached Rome, however, O'Connell cabled Gibbons that the delegation had been established and that Satolli was appointed the first delegate.[45] Immediately Gibbons wrote Satolli congratulating him and within a few days Ryan, Corrigan, and Ireland followed suit. Ireland wrote of his surprise at the "obstinacy" and "spirit of rebellion" among the bishops in opposing the delegation and said that he had already sent Rome the documents on Corrigan's conspiracy.[46] But if Corrigan's opposition to Satolli was to be construed as part of his conspiracy against an apostolic delegation, what were the liberals to do with Gibbons' letter of January 3? The cardinal consulted the other archbishops and all but two thought the letter should be withheld. On January 31, he wrote a second letter thanking the pope for establishing the delegation and for appointing Satolli.[47] Since both of Gibbons' letters were consigned to O'Connell for presentation to the pope, he now devised the strategy of immunizing Gibbons from any Roman reaction to the "obstinacy" of the other bishops against a delegation. In an audience with the pope, O'Connell presented both letters saying that Gibbons had written the earlier one out of deference to the other archbishops, except Ireland. The pope, according to O'Connell, then said, "I am surprised that he allows himself to be impressed by those people" and promised to support all of Satolli's actions.[48]

From the retrospect of the Second Vatican Council, if Gibbons had in fact been deferring to the will of the majority of the archbishops, he was then acting collegially. To gain their objectives, however, Ireland and O'Connell would destroy collegiality, rooted in the American tradition, and replace it with Roman authority. O'Connell recognized the long-term significance of this strategy. As he told Ireland immediately after the establishment of the delegation, "under the circumstances, I do not see what better could be done, or what other way there was out of it. Some inconveniences may be involved in the plan for the future, but it seems they have to be accepted under the present stress. È poi – 'après nous le deluge', as I used to say to you".

---

[44] AAB 91 A 3/1, Gibbons to Leo XIII, Baltimore, Jan. 3, 1893; cited in ELLIS: *Gibbons,* I, 630–631.

[45] AAB 91 B 4, O'Connell to Gibbons, Rome, Jan. 14, 1893.

[46] ASV, DAUS, "Delegazione Apostolica," doss. 4, Gibbons to Satolli, Baltimore, Jan. 14, 1893; Ryan to Satolli, Philadelphia, Jan. 16, 1893; Corrigan to Satolli, New York, Jan. 16, 1893; Ireland to Satolli, St. Paul, Jan. 23, 1893.

[47] APF, APNS, Rub. 153, vol. 74 (1895), 105^r–106^v, Gibbons to Leo XIII, Baltimore, Jan. 31, 1893; copy in AAB 91 D 12. Cf. also AANY, Gibbons to Corrigan, Baltimore, Jan. 19, 1893; AAB 91 C 12, Ireland to Gibbons, St. Paul, Jan. 13, 1893 (telegram); ELLIS: *Gibbons,* I, 633–635.

[48] AAB 91 E 6, O'Connell to Gibbons, Rome, Feb. 13, 1893.

O'Connell and Ireland, however, had themselves opened the floodgates which would deluge them. The liberals enjoyed papal favor and Rome accepted their argument that the conservatives' opposition to the school propositions was really opposition to the delegation. It was when Rampolla heard of the opposition to Satolli, according to O'Connell, that he decided to make the delegation permanent. But the flood which would overwhelm them was already welling up. At the head of Roman opposition to the delegation was Cardinal Lucido Parocchi followed by the Jesuits. Moreover, the tension between the Vatican and Propaganda continued to grow. While Leo and Rampolla envisioned the American delegation as part of their movement toward republican France and America, Ledochowski had broken with Rampolla and "returned, as they say, 'to his first love' i.e. to Prussia".[49]

The friction between the Secretariat of State and Propaganda had a direct bearing on the liberals' future relationship with the delegation. One motive for their agreeing to the delegation was to be independent of the missionary congregation, but when it was once established it was made subject to Propaganda. In announcing Satolli's appointment as permanent delegate, Rampolla told him that he would receive his instructions from Propaganda to which he was to refer all ecclesiastical matters, while he was to report on political affairs and matters of general Church interest to the Secretariat of State.[50] Satolli's own relations with the congregation were strained because of the rapidity with which he restored McGlynn. That action, reported O'Connell, caused more Roman consternation than Satolli's fourteen points.[51] For some time, Ledochowski would complain to Rampolla about Satolli's precipitous action in attempting to hear appeals from priests.[52] The liberals received an early indication that the delegation would not be totally of their own design. O'Connell had hoped to have his vice-rector, Frederick Z. Rooker, appointed as Satolli's secretary, but, instead, Ledochowski chose Donato Sbarretti, a *minutante* at Propaganda specializing in American affairs, and Hector Papi, vice-rector of the Urban College. This had "demoralized" O'Connell and Rooker, Brandi wrote gleefully, and "has struck their party a very hard blow".[53] O'Connell interpreted the appointments as expressing Ledochowski's anger at being ignored in the establishment of the delegation.[54] Ledochowski's anger at the liberals increased still more when he discovered how much they had misled him on the school question.

[49] AASP, O'Connell to Ireland, Rome, Jan. 25, 1893.

[50] ASV, DAUS, "Delegazione Apostolica", doss. 2, Rampolla to Satolli, Vatican, n.d.

[51] AASP, O'Connell to Ireland, Rome, Jan. 25, 1893.

[52] ASV, SS, 280 (1897), fasc. 2, 121^{r-v}, Ledochowski to Rampolla, Rome, June 27, 1894.

[53] AWC, Brandi to Sabetti, Rome, Apr. 17, 1893.

[54] AASP, O'Connell to Ireland, Rome, Feb. 7, 1893.

Independently of the personality and ideological disputes between Ledochowski on the one hand and Rampolla and the liberals on the other, the permanent delegation most of all represented the most definitive step that the Holy See had taken in the Romanization of the American Church. In its instructions to Satolli for his temporary mission, Propaganda had spoken of the differences between immigrant groups. They should become "politically and socially homogeneous with the nation", said the congregation.[55] But an interlinear reading might suggest that in order to overcome their heterogeneity of national origin, American Catholics should first become Roman. In the congregation's instructions to Satolli after his permanent appointment, it charged him with promoting "the most intimate union of the bishops among themselves and with the Apostolic See". When an episcopal see was vacant, he was to see to it that the proper mode of electoral procedure was followed and to take "care to collect with reserve and prudence accurate information on the candidates to transmit it to the Sacred Congregation".[56] In the selection of bishops, therefore, the balance of power began gradually to shift away from the American bishops toward the delegate – a trend which would continue over the following decades.

But the full effect of the delegation on the American Church was still several years in the offing. For the moment, the liberals were triumphant. That summer it was the turn of the Jesuits to be demoralized. When the pope learned from Satolli of *Civiltà's* opposition to him, he ordered Brandi to write an article praising the delegation. The charges against the journal were false, Brandi wrote Holaind, but he admitted he wrote the article "*in timore et tremore*, thanks to God, it has pleased His Holiness, who after reading it, sent it back to me with His imprimatur".[57]

In the United States during the summer and early fall of 1893, the liberals seemed still to be consolidating their victory. Rampolla had requested Gibbons' mediation to bring about a reconciliation between Corrigan and Satolli.[58] But in preparation for it, Satolli had demanded that Corrigan publicly state that he was not inspiring the articles in newspapers attacking the delegate. As Satolli remarked to Rampolla, he was certain that some of the responsibility for the articles lay with Corrigan since one of the most offensive newspapers was the *Catholic Herald* of New York.[59]

---

[55] ASV, DAUS, "Delegazione Apostolica", doss. 3 a, Istruzioni speciali a Satolli.

[56] *Ibid.*, Ledochowski to Satolli, Rome, Feb. 6, 1893.

[57] AWC, Brandi to Holaind, Naples, July 26, 1893.

[58] ASV, SS, 280 (1897), fasc. 2, 32ʳ–33ʳ, Rampolla to Gibbons, Vatican, June 15, 1893 (draft); 42ʳ, Gibbons to Rampolla, Baltimore, June 29, 1893; 49ʳ–51ʳ, Satolli to Rampolla, St. Paul, July 28, 1893.

[59] *Ibid.*, 57ʳ–58ᵛ, Satolli to Rampolla, Washington, Aug. 8, 1893.

The reconciliation occurred at a pontifical Mass on August 15 in St. Patrick's Cathedral. Corrigan preached and denied his association with the articles.[60] Shortly later, however, Corrigan wrote Rampolla swearing that he had neither written nor inspired the articles and his letters of protest to the New York *Sun* and *Catholic Herald* failed to have the editors divulge the authors.[61] How truthful Corrigan was is difficult to determine. Michael Walsh, the editor of the *Catholic Herald*, later broke with Corrigan and sent Rampolla an avalanche of letters asserting that the archbishop had inspired all the articles against Satolli.[62] In the meanwhile, as Corrigan was preparing to meet Satolli, Bishop Chatard was defending Corrigan to Rampolla. He complained about Satolli's close association with Ireland and the Catholic University of America, and enclosed an article from a Minneapolis newspaper stating that Corrigan would be removed. But this was not the time for the Vatican to be dissuaded from its support of Ireland. Rampolla replied to Chatard that the delegation was established to end debate on the school question, that Satolli's friendship with Ireland had begun in Rome, that his association with Keane and the Catholic University was necessary as long as he lived there, and that, if Chatard could cite one newspaper against Corrigan, there were others which claimed Corrigan's support and denigrated the delegate.[63] It must have been difficult even for the conservatives like Chatard or Corrigan to see the storm clouds gathering against the liberals.

B. SATOLLI TURNS AGAINST THE LIBERALS

But there were storm warnings and Satolli was advancing toward his autumn of disillusionment. At the Catholic Congress held in Chicago from September 4 to 8, 1893, he delivered a speech, translated for the audience by Ireland. "Go forward, in one hand bearing the book of Christian truth and in the other the constitution of the United States", he told the crowd. "Christian truth and American liberty will make you free, happy and prosperous".[64] O'Connell dutifully told

---

[60] *Ibid.*, 71^r–72^v, Satolli to Rampolla, New York, Aug. 15, 1893.

[61] *Ibid.*, 53^r–54^v, Corrigan to Rampolla, New York, Sept. 4, 1893.

[62] Cf. *ibid.*, 127^r, Walsh to Rampolla, New York, July 10, 1894. See also CURRAN: *Corrigan*, pp. 442–445.

[63] *Ibid.*, 61^r–62^v, 65^r–66^v, Chatard to Leo XIII, Indianapolis, Aug. 6, 1893; 67^r–70^v, Rampolla to Chatard, Vatican, Aug. 26, 1893 (draft); 63^r–64^v, Chatard to Rampolla, Indianapolis, Sept. 30, 1893. In this last letter, Chatard again explained why Corrigan had not met Satolli's ship and continued to protest against Satolli's association with Ireland.

[64] Francesco SATOLLI: *Loyalty to Church and State,* edited by John R. Slattery, Baltimore 1895, p. 150.

Rampolla of the speech, especially "that magnificent sentence at the close".[65] But how limited Satolli's notion was of "American liberty" soon became apparent in his reactions to two other events held in Chicago shortly after he gave his speech, the Parliament of Religions and the fourth annual meeting of the archbishops.

The archbishops had agreed in 1892 to take part in the Parliament of Religions, held in conjunction with the Chicago Exposition, and delegated Keane to make arrangements for Catholic participation. At the Parliament, held from September 11 to 28, 1893, Keane, Gibbons, and Ireland all took prominent roles. When it was over, Gibbons submitted a report to Rampolla stating that the opportunity for explaining Catholic doctrine overweighed the danger of religious indifferentism. The gathering, he said, was "a solemn affirmation of religious principles against the great evil of our days, materialism, agnosticism, atheism ...". To have refused to have participated would have done harm, he concluded. But his tone obviously implied that he was well aware that the Vatican might not understand this particular expression of American religious liberty.[66] Rampolla's reply was less than enthusiastic. He had shown the report to the pope, he wrote, and Leo recognized the good intention of those who had taken part.[67]

Even less enthusiastic was Satolli. The whole idea of the Parliament of Religions was an unhappy one from the beginning, he wrote Ledochowski, for the president was a Protestant and at the gathering, all religious errors were voiced. Keane, he thought, handled the situation well, but many of the bishops had expressed their fear that Catholic participation would foment religious indifferentism.[68] Nor did the delegate keep his feelings secret from Keane, who wrote O'Connell that Satolli "looks askance at our part in the Parliament of Religions, as do, no doubt, all the ultra conservatives". He recalled how he himself had become involved in the Parliament first at the request of Ireland and then of the other archbishops and remained "confident that the result is an enormous advantage to the Church. But I take it for granted that I shall be denounced for it. So be it".[69] Thus Keane, at least, had an inkling within a year of Satolli's arrival that the delegate would not wholeheartedly support the endeavours of the liberals.

---

[65] AASP, O'Connell to Ireland, Rome, Sept. 25, 1893.

[66] ASV, SS, 262 (1896), fasc. 3, 101r–111r, Gibbons to Rampolla, Baltimore, Oct. 27, 1893, with attached report. The previous year, the Rev. John Henry Barrows, a Presbyterian and chairman of the committee making the arrangements, had written Rampolla asking for the pope's blessing on the Parliament and sending the first report on the Parliament, which contained Gibbons' name first among the religious leaders who supported it; cf. *ibid.* 92r–v, Barrows to Rampolla, Chicago, Mar. 17, 1892. As one of the avowed purposes of the gathering, Barrows mentioned the "ultimate reunion of Christendom".

[67] *Ibid.,* 115r, Rampolla to Gibbons, Vatican, Nov. 20, 1893.

[68] APF, APNS, Rub. 5 (1894), vol. 31, 89r–90v, Satolli to Ledochowski, Washington, Oct. 6, 1893.

[69] ADR, Keane to O'Connell, Washington, Oct. 10, 1893.

If Satolli was becoming alarmed about the liberals' urging participation of the Church with non-Catholics, he likewise had difficulty understanding their tolerant attitude toward secret societies, which not only seemed to him to be Masonic in inspiration but also allowed Catholics to join non-Catholics in prayer. In 1892, Gibbons had appointed a committee consisting of Ireland, Riordan, Corrigan, Katzer, and Ryan to report on two such societies, the Knights of Pythias and the Order of Odd Fellows. At their meeting on September 12, 1893, the archbishops failed to gain unanimity in favor of either of these societies, but all hoped that the Holy See would be lenient in forming its judgment of them.[70] In the same letter in which he gave his reactions to the Parliament of Religions, Satolli commented that the actions of the archbishops did not seem in accord with what the Holy Office had decreed about such societies in Norway.[71] In retrospect, this was the wedge which gradually created a breach between Satolli and the liberals, as will be seen below. Then too, Satolli seemed to begin to have second thoughts about the wisdom of Ireland's school plan, which in any case remained an empty theory since the school boards rescinded their agreements in the fall of 1893.[72] But for the moment at least Satolli seemed firmly on the side of the liberals.

The first clear sign of the coming break between the delegate and the liberals, however, came not from Satolli but from Rome. Archbishop Agostino Ciasca, who had succeeded Jacobini as Secretary of Propaganda, said that Corrigan had actually written in favor of establishing a permanent delegation but had voted against it in 1892 only out of fear of incurring the wrath of the other archbishops.[73] Corrigan's reconciliation with Satolli had now played into the hands of the Roman conservatives.

For most of 1894 there was no open sign of a split between the liberals and Satolli, in part because they were engaged in mutual defense. When the Catholic University came under attack from the conservatives, Satolli urged Gibbons to go to Rome to defend it. When he became discouraged at Propaganda's continued hostility to him while it maintained cordial relations with Corrigan who invested its funds, he received encouragement from the liberals.[74] He had himself complained bitterly to Rampolla that Propaganda had diminished his faculties by not

---

[70] APF, APNS, Rub. 153, vol. 27 (1893), 598^r–608^v, Minutes of the Meeting of Archbishops, Sept. 12, 1893; 596^r, Gibbons to Ledochowski, Baltimore, Oct. 6, 1893.

[71] *Ibid.*, Rub. 5, vol. 31 (1894), 89^r–90^v, Satolli to Ledochowski, Oct. 6, 1893.

[72] CURRAN: *Corrigan,* p. 432.

[73] ADR, Ireland to O'Connell, Chicago, Oct. 4, 1893. No record can be found in Propaganda of such a request from Archbishop Corrigan, but there were requests from Father Patrick Corrigan of Newark, who was urging a delegation to guarantee priests' rights. It seems possible, therefore, that Ciasca might have confused the two Corrigans.

[74] ADR, Ireland to O'Connell, St. Paul, Feb. 16 and Apr. 29, 1894.

allowing him to hear an appeal of a priest from a formal sentence of his ordinary.[75] Sometime in June, O'Connell registered his own protest with both the pope and Rampolla. Propaganda's attitude, he said, had reduced the delegation to "an impotent dignity, useful only to assist at religious functions and the delegate is discouraged". Moreover, since Satolli had such limited faculties, appeals to Rome were increasing rather than decreasing.[76] The pope promised soon to speak on the American situation. This, Ireland hastened to assure Satolli, would invest the delegate with "exceptional powers & new splendor".[77]

But the liberals had to defend Satolli from more than his conservative enemies in the Church. In 1893, the APA had experienced unprecedented growth as it sought to blame the economic depression that year on Catholics.[78] Several bishops, foremost among whom was Spalding, publicly stated that the delegation increased the bigotry. Those prelates who claimed the delegation gave an impulse to the APA, Ireland told Satolli, failed to see "that such an impulse is entirely due to their narrowness, and that the association has not had greater effect. This is to be attributed to the Apostolic Delegation".[79]

No one could deny, Ireland said later, that the permanent delegation had actually hindered the development of the APA.[80] But Spalding, who had written publicly against the delegation in December, 1892, did deny it. "That the Delegate has been and is a source of strength to the A.P.Aists there can be no doubt", he wrote in an article.[81] Satolli had been chafing at Spalding's criticism for some time. On a visit to the Catholic University the previous June, the bishop had avoided even paying his respects to the delegate.[82] Satolli had already complained of this to Rampolla and now forwarded a copy of Spalding's article to the cardinal. On the pope's orders, Rampolla informed Ledochowski of the matter and on October 17 the pope issued Spalding a strong reprimand.[83] The opposition of the

---

[75] ASV, SS, 280 (1897), fasc. 2, 122^r–123^v, Satolli to Rampolla, Washington, June 15, 1894. According to Ledochowski, however, Satolli had no right to set up such appeals; *ibid.*, 121^{r-v}, Ledochowski to Rampolla, Rome, June 27, 1894.

[76] ADR, O'Connell to Rampolla, n.p., n.d. (draft).

[77] ASV, DAUS, "Delegazione Apostolica", doss. 1, Ireland to Satolli, St. Paul, Sept. 11, 1894.

[78] John HIGHAM: *Strangers in the Land: Patterns of American Nativism*, New York 1965, pp. 81 ff.

[79] ASV, DAUS, "Delegazione Apostolica", doss. 1, Ireland to Satolli, St. Paul, Aug. 3, 1894.

[80] *Ibid.*, Ireland to Satolli, St. Paul, Sept. 18, 1894.

[81] J.L. SPALDING: *Catholicism and A.P.Aism*, in: North American Review 154 (Sept., 1894) 283, quoted in: SWEENEY: *Spalding*, p. 229; see also pp. 212–215.

[82] ASV, SS, 280 (1897), fasc. 2, 122^r–123^v, Satolli to Rampolla, Washington, June 15, 1894.

[83] *Ibid.*, fasc. 3, 88^r–89^v, Satolli to Rampolla, Washington, Sept. 7, 1894; fasc. 2, 167^r, Rampolla to Ledochowski, Vatican, Sept. 20, 1894 (draft); 193^r, Rampolla to Spalding, Vatican, Oct. 17, 1894 (draft).

independently minded Spalding to the delegation is but one indication of how unpopular the liberals' program was among their fellow bishops. Spalding's known hostility for the delegation may have also cost him the liberals' support for the coadjutorship of St. Louis in 1893.

During the summer of 1894, two events occurred which began to put the brakes on the liberal movement. First, Leo started to write his apostolic letter to the American Church for which he consulted O'Connell and Thomas O'Gorman.[84] But apparently unknown to the liberals, he also consulted Brandi, who later took credit for the letter.[85] Second, the Holy Office condemned the two secret societies, the Odd Fellows and the Knights of Pythias, referred to it by the archbishops in 1893, and also the Sons of Temperance, which had not even been discussed by the metropolitans. The two events became entangled during the fall of 1894.

On August 22, Rampolla sent the Holy Office's decision to Satolli asking his opinion.[86] On September 4, Satolli promised to communicate the decree to the archbishops at their annual meeting in October. While he felt that each of the societies was Masonic in one way or the other and that they encouraged religious indifference, he nevertheless observed that it might be better to inform every bishop and priest who exercised the ministry of the confessional of the decree than "to give it the pomp of promulgation".[87] Only a few days later, he made the first of a series of reversals on the issue. Because of the great number of Catholics who belonged to the societies and found nothing contrary to Catholic doctrine, he felt that promulgation of the decree would be a moral impossibility and provoke ill feeling against the Church, the Holy See, and the delegation. Quoting Thomas Aquinas, he argued that both human and ecclesiastical law had to permit for the imperfect what it could not tolerate for the virtuous. Finally, he recommended that the decree be suspended until Gibbons had a chance to come to Rome in either October or November. The cardinal, he reminded Rampolla, had earlier argued against condemning the Knights of Labor and that decision had proved beneficial to the Church. In the meantime, bishops and preachers could point out the dangers of these societies to their people.[88] On September 22, Rampolla responded to both of Satolli's letters telling him to communicate the decree to the archbishops but "to leave the application to their conscience and pru-

---

[84] AAB 93 J 7, Keane to Gibbons, Pegli, July 31, 1894; 93 K 7, O'Connell to Gibbons, Grottaferrata, Sept. 9, 1894.

[85] ARCSJ, Maryl. 12–X 26, Brandi to Meyer, Rome, Nov. 29, 1894.

[86] ASV, SS, 280 (1897), fasc. 3, 83^r, Rampolla to Satolli, Vatican, Aug. 22, 1894 (draft).

[87] Ibid., 85^r–86^r, Satolli to Rampolla, Washington, Sept. 4, 1894.

[88] Ibid., 88^r–89^v, Satolli to Rampolla, Washington, Sept. 7, 1894.

dence".[89] Rampolla's response and Satolli's vacillation were now to cause further confusion.

On October 10, the archbishops assembled in Philadelphia for their annual meeting. In view of Rampolla's letter to Satolli, they unanimously voted "that it was inopportune under the present circumstances to publish said condemnation; they moreover agreed not to communicate this condemnation even to their suffragans; and in fine they resolved that no individual Archbishop or Bishop should promulgate it, unless its promulgation were expressly ordered by the Holy See or by the Archbishops in convention assembled".[90] The archbishops were hoping to ward off an anti-Catholic attack from the APA which the promulgation of the decree would provoke. They also had every reason to believe they were acting in accord with Rampolla's instructions leaving "the application to their conscience and prudence".

Satolli, however, changed his opinion. He seems to have been a man swayed by flattery whose own opinion reflected that of those with whom he last spoke. As his position up to the archbishops' meeting seems to have been influenced by Gibbons, his *volte-face* in less than a month seems to have been due to Corrigan. On October 16, he informed Rampolla that Gibbons had notified the other archbishops of the decree. But he also said that the day before he had received a visit from Corrigan who expressed his sorrow for the continued attacks on the delegation and stated that the archbishops were in accord with the decree.[91] This information Rampolla passed on to the Holy Office.[92] Corrigan's opinion of the decree's meeting with the favor of the archbishops and Satolli's wavering may have solidified the Vatican attitude toward promulgating the decree. Whether or not to publish the decree, wrote Rampolla, was not left to the "prudence of the bishops, but only ... the mode of its publication". If a bishop found some difficulty with the decree, he could suspend its promulgation for two months while he explained the difficulty to Rome.[93] Rampolla's new instructions to Satolli now caused further controversy.

On December 21, Satolli informed Rampolla that the decree had been sent to all the bishops and that Ireland had publicly urged adherence. While some bishops feared there would be damage to the Church, Satolli thought the decree was "opportune, necessary, and highly advantageous for the spiritual good of souls".[94] Satolli had clearly fallen from Gibbons' influence. On December 25, the

[89] *Ibid.*, 87ʳ, Rampolla to Satolli, Vatican, Sept. 22, 1894 (draft).
[90] AAB 93 L 4/1, Minutes of the Meeting of Archbishops, 1894.
[91] ASV, SS, 280 (1897), fasc. 3, 100ʳ⁻ᵛ, Satolli to Rampolla, Washington, Oct. 16, 1894.
[92] *Ibid.*, 103ʳ⁻ᵛ, Rampolla to Satolli, Vatican, Nov. 8, 1894 (draft).
[93] *Ibid.*, 106ʳ, Rampolla to Satolli, Vatican, Nov. 21, 1894 (draft).
[94] *Ibid.*, 107ʳ⁻ᵛ, Satolli to Rampolla, Washington, Dec. 21, 1894.

American cardinal, acting as he thought in accordance with Rampolla's earlier instructions, wrote Rampolla that, while he had sent the decree to his suffragans, he felt it inopportune to publish it in his own diocese. While not demeaning the wisdom of the Holy Office, he regretted its decision. Priests in the confessional, he thought, could persuade people to leave the societies without the publication of the decree.[95] Thus Gibbons asserted the same position which Satolli took in September.

Ireland's response was filled with his usual persuasive rhetoric. Most Catholics, he wrote, regarded these societies as for mutual aid only and the condemnation of them would now resurrect the anti-Catholic prejudice of the past. The old attitude was dying due "entirely to the generous, liberal, and foreseeing action of Leo XIII, whom Americans regard as the Morning Star of a new era for the Church and humanity". Ireland had only to contrast the favorable response to *Praeclara*, which would have been greeted with insult twenty years earlier. The establishment of the apostolic delegation would also have been impossible, had Satolli not "come as the messenger of Leo and the representative of the ideas of progress, of liberty, of moderate and reasonable authority, of social and religious peace". With the condemnation of the three societies, all of this would be ended. The hierarchy was divided on the issue with the majority favoring toleration, he continued. At the archbishops' meeting in 1893, only the Knights of Pythias and Odd Fellows were considered, but the Holy Office condemned the Sons of Temperance as well, "the most innocent" of the societies. At their meeting in 1894, twelve of the fourteen archbishops, he thought, had voted against the promulgation of the decree.[96] A short time later, Ireland and his suffragans wrote Leo giving their difficulties in promulgating the decree.[97]

From the documentary evidence, Ireland, as could have been expected, was the most outspoken against promulgating the decree, but it was not against him that Satolli levelled his criticism. He was displeased at "the negative conduct" of Gibbons, he wrote, and it seemed to him he did not "have the correct idea of what a cardinal ought to be in his own province and nation".[98] Satolli's criticism was unfair and may well have been due to Corrigan's increasing influence on him. Before the delegate's letter could have reached Rome, Rampolla informed him that he had written to both Ireland and Gibbons and that he had instructed the latter to have recourse to the delegate for any suggestions about the decree.[99] Subse-

---

[95] *Ibid.,* 63ʳ−64ʳ, Gibbons to Rampolla, Baltimore, Dec. 25, 1894.

[96] *Ibid.,* 65ʳ−77ʳ, Ireland to Rampolla, St. Paul, Dec. 30, 1894.

[97] *Ibid.,* 117ʳ−120ᵛ, Ireland and suffragans to Leo XIII, St. Paul, Jan. 6, 1895.

[98] *Ibid.,* 112ʳ−113ᵛ, Satolli to Rampolla, Washington, Jan. 15, 1895.

[99] *Ibid.,* 111ʳ, Rampolla to Satolli, Vatican, Jan. 18, 1895 (draft).

quently the cardinal secretary instructed Satolli to use all due courtesy to have Gibbons conform.[100] But the issue of promulgating the decree was closed as far as both the Holy Office and Rampolla were concerned. By mid-February, Satolli reported that Gibbons had accepted his advice and that all the bishops had promulgated the decree.[101] As will be seen, however, Gibbons did make one more personal appeal in Rome for a suspension of the decree.

The insistence on promulgating the decree reflected the changing attitude of Satolli and of the Holy See toward the American liberals. While Satolli in the United States began to fall under the increasing influence of Corrigan and the conservatives, Leo and Rampolla seem to have fallen under the increasing influence of the Jesuits. As was noted above, Brandi took credit for the apostolic letter, *Longinqua Oceani,* addressed to the American Church and issued on January 5, 1895. It specifically alluded to the necessity of shunning "not only those associations which have been openly condemned by the judgment of the Church, but those also which, in the opinion of intelligent men, and especially of the bishops, are regarded as suspicious and dangerous".[102] On a topic dear to the liberals, the pope said: "it would be erroneous to draw the conclusion that in America is to be sought the type of the most desirable status of the Church, or that it would be lawful or expedient for State and Church to be as in America, dissevered and divorced".[103] Leo then turned to his motive in establishing the apostolic delegation, the "proper and becoming crown upon the work" of the Third Plenary Council. In patronizing language, he said that his action was "to certify that, in Our Judgment and affection, America occupies the same place and rights as other States, be they every so mighty and imperial ... [and] to draw more closely the bonds of duty and friendship which connect you and so many thousands of Catholics with the Apostolic See".[104]

Leo XIII had clearly given an ominous warning to the American liberals. His letter manifested his suspicion of the American Church and its particular form of freedom and his desire to increase its dependence on Rome. Satolli regarded it as elevating the juridical status of the delegation and hoped to see his office elevated still more to a tribunal of appeal from metropolitan courts.[105] Satolli's general reaction seemed to center solely on his own increased importance; at this point he

---

[100] *Ibid.*, 114^r, Rampolla to Satolli, Jan. 31, 1895 (draft).
[101] *Ibid.*, 121^{r-v}, Holy Office to Riordan, Rome, Feb. 19, 1895 (draft); 123^{r-v}, Rampolla to Ireland, Vatican, Feb. 20, 1895 (draft); 126^r–129^r, Satolli to Rampolla, Washington, Feb. 12, 1895.
[102] ELLIS: *Documents,* II, 508.
[103] *Ibid.*, p. 502.
[104] *Ibid.*, p. 505.
[105] ASV, SS, 280 (1897), fasc. 3, 126^r–129^r, Satolli to Rampolla, Washington, Feb. 12, 1895.

ignored the other issues raised by the letter. His conversion to the conservative party was by no means yet complete. While he seems to have remained cool toward Gibbons, he continued to support Ireland. This he showed openly during the very period when he was wavering on whether the Holy Office decree should be published.

After the meeting of the archbishops in October, Ireland went to New York on business. While there he met former President Benjamin Harrison and other prominent Republican leaders. They invited him to give a speech during a banquet and Ireland took the opportunity to state that the Catholic Church was not identified with either of the two political parties. His speech occurred in New York where Catholics were heavily identified with the Democratic Party and where, according to Ireland, some priests in the pulpit were urging their people to vote for the Democrats. Moreover, he spoke just as a New York State committee was investigating the New York City Democratic machine, Tammany Hall, with which Corrigan was rumored to be involved. Finally, Ireland supported the candidacy of Father Sylvester Malone of Brooklyn for the state Board of Regents, which supervised education. Unfortunately, he did not know that Malone's opponent in the campaign was Bishop McQuaid. On November 25, McQuaid ascended his pulpit and delivered a denunciation of Ireland for travelling in the entourage of politicians and meddling in affairs outside his own diocese. McQuaid's reaction to Ireland, taking the form of a sermon from the pulpit, won him a strong rebuke and Ireland an apology from Rampolla.[106] McQuaid apologized for any pain which he had caused the pope, but suggested that Ireland too deserved a reprimand.[107]

Curiously this controversy won Satolli's complete sympathy for Ireland. Alluding to the dispute in the same letter in which he recounted Gibbons' promulgating the Holy Office decree, Satolli told Rampolla: "I hold firmly that posterity will know Mons. Ireland as an archbishop most active, correct, and loyal, disloyally assaulted by implacable adversaries, while he is openly and constantly devoted to the Holy See and to the person of the Holy Father".[108] It would seem, then, that if Satolli was falling under the influence of Corrigan, the latter was wise enough to turn the delegate against Gibbons but not to criticize Ireland directly. During the next few months, however, Satolli was openly consorting with the conservatives.

---

[106] *Ibid.*, 20^r–v, Rampolla to McQuaid, Vatican, Dec. 16, 1894 (draft); 22^r–23^v, Gibbons to Rampolla, Baltimore, Nov. 29, 1894; 28^r, Rampolla to Gibbons, Vatican, Dec. 16, 1894 (draft); 44^r–52^v, Ireland to Rampolla, St. Paul, Dec. 13, 1894; 54^r–v, Rampolla to Ireland, Vatican, Jan. 17, 1894 (draft); for McQuaid's speech, see ZWIERLEIN: *McQuaid,* III, 207–210.

[107] ASV, SS, 280 (1897), fasc. 3, 79^r–80^r, McQuaid to Rampolla, Rochester, Jan. 12, 1895.

[108] *Ibid.*, 126^r–129^r, Satolli to Rampolla, Washington, Feb. 12, 1895.

On April 21, 1895, he accompanied Monsignor Joseph Schroeder, the arch-conservative theology professor at the Catholic University, to the laying of a cornerstone of a German parish in Pottsville, Pennsylvania. Also in attendance was Augustine Schulte, then a professor at St. Charles Borromeo Seminary in Philadelphia. That evening, Satolli gave a banquet address in which he praised the work of German Catholics, some of which, he said, were the "subject of false charges and accusations".[109] By June, Schroeder, whether or not with Satolli's knowledge or encouragement, wrote the Vatican protesting that several professors at the university, with Keane's knowledge, were teaching heresy.[110]

Satolli's shift toward the conservatives coincided with their efforts to undermine the liberals. In May, 1895, Gibbons went to Rome in an effort to repeat his victory of 1887 and have the three secret societies tolerated. This time, however, his overture was rejected and he was further informed that Leo XIII had demanded the resignation of Denis O'Connell as Rector of the American College. This was Corrigan's doing. The archbishop had known that O'Connell had engineered the confrontation with Satolli in 1892 and began collecting a dossier against the rector. This he submitted to Propaganda, with which O'Connell was not on good terms and which, in turn, informed the pope.[111] Because of this and other issues, Leo demanded O'Connell's dismissal and then recalled all the papers.[112] "Dr. O'Connell's resignation", Brandi happily wrote Corrigan, "has surprised nobody in Rome. It was given *spinte* and not *sponte* at the demand of the Holy Father, to whom complaints against the Rector had been made by the Cardinals of Propaganda. The principal complaints were first: neglect of duty by frequent and long absences from Rome; second: want of confidence in the Rector on the part of the great majority of American bishops. Besides these reasons, the Holy Father, I think was displeased with the Rector because of his relations with Miss [Virginia Scott]M[a]cTavish of Baltimore with whom the Rector has travelled very extensively and whom he has often visited at the Hotel. Miss M[a]cTavish, at the request of the Rector, was received by the Holy Father, and the day *after* the pontifical audience was received at the Quirinal by the Queen".[113] Brandi's insinuations that O'Connell's relations with Virginia MacTavish were irregular are unsupported by any other evidence, but in any case the Jesuit seems to have been more concerned about the implicit recognition of the legitimacy of the Kingdom of Italy. O'Connell himself had formed a close friendship with the

---

[109] Quoted in BARRY: *German-Americans,* pp. 320–323.

[110] ASV, SS, 43 (1903), fasc. 2, 78ʳ–80ᵛ, Schroeder to Rampolla, Washington, June 18, 1895.

[111] AANY, transcripts of letters concerning O'Connell; ADR, Charles H. Meltzer to O'Connell, New York, Nov. 25, 1896.

[112] FOGARTY: *Vatican,* pp. 253–254.

[113] AANY, Brandi to Corrigan, Rome, July 8, 1895.

Cardinals Serafino and Vincenzo Vannutelli who were known to favor the recognition of the Kingdom of Italy and the settlement of the Roman Question.

In the fall of 1895, O'Connell left Rome for a few months and then returned as vicar of Gibbons' church, Santa Maria in Trastevere. Soon his apartment would become the gathering place for a number of European liberals. As Rector of the American College, he was replaced by William O'Connell, later the Cardinal Archbishop of Boston. In view of William O'Connell's later prominence, it is curious to note that in 1895, Satolli knew nothing about him.[114]

Satolli was responsible for yet another papal warning to the American Church. The Parliament of Religions, at which the delegate had looked askance, had by 1895 captured the imagination of French intellectuals and the *néo-chrétien* movement in particular. Henri Berenger, Georges Goyau, Georges Fonsegrive, Abbé Félix Klein, and Abbé Victor Charbonnel had each on different occasions proposed that a similar gathering be held in conjunction with the World's Exposition to be held in Paris in 1900.[115] The French enthusiasm for one more facet of the American liberal program drew Rome's attention back to the Parliament. Whether prompted by the French discussion or by the American criticism of the liberals' participation in the Parliament, Satolli on August 12, 1895, requested that Leo XIII issue a letter calling for Catholics to hold their own assemblies with Protestants admitted as guests. He also asked the pontiff to praise the work of the Paulists.[116]

On September 18, the pope responded. He was well aware, he said, that there had been meetings in the United States at which "Catholics and dissenters from the Catholic Church assemble to discuss together religion and right morals". He recognized that the motive for these gatherings was "zeal for religion", but he continued, "now, although those general meetings have been tolerated by a prudent silence to this day, it would seem, nevertheless, more advisable for Catholics to hold their assemblies apart. However, not to confine their usefulness to themselves alone, they may be announced as open to all, even to those separated from the Catholic Church." The pontiff concluded by commending the work of the Paulists in addressing "dissenting brethren" to explain Catholic doctrine and answer questions.[117]

[114] APF, Acta, 265 (1895), 521^r–524^r, V. Vannutelli Ponenza with sommario, Nov., 1895.

[115] McAvoy: *Great Crisis*, pp. 123–127.

[116] *Ibid.*, p. 127; James F. Cleary: *Catholic Participation in the World's Parliament of Religions, Chicago, 1893,* in: Catholic Historical Review 55 (Jan., 1970) 605. Both Cleary and McAvoy cite the Soderini Ms. for Satolli's letter which was not found in ASV.

[117] ASV, SS, 280 (1897), fasc. 4, 58^{r-v}, Leo XIII to Satolli, Vatican, Sept. 18, 1895 (draft); text is given in Cleary: *Catholic Participation,* pp. 605–606.

Satolli immediately published the letter throughout the United States. The reaction was as could have been expected. The conservatives saw in the letter a condemnation of ecumenical gatherings and of those Catholics who had participated in the Parliament. The liberals sought to interpret the papal action as merely stating the conditions under which Catholics could take part in such meetings. In Rome, *Civiltà Cattolica* charged the liberals with "neo-pelagianism" in proclaiming "the goodness, the honesty, the purity, and the sanctity of people who live outside the fold of the Catholic Church".[118] For the conservatives in either the United States or Europe, the recognition of partial truth existing in other denominations was tantamount to a denial of truth being the exclusive preserve of the Catholic Church.

Within a year the liberals received another blow. For some time, the Catholic University of America and its professors had been under attack for liberalism from both American and Roman quarters.[119] On August 11, 1896, Satolli, who had been named a cardinal the previous November but remained in the United States as pro-delegate, wrote Rampolla that Keane should be removed as rector for the sake of the discipline, intellectual life, and economic welfare of the university. He suggested that Keane could perhaps be made an archbishop.[120] On September 15, Leo asked for Keane's resignation. For his reason, the pontiff simply cited the custom of limiting the terms of office of university rectors. He then promised Keane either an American archdiocese or a position in Rome as consultor of Propaganda and of the Congregation of Seminaries and Universities.[121] Keane chose the latter and late in 1896 arrived to take up residence in the Canadian College,[122] for the American College under William O'Connell was no longer a place of welcome for the liberals.

Satolli, in the meantime, had also returned to Rome. The arrival of his successor, Archbishop Sebastian Martinelli, O.S.A., and his own departure from the United States stood in symbolic contrast to his reception four years before. On October 6, 1896, Martinelli arrived in New York to be greeted by Archbishops

---

[118] In: CLEARY: *Catholic Participation,* pp. 606–607.

[119] On Oct. 16, 1893, an article appeared in the New York *Herald* about the attacks on the University. It printed correspondence from Rome which supposedly reflected the opinion of an unnamed highly placed Jesuit. The Washington correspondent added to this the name of Brandi. Brandi demanded a retraction from Keane, who refused on the grounds that he had never made the erroneous statement; ACC, Brandi to Keane, Rome, Oct. 30, 1893; Keane to Brandi, Washington, Nov. 15 and Dec. 14, 1893. On the issues leading to Keane's dismissal see AHERN: *Keane,* pp. 120–178.

[120] ASV, SS 43 (1903), fasc. 1, 79^r–81^r, Satolli to Rampolla, Washington, Aug. 11, 1896.

[121] *Ibid.,* 86^{r-v}, Leo XIII to Keane, Vatican, Sept. 15, 1896; AHERN: *Keane,* p. 179.

[122] AHERN: *Keane,* pp. 203–204.

Corrigan and Ryan, Bishop Thomas Burke of Albany, members of the delegation staff, and prominent lay Catholics. The same day, Satolli left Washington in order to pay a last visit to Corrigan and Bishops Winand Wigger of Newark and Charles McDonnell of Brooklyn before sailing for Rome.[123] Gone were the days when the delegation could be seen as the liberals' institution.

By the beginning of 1897, the liberals were in disarray largely through problems of their own manufacture. They had taken the initiative in supporting the Knights of Labor and thus wedded the American Church to the workingman, but then they over-extended themselves in supporting other secret societies in an era when such associations were subject to misunderstanding in Rome. Their program called for an alliance of the Church with the people, and it seems that as time went on they began to see the logic of their own position and began to support priests' rights. To illustrate this they worked for the restoration of Edward McGlynn. This served to strengthen still more the forces mustered against them: Corrigan and the Jesuits. To win their victory on the school question and the McGlynn issue, however, they had had to introduce what their program required to be excluded – the apostolic delegation with its first steps toward Romanization. Easily flattered by their initial support and dependent on them for translation into English, Satolli gradually turned against them on the issue of interreligious cooperation, a major point of contention between the Vatican and the American Church for another seventy years. They suffered defeats in the forced resignations of O'Connell and Keane, but they were still ready for one last try at victory by appeal to the European world in their program of Americanism.

---

[123] APF, APNS, Rub. 153, vol. 98 (1896), 148^r–149^r, Martinelli to Ledochowski, Washington, Oct. 6, 1896.

CHAPTER VI

AMERICANISM EXPORTED TO EUROPE

A. Internationalizing Americanism

Controversy in the American Church might well have ended with Keane's obtaining a sinecure in Rome, had it not begun to spread to Europe. The liberals, or Americanists as they now began to call themselves, consciously nurtured the international dimension of their movement and allied themselves with Catholic liberals in France, Germany, and Italy. At the same time that they commenced exporting their ideals of the American Church, however, the United States began emerging as a world power. Religious and political Americanism became inextricably intertwined. Rome's reaction was guarded but swift and after 1900 the Romanization of the American Church began in full measure.

Catholic supporters of the Third French Republic had already been enamoured with American republican ideas. Had not Archbishop Ireland himself in 1892 spoken in favor of the pope's new policy of *ralliement*? Ireland, however, planted his seeds of the compatibility of republicanism and Catholicism in ground which had been well prepared by Lamennais, Dupanloup, Lacordaire, and Montalembert. Moreover, many of the American secular clergy, but especially the liberals, as has been seen, had attended seminaries run by the Sulpicians. This religious society, according to Albert Houtin, a French Americanist and later modernist, preserved the older French liberal tradition and inculcated it in its students.[1] John Ireland himself referred to France as the "mother of my ideas" and the "father of my youth".[2] Ireland was well aware of the potential French sympathy for his Americanist movement and he played upon it. Soon the Abbé Félix Klein, professor of French literature at the Institut Catholique de Paris, was translating the archbishop's American speeches into French. Despite the warnings of *Longinqua Oceani* against the exporting of the American notion of the separation of Church

---

[1] Albert HOUTIN: *L'Américanisme*, Paris 1904, pp. 212–213.

[2] LECANUET: *La vie*, pp. 547–550, cited in Ornella PELLEGRINO CONFESSORE: *Conservatorismo politico e riformismo: La Rassegna nazionale dal 1898 al 1908*, Bologna 1970, p. 103 n. But Ireland's Francophilia and progressive ideas were not typical of his writings and sermons as a young priest; see Thomas E. WANGLER: *John Ireland and the Origins of Liberal Catholicism in the United States*, in: Catholic Historical Review 56 (1971) 617–629.

and State and the forced resignations of O'Connell and Keane, the liberals were encouraged to proceed ahead to internationalize their domestic quarrel.

Shortly after Keane arrived in Rome O'Connell turned his apartment, dubbed "Liberty Hall," into the Tuesday evening meeting place for the "Club" or "Lodge," a thinly disguised reference to the secret societies so dear to the liberals. Besides O'Connell and Keane, the membership came to include a group of clergy and laymen either living in or visiting Rome, who were dedicated in a variety of ways to the modernization of the Church, Father John A. Zahm, C.S.C., had been professor of science at the University of Notre Dame and subsequently wrote on the compatibility of evolution and Christian doctrine. In the spring of 1896 he had come to Rome as the procurator for the Congregation of the Holy Cross. European members of the "Club" included the conciliationist cardinals Vincenzo and Serafino Vannutelli, the Abbé Louis Duchesne, former professor of Church history at the Paris Institut Catholique and then Director of the École Française in Rome, the Baron Friedrich von Hügel from England, and Father David Fleming, O.F.M., an English consultor to the Holy Office. Félix Klein kept in close touch with the group and O'Connell also maintained an occasional correspondence with the Abbé Alfred Loisy and later, through the Baroness Augusta d'Eichthal, made contact with the German liberals, especially Franz X. Kraus.[3]

Up to this point, the liberal movement in the United States had primarily focused on the Americanization of the immigrants and the accommodation of the Church to American culture. With the formation of the "Club", it became not only international but also more universal in its concerns. The benefit to the Church of the American separation of Church and State and the corollary, religious liberty, were the peculiar American contributions to worldwide Catholicism. But this was now blended with progressive European views on biblical and historical scholarship, theology, and science. There was already an affinity between the American liberals' praise of religious liberty and the European progressives' support of a valid subjectivity in theology, between the former's rapprochement with democracy and scientific progress and the latter's program to reconcile the Church with the modern age. All that was needed was a catalyst to bring that affinity into the open and meld together those divergent interests.

---

[3] FOGARTY: *Vatican*, p. 257; Ralph E. WEBER: *Notre Dame's John Zahm: American Catholic Apologist and Educator*, Notre Dame 1961, pp. 92–218. O'Connell had earlier recommended Loisy for Ireland's seminary saying he was "the leading Biblical scholar in the church"; AASP, O'Connell to Ireland, Rome, Sept. 21, 1890. Brandi was annoyed that Zahm had not been to see him upon his arrival in Rome and was "afraid that his recent utterances on transformism, and his relations with the liberal party, well known in the Vatican and Propaganda, will interfere somewhat with his work of Procurator. ..."; AANY, Brandi to Corrigan, Rome, June 13, 1896.

The catalyst came in the latter part of 1896. In France, the conservative Catholic *La Vérité* published a series of articles by George Périès writing under the pen-name "St. Clement". Dismissed earlier that year as professor of canon law at the Catholic University of America, Périès linked the American liberals with the *néo-chrétiens* in France. He then stated that Keane's was the first of several forthcoming dismissals from the university, that Ireland would be summoned to Rome for his liberalism, and that Gibbons would soon receive a coadjutor.[4] These attacks on the liberals in the European press were also picked up in the United States. They occurred, moreover, during the heated presidential election campaign with the Republican candidate William McKinley opposing the Democrat William Jennings Bryan, whose platform called for the rejection of gold and the increased coinage of silver. Ireland had publicly repudiated Bryan and declared his unconditional support for McKinley.

In October, the editor of the New York *Examiner* cabled Rampolla asking if Ireland was speaking with the authority of the Church. The cardinal secretary immediately cabled Archbishop Sebastian Martinelli, the new delegate, requesting information. Martinelli, in turn, contacted Ireland who explained that, at the request of several prominent citizens, he had spoken for McKinley and "expressed his opinion not as Archbishop nor as reflecting the views of the Catholic Church, or of the Holy See in regard to the presidential campaign, but simply as a private citizen". The severity of Ireland's attack on Bryan, said the delegate, was in part due to the well-known fact of his being a Republican. But Martinelli took the opportunity of defending Ireland to explain the American two-party system to Rampolla. The parties, he wrote, differed in regard to economics and their conception of the central government. Then he added: "Catholics belong indistinguishably to both parties; and it is good".[5]

After McKinley's election, Périès continued his attacks on Ireland and the liberals. More disturbing were two articles in the *New York Journal* stating that Satolli had reported to Rome that Ireland was an apostle of heresy and should be called to Rome and that the liberal tendencies of the university had now been tempered by Keane's removal.[6] Here for the first time, Ireland was reported as under attack by his former friend, then a curial official. On November 16, he protested to Rampolla about these attacks printed in American and European newspapers. Unlike his previous letters to the cardinal secretary, however, this one lacked his usual confidence, was somewhat apologetic in tone, but still man-

---

[4] McAvoy: *Great Crisis*, pp. 143, 149–152.

[5] ASV, SS, 280 (1898), fasc. 2, 57ʳ, Rampolla to Martinelli, Vatican, Oct. 15, 1896 (draft of cable); 58ʳ⁻ᵛ, Martinelli to Rampolla, Washington, Dec. 20, 1896.

[6] New York *Journal*, Nov. 12, 1896, *ibid.*, 64ʳ. See McAvoy: *Great Crisis*, p. 143.

ifested his high self-esteem. The journalistic attacks, he said, had provoked discussions "in the streets, in business offices, and in private salons" and as a result "I have suffered; religion has suffered". One story said that his letter in support of McKinley had displeased the pope; yet it was acknowledged "by Mr. McKinley as having greatly contributed to his success". Rampolla would readily understand, he continued, "how much my influence, both as a citizen and as a bishop, has suffered" and that the controversy arising from these stories could "not turn to the profit of the Church". If he had done anything to offend the Holy Father, he added, "I ask you to tell me his will directly, instead of leaving the task of informing me to Roman Gossip".

Ireland was nevertheless confident that the stories were false and that he was still in Leo's good graces. He, therefore, requested that the Holy See say something "to destroy the calumnies of which I am the victim". Were it not for the bad interpretation which would be placed upon a trip to Rome, he would immediately go, but he promised to make the trip within a year. Finally, he defended his letter supporting McKinley. The last election, he asserted, was "far from being purely political", since the Democrats were advocating "dangerous socialism" and attacking "the honor of the nation", commercial agreements, and "the most venerable rights of the federal government". Since many Catholics supported Bryan, Ireland believed he had to speak out. Millions of Americans could now attest that his letter had benefitted the Church. He then maintained: "An immense public influence accrues to me; Mr. McKinley avows himself indebted to me for his election; never has a Catholic bishop had the influence in America which is mine. And this influence will be used entirely and always for the Church and for the honor of its head. I do not believe that Leo XIII blames me if I succeed in raising the holy candlestick from the darkness and placing it on the mountaintop".[7]

It was always difficult to determine beneath Ireland's rhetoric whether he was arguing for himself or for the Church. But in this case his protest was successful. Rampolla cabled him in December that he not only enjoyed the pope's favor but also his enemies knew it.[8] Martinelli, in the meantime, had also written Rampolla about the newspaper stories and received the instructions publicly to contradict them as "lies" and the product of a "reproachable maneuver".[9] For the moment the attacks on the liberals, instead of throwing them on the defensive, won them new Vatican support. This support, in turn, formed the backdrop for O'Connell to form the "Club" as the counter-poise to the growing European opposition to the liberals.

---

[7] ASV, SS, 280 (1898), fasc. 2, 60^r–63^r, Ireland to Rampolla, St. Paul, Nov. 16, 1896.
[8] *Ibid.*, 65^r, Rampolla to Ireland, Vatican, Dec. 5, 1896 (draft).
[9] AAB 94 U 2, Martinelli to Gibbons, Washington, Dec. 3, 1896.

What the liberals needed to construct the international dimensions of their movement was a broader ideological base. Here O'Connell was the strategist and early in January, 1897, he outlined for Ireland the first phase of their tactic to ally with the German progressives and neutralize or isolate the German-American and other conservatives. He stated: "With Germans as Germans, you have no contention whatever. You never failed in all your life to express yr. repulsion for war of race on race, and you never intended to promote such medieval vulgarity. Your contention is for an idea. That idea is progress, and that's yr. battle cry. You have as many & more friends in Germany as in Ireland. Your only opponents are the reactionaries, wherever they be. In America, some of your most bitter opponents are among the Irish. The little clique of Germans that attacked you in America do not represent the Germans. Your only made war on that narrow clique because they attacked you when you spoke for progress. Even among the Jesuits you have sympathising friends. Your war then is not a war of race on race of community on community on community [sic] but of progress vs stagnation. ... Honor compelled every German to arm against you, as long as he thought you made war on his fatherland. Make him understand you make war only on the medievalist, and the German is with you, and your victory is won. The question in the U.S. was only incidental, and was not fairly represented by your enemies. Now make yourself known. I am sure you have millions of sympathisers for your ideas in Germany. Now what I write you in this letter is already a reality in Rome and the platform is adopted by both parties, and both parties are delighted with it. Keane is enthusiastic, so is d'Eichthal, so too Zahm, and I have written Boeglin to sound the idea from Paris. Now one thing remains to be done. On a suitable occasion, and that very near, you must seek an opportunity of publishing your real program to the world, i.e., not war of race on race, but idea on idea, of progress on stagnation. Do it, and in consistency you can do it and in duty you ought to do it, and you will lead the world. ... Then send the discourse over here, and d'Eichthal says she will do the rest".[10]

A few weeks later O'Connell wrote to say that he and his friends had determined on a name for their party: "It is this: we are to have no name at all, we are the same old thing all the time. We are no party at all. We are the Church. All the other fellows the opposition are a party, a party in the Church as there always was, and they are the 'Réfractaires'." Noting that the pope had used "Réfractaires" to describe those who opposed his policy in France, O'Conell suggested that Ireland extend it "to the whole world and to the past".[11] Finally, he told Ire-

---

[10] AASP, O'Connell to Ireland, Rome, Jan. 7, 1897; cf. AASP, Keane to Ireland, Rome, Jan. 11, 1897.

[11] AASP, O'Connell to Ireland, Rome, Jan. 28, 1897. Keane again supported the proposal and added that Boeglin believed the use of "réfractaires" would make the American position intelligible in Rome; AASP, Keane to Ireland, Rome, Jan. 31, 1897.

land not to limit himself to papal political policy in France, but to "enlarge the idea, by assuming that the Pope is laboring for the advancement of civilization & science, to put the Church at the head of the age".[12]

Soon after McKinley's inauguration, Ireland found the occasion to express O'Connell's ideas. On March 28, at St. Patrick's Church in Washington, he delivered a sermon entitled "The New Age". With considerable rhetorical skill, he publicly attacked his critics and extended the notion of *réfractaires* to embrace the American conservatives. Leo had characterized as *réfractaires* those in France who ignored his "repeated invitation to all Catholics to see in the Republican form of government which the people of that country have adopted the representative of law and order" and "to rally around the Government and work loyally and earnestly under it for the welfare of the country and of Mother Church". But "'réfractaires', rebels against Leo, are found outside of France", he continued. "They are found where we should least expect to find them – in America". The divisions among American Catholics, however, were not "in strict matters of faith and morals, but in tendencies and movements". Yet, he continued, "there should be for us but one tendency, one movement, one mode or adaptation – those indicated by Leo. Separation from Leo, opposition to his direction, however much it clothes itself in America as it does, with the specious titles of conservatism and traditional Catholicity, a religious fear of novelties is nothing but rebellion. Those in America who resist the direction given by Leo are rebels and refractaires, however much they dare push themselves forward as the only true and trustworthy Catholics. ... Loyal Catholics have but one name – Catholics. They have but one rule of action, Leo's will and example".

For Ireland the real battle in the American Church was not between nationalities, as some would say, but between defenders and opponents of the pope, who were to be found among all language groups. Verbally retreating from the position he had taken during the German dispute, he represented himself and the liberals as the true champions of Leo: "I speak now for myself, but in what I say, I know I speak for all loyal Catholics. There is for me no race, no language, no color. I rise above all such accidentals. In seeking out my brethren, I wish to find those who work for God and for truth, those who work with Leo. When I move away from Catholics, I move away from the refractaires and from none other. ... I would scorn to draw distinctions among Catholics because of race or language. I am – I must be – as Catholic as is God's Church. I differ from men – I

---

[12] AASP, O'Connell to Ireland, Rome, Feb. 1, 1897. To cap off his appeal O'Connell reported that Lady Mary von Hügel had defended Ireland's liberal program before Count von Bülow, the Prussian ambassador to Italy, and promised that the archbishop would soon clearly define his position on the Germans; AASP, same to same, Feb. 5, 1897.

war with men on account of ideas, not on account of race. And so it is with Leo. And so it is with all loyal Catholics. It is well that this be understood and proclaimed aloud, far and wide. Efforts are being made to identify certain refractaire tendencies with whole races of Catholics. This is wrong. This is an injustice to those races, the great number among which are most loyal to the Pope, most ardent to follow his directions, most earnest in working with him. Self-constituted leaders, in order to advance their own ideas, are often too ready to call around them a whole race of men and blinding them to the real issues, lead them under the banner of nationalism, to follow where true Catholics should not go".[13]

Paradoxically, Ireland had raised the banner of ultramontanism. Just as he was previously so intent on gaining victory in his school question that he agreed to the institution of the delegation, so now he was linking his program to the ideas of Leo. But so dependent did he make his policy for the American Church on the pope's policy for France that, if the latter failed, so would his. In any event, his speech hardly won any German-Americans to his cause, but it did have the desired effect in Europe.

Ireland's sermon had "cleared the atmosphere for us here", O'Connell declared that summer, "and rendered all explanation to Germans superfluous". It had not only enabled the liberals to increase their European allies but also to return to the offensive against the conservatives in the United States, this time by purging the Catholic University of Joseph Schroeder who had been responsible for Keane's removal. Franz Kraus, who had been in the United States when Ireland spoke and had a copy of the text, had begun attacking Schroeder in a series of letters, signed "Spectator", in the Munich *Allgemeine Zeitung*. O'Connell warned Ireland, however, to proceed cautiously with Kraus, lest "anyone suspect any kind of understanding existing between you".[14]

The fact that there was no "understanding" between Ireland and Kraus, however, encouraged the former to take the German's independent support as an incentive to increase his contact with other German liberals. He therefore congratulated Herman Schell, professor of theology at the University of Würzburg, for his book showing "how the Jesuits & their ilk are killing the Church".[15] O'Connell, however, cautioned Ireland against any public alliance with either Kraus or Schell, for "Schell will probably come to grief and Rampolla & Leo hate Kraus". Ireland should, instead, raise the banner of his "Refractaire speech and of themselves all the braves will rally around it".[16] The liberals' overture to the Germans

---

[13] New York *Freeman's Journal*, Apr. 3, 1897, in MCAVOY: *Great Crisis*, pp. 102–103.
[14] AASP, O'Connell to Ireland, Rome, July 24, 1897; cf. AAB 95 P 3, Keane to Gibbons, Rome, May 9, 1897.
[15] ADR, Ireland to O'Connell, St. Paul, July 25, 1897.
[16] AASP, O'Connell to Ireland, Milan, Aug. 12, 1897.

was due not only, as will be seen, to their desire to prepare the way for the removal of Schroeder in the fall of 1897, but also to the continuing internationalization of their movement, a policy which O'Connell was now vigorously pursuing.

Even as he and Ireland were taking the first tentative steps toward the German liberals, O'Connell was establishing rapport with the Italian progressives. The latter sought not only to update clerical education and revitalize the laity but also to reconcile the Church to modern science and culture. Their program included ending the Italian Catholic preoccupation with the Roman Question and achieving conciliation between the Vatican and the Kingdom of Italy. Soon they became enamoured with the Americanists, whom they lauded in the pages of their journal *La Rassegna nazionale*. Early in 1897, O'Connell had established contact with one of the journal's principal contributors, the Countess Sabina Parravicino di Revel of Milan. With the assistance of her husband, Emiliano, during the summer she prepared an Italian translation of Ireland's discourses, including his *réfractaire* address. With Keane's approval, she had omitted some of Ireland's paeans to Republican government, for, as she told O'Connell, "as a monarchist, I could not accept the statement that 'monarchies rest upon guns and bayonets, whereas republics rest on the love of subjects'. Here in Europe rather the opposite occurs". She then planned to obtain the *imprimatur* for the publication from Bishop Geremia Bonomelli of Cremona, who sympathized with the Italian liberals.[17] The publication of the Italian translation was scheduled to coincide with the visit Ireland had promised Rampolla he would make in 1897, a visit which, as will be seen, had to be delayed for over a year.

In establishing an open alliance with Italian conciliationists, either the liberals displayed extraordinary ignorance of Roman sensitivities and of the Vatican's basic pro-French policy; or they suffered from hubris and actually believed that they could win the Vatican over to their entire program. But it was a dangerous gamble in 1897. In the United States, Schroeder continued to excoriate Ireland as a European liberal and to represent himself and the German-American conservatives as the true supporters of the pope. In Rome, Satolli publicly allied with Mazzella and said Gibbons had no love for Leo XIII. Furthermore, the liberals already knew the Vatican's sensitivity to any type of recognition of the Kingdom of Italy. Ireland claimed responsibility for having had McKinley appoint William Draper as ambassador to Italy. But when Draper arrived in Rome, O'Connell could not get him and his wife a papal audience because this would imply recog-

---

[17] ADR, S. Parravicino to O'Connell, Appiano, Aug. 16, 1897; see also letters of June 7 and July 3, 1897.

nition of the government in the Quirinal. Rampolla, nevertheless, seemed impressed with Ireland's influence on the new government.[18]

Ireland, however, within a few months showed how little he understood the Roman Question. Still boasting of the influence he enjoyed with McKinley, he told Rampolla that in a recent conversation the president said that, while Draper was the ambassador to Italy, he would be happy for any services the American representative could render to the Vatican.[19] Rampolla appreciated Draper's "good dispositions" toward the Vatican, but informed Ireland that "it is not possible for a minister accredited to the Quirinal to have direct relations with the Vatican".[20] For Ireland in 1897 to suggest that the American ambassador also deal with the Vatican may have raised the question for the Holy See that not only did he not understand diplomatic protocol but also could not see the issue of papal temporal power, especially when he was openly courting Italian conciliationists.

Ireland may well have profited from his planned visit to Rome in 1897. He could have seen first-hand the complications he and the liberals were creating for themselves. He was forced to delay his trip, however, partly because of the controversy which had meanwhile developed in France over the translation of Father Walter Elliott's *Life of Father Hecker* and partly because of the campaign he decided to wage in the fall for the removal of Schroeder from the university.

B. La Vie Du Père Hecker

Isaac Hecker was born in New York City in 1819. Raised as a Protestant, he toyed with the communitarian settlement of Brook Farm, and finally became a Catholic in 1844. He then entered the Redemptorists and was ordained in 1849. He and several other native-born, convert Redemptorists soon found themselves at odds with their superiors in regard to adapting the order's apostolate to converting American Protestants. In 1857, Hecker decided to present their petition personally in Rome only to find upon his arrival that he had been expelled from the order. Through his friendship with Cardinal Barnabò, the Prefect of Propaganda, and Pius IX, he was restored to the order with permission granted to him

---

[18] AASP, O'Connell to Ireland, Rome, July 21, 1897. Richard C. Kerens, a Republican national committee-man from Missouri, who had helped arrange Foster's invitation for Leo to send a representative to the Columbian Exposition, had earlier told Rampolla that Ireland had influenced McKinley to appoint Joseph McKenna, a Catholic, as Attorney General; ASV, SS, 280 (1898), fasc. 2, 69^r–74^r, Kerens to Rampolla, Washington, Mar. 30, 1897.

[19] ASV, SS, 280 (1898), fasc. 2, 151^r–154^r, Ireland to Rampolla, Washington, Oct. 29, 1897.

[20] *Ibid.*, 155^{r-v}, Rampolla to Ireland, Vatican, Dec. 1, 1897 (draft).

and his fellow petitioners honorably to withdraw and establish their own congregation. Hecker thus founded the Congregation of St. Paul the Apostle, the purpose of which was to carry out his vision for the evangelization of America. So convinced was he that Protestants preserved the basic elements of Christianity that he believed, if Catholicism were presented positively to them, they would become Catholic. This form of apologetics appealed to the later liberals who also found the ideas resonated in Canon Salvatore di Bartolo's *Criterions of Catholic Truth*, which was condemned in 1891. To enable the members of Hecker's new congregation freely to carry out their mission, moreover, they were not to take religious vows; yet they were to be disposed to do so at the command of legitimate ecclesiastical authority. This positive approach toward American Protestants and the lack of formal vows brought Hecker's disciples into conflict with European conservatives.[21]

Hecker died in 1888, and three years later Elliott published his biography. With an *imprimatur* from Corrigan and an introduction by Ireland, *The Life of Father Hecker* drew little attention. The French translation had been done by Countess de Ravilliax who had been enlisted by her cousin, Count Guillaume de Chabrol, a leader of the *néo-chrétien* movement. Since the original work was too long for a French audience, Chabrol convinced Abbé Félix Klein to adapt the translation to the French situation and write a preface. Klein, who had already been translating Ireland's speeches, found in Hecker the embodiment of the archbishop's ideas. His preface transformed Hecker from a deeply spiritual American priest mediating Catholicism to Protestant America to the ideal type of the priest of the future, who harmonized the Church with modern science, who based his spirituality on the interior direction of the Holy Spirit, and who responded to the active virtues which produced the new saints of the marketplace rather than to the passive virtues which produced monks and hermits. For Klein, this spirituality was in total conformity with the contemporary movement toward freedom and personal independence in the natural order; it also expressed the characteristic response to interior forces by the northern races to whom the future belonged.[22]

La Vie du Père Hecker appeared in the early summer of 1897. It fitted in perfectly with the liberals' strategy of broadening their movement both internationally and ideologically. "It is surprising", O'Connell told Ireland, "how circumstances are combining in favor of the new idea. Hecker's Life gives a tremendous impulse. You can hardly imagine it. Klein wrote a masterly preface that is a tour

---

[21] On Hecker's early life, see Vincent F. HOLDEN: *The Yankee Paul: Isaac Thomas Hecker*, Milwaukee 1958. On the liberals' flirtation with di Bartolo, see Robert D. CROSS: *The Emergence of Liberal Catholicism in America* Cambridge, Mass. 1958, pp. 154, 193.

[22] MCAVOY: *Great Crisis*, pp. 153–159.

de force of itself, and that has rec'd a stupendous welcome. Klein is a noble fellow, body & soul in your idea and ready, he writes me, to sacrifice everything to the cause." O'Connell was already making preparations to have Hecker's biography translated into Italian.[23] At this point, moreover, O'Connell was preparing his own contribution to the literature on Americanism, as the movement was now called by friends and foes alike.

O'Connell, Keane, and Zahm, together with Charles A. Grannan and Edward A. Pace, professors at the Catholic University, chose the International Catholic Scientific Congress at Fribourg in August as the setting in which to articulate the Americanist platform. Zahm delivered a paper on evolution and O'Connell gave a discourse on the meaning of Americanism, "A New Idea in the Life of Father Hecker".

He began his address by recalling that Archbishop Corrigan had given his *imprimatur* to the English version of Hecker's biography and that a French translation with Klein's preface was available to his European audience. A "new idea", he said, ran like a "golden thread" through the volume and the name of that idea was "Americanism", which "in the mind of Father Hecker ... bore a double signification: the one *political*, the other, what I may call *ecclesiastical*".

Political Americanism he defined as the "order of ideas" expressed in the Declaration of Independence. Fundamentally, this order could be reduced to the statement: "the remote source of all power and of every right is God, that the immediate source of power is the people, and that the officers of the government do not possess power for themselves, but only for the benefit of each individual among the people and for the community, and that the only limit placed upon the exercise of individual liberty is the obligation to respect the equal rights of others". This idea was in the tradition of British and American Common Law, planted in the Magna Charta and flowering in English-speaking countries. In the Common Law, therefore, no individual was above the law, for "the individual is not the source of law; the immediate source of Law is the people as interpreters of the natural Law of God".

Better to explain the advantages of Common Law, O'Connell contrasted it with the Roman "political code or the public law", which considered man as a

---

[23] AASP, O'Connell to Ireland, Milan, Aug. 12, 1897. Klein's preface had been published separately in *La Revue du clergé français*. O'Connell wrote him: "You seem really to have been raised up by Providence to render justice to a heart broken man, and to give to his work that potency which he always desired for it and for which in his last days he hardly dared any longer to hope"; AUND, Klein Papers, O'Connell to Klein, Rome, July 31, 1897. O'Connell also suggested that the preface be translated into English. Klein agreed and suggested an Italian translation of the life and preface as well; ADR, Klein to O'Connell, Paris, Aug. 6, 1897.

tabula rasa who had rights only as "the free gift of the State made to him in his character of citizen, and these were neither inalienable nor inviolable"; it subordinated the individual to the State which had no obligation to consider individual rights when opposed to itself; and it placed the Emperor above the law as "the sole real source of law ... [and] the embodiment of all judicial and executive powers".

There were, of course, intermediate stages between Roman Law and Common Law, but O'Connell's basic premise was that whenever the former held sway sooner or later it would disclose, "with sad results, the defects of its origin" in paganism. Nor could it be otherwise, for "Roman Law never knew God nor that dignity which in creation God conferred upon His image, to say nothing of the dignity of 'adoption' conferred by Baptism, and the 'participation of the divine nature'". On the other hand, "Father Hecker saw in his *'Americanism'*, in its political aspect, a public acknowledgement of the existence and the reign of the one, only true God, a recognition of the dignity that the Creator conferred upon His creature, and in these two points, his pious heart discovered a broad basis whereon to begin among men the work of the supernatural".

While he acknowledged that the "American idea" was not perfect, he could not see how it was "contrary to Catholic faith". The Church had never approved the political law of the Roman Empire, he noted, "and even as regards the Civil Code or Private Law, if the Church sometimes makes use of it and most wisely, she is nevertheless not dependent upon it, nor blind to its defects". The Church had lived for centuries without Roman Law, but had developed her own laws. These she could take up "again when she will, and her trend is to create eventually an entirely complete code of Christian law, bearing throughout and in every part the imprint of the Incarnation". The Church might do well in her search for that code to examine closely the Common Law, O'Connell implied, for "the principles of American law are nothing else than the first principles of the law of nature, as far as the authors of the Declaration of Independence were able to interpret it". So far was the American system from being incompatible with Catholic teaching, he recalled for his audience, that Pope Leo himself had blessed a copy of the United States Constitution presented to him, and Cardinal Satolli had "recommended the Gospels, and the American Constitution taken together as the complete Charter of human life". It was a skillful turn of phrase, for now he was making the pope and cardinal bear responsibility for their earlier actions and words.

"Ecclesiastical Americanism" or the peculiar relations between Church and State in the United States was a more controverted topic. These relations O'Connell analyzed under two headings: "Philosophically speaking, the just relations between Church and State are the expression in the concrete of the harmony that naturally exists between the two ideas incorporated in these institutions. Historically, these relations have been expressed sometimes in the establishment of the Church as the religion of the State, and sometimes by Concordats. The two latter modes of existence can never obtain in the United States, because contrary to the Amendment of the Constitution which says: 'Congress shall make no law respecting an establishment of religion, or prohibiting the free exercise thereof'". That this did not make the American state "godless", as some Catholics claimed, O'Connell thought was clear from what he said about the Declaration of Independence.

Against this background O'Connell introduced into his argument the "thesis-hypothesis" reasoning on the proposition formulated by Félix Dupanloup, Bishop of Orleans, in response to the Syllabus of Errors in 1864.[24] Unlike Dupanloup, however, he identified the "thesis" with the union of Church and State, but for the moment he passed to the practical consideration that if the majority of Americans declared any religion the religion of the State, it would be Protestant. But then he turned to an actual attack on the "thesis": "however beautiful and true in theory [the thesis] may be the doctrine of the legal union of Church and State, in practice it has unfortunately been found but too often to work to the grave injury of the Church by diminishing her liberty, and giving to laymen sometimes possessed of little piety, the pretext for interfering in the administration of her affairs". Viewing the "hypothesis", or concrete situation in America, he asserted that the First Amendment not only refused to establish a state religion, which would have been Protestant, but also declared the state's incompetence in religious matters. In his mind the "hypothesis" worked at least as well as the "thesis", for "whatever be the theory [the thesis], in practice this system [the American hypothesis] seems to work as well as any other actual system we are acquainted with. Nowhere is the action of the Church more free, and the exercise of Pontifical authority more untrammelled. The Church lives entirely under her own freely made laws; the relations of the bishops with the Holy See are direct and unhampered, and the exercise of the authority of the Pope is immediate and uncontrolled. And though the Church enjoys no patronage under the law, she receives unbounded support from the warm sympathy of a Christian people and from the majestic strength of a favorable public opinion".

Summarizing his address, O'Connell attributed to Hecker his own motivations for accepting "political Americanism". As early as 1890, he had communicated to Ireland his conviction that Roman canon law had little application in America and that America had an evangelical mission to convert the world to democracy. In O'Connell's words, Hecker accepted "political Americanism" because "it rec-

---

[24] See Roger AUBERT: *Monseigneur Dupanloup et Le Syllabus*, in: Revue d'histoire ecclésiastique 51 (1956) 121–122.

ognized as well, if not better than any other prevailing political system, the dominion of God and the natural dignity of man, and at the same time furnished a magnificent foundation for the work of the supernatural. He accepted it because of his great zeal for the conversion of his countrymen. Knowing their profoundly religious character, he believed their conversion to Catholic truth quite easy, but their conversion to Roman political or public law utterly impossible. Further, he accepted it on account of his great love for the Church, because it was his conviction that Roman political law was destined finally in all its traces to pass away, and that the Church was to hold generations yet to come through the power of the democratic, that is to say in a general sense, the American idea". According to O'Connell, Hecker accepted "ecclesiastical Americanism" or the separation of Church and State "because, like a pious and practical Catholic of the nineteenth century, looking the world around and into the future, he could find nothing that served the Church in America better".

In conclusion, O'Connell said that Americanism involved "no conflict with either Catholic faith or morals", that it was "no new form of heresy or liberalism or separatism", but rather it was "nothing else than that loyal devotion that Catholics in America bear to the principles on which their government is founded, and their conscientious conviction that these principles afford Catholics favorable opportunities for promoting the glory of God, the growth of the Church, and the salvation of souls in America".[25]

O'Connell's Fribourg paper was a carefully worded exposition of what he and his friends considered Americanism to be. His explanation of the differences between Common Law and Roman Law may well have been derived from Louis Duchesne. He also attempted to avoid the pitfalls of supporting propositions condemned in recent papal statements. Thus, in accordance with *Longinqua Oceani*, he did not say that he or Hecker believed the American hypothesis was the best situation for anyone but Americans. He did, however, challenge the thesis of the union between Church and State as frequently working to the detriment of the Church; and he did say that Hecker, at least, believed that the future of the Church would rest on the "democratic, that is to say ..., the American idea". In 1897, these were threatening words to European conservatives. They provoked a controversy similar to the one between the American John Courtney Murray, S.J., and Cardinal Alfredo Ottaviani on the eve of the Second Vatican Council.

The afternoon of O'Connell's address, Bishop Charles F. Turinaz of Nancy, who had not been present, proceeded to charge Hecker, according to Klein, "with

---

[25] ADR, "On a New Idea in the Life of Father Hecker", Ms. The address was published in the New York *Freeman's Journal* on Sept. 25, 1897. It is also reprinted in Abbé Félix KLEIN: *Americanism: A Phantom Heresy*, Atchison, Ka. 1951, pp. 71–75 and FOGARTY: *Vatican*, pp. 319–326.

exaggerating the value of individuality, with distorting the ideas of the supernatural, with speaking in an almost Protestant fashion of the inner guidance of
the Holy Spirit in the soul". After consultation with O'Connell and some other
friends, Klein rose in Hecker's defense saying that the bishop's accusations could
not be substantiated either in Hecker's thoughts or in Klein's own preface.[26] But
in general the reaction to the address was positive and O'Connell reported the
numerous toasts made to Ireland. He also hoped to enlist the aid of Baron von
Hertling, President of the Congress and leader of the German Center Party. Germany or at least the liberal German thinkers seemed to be in the camp of the
American liberals.[27]

O'Connell's address was given wide circulation, a publicity effort made neces-
sary by Klein's information that the Jesuits in Rome were intent on placing the
Vie du Père Hecker on the Index. The publication was intended to transfer the
controversy from the theological to the political level. To condemn Hecker,
O'Connell assured Klein, would be "to condemn our government and that could
create too great a controversy". He therefore urged Klein in reviewing "A New
Idea" to show that political Americanism was "nothing else than the policy the
Pope recommends for France".[28] O'Connell's paper received accolades from the
principal Americanists: Gibbons, Ireland, Keane, Walter Elliott, and Alphonse
Magnien, S.S., and from European intellectuals as well, for example, Dom Aidan
Gasquet and Baroness d'Eichthal. Gibbons' statement was typical of the liberal
American reaction. The address, he wrote, was "clear, precise in terms, giving a
definition of 'Americanism' to which every honest Catholic must subscribe. Every sentence conveys a pregnant idea, & the relations of Church & State are ad-
mirably set forth especially for the eye of Rome. 'If this be treason, let them make
the most of it' to use the words of Patrick Henry".[29]

A week after the Fribourg address, O'Connell and Zahm attended the Zurich
Social Congress at the invitation of Gaspard Decurtins. After that they visited
Hermann Schell at Würzburg, further to increase German support for the
Americanist program. O'Connell explained to Schell that in the German con-
troversy Ireland and the Americanizing bishops had to choose between the un-
changing and changing elements in the Church, between the English-speaking
American environment and immigrant culture. Ireland therefore was concerned
with the future freedom of children of German immigrants who might wish to at-

---

[26] KLEIN: *Americanism*, pp. 63–64.
[27] AASP, O'Connell to Ireland, Freiburg im Br., Aug. 26, 1897.
[28] Klein papers, AUND, O'Connell to Klein, Freiburg im Br., Sept. 3, 1897; cf. FOGARTY: *Vatican*,
p. 270.
[29] ADR, Gibbons to O'Connell, Baltimore, Sept. 27, 1897. For other reactions, see FOGARTY: *Vatican*, pp. 270–271.

tend English-speaking churches. When Schell asked if the Jesuits were behind the opposition to Ireland, O'Connell replied that a few old German pastors resisted Americanization in practice because they feared losing their parishioners, but, he said, "the men who worked the theory, both in America & Europe, were the Jesuits, saying to enter American ways was to abandon the church or to go towards indifferentism ...".[30] The rapprochement with liberals in Germany and elsewhere in Europe was the backdrop for Ireland and the Americanists to pass to the offensive in what the Archbishop of St. Paul called his "War of 1897" for Schroeder's removal from the Catholic University faculty.

From the time of his appointment as professor of dogmatic theology at the university, Schroeder had antagonized the liberals. He had spoken openly in Cahensly's behalf and had befriended Corrigan.[31] But after he was instrumental in winning Satolli to the conservatives and in gaining Keane's dismissal, he became a powerful enemy. In the early part of 1897, as was seen, he attacked Gibbons, Ireland, and Keane for their liberalism. During the summer, the liberals planned their strategy for his removal. Grannan, Pace, and Thomas J. Shahan, members of the university faculty, discussed the issue with O'Connell at Fribourg. Ireland, of course, was ready for the fight. Feeding into their plans were Kraus' "Spectator" letters attacking Schroeder and making it appear that the opposition to him was not simply a matter of a conflict of nationalities.[32]

Once back in Washington, the liberal professors gathered sworn affidavits from witnesses charging that Schroeder frequented public saloons, was often seen drunk, returned to his university residence early in the morning, and was perhaps guilty of other moral failings. These affidavits, together with Italian translations, O'Connell then presented to Rampolla.[33] The difficulty was winning over the other liberal and moderate members of the Board of Trustees. "Williams & Gibbons want peace", Ireland told O'Connell urging him to "write the Cardinal ... giving him an idea of the support we have in Germany & saying that Germans wonder we hold on to such a man as Schroeder. All America is laughing at us, deriding us for being kept in awe by a Dutch beerguzzler ...".[34]

On October 20 and 21, the Board of Trustees met and prepared a resolution demanding Schroeder's dismissal. Gibbons then received a cable from Rampolla stating that it was the pope's wish that the priest not be dismissed. The board,

---

[30] AASP, O'Connell to Ireland, Munich, Sept. 14, 1897.
[31] CURRAN: *Corrigan*, p. 434; Peter E. HOGAN: *The Catholic University of America: 1896–1903: The Rectorship of Thomas J. Conaty*, Washington 1949, pp. 148–151.
[32] MCAVOY: *Great Crisis*, pp. 188–189.
[33] ASV, SS, 43 (1903), fasc. 2, 30^r–67^r.
[34] ADR, Ireland to O'Connell, St. Paul, Sept. 13, 1897.

nevertheless, voted ten to four to dismiss Schroeder but postponed action until the case could be placed before the Holy See.[35] Gibbons then suggested that Schroeder be persuaded to submit his resignation, but this Schroeder refused to do, arguing that he was remaining at the university at the explicit desire of both the pope and Cardinal Andreas Steinhuber, S. J., Prefect of the Congregation of the Index. He did, however, offer to resign if the pope gave his permission. Notice of the trustees' action must then have been forwarded to Rome by cable, for, on October 23, Rampolla cabled Martinelli saying that the trustees had premised their decision to dismiss Schroeder on his moral character. He therefore asked the delegate to gather more information.[36] Rampolla must have been satisfied with Martinelli's information, for on November 13 he informed the delegate that the pope gave his permission for Schroeder to resign provided that he could preserve his reputation.[37] He sent his letter just in time for only four days later he received a letter from Steinhuber strongly defending Schroeder.[38] At the end of the year the latter found a face-saving way of profferring his resignation by accepting a post at the Catholic Academy of Münster.[39]

Ireland was elated with his victory. "The greatest & last battle of the war has been fought and won. The German papers are quiet: they feel their power is gone".[40] Ireland could not have been more mistaken. As he and O'Connell were seeking to internationalize their movement, they were further antagonizing a group which was already internationalized, namely the Jesuits. Even as the Schroeder case was coming to an end, O'Connell warned Ireland of the anger against him in curial circles for Schroeder's dismissal; yet he remained sanguine that the Vatican would have to see their viewpoint. "The whole atmosphere of Europe", he wrote, "is now redolent of Americanism ... [which] now means no longer provincialism but modern society, modern law in contrast with the ancient law". Americanism in France was particularly strong and came at a time when Leo and Rampolla had "not made a success of their plans in France where now everything like a Catholic party is a lot of scattered fragments". What seemed to

---

[35] HOGAN: *Catholic University*, p. 154. Rampolla's cable to Gibbons was dated Oct. 16, 1897, but he had also cabled Martinelli that Schroeder was not to be dismissed; ASV, SS, 43 (1903), fasc. 1, 187ʳ, Rampolla to Martinelli, Vatican, Oct. 20, 1897 (draft).

[36] ASV, SS, 43 (1903), fasc. 1, 188ʳ, Rampolla to Martinelli, Vatican, Oct. 23, 1897 (draft). There was a brief account in O'Connell's handwriting, of the trustees' action, giving the accusation of the other professors against Schroeder's character, but saying nothing about his nationality; *ibid.*, 189ʳ–190ᵛ.

[37] HOGAN: *Catholic University*, p. 156.

[38] ASV, SS, 43 (1903), fasc. 2, 68ʳ, Steinhuber to Rampolla, Rome, Nov. 17, 1897.

[39] HOGAN: *Catholic University*, p. 156.

[40] ADR, Ireland to O'Connell, St. Paul, Jan. 8, 1898.

be needed was "centralization" among the Americanists of all nationalities in order to win over the Vatican.[41]

Ever lurking in the background of the Americanists' ambitious scheme, however, was the specter of the Roman Question. On November 26, 1897, the New
York *Sun* published a story, probably written by Ella B. Edes, that O'Connell was
trying to influence the outcome of the next papal election by inviting foreign cardinals to banquets in honor of Serafino Vannutelli. Early the next year, the St.
Louis *Globe-Democrat* reported that "Vannutelli is once more in deep disgrace,
thanks ... to his American friend, Mgr. Denis O'Connell", who had invited him
to a dinner in honor of Draper. The cardinal's presence was construed as his implicit recognition of the Kingdom of Italy.[42] O'Connell's canvassing of votes and
support for Vannutelli may well have represented a sincere effort to shore up the
pope's crumbling French policy by broadening the Americanist's influence, but to
fail to see the essential link between that policy and the Roman Question was
sheer naïveté.

In the meantime, Klein was preparing to consolidate the Americanist party in
France by delivering an address at the Institut Catholique of Paris entitled "True
and False Americanism". Keane urged him to use O'Connell's address as the
basis of his discourse and show that Americanism "is no new form of heresy, of
Liberalism, or separatism". But Keane's view of Americanism differed from that
of O'Connell and Ireland who wished the universal Church to adopt the principles of the American Church, derived from the separation of Church and State.
For Keane, "Americanism does not mean a Propaganda, aiming at imposing
American conditions on the rest of the world". To do so, he said, would be
counter to "the wisdom of Leo XIII in saying that our conditions are not to be regarded as a rule for the rest of the world".[43] But Klein never got to give his speech
due first to ill health and then to the increased controversy over Americanism in
France.

C. THE CONSERVATIVE REACTION

1. *Charles Maignen, Le Père Hecker est-il un Saint?*

From March 3 to April 19, 1898, there appeared in *La Vérité* a series of eighteen articles entitled "L'Américanisme Mystique" and signed "Martel". The author was Father Charles Maignen of the Society of the Brothers of St. Vincent de

[41]AASP, O'Connell to Ireland, Rome, Dec. 2, 1897.
[42] FOGARTY: *Vatican*, pp. 275–276.
[43] ACSP, Keane to Klein, Jan. 18, 1898, in MCAVOY: *Great Crisis*, pp. 184–185.

Paul who had earlier gained notoriety as an opponent to the *ralliement*. He originally intended to write a series of review articles of *La Vie du Père Hecker*, but then began expanding his treatment with the collaboration of George Périès. Maignen gave a strident critique of Hecker, his life as a Redemptorist before being allowed to found the Paulists, his emphasis on the interior guidance of the Holy Spirit to the detriment of the exterior authority of the Church, his teaching on the active virtues which seemed appropriate for republicans and on the passive virtues which were more suited to monarchists, his denigrating religious vows, and his watering down the doctrine of the Church to gain converts.

Maignen then turned to attack the Americanists in general. The controversy, he said, was really between the liberals, Ireland, Keane, and O'Connell who, like Hecker, claimed superiority for the Saxon races and wished to replace monarchy, a proven form of government, with republicanism, which hardly had a history. O'Connell's Fribourg address was nothing more than a new edition of Montalembert's cry for "A Free Church in a Free State" and a revision of the teachings of the 1863 Congress of Malines, which Hecker had attended. O'Connell had praised the thesis that the State should be united to the Church or at least accord it special privileges, but then hastened "to affirm that 'in practice' it has produced detestable effects". The logic of the Latin races, said Maignen, would conclude that the thesis was bad and should be rejected, whereas O'Connell, using the logic peculiar to the Anglo-Saxon races, concluded that "better effects are obtained from a theory which is admitted to be false and bad". O'Connell's replacement of the thesis with the American hypothesis was clearly condemned by Proposition LXXX of the Syllabus of Errors. Keane, moreover, had fallen under the condemnation of Proposition XVIII for calling Protestants fellow Christians and for his support of the Parliament of Religions. All of these Americanists, concluded Maignen, were directly influenced by Hecker and had a program for carrying their campaign from the New World into the Old.[44]

If Americanism had remained a war over conflicting ideas, it may never have been condemned. But in April it also became a fighting war between the New World and the Old, as the United States went to war with Spain. On February 15, the American battleship *Maine* had been sunk in the harbor of Havana, Cuba. On March 25, Raffaele Merry del Val, the Spanish ambassador to the Holy See, requested Leo XIII's intervention to prevent war. Two days later, at Rampolla's request, Keane wrote Ireland asking him to use his well-known influence with President McKinley to avert war.[45] If Ireland had been successful, he might still have

[44] McAvoy: *Great Crisis*, pp. 189–198.
[45] ASV, SS, 249, Protocol no. 43157, Merry del Val to Rampolla, Rome, Mar. 25, 1898; Protocol no. 43158, Rampolla to Merry del Val, Vatican, Mar. 27, 1898.

obtained his long-desired red hat, for which his friends had long been working. Despite a flurry of cablegrams back and forth between Ireland in Washington and Rampolla in Rome, however, Ireland's mission failed.[46] On April 25, Congress declared that a state of war had existed since April 2. The hostilities, which introduced the United States to the world scene as a colonial power, ended with an armistice on August 12. The outbreak of war also brought initial charges that American Catholics would be loyal to Catholic Spain rather than their own nation. But on this issue, liberals and conservatives stood united in their displays of patriotism. When the conflict was over, they then had to combat the anti-Catholic attitude of those, including President McKinley, who then wanted to "Christianize" the former Spanish colonies.[47]

Ireland, who seems sincerely to have wished to prevent the war, believed that he could have prevented it if the pope had sought his services two months earlier. But once war was declared, he was "for war – for the Stars & Stripes". Furthermore, in what from the perspective of the twentieth century seems like a prophecy, he wrote O'Connell: "Evidently, you wish America to be in a situation to frighten Europe. Well, she is in that situation. And henceforward she will be more so. The result of this war will be to strengthen & enlarge our navy – & reach out for new territory. If the Pope in the future is to have any world-wide prestige, he must deal as never before with America. Tell all this in Rome. And even if we do not hold Cuba & the Philippines – the church there will be organized on the lines of Americanism".[48] He had submitted his report to the pope on his unsuccessful mission and when he learned that the Vatican was indignant, he could only comment: "What those people want is success, & when success does not come they make no allowance".[49]

In reply, O'Connell contributed an important statement on the type of Americanism he shared with Ireland. He was confident of the inevitable victory of the United States and of the consequent impossibility of a condemnation of Americanism. With that victory Ireland's prestige in Rome and America would be enhanced and he would, said O'Connell, "be the instrument in the hands of Providence for spreading the benefits of a new civilization over the world". The war and Americanism were inextricably intertwined as O'Connell told his friend: "And now only one word more: All doubts & hesitation to the wind, and on with the banner of Americanism, which is the banner of God & humanity. Now

---

[46] These are contained in ASV, DAUS, "Stati Uniti", doss. 25.
[47] See Frank T. REUTER: *Catholic Influence on American Colonial Policies: 1898–1904*, Austin 1967, pp. 3–19.
[48] ADR, Ireland to O'Connell, St. Paul, May 2, 1898.
[49] ADR, Ireland to O'Connell, St. Paul, May 11, 1898.

realize all the dreams you ever dreamed, and force upon the Curia by the great triumph of Americanism that recognition of English speaking peoples that you know is needed".

O'Connell continued: "For me this is not simply a question of Cuba. If it were, it were no question or a poor question. Then let the 'greasers' eat one another up and save the lives of our dear boys. But for me it is a question of much more moment: – it is the question of two civilizations. It is the question of all that is old & vile & mean & rotten & cruel & false in Europe against all this [sic] is free & noble & open & true & humane in America. When Spain is swept of [sic] the seas much of the meanness & narrowness of old Europe goes with it, to be replaced by the freedom & openness of America. This is God's way of developing the world. And all continental Europe feels the war is against itself, and that is why they are all against us, and Rome more than all, because when the prestige of Spain & Italy will have passed away, and when the pivot of the world's political action will no longer be confined within the limits of this continent, then the nonsense of trying to govern the universal Church, from a purely European standpoint and according to exclusively Spanish and Italian methods, will be glaringly evident even to a child. 'Now the axe is laid to the root of the tree'. Let the wealth of the Convents & Communities in Cuba & the Philippines go: it did nothing for the advancement of religion. No more patching of new pieces on old garments: it serves neither one nor the other, and the foundations of religion must be laid anew 'in spirit and in truth'. Begin these anew with the Gospel and with such accessories & Canon Law as the Gospel requires without making paramount the interests of comfortable-living personages or communities".

Yet it was not just the Church that O'Connell considered. From what he heard from European diplomats, the continent would try to bar American trade. Therefore America should become a powerful naval power like England or Russia "and then no continent would be strong enough to conspire against her". The nation had to cast off the isolation of its childhood and compete with European powers with possessions throughout the world without dependence on any other nation for markets or resources.

Behind this expansion, however, O'Connell saw America's divine mission to humanity. "Again it seems to me that above all nations, moving them on along the path of civilization to better and higher & happier modes of existences is the constant action of a tender divine Providence, and that the convergent action of all great power, is toward that common & destined end: – to more brotherhood, to more kindness, to more mutual respect for every man, to more practical and living recognition of the rule of God. At one time one nation in the world, now another took the lead, but now it seems to me that the old governments of Europe will lead no more, and that neither Italy nor Spain will ever furnish the principles of the civilization of the future. Now God passes the banner to the hands of America, to bear it, in the cause of humanity, and it is your office to make its destiny known to America and become its grand chaplain. Over all America there is certainly a duty higher than the interest of individual states or even the National government. The duty to Humanity is certainly a real duty and America cannot certainly, with honor, or fortune, evade its great share in it. Go to America and say: thus saith the Lord. Then you will live in history as God's Apostle in modern times to Church & to Society. Hence I am a partisan of the Anglo-American alliance. Together they are invincible and they will impose a new civilization. Now is your opportunity, and at the end of the war, as the Vatican always goes after strong men you will likewise become again her intermediary".[50]

O'Connell's long letter was a mixture of chauvinism and social Darwinism. But it was also more than that. From the time of the school question and the Cahensly dispute, he and Ireland were convinced that before Rome would take the American Church seriously, the United States would have to gain universal recognition as a world power. Ultimately they were correct, but in 1898 an American victory was regarded as more of a threat than an opportunity for the Vatican to ally itself with the important western democracy. This European mindset conditioned the final act in the unfolding drama of Americanism.

2. Lepidi's imprimatur

La Vérité had announced that Maignen's articles would appear in book form, but Cardinal François-Marie Richard of Paris, apparently under the influence of the Sulpicians, refused to grant his *imprimatur*. The cardinal in no way was sympathetic with Americanism, but he refused his permission because the book, entitled *Le Père Hecker: est-il un Saint?* attacked members of the American hierarchy. Maignen, now with the overt support of Périès, then obtained a Roman publisher and the necessary *imprimatur* from Albert Lepidi, O.P., Master of the Sacred Palace.[51]

Le Père Hecker reprinted the original articles from *La Vérité* and added some new essays. In one of the latter, Maignen spoke of the Americanist attempt to create a pro-American climate of opinion in Rome with Americans in the Curia and of the use by the United States of the Church to further its own ends during

---

[50] AASP, O'Connell to Ireland, [Rome], May 24, 1898. This letter is printed in its entirety in McAvoy: *Great Crisis*, pp. 206–210.

[51] ADR, Klein to O'Connell, Paris, May 14, 1898, and Le Bruill St. Michel par Chambourg, May 28, 1898.

the Spanish-American War. As an example, he reported how O'Connell and Keane entertained Roman and foreign cardinals, the Roman aristocracy, and diplomats at O'Connell's apartment. At one such dinner in honor of Cardinal Vincenzo Vannutelli, Archbishop John J. Kain of St. Louis, and other sympathizers, Ferdinand Brunetière, editor of the *Revue des deux mondes,* proposed a toast to the United States. To this Keane replied by eulogizing the American Revolution which produced happier results than the French because it was founded on ideas which were truer and wiser.[52] Maignen was clearly playing to the fears of the Old World at what would happen to the Church now that the young American Republic had emerged onto the world scene as a military power.

On June 2, Keane protested to Rampolla and demanded "reparation" for Lepidi's giving the *imprimatur* which Cardinal Richard had refused. He listed the book's calumnies against himself, Ireland, and Gibbons, and said, "naturally Cardinal Gibbons and Msgr. Ireland will present their complaints, when they have learned of the attack and its Roman authorization".[53] O'Connell then immediately notified Gibbons, Ireland, and Elliott to protest the Lepidi *imprimatur.* But he harbored the fear that Lepidi had acted with explicit authorization. If this was true, he drew for Ireland some conclusions about the Roman Curia and the form the Americanists' protest should take: "Now comes the considerations: for the past six years the Curia Romana has been playing a double part with us. While openly given [*sic*] us smiles & fair words it has covertly given every encouragement in its power to our enemies, and never lost an opportunity of hurting us. ... This patronage of Périès & Co. is nothing but a continuation of the same false system and now that the Curia has publicly shown its hand, it is in order for us to ask it: where we stand, and what are its intentions. They don't own the Church. For hundreds of years history shows that the Curia Romana has been in constant conflict with the Church, and now let us know openly where we are and not await any more dark lantern policy. If we are not Catholics, let them frankly say so. It is our business. Abp. Keane has protested for himself and bade them expect protests from you and Gibbons".[54] Keane's protest drew Rampolla's denial of any prior knowledge of Lepidi's action. While O'Connell doubted the complete veracity of the cardinal's statement, he planned on having the account of Keane's meeting published in the London *Tablet* and in the *Univers.*[55] The

---

[52] Maignen: *Études sur l'Américanisme: Le Père Hecker, est-il un saint? pp. 274–276.* For analysis see McAvoy: *Great Crisis,* pp. 211–217.

[53] ASV, SS, 280 (1900), fasc. 2, 11^r–12^v, Keane to Rampolla, Rome, June 2, 1898.

[54] AASP, O'Connell to Ireland, Rome, June 3, 1898; Keane reported that he had received Cardinal Serafino Vannutelli's endorsement of his protest; AASP, Keane to Ireland, Rome, June 4, 1898.

[55] ACSP, Klein Papers, O'Connell to Klein, Rome, June 5, 8, 9, 1898.

French paper, however, refused to become involved in the quarrel,[56] but then on June 14, *La Croix* published a story that Lepidi acted with the pope's explicit authorization. Cardinal Richard, who desired peace, enjoined Klein to keep silent, but the latter did, however, protest to *La Croix* stating that Keane's interview with Rampolla discounted its story.[57] Keane too, protested the articles to Rampolla repeating his request for an official declaration from the Vatican putting an end to the charges.[58]

The question of whether Lepidi acted with authorization is further complicated by a statement from Brandi that "it *may be* that Cardinal Rampolla using diplomatic language told his Grace [Keane], that he (Rampolla) and the Holy Father knew nothing of the *Imprimatur* given by Fr. Lepidi to Abbé Magnien's [*sic*] book; but it is a fact that the Holy Father knew everything about it, and that the Imprimatur was given with the *express* consent of His Holiness. On this point there is no doubt whatever".[59]

In the meantime, Lepidi, whom Rampolla informed of Keane's protest, replied that the function of the office of Master of the Sacred Palace was to "safeguard faith and morals", but to remain aloof from judging opinions on doctrines or on persons. It thus tolerated in a controversy "some lively words, insinuations, and interpretations". He thought that the publication would do some good, "in provoking declarations on what is called Americanism". For the movement, he concluded, needed explanation.[60] This was not the answer Keane expected: "His Eminence, Cardinal Rampolla, expressly told me that the granting of the imprimatur was most regrettable. Your letter says exactly the opposite". He could not comprehend, he said, "how the limitations on the office of Master of the Sacred Palace to 'safeguard faith and morals' could excuse the permission accorded to a heinous attack" on bishops respected by the Holy See and on the entire body of American Catholics, "characterized in the book as 'the quasi-schismatic Church of the United States'". For Keane, "this incendiary act appears to be clearly *against good morals*".[61]

Keane then made copies of Lepidi's letter and his own reply and sent them to Rampolla. Recalling the cardinal's own statement that the *imprimatur* was "most regrettable", he charged that "Father Lepidi's letter is far from expressing any regret". He saw Lepidi's hostility to Americanism as but a general expression of the

---

[56] ADR, Klein to O'Connell, Paris, June 10, 1898.

[57] ADR, Klein to O'Connell, Paris, June 14, 1898; Klein to Director of La Croix, Paris, June 15, 1898 (copy).

[58] ASV, SS, 280 (1900), fasc. 2, 3^r, Keane to Rampolla, Rome, June 18, 1898.

[59] AANY, Brandi to Corrigan, Rome, Sept. 3, 1898.

[60] ASV, SS, 280 (1900), fasc. 2, 7^{r-v}, Lepidi to Keane, Vatican, June 12, 1898 (copy).

[61] *Ibid.*, 8^{r-v}, Keane to Lepidi, Rome, June 13, 1898 (copy).

hostility of Dominicans, including their general, not only toward Americanism but toward the United States, especially during the recent war with Spain. Keane clearly saw how much the Church's positions and politics were intertwined. "Now, in such an era", he said, "when political prejudices are so easily mixed up with all perceptions, six million Catholics in the United States will not be very content that the judges of America and of 'Americanism' are the Dominicans; sixty million of their fellow citizens will think the same; they will therefore ask me: 'Does their judgment express the judgment of the Holy See?'"

Keane then stated again the very moderate view of Americanism he personally espoused: "Americanism is only the sentiment of Catholics of the United States toward their country, – a sentiment of contentment, of recognition, of devotion, expressed in the first place by our great Archbishop Carroll, and which is, following him, the sentiment of the large body of Catholic Americans. It is not a system or doctrinaire 'program'; it is not a propaganda. If the people of Europe seek to study the lives and writings of some of our distinguished men, and if they find there something to admire, it is not our fault. The tableau of 'Americanism' presented in Father Maignen's book is an infamy; likewise what is presented in Father Lepidi's letter is perverted and unjust". As for Lepidi's statement that the publication would do good because it would provoke "declarations", Keane could only say that none of the bishops maligned in the book had any obligation to make "declarations" to Lepidi either in his personal or official capacity and "assuredly no bishop will offer any to Father Maignen". If, however, either Pope Leo or Rampolla desired them, Keane concluded, "they will be given wholeheartedly, with sincerity and absolute frankness".[62]

It was a remarkably blunt protest from the otherwise gentle Keane, but it only evoked Rampolla's response that he could do nothing.[63] At about this time, moreover, Bishop Sebastian Messmer of Green Bay arrived in Rome. In his audience with the pope, he said that many of his fellow bishops did hold the theories attributed to them by Maignen and that he himself had resigned his post at the Catholic University, just as his friend Schroeder did later, because of its liberalism. The dispute was not over nationalities, he concluded, but over religion.[64] Here was a strong accusation of the heterodoxy of the Americanists coming from one who had been a relative moderate in the German question.

In the meantime, some preliminary protests from the American liberals began to reach Rome. Gibbons, who delayed his official protest for another two months, wrote O'Connell on June 16 that he had read enough of Maignen's book

---

[62] *Ibid.*, 9ʳ–10ᵛ, Keane to Rampolla, Rome, June 13, 1898.

[63] AASP, O'Connell to Ireland, Rome, June 16, 1898.

[64] AASP, O'Connell to Keane, Rome, July 12, 1898; O'Connell to Ireland, Rome, July 20, 1898.

"to perceive its venom". He continued: "I regard the attacks of Protestantism as mild compared with the unprincipled course of these so-called Catholics. Our mission is surely a hard one here. While trying to exhibit the church in all her beauty, we are assailed by those who would exhibit her in an odious light. But truth will prevail".[65] Walter Elliott, C.S.P., also assured O'Connell that a protest from the Paulists would be forthcoming.[66]

Father George Deshon, the Superior General of the Paulists, had, in fact, asked Corrigan, the ordinary of the place in which they had their headquarters, to defend Hecker. Corrigan had received a copy of Maignen's book with a request for an endorsement and he now began to read for the first time Elliott's biography to which he had given his *imprimatur*. On both these books he then asked the opinion of Father Edward I. Purbrick, S.J., the Provincial of the Maryland-New York Province. While reading Maignen, Purbrick happened to meet Deshon, who gave him a totally different view from Maignen on Hecker's attitude toward religious vows and the inner guidance of the Holy Spirit. Nevertheless, he felt "that on the whole Maignen has sufficiently established his position or thesis" and "is not wrong in looking upon what is called 'Americanism' as a real and not unimportant danger". As for advice to Corrigan, he wrote: "I venture to suggest silence and non-committal. I presume the Life of Fr. Hecker has been or soon will be delated to the S. Cong. of the Index, and therefore think it best simply to await the action of the Holy See". In response to Elliott's request for a statement, Purbrick advised the archbishop to congratulate the Paulists on their spirit of obedience to the Holy See and urged them to suspend "public discussion of the matter until a decision should be forthcoming".[67]

Corrigan was in a curious situation. He had given the original *imprimatur* to a book which was now in danger of being placed on the Index. Yet he followed Purbrick's advice and remained silent, for Americanism had not provoked heated newspaper controversies like either the school question or the McGlynn case. While he neither wrote to Rome defending Hecker or Elliott's biography nor did he publicly endorse Maignen, he was rumored, however, to have written to Lepidi commending his granting the *imprimatur* to Maignen.[68]

No documentary evidence has been found to indicate that Corrigan officially wrote the Holy See asking for a condemnation of Hecker's ideas or the Americanists. He was, however, in correspondence with Brandi, who like his American confrère counselled silence and told of the positive Roman response to

[65] ADR, Gibbons to O'Connell, Baltimore, June 16, 1898.
[66] ADR, Elliott to O'Connell, St. Louis, June 25, 1898.
[67] AANY, Purbrick to Corrigan, New York, June 26, 1898.
[68] CURRAN: *Corrigan*, pp. 491–492; MCAVOY: *Great Crisis*, p. 281.

Maignen.[69] He may well have been content to watch from the side-lines as his arch-enemies, Ireland, Gibbons, and Keane, were condemned first by European adversaries and then by the Holy See itself. For, even as the Americanists were trying to muster their forces, the European literature against them continued to grow. Alphonse J. Delattre, S.J., professor of Hebrew at the Jesuit scholasticate at Louvain, published *Un Catholicisme Américain*, renewing the attacks on Hecker made by Maignen, suggesting that the Spiritual Exercises of Ignatius Loyola were a better cure for American materialism than Hecker's discovery in American culture of a quest for the supernatural, and stating that the separation of Church and State was a product of the Reformation and a break from the early centuries of the Church, when it was subject to Roman Law and when supernaturally it enjoyed its golden age.[70]

On July 11, 1898, Ireland sent his official protest to Rampolla. (So angry or nervous was he that he addressed the letter to Ledochowski as Secretary of State!) American newspapers, he said, took Lepidi's *imprimatur* as official Vatican approval and accordingly announced: "Americanism condemned – Paulists under anathema – Gibbons, Keane, Ireland and their friends under papal censure." "Americanism" for the American people, he explained, "is a sacred word: it symbolizes for them all that is most dear – their institutions, civil and political". Maignen could not have chosen a better means "to antagonize all the American people, and to strengthen their prejudices against the Church" than by attacking American institutions and a prelate so respected as Gibbons. As a result, "Americans will say, Americanism, that is to say their institutions, have been condemned by Rome: therefore Rome is opposed to America. The prelates who have worked with all their energies to show that the Catholic faith is entirely compatible with the civic duties of an American citizen are placed under censure: therefore the Church and America cannot live together in harmony". Was it "part of wisdom and prudence", he asked, to allow this impression to be given just when the United States was determining "on the fate of twelve million Catholics belonging to the former colonies of Spain?"

As he had done in his defense of his support of McKinley and in his réfractaire discourse, Ireland now made himself to be the papal loyalist and reminded Rampolla of the service he and the other liberals had rendered to the Holy See. "The prelates whom they attack have but one system – that of the Holy See: they maintain but one class of ideas – those of the Holy See. These prelates give an ear to the least word coming from the Holy See and are eager to follow it. When the Sovereign Pontiff sent a delegate to the United States, who, except these prelates,

---

[69] AANY, Brandi to Corrigan, Poppi, July 11, 1898.
[70] McAvoy: *Great Crisis*, pp. 224–226.

overwhelmed him with their good offices and public influence? Was there ever a single occasion when these prelates did not follow the will of the Holy See with the liveliest enthusiasm? And at this moment, Father Lepidi and Mgr. Cassetta proclaim to the world that the Holy See has to defend itself against these prelates, who wish to dominate the Holy See – who are on the point of becoming heretics and schismatics, if they are not already such".

It was even more ironic for Ireland that he and the other liberals were attacked in a book granted a Roman *imprimatur* but written by a man who had attacked "Count de Mun because the Count had rallied to the French policy of the Holy Father". Recalling the words he used in defending his support of McKinley, Ireland concluded by saying that, if Lepidi represented the Holy See, he and the other liberals would make a submission; if, as he believed, Lepidi did not speak for the pope, then the Vatican should speak "to clarify public opinion".[71] Rampolla encouraged Ireland "to be tranquil" and not place any weight on the polemics against him.[72]

In the meantime, O'Connell in Rome made the first of a series of miscalculations which in retrospect illustrated the forces aligned against the Americanists. Early in July he had an interview with Lepidi to whom he gave a copy of his Fribourg address. After reading it, said O'Connell, Lepidi realized that there was a difference between European and American Americanism, that the former was religious and the latter only political. At O'Connell's suggestion, Lepidi agreed to review the life of Hecker and make any corrections he felt were necessary. O'Connell, therefore, asked him not to grant an *imprimatur* for a second edition of Maignen's book. A few days later, O'Connell returned to Lepidi who could not provide the list of corrections, he said, because the pope had reserved the matter to himself. In the meantime, a new edition of Maignen was to appear. O'Connell was impressed with Lepidi's open-mindedness, but he concluded to Keane: "Poor Lepidi can do almost nothing and on certain authority I hear the Pope compelled him to give the imprimatur, in the first instance".[73]

While reporting this to Keane, he did not note that he had already written one letter to Lepidi on July 11 and would write two more on July 14 and 16 repudiating in his own name and in that of "every good Catholic in America" any sympathy with so-called "religious Americanism" which he termed "a peculiar kind of religious subjectivism" and which its adherents called "Heckerism". In regard

---

[71] ASV, SS, 280 (1900), fasc. 2, 16ʳ–21ʳ, Ireland to Ledochowski [*sic*], St. Paul, July 11, 1898. This is given also in AUND, Soderini Ms., cited in AHERN: *Keane*, pp. 264–265 and MCAVOY: *Great Crisis*, pp. 231–233.

[72] ASV, SS, 280 (1900), fasc. 2, 22ʳ⁻ᵛ, Rampolla to Ireland, Vatican, Aug. 6, 1898 (draft).

[73] AASP, O'Connell to Keane, Rome, July 12, 1898.

to his own Fribourg address he pointed out that he had made explicit the distinction "between the thesis and the hypothesis". He then declared, "as regards the thesis, I admit it fully; I was treating only the hypothesis, taking into account all the circumstances and conditions in the midst of which the Catholic Church lives in America".[74] O'Connell was surprised to find selections from his letters from Lepidi, carefully edited and taken out of context, published by Maignen in *La Vérité* on August 15. "I imagined I was drawing up an official note for the Vatican official", he wrote Elliott, "to appear in the 'Osservatore Romano' or the 'Voce', and never dreamed I was being fooled to furnish an appendix for the man I was protesting against; I don't call that 'fides punica'. These men are not honest, and it is an illusion to treat them so".[75]

That summer, clerical Rome was in reaction. Leo XIII was in poor health and the Jesuits, particularly Mazzella, seem to have wielded an extraordinary influence over him. Late in June, Brandi informed Corrigan that the pope would soon issue a statement on Americanism, but he was not free to say anything more.[76] A few weeks later O'Connell learned that the pope had appointed a commission to study the question and conjectured that, since Lepidi had quoted the English version of the life of Hecker, Mazzella, Brandi, and Satolli, all of whom spoke English, were being consulted. But other issues were also being examined. There were rumors that the Holy Office might soon issue a statement on evolution and that it was investigating Marie-Joseph Lagrange, O.P., and the *Revue biblique*. One scripture scholar had already been silenced. Reporting these events, O'Connell noted: "Duchesne says he always observes the H. Office is worse during the months of June & July".[77] The reactionary mood of Rome and the resulting confusion may explain the events which followed, in which Rampolla seems not to have been involved in the discussions.

On August 26, Gibbons finally sent his long awaited protest against Lepidi's *imprimatur*. He felt the prelates attacked by Maignen could defend themselves, but he spoke strongly in favor of Hecker and his spirituality. The original biography with Corrigan's *imprimatur*, he told Rampolla, had not created any controversy in the United States. The controversy was entirely the creation of Maignen who wished others to think "of a perverse tendency, of a doctrine not only suspect, but clearly erroneous and even heretical, as one speaks of liberalism, of Gallicanism, and other qualifications of this kind". Whatever may be the formal

---

[74] Charles MAIGNEN: *Father Hecker: Is He a Saint?* Rome 1898, pp. 406–407.

[75] ACSP, O'Connell to Elliott, Freiburg im Br., Aug. 22, 1898.

[76] AANY, Brandi to Corrigan, Rome, June 25, 1898.

[77] AASP, O'Connell to Keane, Rome, July 12, 1898. See also PELLEGRINO CONFESSORE: *Conservatorismo politico*, pp. 101 n. and 106 n.

function of an *imprimatur*, he said, Protestants and Catholics alike now had the impression "that it was not just the Abbé Maignen, but the Holy See itself which publicly accuses us of errors in the faith and of schismatic tendencies". Reiterating many of Ireland's arguments, he stated that the approbation of Maignen would ruin the Church's influence in the United States and feed the Protestant prejudice that the Church was "necessarily opposed to our political and civil institutions and that a Catholic cannot but be an American citizen disloyal to his country". He now heard that an English translation of Maignen was being prepared and that it would receive "the pontifical imprimatur". This would be disastrous to the American Church and the Holy See, he concluded, and would be construed "as a more or less intentional attack on the United States, and a form of revenge taken by Spain after its defeat at our arms". He closed by asking that the original *imprimatur* be withdrawn.[78]

What happened next is mysterious. Lepidi was given Gibbons' letter to help him formulate his position, which he presented to the pope. Gibbons' letter, together with the earlier protests of Keane, Ireland, and O'Connell, seemed to have influenced him in designating a third type of Americanism besides the political and religious. Maignen, he said, had not impugned "political Americanism", the attitude which American citizens should have toward their national customs; nor did he attack "political-religious Americanism", the relations which *de facto* existed between Church and State in the United States. Had Maignen done so, Lepidi would have refused the *imprimatur* "without hesitation". But Maignen had primarily written about "religious Americanism". This was "a new direction, which some, principally in Europe, informed by certain thoughts and aspirations of Father Hecker, would like to give the Church". In this, there was dominant "a dangerous tendency with the accent on individualism, or subjectivism".

Lepidi then listed six areas of concern in this "new direction". First, it contrasted the external discipline of the Church with the internal direction of the Holy Spirit and stated that in the present time "the dominant influence ought to be the docility to the inspiration of the Holy Spirit, dwelling in each regenerated soul". Second, it so emphasized the divine action within souls that it diminished the external authority of the Church. Third, the active virtues, "inspired by one's individual initiative", were of more value than the passive ones. Fourth, religious orders with their vows "no longer respond to the actual state of souls, or to the needs of the times". Fifth, this movement proclaimed certain maxims, which, though inspired by generosity and good intentions, "could in time lead to religi-

---

[78] ASV, SS, 280 (1900), fasc. 2, 23ʳ–27ᵛ, Gibbons to Rampolla, Baltimore, Aug. 26, 1898. There is a copy in AAB 96 M 6, which differs slightly and is dated Aug. 27. See also ELLIS: *Gibbons*, II, 59–62 and McAVOY: *Great Crisis*, pp. 236–237.

ous indifference". Finally, it held out "as a practical ideal, the only one truly possible, the relations between Church and State which exist in America".

After listing these dangers, Lepidi concluded by saying: "the book of Father Maignen is good in regard to its substance, and came to light at an opportune moment; because it combats dangerous maxims and tendencies". Using words similar to those he had written to Keane earlier in the summer, Lepidi argued that Maignen's book contained nothing against faith or morals, even though it was heated in its polemic against certain persons. He therefore asked Leo not to withdraw the *imprimatur* and hoped his explanation would satisfy the American bishops.[79] Lepidi saw nothing wrong with Maignen's character assassinations. On the other hand, he said nothing about condemning the biography of Hecker.

Lepidi's explanation had basically outlined the errors of "Religious Americanism" which became the focus for discussion during the coming months. It also provided the draft for Rampolla's reply to Gibbons' protest. Rampolla made his own Lepidi's declaration that the *imprimatur* in no way implied "approval of what is contained in the book, and even less of the irreverence ... toward episcopal authority", but was "simply a negative declaration" that the book contained nothing against faith or morals. Citing Lepidi almost *verbatim*, the cardinal expressed the hope that this would convince the bishops that "there was no ground for the fear and sorrow" which had been reported to Rome. Still borrowing from Lepidi, Rampolla said the pope trusted that "the bad impression would not last, and that those bishops, so zealous, so hard working and serving so effectively in the Church of Jesus Christ, will draw comfort from the assurance that there is no diminishing of the pope's esteem and good will toward them. In addition, it pleases me to let Your Eminence know that in regard to the doctrines of Father Hecker, His Holiness has reserved to himself to write Your Eminence a Pontifical letter".[80] While relying heavily on Lepidi's justification for the *imprimatur*, Rampolla had given none of the reasons Lepidi felt Maignen's treatment of religious Americanism merited an *imprimatur*. He did, for the first time however, indicate officially that the pope would soon speak on the question, but gave no clue as to the contents of the forthcoming letter.

The Americanists were in retreat, relying now on a statement from the pope, whom they felt they had defended and who had defended them so frequently in the past. Ireland had interpreted Rampolla's response to his protest as enjoining him "to preserve silence and to say nothing publicly to defend myself from the accusations launched against me by the Abbé Maignen and his allies". But he was

---

[79] ASV, SS, 280 (1900), fasc. 2, 41ʳ–44ʳ, Lepidi to Leo XIII, Vatican, Sept. 15, 1898.

[80] AAB 96 N 6, Rampolla to Gibbons, Vatican, Sept. 23, 1898; draft in ASV, SS, 280 (1900), fasc. 2, 47ʳ–48ʳ.

indignant to learn that a new edition of Maignen's book with a congratulatory letter from Satolli was being translated into English.[81] If silence had been enjoined on both sides in the controversy, the anti-Americanists did not know it, said Brandi. Further to support his argument that Leo had approved Lepidi's *imprimatur*, he reported of the "'Vatican pamphlet' against Americanism", probably written by Cardinal Francesco Segna, Prefect of the Vatican Archives, and published with Lepidi's *imprimatur*. In addition, Delattre's book was being openly sold in Rome.[82]

As speculation mounted on the contents of the pope's forthcoming letter, the Americanists received conflicting signals from Rome. On the one hand, their protests seem to have been effective in preventing the publication of the condemnation, if not the condemnation itself, of the life of Hecker.[83] On the other hand, John Zahm's *Evolution and Dogma* was placed on the Index, but the decree of condemnation was not published. Zahm, who had returned to the United States to become Provincial of the Congregation of the Holy Cross, was told by his general and others that the issue was not so much his theories on evolution as his association with O'Connell and the other Americanists.[84] The American liberals were beginning to bear the full brunt of the conservative reaction to the program they had so carefully put together over the previous decade and a half.

On October 12, Brandi told Corrigan that "'Americanism' will soon receive a blow in a more solemn and perhaps more telling manner [than the publication of the condemnation of the *Life of Father Hecker*] in the shape of a pontifical document addressed to the Bishops of the U.S. This letter is now being prepared and it will not be long before it is ready to be made public".[85] The same day Brandi wrote, the archbishops assembled at the Catholic University for their annual meeting. Ireland, for unexplained reasons and despite O'Connell's advice to initiate a protest, was absent giving a speech in Chicago, but he assured O'Connell he would soon come to Rome to discuss Americanism.[86] The Paulists, in the meanwhile, had submitted a protest against Maignen to the archbishops. But,

---

[81] ASV, SS, 280 (1900), fasc. 2, 50^r, 51^r, Ireland to Rampolla, St. Paul, Aug. 29, 1898.

[82] AANY, Brandi to Corrigan, Rome, Sept. 3, 1898.

[83] McAvoy: *Great Crisis*, p. 219, claims the condemnation was prevented. Brandi, however, told Corrigan the *Life* had been condemned by the Index, but that the decree was not published; AANY, Brandi to Corrigan, Rome, Oct. 12, 1898.

[84] Fogarty: *Vatican*, pp. 286–287; Weber: *Zahm*, pp. 108–114.

[85] AANY, Brandi to Corrigan, Rome, Oct. 12, 1898.

[86] ADR, Ireland to O'Connell, St. Paul, Oct. 27, 1898. McAvoy cites Rampolla's letter to Ireland on Aug. 6, as telling Ireland not to come to Rome, but this is not in the draft in ASV, cited above, n.72; cf. McAvoy: *Great Crisis*, p. 266 n. Brandi, however, later said that Rampolla advised Ireland against the trip; AANY, Brandi to Corrigan, Rome, Jan. 2, 1899.

with Ireland absent, Corrigan unwilling to discuss the matter, and Gibbons expecting Americanism to be handled in the papal letter, they did not bring up the question.[87]

Brandi's information to Corrigan seems to have reflected what he learned from Mazzella, for some time in October the pope apparently appointed a special commission to investigate Americanism. From the available evidence, it was subject neither to the Secretariat of State nor the Holy Office.[88] Mazzella, at least, seems to have been privy to the investigation. A few days after Brandi wrote Corrigan, O'Connell reported that Mazzella was dominating the discussions and that the Dominicans were openly allied with the Jesuits against the movement.[89] But who comprised the commission remains a mystery. O'Connell subsequently said the commission consisted of Ledochowski, as president, Serafino Vannutelli, as vice-president, Satolli, Domenico Ferrata, and Angelo di Pietro.[90] He later learned, however, that Vannutelli was no longer intimate to the discussions. But other lists included Mazzella.[91] The topics actually treated in the pope's letter and the rumors making the rounds before its publication bear a striking resemblance to Lepidi's outline of the errors of religious Americanism the previous September. In the light of this, what seems probable is that Lepidi, perhaps with Mazzella's assistance, drew up a series of dangerous propositions in religious Americanism which were then submitted to a broader commission.

Whoever comprised the commission examining Americanism, O'Connell and Keane seem to have relied on information obtained from Vannutelli in sending their optimistic reports back to the United States in November and December.[92] Moreover, in November, Ferdinand Brunetière published a sympathetic article in the *Revue des deux mondes*, placing Hecker and Americanism in the proper American context. He concluded by saying the French Church could learn from the remarkable growth of the American Church what could be done in a democracy.[93] Brunetière forwarded a copy of his article to Rampolla, who expressed his

---

[87] McAvoy: *Great Crisis*, pp. 266–269.

[88] There is no record of the commission in the Secretariat of State archives in ASV. Through the kindness of Father Karlheinz Hoffmann, S.J., I received the written assurance of Archbishop Jerome Hamer, O.P., Secretary of the Congregation for the Doctrine of the Faith, that the Holy Office never dealt with the question. Nor was the commission under the Index; cf. ASV, SS, 1 (1899), fasc. 5, 211^{r-v}, Essen to Trepepi, Vatican, Feb. 16, 1900. An examination of the papers of the Congregations of Latin Letters and of Letters to Princes for the period also failed to turn up any information.

[89] ACSP, Klein Papers, O'Connell to Klein, Rome, Oct. 15 and 31, 1898.

[90] ACSP, O'Connell to Elliott, Paris, Dec. 10, 1898.

[91] McAvoy: *Great Crisis*, p. 239.

[92] Fogarty: *Vatican*, p. 287.

[93] McAvoy: *Great Crisis*, pp. 254–256.

agreement with its premises and promised to give it to the pope.[94] In view of Rampolla's response, it seems likely that he was being excluded from the full discussions on Americanism.

In early December, Keane filed another protest to Leo. Satolli, he said, had been responsible for his removal from the Catholic University rectorship and had told the superior of the Canadian College that he would be compromised if Keane were allowed to live there. This was part of a "persecution" directed not only at him, but at Gibbons, Ireland, and O'Connell, in which they were proclaimed, "with the grossest injustice, to be liberals, neo-Pelagians, dangerous innovators". This campaign had been waged "not only with the knowledge but with the consent of the Holy See". After the protests which he himself and others had made during the summer, how could the pope allow Lepidi to give his *imprimatur* both to the English translation of Maignen and to the pamphlet against Americanism published at the Vatican? Rehearsing the implications for the American Church, which had characterized the other protests, Keane now requested a personal audience with the pope.[95] There is no evidence, however, that the pope granted him one.

The day after he wrote the pope requesting an audience, Keane wrote Rampolla enclosing a copy of a letter he had just received from Brunetière. Any hostile move "against the Abbé Klein and the Americanist movement", said Brunetière, "will be interpreted in France as a joining together of *Catholicism* with the *Society of Jesus*". For him true Americanism showed that Catholicism was totally compatible "with democracy, the republic, and liberty".[96] This the Jesuits and their followers rejected. Keane's was the last protest before the final condemnation.

---

[94] ASV, SS, 280 (1900), fasc. 2, 52^r–53^v, Brunetière to Rampolla, Paris, Oct. 30, 1898; 56^{r-v}, Rampolla to Brunetière, Vatican, Nov. 3, 1898 (draft).

[95] *Ibid.*, 35^r–38^v, Keane to Leo XIII, Rome, Dec. 6, 1898.

[96] *Ibid.*, 39^r–40^v, Keane to Rampolla, Rome, Dec. 7, 1898, enclosing copy of letter: Brunetière to Keane, n.p., Dec. 2, 1898.

CHAPTER VII

AMERICANISM CONDEMNED: THE END OF INTELLECTUAL LIFE

A. Testem Benevolentiae

The American liberals had lined up against them an impressive array of enemies both in the United States and in Europe. Both sides waited eagerly for the pope to speak. For the events of the last few days before Pope Leo XIII issued his letter, the only source is Denis O'Connell, who had gone to Paris at Boeglin's request. He seems to have depended for his information on S. Vannutelli. Writing Elliott on December 10, he said that a decree condemning Hecker had been ready for the pope's signature at the end of the summer vacation, but Leo decided instead to issue a letter, which, he maintained, "at first conception, was to have been composed of three points 1) the relations existing in America between Church & State are very good there, but they are not to be elevated to the dignity of a principle, 2) as regards 'individuality' and the dispensing with the services of a Director, he would have said that a director cannot be entirely dispensed with, as v.g. in the sacrament of penance. 3) As to vows, 'the doctrine of St. Thomas that vows are not an act of weakness but of heroism.' That was the substance. Our enemies were angry not to have had more, tho some of us thought even these concessions were not necessary". O'Connell thought that the pope would most likely not issue an "encyclical" and would actually like to have said "something pleasing to the Americans", but had to ask "himself what Spain would think of him if at this moment of her humiliation he were to pay compliments to her conquerors". Religious Americanism, said O'Connell, was now regarded as a fiction, although the cardinals on the committee investigating it were divided. "The strongest argument adduced in favor of the calumnies of Maignen", he concluded, "were [sic] the congratulations sent by Abp. Corrigan on his publication 'Pere Hecker est-il un Saint' but he desired that his congratulations be kept secret".[1] O'Connell's description of the topics to be included in the papal letter bore a marked resemblance to those about which Lepidi had written to Leo. But

---

[1] ACSP, O'Connell to Elliott, Paris, Dec. 10, 1898; given in McAvoy: *Great Crisis*, pp. 273–274 and Fogarty: *Vatican*, pp. 287–288. See also ACSP, Klein Papers, O'Connell to Klein, Rome, Dec. 1, 1898.

O'Connell and his informants were unduly optimistic that the issue of Americanism was dead.

On January 2, 1899, Brandi informed Corrigan that a letter against Americanism was ready for publication.[2] Ten days later, Ireland sailed for Rome ostensibly on his *ad limina* visit. On January 27, he met with Rampolla and, on February 1, with the pope. But this visit had none of the triumph of his last one in 1892. On January 31, Leo had already dispatched his apostolic letter *Testem Benevolentiae* to Cardinal Gibbons. Notified by cable of the coming letter, Gibbons cabled back asking that its Roman publication be delayed until he was able to submit his views.[3] Rampolla replied, however, that the pope could not wait because of the "deep dissension and dangerous divisions" which existed on the question among the Catholics of France. Due to the miscarriage of the copies of the letter sent to Martinelli for the other bishops, Gibbons was the first to receive it. On the advice of Frederick Rooker, Martinelli's secretary, Gibbons had a translation made and published in the Baltimore *Sun* on February 23 to prevent its being picked up first by the Associated Press.[4]

In his apostolic letter *Testem Benevolentiae*, dated January 22, Leo wrote that his intention was "to put an end to certain contentions which have arisen among you", but then he immediately added that the contentions arose from the French translation of the *Life of Father Hecker*. On the one hand, he condemned the watering down of doctrine in order to win converts. On the other hand, he declared the Church's willingness to accommodate its "rule of life" to various ages and customs, "if required for the salvation of souls", but this was to be determined by proper ecclesiastical authority and not "by the will of individuals". "Religious Americanism", the pope continued, "involves a greater danger and is more hostile to Catholic doctrine and discipline, inasmuch as the followers of these novelties judge that a certain liberty ought to be introduced into the Church, so that, limiting the exercise and vigilance of its powers, each one of the faithful may act more freely in pursuance of his own natural bent and capacity. They affirm, namely, that this is called for in order to imitate that liberty which, though quite recently introduced, is now the law and foundation of almost every civil community. On that point We have spoken very much at length in the letter

---

[2] AANY, Brandi to Corrigan, Rome, Jan. 2, 1899.

[3] ASV, SS, 280 (1900), fasc. 2, 62^r, Rampolla to Gibbons, Vatican, Jan. 31, 1899 (draft of cable); 64^r, Gibbons to Rampolla, Baltimore, Feb. 1, 1899 (cable).

[4] *Ibid.*, 65^r, Rampolla to Gibbons, Vatican, Feb. 2, 1899 (draft of cable); ADR, Rooker to O'Connell, Washington, Feb. 24, 1899. The apostolic delegate seems not to have received his copies until Feb. 24; see ASV, SS, 280 (1900), fasc. 3, 45^r, Martinelli to Rampolla, Washington, Feb. 24, 1899 (cable).

written to all the bishops about the constitution of States; where We have also shown the difference between the Church, which is of divine right, and all other associations which subsist by the free will of men". Here was the European fear that accommodation of the Church to democracy as a form of government entailed introducing democracy into the Church. Indirectly, it was also a sharp blow at those who wished to assert the novel principle of religious liberty, not only in the Church, but also within nations.

The pope then proceeded to condemn the notion that external guidance was unnecessary if one responded to the impulses of the Holy Spirit. The result of this was the exaltation of the natural over the supernatural virtues. Parallel to this, Leo rebuked those who preferred "active" to "passive" virtues and who accordingly denigrated religious vows as more suitable to the past than to the present.

In conclusion the encyclical distinguished between religious and political Americanism. "Hence, from all that We have hitherto said, it is clear, Beloved Son, that We cannot approve the opinions which some comprise under the head of Americanism. If, indeed, by that name be designated the characteristic qualities which reflect honor on the people of America, just as other nations have what is special to them; or if it implies the condition of your commonwealths, or the laws and customs which prevail in them, there is surely no reason why We should deem that it ought to be discarded. But if it is to be used not only to signify, but even to commend the above doctrines, there can be no doubt but that our Venerable Brethren the bishops of America would be the first to repudiate and condemn it, as being unjust to them and to the entire nation as well. For it raises the suspicion that there are some among you who conceive of and desire a church in America different from that which is in the rest of the world. One in the unity of doctrine as in the unity of government, such is the Catholic Church, and, since God has established its centre and foundation in the Chair of Peter, one which is rightly called Roman, for where Peter is there is the Church".[5]

The praise of legitimate Americanism seems to have been derived from the protests made by Keane, Ireland, and Gibbons the previous summer. The suspicion that some would want a separate American Church was totally derived from Maignen and the other anti-Americanists. The general topics condemned reflected those presented by Lepidi. While the pope thus praised political Americanism and never said the errors actually existed in the United States, the fact remains that he sent his letter to the lone American cardinal. By the time he wrote, it was difficult for conservative Europeans to distinguish between political and religious Americanism, for in their eyes the victory of the United States over

---

[5] Given in ELLIS: *Documents*, II, 538–547 and in McAVOY: *Great Crisis*, pp. 379–391; cf. *ibid*, pp. 275–279 for an analysis of the apostolic letter.

Spain meant the diffusion of political Americanism throughout Europe; with it, they feared, would come religious Americanism as well.[6]

1. Responses: American and European

The *Osservatore Romano* published *Testem Benevolentiae* on February 22, 1899, George Washington's Birthday. The indirect language of the letter allowed the Americanists readily to submit. As a result, a new controversy arose over the interpretation of what was condemned. Ireland immediately wrote the pope to "repudiate and condemn ... all those false and dangerous opinions to which, as the Letter says, 'certain people attribute the name of Americanism'". The use of the term "Americanism" to designate "errors and extravagances of this sort" was, for Ireland, an insult to the American Church; and those who espoused them were "enemies of the Church of America and false interpreters of the faith, who 'imagine' that there is, or who wish to establish in the United States, a church which differs one iota from the Universal Church ...".[7] Ireland's letter was published in the *Osservatore Romano* on February 24. At the same time the works of Hermann Schell were also condemned. Keane and George Deshon, General of the Paulists, wrote letters similar to Ireland's. Klein wrote Leo declaring his total adherence to the letter and his withdrawal of *La Vie du Père Hecker* from sale. So impressed was Cardinal Richard at the priest's humility that he begged a special papal blessing on him.[8]

Ireland's repudiation was "timely", Gibbons wrote O'Connell in early March, "& I am glad he so cordially accepted it. But it is very discouraging to us that the American church is not understood abroad & that its enemies are listened to & that they can lie with impunity. I do not think that any of the questions discussed was a living question here".[9] Gibbons himself, however, waited until March 17 before writing the pope to deny that anyone in the United States ever held the "extravagant and absurd doctrine".[10] Unlike the other letters of adherence to

---

[6] PELLEGRINO CONFESSORE: *Conservatorismo politico*, pp. 88–91.

[7] ASV, SS, 280 (1900), fasc. 3, 32ʳ–35ʳ, Ireland to Leo XIII, Rome, Feb. 22, 1899; given in McAVOY: *Great Crisis*, pp. 282–283.

[8] ASV, SS, 280 (1900), fasc. 2, 45ʳ–46ʳ, Keane to Leo XIII, Rome, Feb. 24, 1899; fasc. 3, 39ʳ–40ʳ, Richard to Leo XIII, Paris, Mar. 1, 1899; 43ʳ–44ʳ, Klein to Leo XIII, Paris, Feb. 28, 1899; 50ʳ–51ᵛ, Deshon to Leo XIII, New York, Feb. 28, 1899. See McAVOY: *Great Crisis*, pp. 282–285.

[9] ADR, Gibbons to O'Connell, Baltimore, Mar. 2, 1899.

[10] AAB 97 E 8/1, Gibbons to Leo XIII, Baltimore, Mar. 17, 1899 (draft); given in McAVOY: *Great Crisis*, p. 286.

Testem, Gibbons' was not published in the *Osservatore Romano* and, in fact, cannot be located in either the Vatican or Propaganda Archives. The Countess Parravicino, who may have received her information from O'Connell, believed that the cardinal's letter was never published because, after the response to Ireland's letter, Gibbons' would make it all the more clear that the condemned Americanism had never existed. Some of the French liberals were of the same opinion.[11]

The responses of the other archbishops reflected the attitudes they had taken on the devisive issues over the previous decade. Patrick Feehan of Chicago, John Hennessy of Dubuque, and Peter Bourgade of Santa Fe said nothing. Elder of Cincinnati, Chapelle, who had been transferred to New Orleans, Alexander Christie of Oregon City, and Ryan of Philadelphia thanked the pope for the letter, but did not acknowledge the existence of the heresy.[12] Riordan of San Francisco, Kain of St. Louis, and Williams of Boston joined Gibbons, Ireland, and Keane in denying emphatically that the heresy existed.[13]

The conservatives, however, would not allow the liberals and neutrals to dismiss Americanism as a chimerical invention of French *réfractaires*. They hastened to assure Leo how opportune his condemnation had been for their country. Corrigan, who may have encouraged the condemnation by writing Lepidi with approval of his *imprimatur* to Maignen, addressed the pope in the name of his suffragans on March 10. Leo had accurately identified "the multiplicity of fallacies and errors" which passed "under the specious title of 'Americanism'", he said, and "by reason of your infallible teaching we will not have to transmit to our successors the ungrateful task of having to struggle with an enemy which perhaps would never die".[14] Katzer and his suffragans went even beyond Corrigan. Con-

---

[11] PELLEGRINO CONFESSORE: *Conservatorismo politico*, p. 95 n. It was in an effort to locate Gibbons' original letter and possibly other material on Americanism that I approached Archbishop Hamer; see p. 175, n. 88 above.

[12] Elder's suffragan, Ignatius Horstmann of Cleveland, wrote, however, that while the controversy over the life of Hecker was limited to France, there was a danger in the United States of "minimizing" Catholic teaching to win converts and by declaring that only those truths had to be held which had been formally defined. He himself had noticed this tendency and had condemned it in the writings of Canon Salvatore di Bartolo who was later condemned by the Index. The liberals in America also presented certain dangers in their support of cooperation with public schools and of membership in secret societies. As a result of this liberal program, the children of wealthier Catholics, wishing to enter the mainstream of American society, entered mixed marriages which were detrimental to the faith of their children; APF, APNS, Rub. 1, vol. 147 (1899), 86ʳ, Horstmann to Ledochowski, Cleveland, Mar. 7, 1899.

[13] McAVOY: *Great Crisis*, pp. 290–291.

[14] ASV, SS, 280 (1900), fasc. 3, 64ʳ–66ᵛ, Corrigan to Leo XIII, New York, Mar. 10, 1899, given in McAVOY: *Great Crisis*, pp. 292–293.

gratulating Leo for "condemning the errors", the Milwaukee bishops were indignant to find Americans, "who indeed affirmed that they reprobated the aforesaid errors, but did not hesitate to proclaim again and again, in Jansenistic fashion, that there was hardly any American who had held them and that the Holy See, deceived by false reports, had beaten the air and chased after a shadow, to use a popular expression. It can escape no loyal Catholic how injurious to the Infallible See and how alien to the orthodox faith such conduct is, since those erroneous opinions have been most assuredly and evidently proclaimed among us orally and in writing, though perhaps not always so openly; and no true Catholic can deny that the magisterium of the Church extends not only to the revealed truths, but also to the facts connected with dogma, and that it appertains to this teaching office to judge infallibly of the objective sense of any doctrine and the existence of false opinions".[15]

Katzer's letter in particular was, of course, a direct insult to Gibbons, Keane, and Ireland, and, as will be seen, Ireland attempted to get a protest against it. But Katzer's drawing the parallel between the Americanists and Jansenists had but echoed *Civiltà Cattolica's* reaction. Ireland protested to Rampolla, reminding him of the journal's role in the earlier school controversy and saying that for either side to resurrect the Americanist controversy would simply result in a "war, which can be nothing but regrettable".[16]

Civiltà's view of Americanism, however, was characteristic of several of the European responses. Immediately upon the publication of *Testem*, Bishop Louis Isoard of Annecy, who was then in Rome, wrote the pope saying that the letter would increase still more the esteem of the French bishops for the Holy See.[17] Bishop Ignatius Senestrey of Regensburg, the old warhorse of the infallibilists at Vatican I, congratulated Leo both for the letter and for the condemnation of Schell.[18] One of the most interesting of the European responses, however, came from the bishops of the provinces of Turin and Vercelli. Writing in the names of their suffragans, Cardinal Agostino Richelmy of Turin and Archbishop Lorenzo Carlo Pampirio, O.P., of Vercelli expressed their consolation at the pope's combatting the errors which were penetrating the hearts of the clergy and faithful alike. Like Corrigan and Katzer, they linked the letter with papal infallibility.

---

[15] APF, APNS, Rub. 1, vol. 147 (1899), 144^r–146^v, Katzer to Leo XIII, Milwaukee, Pentecost, 1899; given in McAvoy: *Great Crisis*, pp. 296–297.

[16] ASV, SS, 280 (1900), fasc. 3, 47^r–48^r, Ireland to Rampolla, n.p., n.d. For *Civiltà's* article, see McAvoy: *Great Crisis*, pp. 294–295.

[17] ASV, SS, 280 (1900), fasc. 3, 36^{r-v}, Isoard to Leo XIII, Rome, Feb. 22, 1899.

[18] *Ibid.*, 54^{r-v}, Senestrey to Leo XIII, Ratisbon, Mar. 2, 1899.

"The expression of paternal kindness", they wrote on February 28, "with which Your Holiness so wonderfully joins firmness of principles and condescension of means, the just praise for the discoveries of true science and the reprobation of the insane pretexts of a false and proud doctrine have penetrated our hearts; and for our part we will have to repeat to all those, who are committed to our care, that, as the solemn definition of the Vatican Council in regard to the infallible magisterium of the Vicar of Jesus Christ is far from favoring the spirit of independence, it ought to increase in all humble subjection and faithful submission to the Apostolic See". In a day when license was frequently confused with liberty, they wrote, when there was a passion to speak, think, and publish whatever one wanted, "a magisterium is, more than ever before, useful and necessary, in order not to go counter to conscience and duty". With the pope the bishops of the Piedmont condemned the error of those who denied the necessity of external guidance and they joined him in praising religious orders. They were grateful for the pope's praise of preaching the Gospel and condemnation of those "who would elude the authority of bishops and put away all effectiveness, for the conversion and sanctification of the world", in preference for private opinions and "profane learning".[19] The Piedmontese bishops had reacted to a caricature of what the American liberals actually held, but the points they singled out for praise indicate the pastoral concerns of the Piedmont where the *risorgimento* had begun. They also exemplified how little Europe could understand the American Church with its eulogy of liberty.

In the immediate aftermath of the letter, Ireland still hoped to continue the movement. Before offering his submission to *Testem*, he even toyed briefly with the notion of having Satolli's speeches as delegate published in Italian, to "let Rome know what Satolli said when he was in America, so different from what he says to-day".[20] For much of the controversy leading to the condemnation he blamed O'Connell and urged him not to speak openly and to "give up your Liberty Hall". He rested his hopes on gaining a successor to Leo friendly to the Americanist program. "My heart is in Vannutelli's election: not my expectation", he wrote O'Connell. "You need not give him up, but don't anger Rampolla".[21] But Ireland was being unfair in his criticism of O'Connell, for he himself had beat a hasty retreat from the charge of Americanism and allowed to be introduced what he had resisted in Cahenslyism—European political influence on American ecclesiastical affairs.

---

[19] *Ibid.*, 57^r–58^v, Richelmy and Pampirio to Leo XIII, Turin, Feb. 28, 1899.
[20] Archives of the Josephite Fathers, 25 B 7, Ireland to John R. Slattery, Rome, Feb. 18, 1899.
[21] ADR, Ireland to O'Connell, "The Ocean", July 24, 1899.

The Ruthenian Question: Ireland's Retreat

For some years the Austro-Hungarian ambassador to the Holy See, Friedrich Graf Revertera, had been discussing the plight of Ruthenians in the United States with Propaganda. Requested by his government to treat the situation with Ireland during the latter's stay in Rome, the ambassador reported the archbishop's desire "to wash himself clean of the reproach of Americanism" and promise in "repeated conversations" to propose the appointment of a vicar-general for Ruthenians at the next meeting of the archbishops. There is no record that Ireland did introduce the measure at the meeting,[22] but on July 2, 1900, Rampolla sought Martinelli's opinion of the Austro-Hungarian Emperor's request that the Holy See accredit a Ruthenian priest to the apostolic delegation to handle Ruthenian affairs. The pope, he noted, did not oppose the request.[23]

Martinelli opposed the suggestion, arguing that this would increase the American criticism that the Church was subject to foreign political influence and recalling the issues of the Abbelen memorial and Cahenslyism and the bishops' desire to assimilate the Ruthenians to American culture. If the Austro-Hungarian Empire could have a priest appointed to the delegation, he concluded, then the German Empire would also request one.[24] A year and a half later, however, Ledochowski informed Martinelli that Leo had acceded to the Emperor's request and was appointing a Ruthenian priest, subject to both the delegation and to the local ordinaries, to conduct a visitation of the Ruthenians.[25] This visitation, conducted by Father Andrea Hodobay, ultimately led in 1907 to the appointment of Bishop Soter Stephan Ortynsky, who was to be immediately subject to the Holy See under the direction of the delegation but was to receive only delegated jurisdiction from the Latin-rite bishops in whose dioceses Ruthenians resided.[26] This episode regarding Oriental-rite Catholics was a relatively minor one in the complicated affair of Americanism. Ireland's compliance with the Austro-Hungarian ambassador in Rome and his later silence at the Holy See's sending a visitor to the United States at the Emperor's request is an indication of how far he had re-

---

[22] Gabriel ANDRIANYI: *Friedrich Graf Revertera, Erinnerungen*, in: Archivum Historiae Pontificiae 10 (1972) 268. See FOGARTY: *Oriental Rite Catholics*, p. 24.

[23] ASV, DAUS, "Stati Uniti", doss. 32, Rampolla to Martinelli, Vatican, July 2, 1900.

[24] *Ibid.*, Martinelli to Rampolla, Washington, July 24, 1900 (draft).

[25] *Ibid.*, Ledochowski to Martinelli, Rome, Feb. 2, 1902.

[26] See Bohdan P. PROCKO: *Soter Ortynsky: First Ruthenian Bishop in the United States, 1907–1916*, in: The Catholic Historical Review 58 (1973) 513–533. In 1913, Ortynsky was named ordinary of all Ruthenian Catholics in the United States. After his death in 1916, however, dissension among oriental Catholics continued and delayed the appointment of a successor until 1924 when the Holy See divided the jurisdiction and appointed Constantine Bohachevsky exarch of Philadelphia for Ukrainians and Basil Takach exarch of Pittsburgh for Ruthenians.

treated from his position of the early 1890s. Rampolla's own role in the episode seemed to manifest his vision of the United States, not as a nation but as a series of colonies of foreign settlers. It was but one of the areas into which the Holy See would begin to intervene regardless of the sentiments of the bishops.

2. The Last Act

In the meantime, on October 12, 1899, the archbishops held their first annual meeting since *Testem Benevolentiae*. Katzer's letter to Leo comparing those who denied the heresy existed with the Jansenists had been a direct affront to Ireland and Gibbons. Katzer himself was absent from the meeting. Riordan opened the attack by declaring that the letter from the Milwaukee bishops was "a direct charge of heresy against some of ourselves". Kain seconded him and then Ireland introduced the resolution that the bishops be polled as to whether the errors existed and where and by whom they were held. Such a resolution Corrigan deemed to be disrespectful to the pope who had pointed out those errors. Ryan then attempted to substitute a resolution calling upon all the archbishops who had not done so to write to Rome acknowledging the apostolic letter. Ryan's substitute lost by a tie vote. Ireland's resolution was then rejected by a vote of five to four with Gibbons voting to break the tie.[27] Ireland reported to O'Connell how he, Riordan, Kain, and Christie had "tried to get a joint protest against the idea of existence of errors. Philadelphia almost joined in but Baltimore cried 'peace, peace – death for the sake of peace', and nothing was effected".[28] By the end of the year, he wrote: "nothing is heard of 'Americanism' – No one seems to know that the Pope ever wrote – outside of Corrigan and the Jesuits – who gloat over their supposed triumph. Corrigan imagines he is forever 'cock of the walk'. Can you with any kind of stick haul him down? Try".[29]

Death and not the Americanists would ultimately haul Corrigan down and Ireland seems to have understood that the movement of Americanism was ended. But before the movement ended, it emitted a few last dying gasps which caused comment and clarified just what it was that Europeans had against Ireland's vision of the role of the Church and the age. In the spring of 1900, Spalding paid a visit to Rome. Silent during the controversy, if not, as was seen, actually hostile to Ireland at times, he now threw himself wholeheartedly into the Americanist camp. He first had an audience with Leo and strongly defended the orthodoxy of

---

[27] AAB 97 M 5, Minutes of the Archbishops' Meeting, 1899; see McAVOY: *Great Crisis*, p. 332.
[28] ADR, Ireland to O'Connell, St. Paul, Oct. 21, 1899.
[29] ADR, Ireland to O'Connell, St. Paul, Dec. 23, 1899.

Hecker against the errors the pope thought the priest had held. Then on March 21, he picked for the enunciation of his ideas a pulpit certain to gain them notoriety, the Church of the Gesù, the principal Jesuit church in Rome. He urged that the Church assimilate to its teaching the movements of the modern age just as Augustine and Thomas Aquinas had baptized Plato and Aristotle. Priests should be not only ministers of the sacraments but also cultured men of their age not hiding behind monastic walls. He praised higher education for women and called for unhindered freedom of inquiry within the Church. American Catholicism was the wave of the future for the English-speaking Church, he said, and with the spread of the British Empire and the American Republic there would come democracy and, except for Great Britain itself, the separation of Church and State.[30] Spalding's was almost a Quixotic gesture. Leaving Rome, he journeyed to Milan, where Sabina Parravicino arranged for the Italian translation and publication of his speech, and then to Paris, where Klein translated it into French.

But such statements were what had alarmed the European conservatives all along. Benedetto Lorenzelli, the Nuncio to France, wrote Rampolla in May asking instructions. Ireland was scheduled to arrive in July as President McKinley's delegate to the dedication of a statue of Lafayette. "As is known to Your Eminence", he wrote, "the Archbishop of St. Paul is an orator and loves to talk a lot". He had heard that Ireland had written the Duke of Norfolk that the future belonged to the Anglo-Saxons and that it would be to the papacy's self-interest "to divest itself of its Latin dress, dis-Italianize itself and abandon the claim to the temporal sovereignty of the Holy See". Riordan had already been in Paris and assured the students of the Seminary of San Sulpice that "Americanism does not exist outside of the imagination of three or four Frenchmen". Then Spalding had arrived and his conversations increased Lorenzelli's fear still more that Americanism continued to be a live and dangerous heresy. The bishop, he wrote, had "proclaimed the necessity of reforming the Church in the sense understood by all those pseudo-intellectual ecclesiastics" who comprised "the band, Bonomelli, Kraus, O'Connell, former rector of the North American College, Duchesne, and similar people", who publicized their views in various European journals and did "not know how to present any other remedy for the complex evils of the present-day situation than the submission of the Holy See to the Kingdom of Italy, the levelling, more or less veiled, of the heresies to the Catholic Faith, the separation of the Church from the State and the transfer of the Papacy to the Anglo-Saxons". Lorenzelli was concerned that Ireland's arrival would simply "repeat the aberrations of our pseudo-intellectuals".[31]

---

[30] SWEENEY: *Spalding*, pp. 226–272.
[31] ASV, SS, 280 (1900), fasc. 3, 133ʳ–134ᵛ, Lorenzelli to Rampolla, Paris, May 24, 1900.

Lorenzelli's was one of the most clear official statements of the curia's fear that the American praise of the separation of Church and State was linked with the Roman Question. He received only the vague instructions that, should Ireland come to the nunciature, he was to be treated with "courtesy and benevolence".[32] In the meantime, Ireland wrote Rampolla protesting against the statements attributed to him in the Italian press that he had written the Duke of Norfolk denigrating papal temporal power.[33] Ireland was desperately trying to rid himself of the taint of Americanism. Upon his arrival in Paris, Lorenzelli found him fearful that he no longer enjoyed the confidence of the Holy See and that the term Americanism would increase the charge against American Catholics that they were disloyal to their country. Lorenzelli sought to assure him that Rome had not forgotten his role in establishing the delegation and that the Holy See was not "ascribing to him those heterodox tendencies and aberrations, which certain pseudo-intellectuals" were proposing. He then explained to him the reasons for papal sovereignty and warned him "to be on guard against the anti-Latin and anti-theological theories of certain German professors such as Schell, and against the proposals of certain Powers, allied with the Quirinal, directed to nationalizing and atrophying the Papacy and to offering pretext for schisms or secessions".

If Lorenzelli's account can be trusted, Ireland was then "on guard against that Italian-German-French-American ecclesiastical group which is rationalistic in dogmatics, laxist in morals, innovative in discipline, liberal and in favor of the Triple Alliance in politics". In other words, Ireland was on guard against O'Connell's "Liberty Hall". Overall, the nuncio found Ireland well-disposed and praised his continuing support of the pope's French policy.

But if Ireland had removed himself from Lorenzelli's suspicion, such was not the case with Archbishop John J. Kain of St. Louis, who had also come to Paris. Kain had spoken with him "about the condemnation of *Americanism*, as an ensemble of errors which did not exist in America. But in the course of the discussion he showed himself to be an *Americanist* without knowing that he was one ...". For the nuncio, Kain's advocacy of "the gradual instruction of catechumens" and his positive assessment of the Christian truths already held by Protestants in approaching the Church were attitudes clearly condemned in *Testem*. One of the most surprising revelations of Lorenzelli's report to Rampolla was Corrigan's attitude toward Ireland. The Archbishop of New York not only "paid homage to the rectitude, sincerity, talent and good influence of Mgr. Ireland in America", but also observed that, while it was not desirable that all the bishops share in his "whim", Ireland was "most useful" in serving as "the most au-

---

[32] *Ibid.*, 135^{r-v}, Rampolla to Lorenzelli, Vatican, June 4, 1900 (draft).
[33] *Ibid.*, 136^r–137^r, Ireland to Rampolla, St. Paul, May 25, 1900.

thoritative mediator between Protestants and Catholics".[34] Corrigan, it seems, was far more open to the pluralism of opinions among the bishops than his enemies would have assumed. But such pluralism was to be squelched, partly because of the Vatican's fear of the international "ecclesiastical group" or "band", which seemed to link the American praise of the separation of Church and State and religious liberty with the Roman Question and decentralization of the Church. Immediately after *Testem*, Ireland had chastized O'Connell for speaking too openly and told him to disband "Liberty Hall". Over a year later, Lorenzelli continued to see the group as a threat to the Church he knew. Ireland could try as he might to dissociate himself from that side of Americanism, but he would fail. With that failure ended some of the most exciting years in the history of American Catholicism.

Did Americanism Exist?

Before leaving the subject of Americanism, the question must be raised whether the American liberals actually held what was condemned. Many years after the controversy, the Abbé Félix Klein published his *l'Americanisme: une hérésie fantôme*, the name by which the issue has since been known. First of all, in view of the Piedmontese bishops' response and of Leo's interrogation of Spalding, it seems certain that the European Church actually did believe that Hecker held the heresy. For Europeans in general and for the pope and Vatican officials in particular, the American Church was a Church of immigrants and the preservation of their faith was the Church's primary goal.

But Hecker had a different goal — the conversion of Protestants. Devoted to the truth of Catholicism, he saw American Protestants as unhampered with the historical and theological baggage of Europe where religious wars rather than persuasion had brought about toleration but not liberty. An optimist, he was convinced that emphasizing the positive aspects of Catholicism within the context of American religious freedom would lead religious Protestants to the Church. In this, he influenced all the other American liberals. But so divergent was this from the European experience that the Vatican rejected it. When Hecker and the Americanists spoke of presenting Catholic truth positively, it smacked of watering down doctrine. When they spoke of personal initiative and "active" virtues, they raised the specter of Pelagianism. When they praised religious liberty, it sounded like religious subjectivism. When they spoke of the advantage to the Church of the separation of Church and State, they found themselves in the eye of Italian conservatives and liberals alike advocating the surrender of papal tem-

---

[34] *Ibid.*, 139ʳ–141ᵛ, Lorenzelli to Rampolla, Paris, July 21, 1900.

poral power. The condemnation of Americanism arose not only from the translation of Hecker's biography into French but also from the impossibility of translating American ideas into a nineteenth-century European setting.

The reaction against Americanism must also be seen in the context of the pontificate of Leo XIII. The encyclicals of his early reign on Church-State relations
led the liberals to see themselves on the cutting edge of implementing papal policy
in the United States. In this they may well have been misled and deceived.[35] Those
same encyclicals a half century later provided the locus for John Courtney Murray's theological analysis and argument for the development of doctrine on
Church-State relations; like the Americanists, he too would be suspect of heresy.
For the end of Leo's pontificate was characterized by growing conservatism
which ultimately resulted in the election of Pius X. In that conservative atmosphere, some of the liberals' statements when reduced to philosophical abstrac-
tions could have been construed as the type of Americanism condemned in *Testem*.[36] But such a construction of Americanism was possible only according to the
integrist mentality which led to the condemnation of Modernism a few years later.

Just how little the Vatican understood American religious pluralism can be illustrated by the reaction to the assassination of President William McKinley in
September, 1901, when Rampolla instructed Martinelli to prohibit the Catholic
clergy from participating in any religious memorial services.[37] Catholics joining
in prayer with non-Catholics had been the issue on which Satolli had turned
against the liberals. It remained an issue and cause of suspicion for the Vatican
until the Second Vatican Council. At the turn of the century, however, it was
cause for alarm, for the Holy See had to deal with the settlement of Church lands
in the former Spanish colonies of Cuba, Puerto Rico, and the Philippines and the
replacement there of Spanish with American bishops. The Holy See appointed
Archbishop Placide Chapelle of New Orleans as apostolic delegate to Cuba and
Puerto Rico in 1898 and it extended his authority the following year to cover the
Philippines. Chapelle, however was frequently at odds with William Howard

---

[35] Margaret M. REHER: *Leo XIII and "Americanism"*, in: Theological Studies 34 (1973) 679–689.

[36] For example, some of Ireland's rhetorical statements, when taken out of context, could be construed as denying the need for external guidance in the Church. "Let there be individual initiative",
he told the second Catholic Congress in Chicago in 1893; "layman need not wait for priest, nor
priest for bishop, nor bishop for pope"; in: IRELAND: *The Church*, p. 72. For an analysis of the position of the Americanists in relation to *Testem*, see Margaret M. REHER: *The Church and the Kingdom of God in America: The Ecclesiology of the Americanists*, unpublished Ph. D. dissertation,
Fordham University, N. Y. 1972, especially, pp. 175–238.

[37] ASV, SS, 280 (1902), fasc. 3, 9ʳ, Martinelli to Rampolla, Washington, Sept. 14, 1901 (cable); 8ʳ,
Rampolla to Martinelli, Vatican, Sept. 15, 1901 (draft of cable).

Taft, Governor General of the Philippines, and with other government officials and in 1901 he was replaced by Donato Sbarretti, former secretary in the delegation in Washington.[38] In the on-going negotiations, Ireland was frequently summoned to Washington to consult with the government and he attempted to use his association with President Theodore Roosevelt to gain a red hat.[39] But his very influence with the government which renewed the hopes of his friends to make him a cardinal also caused his rejection, for Rome was simply too frightened that by accepting his role in political Americanism it would encourage the spread of religious Americanism.

After the First Vatican Council, Americanism was the first introduction of the American Church and its ideas onto the European scene. The American liberals reflected the growing feeling of liberalization during the pontificate of Leo XIII. But the movement came at a time when the United States emerged on the world scene as a political and military power and a threat to the old order. Neither the Vatican nor European political powers were quite ready to accept the vibrant young republic. With the condemnation of Americanism a new spirit was breathed into the American Church, a spirit of Roman authority and discipline, of loss of American independence and episcopal collegiality. With it also came the stifling of intellectual life in the new nation.

B. THE END OF AMERICAN CATHOLIC INTELLECTUAL LIFE: THE MODERNIST REACTION

The condemnation of Americanism conditioned the overreaction of the American Church to Modernism. In their haste to cleanse themselves of any taint of heterodoxy, some of the old-guard liberals were dragged into the integrist movement. The prime example of this was the erstwhile theologian of Americanism, Denis O'Connell. He was the only one of the Americanists who did not formally submit to the condemnation; he apparently thought that his letters to Lepidi were explanation enough of his position. He was also the only one of the liberal leaders who was not a bishop and Klein said he wanted to be one.[40] With the support of Charles Grannan, Edward A. Pace, and other liberal professors at the Catholic University and through the influence of Satolli, with whom he was again on good terms, he was named rector of the university on January 5, 1903.

---

[38] REUTER: *Catholic Influence*, pp. 17, 99–101, 115, 131. On Taft, see John T. FARRELL: *Background of the 1902 Taft Mission to Rome*, in: Catholic Historical Review 36 (1950) 1–22.

[39] FOGARTY: *Vatican*, pp. 294–295.

[40] Klein made this remark to Thomas T. McAvoy in an interview on May 25, 1951; see FOGARTY: *Vatican*, p. 296.

Intellectually, his rectorship could be described as cautious at best. His style of leadership was Roman. Because of this he alienated one of his former supporters, Charles Grannan, professor of scripture, who was chosen vice-rector in 1905 only to resign a year later. O'Connell's antipathy for Grannan and apparently his desire to appear orthodox after the condemnation of Modernism led to one of the few instances of academic repression in the United States. In 1907, Henry Poels, associate professor of scripture, obtained an audience with the pope during which he stated that he did not feel he could abide by the Biblical Commission's decree that Moses was the author of the Pentateuch. Poels was led to believe that the pope wished him to teach some other branch of scripture than the Old Testament. He gained a contrary opinion from Giovanni Genocchi, who was present as an interpreter, which was sustained by a letter from Lawrence Janssens, O.S.B., Secretary of the Biblical Commission in May, 1908. Shortly thereafter O'Connell had an audience with the pope. Alluding to but not naming Grannan, O'Connell said that a scripture professor raised too many questions without providing answers. Naturally assuming O'Connell meant Poels, the pope said that he had already ordered him to depart.

The Poels case rested there until the following meeting of the university Board of Trustees in April, 1909, at which Gibbons had Poels explain his position and the board exonerated him. That summer, however, the new rector of the university, Thomas Shahan, had an audience with Pius X, whose memory of his interview with Poels three years before differed from the professor's. This began a long and complicated series of negotiations at the end of which Poels was instructed that his contract with the university would expire in June, 1910.[41] Poels returned to his native Holland to a fruitful career in the social apostolate, but still angry at his treatment at the university. His dismissal for a time ended the liberals' original hope that the university would be on the cutting edge of American intellectual life.

Properly speaking, there was no real Modernism in the United States. American Catholic scholarship at the beginning of the twentieth century was in its infancy and tended to reflect European scholarship rather than to be creative. The foremost example of this was the fascinating journal, *The New York Review*, which began publication at St. Joseph's Seminary, Dunwoodie, New York, in 1905. Under the editorship of James Driscoll, S.S., the rector of the seminary, it had the explicit encouragement of Archbishop Farley. But such was not the response from Edward Dyer, S.S., the vicar general of the American Sulpicians, as a result of which Driscoll and several other Dunwoodie Sulpicians withdrew from

---

[41] ELLIS: *Gibbons*, II, 172–184. Colman J. BARRY: *The Catholic University of America: 1903–1909: The Rectorship of Denis J. O'Connell*, Washington 1950, pp. 177–181.

the society and were incardinated in the Archdiocese of New York. For the three years of its publication, The *Review* presented articles by some of the leading European intellectuals, some of whom were subsequently considered to be Modernists, as well as by some American scholars. What brought the demise of the *Review* were a series of articles by Edward J. Hanna and an advertisement for a book by George Tyrrell after he had been placed on the Index.

Edward J. Hanna was a professor at St. Bernard's Seminary, Rochester, New York, where he had taught after receiving his doctorate by acclamation at the Urban College of Propaganda. He contributed to the *Review* four articles on the human knowledge of Jesus. The first three raised the question of the limitations of Jesus' knowledge and attracted the attention of Rome. The fourth was virtually a retraction of the first three and had been written under the direction of Satolli. The Hanna case was all the more complicated because at that time Riordan was asking for him as his coadjutor in San Francisco. Hanna's rejection for the coadjutorship led to Riordan's having thrust upon him Denis O'Connell as auxiliary bishop. McQuaid, who had been a conservative on other issues, resented the implication that one of his professors was heterodox and demanded that each of them swear an oath that he had not delated Hanna to Rome. One, Andrew E. Breen, admitted that he had written to Rome against Hanna and was dismissed from the seminary faculty.[42] Hanna remained in the limbo of suspicion of heresy for several more years.

The Hanna case seemed to have drawn Roman attention to the *Review*. On January 15, 1908, Archbishop Diomede Falconio, the apostolic delegate, wrote Farley about an advertisement for George Tyrrell's *Lex Credendi* which had appeared in the journal after the book was placed on the Index. Falconio also charged that the *Review* had published several articles by known Modernists and that several New York priests were intimate with Genocchi, who was no longer on the Biblical Commission and was then suspect. Farley defended the *Review* and explained that the advertisement had appeared by accident, that some of the Modernists Falconio cited had written in the *Review* when the Catholic world still considered them orthodox, and that the others cited had not written at all. In regard to his priests' friendship with Genocchi, he pointed out that they wished to have an English-speaking confessor in Rome. Farley's defense seems to have been to no avail, however, and the *Review* ceased publication in 1908, giving the official reason that it had not received adequate financial support.[43] The American

---

[42] Michael J. DEVITO: *Principles of Ecclesiastical Reform According to the New York Review*, New York 1977, pp. 260–276; GAFFEY: *Riordan*, pp. 282–310.

[43] DEVITO: *New York Review*, pp. 276–296; Joseph T. LIENHARD: *The New York Review and Modernism in America*, in: Records of the American Catholic Historical Society 82 (1971) 67–82.

Catholic reader, whether clerical or lay, was not yet in a position to support such an endeavor, but the stifling atmosphere following the condemnation of Modernism had perhaps more effect in the United States than in Europe. In Europe critical scholarship went underground; in the United States it was nipped in the bud. Not until 1940 with the founding of *Theological Studies*, ironically by the Jesuits at Woodstock College, formerly the citadel of conservatism, did a scholarly journal again appear.[44]

One final episode of Modernism occurred in Gibbons' own St. Mary's Seminary. Joseph Bruneau, S.S., had taught at Dunwoodie and had contributed to the *Review*. During the 1890s he had written on biblical questions for the *American Ecclesiastical Review* and had sided with the opinions of M.-J. Lagrange, O.P. and Alfred Luisy. Leaving Dunwoodie when the Sulpicians withdrew, he went to St. John's in Boston where he translated into French Henry N. Oxenham's *Catholic Doctrine of the Atonement*. He then became a professor at St. Mary's Seminary in Baltimore. On information received from Cardinal Raffaele Merry del Val, the Secretary of State, Falconio reported to Gibbons on March 8, 1910, that both *Civiltà Cattolica* and *Osservatore Romano* had criticized several errors in the book and that the cardinal should investigate Bruneau's orthodoxy. Gibbons immediately wrote Bruneau, who replied on March 13 that he, like Oxenham, would most willingly submit his teachings to the Holy See. Gibbons forwarded this to Merry del Val with the statement, possibly aimed at Merry del Val's protégé in Boston, Archbishop William O'Connell, that the Sulpicians since their arrival in Baltimore in 1791 had never been anything other than pious, orthodox, and loyal to the Holy See.[45]

With the condemnation of Modernism following so closely on the condemnation of Americanism, the American Catholic Church lapsed into an intellectual slumber from which it did not awaken until the 1940s. The question, of course, arises whether Americanism and Modernism were related. Some later European Modernists were identified with Americanism, such as Albert Houtin, who wrote the first history of the latter movement. But no Americanist in the United States was associated with Modernism, except Denis O'Connell, who was a reactionary against it. In fact, only three Americans, all priests, left the Catholic Church over Modernism: William L. Sullivan, C.S.P., director of the Catholic chapel at the

---

[44] Michael V. GANNON: *Before and After Modernism: The Intellectual Isolation of the American Priest*, in: John Tracy ELLIS (ed.): The Catholic Priest in the United States: Historical Investigations, Collegeville, Minn.: 1971, pp. 343, 362.

[45] AAB 107 D 2, Falconio to Gibbons, Washington, Mar. 8, 1910; 107 D 3, Gibbons to Falconio, Baltimore, Mar. 9, 1910 (copy); 107 D 5, Bruneau to Gibbons, Baltimore, Mar. 13, 1910; and 107 D 8, Gibbons to Merry del Val, Baltimore, Mar. 15, 1910 (copy). See also ELLIS: *Gibbons*, II, 475–476.

University of Texas in Austin, John R. Slattery, S.S.J., first Superior of the Society of St. Joseph for Colored Missions (Josephites), and Thomas J. Mulvey, an assistant pastor in Brooklyn. Of these, only Slattery had any direct connection with the Americanists and that had principally consisted in a correspondence he maintained with O'Connell on various liberal endeavors to update the Church.[46]

Pope Pius X, nevertheless, seemed to see a relationship between Americanism and Modernism. In *Pascendi Dominici Gregis*, he condemned the Modernists because, among numerous other subjective and immanent tendencies, "with regard to morals, they adopt the principle of the Americanists, that the active virtues are more important than the passive, both in the estimation in which they must be held and in the exercise of them".[47] The American liberals had of course denied their acceptance of such principles in 1899, but here again was raised the specter of the "phantom heresy". Moreover, some of the condemnations and prescriptions of *Pascendi* were at variance with some of the principles the American liberals held in their recognition that the separation of Church and State in the United States was beneficial to the Church and that the Church could well use Anglo-American Common Law to assure due process in the Church. Americanism, as condemned, was espoused by no one in the United States and Modernism was primarily a European movement, but the juxtaposition of them in the reactionary days of Pius X had its effect on the American Church. Regardless of its denials, the Church in the United States was under suspicion. The Romanization of intellectual life was reinforced by the Romanization of the hierarchy, for Rome not only spoke to America; it acted.

---

[46] GANNON: *Before and After Modernism*, pp. 338–339.
[47] Acta Sanctae Sedis 40 (1907) 631.

CHAPTER VIII

FROM ROMANIZATION TO THE FIRST WORLD WAR

A. ROMANIZATION OF THE HIERARCHY

Integrism in the American Church took place not through the repression of scholarship, which was virtually non-existent, but through the gradual Romanization of the American hierarchy. The development of this new American ultramontane spirit was not, however, immediately obvious at the turn of the century. Keane, who had been rejected as Archbishop of Oregon City in 1899 — Satolli had presented the *ponenza* — was finally named Archbishop of Dubuque in the summer of 1900. Katzer, who continued to hold that Americanism really existed, opposed him as one of the "liberal Americanists," but Gibbons' strong advocacy of him with Rampolla and Riordan's personal Intervention in Rome ultimately won his appointment. Cardinal Lucido Parocchi, who had been relatively neutral during the liberal-conservative dispute, had drawn up the *ponenza* for Propaganda on the succession.[1] The full-fledged Romanization, however, occurred as Satolli and later Martinelli, as a cardinal, were given increasing roles in preparing the *ponenze* for episcopal nominations.

1. Appointment of William O'Connell as Bishop of Portland

The first sign of the new order came with the appointment of a new Bishop of Portland, Maine, in 1901. Both the priests of the diocese and the bishops of the Province of Boston agreed on the same three names, but not on the order of preference. Father Michael O'Brien, the administrator of the diocese, then informed Rome that the priests' list was invalid because the consultors' term of office had expired. Other priests in the diocese subsequently wrote Propaganda in favor of

---

[1] APF, Acta, 271 (1900), 410ʳ–420ʳ, Parocchi Ponenza, July, 1900; GAFFEY, *Riordan*, pp. 339–341. The priests of Dubuque had listed in order: Father John Carroll, Keane, and Father Edward John McLaughlin; the bishops had named Keane first followed by Bishop Thomas O'Gorman of Sioux City and Bishop Laurence Scanlon of Salt Lake City; AABo, Martinelli to Williams, Washington, Apr. 6, 1900.

O'Brien, who was not on the lists. The congregation, therefore, decided to postpone a decision and to seek more information from Martinelli and through him from Archbishop Williams about O'Brien and Father Edward Hurley, one of the original candidates.[2]

Martinelli responded that he knew some of the clergy had reservations about Hurley, because he liked to play cards and drink wine and would be manipulated by a group of priests who ran the diocese during the last days of Bishop James A. Healy. O'Brien, he said, had himself initiated the move for his promotion and the bishops of the province had refused to consider him because he had earlier been a known drunkard, had been deprived of his faculties, and his appointment would create a scandal. Satolli placed all this information in his second *ponenza* for the Portland succession. On April 22, 1901, the cardinals of Propaganda again met, rejected all the candidates, and nominated William O'Connell, Rector of the American College.[3] Conflicting reports, a poor choice of candidates, and fear of scandal in the American Church provided the Vatican with the opportunity to take episcopal appointments solely into its own hands.

O'Connell signalled the new style of American bishop who depended on Roman rather than American patronage for advancement. In his case, his patron was the rising young power in the Vatican, Archbishop Raffaele Merry del Val, son of the Spanish ambassador to the Holy See. O'Connell's style irritated even the old conservatives. Ella B. Edes, who seems to have been quiet during the Americanist crisis, unsheathed her tongue about O'Connell early in 1900. "Monsignor Pomposity", as she dubbed him, "is so invariably rude, ill-bred, and disobliging. ... I do not suppose he knows any better, being low-born and common, pitch-forked, suddenly, to a position which has turned his head. Like all underbred Paddies, I am not, in his eyes, sufficiently rich, or fashionable to be treated with even ordinary courtesy".[4] His nomination to Portland prompted her acerbic comment that the rapidity of his consecration by Cardinal Satolli, assisted by Archbishop Edmund Stonor, Rector of the English College, and Archbishop Merry del Val, had made "people laugh and ask if he were not, possibly, afraid the Powers that Be might change their minds and not permit the mitre to rest on his head, after all".[5] O'Connell was in place in the American hierarchy ready to implement the policy of Romanization of the American Church which occurred

---

[2] APF, Acta, 272 (1901), 41ʳ–48ʳ, Satolli Ponenza, Jan., 1901.

[3] *Ibid.,* 352ʳ–353ʳ, Satolli Ponenza, Apr., 1901. On O'Connell's appointment to Portland, see James P. GAFFEY: *The Changing of Guard: The Rise of Cardinal O'Connell of Boston,* in: Catholic Historical Review 59 (1973) 225–228.

[4] AANY, Edes to Corrigan, Rome, Jan. 6, 1900.

[5] AANY, Edes to Corrigan, Rome, May 17, 1901.

in earnest after the death of Leo XIII in 1903. But that policy was still two years off and in the meantime five new archbishops were appointed to replace the "old guard" which had reached its ascendancy in the years after the First Vatican Council.

2. The Appointment of New Archbishops

During the summer of 1902, two archdioceses were vacant: New York and Chicago. Corrigan had died on May 5. The priests' list named in order John Farley, the auxiliary bishop, Monsignor Joseph Mooney, and Father Patrick McSweeny, McGlynn's old supporter. McSweeny's name on the list indicated the continued pro-McGlynn sentiment among the clergy. When the bishops met to draw up their list, they unanimously rejected McSweeny for his lack of loyalty to Corrigan during the McGlynn affair. Having received a letter from Mooney that he wished his name withdrawn, they then turned to formulate their list. Unanimously they placed Farley first, followed in second and third places by Bishop James E. Quigley of Buffalo and Father Charles E. Colton, McGlynn's successor as rector of St. Stephen's Church.[6] Corrigan is rumored to have preferred Colton as his auxiliary in 1895, but then he turned instead to the moderate Farley, who also had Satolli's support.[7] Since Farley's name was in first place on both lists and he continued to enjoy Satolli's favor, he was the logical choice for the cardinals of Propaganda to make when Martinelli submitted the *ponenza* to them. On September 25, 1902, Farley was named fourth Archbishop of New York.[8]

But Chicago presented a more complicated picture. For some time the archdiocese had been beset with turmoil and scandal because of the weak administration

---

[6] APF, Acta, 273 (1902), 541^r–543^r, Martinelli Ponenza, Sept., 1902.

[7] CURRAN: *Corrigan,* p. 474. Actually, the concept of an auxiliary bishop was relatively new and created some confusion in Rome. Corrigan petitioned that Farley be named his auxiliary, but Propaganda sent briefs naming him coadjutor with right of succession. This of course created a canonical irregularity, since Corrigan had not had the consultors and irremovable rectors of the archdiocese and the bishops of the province submit *ternae.* He, therefore, kept the first set of briefs secret and requested new ones; APF, APNS, Rub. 153, vol. 97 (1896), 564^r–565^r, Corrigan to Ledochowski, New York, Sept. 14, 1895; 571^{r-v}, Satolli to Ledochowski, Washington, Sept. 20, 1895; 576^{r-v}, Corrigan to Ledochowski, New York, Dec. 17, 1895.

[8] APF, Acta, 273 (1902), 544^r, Audience of Sept. 5, 1902. Some of the pro and anti-McGlynn tension remained even in regard to Farley. Henry Brann, a New York priest who had been a principal in getting the clergy's declaration of loyalty to Corrigan during the McGlynn affair, reminded Propaganda officials that Farley had originally refused to sign the declaration; *ibid.,* Sommario, 553^{r-v}, Brann to "Monsignor", n.p., June 9, 1902. On Brann and the declaration of loyalty to Corrigan, see CURRAN: *Corrigan,* pp. 237–239.

and failing health of Archbishop Feehan. Sebastian Martinelli had been monitoring the situation early in 1902 and reported that there was rebellion against the archbishop and that other prelates were involved; he suspected that Ireland was intruding out of personal ambition.[9] On July 12, Feehan died; on July 24, the eligible priests of the archdiocese and the bishops of the province met to draw up their *ternae*. In order of preference, the priests named Spalding, Peter Muldoon, the auxiliary bishop, and Bishop James E. Quigley of Buffalo. The bishops listed Spalding, Bishop Montgomery of Monterey, and Father Daniel J. Riordan of Chicago, the brother of the Archbishop of San Francisco.[10] In the additional information which they sent to Rome, the bishops noted that they had rejected Muldoon because of doubts of his moral conduct and danger of factionalism. Quigley they had excluded because they feared he would be too weak.[11]

Archbishop Riordan, whose name had also been mentioned as a candidate for Chicago, was then in Europe and decided to go personally to Rome to work for Spalding's promotion and for Denis O'Connell's appointment as Rector of the Catholic University. Once in Rome, Riordan, with Denis O'Connell's assistance, drafted two reports for Cardinal Girolamo Gotti, who had succeeded Ledochowski as Prefect of Propaganda. Feehan, reported Riordan, had adopted a "live and let live" attitude, as a result of which grave scandals had arisen including priests living in concubinage. Protestants, he continued, regarded the archdiocese as the "bilge of corruption" and agreed with their forebears' assessment of the Catholic Church as "the whore of Babylon". To bring order out of this chaos, there was needed a strong bishop and there was no more suitable candidate than Riordan's old friend from Louvain, Spalding of Peoria. Of the other two names on the bishops' list, Montgomery had just been named coadjutor of San Francisco and had withdrawn his name from consideration for Chicago; and Daniel Riordan was too ill to assume the administrative responsibilities.[12] Spalding, then seemed the clear choice.

But at this juncture, Riordan received disturbing information about his friend in Peoria. The Baroness von Zedtwitz, the former Elizabeth Caldwell, had written to both Gotti and Satolli impugning Spalding's moral character and threatening to create a scandal if he were named to Chicago. Since she had not specified her charges, Propaganda asked Riordan to interview her on his way back to the

---

[9] ASV, SS, 280 (1902), fasc. 2, 83ʳ–84ʳ, Martinelli to Rampolla, Washington, Mar. 14, 1902; 87ʳ–88ʳ, Martinelli to Ledochowski, Washington, Mar. 21, 1902 (copy).

[10] AABo, Spalding to Williams, Peoria, July 25, 1902.

[11] APF, Acta, 273 (1902), 598ᵛ, Satolli Ponenza, Dec., 1902.

[12] *Ibid.*, 610ᵛ–612ᵛ, Sommario, Riordan to Gotti, n.p., Oct. 28 and Oct. 29, 1902; cited also in GAFFEY: *Riordan*, p. 344.

United States. Seeing her in Geneva, Riordan remained unconvinced of her charges; he later noted that both she and her sister Mary Gwendolen, then the Marquise des Monstiers-Merinville, both had reputations for erratic behavior. But the Baroness remained adamant and again wrote Satolli offering to come personally to Rome with witnesses to confront Spalding. Riordan, in the meantime, had gone to London where he found convincing evidence of Spalding's intimacy with Mary Gwendolen and accordingly wrote Satolli withdrawing his support for Spalding's nomination to Chicago.[13]

On December 15, 1902, the cardinals of Propaganda met on the Chicago succession. Satolli presented the *ponenza*, which incorporated the pertinent information about Spalding. While even now the veracity of the charges against the bishop remain uncertain, Satolli would have been well-disposed to accept them in view of Spalding's earlier opposition to the apostolic delegation. The cardinals then turned to Quigley and proposed him to Leo XIII for confirmation as Archbishop of Chicago[14] – an appointment, which incidentally paved the way for Colton, on the bishops' *terna* for New York in 1901, to be named Bishop of Buffalo. From San Francisco, Riordan wrote O'Connell: "The Chicago affair is settled and a great scandal avoided. You must advise the B[aroness]. for the sake of her family and especially for the sake of her child to say no more about it to anyone. He has no chance for a promotion. Let him remain where he is until God calls him".[15] Spalding's rejection was due to the charges of immorality brought against him, but it also indicated the increasing initiative which Rome would take in the appointment of bishops.

The last two archbishops named before the death of Leo XIII were coadjutors to St. Louis and Cincinnati. The *ternae* for both sees were relatively simple. The consultors and irremovable rectors of St. Louis named Bishop John J. Glennon, coadjutor of Kansas City, second on their list and the bishops of the province placed him first. Satolli presented the information to the cardinals of Propaganda who recommended Glennon to the pope for confirmation in April, 1903.[16] Glennon succeeded to the archiepiscopal see of St. Louis on October 13, 1903, upon the death of Kain. His would be a long episcopate – he died in 1946 – but he remained aloof from national affairs and concentrated on the management of his archdiocese.

---

[13] GAFFEY: *Riordan,* pp. 345–346; SWEENEY: *Spalding,* pp. 308–309.

[14] APF, Acta, 273 (1902), 598^r–600^v, Satolli Ponenza, Dec., 1902.

[15] ADR, Riordan to O'Connell, San Francisco, Dec. 30, 1902.

[16] APF, Acta, 274 (1903), 267^r–271^v, Satolli Ponenza, Apr., 1903. The priests had named in first and third place respectively Bishop Edward J. Dunne of Dallas and Bishop Sebastian Messmer of Green Bay. The bishops placed Bishop Dunne second and Bishop John J. Hennessy of Wichita third.

Cincinnati was only slightly more complicated. The priests named Bishop Henry Moeller of Columbus in first place and Bishop Camillus Maes of Covington in second. The bishops split evenly on their votes for both Moeller and Maes in first place. Moeller was chosen to be coadjutor to Archbishop Elder.[17]

New men were thus taking their places among the ranks of the archbishops. Late in 1902 and early in 1903 the full implementation of the Romanization of the American hierarchy was still months away, but the old liberals were in disarray. Nothing indicated this more than a letter Frederick Z. Rooker sent Denis O'Connell. Rooker, then the secretary of the apostolic delegation, was ambitioning to become Archbishop of Manila – he was eventually named Bishop of Jaro – at the same time that O'Connell was under consideration as Rector of the Catholic University. Rooker felt that he and O'Connell had "both been fools to tie ourselves" to Ireland and his friends. If O'Connell were to come to the university, he warned, he would have to "cut absolutely loose from them", for "it is Irelandisme that has ruined that place after Keanism had made it the spectacle of slop that it was". If O'Connell were to make the university great, he concluded, he would have to "show the country and the world that it is no longer a mere instrument of Ireland", for American Catholics "have no use for him …".[18] This may well have been the advice O'Connell followed as he was first restored to Satolli's good graces and then was appointed rector of the university in 1903.[19] Yet he still had not broken completely with Ireland.

In the summer of 1903, O'Connell returned to Rome on a mission for the university and in one more effort to get Ireland a red hat. While there, however, Leo XIII died and some newspapers reported that he was ordered to leave Rome during the ensuing conclave, lest he swing votes toward Gibbons.[20]

The conclave of 1903 was the first at which an American cardinal voted. On the first four ballots, Cardinal Rampolla received a plurality, but then Cardinal Jan Kozielsko Puzyna, Archbishop of Cracow, cast a veto against him in the name of the Austrian emperor. The balloting then gradually shifted to Cardinal Giuseppe Melchior Sarto of Venice who was elected Pius X on the seventh

---

[17] *Ibid.*, 272[r]–280[v], Martinelli Ponenza, Apr., 1903. In third place the priests had named Denis O'Donaghue, auxiliary bishop of Indianapolis, and the bishops named Bishop Henry Richter of Grand Rapids. Archbishop Williams wrote Archbishop Falconio, the apostolic delegate, that he knew only Maes and recommended him; AABo, note on Elder to Williams, Cincinnati, Jan. 27, 1903.

[18] ADR, Rooker to O'Connell, Washington, Oct. 10, 1902; see also Rooker to O'Connell, Washington, Sept. 8, 1902.

[19] FOGARTY: *Vatican*, pp. 296–300. Ireland likewise regarded O'Connell with suspicion, as he told his friend Maria Longworth Storer; see *ibid.*, pp. 294–295.

[20] ACUA, Shahan to O'Connell, Chester, Nova Scotia, Aug. 4, 1903.

scrutiny. "Pope man of God", Gibbons immediately cabled Ireland, who subsequently wrote O'Connell that either Rampolla or Vannutelli "would have done me for 'a man of God'".[21] With Pius X's election, it was obvious to the liberals that he would appoint as Secretary of State, the thirty-eight year old Archbishop Merry del Val, the secretary of the conclave. As Merry del Val presided over the integrist mentality in Europe, he saw to the continued Romanization of the American Church. What was needed was an important see to be Romanized.

3. Appointment of William O'Connell as Archbishop of Boston

The first American metropolitan see to be filled in the new pontificate was Milwaukee, where Archbishop Katzer had died in July, 1903. Second on the priests' list and first on the bishops' list was Bishop Sebastian Messmer of Green Bay who was named Archbishop of Milwaukee in November.[22] That Messmer was already a bishop, was on both lists, and had been a strong opponent to Americanism made him the most likely candidate for the cardinals of Propaganda. But within a few months they began discussing a yet more important metropolitan see.

In April, 1904, the consultors and irremovable rectors of the Archdiocese of Boston and the bishops of the province met to nominate a coadjutor to the aging Archbishop John Williams. In first place on both *ternae* was Matthew Harkins, Bishop of Providence, who also received the overwhelming endorsement of the other metropolitans.

Bishop O'Connell of Portland, the secretary of the bishops' meeting, expressed in his minutes a disapproval of all the candidates, without specifying his reasons. Before the meetings he had consulted with Satolli about the coadjutorship; and afterwards he wrote to Archbishop Diomede Falconio, the apostolic delegate, about a conspiracy among the Boston clergy to obtain a malleable successor to Williams. To his friend Merry del Val, he amplified his views on the men nominated and on the type of man who should be appointed. "The one frank and a-vowed motive actuating" the bishops and priests who drew up the lists, he declared, "was to keep off the *terna* at all costs any name which stood for Rome, for Roman views and for Roman sympathies. This is a well known and well proven fact. Threats, criminal promises, published calumnies – these were the means re-

---

[21] ACUA, Ireland to O'Connell, St. Paul, Nov. 15, 1903.
[22] The priests had named Father Augustine F. Schinner, administrator of the archdiocese, in first place and Father Joseph Rainer, rector of the archdiocesan seminary, in third; AABo, Falconio to Williams, Washington, Aug. 3, 1903.

sorted to for the success of this plot, which in the face of protests of all good and respected priests of the diocese has thus far succeeded. As God will one day judge me, He knows now that my only thought is to save in this awful hour of peril, the honor of His Church and the very life of that unity with the Apostolic See which again and again is threatened and which at this juncture is in awful peril here. Boston is at this moment in the balance between Rome and her enemies". He begged Merry del Val to delay the appointment and offered personally to come to Rome.[23]

While O'Connell was thus writing to Rome, appeals also went from some Boston priests and laity in his favor – an approach which seems to have been used later in New York. Several Italian laymen wrote of how gratifying his appointment would be to their fellow countrymen. One pastor argued that O'Connell's name was omitted from the *ternae* because the bishops were seeking revenge for his appointment to Portland three years previously. Two others, however, raised the specter of "Jansenistic Americanism" as inspiring those opposed to O'Connell and in favor of Harkins. So soon after the condemnation of Americanism it would be disastrous for the Holy See to appoint an Americanist to the See of Boston.[24]

Owing to these conflicting reports, Propaganda delayed the appointment in August. In the meantime, Satolli visited the United States during the summer and stopped off in Portland. Later that fall, O'Connell left for his first *ad limina* visit to Rome. During this time he received his sole support from a Boston suffragan, John B. Delany, Bishop-elect of Manchester, New Hampshire. That December, Williams and his suffragans, not knowing of the congregation's decision to delay the appointment, petitioned Propaganda to make it. O'Connell had no sooner returned to the United States in early 1905 when he was given the commission as papal envoy to Japan to investigate Church conditions there and report on possibilities for establishing diplomatic relations with the Holy See. In October, he left on his mission accompanied by two Boston priests known to support his candidacy. In his absence, Williams and his suffragans again petitioned Propaganda to make an appointment, now delayed for almost two years. This letter had probably no sooner reached Rome than O'Connell arrived there to give his report on Japan. On January 22, 1906, the cardinals of Propaganda named him coadjutor to Williams and on February 1, Pius X confirmed him.[25]

O'Connell's appointment was a gross violation of the canon law then prevailing in the United States. Rome's action was also markedly inconsistent, for,

---

[23] O'Connell to Merry del Val, Portland, Apr. 17, 1904, in: GAFFEY: *O'Connell*, p. 230.
[24] *Ibid.*, pp. 231–232.
[25] *Ibid.*, p. 235.

whereas in 1884 it had insisted on giving priests some say in nominating bishops, it now began the trend of ignoring both them and the bishops. Riordan of San Francisco commented that the appointment was "the most disastrous thing that has happened to religion in a century".[26] There was for a while a movement to have the archbishops protest to Rome about the appointment which Falconio reported had made a "most painful impression within the Episcopate in general, especially among the Archbishops and Bishops of the ecclesiastical province of Boston, excepting Msgr. Delany ...".[27] Falconio himself seems to have been suspicious of O'Connell and strongly defended Williams against efforts to have him retire early.

Ella B. Edes, however, reported another version of Falconio's role in O'Connell's promotion. The delegate, she informed McQuaid, had worked in Rome against Harkins and "I have no doubt that Pomposity paid well, Falconio, Merry del Val, and especially, Satolli, and that they seized the moment when Cardinal Gotti is lying at point of death, to carry out their design". In her opinion, the bishops of the Boston Province should "resolutely show their teeth, and not suffer their noble Metropolitan to be thus grossly insulted & shamefully treated, simply to promote the selfish aims and inordinate ambition, and gratify the shameless cupidity of Italian cardinals & Roman officials! Denis did a grand work, indeed, when he promoted that Apostolic Delegation at Washington, which he so proudly claimed as 'his work'". Her one remedy was that applied by an Irish bishop who mentally placed the names of recalcitrant priests in the chalice he offered at Mass and left them to God's disposition "& they die-off like flies!" "What a pity", she concluded, "one could not put Pomposity, Satolli, Merry del Val, Falconio, & a few others, in that celebrated chalice & leave them at God's disposition & will!"[28] The new order was hardly pleasing even to the old conservatives.

Wishing for peace, Williams never protested to Rome. Gibbons congratulated the new archbishop with the remark: "I little thought when I recommended you as Rector of the American College that your rise would be so rapid". He hoped that O'Connell would act toward Williams as "a loving son or younger brother".[29] It was a cordial letter but cool. In August, 1907, Williams died and O'Connell became Archbishop of Boston. Gibbons declined the invitation to preach at the funeral, but did preside. Williams' old friend, McQuaid, likewise asked to be excused from preaching because of his ill health. In O'Connell's memoirs, he re-

---

[26] Riordan to Stang, Mar. 5, 1906, in: *ibid.*, p. 236.
[27] Falconio to Gotti, Washington, Feb. 21, 1906 in: *ibid.*, p. 237.
[28] ADRo, Edes to McQuaid, Rome, Jan. 24, 1906.
[29] AABo, Gibbons to O'Connell, Baltimore, Mar. 11, 1906.

corded that both Gibbons and McQuaid had declined invitations to preach, but made no mention of the cardinal's presence at the funeral. He said only: "I decided that I, myself, with God's help, would undertake to sing the Mass and preach the sermon".[30] As on so many other occasions, O'Connell's memory would be somewhat faulty where facts were concerned – a trait which served further to alienate him from the rest of the hierarchy.

O'Connell's first task was to bring "Roman" discipline to his province. When the diocese of Hartford was vacant in 1908, he strongly urged the appointment of one candidate because, in part, "he is the only one of the three educated in Rome". In regard to the coadjutorship of Burlington, Vermont, he opposed one candidate, D. J. O'Sullivan, because of his poor administrative ability and disobedience to his bishop, but more particularly because he was "an Americanist who would inevitably cause trouble". His rejection was essential if "the Holy See ... expects a renewal of the Catholic spirit here and an elimination of certain tendencies which in the late past have been dangerously obvious".[31] A year later John J. Nilan was appointed Bishop of Hartford, which Archbishop Riordan took as a rebuke to O'Connell, but the latter expressed his pleasure at the appointment to Merry del Val and seemed to console himself by the realization that "he is at least not a Sulpician. Anything which breaks that blighting tyranny in this Province is a thing to be grateful to God for. It was true – further propagation of it meant a speedy misfortune to the Church here and its relations with Rome".[32] O'Connell's detestation for the Sulpicians, who operated his own seminary and St. Mary's Seminary in Baltimore and who had aided Gibbons during the Americanist crisis, was well known. At the end of the academic year 1910–1911, he ordered them to leave St. John's, the archdiocesan seminary of Boston.[33]

In the meantime, in June, 1908, Pius X had issued his constitution *Sapienti consilio* which, among other things, removed the American Church from the jurisdiction of Propaganda and placed it under the Sacred Consistorial Congregation.[34] This reflected, however, the pope's reorganization of the Roman Curia rather than the independence of action for the American Church that Ireland had thought would result from separation from the missionary congregation. The division among the bishops in the previous decade had cost them the ability to take

---

[30] William Cardinal O'CONNELL: *Recollections of Seventy Years,* New York 1934, p. 267. See ELLIS: *Gibbons,* II, 421.

[31] AABo, O'Connell to Merry del Val, Satolli & Martinelli, Boston, Dec. 8, 1908 (copy).

[32] AABo, O'Connell to Merry del Val, Boston, Feb. 26, 1910 (copy).

[33] GAFFEY: *O'Connell,* p. 240.

[34] Acta Sanctae Sedis 41 (1908) 425–440.

the initiative in certain areas. One example of this was the continuing problem of secret societies. With the opposing voice of Corrigan now silent, Ireland had succeeded by 1908 in gaining the unanimous support of the archbishops to request the Holy See to reopen the case of the societies condemned in 1894. In February, 1910, however, Rampolla, then the Secretary of the Holy Office, responded that, in issuing the original condemnation, Rome had "made a full and thorough examination of the question ...". One of the issues remained "communication *in divinis* with non-Catholics".[35] The Vatican's acceptance of American religious pluralism was still a long way off.

The American Church, nevertheless, was no longer regarded as a mission; in fact, it had already been sending missionaries to foreign countries for some time. In the late 1880s, American Jesuits and Sisters of St. Anne went to the Alaska mission. The Bahamas, for a time under the charge of the Bishop of Charleston, were transferred in 1885 to the ecclesiastical jurisdiction of the Archdiocese of New York, from which came diocesan priests and Sisters of Charity. In 1891, however, the islands became the responsibility of Benedictine monks from St. John's Abbey in Minnesota. In 1893, American Jesuits opened a mission in Belize where they collaborated with Holy Family and Mercy sisters. The same year, other American Jesuits began their mission in Jamaica.[36]

One of the most exciting examples of this new missionary spirit was the founding in 1911 of the first American congregation strictly for the purpose of the foreign missions. With the support of Cardinal Gibbons and at the request of Archbishop Diomede Falconio, the archbishops gave their approval to the plan of two American priests, James Anthony Walsh and Thomas Frederick Price, to found the Catholic Foreign Mission Society of America, more familiarly known as Maryknoll. In 1918, the first Maryknoll missionaries arrived in Kwantung Province, China. Other Americans would soon follow them to China and other mission fields.[37] Although the American Church was now recognized as and had all the characteristics of a mature Church, its older spirit continued to decline.

In 1911, O'Connell rose yet higher when his friend Pius X raised him together with the moderate Farley to the College of Cardinals. On hearing the news, Gibbons wept. The old liberals still hoped to see their hero in St. Paul rewarded.

---

[35] Rampolla to Falconio, Rome, Feb. 7, 1910, in: AANY, Minutes of the Meeting of Archbishops, Apr. 7, 1910. See also the minutes for their meetings in 1905–1909.

[36] James HENNESEY: *American Catholics: A History of the Roman Catholic Community in the United States,* New York 1981, p. 245; Colman J. BARRY: *Upon These Rocks: Catholics in the Bahamas,* Collegeville, Minn. 1973, pp. 59–97.

[37] ELLIS: *Documents,* II, 576–580. See also Thomas A. BRESLIN: *China, American Catholicism, and the Missionary,* University Park, Pa. 1980 and Robert CARBONNEAU: *The Passionists in China, 1921–1929: An Essay in Mission Experience,* in: Catholic Historical Review 66 (1980) 392–416.

Riordan thought O'Connell's elevation was "above all understanding, and it is better to keep silence than to express my views on it. Our old friend of St. Paul would have been the choice, I think, of nearly all the best minded of our people ...".[38] That same year, the other O'Connell began the last stage of his now plummeting career by becoming Bishop of Richmond, the diocese for which Leo XIII rejected him twenty-four years before because of his value in Rome.[39] The old guard was fading, but the new one, represented by Cardinal O'Connell, never completely took over. The process of Romanization which continued over the twentieth century was never a univocal term. Rather Romanization reflected a particular Roman patron and depended on who was prominent in Rome in a given era. Indeed, O'Connell's brand of Roman authority began to fade in 1914 with the death of Pius X.

Prior to the conclave of 1914, the anti-modernists drew up a list of the College of Cardinals with a description of each one's theological and ecclesiastical leanings. There were at the time three American cardinals. Gibbons was described as an "old-style liberal American", and Farley as "liberal for an American". O'Connell was dubiously characterized as a "friend of Merry del Val from boyhood, was consecrated by him, became Roman, represents Romanism in America, very shady, a careerist because of his money".[40] Both O'Connell and Farley had been in Europe early in the summer of 1914 and had heard rumors of Pius X's failing health. After Sarajevo, however, Farley fled to Switzerland and O'Connell, assured that the pope's health was improving, returned to the United States. On August 20, he was informed of the pope's death and set about immediately to book a passage on a ship to Italy. In Baltimore, however, arrangements were made for the ship on which O'Connell was sailing to be diverted from Boston to New York to pick up the eighty-year old Cardinal Gibbons. The law at the time stated that the cardinals were to assemble in conclave ten days after a pontiff's death. Irritated at the delay, O'Connell abandoned Gibbons in Naples to make his own way to Rome in a hired automobile. But his car broke down and he war forced to delay for repairs. On September 3, therefore, he and Gibbons arrived together in Rome to the sound of the rejoicing at the election of Cardinal Giacomo della Chiesa, Archbishop of Bologna, who took the name Benedict XV. O'Connell was livid. It was well known that, had he arrived on time, he would have cast his ballot for Merry del Val.[41]

---

[38] AAB 107 V, Riordan to Gibbons, San Francisco, Nov. 29, 1911, in: ELLIS: *Gibbons*, II, 422.

[39] APF, Acta, 258 (1888), 692ʳ–696ʳ, Mazzella Ponenza, Dec., 1888; FOGARTY: *Vatican*, pp. 309–311.

[40] Émile POULAT: *Intégrisme et catholicisme intégral: un réseau secret international antimoderniste: La "Sapinière" (1909–1921)*, Tournai 1969, pp. 329–330.

[41] Dorothy G. WAYMAN: *Cardinal O'Connell of Boston: A Biography of William Henry O'Connell, 1859–1944*, New York 1955, pp. 172–176.

Della Chiesa's election for a while buoyed the hopes of the old American liberals. He removed Merry del Val as Secretary of State and replaced him with Cardinal Pietro Gasparri. Moreover, he had supported Ireland's school plan back in 1892, which drew from Corrigan the comment that he was "a gentlemen without any influence whatever in theological circles, and whose name consequently, if published, would carry absolutely no weight with it".[42] He had continued a friendship with Ireland and had spoken of him during his audience with Gibbons immediately after the election. Ireland was not surprised, he wrote, for "of Della Chiesa it could not be said, as it could be of Sarto – non cognoverunt Joseph". He had prayed for della Chiesa's election, he concluded, for "I felt that the pendulum would swing to Leo & Rampolla – and that meant Della Chiesa".[43] At the end of the year, he was again enthusiastic that Benedict would soon name him a cardinal,[44] as Gibbons reportedly urged during his audience. Again Ireland's hopes were to be dashed and with them the hopes of the old guard. But this time the reason was less the opposition to him in the American hierarchy and more the world war which occupied the pope's attention.

B. The First World War

The United States remained a nation of immigrants. As it approached entry into the First World War, its citizens were divided in opinion. Irish and German Americans alike favored neutrality – the former because of their antagonism for the British and the latter because of their continued loyalty to the land of their forebears. But the war was particularly difficult on German-Americans who found their loyalty to the United States regarded with suspicion.[45]

1. Appointment of George Mundelein as Archbishop of Chicago

On the eve of American participation in the war, German-American loyalties even influenced at least one episcopal appointment. On July 10, 1915, Archbishop Quigley of Chicago died. The priests nominated in order of preference: Edmund M. Dunne, Bishop of Peoria, Peter J. Muldoon, Bishop of Rockford, Illinois, and Alexander J. McGavick, Auxiliary Bishop of Chicago. The bishops of

---

[42] AANY, Corrigan to "dear Bishop", New York, June 21, 1892 (copy of form letter to McQuaid).

[43] AAB 114 F 1, Ireland to Gibbons, St. Paul, Sept. 27, 1914.

[44] AAB 114 S 8, Ireland to Gibbons, St. Paul, Dec. 31, 1914.

[45] See Philip GLEASON: *The Conservative Reformers: German-American Catholics and the Social Order*, Notre Dame 1968, pp. 159–171.

the province rejected this list in favor of John P. Carroll, Bishop of Helena, Montana, John J. Glennon, Archbishop of St. Louis, and Thomas F. Lillis, Bishop of Kansas City.[46] Gibbons and Sebastian Messmer favored Muldoon.[47] Rumors began making the rounds of Chicago, however, that the Holy See would reject the lists altogether and appoint Dennis J. Dougherty, Bishop of Jaro in the Philippine Islands. In the meantime, the See of Buffalo was also vacant and the Holy See intended to appoint George Mundelein, then Auxiliary Bishop of Brooklyn, when the British Foreign Office requested that a bishop of German ancestry not be appointed to a see on the border between the United States and Canada during the hostilities. Dougherty was then sent to Buffalo with the promise of being named to the first available metropolitan see, while Mundelein was appointed Archbishop of Chicago.[48]

But Mundelein also owed his rise to prominence to his close friendship with Archbishop Giovanni Bonzano, then the apostolic delegate, with whom he had become acquainted when he was attending the German College in Rome.[49] Bonzano's promotion of Mundelein may have contributed to the reputation he had with the British of promoting German interests in the American Church.[50] Mundelein's installation as archbishop was itself a newsworthy event, for, according to the official story, an anarchist poisoned the soup at the luncheon following the ceremony. The bishops and other guests were saved from mass assassination only because so many had arrived that the caterer had to dilute the soup at the last moment.[51] Mundelein was off to a good start in his ascent in the American hierarchy. Within a few years, he would surpass O'Connell as the most powerful figure in the American Church. That the Holy See chose to ignore the *ternae* for Chicago indicated its desire to alter the direction of the American Church. Such a redirection became easier by a decree of the Consistorial Congregation in 1916 changing the method of selecting bishops. Henceforth, each bishop was to submit

---

[46] AANY, Bonzano to Farley, Washington, Aug. 18, 1915.

[47] ELLIS: *Gibbons,* II, 418.

[48] For a summary of the succession to Chicago, see James P. GAFFEY: *Francis Clement Kelley & the American Catholic Dream,* Bensenville, Ill. 1980, I, 151–155. See also Hugh J. NOLAN: *Native Son* in: The History of the Archdiocese of Philadelphia, edited by James F. CONNELLY, Philadelphia 1976, pp. 343–344.

[49] In ACC, there are several letters from Bonzano while Mundelein was still in Brooklyn. Father Francis E. Keenan, S.J., who was Bishop McDonnell's secretary in Brooklyn in 1915, also attested to Mundelein's long-standing friendship with Bonzano.

[50] Thomas E. HACHEY: *British War Propaganda and American Catholics, 1918,* in: Catholic Historical Review 61 (1975) 58.

[51] GAFFEY: *Kelley,* I, 154. Father Keenan, who was present, told this writer that he believed that the incident may have been a simple case of food poisoning, but that the caterer cast the blame on an anarchist.

to his metropolitan every two years the names of one or two priests he thought worthy of being made a bishop. To arrive at his two names, the bishop was to seek the opinion of his consultors and irremovable rectors, but individually and under the bond of secrecy. The bishops of each province would then discuss the names submitted and determine on the ones to be forwarded to the Consistorial Congregation through the apostolic delegate. When a see was vacant, the Holy See would then seek the opinion of the bishops on the most likely candidates, "through the Most Reverend Apostolic Delegate or in some other manner".[52] The priests thus lost their consultative vote which the Holy See had demanded the Third Plenary Council give them and now the apostolic delegate received an increasing role in the naming of American bishops.

2. The Vatican and the American Church in the First World War

For the time being, however, the Holy See was less concerned with Romanizing the American Church than with attempting to end the First World War. In 1916, the United States was still neutral, but its policies favored the Allies. Ireland had earlier predicted that the Vatican would take the American Church seriously only when it realized that the United States was a world power. Yet, the emergence of the nation on the world scene, if anything, hampered that Vatican realization, for the American President at the time, Woodrow Wilson, was not well-disposed toward Catholics. As a historian, he had earlier written disparagingly of immigrants to the United States, particularly from Italy and eastern Europe. During the Mexican Revolution in 1915, he had ignored Gibbons' pleas to remain neutral toward either Francesco "Pancho" Villa or Venustiano Carranza and gave de facto recognition to Carranza who continued to persecute the Church.[53] Any attempt to win Wilson to support Benedict XV's peace overtures, therefore, was going to be difficult, especially with the American government's suspicion that the pope leaned toward the Central Powers.

There were also factors internal to the American Church which militated against a clear-cut American Catholic attitude toward the war. According to the British Foreign Office, the Vatican efforts to destroy Americanism had met with "sustained opposition, which shows no sign of dissipating itself in the immediate future". Such a block of American Catholic thought would support Wilson's policies.[54] Gibbons was still the leader of the American hierarchy and to him fell the task of conveying papal messages for peace. But he also maintained an inde-

---

[52] Acta Sanctae Sedis 8 (1916) 400–404.
[53] ELLIS: Gibbons, II, 205–217. Dragan R. ŽIVOJINOVIĆ: The United States and the Vatican Policies: 1914–1918, Boulder, Colorado 1978, pp. 17–19.
[54] HACHEY: British War Propaganda, pp. 51–52.

pendent position. In general, he supported Wilson's attempts at mediation, but, after the sinking of the *Lusitania* on May 7, 1915, he recommended that Americans not travel on ships owned by belligerents; in August, he carried out Gasparri's instructions to inform Wilson of the German assurance not to sink belligerent passenger ships without prior warning.[55] Yet he praised Wilson's preparedness speech and once the United States declared war on Germany on April 4, 1917, he and the rest of the hierarchy stood firmly behind the president.

Even after American entry into the war, Gibbons continued to act as intermediary between the Vatican and the United States government. In August, 1917, he sought to use his influence indirectly to have the president cooperate with Benedict's new peace initiative to have the belligerents return to the *status quo ante bellum*; yet, there is no evidence that he saw Wilson personally.[56] Shortly after the United States declared war on Austria-Hungary in December, 1917, he urged Wilson to cooperate with the pope in seeking to detach the Empire from Germany. Denying that the pope wished to introduce the Roman Question at the peace conference, planned by the Allies, he sought the president's aid in countering the British initiative to exclude the Holy See from participation. On the other hand, he would neither call for public demonstrations in favor of the Holy See's participation nor join bishops in the British Empire in protesting the British exclusion. He refused to allow himself and the American Church to be dragged into a situation which would increase American anti-Catholic prejudice. He was faced with the familiar dilemma of American Catholicism – to display loyalty to Rome and to the United States. He still believed that Rome misunderstood the American Church and thus sought to cooperate with the British in presenting his views to the Vatican. He also quietly refused to comply with Gasparri's request in October, 1918 to see Wilson personally about accepting a separate Austro-Hungarian armistice.[57]

The war was a test of American Catholic loyalty. While Benedict XV may have been sympathetic toward Austria-Hungary with its large Catholic population, his overtures for peace were construed in the United States as favoring only the Central Powers. In this context, Gibbons followed the best strategy possible in faithfully presenting papal views while encouraging Catholic loyalty to the nation.[58]

---

[55] ŽIVOJINOVIĆ: *The United States,* pp. 48–50.
[56] ELLIS: *Gibbons,* II, 243–246.
[57] ŽIVOJINOVIĆ: *The United States,* pp. 147–149, 169.
[58] ELLIS: *Gibbons,* II, 250–258. Gibbons' own view of the American Church was further jeopardized by an effort, encouraged by the British, to have Wilson send a diplomatic representative to the Holy See – a proposition to which the hierarchy was not party and which Wilson ultimately rejected in 1918 because of the difficulties it would raise for him with the American public; see ŽIVOJINOVIĆ: *The United States,* pp. 141–156.

In the final analysis, the Vatican had little influence on American Catholic participation in the war, but the war influenced Catholic participation in American society.[59]

3. The Polish Question

The war had accelerated the Americanization of Irish and German-Americans. Yet, reminiscent of the charges and counter-charges of the Cahensly controversy, tension remained with other ethnic groups, notably the Poles. As early as 1897, a group of Poles had gone into schism to form the Polish National Church.[60] In 1920, a group of Polish-American priests protested directly to the Polish government about their treatment in the American Church. Calling for Polish auxiliary bishops to be appointed in several dioceses and for Bishop Paul P. Rhode of Green Bay to be made an archbishop, they predicted grave losses to the faith if their plea was not heeded.[61] Furthermore, they accused the American hierarchy of attempting to Americanize the Poles. On June 23, 1920, the Polish Legation to the Holy See submitted the petition on behalf of its government. Gasparri then forwarded it to Gibbons and also seems to have shown the Polish ambassador a letter Mundelein had written complaining of the Poles. At their annual meeting on September 22–23, the bishops unanimously resolved to "enter protest ... against the interference of any foreign government in the ecclesiastical affairs of the United States, and ... [against] the unwarranted assumption on the part of laymen to dictate the nomination of bishops". They furthermore condemned the group of Polish-American clergy for appealing "to laymen or to a foreign government, for the purpose of coercing the Episcopate in the selection of candidates for the episcopal office".

Gibbons then appointed a committee of Dougherty, Mundelein, and Messmer to draft a more detailed response to Gasparri's letter. Each of them were the ordinaries of archdioceses which were said to need Polish auxiliaries. They divided the letter among themselves. Dougherty treated the problem of foreign interference. This, he said, would not only "restrict the liberty of the Holy See" in select-

---

[59] For an analysis of Irish and German-American attitudes toward the war, see Edward CUDDY: *Pro-Germanism and American Catholicism, 1914–1917,* in: Catholic Historical Review 44 (1968) 427–454.

[60] William GALUSH: *The Polish National Church: A Survey of Its Origins, Development and Missions,* in: Records of the American Catholic Historical Society of Philadelphia 83 (1972) 131–149.

[61] The dioceses for which they requested Polish auxiliaries were Chicago, Boston, Detroit, Philadelphia, Scranton, Pittsburgh, Buffalo, and Milwaukee; AAP, Dougherty, notes on the Polish memorial.

ing bishops but would lend credence to the unjust charge leveled against American Catholics "of disloyalty to the American Government and of subservience to
foreign potentates". If the proposal were acted upon, he continued, "non-
Catholics would calumniate us as hindering the unification of the Nation" and
would set a precedent for appointing bishops for every other national and racial
group, with "resultant confusion [which] would surpass any discord recorded in
history". As for the "prophetic warnings of the Polish Legate", Dougherty recalled that "years ago, they were employed by other nationalities for political and
selfish purposes similar to those now harbored by the Polish Government".[62]

Messmer's notes had called for a protest against a letter from an American
bishop to the Holy See being shown to a diplomatic representative without either
the bishop's or the pope's permission, but Dougherty refused "to be a party to
any censure upon the Holy See for its behavior in the matter of disclosing Archbishop Mundelein's letter regarding the Poles".[63] Mundelein's own notes for his
section bristled with sharp comments about the Poles and the attempts to have
Rhode promoted, but in his final draft he confined himself to comment only on
the specific charges and recommendations of the petition.

There was no evidence, he asserted, that any bishop had ever discriminated
"against any Polish Priest or layman because of his nationality". While he favored retention of teaching Polish in some seminaries to students of Polish descent, he believed that "the greatest danger ... for the future would threaten the
Church in this country did we ever attempt to propagate the study of the history
and traditions of every element that goes to make up our population, and even
greater danger lies in any attempt to show favoritism to one people like the Poles".
He denied that there was any attempt "to 'Americanize' any of the existing
Polish parishes". Whenever French and German-speaking parishes had adopted
English, he said, it was at the request of the pastors who saw their young people,
American-born, deserting their own parishes for English-speaking ones; this was
now the case with the Poles. The patriotism of the American bishops had also
been called into question, to which Mundelein responded that if it had not been
for "the so-called Americanism of the American Bishops" many priests and
seminarians would have been drafted for military service and alien priests and sisters would not have been given "generous treatment".[64]

The section prepared by Messmer indicated not only how far he had come
from the 1890s when he was an opponent to Ireland's Americanization but also

---

[62] AAP, [Gibbons] to Gasparri, n.d., Dougherty's draft.
[63] AAP, Messmer's notes on the Polish Question, Nov. 11, 1920; Dougherty to Messmer, Philadelphia, Nov. 15, 1920 (copy).
[64] AAC, Gibbons to Gasparri, n.p., n.d. (draft) with Mundelein's notes attached.

reflected the experiences he had had with Poles in Milwaukee. Appointing Polish bishops would isolate "the Polish Catholics from their American Catholic Brethren", he said, and would "preserve a distinct and separate Polish nationality in the United States". Such a policy would be "injurious both to the Church and to the Country". Far from helping Poles preserve their faith, such isolation, said Messmer, would render them incapable of explaining and defending their faith before non-Catholics. He then concluded with words which would have branded him as an Americanizer thirty years earlier: "It is of the utmost importance to our American nation that the nationalities gathered in the United States should gradually amalgamate and fuse into one homogeneous people and, without losing the best traits of their race, become imbued with the one harmonious national thought, sentiment, and spirit, which is to be the very soul of the nation. This is the idea of Americanization. This idea has been so strongly developed during the last war that anything opposed to it would be considered as bordering on treason. The American people and government are today fully determined that nothing shall stand in the way of promoting, in every section of the country and in every portion of the people, this work of Americanization. It will be a real disaster for the Catholic Church in the United States if it were ever to become known that the Polish Catholics are determined to preserve their Polish nationality and that there is among their clergy and leaders a pronounced movement of Polonization".[65]

Mundelein put together the various sections of the letter and sent it to Gibbons with the comment that "while temporate and respectful, [it] will constitute one of the strongest and most forceful documents ever presented by us to the Holy See".[66] On November 18, Gibbons signed it in the name of the American hierarchy and sent it to Gasparri.[67] Had the joint authors been known, the Vatican may have gotten a clear indication of just how Americanized earlier immigrant groups had become. The letter and the previous resolutions also indicated the sensitivity of the hierarchy to anti-Catholicism.

---

[65] AAP, Messmer, "Notes on the Polish Memorial", Milwaukee, n.d. Messmer had given a copy of these same notes to Mundelein; AAP, Messmer to Dougherty, Milwaukee, Nov. 19, 1920. With a few minor changes they constitute the third part of Gibbons' letter to Gasparri. For Messmer and the Poles, see Anthony J. KUZNIEWSKI: *Faith and Fatherland: The Polish Church War in Wisconsin, 1896–1918*, Notre Dame, Ind. 1980.

[66] AAC, Mundelein to Gibbons, Chicago, Nov. 16, 1920 (copy).

[67] AAB 137 N 2, Gibbons to Gasparri, Baltimore, Nov. 18, 1920 (copy).

CHAPTER IX

THE NATIONAL CATHOLIC WELFARE CONFERENCE

A. FORMATION OF THE WELFARE COUNCIL

Anti-Catholicism had continued to play a part in American culture. Partly to counteract this, Father John J. Burke, C.S.P., editor of *The Catholic World,* saw the war as an opportunity to realize Hecker's goal of influencing American society. Recognizing the danger of parochialism, he saw the need for a national organization to coordinate Catholic activity similar to the role filled by the Federal Council of Churches for Protestant denominations. With the approval of Gibbons and the support of Farley and O'Connell, he called a meeting of all Catholic organizations and asked each diocese to send representatives. On August 11–12, 1917, the delegates of fifty-eight dioceses and of the larger Catholic societies met at the Catholic University, where Burke and his supporters drafted plans for the National Catholic War Council. In November, these plans were approved by the archbishops who comprised the trustees of the university, and, in January, 1918, received the approbation of the rest of the archbishops who continued their annual meetings. The War Council was placed under the metropolitans with its immediate direction given to Bishops Peter Muldoon, William Russell of Charleston, Joseph Schrembs of Toledo, and Patrick Hayes, auxiliary to Cardinal Farley. It was to cooperate with other denominational groups under the general supervision of the government to coordinate Catholic activities ranging from providing military chaplains to financing the work of the Knights of Columbus in the training camps, from supplying religious literature to the armed forces to safeguarding the morals of the Catholic troops. Its success convinced Burke and his supporters of the necessity of retaining such a national organization during peacetime to act as a lobby for Catholic interests in Washington and to advise bishops on legislation pending before state governments.[1]

Burke and Muldoon, who was the episcopal liaison with the archbishops, both now set about to design a permanent organization to promote Catholic welfare. Their movement received impetus at the celebration of the Golden Jubilee of

---

[1] Elizabeth McKeown: *The National Bishops' Conference: An Analysis of Its Origins,* in: Catholic Historical Review 66 (1980) 565–575; Ellis: *Gibbons,* II, 293–297.

Gibbons' episcopate on February 20, 1919, which was held at the Catholic University. The cardinal was the last surviving participant of the First Vatican Council and of the Third Plenary Council; he was, in fact, the senior bishop in the universal Church. Benedict XV sent as his representative to the celebration Archbishop Bonaventura Cerretti, Secretary of the Congregation for the Extraordinary Affairs of the Church. Noting the pope's neutrality during the war, Cerretti called on the American hierarchy to unite for the work of peace, particularly in the areas of education and social justice. Gibbons immediately appointed a committee of three archbishops and four bishops, including Muldoon, Schrembs, and Russell, to devise a proposal for complying with the pope's wishes. The proposal, submitted to the bishops assembled the next day, called for an annual meeting of the entire hierarchy and for a standing committee appointed by the bishops to coordinate Catholic activities between meetings. Benedict XV gave his approval to what would become known as the National Catholic Welfare Council on April 10, 1919.[2]

In notifying the bishops of the papal approval of the new organization, Gibbons noted that because of the favor he had enjoyed in the hierarchy and of the location of Washington within his archdiocese, he alone had been responsible for dealing with the government and for some time had been convinced of the need for "such a committee which with adequate authority and the aid of sub-committees could accomplish more than any individual, however able or willing he might be". The American Church, he argued, "has been suffering from a lack of a unified force" and needed to enter the political process to prevent the passage of hostile laws.[3] In response to Gibbons' call, nearly one hundred bishops met at the Catholic University on September 24, 1919, to consider the proposals to be presented by the bishops of the War Council.

At the meeting, Muldoon proposed that the new Welfare Council be composed of an executive committee of seven prelates who would supervise five permanent departments: education, social action, the laity, press, and home and foreign missions. These departments under the executive committee would speak for the hierarchy and represent Catholic interests between the annual meetings of the bishops. There was immediate opposition to the proposal. Bishop Charles McDonnell of Brooklyn objected that it would allow one bishop to intrude into the internal diocesan affairs of another, which was a violation of canon law; he feared that the administrative committee would dictate policy to the rest of the hierarchy. He implied, moreover, that the pope's letter of approval may have

---

[2] MCKEOWN: *Bishops' Conference*, pp. 575–576.

[3] ANCWC, War Council File, Gibbons to the American Bishops, Baltimore, May 1, 1919, in: MC-KEOWN: *Bishops' Conference*, pp. 576–577.

been a forgery. Supporting McDonnell's position were Cardinal O'Connell and Archbishop Messmer. In favor of accepting Muldoon's report were Edward J. Hanna, Mundelein, John Glennon of St. Louis and James Keane of Dubuque. The bishops postponed the discussion of financing the organization and voted to establish the NCWC. They then elected an administrative committee consisting of Hanna as Chairman, Archbishops Dennis Dougherty of Philadelphia and Austin Dowling of St. Paul and Bishops Muldoon, J. Regis Canevin of Pittsburgh, Russell and Schrembs, who had been transferred from Toledo to Cleveland. John Burke was chosen to be secretary as he had been of the old War Council.[4]

The New York Succession and Other New Figures in the Hierarchy

Much of the peace which seemed to prevail during this period was due to the presence of Gibbons, whose death William O'Connell seemed eagerly to await so that he would be the senior cardinal. Indeed O'Connell may have been trying to engineer a plan to increase his prominence in American affairs. On September 17, 1918, Cardinal Farley died. Two months later, Irish-Americans held a rally at Madison Square Garden in New York to support the movement for Irish independence in the forthcoming British elections. Since the See of New York was vacant, O'Connell was invited to speak. In his view, the primary purpose of the First World War was to gain Irish freedom.[5] John J. Dunn, chancellor of the archdiocese and later auxiliary bishop, described the scene: "The centre of attraction naturally was the Czar of all the Russias and he sure did look the part. Dressed in full uniform and with his usual bearing of lofty virtue and pained tolerance of plebeian conditions, he stood out the central figure in the moving drama. The preparations for his reception, however, were not up to the part he played. Someone missed his cue and as a consequence, his Eminence was ushered into the bar room, which had been spoken of as the reception room." Dunn thought that "his presence [was] impressive just as an elephant is impressive", and that "there would never be demand for his presence outside Boston, where they receive anything and everything that bears the stamp of learning. He reads like a dictionary and talks like a high priced phonograph, – you know I have a victrola and can, therefore, judge".[6] What Dunn was concerned about was the rumor that O'Connell would be transferred to New York.

How serious was any intention on O'Connell's part to be transferred to New

---

[4] *Ibid.,* 579–580; ELLIS: *Gibbons,* II, 298–308.
[5] *New York Times,* Dec. 11, 1918.
[6] AANY, O-6, Dunn to John J. Donovan, New York, Dec. 11, 1918.

York is unknown. He did, however, write to Cardinal Gasparri about the New York succession sometime early in 1919. The man appointed, he said, had to have more than "amiability and piety" in order to arrest the deterioration of the previous twenty years, "the chief cause of which has been that those who were in office there had no powerful voice which could be heard throughout the country". If "the right man" were not chosen, he continued, "it will be nothing short of a catastrophe for the Church in America", for Rome now had the opportunity "to fill the See with a personage who must be a directing force in the moral life of the whole nation, for after all New York is the metropolis of America". He was, he assured Gasparri, writing "in a most disinterested way", but "the people are expecting the appointment of a Prelate who will stand well above the ordinary".[7] It would be reading too much into this letter to suggest that O'Connell himself wanted the post, but he mentioned no candidates and the description he gave of "the right man" fitted his own self-image.

Whatever may have been the possibility of O'Connell's being transferred to New York, on March 10, 1919, Patrick Hayes, Auxiliary Bishop of New York and a member of the episcopal committee of the War Council, was appointed Archbishop of New York. Almost immediately, O'Connell wrote him apparently denying any attempts to have himself transferred to New York and asking for full harmony in the hierarchy. Hayes replied that he had indeed heard various rumors, but paid them no heed since he was engaged with the war work. He added: "Some of our Irish leaders here, of the radical type (I learned only recently) seem to have been responsible for using your Eminence's name in a way, I know, you would not sanction, in connection with the vacancy in New York". He concluded by promising in an almost subservient fashion "the unity of purpose and harmony of action you desire", for he remembered the scandal of the open breach within the hierarchy over the school question in the 1890s.[8]

Whatever may have been O'Connell's desires for being transferred to New York, there is a striking parallel between the New York Irish protests in 1918 and the earlier Boston Italian petitions which helped bring him to the coadjutorship. Hayes, on the other hand, had important supporters within the American hierarchy. His old schoolmate from Manhattan College, Mundelein, admitted that "I did consistently and perhaps persistently advocate your appointment to the New York vacancy", even though he ordinarily favored bringing in a bishop from outside. He assured the new archbishop that he had "no critics out here in the West, but only well-wishers (whatever you may have in the east) ...".[9] It is, of course,

---

[7] AABo, O'Connell to Gasparri, Boston, n.d., but sometime after Jan. 20, 1919 (copy).

[8] AABo, M-1498, Hayes to O'Connell, New York, Mar. 28, 1919; a draft of a slightly different version is in AANY.

[9] AANY, Mundelein to Hayes, Chicago, Apr. 20, 1919.

impossible to determine whether Mundelein was alluding to O'Connell and the Irish.

Yet O'Connell and the radical Irish continued to be a problem for Hayes. A year after his installation, he wrote to Cerretti: "As you know, I found, on becoming archbishop, the Irish situation a very delicate and difficult one, – due no doubt to the disappointment experienced by a few radicals who have little regard for the Church, but who were hoping for the transfer of Boston to this See. At the very outset of my administration, even at the risk of doing something very unpopular, I had to assert my authority as archbishop with regard to the use of the pulpit for Irish political propaganda. Some of our priests also were identified and presiding at very radical meetings which approved Bolshevism etc."[10] It is difficult to see how Hayes could mix together radical Irishmen with Bolsheviks, but it is clear that he did feel O'Connell was an irritation. O'Connell would soon have a chance to play his last grand act on the national scene, but then he overplayed his role and ceased to be a national leader. Hayes, for his part, would be a pastoral bishop, not concerned with assuming national leadership, and would win the epithet "Cardinal of Charity".

The year 1918 was eventful in terms of restructuring the American hierarchy. On June 27, John Keane, who had already resigned the See of Dubuque in 1911, died; his successor was James J. Keane. On September 25, John Ireland died to be replaced on March 10, 1919, the same day Hayes was named to New York, by Austin Dowling. St. Paul was never again to assume the national prominence it had enjoyed through the personality of the "Consecrated Blizzard of the Northwest". Of the old liberals, only Gibbons and Denis O'Connell held on, and the latter's age now made it impossible for him to realize his goal of succeeding his friend in Baltimore. New men, Roman-trained and Roman in orientation, were taking up the leadership. On May 1, Dennis Dougherty was transferred from Buffalo to Philadelphia. He was popular in Roman circles, but never sought to extend his influence beyond Philadelphia. On March 7, 1921, he was named a cardinal and for another two weeks the American Church again had three cardinals. On March 24, however, the old order came to an end. Cardinal James Gibbons died at the age of 86. As was the case of St. Paul, Baltimore received an archbishop who was pastoral but not a national leader, Michael J. Curley, former Bishop of St. Augustine, Florida. With Gibbons' death, the stage was set for O'Connell, as the senior cardinal, to make his bid for national leadership.

Hardly had O'Connell assumed his new role, however, when he seemed depressed. He poured out his heart to Merry del Val, whose own fortunes in Rome were falling. "There is", said O'Connell, "all around about an intangible some-

---

[10] AANY, Hayes to Cerretti, New York, Mar. 20, 1919 (copy).

thing which would seem to emanate from too much politics, diplomacy and intrigue – too much mingling with affairs which don't concern us. But thank God it
does not exist around me. How different in the wonderful days of Pio X when the
chief concern was God and when cheap politics and free-masons were kept in
their place. The memory of those days is a rare possession – conditions then were
as near ideal as they ever can be. Will they ever return? For one thing I shall live in
the spirit of that holy time and rate intrigue at its true value – just zero".[11]
O'Connell, of course, was considered by his contemporaries to be a master of intrigue, but apparently that did not count.

Merry del Val was struck at his friend's "realizing from a distance the preva-
lence of too much politics, worldly diplomacy and intrigue that are hardly in
keeping with the lofty ideals of our mission, nor profitable to the best interests of
God and of his Church. Here, alas! we come up against it at every step, all day
and every day." The Roman cardinal was obviously critical of the policies of Benedict XV and Gasparri to work for world peace. "We are drifting", wrote Merry
del Val, and "how far we may drift I dread to think: and how hard it will be later
on to get back to our only safe tracks, if we are to regain what we have lost.
Surely at a time when the world has lost its bearings and is anxiously seeking for
an anchorage which we alone are able to provide, we should not drift ourselves or
appear to juggle with principles, but hold up the lesson of light as God gave it to
us and refrain from the tactics of human politics".[12] The chance to recreate the
Church of Pius X and to cease using "human politics" soon came. On January 22,
1922, Benedict XV died.

Again O'Connell made hasty plans to attend a conclave. Accompanied by
Dougherty, he arrived at the railroad station in Rome on February 6. He had a
smile on his face, which turned to a frown when he was informed that a half-hour
previously, after the sixteenth scrutiny, Achille Ratti, who had just been elected
Pius XI, had given his blessing in St. Peter's. He replaced his smile for waiting
photographers and then was driven off to the Vatican. There he confronted Gasparri, the camerlengo of the conclave, arguing that he could have either given the
Americans some warning of Benedict's failing health or delayed the conclave to
give them time to arrive. There was a certain irony in O'Connell's failure to be
present for the conclave. If the reports are true, on the first ballot Gasparri received twenty-four votes and Merry del Val twenty-three. The vote of O'Connell
would certainly have gone to his friend as would probably that of Dougherty.[13]
It is highly doubtful, however, if this would have been sufficient to swing the

---

[11] AABo, M-850, O'Connell to Merry del Val, Boston, sometime after Oct. 24, 1921 (copy).
[12] AABo, M-850, Merry del Val to O'Connell, Nov. 24, 1921.
[13] WAYMAN: O'Connell, pp. 178–181.

votes of the other cardinals toward Merry del Val, who together with Cardinal Gaetano De Lai represented the old order they had rejected in 1914. O'Connell did, however, win the concession from the new pope that future conclaves would be delayed to allow distant cardinals to arrive.

B. O'CONNELL AND DOUGHERTY WORK FOR THE CONDEMNATION OF THE NCWC

Even before the death of Benedict, O'Connell, probably in conjunction with Dougherty, had contrived a plot to thrust him into the position of national leadership left vacant by Gibbons' death. The American Church had virtually meant Cardinal Gibbons. The Vatican consulted him on all American affairs and through him went most correspondence with the Holy See. He was in fact, though not in name, the Primate of the American Church. But to assume his role O'Connell had first to undo some of Gibbons' actions, notably the NCWC.

As Dougherty was leaving Rome after the conclave, he was handed a decree of the Consistorial Congregation, signed by De Lai and dated February 25, ordering the NCWC to disband immediately. The administrative committee met in a special session at Schrembs' residence in Cleveland on April 6. All were present except Hanna and they elected to send a cablegram to Pius XI saying that it would be impossible to cease operations with the federal government, especially in regard to immigration and Russian relief, and asking that the decree of the Consistorial not be published until a representation could be made. Gasparri cabled back the necessary permission. Next they delegated Schrembs to take the case of the NCWC personally to Rome.[14]

Late on the night of April 25, the committee met in Washington. All the members were present, except Schrembs who had left that morning for New York on his way to Rome. They resolved to consult with the bishops on the Board of Trustees of the Catholic University and propose that a petition be sent to Rome asking for the suspension of the decree and giving reasons for continuing the NCWC. The next day, they met with the trustees, except Cardinal Dougherty, who absented himself soon after the meeting began, to keep an appointment with Bonzano. The bishops present unanimously supported the petition to Rome. The committee then went to see Bonzano who said the decree had been issued without his knowledge or consultation. The committee then resolved to circulate to the rest of the hierarchy for additional signatures the petition already signed by the

---

[14] ANCWC, Administrative Board, Apr. 6, 1922, pp. 32–33; Apr. 25, p. 34.

university trustees.[15] Finally, at a meeting on April 27, the administrative committee resolved to have the pertinent documents translated into Italian by Filippo Bernardini, professor of canon law at the Catholic University, a consultant to the apostolic delegate, and also Cardinal Gasparri's nephew. They then entrusted the documentation to Archbishop Henry Moeller of Cincinnati who was to join Schrembs in Rome.[16]

As the administrative committee of the NCWC mobilized to prevent its condemnation, it was no secret who was behind the decree. Immediately after the meeting of the committee on April 6, one of its members, Bishop Louis Walsh of Portland, gave his "personal opinion" to Hayes that "this Decree is a dangerous underhand blow from Boston, aided by Philadelphia, who both realized at our last meeting that they could not control the Bishops of this country and they secured the two chief powers of the Consistorial, Cardinals De Lai and Del Val [sic] to suppress all common action". Walsh believed that if both Hayes and Curley took "a firm and clear stand to vindicate the honor and rightful influence of the hierarchy of our country, they will have the other Archbishops and Bishops of the country behind them and give a fine and perhaps really needed object lesson". The Cardinal of Boston, according to the bishop's information, had managed in Rome to discount some of the charges made against his nephew, Monsignor James P. O'Connell, who had served as his chancellor and had left the priesthood. Having vindicated himself in Rome, thought Walsh, "perhaps he will attempt to turn the tide over here and call to account some of his hierarchical opponents, hence perform some more ecclesiastical acrobatic stunts, but, as far as I am concerned he is welcome to begin anywhere and at any time in open or secret session, and then *videbimus*".[17]

Walsh had accurately summarized the fears of the majority of the American bishops that O'Connell would impose himself on them as the sole representative of Roman authority. On May 3, the cardinal wrote Muldoon asking for an explanation for the use of the term "consternation" at the "condemnation" of the NCWC. Against Archbishop Dowling's advice not to answer, Muldoon responded on May 22, saying that the news reports of a condemnation were false and that there was indeed consternation among both the bishops and the laity. No bishop had seen fit to publish the decree, Muldoon noted, and information gleaned from the National Conferences of Catholic Women and Men showed the

---

[15] *Ibid.*, Apr. 26, 1922, pp. 35–36.

[16] *Ibid.*, Apr. 27, 1922, p. 36. For the text of this petition, see Elizabeth McKeown: *Apologia for an American Catholicism: The Petition and Report of the National Catholic Welfare Council to Pius XI, April 25, 1922,* in: Church History 43 (1974) 514–528.

[17] AANY, Q-9, Walsh to Hayes, n.p., Apr. 9, 1922.

confusion among the laity that the organization, blessed by Benedict XV, was now condemned.[18]

In the meantime, Archbishop Bonzano had been requested by De Lai to seek Dougherty and O'Connell's opinions regarding the suspension of the decree.[19] Dougherty replied that the Holy See should not rescind its condemnation, but should empower the Welfare Council or a committee of bishops "to continue such works only that cannot, without discredit or injury to the Church, cease at once". More particularly, he said, the decree forbade the annual meetings of the hierarchy because they violated canon law and "it would, therefore, be a sign of weakness on the part of the Holy See if it were now to reverse its ruling". More strongly than the meetings of the bishops he opposed the Welfare Council itself for it was a "small group of bishops, priests and laymen" who "have been usurping the place of the hierarchy". Furthermore, with the knowledge of only one or two members of the Welfare Council, "laymen have been appointed at extravagant salaries to do work which, in some instances, is of very little importance to Religion", particularly the establishment of a press department. Finally, he complained about laymen issuing statements on education, which many bishops condemned, and about John A. Ryan, director of the Social Action Department, having "published works which I know many of the bishops would not sponsor". He concluded that "from what I could gather at the meeting of the University Trustees, those who wish to suspend the Decree so act more because their pride has been hurt, than for the good of Religion".[20]

O'Connell's reply to Bonzano cannot be found, but he also communicated directly to both Merry del Val and De Lai. To the latter he wrote that "the *group*" was making all the commotion "in order to annul the wise and just decree abolishing the famous N.C.W.C. great in pretense and gigantic in cost". But, he continued:

"I hope and remain certain that Your Eminence and the other Roman authorities will not allow yourselves to be *intimidated* by this 'bluff'.

"The fact is that the telegram they sent to Card. Gasparri is nothing else than an attempt at intimidation – by asserting certain phrases which are a *long way from the truth*. They speak in that telegram of the 'consternation of America'. The people feel no disturbance at all as a consequence of the decree, do not know that such a decree exists, and do not care at all. The 'consternation' is found among

---

[18] AABo, Muldoon to O'Connell, Rockford, Ill., May 22, 1922; John B. SHEERIN: *Never Look Back: The Career and Concerns of John J. Burke,* New York 1975, p. 71.

[19] AABo, Bonzano to O'Connell, Washington, May 4, 1922; AAP, Bonzano to Dougherty, Washington, May 4, 1922.

[20] AAP, Dougherty to Bonzano, Philadelphia, May 5, 1922 (copy).

those who have to render an account of the immense sums they have thrown away on huge salaries and futile and useless works.

"Now they are taking a 'plebiscite' among the bishops in order to annul the force of the decree. The customary maneuver demonstrates again more evidently the wisdom of the decree. Today we are in full 'Democracy, Presbyterianism, and Congregationalism'.

"If this maneuver succeeds, good-by to the authority of the Roman congregations. We will make all the laws and decrees through means of 'plebiscites', a method which naturally has more popularity, the idol of the day.

"And now it seems more than ever that this N.C.W.C. shows more clearly that not only does it tend little by little to weaken hierarchical authority and dignity, but also wishes to put into operation the same tactics against the Consistorial.

"It is incredible that Rome does not see the danger of conceding today in order to have to concede *much more tomorrow.*

"Your Eminence will see in the letter to the Delegate my position which I am certain will be also that of Rome. In the meantime, here I say not a word. The plebiscite certainly will have many names of *those who profit.* But Your Eminence is there and watches out for God and the Faith in Rome. I am nothing, but I am here and faithful".[21]

O'Connell seems almost to have regarded himself as a *legatus natus.* As the senior American cardinal, he saw himself as at the apex of a hierarchical pyramid in contrast to the more horizontal structure favored by the majority of other American bishops – a structure which retained vestiges of the earlier American tradition of collegiality.

In the meantime, Schrembs was on his way to Rome both for his *ad limina* visit and to present the case for the NCWC. In Paris, he met Cerretti, who was then nuncio to France. The archbishop reinforced the suspicion that O'Connell and Dougherty were responsible for the condemnation and promised his assistance. In Rome, Schrembs had the first of several audiences with Pius XI who assured him that he had not fully understood the meaning of the decree of the Consistorial Congregation, but that it had been presented for his signature as unfinished business from the pontificate of Benedict XV. Schrembs also found that the fear of schism – the specter of Americanism – seemed to have swayed the Consistorial Congregation in accepting O'Connell and Dougherty's protest against the NCWC. The condemnation, moreover, reflected the tension between Gasparri and the cardinals favorable to the policies of Pius X, notably Merry del Val, De Lai, William Van Rossum, and Pompili.[22] Indeed, the opposition against Gas-

---

[21] AABo, O'Connell to De Lai, Boston, May 10, 1922 (copy); the letter to Merry del Val of the same date is slightly briefer, but covers the same arguments.

[22] SHEERIN: *Burke,* pp. 72–74.

parri was so great that summer that Pius XI sent him a letter of support, a copy of which the cardinal sent to O'Connell.[23]

Schrembs, who had been joined by Moeller late in May, now began canvassing Roman officials. At an audience with the pope on May 30, he presented the petition of the bishops in favor of the NCWC, signed by ninety percent of the hierarchy, including all the archbishops except O'Connell, Dougherty, and James Keane of Dubuque. Schrembs then spoke with Father Vladimir Ledochowski, General of the Jesuits, who said that many of the cardinals, but especially Merry del Val, continued to find modernism everywhere. Cardinal Tommaso Pio Boggiani, O.P., a member of the Consistorial Congregation, said he had not heard of the decree before it was published, but he remained somewhat sceptical until he saw as one of the signators of the petition his protégé, John T. McNicholas, O.P., then Bishop of Duluth. To win over Gasparri, the Americans seemed to have relied on Bernardini. The problem remained De Lai. When the cardinal told Schrembs that one objection to the NCWC was the size of the American hierarchy, the bishop sharply retorted that Rome's mentality was that it was easier to deal with bishops individually than with an entire hierarchy.[24]

The petition of the overwhelming majority of the hierarchy and the canvassing in Rome were ultimately successful. Gasparri was won over and on June 20 was instructed by the pope to tell the Consistorial Congregation that he too was in favor of suppressing the decree and of continuing the NCWC. On June 22 the congregation met and decreed that the NCWC was to remain and that the bishops could assemble in September in accordance with instructions soon to be issued.[25] The instructions, dated July 4, 1922, recommended among other things that perhaps the meetings of bishops not take place every year, that attendance at them be voluntary, that decisions of the meetings not be binding and not be in any way construed as emanating from a plenary council, and that the name "Council" in the title of the organization be changed to something like "Committee".[26]

The new decree was one among several signs of O'Connell's declining influence in Rome, but he was not a gracious loser. Bonzano sent the Consistorial Congregation's instructions to O'Connell on August 1, asking for his observations.[27]

---

[23] AABo, Gasparri to O'Connell, Vatican, July 16, 1922. O'Connell said he had already had the letter published in *The Pilot* assuring its dissemination "through the English speaking world". The opposition to Gasparri, he said, was simply the result of being in a high position and of Bolshevism in the Church; O'Connell to Gasparri, Boston, Aug. 7, 1922 (copy).

[24] SHEERIN: *Burke*, pp. 74–78.

[25] *Ibid.*, pp. 78–82.

[26] AABo, Decree of Consistorial Congregation, June 22, with instructions of July 4, 1922.

[27] AABo, Bonzano to O'Connell, Chicago, Aug. 1, 1922.

The cardinal was delighted "to see from this decree that we are to return to the traditional method of meeting, which will now be safeguarded as it should have been from the beginning". He furthermore trusted "that the Bishops will decide to meet not oftener than once in three years". Then he sought the delegate's advice as to "who will call the meeting in September", for he did not "want to overstep my authority in the least measure; neither, on the other hand, do I wish to neglect my duty".[28] Quite clearly O'Connell was still hoping to weaken the force of the decree preserving the NCWC by noting in the instructions the advice that the bishops not meet annually, and the statement that the purpose of the meetings was for friendly consultation and not legislation. But he especially appealed to his role as the senior cardinal in the American Church. Bonzano responded that according to the instructions those who had charge of the meeting were to communicate the agenda before time to each bishop and the "chairman of the meeting was to be whoever had the right according to canon law". This, Bonzano thought, clearly gave O'Connell the right to convoke the meeting and he further believed that this was the intention of the administrative committee.[29]

On August 11 and 12, the administrative committee met in Chicago to draw up the agenda for the meeting scheduled for September 27 and 28. It sent telegrams informing O'Connell and Dougherty of the dates, but before adjourning had received no reply from O'Connell. After the committee had left Chicago, Muldoon received a telegram O'Connell had addressed to Hanna, which read: "Dates acceptable to me. Question is now who will call meeting." Muldoon communicated this to the members of the committee who resolved that the letter convoking the meeting would be sent out over O'Connell's name.[30]

The next crisis developed over the proper title for the NCWC. At its Chicago meeting the executive committee had suggested that, if a change in title were necessary, "Conference" be substituted for "Council", on the grounds that "the instructions of July 4th use this word".[31] The instructions had, however, suggested the word "Committee" which was O'Connell's next point of attack. At their meeting on September 28, the bishops discussed the matter and Bishop Walsh of Portland made the motion which was carried that the title be changed to the National Catholic Welfare Conference. O'Connell wrote De Lai protesting this action.[32] In his reply De Lai said Pius XI had read O'Connell's letter and was disturbed. He concluded that "The Holy Father's mind and my own is that in

---

[28] AABo, O'Connell to Bonzano, Boston, Aug. 5, 1922 (copy).
[29] AABo, Bonzano to O'Connell, Washington, Aug. 9, 1922.
[30] ANCWC, Administrative Committee, Aug. 11–12, 1922, pp. 37–43.
[31] *Ibid.,* p. 39.
[32] ANCWC, Minutes of Bishops' Meeting, Sept. 27–28, 1922, pp. 6–7.

place of Council, the Welfare [sic] should take the name Committee". He then asked O'Connell to consult Dougherty and report back to him.[33] O'Connell immediately passed on this information to Dougherty and added "the few who seem to be running this machine – especially at present – Muldoon and Walsh especially resent even a suggestion about any change – even of the name …".[34] Dougherty agreed and added some ammunition of his own. He recounted a conversation he had once had with Burke and Edward A. Pace of the NCWC's education department in which "they pertinaciously upheld that the 'Welfare Council' is the hierarchy; which I indignantly denied. The few bishops who constituted the NCWC should therefore properly be designated a committee".[35]

Armed with this assurance of his fellow cardinal, O'Connell wrote Archbishop Hanna a sharp letter demanding that a distinction be made between the meetings of the bishops and the executive committee and that the name National Catholic Welfare Committee be used to designate only the latter. He felt that the refusal of a few bishops "to change the name to anything but 'Conference'" expressed an "attitude" which "seemed to me rather typical". O'Connell continued: "I have now received a communication from the Holy See in which it is plainly said that the Holy Father himself wishes the word 'Committee' to take the place of 'Council' or 'Conference' or any other word. This is what might have been well expected by those who could not see that a polite recommendation to any or all of us Bishops is equivalent to a command".[36] O'Connell then reported all he had done to De Lai.[37] But even on this issue O'Connell was not to be successful. It is somewhat mysterious that, if De Lai was truthful in saying that Pius XI wanted the change in name, the pope never seems to have insisted on it. The title National Catholic Welfare Conference continued to designate the standing secretariat of the American bishops with its various departments representing various aspects of national Catholic concern until the agency was reorganized after the Second Vatican Council as the United States Catholic Conference. The bishops likewise continued to meet annually and assumed the corporate title of the National Conference of Catholic Bishops in 1966.

The failure to have the NCWC condemned was O'Connell's last grand act on the national stage. After 1922 he concerned himself more and more with strictly diocesan affairs. Neither he nor Dougherty contributed to the National Catholic

---

[33] AABo, De Lai to O'Connell, Rome, Nov. 18, 1922.
[34] AAP, O'Connell to Dougherty, Boston, Dec. 13, 1922.
[35] AAP, Dougherty to O'Connell, Philadelphia, Dec. 15, 1922 (copy).
[36] AABo, O'Connell to Hanna, Boston, Dec. 16, 1922 (copy).
[37] AABo, O'Connell to De Lai, Boston, Dec. 22, 1922, (copy).

Welfare fund.[38] But neither gave up the fight gracefully. O'Connell was angry at the re-election of the seven bishops who composed the administrative board of the NCWC at the bishops' meeting in 1923 which he saw as a plot of his old enemies, the Sulpicians. Writing to Dougherty, he said:

"The usual bombast on the part of *Dowling, Walsh* and *Muldoon* flooded the reports and the interminable orations. The first two were professors (or at least that was the title) with the Sulpicians here, and were made by the Sulpicians. Muldoon has always been a great favorite with them and has always been slated for higher honors, which however do not materialize. That is distinctly the central force of all the planning and scheming. Hanna and [Edmund] Gibbons [Bishop of Albany] are merely tolerated but count for nothing. It is unquestionably the continuation in a condensed form of Sulpicianism contra mundum but especially contra nos.

"Generally the little clique work in secret and in the dark. But Fenelon [*sic*, John F. Fenlon, S.S., secretary of the administrative committee] is beginning to give the trick away.

"It will interest you to know that while the Delegate was addressing the meeting and Y.E. and I were busy there, Fenelon seated in the corridor outside was regaling my Chancellor Mgr. Haberlin and Waring of N Y of the *duplicity* of the *Roman Curia* illustrating his remarks by several recent instances. He finished his instructive discourse by these words – 'You can make Rome do what ever you want if you get a *crowd* behind you'. This from an officer of N.C.W.C. and from the *Spiritual* Director of the University. The centre of all these things, say what they will, is S. Sulpice and the purpose is obvious – to keep the power in their hands by demolishing us and our prestige. We are obviously intruders and must be kept in our place – by the crowd.

"I am genuinely and eagerly desirous of being and acting in all things in harmony and unity with Y.E. If I could know before these or similar meetings in which we have to take a stand just what was in the mind of Y.E. it will be of great help. For with S. Sulpice we can see only an enemy not merely personal but in principle. And any sign of lack of unity between us would of course only strengthen them and their clique. I have entire confidence in Y.E. and your judgement. I have absolutely none in them, their principles or rather their schemes. We know them and they will never change. Fenelon was clearly voicing them, not originating them".[39]

---

[38] AAP, List of Allotments and Payments to the NCW Fund for 1920–1925; cf. also Dowling to Dougherty, St. Paul, Aug. 27, 1922, Nov. 23, 1922, Dec. 12, 1923, and Nov. 24, 1924, and Dougherty to Dowling, Philadelphia, Aug. 30, 1922, Dec. 1, 1922, Dec. 17, 1923, and Nov. 28, 1924.

[39] AAP, O'Connell to Dougherty, Boston, Oct. 2, 1923.

Still another issue annoyed both Dougherty and O'Connell. At the last session of the bishops' meeting in 1923, they discussed the matter of Ruthenian Catholics and asked Hanna, the chairman of the administrative committee, to present their sentiments to the apostolic delegate. The delegate asked that the bishops who were concerned express their opinions to him particularly in regard to whether an Oriental-rite bishop with full jurisdiction should be appointed or whether some other arrangement should be made. Hanna then communicated this to the hierarchy.[40] Dougherty replied that since he was a member of the Congregation for the Oriental Church he should not express his opinion. Moreover, he believed "that the Holy See would prefer to be entirely at liberty in the matter and not be in any way pressed from without to take a course of action which it has hitherto not deemed advisable".[41] To O'Connell he wrote that the duty of sending out such a letter "would devolve upon the ranking Cardinal".[42] O'Connell was livid. The bishops had designated him to lay the matter before the delegate, he wrote, and he had done so by letter. But more to the point: "Archbishop Hanna had absolutely no business in this matter at all, and I shall write this to the Delegation. It is simply a trick, and a contemptible one at that, to attempt to force the recognition of the N.C.W.C. by the Delegation, which has never been given before".[43] This protest, too, would fail and in the years to come the Holy See relied more heavily on the NCWC for influencing American affairs. Some years after he undertook his mission to Rome on the NCWC's behalf, Schrembs noted to Giuseppe Pizzardo, then in the Secretariat of State, that the decision of the United States Supreme Court in favor of the right to parochial schools in Pierce *vs.* Society of Sisters was "the best vindication of the National Catholic Welfare Conference".[44] The Holy See soon acknowledged even more benefit from the NCWC by using it as an agency for influencing the United States government, notably in the case of regularizing the status of the Church in Mexico.

C. THE RISE OF CARDINAL MUNDELEIN

O'Connell's decline from national power was evident after 1922. The other men who rose to power were also Roman in orientation, but they reflected different Roman patrons for their advancement. As Romanization increased, so did re-

---

[40] AAP, Hanna to Dougherty, Washington, Oct. 6, 1923.
[41] AAP, Dougherty to Hanna, Philadelphia, Oct. 16, 1923 (copy).
[42] AAP, Dougherty to O'Connell, Philadelphia, Oct. 16, 1923 (copy).
[43] AAP, O'Connell to Dougherty, Boston, Oct. 17, 1923.
[44] ADC, Schrembs to Pizzardo, Cleveland, n.d., but sometime in 1925 or early 1926 (copy).

gionalization as the formerly all-important eastern sees gave way to the rising mid-western ones. Among the Catholic University trustees to sign the petition in favor of the NCWC was Archbishop George Mundelein of Chicago. His signature may well have influenced his close friend Giovanni Bonzano, who returned to Rome to become a cardinal in December, 1922. On March 24, 1924, Mundelein, too, together with Hayes, was named a cardinal. It was a sign of the growing importance of the mid-west and Mundelein turned it to his advantage to assume national leadership among the hierarchy. No sooner had the first cardinal in the west received his red hat than he arranged to have the first international Eucharistic Congress held in the United States scheduled for his see. On the eve of the event, Filippo Bernardini sarcastically remarked to Dougherty that "the beautiful soul of Cardinal O'Connell like the dove of the Canticles hat sent forth a sweet lament".[45]

Mundelein spared no trappings for making the congress as splendid as possible. He arranged for the cardinals arriving from Europe to be housed in New York as guests of Hayes. From there they would all be conveyed to Chicago by a special train provided by the Pullman Company. Each car was to be painted cardinalatial red and bear the name of the pope, cardinal legate "and other well-known sons of Holy Church of every grade". The train would carry no one but cardinals and their suites with the only laymen being those appointed to accompany the legate. It would schedule its arrival in various cities to coincide with contingents of priests and laity who would be unable to attend the congress itself. It would "probably be a unique demonstration of Catholic faith, and incidentally Catholic strength, in the eastern and middle-west section of our country", Mundelein wrote Dougherty coaxing him to join the trip.[46] But Dougherty was not to be outdone by the younger prince of the west. The Pennsylvania Railroad, he replied, had already placed at his disposal a special car to and from Chicago.[47]

The Eucharistic Congress held from June 18 to June 25 was partly a show of the importance of the growing American mid-west in universal Catholicism and partly an exhibit of the strength of Catholicism in the United States which was then experiencing a resurgence of anti-Catholicism, notably in the Ku Klux Klan, which would be fully manifest in the election of 1928. Cardinal Bonzano, Mundelein's old friend, was named by Pius XI to be the legate for the congress. He was received with full courtesy by both civil and ecclesiastical officials in New York on June 11. On June 16, the "Cardinals' Special", seven cars all painted red, left New York for Chicago. On board besides Bonzano were nine cardinals, two

---

[45] AAP, Bernardini to Dougherty, Washington, Apr. 24, 1926.
[46] AAP, Mundelein to Dougherty, Chicago, May 19, 1926.
[47] AAP, Dougherty to Mundelein, Philadelphia, May 24, 1926 (copy).

apostolic delegates, four archbishops, and seven bishops. Altogether there were seventy-four passengers, including only four laymen. It had the right of way a-cross the country to its destination at a special station built at Michigan Boulevard and 11th Street in Chicago.[48] The reception on June 17 in Chicago was tumultu-ous. Never before had ten cardinals been assembled in the United States and more were yet to come. That evening Dougherty was due to arrive from Philadelphia and the next morning O'Connell with 500 pilgrims from Boston arrived by a spe-cial boat from Buffalo.[49] At the opening session on June 18, James J. Davis, Sec-retary of Labor, presented the greetings of Calvin Coolidge, President of the Un-ited States. Next Samuel Insull, a Chicago magnate, spoke in behalf of non-Catholics.[50] The celebration drew one million people, a Catholic gathering not to be surpassed until the visit of Pope John Paul II to the United States in 1979. The closing ceremonies took place at St. Mary of the Lake Seminary in Mundelein, Il-linois, where Mundelein had begun his impressive seminary of Georgian-style buildings around an artificial lake.[51] The seminary may have been the realization of Corrigan's hope for establishing a pontifical university under the Jesuits, for Mundelein had it chartered as a pontifical faculty and placed under the direction of the Jesuits.

Mundelein was quite conscious of proving to Rome the uniqueness and impor-tance of the mid-west – he sent Pius XI a gift of $1,000,000 to build the new Ur-ban College of Propaganda on the Janiculum in Rome. At the same time, his prominence in the American hierarchy was one sign of the growing regionalism which flowed from Romanization. But, as much as anything, the Eucharistic Congress was a statement to the American people of the faith and strength of American Catholics. This strength was to be of critical importance in the settling of one of the most threatening situations confronting the whole Church – the per-secution of the Catholic Church in Mexico. During Bonzano's visit, he had told President Calvin Coolidge "that the Vatican hoped to see the United States de-liver Mexico from President Calles".[52]

D. MEXICO AND THE *MODUS VIVENDI*

Since the Mexican Revolution had begun in 1911, it had become more and more anti-clerical. Because the government had initially confiscated American

---

[48] *New York Times,* June 17, 1926.

[49] *Ibid.,* June 18, 1926.

[50] *Ibid.,* June 19, 1926.

[51] *Ibid.,* June 25, 1926.

[52] In: M. Elizabeth Ann RICE: *The Diplomatic Relations between the United States and Mexico, as Affected by the Struggle for Religious Liberty in Mexico, 1925–1929,* Washington 1959, p. 93.

property, the United States seemed for a time to be on the brink of war with Mexico. The advent of the First World War, however, caused the American hysteria to die down; with peace, the pleas for mediation or intervention were muted by the growing anti-Catholic sentiment in the United States.[53]

Mexico's new constitution in 1917 was decidedly anti-Catholic, but only gradually was it vigorously enforced. President Álvaro Obregon (1920–1924) expelled the apostolic delegate, Bishop Ernesto Filippi. President Plutarco Elias Calles (1924–1928) then began the persecution of the Church in earnest. Bishops and foreign-born priests were banished; many native-born priests were imprisoned. Partly in the belief that an American citizen would be immune to Mexican reprisals, the Holy See then named Archbishop George Caruana, a naturalized American citizen of Maltese birth, as apostolic delegate. But his sojourn in Mexico lasted only for a few months in early 1926 before he too was expelled. During his stay, however, he appointed Bishop Pascual Diaz, S.J., of Tobasco to organize a committee of Mexican bishops from whom would emanate all official episcopal statements. Late in 1926, Diaz too was arrested and then deported, and he and other Mexican bishops went into exile in the United States. Diaz took up residence in New York where he could gain access to American government officials. Back in Mexico militant Catholics turned the *Liga de Defensa de la Libertad Religiosa* from peaceful opposition into armed rebellion.[54]

To mediate in the Mexican situation, the Vatican increasingly turned to the American Church. But Catholic sentiment was divided as to what form that mediation should take. Some like Archbishop Curley of Baltimore and the leaders of the Knights of Columbus urged that American Catholics publicly protest against the American government's silence and encouraged armed rebellion in Mexico. Others, like John Burke, the administrative committee of the NCWC, and the majority of Mexican bishops deplored the use of violence. The United States government, for its part, feared that if it made too strong a protest it would have to be ready to invade Mexico. It was in this context that the first overtures toward a solution were made.[55]

For some time, the NCWC had been involved in the Mexican situation. It combatted anti-Catholic propaganda, disseminated by Mexican officials in the United States, by informing the secular press of the true state of the Church in Mexico. It also protested about this propaganda to the State Department, which

---

[53] ELLIS: *Gibbons*, II, 205–221; GAFFEY: *Kelley*, II, 3–57.
[54] See Jean A. MEYER: *The Cristero Rebellion: The Mexican People between Church and State, 1926–1929*, translated by Richard SOUTHERN, Cambridge 1976, and Robert E. QUIRK: *The Mexican Revolution and the Catholic Church: 1910–1929*, Bloomington, Ind. 1973.
[55] SHEERIN: *Burke*, pp. 110–112.

was also being pressured by telegrams sent by the National Council of Catholic Men and the National Council of Catholic Women. It then notified the Holy See of these efforts through the apostolic delegate.[56] At the annual meeting of the hierarchy in September, 1926, the bishops addressed a statement of concern to the Mexican Church.[57] In December, they made the Mexican persecution of the Church the subject of their pastoral letter to American Catholics.[58] For these efforts, the NCWC received a letter of commendation from Cardinal Donato Sbarretti, Prefect of the Congregation of the Council and former secretary to the American apostolic delegation.[59] The stage was now set for the NCWC's more direct involvement in the Mexican situation, through its administrative secretary, Father John Burke.

In October, 1927, Dwight Morrow was named the new American ambassador to Mexico. Before taking up his post he had been approached by Cardinal Hayes, Father Burke, and several laymen, Nicholas Brady, John D. Ryan, and Judge Morgan O'Brien, to use his influence to effect a settlement.[60] In November, the administrative committee of the NCWC instructed Burke to meet with both President Coolidge and with Secretary of State Frank Kellogg, but both refused to commit the United States government to an official protest. Kellogg did, however, agree to forward the NCWC protests to the Mexican ambassador. Then in January, 1928, Burke received from Morrow an overture to join him in Mexico City for possible conversations with Calles. At first sceptical about negotiating with the Calles government and about the motivations of the American government, Archbishop Pietro Fumasoni-Biondi, the apostolic delegate, finally gave his approval to Burke's mission.

Burke's own agenda for a settlement was that Calles agree to accept an apostolic delegate and to allow the exiled bishops to return. On April 4, 1928, Burke had his first meeting with Calles, who agreed to the return of the bishops and to an apostolic delegate, provided that he be Mexican. This agreement Burke communicated to Archbishop Leopold Ruiz y Flores, who then presided over a meeting of the Mexican bishops in San Antonio, Texas, where they drafted a proposal similar to the Burke-Calles agreement. On May 17 and 18, Burke and Ruiz met

---

[56] ANCWC, Administrative Committee, Sept. 13, 1926, pp. 111–113.

[57] *Ibid.*, Minutes of Bishops' Meeting, Sept., 1926, pp. 8–9. The text of the letter is given in Raphael M. HUBER (ed.): *Our Bishops Speak: National Pastorals and Annual Statements of the Hierarchy of the United States, 1919–1951,* Milwaukee 1952, pp. 188–189.

[58] Text is in: *ibid.*, pp. 66–97 and Hugh J. NOLAN (ed.): *Pastoral Letters of the American Hierarchy, 1792–1970,* Huntington, Ind. 1971, pp. 262–286.

[59] ANCWC, Administrative Committee, Sbarretti to Hanna, Rome, Feb. 7,1927(translation),p,131.

[60] Wilfrid PARSONS, S.J.: *Mexican Martyrdom,* New York 1936, pp. 102–103; SHEERIN: *Burke,* p. 117.

with Calles and Obregon, the president-elect. Ruiz and Calles then exchanged letters of agreement which were cabled to Fumasoni-Biondi requesting Roman approval. A settlement seemed imminent when, on May 26, the delegate ordered the negotiators back to the United States.[61]

Burke was demoralized. Ruiz headed for Rome and in Paris gave an interview — which he later denied — in which he was reported as saying that Obregon, as Calles had already seen, would need to reconcile the Church with the State. The secret negotiations were now public, just at a time when the settlement was further jeopardized. On July 17, Obregon was assassinated by a staunch Catholic. While Calles blamed the assassination on the clergy universally, Ruiz stated that it was understandable that those whom Obregon had oppressed would retaliate. Bishop Diaz and Archbishop Hanna, chairman of the administrative board of the NCWC, however, deplored the slaying. Burke succeeded in having Calles modify his statement and say that only some priests were responsible. At this juncture, among many, the Vatican's position was incomprehensible. The *Osservatore Romano* published a series of articles claiming that Morrow was only a financial tool for American interests and that Calles had himself engineered Obregon's death in order to increase his own power and to continue the persecution of the Church.[62]

Morrow, understandably confused, wrote to Bishop Diaz, who responded that Fumasoni-Biondi was apostolic delegate both to the United States and to Mexico, that the delegate appointed him as the liaison with the Mexican bishops, and that Burke was the delegate's agent for settling the Mexican situation. Fumasoni-Biondi, for his part, was despondent because, aside from Diaz and Ruiz, none of the other Mexican bishops recognized his authority and the Jesuits, who advised the *Liga Nacional,* were telling Rome to hold out on a settlement. Burke's own role in the negotiations also seems to have come under fire in Rome. At the meeting of the NCWC's administrative committee on November 12, 1928, Archbishop Dowling suggested that the NCWC as such not be involved in further negotiations and that whatever Burke undertook in the future "would be at the specific request of the Apostolic Delegate, inasmuch as the present attitude of the higher authorities in the Church indicated resentment at the intrusion of the American hierarchy into a matter that was not their affair". Burke pointed out, however, that it was "to keep faith with the State Department ... that the N.C.W.C. put itself at the disposition of the Apostolic Delegate".[63]

Since there were no diplomatic relations between the United States and the

---

[61] SHEERIN: *Burke,* pp. 118–130.
[62] *Ibid.,* pp. 130–134.
[63] ANCWC, Administrative Committee, Nov. 12, 1928, p. 168.

Holy See, there was no Vatican official who could have direct and official access to the State Department. Burke, as the secretary of the administrative committee of the NCWC, could act as liaison for American Catholics and the delegation with the State Department.

Calles was due to leave office on November 30, 1928, to be replaced by Portes Gil, who had been elected provisional president. Morrow had still hoped to complete the settlement with Calles, when yet another confusing note was added to the negotiations. As Calles' term was coming to an end, Morrow received word that several months earlier the Vatican had appointed Father Edmund A. Walsh, S.J., of Georgetown University, to negotiate a settlement. While no documentary evidence has yet been found for Walsh's appointment, he was a friend of Pius XI's. But his presence in Mexico City endangered the proceedings. Ultimately the breakthrough came when Gil issued a statement that a religious settlement would be possible if there was good will on both sides. Ruiz publicly commended Gil and offered to confer with him. In consultation with Morrow, Ruiz asked only that there be a promise of religious toleration and not a change in the constitution. The archbishop was then appointed apostolic delegate to Mexico and, together with Diaz, went to Mexico City where, on June 21, 1929, they concluded with Gil the *modus vivendi,* which was fundamentally the agreement which Calles and Burke had reached over a year earlier.[64]

In the settlement of the Mexican situation, temporary though it turned out to be, the NCWC proved to be a valuable asset to the Church. The Vatican, nevertheless, expressed misgivings to Curley about the undue influence it felt Burke had on Fumasoni-Biondi. The archbishop was asked to report on this during his *ad limina* visit in July, 1929. In December, he wrote Cardinal Carlo Perosi, Secretary of the Consistorial Congregation, that all such influence was "grossly exaggerated" and had grown out of the extensive contacts Fumasoni-Biondi had had with Burke during the Mexican "imbroglio". In Curley's mind, Fumasoni-Biondi was wise in making use of Burke, for he "could not very well approach in person high officials of our government". The archbishop made it clear that he felt it necessary to defend the delegate from any charges of "weakness", but on the other hand, he expressed vague reservations about the NCWC as such.[65] Curley, of course, could have been merely voicing his feeling that the NCWC had not been militant enough in calling for direct intervention in Mexico. Yet, he could

---

[64] SHEERIN: *Burke,* pp. 151–152. Sheerin also treats here the confusing role played by Walsh, who, Gasparri said, had only authority to report on Mexican affairs and not to negotiate a settlement. On the role of Morrow and of American diplomacy in this issue, the best study is RICE: *United States and Mexico.*

[65] AAB, Curley to Perosi, Baltimore, Dec. 17, 1929 (copy).

also have been reflecting continued Roman suspicion of the NCWC, which had sought to tread a delicate line in the Mexican situation especially as it became intertwined with the Catholic issue in the presidential election of 1928.

The nomination of Alfred E. Smith, the Catholic Governor of New York, by the Democratic Party placed American Catholics in a delicate position. The issues in the election were manifold. Smith favored the repeal of the constitutional amendment prohibiting the sale of alcohol and thus met the opposition of certain religious groups intent on preserving prohibition. The nation was also experiencing a superficial prosperity and saw no need to change the party in control of the presidency. But these political issues became more charged by Smith's Catholicism. American opponents challenged whether as a Catholic he would not seek the union of Church and State. Mexican propaganda simply added to the growing body of American anti-Catholic literature of the period. Moderates like John Burke and the leadership of the NCWC, therefore, sought to avoid fanning the flames of prejudice which would only be increased by calls for armed intervention or rebellion in Mexico. The Vatican, on the other hand, may well have hoped unrealistically that, if Smith were elected, the United States would intervene in Mexico. This hope may account for Rome's sudden decision to have the delegate recall Burke and Ruiz from Mexico in May, 1928.[66]

Throughout the campaign, however, the bishops remained silent on Smith's candidacy. From archival sources, moreover, there is no mention of the campaign in correspondence between American bishops or between them and the Vatican. Only Dougherty broke this silence in private correspondence with Bernardini. Smith's nomination, he wrote, "had been, generally speaking, well taken throughout the country. His opponents will be the prohibitionists and the ultra-Protestants. He is personally popular; Hoover is not".[67] In November, he reported that rumors were spreading that he, Mundelein, and several southern bishops were in favor of Hoover. "I am convinced", he said, "that there has been concerted movement from the higher-ups among the Republicans to affect the Catholic vote by these representations".[68] But these were private remarks with no influence on the outcome of the election. Smith was overwhelmingly defeated and Catholics were convinced that they would always be second-class citizens, a conviction which was shared by Vatican officials.

Yet the road was already being paved for the full-scale acceptance of Catholics as Americans. Since the days of Gibbons' defense of the Knights of Labor, the

---

[66] On the relationship between the Smith campaign and the Mexican situation, see RICE: *United States and Mexico* p. 152.

[67] AAP, Dougherty to Bernardini, Philadelphia, July 15, 1928 (copy).

[68] AAP, Dougherty to Bernardini, Philadelphia, Nov. 5, 1928 (copy).

American Church had been developing a strong program of social action which would enable it to ally with President Franklin D. Roosevelt's "New Deal". As the nation moved into the decade of the 1930s and recovery from the depression of 1929, Roosevelt increasingly shored up his alliance with Catholics. His policy had international repercussions. First, the Mexican persecution of the Church again broke out in 1932 and some bishops returned to their American exile. American Catholics again brought pressure on the government and sought to counter the anti-Catholic propaganda. In this effort, Bishop Francis C. Kelley of Oklahoma City, founder and first president of the Catholic Church Extension Society, contributed his *Blood-Drenched Altars* and Wilfrid Parsons, S.J., his *Mexican Martyrdom*. In 1935, President Lazaro Cardenas, not wishing to embarrass Roosevelt with his Catholic constituents, called for a less strict interpretation of the constitution of 1917; basically he returned to the Ruiz-Calles agreement of 1929.[69]

The second repercussion was more lasting. As Europe moved toward the Second World War, Roosevelt sought closer relations with the Church and the Vatican sought closer contact with the United States, which it now realized held the balance of power in world affairs.

---

[69] Frank TANNENBAUM: *Mexico, The Struggle for Peace and Bread,* New York 1950, p. 135. Tannenbaum is friendly toward the Mexican revolution, but he makes the American Catholic pressure on Roosevelt monolithic. When Senator William Borah of Idaho, a Protestant, introduced a bill in the Senate calling for an investigation of the persecution in Mexico early in 1935, his bill received the endorsement of Curley, but no support from the NCWC; SHEERIN: *Burke,* pp. 164–171. When Curley attacked Roosevelt for not taking action and the Knights of Columbus held a mass meeting against Roosevelt's refusal to intervene, Archbishop John T. McNicholas of Cincinnati stated that the Knights did not speak for all Catholics; *New York Times,* Mar. 26, July 9, Nov. 4, Nov. 20, 1935. On Kelley, see GAFFEY: *Kelley:* II, 86–92.

CHAPTER X

THE AMERICAN CHURCH, ROOSEVELT AND THE VATICAN

A. CATHOLIC SOCIAL TEACHING: LAYING THE GROUNDWORK FOR RAPPORT WITH ROOSEVELT

1. Two Approaches to Social Justice: John A. Ryan and Charles E. Coughlin

The American Church had almost no area of thought which could be described as liberal, except its attitude toward labor and social questions – an attitude which could be construed as a continuation of the social dimension of Americanism. At the end of the First World War, the administrative committee of the War Council sought to issue a suitable statement on the problems of reconstruction after the war. The members turned to Father John A. Ryan, professor of moral theology at the Catholic University of America. Ryan had prepared a draft for a speech on the topic, but had then laid it aside. He was encouraged to complete it; the committee issued it still in fragmentary form, as "The Bishops' Program for Social Reconstruction". It presented a far-reaching series of proposals, which later became the virtual platform for social reform of the Social Action Department of the NCWC. It called on the government to retain certain wartime agencies, notably the United States Employment Service and the National War Labor Board which supported the rights to a living wage, to organized labor, and to collective bargaining. It asked for government loans to returning servicemen, for prevention of monopolies in commodities, for government regulation of monopolies of privately owned public services, and for heavy taxation of incomes and inheritances. It went on to propose government competition with private industry, if anti-trust laws failed, wider distribution of stock among employees, the elimination of child labor through government taxation, and, while not favoring women in the labor force, equal pay for equal work for both men and women.[1]

---

[1] Francis L. BRODERICK: *Right Reverend New Dealer: John A. Ryan,* New York 1963, pp. 104–106. The Bishops' Program is given in ELLIS: *Documents,* II, 589–603.

The "Program" was issued over the signatures of Bishops Muldoon, Schrembs, Hayes, and Russell. Almost immediately it received the protest of the National Association of Manufacturers as "partisan, pro-labor union, socialistic propaganda".[2] It was subsequently branded by a committee of the New York State Senate investigating seditious activity as emanating from "a certain group in the Catholic Church with leanings toward Socialism".[3]

The author of the pamphlet, John A. Ryan, was not without enemies within the Church. At the inception of the Social Action Department of the NCWC in 1919, he became its director, a post he held until 1944. At the time of the condemnation of the NCWC in 1922, there was some rumor that one cause was Ryan's position on social reform. Perhaps his most bitter opponent was Cardinal O'Connell. In 1924, Ryan supported an amendment to the United States Constitution prohibiting child labor. O'Connell and others saw this as an intrusion of the federal government into the family. It was "Soviet legislation", fumed the cardinal to Archbishop Curley, and its correct interpretation seemed to be "the special privilege of J. A. Ryan, Jane Addams and a few more socialistic teachers and writers". For O'Connell it was a matter either of the hierarchy's abandoning "weakly our duty and turn it all over into the hands of the Ryans ...". Or of demanding "that these servants of the University and paid agents of the N.C.W.C.either cease their crooked and false activities or leave the University and the offices of the N.C.W.C.".[4] Archbishop Curley, who was also Chancellor of the Catholic University, at this point defended Ryan and his fellow workers and adroitly fended off the cardinal.[5]

Controversial though the "Program" and its author may have been in 1919, most of its salient points became legislation under Franklin D. Roosevelt. During the presidential campaign of 1932, the crucial issue was the depression. Ryan, with most of the rest of the country, had given up hope that President Herbert Hoover could restore the economy, but he was unenthusiastic about Roosevelt. Not so Father Charles Coughlin, pastor of the Shrine of the Little Flower in Royal Oak, Michigan. Coughlin had originally broadcast a children's program over a local Detroit radio station, but by 1931 he had his own private network reaching a weekly audience of millions. He amply sprinkled his texts with citations from the papal social encyclicals, but he was neither a theologian nor an economist.

---

[2] Mason to Gibbons, Feb. 25, 1919, quoted by ELLIS: *Documents*, II, 589.
[3] RYAN: *Social Doctrine in Action*, p. 147, quoted *ibid*.
[4] AAB, O'Connell to Curley, Boston, Nov. 2, 1924; see also O'Connell to Curley, Boston, Oct. 24 and Nov. 12, 1924.
[5] AAB, Curley to O'Connell, Baltimore, Nov. 10, 1924 (copy).

Pro-labor, he cast the blame for the depression on the bankers. Basically a populist idealist, he had no practical program.[6]

By April, 1932, he openly endorsed Roosevelt. He even implied in a conversation with Senator David I. Walsh of Massachusetts that Roosevelt "had promised him something for his support".[7] The issue before the country for the rest of the decade was whether Coughlin spoke for the Church. Cardinal O'Connell took the matter in hand in his inimitable way by stating that Coughlin had no authority whatsoever. This provoked the comment from Archbishop McNicholas of Cincinnati that "the blast of Boston about Father Coughlin is very interesting. His Eminence is eminently clever. He is speaking, he says, as a Catholic citizen. He objects to a parish priest speaking beyond the limits of the parish. It is just a bit strange to have him speak as a citizen to all the Bishops and people of the United States on a matter which belongs strictly to episcopal supervision. His words, of course, are those of a Bishop, and he transgresses the very rules that he lays down of speaking to other Bishops and dioceses". There was indeed some confusion, for the American people did not understand the hierarchical structure of the Church and believed that a cardinal — and the senior cardinal at that — somehow had jurisdiction over Coughlin's own bishop. For his own part, McNicholas could not agree with the conservative Senator Walsh that agitation among the poor was dangerous, but he simply felt "fearful of Father Coughlin" who was "not grounded in the fundamentals" of Catholic theology and philosophy.[8]

For the rest of the decade Coughlin would be a worry to the hierarchy, especially since he counted his own bishop among his supporters. Whether there was any agreement between Roosevelt and the priest, however, Coughlin — inaccurately — took credit for Roosevelt's election in 1932. For approximately half of Roosevelt's first term, Coughlin was his ardent supporter — "Roosevelt or Ruin" was his plea to his listeners. But as the president gradually unfolded his programs, Coughlin became increasingly suspicious. He now loosed his venom on Roosevelt and his public criticisms caused concern for the hierarchy.[9] Ryan, on the other hand, initially lukewarm toward Roosevelt, found himself openly espousing the new social programs, so similar to what he had proposed in "The Bishops' Program". The similarity between Catholic social teaching and New Deal legislation forged one of the closest associations between the Church and the government since the days of Ireland and Gibbons in the 1890s. The association was nurtured not only by old leaders in the hierarchy but also by new ones who joined their ranks in paying homage to Roosevelt.

---

[6] Charles J. TULL: *Father Coughlin and the New Deal,* Syracuse 1965, pp. 1–14.

[7] AACi, Noll to McNicholas, Huntington, Ind., Apr. 14, 1932.

[8] AACi, McNicholas to Noll, Cincinnati, Apr. 21, 1932 (copy).

[9] TULL: *Coughlin,* pp. 18–58.

2. *Rise of New Leaders: Francis Spellman, Amleto Cicognani, and Edward Mooney*

On September 8, 1932, Monsignor Francis Spellman was consecrated in St. Peter's Basilica by Cardinal Eugenio Pacelli and was named Auxiliary Bishop of Boston to replace Bishop John Peterson who had been appointed Bishop of Manchester. There was a certain poetic justice in Spellman's new post. After his ordination in Rome in 1916, he served as the vice-chancellor of Boston until O'Connell relegated him to relative obscurity as a member of the staff of *The Pilot*, the archdiocesan paper. But Spellman ably nurtured his Roman contacts. He translated into English two works by his old friend and professor in Rome, Monsignor Francesco Borgongini-Duca. In gratitude for this, early in 1924, the monsignor requested of O'Connell that Spellman be named a papal chamberlain.[10] The cardinal's reply was cold, but not without ironic implications. Spellman, he wrote, did "not yet have a position to be raised to the purple".[11] Spellman, however, now obtained a position which merited the purple.

Well aware of O'Connell's antagonism for him, in 1925, Spellman took advantage of his Roman connections to have himself made director of the Knights of Columbus playgrounds in Rome, subject to the Congregation for the Extraordinary Affairs of the Vatican Secretariat of State. There he continued his friendship with Borgongini-Duca and began one with Monsignor Eugenio Pacelli, whose rise to power he carefully recorded in his diary. For the next seven years, he gained personal experience working in the curia. Late in 1929, he recorded his sorrow at Cardinal Gasparri's having to resign his office and his happiness at the appointment of Pacelli, soon to be made a cardinal, to replace him.[12] With Pacelli's promotion, he continued to enjoy the cardinal's complete confidence. He was a witness to Mussolini and his Fascists' attempts to destroy Catholic action and actual suppression of papal protests. It was Spellman whom Pacelli recommended to Pius XI in the summer of 1931 to smuggle the encyclical against Fascism, *Non abbiamo bisogno,* out of Italy to be published in France.[13]

If O'Connell owed his rise to power to Merry del Val, the priest he shunned now had gained a more important Roman patron in Pacelli. As O'Connell was foisted on Archbishop Williams as coadjutor, Spellman was now imposed on O'Connell, for the cardinal had not asked for Spellman or anyone else as his aux-

---

[10] AABo, Borgongini-Duca to O'Connell, Rome, Jan. 5, 1924.
[11] AABo, O'Connell to Borgongini-Duca, n.p., Apr. 9, 1924 (copy).
[12] AANY, Spellman Diary, Nov. 24–25, 1929.
[13] *Ibid.,* June 30–July 3, 1931; Robert I. GANNON: *The Cardinal Spellman Story,* Garden City, N.Y. 1962, pp. 75–77.

iliary. The new bishop had, furthermore, received the assurance of Pius XI that he would ultimately succeed O'Connell, provided, of course, that the pope outlived the cardinal.[14]

Spellman boarded the *Rex* in Genoa on September 27, 1932, for his voyage to Boston. As one of his travelling companions, he had Monsignor Egidio Vagnozzi, who was to join the Apostolic Delegation in Washington. While at sea he received the curt telegram: "Welcome to Boston. Confirmations begin on Monday. You are expected to be ready. Cardinal O'Connell".[15] An official press release from the cardinal's office dispelled any rumors that Spellman was coadjutor and stated that he was returning "to Boston to take up whatever work Cardinal O'Connell designates for him to do in regard to the confirming of the children of the archdiocese".[16] Upon arrival in Boston, Spellman recorded: "Mass at Cathedral. Cardinal not here to receive me. Mons. Burke gave me my instructions, said I was to live in Seminary".[17]

The relationship between O'Connell and Spellman was, at best, publicly civil, never cordial, and frequently hostile. In December, 1932, McNicholas wrote Pizzardo that Spellman seemed "happy despite the unnecessary trials to which he has been subjected since his return. I am sure his love for the Church and his devotion to the Holy See will make even his present uncongenial surroundings profitable to him".[18] It was one of the ironies of American Catholic history that within the decade both McNicholas and Spellman would have to prove their love for the Church, as both were in contention for the Archdiocese of New York. But Spellman was Pacelli's man and would be increasingly used for contact with the American government.

Spellman's ascent in the American hierarchy coincided with a period of transition in the American Church. In March, 1933, Archbishop Amleto Cicognani was named apostolic delegate to succeed Fumasoni-Biondi, who had been named Cardinal Prefect of Propaganda. A skilled canonist, he began his twenty-five years of tenure in the office – the longest of any American delegate. His presence partially prompted McNicholas to suggest that it was opportune to hold a Fourth Plenary Council.[19] Although McNicholas did not specifically suggest that Cicog-

---

[14] For Spellman's early career, see GANNON: *Spellman* pp. 31–89.

[15] Quoted *ibid.*, p. 90.

[16] *Ibid.*

[17] AANY, Spellman Diary, Oct. 8, 1932.

[18] AACi, McNicholas to Pizzardo, Cincinnati, Dec. 28, 1932 (copy).

[19] ADC, McNicholas to Schrembs, Cincinnati, Aug. 28, 1934; Schrembs to McNicholas, Cleveland, Sept. 6, 1934 (copy). The only other reference found to the possibility of holding another plenary council was in the annual meeting of the bishops in 1935 when Glennon suggested that certain issues be referred to a council; ANCWC, Minutes of Bishops' Meeting, 1935, p. 23.

nani preside over the council, his attitude indicated how far removed the bishops of the 1930s were from the earlier collegial spirit of the American Church.[20]

Shortly after Cicognani's appointment another American prelate with Roman connections returned to the United States. In August, 1933, Edward Mooney was appointed Archbishop-Bishop of Rochester. He had been the principal of the Cathedral Latin School in Cleveland from 1916 to 1922, when Schrembs turned the school over to the Marists and named him a pastor. A year later he was named the spiritual director at the North American College in Rome. This appointment caused Schrembs to bristle. When Cardinal Luigi Sincero suggested in November, 1932,[21] that Mooney's position merited his being made a domestic prelate, Schrembs promised to place no obstacle in the way, but he expressed strong reservations. Mooney, charged the bishop, had obtained his appointment "through some intrigue"; Monsignor Charles A. O'Hern, the rector of the college, had falsely claimed that Mooney was the choice of the archbishops who comprised the college's board of directors. While Schrembs believed Mooney to be "a clean, good priest", he objected to "his association of quasi leadership with a bad crowd in the Diocese and ... his lack of straight-forward loyalty to me, his bishop". All of this information Schrembs had already sent to the apostolic delegate and to the Consistorial Congregation.[22]

Mooney, however, had powerful friends in Rome who were able to counter whatever negative statements Schrembs had made to the Consistorial Congregation. In 1926, he was named Apostolic Delegate to India and consecrated Archbishop of Irenopolis. A few years later, he seems to have been restored to Schrembs' friendship.[23] In 1931, he was transferred as Apostolic Delegate to Japan. He was, incidentally, succeeded in Japan in 1933 by Paolo Marella who had served in the American delegation since 1922 and had been chargé d'affaires from February, 1933, until Cicognani's arrival in September. Mooney thus brought into the American episcopate a background similar to Spellman's, but he enjoyed greater confidence among his fellow bishops who elected him chairman of the administrative board of the NCWC from 1936 to 1939 and again from 1941 to

---

[20] When the NCWC was condemned in 1922, Bishop William Russell thought it was part of an attempt to gain an accredited American diplomatic representative to the Holy See and to have the delegate preside over the meetings of the hierarchy; SHEERIN: *Burke,* p. 71.

[21] ADC, Sincero to Schrembs, Rome, Nov. 29, 1923.

[22] ADC, Schrembs to Sincero, Cleveland, Feb. 2, 1924 (copy). At this time, Mooney seems to have been under consideration for Rector of the North American College which provoked Schrembs to express his reservation to Archbishop Curley, a member of the college's board of directors; ADC, Schrembs to Curley, Cleveland, Jan. 12, 1924 (copy).

[23] ADC, Schrembs to Mooney, Cleveland, Jan. 10, 1927, Aug. 23, 1929, Dec. 7, 1929, Mar. 14, 1930 (copies); Mooney to Schrembs, Bangalore, Jan. 23, Sept. 11, 1929, Apr. 30, 1930.

1945. While documentary evidence is lacking, the bishops may well have elected him to this post because he had been an apostolic delegate and could thus deal more effectively with Cicognani.

3. Roosevelt and Mundelein: the continuing problem of Coughlin

In 1933, however, Spellman may have been Pacelli's man in the hierarchy, but Roosevelt's man was Mundelein. On April 22, 1933, one month after his inauguration, the president wrote Mundelein on the feast day of St. George. Delighted at the letter, the cardinal congratulated Roosevelt "on the remarkable record for achievement you have made in the past few weeks you have been our national leader and chief executive".[24] The cardinal and the president then began a long friendship which had as its basis their mutual concern over social reform. Roosevelt's advisers recognized the conservatism of the eastern bishops, but they became increasingly enamoured of Mundelein's progressive social programs, especially under the direction of his auxiliary bishop, Bernard J. Sheil.[25] Roosevelt made no secret of his admiration for the cardinal; on May 5, 1933, Mundelein made the first of several calls to the White House.[26]

As Roosevelt gradually unfolded his New Deal legislation, he won the support of most rank and file Catholics, notably John A. Ryan, who had been named a monsignor in 1933. But whether from personal pique at not being rewarded for his early support or from ideological differences, Charles Coughlin became more and more an arch-critic of Roosevelt. In 1934, he founded the National Union of Social Justice to lobby in Washington for legislation. The only ecclesiastical restriction placed on him was that Cicognani told him not to broadcast his speeches from his church.[27] Dougherty found him "aided and abetted by his Most Reverend Ordinary, Bishop [Michael J.] Gallagher" and "now quite beyond control". He was, said the cardinal of Philadelphia, "a hero in the minds of the proletariat and especially those members of that rabble, who are of Jewish extraction or belong to the Socialists or Communists".[28] As Coughlin continued his campaign, however, he became increasingly anti-Semitic and found communism everywhere, especially in Roosevelt's New Deal.

---

[24] FDRL, PPF 321, Mundelein to Roosevelt, Chicago, Apr. 26, 1933.
[25] Cf. Harold L. ICKES: *The Secret Diary of Harold L. Ickes,* New York 1954, II, 349–350.
[26] George Q. FLYNN: *American Catholics and the Roosevelt Presidency, 1932–1936,* Lexington, Ky. 1968, p. 38.
[27] AAP, Dougherty to Fumasoni-Biondi, Philadelphia, Feb. 11, 1935 (copy).
[28] AAP, Dougherty to Bernardini, Philadelphia, May 7, 1935 (copy).

But Roosevelt continued to win Catholic support. On December 9, 1935, the University of Notre Dame awarded him an honorary degree. Mundelein presided over the ceremonies and praised the president's "indomitable persevering courage". Roosevelt was moved by this unexpected endorsement and went on to speak of the national life depending on the rights of man, supreme among which were "the rights of freedom of education and freedom of religious worship".[29]

While the liaison between Roosevelt and Mundelein increased, however, Coughlin became a greater embarrassment to the Church. Early in 1936, Cicognani consulted with McNicholas about the possibility of having the administrative board of the NCWC issue a statement on Coughlin. McNicholas, with some reservation, proposed to Archbishop Edward Mooney, chairman of the administrative board, a statement like the following: "Father Coughlin's discourses on a variety of subjects over a period of several years show the liberty of opinion permitted in the Catholic Church and among Catholic priests. One may not agree with Father Coughlin, but Catholics recognize his right as a citizen, as an individual and as a student of social questions, to express his opinion. Father Coughlin, naturally, is not speaking for the Catholic Church of the United States, nor for the American Hierarchy. As his own Bishop has publicly stated, he is speaking with his approval, etc., etc."

McNicholas felt that the Holy See should not bear the brunt of censuring Coughlin, but on the other hand "it has seemed to me that if Father Coughlin is to be censured, a formula must be found by which an American Bishop, or Bishops, can do it. This will not be so easy". To ban Coughlin's radio broadcasts for a given diocese, McNicholas believed, would only turn the acrimony of the people against the bishop and the same thing would occur if the administrative committee issued a statement. He would have no hesitation in disapproving Coughlin's preaching for Cincinnati, he continued, if the priest "should transgress in the domain or [sic] faith or morals". When McNicholas had chided Bishop Gallagher for allowing Coughlin "to violate charity in denouncing people by name", however, the bishop replied: "Well, St. John the Baptist denounced Herod and his wife because of their adulterous union!"[30] McNicholas clearly saw the difficulties of issuing a censure of Coughlin, but he thought perhaps Mooney and Archbishop Samuel Stritch of Milwaukee and Bishops John Peterson of Manchester and John Duffy of Syracuse could discuss all the aspects of the question before submitting it to the administrative committee.

The American hierarchy was clearly in a dilemma in regard to Coughlin. If Church authorities silenced him, they would be accused of restricting free speech

---

[29] Quoted in FLYNN: American Catholics, pp. 184–185.
[30] AACi, McNicholas to Mooney, Cincinnati, Feb. 28, 1936 (copy).

– a standard American charge against the Church. If they remained silent, they would be accused of countenancing what he said. Mooney's response to McNicholas summed up the dilemma and perhaps also expressed the policy he would follow when he inherited the Coughlin problem upon his transfer to Detroit in 1937. Cicognani's suggestion, he wrote, "does, indeed, raise a delicate and difficult question". Then he continued: "It is unwise, perhaps, for me to start with this thought (or "hunch["]), but I am wondering whether, when all concerned, including the Delegate, see the only kind of statement which they feel can be made, they will not all conclude that it is not worth making. After all, there are just two authorities who can, with clear right, step into this affair, his own Bishop and the Holy See. His own Bishop has spoken – and how! Evidently the Holy See does not care to speak – and in this, as in so many other things, it is probably very wise. Where then do we come in and how? Of course, if there is any transgression of faith or morals, then, as you say, anyone of us can step to the front, but, short of that, what can we say that will not result in greater confusion? If supreme authority wishes to exercise some indirect control, could that not better be done by bringing pressure to bear on the Ordinary than through the medium of a necessarily vague statement of a group whose competence is not clear enough to defy a challenge – perhaps on the part of the proper Ordinary who is something of a challenger? I very much fear that any statement which stops short of condemnation – and it must do that – will almost inevitably be taken as some sort of approbation".[31] It is unknown whether the group of bishops McNicholas suggested ever considered a resolution regarding Coughlin. Mooney's opinion seemed to prevail that there was little they could do – an opinion which would be later strengthened by the popular attack on Mooney after he disagreed with Coughlin.

In the summer of 1936, Coughlin became still more controversial by announcing the formation of a third party with Congressman William Lemke of North Dakota as its presidential candidate to counter the two major parties. In July, Bishop Gallagher went to Rome amid newspaper reports, which he denied, that the Vatican wished to discuss Coughlin. Early in September, the *Osservatore Romano* rebuked Coughlin for his violent attacks on Roosevelt. It further stated that Gallagher was in error in saying that Coughlin spoke with Vatican approval and had been given directives in Rome on the matter.[32] Later that month, Spellman first wrote and then personally visited Cicognani to convey Roosevelt's displeasure about Coughlin. When the delegate replied that he could do nothing, the bishop responded that "he could at least rebuke Gallagher or demand that he keep Coughlin in Detroit". In Spellman's eyes, however, Cicognani was "weak

---

[31] AACi, Mooney to McNicholas, Rochester, Mar. 5, 1936.
[32] TULL: *Coughlin,* pp. 143–144.

and frightened and I am sure that he is suspicious and too cautious". Spellman added to his diary: "I did not tell him of Cardinal Pacelli's visit".[33]

B. VATICAN-AMERICAN RAPPROCHEMENT

1. The Visit of Cardinal Pacelli

Spellman had known of Pacelli's forthcoming visit to the United States since early August when Genevieve Garvin Brady, the widow of Nicholas Brady and a papal duchess, telephoned him from Paris. The cardinal was to come as Mrs. Brady's guest, but Spellman soon interposed other plans. He first wrote several letters of protest to Rome and received, on September 16, the assurance from his friend Enrico Galeazzi, an architect and engineer, confidant of Pacelli, and Roman representative of the Knights of Columbus, that "my suggestions are being followed".[34] The precise nature of these suggestions is unknown, but they may well have concerned Coughlin, at least in part, for the day after Spellman visited Cicognani he paid a visit to Roosevelt at Hyde Park, New York. Among the topics they discussed were Coughlin and Pacelli's forthcoming visit.[35]

But Coughlin seems not to have been the major reason for Pacelli's American tour. The radio priest was, of course, an irritation in the growing rapprochement between the New Deal and the American Church, but he was not the primary concern of the Vatican. He was, however, a source of concern to the advisers of Roosevelt who was then campaigning for a second term. James A. Farley, a Catholic and chairman of the Democratic National Campaign Committee, urged that Roosevelt seek from Mundelein, not an endorsement, but a statement saying "that he sees no communistic tendencies in the present administration". This, he thought, would neutralize Coughlin's charges which were being used by the Republicans.[36] Actually Mundelein had already issued a statement which fell just short of an endorsement of Roosevelt. In September, while registering to vote, the cardinal gave a newspaper interview calling Roosevelt "his friend" and speaking of the gratitude the American people should feel "for the prosperity, the happiness, and the freedom now abroad in our land".[37] Democratic leaders also prevailed on John A. Ryan to make one radio broadcast defending Roosevelt's legislative programs. This won for Ryan the epithet from Coughlin of "Right Rev-

---

[33] AANY, Spellman Diary, Sept. 25, 27, 1936.
[34] *Ibid.*, Aug. 6, Sept. 7, 8, 16, 1936.
[35] *Ibid.*, Sept. 28, 1936.
[36] FDRL, PPF 321, Farley to Roosevelt, New York, Oct. 23, 1936.
[37] *Ibid.*, *The Times* (Chicago), Sept. 15, 1936.

erend New Dealer" and the permission from Archbishop Curley, who had no love for Roosevelt, for his diocesan newspaper to publish an attack on both Coughlin and Ryan.[38] But the presidential campaign was peripheral to Pacelli's real motive in coming to the United States.

On September 30, Pacelli's visit became public. For the next week, Spellman, who may have been acting on the cardinal's private instructions, alienated Cardinal Hayes, Cicognani, and Mrs. Brady.[39] He was in the group which met Pacelli's ship at quarantine, but immediately afterwards he was attacked by Mrs. Brady, "aided and abetted by Cardinal Hayes and Apostolic Delegate". He suspected he knew the reason. A few days before the ship docked, he had phoned Pacelli and had also written to Galeazzi who accompanied the cardinal. He then misplaced his memorandum of the conversation while visiting Cicognani in New York. The discovery of his notes, he was convinced, precipitated the hostility toward him.[40]

The day after Pacelli's arrival, Spellman "decided to go to Cardinal Hayes and Apostolic Delegate and ask my lost memorandum card back. Both denied having it or knowing anything about it". Several years later, Spellman added to the diary entry: "They are both liars & so is Mons. [James] McIntyre [Chancellor of the Archdiocese of New York]." One source of the tension between him and Mrs. Brady, he felt, was the discovery of the letter he had written to Galeazzi "in which I told him my opinion of the dangers of following the Duchess to [sic] closely & ignoring the Cardinals!!"[41]

It was an ill-starred introduction for Spellman to the ecclesiastical stage of New York which he would come to dominate. And the tension remained for the duration of Pacelli's tour of the United States during which Spellman was his constant travelling companion. They first visited New York, Philadelphia, Baltimore, and Washington. Then on October 25, they left New York on a chartered plane for an extended tour of the country which included Cleveland, the University of Notre Dame, Chicago, St. Paul, San Francisco, Los Angeles, St. Louis, and Cincinnati.[42] There, on October 30, if Coughlin's later testimony can be trusted, Pacelli discussed his case with McNicholas and refused to grant an audience to Bishops Gallagher and Schrembs who had gone to Cincinnati to see him. The next day Pacelli supposedly instructed Gallagher to forbid Coughlin to engage in further political activities after the election of 1936.[43] Spellman, however, who

---

[38] BRODERICK: *Ryan,* pp. 225–228.

[39] AANY, Spellman Diary, Oct. 2, 3, 6, 7, 1936.

[40] *Ibid.,* Oct. 8, 1936; Spellman noted that he wrote part of this six weeks later.

[41] *Ibid.,* Oct. 9, 1936.

[42] *Ibid.,* Oct. 18–29, 1936.

[43] Marcus SHELDON: *Father Coughlin: The Tumultuous Life of the Priest of the Little Flower,* Boston 1973, p. 131.

was otherwise garrulous in recording every detail of the trip, made no reference to this episode in his diary. Pacelli arrived back in New York on October 31 and three days later Roosevelt was elected to a second term by an overwhelming majority. Coughlin's attempt to throw the election into the House of Representatives was a disaster. Moreover, with the election over, Pacelli was able to realize one of the principal goals of his trip – a meeting with the president.

Arranging a meeting between the president and the Cardinal Secretary of State involved a delicate matter of protocol. As soon as news of Pacelli's coming was made public, Cicognani enlisted the aid of John Burke and the NCWC, to arrange a meeting at the White House. Burke, as the Secretary General of the NCWC, was to accompany the cardinal to the meeting. Burke had just about completed the arrangements when Cicognani summoned him to report that Pacelli would not meet with Roosevelt in Washington but in his mother's home at Hyde Park, New York. This had probably been prearranged, the delegate angrily told Burke, through Spellman. For one bishop, with the aid of the cardinal, to act alone on such a matter, Burke protested to Mooney, was a snub both to the apostolic delegate, the pope's official representative to the hierarchy, and to the NCWC, the officially established organization of the bishops.[44] It was one more issue which created tension between Spellman and Cicognani.

2. Mundelein, Spellman and Diplomatic Relations with the Holy See

Spellman had arranged for Pacelli to meet Roosevelt through Joseph P. Kennedy, a prominent Catholic and later ambassador to the United Kingdom. On October 25, the cardinal received the president's formal invitation to come to Hyde Park on November 5, two days after the election.[45] Newspapers speculated at the time that the topic of discussion between the president and the cardinal was the establishment of diplomatic relations between the Holy See and the United States. This apparently had been one of the tasks assigned to Spellman during his tenure in Boston, for, in November, 1935, he had reported to Pacelli that Kennedy had spoken to Roosevelt, found him open on the question, and believed "that the president will do something in this direction during 1936". James Farley shared this opinion, but Spellman had communicated nothing about it to Cicognani.[46] A few weeks after the Roosevelt-Pacelli meeting, Spellman recorded

---

[44] SHEERIN: Burke, pp. 217–218.
[45] AANY, Spellman Diary, Oct. 24, 25, 1936.
[46] AANY, Spellman to Pacelli, Boston, Nov. 27, 1935 (copy).

that a friend "told me that President wanted me to represent the Church in Washington. It was of course impossible or impractical".[47]

In February, 1937, he stayed overnight at the White House helping James Roosevelt, the president's son, draft a speech in favor of a constitutional amendment prohibiting child labor. But he recorded no discussion about diplomatic relations.[48] The topic was again broached late in the summer when Roosevelt began building Catholic support for a revision of the neutrality laws. First, Thomas Corcoran, a White House aide, and later James Roosevelt discussed Holy See-American diplomatic relations with Spellman.[49] But the president's direct initiative on the subject was taken through his old friend, George Mundelein.

Mundelein's support not only for Roosevelt's domestic policies but also for his foreign ones must be seen in the context of the division of sentiment in the American nation and Church toward German designs in Europe. American Catholic attitudes toward neutrality or intervention in part reflected their ethnic backgrounds. Those of Irish ancestry in general, and Coughlin in particular, filtered anti-German propaganda through their own anti-British prejudice. What was therefore more useful to Roosevelt than to cultivate a prelate of German ancestry who was decidedly American? In May, 1937, Mundelein had publicly branded Adolf Hitler "an inept paper hanger".[50] His statement elicited the support of many other bishops, but it also caused Germany first to protest and then to withdraw its ambassador to the Holy See.[51] German persecution of the Jews was the stimulus for American Catholic leaders to call on Roosevelt to become involved in European affairs without direct intervention. The president, for his part, had to steer a course between openly siding with the Allies and ignoring the conflict altogether.

On October 5, 1937, Roosevelt delivered a speech in Chicago calling for a pact of nations committed to isolating and severing all communications with aggressor nations. After the speech, he dined at Mundelein's residence, where the two discussed inviting the Holy See to participate in a "movement", the purpose of which would be "establishing permanent peace in a war-torn old world". Roosevelt's overture to the Holy See was a far cry from Wilson's aloofness and received Mundelein's immediate encouragement. The cardinal then wrote Cicognani that the president's "intention would be to send a special envoy to the Vati-

---

[47] AANY, Spellman Diary, Nov. 20, 1936.
[48] *Ibid.*, Feb. 16–17, 1937.
[49] *Ibid.*, Aug. 30, Sept. 18, 1937.
[50] George Q. FLYNN: *Roosevelt and Romanism: Catholics and American Diplomacy, 1937–1945*, Westport, Conn. 1976, p. 13.
[51] *New York Times*, May 21, 26, June 2, 1937.

can, not an ordinary priest or layman, but the man he had in mind is a man of ambassadorial rank. It was his own suggestion that the approach might be made through Your Excellency and I agreed with him in this and promised I would write to you and prepare the way. If you think well, I would suggest that you communicate by code with the Holy See, placing before the Holy Father a brief resume of the President's plan".[52] Enclosing a copy of his letter to Cicognani, the cardinal wrote Roosevelt that: "I feel quite certain you will have the assurance of most cordial cooperation in your efforts to arrest the spread of this gangster spirit in nations which is menacing present and future generations".[53]

Less than a week after receiving Roosevelt, Mundelein had a visit from Spellman who, unfortunately, recorded nothing in their conversation regarding diplomatic relations.[54] On September 21, however, Spellman had written to Pacelli apparently about his conversation with James Roosevelt. On November 26, Pacelli responded asking Spellman's advice on a pro-memoria to be submitted to Pius XI. Alluding to the bishop's earlier letter, Pacelli noted that "the Holy See always required that its representative be recognized as the Dean of the diplomats of the same grade" and that the American ambassador to Italy could not be accredited also to the Holy See – a point on which Rampolla had warned Ireland in 1896. The cardinal saw no other points at issue against establishing diplomatic relations and concluded: "The practical procedure to arrive at the establishment of relations is simple, it would be enough that the Government express a desire so that everything can be easily prepared".[55]

Spellman drafted a response to Pacelli on January 7, 1938. Joseph Kennedy, he said, had suggested he discuss the issues with James Roosevelt, who requested that he draw up a pro-memoria for submission to the president stating what was essential and what was only desirable from the Vatican's point of view. The president's son saw difficulties with having the nuncio recognized as the dean of the diplomatic corps and Spellman knew that this was also the opinion of Cordell Hull, the Secretary of State. From the American point of view, having the American ambassador to Italy also accredited to the Holy See had the advantage that the president could avoid opposition to the establishment of diplomatic relations, for he would not have to appeal to congress for special appropriation of funds. Spellman, however, was not "too optimistic about the eventual success" of his

---

[52] FDRL, PPF 321, Mundelein to Cicognani, Chicago, Oct. 6, 1937.
[53] *Ibid.*, Mundelein to Roosevelt, Chicago, Oct. 6, 1937; cf. Roosevelt to Mundelein, Washington, Oct. 22, 1937.
[54] AANY, Spellman Diary, Oct. 11–12, 1937.
[55] AANY, Pacelli to Spellman, Rome, Nov. 26, 1937.

endeavours, but he planned to submit his memorandum to the president.[56] From the documentary evidence available, it is unclear whether Spellman actually sent this report to Pacelli.

On January 12, he went to Washington at James Roosevelt's request, visited Cicognani and informed him that he was going to the White House. The next day, he met with James Roosevelt, who, Spellman recorded, "liked the memorandum I prepared and I think I am making progress in persuading the President that it would be a good thing all around".[57] On January 26, he reported his actions to Pacelli, who responded that while "it would be more dignified for the United States to have a true and proper Ambassador, nevertheless the Holy See could not raise a difficulty if it preferred to give to the Representative only the designation of Minister".[58] Pacelli made no allusion to the status of the Holy See's representative to the United States. Obviously sensitive to the American situation, he was open to further discussion. For several months, however, nothing further was discussed.

3. Mooney appointed First Archbishop of Detroit

In the meantime, Coughlin continued to be a major problem. After the defeat of his Union Party in 1936, he announced that he was abandoning his radio broadcasts. Then in a special New Year's broadcast to his followers, he said he would return to the radio if his supporters doubled the subscriptions to his journal *Social Justice* to one and a quarter million – a figure he later lowered. Next, on January 20, 1937, Bishop Gallagher died. Within a few days Coughlin resumed his regular broadcasts saying that it had been the bishop's dying request. On May 26, the Holy See announced the establishment of Detroit as an archdiocese and named Edward Mooney, then Bishop of Rochester, as the first archbishop. Coughlin would not find in Mooney the tractable supporter he had had in Bishop Gallagher, but he would put the new archbishop's immense diplomatic skill and prominence in the hierarchy to the strongest test.[59]

Coughlin's radio broadcasts became increasingly strident not only against Roosevelt but also against the Congress of Industrial Organizations (CIO) and its

---

[56] AANY, Spellman to Pacelli, New York, Jan. 7, 1938 (draft).

[57] AANY, Spellman Diary, Jan. 12–13, 1938.

[58] AANY, Pacelli to Spellman, Rome, Feb. 26, 1938.

[59] It is regrettable that at the time of the research for this book Mooney's papers were not available. The papers on the Coughlin case are in the archives of the Archdiocese of Detroit, but are not yet open to research. For Mooney's handling of Coughlin, therefore, it has been necessary to rely either on published studies or on his correspondence with McNicholas.

leader John L. Lewis. In October, 1937, just before he began his new broadcast season, he gave an interview in which he referred to Roosevelt's "personal stupidity" in appointing Hugo Black, a former member of the Ku Klux Klan, to the Supreme Court. He also inveighed against Catholics joining the CIO because he believed the organization leaned toward communism. On October 7, Mooney issued a public statement dissociating the archdiocese from Coughlin's pronouncements on the CIO. After Mooney refused Coughlin permission to publish a statement of his position, the priest announced he was cancelling his radio series for 1937–1938. Mooney was immediately swamped with letters of protest. Coughlin's followers even threatened a direct appeal to the pope. When Cicognani issued a statement defending Mooney's actions, Coughlin's defenders said the delegate did not speak for the Vatican. Bowing to pressure, Mooney allowed Coughlin to resume his broadcasts in January, 1938. The archbishop found himself living out what he had predicted to McNicholas in 1936 – any ecclesiastical authority which censured Coughlin would itself become the object of censure.[60] Mooney was himself powerless to do anything about Coughlin, except repudiate what was clearly not the stance of the Church. As he wrote in frustration to his friend McNicholas early in 1940, "I am still busy trying to write straight answers to his dodging letters. There is no telling yet what the outcome will be".[61]

During the summer Coughlin again made an attempt to form a national association, the Christian Front, to espouse, among other things, the cause of American non-intervention in the approaching European war. His broadcasts became increasingly anti-Semitic and his journal, *Social Justice,* devoted more space to foreign affairs. His general program was a confused mixture of isolationism, anti-Semitism, and anti-communism. After the German invasion of Poland on September 1, 1939, Roosevelt called for the repeal of the Embargo Act forbidding the sale of arms even to a nation which was the victim of aggression. Coughlin, now joined publicly by Archbishop Francis J. Beckman of Dubuque, called for retention of the act and total neutrality and mobilized his followers to influence the Senate. In the midst of this controversy, the National Association of Broadcasters finally did what Mooney could not do. It issued a new code which forbade controversial broadcasters unless they were part of a panel. Coughlin then had to cancel his radio series for 1940–1941.[62] Though apparently subject to Mooney's increasing restrictions, Coughlin continued his crusade in the pages of *Social Justice,* until it was suppressed by the government.

---

[60] TULL: *Coughlin,* pp. 173–185.
[61] AACi, Mooney to McNicholas, Detroit, Feb. 29, 1940.
[62] TULL: *Coughlin,* pp. 188–227.

4. Vatican American Relations: Mundelein's Visit to Rome

While Coughlin continued his vicious attacks on Roosevelt in his effort to retain American isolationism, the Vatican and the United States renewed their efforts to establish some means of communication during the conflict which was becoming inevitable. What would bring about this communication, however, was not a political but an ecclesiastical event. On September 4, 1938, Cardinal Patrick Hayes of New York died. The same day, Spellman, who had his own private source of information about the New York succession, received a telegram stating "Fight Starts" to which he added the comment: "The battle is certainly starting soon but with all the opposition I believe it is impossible".[63] Even at this date, the bishop knew he was a contender for the important See of New York and his appointment was directly related to the Vatican's desire for closer ties with the United States.

On September 9, Cardinal Hayes was buried. Before the funeral, Spellman was contacted by several friends of the president who had instructed them to speak with both him and Mundelein about diplomatic recognition of the Vatican. After the funeral, Spellman spoke with Mundelein, a conversation in which both diplomatic relations with the Vatican and Spellman's chances for being appointed Archbishop of New York were intertwined.[64] On October 12, the bishops opened their annual meeting in Washington and Spellman had a "momentous meeting with Tom Corcoran".[65] Two days later, he had dinner with Roosevelt who discussed the European situation.[66] On October 19, he went to New Orleans for the Eucharistic Congress to which Mundelein had been named legate, and there he and Mundelein used the opportunity to discuss diplomatic recognition of the Holy See.[67] After the congress, Mundelein was to go to Rome to report on both the congress and the negotiations with Roosevelt.

On October 1, Roosevelt wrote Mundelein a brief note informing him that Ambassador William Phillips had been notified of his expected arrival in Naples.[68] On October 5, Mundelein responded assuring the president that "of course, I shall see you personally before I leave, and to place myself at your service in any way I can be helpful. Thanks to your efforts in behalf of the peace of

---

[63] AANY, Spellman Diary, Sept. 4, 1938.

[64] *Ibid.*, Sept. 9–10, 1938.

[65] *Ibid.*, Oct. 12, 1938.

[66] *Ibid.*, Oct. 14, 1938.

[67] *Ibid.*, Oct. 19, 21, 1938.

[68] FDRL, PPF 321, Roosevelt to Mundelein, Washington, Oct. 1, 1938; Roosevelt to Phillips, Washington, Oct. 1, 1938.

the world, I need not either postpone my trip – which for a time seemed probable – or to anticipate any dangers at sea, outside of unquiet winds and seas".[69] Before leaving for Rome, Mundelein stayed overnight at the White House, and then on October 29, he sailed from New York.[70]

Roosevelt had wished to impress the Holy See and Italy with the respect with which Mundelein was held by the United States government. Ambassador Phillips met Mundelein's ship in Naples. After a dinner on the *U.S.S. Omaha*, Mundelein was escorted to the dock where he was accorded by the Italian government the honors due to a legate. Then Phillips escorted the cardinal to a special train which he had asked the government to provide. Once in Rome, where the cardinal was again saluted by the Italian government, Phillips escorted Mundelein to a Vatican car where he turned him over to Vatican officials. Phillips subsequently gave a reception and a dinner in honor of Mundelein who was also feted at several other functions, including one held by the Irish ambassador to the Holy See, who was then married to Nicholas Brady's widow.[71] If Roosevelt had hoped to create the impression that Mundelein enjoyed the full support of the United States government, he was successful. German newspapers were soon reporting that Mundelein was going to announce the establishment of diplomatic relations which was Roosevelt's reward for his role in delivering the Catholic vote in 1936, a charge which the cardinal denied in such a way as to leave the impression that such recognition by the United States was indeed part of his mission.[72]

5. Spellman Appointed Archbishop of New York

But no such recognition was to be granted at this time and Mundelein was to play no further role in drawing Roosevelt and the Vatican closer together. For the time, the succession to the Archdiocese of New York became the Vatican's paramount preoccupation in the American Church. The maneuvering for Hayes' replacement had begun immediately after his death, as Spellman had recorded in his diary. Mundelein presided at Hayes' funeral which drew from Dougherty the sarcastic remark to Bernardini, then the nuncio to Switzerland, that "Cardinal Mundelein made a public statement that he [Hayes] (not himself) was the outstanding prelate of the American Church. Do you think there was any mental re-

---

[69] *Ibid.*, Mundelein to Roosevelt, Chicago, Oct. 5, 1938.

[70] AANY, Spellman Diary, Oct. 29, 1938.

[71] FDRL, PSF 58, Phillips to Roosevelt, Rome, Nov. 10, 1938, with enclosed memorandum for State Department.

[72] FLYNN: *Roosevelt and Romanism,* p. 100.

servation?"[73] In the meantime, it was fully expected that Mundelein would use his influence during his trip to Rome to have a successor appointed to Hayes.

Mundelein discussed the New York succession with Spellman on at least two occasions, at the time of Hayes' funeral and just before leaving for Rome. During the vacancy, Bishop Stephen Donahue, the auxiliary bishop, had been named administrator of the archdiocese and was the favorite candidate among New Yorkers. As Spellman, Donahue, and Cicognani gathered on the dock to see Mundelein off, the delegate monopolized most of the cardinal's time, leaving Spellman time for only a five-minute conversation. As Mundelein departed, Spellman commented: "It was funny, the Delegate, Bishop Donahue and I standing on the dock. The Cardinal must have laughed as he looked at us".[74]

What Mundelein said about the New York succession in Rome remains a mystery. While the cardinal was in Rome, Bernardini commented that Mundelein's "senility and megalomania" had increased, but he revealed nothing about what the cardinal had said regarding New York.[75] At the same time, Enrico Galeazzi cabled Spellman on November 8 that Mundelein showed a "good disposition", but then Spellman received a later letter saying that Pius XI and the cardinal had not discussed New York.[76] Subsequently, however, Mundelein was known to favor the transfer of Archbishop Joseph Rummel of New Orleans to New York. Dougherty bristled at the recommendation of the "Prince of the Church of Chicago". "I wouldn't be surprised", he wrote Bernardini, "if it was someone with a Teutonic name, especially if he recommends anyone living outside New York. At a large gathering of Bishops and Clergy in New Orleans he preconized Archbishop Rummel for New York and Rummel designated him for the next Pope, after Pius XI. In other words, one good turn deserves another".[77] Bernardini could only wonder how "a man 'of sound mind'" could think of suggesting a German-born prelate for New York as the world moved toward war.[78] "Deutschland über alles" was Dougherty's last retort to Mundelein's machinations.[79] More than likely Rummel's German birth was one of several reasons for his rejection; yet that same factor may have been a motive for Mundelein to support his candidacy in order to show that German-Americans had become Americanized.

---

[73] AAP, Dougherty to Bernardini, Philadelphia, Sept. 19, 1938 (copy).
[74] AANY, Spellman Diary, Oct. 29, 1938.
[75] AAP, Bernardini to Dougherty, Bern, Nov. 9, 1938.
[76] AANY, Spellman Diary, Nov. 8, and 26, 1938.
[77] AAP, Dougherty to Bernardini, Philadelphia, Dec. 26, 1939 (copy).
[78] AAP, Bernardini to Dougherty, Bern, Dec. 4, 1939 and Jan. 16, 1940.
[79] AAP, Dougherty to Bernardini, Philadelphia, Mar. 9, 1940 (copy).

Archbishop Mooney of Detroit was also mentioned, but in retrospect it seems highly unlikely that there was any real chance of moving him so soon after his arrival in his see where Coughlin continued to be a problem. Locally in New York the favorite candidate remained Bishop Stephen Donahue, who seems, unrealistically, to have expected the appointment. The candidate who seemed most likely was John T. McNicholas of Cincinnati. His name was frequently mentioned in newspaper accounts and, late in November, even Spellman heard that he was "cleaning his desk preparing to go to N.Y. as Archbishop".[80] According to some sources, McNicholas was actually named Archbishop of New York, but Pius XI died before confirming him.[81]

Pius XI's death, on February 10, 1939, left little doubt as to his successor. As on previous occasions, Cardinal O'Connell was in the Bahamas when he received word of the coming conclave, but he arrived in time for the brief conclave which elected Cardinal Eugenio Pacelli as Pope Pius XII. If other American prelates had achieved their prominence through powerful Roman patrons, Spellman now had the most powerful one of all. Moreover, Pius XII desired to remain on good terms with the United States as it became increasingly evident that war could not be averted. To do this, it was imperative that the Archbishop of New York be close to the president. This among others might have been one reason for rejecting McNicholas, known not to favor Roosevelt. On June 29, 1938, McNicholas had written to Domenico Tardini, Secretary of the Congregation of the Extraordinary Affairs of the Church: "Our political situation here grows more perplexing. Our President has been given unprecedented powers by Congress. I cannot think that he is a serious-minded man or that he studies any questions profoundly. He has no prejudice whatever against the Catholic Church. On the contrary, he is very kindly disposed to things Catholic. He is an opportunist. Consistency means nothing to him. What seems to me the most serious objection to be made to the Federal Administration of our Government during six years is that radical and subversive teachings have everywhere been tolerated and even encouraged".[82] If Pacelli did not already personally know McNicholas' sentiments toward the president, he certainly would have learned them from Tardini. Once elected pope, he would have found McNicholas unacceptable as Archbishop of New York even if he did not have his own candidate.

---

[80] AANY, Spellman Diary, Nov. 26, 1938.

[81] Interview with John McMahon, S.J., June 30, 1974. McMahon was the librarian at the Gregorian University in Rome at that time and heard the report from Robert Leiber, S.J., later a confidant of Pius XII. Bishop Clarence Issenmann, who was McNicholas' secretary, confirmed this story in an interview on Jan. 8, 1981.

[82] AACi, McNicholas to Tardini, Cincinnati, June 29, 1938 (copy).

After the election of Pius XII, however, there was some delay in naming Spellman. In an unprecedented move, Roosevelt named Joseph Kennedy, then American ambassador to the United Kingdom, to represent him at the coronation of the new pope – an appointment which drew protests in the United States as a violation of the separation of Church and State. Kennedy reported to Spellman that Galeazzi was working hard for his appointment.[83] Spellman also knew that Bernardini had been supporting him;[84] Cardinal Dougherty, too, may have favored him.[85] But Spellman continued to receive contradictory information. On March 30, he was "feeling relieved to know what the 'serious reasons' were that prevented my appointment to New York". On April 1, he learned "that three cardinals are against me going to New York. That is one reason why I should think I might go".[86] At last on the morning of April 12, he received word that he had been nominated Archbishop of New York. He intended to fly to Washington to the apostolic delegation and then cable Rome: "Father, if it is possible, let this chalice pass from me". Weather conditions at the Boston airport, however, prevented the departure of his flight, so he cabled Cicognani his acceptance.[87] Only on April 24, however, did Rome make the official appointment. The first person whom Spellman notified was Roosevelt.[88]

Spellman immediately went to Cardinal O'Connell, who was gracious and who subsequently issued a statement – "quite a contrast to the statement issued when I was made a bishop six years ago", Spellman noted.[89] Before leaving his former ordinary he received the advice "not to be 'so humble'. 'That doesn't get you anywhere.' I said to myself 'O, Yes'".[90] Spellman was officially installed as Archbishop of New York on May 23, 1939, at a Mass celebrated by Bishop Donahue.

Spellman was destined to be the most powerful figure in the American hierarchy, not only because of his close personal friendship with Pius XII but also because of his role in negotiating with the United States government over the next two decades. At the time of Pius' coronation Kennedy phoned Spellman and mentioned that Cardinal O'Connell opposed the establishment of diplomatic rela-

---

[83] AANY, Spellman Diary, Mar. 15, 1939.

[84] *Ibid.,* Feb. 5, 1939.

[85] Cf. AAP, Bernardini to Dougherty, Bern, Dec. 12, 1939, in which Bernardini made a vague reference to the Holy Father's appreciation for "the advice and encouragement" Dougherty gave on the New York succession.

[86] AANY, Spellman Diary, Mar. 30, Apr. 1, 1939.

[87] *Ibid.,* Apr. 12, 1939.

[88] *Ibid.,* Apr. 24, 1939; FDRL, PPF 4404, Spellman to Roosevelt, Apr. 23, 1939.

[89] AANY, Spellman Diary, Apr. 25, 1939.

[90] *Ibid.,* June 29–30, 1939.

tions. It is difficult to determine whether Roosevelt himself actually wanted official diplomatic relations. But whatever his desires on the subject, in the future he would have to deal with Spellman for, on October 2, 1939, Cardinal Mundelein died of a heart attack. His unexpected death was by no means universally mourned. Bernardini commented that in recent days the cardinal "was dangerous, more dangerous than his colleague of Boston". Bernardini was hostile because of Mundelein's outspoken support of Roosevelt and because of his statement, published posthumously by Bishop Bernard Sheil, calling on American Catholics "to sustain the policies of the President on the grave question of neutrality because it coincides with the idea of the Holy Father". For Bernardini, the statement was "erroneous in its premises and imprudent in its conclusions. Who gave instructions to Card. Mundelein to indicate political directives to American Catholics?"[91]

Mundelein's open advocacy of Roosevelt had antagonized some people in curial circles. Furthermore, Sheil, who was the administrator of the vacant see, was very probably Roosevelt's preferred candidate to succeed Mundelein. In this, the president may have received Spellman's assistance.[92] Whatever may have been Roosevelt's – and Spellman's – preference, on December 27, 1939, the Holy See transferred Archbishop Samuel Stritch from Milwaukee to Chicago. For any further negotiations with the Vatican, Roosevelt would now have to use Spellman, who, in turn, seems to have striven, unsuccessfully, to inherit the mantle of Mundelein's close friendship with and influence over the president.

---

[91] AAP, Bernardini to Dougherty, Bern, Oct. 10, 1939.

[92] AANY, Galleazzi to Spellman, Rome, Dec. 14, 1939. Galleazzi's references to the Chicago succession are vague. He noted that he had already thanked Spellman, in a previous letter not found, for his "useful" information about Chicago, but then he added that until that point there had been little reason for haste, "because there is somewhat of an impression that long periods of *sede vacante* are not harmful to administrations, because usually the administrator who remains in office, hopeful for the succession, tried to do better than he would and everything therefore works to the advantage of that institution".

CHAPTER XI

THE UNITED STATES MOVES TOWARD WAR

A. ROOSEVELT, SPELLMAN, AND THE MYRON TAYLOR MISSION

In some ways, Joseph Kennedy's presence at Pius XII's coronation was a trial balloon to test the American public's reaction to establishing diplomatic relations, which became all the more important as European political tensions increased. Roosevelt tried his own hand at preserving the peace by sending telegrams to Mussolini and Hitler, asking their guarantee against further aggression. At the same time, he had Sumner Welles, Assistant Secretary of State, approach Monsignor Michael J. Ready, the General Secretary of the NCWC, to seek the Vatican's endorsement. Unfortunately, the dispatch of the telegrams coincided with German annexation of Czechoslovakia. Roosevelt's simultaneous approach to the Vatican to endorse his initiative also met with difficulty. Since his statement singled out the Axis leaders for bearing responsibility for ceasing aggression, the Vatican could not endorse it without surrendering its own neutrality. In May, Pius XII launched his own peace initiative suggesting that five major European powers hold a conference; he deliberately excluded both the United States and Russia. When Monsignor Joseph P. Hurley, an American in the Secretariat of State, was approached by the secretary of the American Embassy about the papal initiative, he denied there was any plan.[1]

Roosevelt then encouraged a more direct contact with the Vatican. At his request, Sumner Welles consulted Monsignor Howard J. Carroll of the NCWC and agreed to have dinner with Cicognani on June 29. To Welles' assurance that the president was willing to participate in "a conference of nations to adjust the present cause of world unrest", Cicognani replied that the Vatican had to maintain its independence from any particular nation's initiative. The next day, however, Cicognani left for Rome amid rumors of the impending recognition of the Holy See. But again, nothing happened.[2]

The principal movers within the government for diplomatic recognition were Cordell Hull, the Secretary of State, and Welles. Their approach was pragmatic.

---

[1] FLYNN: *Roosevelt and Romanism*, pp. 102–103.
[2] *Ibid.*, p. 104.

Welles urged on Roosevelt the idea that a mission to the Vatican would provide an important European listening post. Moreover, during the early fall of 1939, after the invasion of Poland, the *Osservatore Romano* had praised Roosevelt's neutrality speech and received the condemnation of Fascist newspapers.[3] Roosevelt then took the first hesitant step toward establishing a mission to the Vatican. On October 2, he wrote Hull suggesting that a "special mission" be established to care for the needs of the numerous refugees.[4] Roosevelt's approach was political. Whereas Hull and Welles, as diplomats, wished as many embassies established as possible, Roosevelt had to consider the political repercussions of formal recognition of the Holy See, especially as another election year was approaching. A mission for humanitarian concerns was a creative substitute. At this point Spellman again entered into his confidence.

On October 24, Roosevelt invited Spellman to the White House and proposed sending a special mission to the pope. The next day, through Cicognani, Spellman submitted his report to Cardinal Luigi Maglione, the papal Secretary of State. Spellman first noted that Roosevelt had agreed to speak on the radio at the same time as Pius XII to commemorate the fiftieth anniversary of the Catholic University. The president, he said, "was looking for a moment and occasion suitable for a persuasive appeal to the American people" about establishing relations. Spellman had pointed out to Roosevelt that both the pope and president had struck "the same theme and the same tone" in their speeches. He encouraged the president to balance any criticism he might receive with the realization that he was helping foster "the association of great moral forces for the good of mankind". Roosevelt said that, after revising the Neutrality Act, Congress would probably adjourn in November and not return to session until January 3. During that period, a "special mission to the Holy See" could be established.

What Roosevelt probably intended was that by acting while congress was not in session he would avoid its immediate hostile criticism. Spellman explained to Maglione that "for the time being the relationship would consist of a mission of the United States Government to Rome accredited to the Holy See, without its being necessary that the mission of the Holy See in Washington should be recognised [sic] as an Apostolic Nunciature". Moreover, such a "special mission" would not require congressional approval for funding, but later "congress could be induced more easily to vote the funds for a permanent mission". Roosevelt had further suggested for his emissary either Myron Taylor, former chairman of the United States Steel Corporation, who was already working on the refugee prob-

---

[3] FDRL, PSF 58, Phillips to Roosevelt, Rome, Sept. 27, 1939.
[4] Cordell HULL: *The Memoirs of Cordell Hull,* 2 vols. New York 1948, I, 713–715; FLYNN: *Roosevelt and Romanism,* p. 105.

lem, or Breckinbridge Long, former American ambassador to Italy. Spellman concluded by saying that he had discussed all this with Cicognani.[5]

Spellman then awaited a reply. It came on November 28, 1939, but it was not in a form he liked and may have indicated that Cicognani felt snubbed, as he had in 1936, at the role Spellman was playing in the negotiations. Maglione, Cicognani wrote Spellman, "notified me of having received my letter of October 27 with which I accompanied the report of Your Excellency". The cardinal secretary had further said: "the Holy Father has learned of the report with pleasure and hopes that Your Excellency as well as I will make opportune overtures to the President, that he may carry out his proposal". The delegate concluded by suggesting that Spellman might want to arrange another confidential meeting with Roosevelt.[6] Spellman immediately asked the president for another appointment.[7] Then he notified Cicognani from whom he received the further advice that "perhaps you can open the discussion by mentioning that the previous conversation was referred to the Holy See, and that His Eminence the Cardinal Secretary is deeply interested in the matter".[8]

Cicognani's advice may have been insulting to Spellman, who now devised a better gambit for opening the discussion. It is difficult to determine whether Spellman was piqued at having Cicognani take part in the initiative with Roosevelt, whether he wished to force the president's hand after four years of negotiations, or whether he simply wished to give Roosevelt a definite sign that the Holy See would accept a "special mission". Whatever Spellman's motive, he completely rewrote Cicognani's letter of November 28 assigning to the new version the original protocol number. Spellman's version now focused on the Holy See's reaction to his report and gave the initiative to him alone. The new rendition read:

"The Holy Father received with great satisfaction the information that the President desires to appoint a mission to the Holy See to assist in the solution of the refugee problem and to treat other matters of mutual interest. The Holy Father was particularly pleased to know that the President has the intention of establishing this mission soon after the adjournment of Congress and before January 5, 1940.

"The Holy Father directs Your Excellency to convey to President Roosevelt an

[5] AANY, Spellman to Maglione, Oct. 25, 1939 (copy), given in *The Holy See and the War in Europe: March 1939–August 1940,* edited by Pierre Blet, Angelo Martini, and Burkhart Schneider, translated by Gerard Noel, Washington 1965, I, 302–305; AANY, Cicognani to Spellman, Washington, Oct. 27, 1939.

[6] AANY, protocol no. 231/39, Cicognani to Spellman, Washington, Nov. 28, 1939.

[7] FDRL, PPF 440, Spellman to Roosevelt, New York, Nov. 30, 1939.

[8] AANY, Cicognani to Spellman, Washington, Dec. 2, 1939.

expression of deepest appreciation on his part and to say that he believes and prays that the resumption of relations between the United States and the Holy See will be most propitious, especially at the present time when both are making parallel endeavors for peace, the alleviation of sufferings, and other charitable and humanitarian purposes. You are further requested to represent to President Roosevelt that in the opinion of the Holy Father the proximate fulfillment of his gracious intention will be most conducive to the welfare of a world sadly torn by misunderstanding, malice and strife.

"After you have been accorded an audience with the President you will please communicate through the facilities of the Apostolic Delegation the approximate time that the President intends to make the announcement.

"I need only add to this message from the Cardinal Secretary of State that I am at the service of the President and Your Excellency".[9]

Spellman's luncheon with Roosevelt was arranged for December 7, "off the record" and he would "come in the back way".[10] He left New York that morning, "went to delegation and prepared letter for delegate to sign which he did at my request", and then went to the White House. After the meeting, he recorded his reactions in his diary: "The President was wonderful to me. Luncheon lasted 1 hour and a half and he agreed to recognize Vatican and send either Myron Taylor or Harry Woodring as Ambassador. He agreed to make announcement himself at Xmas as my letter from the Delegate which I left with President was sufficient to give official assent of the Holy See. It was a wonderful day!! Returned to N.Y. with Frank Walker".[11] Spellman's diary entry was, of course, misleading. In the whole course of his conversation with Roosevelt on October 24 and of his rewriting Cicognani's letter to himself, what was spoken of was a "special mission" and not formal diplomatic recognition. Nevertheless, he saw this "mission" as the first step toward such recognition and would continue to work for it until 1953. At this point, however, he had not communicated the results of his meeting with Roosevelt to Cicognani.[12]

Appointment of Taylor

Spellman's version of Cicognani's letter, embodying Pacelli's observations of 1937 about the procedure to be followed in establishing diplomatic relations, was

[9] AANY, Protocol no. 231/37 [sic], Cicognani to Spellman, Washington, Nov. 28, 1939 (copy); there is also a draft of this letter in Spellman's own hand.

[10] FDRL, PPF 4404, Roberta to Watson, Dec. 4, 1939.

[11] AANY, Spellman Diary, Dec. 7, 1939; cf. FDRL, PPF 4404, Spellman to Roosevelt, New York, Dec. 8, 1939.

[12] AANY, Cicognani to Spellman, Washington, Dec. 12, 1939.

sufficient to move Roosevelt to make the appointment. On December 23, the president again summoned Spellman to the White House and entrusted to him a hand-written letter to Pius XII announcing that he was sending him as a "personal representative" Myron Taylor, already known to the pope. The text of the letter was immediately transmitted by telegraph to the Vatican.[13] The original was sent by mail together with a letter from Cicognani. The delegate narrated the history of the conversations between Roosevelt and Spellman, and added that "this Representation of the President of the United States to the Holy See is not, in itself, of a permanent character; to reach this point an Act of the Federal Congress is required. But everybody understands that, after such a decision, *alea iacta est* and the only thing is to hope that the problem will be settled as it deserves".[14]

Roosevelt's letter to Pius XII was made public on December 24 together with letters to Cyrus Adler, President of the Jewish Theological Seminary, and Dr. George A. Buttrick, President of the Federal Council of Churches. By sending a letter to the Protestant and Jewish leaders also, Roosevelt hoped to provide as broad a base of moral support for his attempts to avoid war as possible. But the fact that he sent a personal representative only to the pope did bring forth the anticipated protests about the violation of the separation of Church and State.[15] His invention of the title "personal representative" for Myron Taylor did little to assuage those opposed to recognition of the Vatican and its ambiguity served to encourage those in favor.

In order to increase his prestige, Taylor was given the personal title of "extraordinary ambassador". On February 27, 1940, he presented his credentials to Pius XII and was received with the usual ceremonies reserved for an ambassador. His instructions for his mission were: freedom of religion, freedom of communication such as that exemplified in the news coverage of the *Osservatore Romano,* reduction of arms, and freedom of trade between nations. On these neutral points Taylor and Vatican officials could agree. On the other hand, the Holy See was not about to accord Roosevelt those privileges which he might enjoy were he to establish full diplomatic relations. The president had also instructed Taylor to discuss ecclesiastical topics. "COUGHLIN" was listed as a topic in bold-faced letters. Roosevelt understood Samuel Stritch "to be somewhat of a Fascist", while "Spellman seems to be very good". The president had also learned that Washington would be erected into an archdiocese and as the first ordinary he stressed that "it is important that he be a reputable and liberal-minded Bishop. Bishop Bernard J. Sheil, who was understudy to Cardinal Mundelein would be an agreeable

---

[13] Cicognani to Maglione, Washington, Dec. 23, 1939, *Holy See and the War,* I, 324.
[14] Cicognani to Maglione, Washington, Dec. 23, 1939, *ibid.,* 327–329.
[15] FLYNN: *Roosevelt and Romanism,* pp. 110–115.

choice".[16] Roosevelt added to the agenda for Taylor's discussion the anti-Jewish sentiment in Baltimore, Brooklyn, and Detroit, which "is said to be encouraged by the church" and which in turn "automatically stirs up anti-Catholic feeling and that makes a general mess".[17]

Taylor waited until his interview with Maglione on March 8, 1940, to bring up some of the topics on the agenda given him by Roosevelt. Omitted from his discussion was Stritch, who seems to have been left to Spellman. Maglione condemned the anti-Semitism Roosevelt claimed existed with Catholic support in Baltimore, Brooklyn, and Detroit and promised that if Taylor drew up a protest Cicognani would be instructed to investigate. On Coughlin, Maglione said he was ready to investigate the question. But on the appointment of Sheil to Washington, Maglione side-stepped the question and stated that the appointment properly belonged to the Consistorial Congregation.[18] The president's mentioning of Sheil as a possible candidate for Washington, however, may very well have left the new archdiocese under the administration of Roosevelt's outspoken foe, Archbishop Curley, until the latter's death in 1947; it may also have prevented Sheil's advancement beyond Auxiliary Bishop of Chicago. The Holy See may have been willing to accept a compromise on establishing full diplomatic relations with the United States, but it would not allow the compromiser to intrude into strictly ecclesiastical affairs.

Taylor next arranged an audience with the pope for Sumner Welles, who was concluding a quick visit to the heads of European states in an effort to preserve peace. Taylor himself demanded to be present "for the prestige of his own mission's sake".[19] At the audience on March 18, the pope stressed that an attempt at a peace conference would be ineffectual, an opinion shared by both Maglione and Welles. Only the day before, Mussolini and Hitler had met, but it was unclear whether Hitler wished to drag Italy into the war or whether he hoped to negotiate a peace through Mussolini.[20] The pope then entrusted to Taylor a letter to Roosevelt to be transmitted through Welles, in which he thanked the president for sending his representative as an indication of his "endeavours for the alleviation of suffering".[21]

---

[16] FDRL, Taylor, Memorandum for Taylor, Feb. 11, 1940.

[17] *Ibid.,* FDR memorandum to Taylor, Feb. 13, 1940.

[18] Notes of Msgr. Hurley, Mar. 8, 1940, *Holy See and the War,* I, 352–353.

[19] Notes of the Secretary of State, Mar. 15, 1940, *ibid.* p. 369.

[20] FDRL, Taylor, Taylor's report on Welles' audience with Pius XII on Mar. 18, 1940; Cardinal Maglione's Notes, Mar. 18, 1940, *Holy See and the War,* I, 375.

[21] Pius XII to Roosevelt, Mar. 16, 1940, *Holy See and the War,* I, 370; subsequently the Vatican asked Taylor whether Roosevelt would make the letter public so that the Vatican could publish it at the same time; FDRL, Taylor, Taylor to State Dept., Mar. 29, 1940 (telegram).

Taylor had also consulted other churchmen in Rome outside the Vatican. On the same day Taylor had his audience with the pope, Vincent A. McCormick, S.J., wrote him a letter. An American and Rector of the Gregorian University, McCormick was responding to Taylor's earlier question about how Roosevelt could prevent the war from spreading. For the Jesuit, there was "no more efficacious means" than for "the President [to] make it clear to the world, that America will not look with indifference on a victory of Germany and Russia. If all the Americas joined in such a declaration, so much the better".[22] For McCormick, Italy was of less importance than either Germany or Russia. Taylor forwarded this letter to Roosevelt probably to give him an indication of the variety of sentiments in Roman circles.

The United States saw Taylor's mission as an attempt to keep Italy out of the war, which coincided with Vatican opposition to any further Italian aggrandizements. As Maglione told Welles, however, while the Italian people did not want war, Mussolini was leaning "toward Germany". The Allies, thought Maglione, would benefit by not antagonizing Mussolini, a position which Roosevelt had already taken.[23] On March 29, Taylor had his third audience with Pius XII, followed by one with Maglione. Again the Vatican thought a peace conference would only draw Mussolini and Hitler closer together, but that a private communication from Roosevelt to Mussolini might keep Italy out of the war.[24] During the next few weeks, Taylor waited for a reply from Roosevelt, while he received encouragement from Maglione and Monsignor Joesph Hurley. At last, on April 24, 1940, his efforts seemed successful, as both Roosevelt and Pius addressed letters to Mussolini urging Italian non-belligerency. But these overtures were to no avail. On June 10, 1940, Italy entered the war as Germany's ally.[25]

While Taylor's endeavour to prevent Italy from entering the war was unsuccessful, the establishment of his mission indicated the growing Vatican-American rapport. The Vatican now regarded the United States as holding the balance of power in world affairs; the United States needed the sources of information which the Holy See possessed particularly in Europe.

Taylor was not in the full sense of the term a diplomatic representative. Independently wealthy, he owned a villa in Florence, from which it was thought he could make trips to Rome from time to time. Only after some hesitation did Sec-

---

[22] FDRL, Taylor, McCormick to Taylor, Rome, Mar. 18, 1940 (copy), attached to account of Welles' audience with Pius XII, Mar. 18, 1940.

[23] Cardinal Maglione's Notes, Mar. 18, 1940, *Holy See and the War*, I, 376.

[24] FDRL, Taylor, Taylor's report of audience, Mar. 29, 1940.

[25] Pius XII to Mussolini, Apr. 24, 1940, *Holy See and the War*, I, 395; FLYNN: Roosevelt and Romanism, pp. 118–119.

retary of State Cordell Hull allow him to use State Department stationery and assign him a temporary assistant, Harold H. Tittmann, a consular official assigned to the American Embassy in Rome. Poor health, however, soon forced Taylor to return for treatment to the United States.[26]

B. DOMESTIC AFFAIRS: SPELLMAN, ROOSEVELT, AND PIUS XII.

In the meantime, the American Church domestically prepared for wartime readiness. Early in 1940, before Taylor arrived in Rome, Roosevelt seems to have thought better of having his representative discuss Stritch with the pope. Instead, he had Frank Walker, the Postmaster General, approach Spellman on "reports that Archbishop Stritch was favorable to Father Coughlin and that he was not in sympathy with some of the measures that ... [the president was] sponsoring and supporting". Spellman phoned Stritch, who was still in Milwaukee, and subsequently wrote him about articles which had appeared in the Milwaukee *Catholic Citizen*.[27] Stritch pointedly denied the accusations, said he had issued rebuttals to some of the reports mentioned, and declared his support for Roosevelt's general policies. To keep the Vatican informed, Spellman sent a copy of Stritch's letter to Galleazzi, who could only comment "that the great city of the West will be far from having the fortune of New York".[28] In what seems to have been a breach of confidence, Spellman forwarded the original letter to Roosevelt.[29] A delighted president replied that Stritch "will prove a great success in the Chicago Diocese, not only along spiritual lines but also in pushing forward with the splendid social policies of the late Cardinal". Then he returned to one of his favorite themes for the organization of the American Church: "Also, I hope that Bishop Sheil will receive recognition for the able assistance which he gave to my old friend".[30]

But if Roosevelt was still lamenting the loss of his old friend in Chicago, Spellman was still having difficulties with his "friend" in Boston. He was to have received from O'Connell the pallium investing him with the full authority of archbishop on March 12, 1940, but then the cardinal pleaded a sore throat as an excuse for not being present. On March 8, Spellman phoned Dougherty, who had

---

[26] FLYNN: *Roosevelt and Romanism,* pp. 109, 119. On the early phase of Taylor's mission, see John S. CONWAY: *Myron C. Taylor's Mission to the Vatican 1940–1950,* in: Church History 44 (1975) 85–89.

[27] FDRL, PSF 185, Spellman to Roosevelt, New York, Feb. 5, 1940.

[28] AANY, Galeazzi to Spellman, Rome, Feb. 28, 1940.

[29] FDRL, PSF 185, Stritch to Spellman, Milwaukee, Jan. 20, 1940.

[30] AANY, Roosevelt to Spellman, Feb. 13, 1940 (copy).

earlier declined an invitation, to preside at the ceremony.[31] Spellman chose the occasion of the ceremony to speak of Roosevelt's sending Myron Taylor to the pope.

Spellman's administration of the Archdiocese of New York was to have effects reaching far beyond the eastern see. As Archbishop of New York, he was also the military vicar. To aid him in that task, especially as the war approached, late in 1940, he chose Father John O'Hara, C.S.C., President of the University of Notre Dame, as his auxiliary bishop. Spellman was also a man who could distinguish between personal feelings and recognition of ability. There had been tension between him and Monsignor James McIntyre, not only during Pacelli's visit but also during the New York interregnum. Cardinal O'Connell even advised his former auxiliary to make some changes in the chancery – apparently an allusion to McIntyre,[32] who seems to have offered his resignation.[33] Instead, Spellman made him his auxiliary bishop. He needed the expertise of the former Wall Street clerk especially when he learned that he had inherited a debt-ridden archdiocese.[34] Both O'Hara and McIntyre would alter the face of the American hierarchy.

In addition to laying the groundwork for reshaping the hierarchy, Spellman was assigned a series of tasks to accomplish immediately upon assuming his office. One of these had been the establishment of some type of diplomatic relations; others included the investments of foreign dioceses and institutions in New York banks. But one of the most interesting and moving of the tasks was the restoration to the active ministry of Bishop Bonaventure Broderick. A native of Hartford, Broderick had been appointed Auxiliary Bishop of Havana after the Spanish-American War. In 1905 he was named the collector of the Peter's Pence collection for the United States by Merry del Val. Gibbons had his authority revoked and the bishop found himself without means of support, except for a pension from the Archdiocese of Havana. He moved to Millbrook, New York, where he purchased a farm and later ran a small business. Cicognani had been told to investigate the case at the time of his appointment as delegate in 1933, but it was Spellman who finally settled it. In September, 1939, he paid a secret visit to the bishop, heard his story and then assigned him as the chaplain of a hospital while the Holy Office completed the investigation which led to his full restoration to the episcopal ministry.[35]

---

[31] AAP, Spellman to Dougherty, New York, Feb. 8, 1940; Dougherty to Spellman, Philadelphia, Mar. 7, 1940 (copy); Spellman to Dougherty, New York, Mar. 8, 1940; Dougherty to Bernardini, Philadelphia, Mar. 8, 1940 (copy).

[32] AANY, Spellman Diary, June 30, 1939.

[33] GANNON: *Spellman*, p. 136.

[34] *Ibid.*, p. 141.

[35] *Ibid.*, pp. 146–151.

Spellman's administration pleased his Roman friends. Late in 1939, Galeazzi strongly hinted to him that he and Archbishop John Glennon of St. Louis would soon be named cardinals. The Second World War, however, caused Pius XII to delay convening his first consistory. In May, 1941, Spellman wrote the pope a lengthy letter detailing his administration. He was proud to report that he was a member of the administrative board of the NCWC and, even when he disagreed with the proceedings, "thus far the other Bishops have accepted my viewpoint". Spellman, however, would never be as dominant an influence in the NCWC as Mooney, Stritch, or McNicholas. If he was successful in gaining the cooperation of the Archbishop of Lima, Peru, in reducing his New York debts, he wrote, "the good Lord will have helped me to have solved all of the ten major problems that the Delegate told me existed in New York prior to my coming, problems – some of them of many years standing". Having recounted his own success, he then went on to give his opinion of other bishops. He characterized O'Hara as "a most extraordinary man" and McIntyre as "invaluable to me" and "a devoted exemplary priest and one of the ablest bishops of the U.S." These two auxiliary bishops of New York and his successor as Auxiliary Bishop of Boston, Richard J. Cushing, were all "preeminent among the Bishops of this country". Spellman was careful to discuss all the financial matters of the diocese with McIntyre and urged that if he himself should die "he would be eminently qualified to succeed me & the appointment should follow quickly".[36] Spellman thus took the initiative in promoting the careers of three bishops, each of whom would become cardinals in the years to come.[37]

In 1940, however, Spellman was known less for his power within the American hierarchy than for his influence in Rome. In August, 1940, the *Regime Fascista* had attacked him as the "agent of Jews in America". Through money he sent to the Vatican, the journal stated, he encouraged the Holy See's anti-Fascist attitude and created an alliance between the Church and the Jews.[38] Informed of this by Cardinal Maglione, Cicognani reported that Spellman had made a formal protest to the Italian consul in New York. The delegate himself asked for instructions as to whether he should see the Italian ambassador to Washington.[39] For the next few weeks, however, the Fascist journal continued to attack the Holy See, the *Osservatore Romano,* and Spellman.[40] While it was extreme to see Spellman as an "agent of the Jews", it was accurate to see him as the Vatican's principal agent for dealing with the United States government.

---

[36] AANY, Spellman to Pius XII, May 3, 1941 (draft).

[37] See AANY, Galeazzi to Spellman, Vatican, May 15, 1941.

[38] Maglione to Cicognani, Sept. 3, 1940, ADSS, IV, 135–136.

[39] Cicognani to Maglione, Washington, Sept. 5, 1940, *ibid.* pp. 137–138.

[40] Maglione to Cicognani, Vatican, Sept. 26, 1940, *ibid.,* p. 163.

C. THE AMERICAN CHURCH PREPARES FOR WAR

1. Taylor's Mission Given Permanency

In the meantime, the Holy See was expressing its concern over the status of Roosevelt's personal representation in Taylor's absence. On January 15, 1941, Maglione cabled Cicognani to probe, with Spellman's assistance, Roosevelt's intentions of having Taylor return to Rome and of appointing a permanent substitute during his absences.[41] Perhaps still chafing from Spellman's earlier snubs, the delegate in this instance had motivation for acting on his own. On the same day Maglione had cabled, Roosevelt had summoned Cicognani to the White House. They discussed the similarity between the pope's Christmas message enunciating five points for peace and the president's January address on "the Four Freedoms". The president condemned the Nazi atrocities in the war and still thought it possible for there to be a separate peace for Italy, "whose alliance with Germany is unnatural".[42] This would cease to be an American objective once the United States entered the war, but it remained a constant plea from the Vatican.

Encouraged by the president's confidence in him, Cicognani, without consulting Spellman, decided to approach the State Department directly about the Taylor Mission. On January 18, he asked Adolf A. Berle, the Assistant Secretary of State, to come to his residence to discuss appointing a permanent substitute for Taylor. Berle told Cicognani that such an appointment was the president's prerogative, but recommended the action to Welles, then the Under-Secretary of State.[43] Welles, in turn, recommended to Roosevelt that Tittmann, then assigned as counselor in the American Embassy at Rome, be detached for service exclusively as Taylor's substitute. For the State Department, such a contact was crucial for gaining information on internal affairs of Italy. Roosevelt, however, preferred first to confer with Taylor before taking any action.[44]

On February 14, Cicognani and Joseph Hurley, who had returned from the Vatican to become Bishop of St. Augustine, visited Taylor recuperating in Palm Beach, Florida. To the delegate's expression of concern that Tittmann was then assigned to the Embassy to the Quirinal, Taylor assured him that Tittmann "would continue his work as 'Chargé d'Affaires'" and would henceforth more

---

[41] Maglione to Cicognani, Vatican, Jan. 15, 1941, *ibid.,* pp. 335–336.
[42] Cicognani to Maglione, Washington, Jan. 16, 1941, *ibid.,* p. 344.
[43] NA, RG 59, DS 121.866A/106, Berle to Welles, Washington, Jan. 21, 1941; Memorandum of Berle to Secretary Hull, Washington, Jan. 21, 1941.
[44] *Ibid.,* 121.866A/105A, Welles to Roosevelt, Washington, Jan. 24, 1941; 121.866A/105 1/2, Roosevelt to Welles, Jan. 31, 1941.

actively contact the Vatican. Taylor's designation of Tittmann as "Chargé d'Affaires", was, of course, misleading since there was no official diplomatic mission. Welles found Taylor's letter "inconclusive", but felt that for the time being Tittmann could be "our temporary contact with the Vatican", until Taylor could come personally to Washington in April to confer with the president.[45] On the basis of Taylor's recommendation and Cicognani's concurrence, the State Department then cabled Tittmann instructions on February 20 to resume contact with the Vatican. On April 20, it designated him officially "Assistant to the Personal Representative of the President of the United States to His Holiness the Pope". Tittmann immediately informed Maglione of his appointment and opened an office in the Hotel Excelsior.[46]

Tittmann now began increasingly important contacts with Vatican and other Church officials. Early in May, he reported a long conversation he had had with Vladimir Ledochowski, S.J., the Jesuit General. "Polish blood ... naturally enhances his own bitterness toward Nazis", Tittmann cabled, "but courageous and fighting attitude of Jesuits in general seems in striking contrast with almost pusillanimous atmosphere encountered at present within Vatican". While the Jesuit said he was ready to face martyrdom because of his opposition to the Axis, Tittmann sought to assure him that the United States was determined to see the struggle through to a successful conclusion. Ledochowski's concern, however, was that there was a "fifth column everywhere but more especially in United States and Latin America". For him, the American hierarchy "was not free from guilt in this respect" and Cardinal O'Connell and Archbishop McNicholas, in particular, did not seem to see that Hitler was out to destroy the Church. The German-American clergy "were likewise luke-warm".[47] While there was thus a wide spectrum of opinions both in Rome and among American Church leaders, the Vatican now sought, while maintaining its neutrality, to have the American hierarchy see the danger of Nazism. Vatican policy coincided with the American government's effort to mobilize Catholic support for greater involvement.

On May 3, 1941, just as Tittmann was reporting to the State Department about his conversation with Ledochowski, Spellman wrote Pius XII. "The tendency of the United States", he said, "is towards greater participation in the war although there is still a strong proportion of the population contrary to direct in-

---

[45] *Ibid.*, 121.886A/106A, Welles to Roosevelt, Washington, Feb. 20, 1941 (copy) enclosing Taylor to Welles, Palm Beach, Feb. 18, 1941 (copy).

[46] *Ibid.*, 121.866A/142, Tittmann to Secretary Hull, Rome, Apr. 25, 1941, enclosing Tittmann to Maglione, Rome, Apr. 21, 1941 (copy).

[47] *Ibid.*, 740.0011 European War 1939/10588, Tittmann to Secretary Hull, Rome, May 2, 1941 (telegram).

volvement".[48] For the government, however, the issue was whether some bishops and other Catholics were isolationists or pro-German. Taylor discussed this with Cicognani in June. He pointed out that many bishops of Irish descent saw only an attack on Britain and not the danger of Nazism. Moreover, on May 23, there had been a demonstration of the isolationist America First Committee in New York at which there was distributed a pamphlet quoting phrases from the statement issued by the administrative board of the NCWC in April. In that statement the bishops had said they were not competent to give directives on the political situation and referred to the pope's five points for peace in his Christmas address of 1940. These sentences, however, were taken out of context and construed as stating that the bishops favored isolationism and opposed the government's foreign policy. Authorized by Mooney, chairman of the administrative board of the NCWC, Ready protested the misuse of the statement by the America First Committee. Explaining these actions to Taylor, Cicognani noted that, while some prelates opposed armed intervention, notably O'Connell and Curley, to whom Taylor had referred, none had spoken corporately or individually in favor of Nazism. It was difficult, Cicognani then repeated to Maglione, for there not to be a divergence of opinion in a Church of 116 bishops and about 30,000 priests. With his overall evaluation, he was careful to mention, Spellman agreed.[49] In the months ahead, however, the Vatican worked to lessen or at least make less public that divergence of opinion.

2. Lend-Lease to Russia: McNicholas' Pastoral Letter

Many American Catholics remained isolationists — a posture reinforced by the bitter dispute which had erupted in the United States over the Spanish Civil War from 1936 to 1939. As reports came in about the murder of bishops, priests, nuns and laymen, the American bishops in 1937 had addressed a letter of sympathy to the Spanish hierarchy.[50] In the eyes of many Catholics, the persecution of the Church by the Loyalists was due to communist influence. While there was notable dissent, with journals like *Commonweal* calling for neutrality in the discussion, Catholic opinion seemed definitely to favor Franco. Fascism seemed a preferable alternative to communism.[51] On this critical issue, so directly involving the interests of the Church, however, the available archival material gives no indica-

---

[48] AANY, Spellman to Pius XII, May 3, 1941 (draft).
[49] Cicognani to Maglione, Washington, June 17, 1941, ADSS, IV, 555–558.
[50] HUBER (ed.): *Our Bishops Speak,* pp. 219–221.
[51] FLYNN: *American Catholics,* pp. 29–62.

tion of any Vatican directives for influencing American opinion. Moreover, the pro-Franco and therefore isolationist sentiment of American Catholic leaders may have been exaggerated. While some leaders, like Hayes and McNicholas had spoken in Franco's favor, others, like Mundelein and Mooney had been more reticent.

Whatever tendency American Catholics may have had for involvement in European affairs seemed threatened when they were confronted with the possibility of having to cooperate directly with communism. On June 22, 1941, Germany had invaded Russia. Roosevelt then immediately announced the extension of Lend-Lease to the Soviets. Catholic opinion was further confused by the division of opinion among the bishops. On July 6, 1941, Bishop Joseph Hurley of St. Augustine broadcast a radio address from Washington. Using material provided by Welles, he stated that lending arms to the Russians was not contrary to papal teaching about cooperation with communists. Furthermore, he said, National Socialism was a more immediate danger than communism. That Hurley was a former Vatican official seemed to give his words greater authority in the public mind. He immediately met with the opposition of Coughlin, Cardinal O'Connell, and Archbishops Curley and Beckman. Curley protested privately that Hurley did not have his permission to speak in Washington. Beckman went on the radio to speak against Hurley. The entire dispute, reported in secular journals, Cicognani wrote Cardinal Maglione, had created an unfavorable impression of the lack of unity among the episcopate. The delegate, therefore, recommended that Hurley not be given a temporary mission to India, for which he was then being considered, because such an appointment would seem to give his speech Vatican approbation.[52] Spellman wrote directly to Pius XII repudiating Hurley's position.[53] On September 15, Tardini responded to Cicognani's letter to Maglione deprecating the public dissent between the bishops and stating that such differences of opinion should be expressed privately.[54]

The issue of support for aid to Russia, however, now began to move beyond the public difference of opinions between Hurley and other bishops. With the subtle maneuvering of some American Catholic leaders, the State Department, and the Vatican, the American Church was being prepared for direct intervention in the war. On August 11, Maglione sent Cicognani new instructions. While the bishops were to enjoy full freedom and were not asked to speak against the war, they were, without compromising the Holy See, to inform American Catholics of

---

[52] Cicognani to Maglione, Washington, Aug. 4, 1941, ADSS, V, 130–131; Aug. 11, 1941, *ibid.*, pp. 140–141; Sept. 1, 1941, *ibid.*, pp. 175–178.

[53] Spellman to Pius XII, New York, Sept. 4, 1941, *ibid.*, pp. 181–182.

[54] Tardini to Cicognani, Vatican, Sept. 15, 1941, *ibid.*, p. 214.

religious conditions in Germany.[55] On September 1, Cicognani reported that, while the United States was moving toward involvement, most Americans would fight only a defensive war. Roosevelt and Churchill, however, were now in a-greement that the purpose of the war was to end Nazi totalitarianism. American Catholics were well aware of what Nazism had done to the Church, but the bishops, except for Hurley and John Mark Gannon of Erie, opposed interven-tion; in this regard, O'Connell, Curley, McNicholas, and Gerald Shaughnessy of Seattle were the most outspoken. The Catholic press likewise remained generally isolationist.

But Roosevelt's proposal of aid for Russia placed Catholics in a quandary, Cicognani continued. If Pius XI's encyclical *Divini Redemptoris* were interpreted literally, were Catholics forbidden to cooperate with Russia? Were they therefore obliged to oppose American foreign policy? This was the question raised by Mooney and Ready, who had consulted with Sumner Welles. Mooney urged that the Vatican issue an interpretation of the encyclical in the sense that cooperation with the Russian people was different from cooperation with communism. He further asked that the clarification be published in the *Osservatore Romano* in time for the bishops' meeting in November to avoid the cleavage in the hierarchy which would surely result from varied interpretations of the encyclical.[56]

This topic became part of the commission Taylor carried with him on his sec-ond visit to Rome. Domenico Tardini privately wrote Cicognani that the pope had no difficulty with the distinction proposed by Mooney, but that, rather than publishing that interpretation in the *Osservatore Romano,* the delegate should make it known to Mooney and any others who inquired.[57] To Taylor, Tardini urged that the United States link its aid to Russia with a plea for religious liberty, for the lack of churches still open demonstrated the continued Russian oppres-sion of religion.[58]

With that interpretation of the encyclical — basically the one for which Hurley had been censured — the way was open for mustering Catholic support for Roosevelt's policy. Cicognani narrated for Maglione the actions he had taken. He had orally communicated Tardini's answer to Mooney through Ready. Ready and Mooney, in turn, suggested the strategy of having McNicholas issue a pas-toral letter embodying the interpretation. The archbishop was ideally suited for

[55] Maglione to Cicognani, Vatican, Aug. 11, 1941, *ibid.,* pp. 139–140.

[56] Cicognani to Maglione, Washington, Sept. 1, 1941, *ibid.,* pp. 163–174.

[57] Tardini to Cicognani, Vatican, Sept. 20, 1941, *ibid.,* pp. 240–241.

[58] Tardini to Taylor, Vatican, Sept. 20, 1941, *ibid.,* pp. 241–245. Taylor assured the pope during an audience that Roosevelt was endeavouring to get a clear declaration of religious liberty from the Russians, but in the meantime he asked that Catholics cease their opposition to Lend-Lease; see CONWAY: *Taylor's Mission,* pp. 88–91.

the task. On the one hand, he was known for his loyalty to the Holy See and, on the other hand, he was not closely identified with the government. McNicholas, accordingly, was summoned to Washington where Cicognani confidentially informed him of the Vatican's desires. Then after speaking with Archbishops Mooney and Stritch and Bishop Peterson, McNicholas wrote his pastoral. Exhorting his people to charity in matters of political opinions, he then turned to Pius XI's encyclical *mit brennender Sorge* which drew the distinction between Nazism and the German people. From this he drew the conclusion that the same distinction could be made between communism and the Russian people. The passages of *Divini Redemptoris* which forbade Catholics to cooperate with communists, he concluded, did not apply "to the present moment of armed conflict". It was then arranged for McNicholas' pastoral to be distributed through the National Catholic News Service, but not to the secular press.

Cicognani then turned in his report to the attitude of other American prelates. Archbishop Beckman may have received advanced word of McNicholas' forthcoming statement and stated his opposition to Lend-Lease on the radio. Cicognani reported that the archbishop's broadcasts recalled the tone of Coughlin and that he himself had not moved to silence him only because of the advice of other bishops who argued that such action would be ammunition for Coughlin's *Social Justice*. The delegate had, however, succeeded in preventing Bishop Gerald Shaughnessy from joining Beckman in his broadcast. He had then written both Shaughnessy and Beckman that the Holy See did not want bishops publicly to air their differences of opinion. Shaughnessy agreed to desist, but Beckman refused and in his broadcast denied the distinction between the Soviet state and the Russian army. Cicognani concluded his report to Maglione by saying that Taylor had visited him and had told him about his conversations with both Maglione and Tardini. The delegate confided to Taylor that he had received instructions on interpreting the encyclical. To Maglione, however, he confessed the fear that some government official might leak the fact that the interpretation had actually come from the Vatican.[59]

In the meantime, while McNicholas was preparing his pastoral, Taylor and Mooney were busy trying to neutralize Coughlin whose *Social Justice* advocated American isolationism on the grounds of the passages in *Divini Redemptoris*, which McNicholas' pastoral was endeavouring to interpret. On October 23, Taylor and Mooney met with Roosevelt secretly, in order to avoid the possible charge by Coughlin that Mooney was acting under the administration's orders.[60]

---

[59] Cicognani to Maglione, Washington, Oct. 28, 1941, *ibid.,* pp. 285–288.

[60] FDRL, PPF 423, Grace Tully to Roosevelt, Oct. 9, 1941; Roosevelt to Tully, Oct. 10, 1941; Welles to Watson, Oct. 20, 1941.

It may have been at this meeting that Roosevelt informed Mooney of the possible action the Justice Department might take against Coughlin. But Mooney, as chairman of the administrative board of the NCWC, was concerned with gaining the united stand of the hierarchy at its annual meeting in November, for which McNicholas' pastoral was a preparation. On October 26, McNicholas informed him that he had forwarded a copy of his letter to Ready. "It is very perplexing", he wrote, "to make statements in these crucial days. It is even difficult for us who have principles on our side, who are disinterested, and who wish to do only what is best for the Church and for the whole human family." He went on to report that Senator Robert Taft of Ohio had written him to express his interest in McNicholas' plea for tolerance and his "description of Sovietism, whose basic principle is atheism". Uncertain of his actions in the future, the senator still felt that the United States "ought not to become involved in foreign war", that the invasion of Russia showed "the conflict in Europe is based largely on national interest, and that we are helpless to solve the European problem if we would".[61]

Three days later, Mooney responded thanking McNicholas for the pastoral, which "tackles a job that needed to be done and you have done it well – 'in pondere et mensura'". He had arranged for it to be published in his diocesan paper with an editorial. In regard to Taft's continued isolationism, however, he offered the following reflection which indicated how closely he and perhaps the majority of American bishops identified the cause of the Church with American involvement in the war: "Of course it is easier for a non-Catholic than for a Catholic to be an isolationist. They have not the world view or the worldwide spiritual interest that is our heritage of faith. Of course, too 'the conflict in Europe is based largely on national interest'. The real question is – on that side – whether or not we have a deep national interest in Hitler's defeat. But the opposition of a sincere and moderate man like Taft may be a providential drag on precipitate action. But – like yourself – 'I do not want to get into the arena of politics' – and I hope we can keep the boys out of the arena in Washington the week after next – and still within the orbit of good Catholic American citizenship. You have helped very much to lay one ghost at any rate".[62]

Mooney's efforts to keep the bishops "out of the arena of politics" and "within the orbit of Catholic American citizenship" were successful. At their annual meeting in Washington from November 12 to 13, the bishops deputed the administrative board to issue a statement on "the crisis of Christianity". While pointing out that Nazism and Communism remained enemies of the Church, the statement drew the now familiar distinction between Nazism and the German people and

---

[61] AACi, McNicholas to Mooney, Cincinnati, Oct. 26, 1951 (copy).
[62] AACi, Mooney to McNicholas, Detroit, Oct. 29, 1941.

between Communism and the Russian people. It recalled Pius XII's Christmas message of 1939 laying down five points "for a just and honorable peace". It rehearsed papal social teachings as a program for social reconstruction after the war. But more importantly, it appealed to Leo XIII's treatment of the different spheres of civil and ecclesiastical power and called for respect for both authorities. In words perhaps aimed at Coughlin and Beckman, it stated: "In the confusion of the hour, we deplore the presumption of those who, lacking authority, strive to determine the course of action that the Church should take within her clearly defined field. Recognizing the liberty of discussion, and even of criticism, which our democratic form of government guarantees, we urge and commend respect and reverence for the authority of our civil officials which has its source in God". They appealed to priests and laymen to exercise restraint and to labor leaders to "refrain from doing anything that is harmful to the general welfare ...". The statement ended with a prayer for guidance for civil officials.[63]

3. *The United States Enters World War II: The Hierarchy Is Forced to Conform*

The statement of the administrative board received favorable comment in the secular press and was published in its entirety in the *New York Times*.[64] But hardly had the American people time to digest the import of the statement than they were called on practically to support civil authorities. On December 7, 1941, the Japanese bombed Pearl Harbor; the next day, the United States declared war on Japan. On December 11, Germany and Italy announced that they were in a state of war with the United States, which immediately took the same action toward the two European Axis powers. But even then there was some doubt as to the unanimity of the American episcopate. On December 23, Mooney, after consulting the members of the administrative board, offered Roosevelt the support of the hierarchy. Beckman still opposed American intervention and threatened to dissent from Mooney's statement. Cicognani finally won his silence by referring him to Tardini's dispatch of September 15, opposing public dissent among the bishops, and by reminding him of the consequences of acting contrary to the unanimous opinion of the episcopate.[65]

Complaints about Curley's attitude toward the declaration of war had also reached the Vatican. Cicognani was asked to investigate. Curley had been unaware of the attack on Pearl Harbor when reporters for the Baltimore *Evening Sun*

[63] HUBER (ed.): *Our Bishops Speak*, pp. 102–109.
[64] AACi, Mooney to McNicholas, Detroit, Nov. 24, 1941.
[65] Cicognani to Maglione, Jan. 5, 1942, ADSS, V, 361–362.

questioned him about the "fighting in the Pacific". He explained to Cicognani that he had "simply stated that I was not interested in the fighting in the Pacific or the Atlantic, but since we were fighting, we might as well fight on all Seven Seas". He did not construe anything he had said or written, he told Cicognani, as being "anti-Government". "I have never", he said, "discussed any matter that was purely political and I might add, at the same time, I have never spoken in my life to gain the favor of anyone and I never gave a thought of incurring the displeasure of anyone". He had already issued a statement on December 9 which stated now that the issue was no longer one of intervention or isolation but one of national defense. He was also queried by Cicognani about a "broadcast from Berlin or some Italian Station" and could only reply: "I was told that the Berlin Radio did take a sentence out of a talk I gave ... and broadcast that talk as a condemnation by me of England and England's policy toward the Church. The Berlin Station did not broadcast what I said about Germany's attitude towards the Church or the attitude of Russia or France. It did not broadcast what I said about the evil condition in our own Nation, having in mind those same conditions referred to by our present Holy Father in his special letter written to the American Hierarchy on the occasion of the 150th Anniversary of the Formation of the Hierarchy in this Country".[66] This typical statement of the blunt Archbishop of Baltimore seemed to satisfy Cicognani who assured Curley that "I shall do everything to present this matter to the Holy See with accuracy and completeness, seeking to illuminate other factors which perhaps were not included in the original source of information".[67]

The Holy See's attitude toward dissent among the American bishops represented a shift from its attitude in 1922. When the National Catholic Welfare Council was condemned in 1922, one reason was the fear that the American episcopate was so large that its united stance on any issue might constitute a threat to its loyalty to the Holy See. In regard to Shaughnessy's speaking against Hurley and especially of Beckman's and possibly Curley's dissent from the war, the Holy See virtually demanded their public conformity to the statement of support of the government issued by Mooney in the name of the administrative board of the NCWC. The exigency of war, in which the United States would hold the balance of power, led the Vatican to demand corporate action from the bishops.

The final obstacle to the American Church's support of the government remained Coughlin. Mooney may have discussed the government's intended course of action against the priest when he and Taylor met with Roosevelt in October of 1941. *Social Justice,* after the declaration of war, continued to challenge

---

[66] AAB, Curley to Cicognani, Baltimore, Jan. 14, 1942 (copy).
[67] AAB, Cicognani to Curley, Washington, Jan. 18, 1942.

Roosevelt's administration for getting into the war. Francis Biddle, the Attorney General, consulted with Frank Walker, the Postmaster General, about revoking the journal's mailing privileges on the grounds that it was obstructing the war efforts. Walker, accordingly, called for a hearing on April 29, 1942, and in the meantime ordered the Royal Oak postmaster to withhold the journal. Roosevelt then dispatched a Catholic friend, Leo Crowley, to Mooney. On May 1, 1942, the archbishop in an interview ordered Coughlin to cease all non-religious activities or be suspended. The hearing, in the meantime, was postponed until May 4, but on that date no representative of *Social Justice* appeared.[68] At long last the troublesome priest was silenced, but only with the threat of government investigation. The United States and the American Church were now ready for the war.

---

[68] MARCUS: *Coughlin*, pp. 211–217.

CHAPTER XII

THE SECOND WORLD WAR: THE VATICAN RECOGNIZES THE UNITED STATES IN WORLD EVENTS

A. THE AMERICAN CHURCH AND VATICAN NEUTRALITY

1. *Tittmann Named Chargé d'Affaires*

American entry into the war occasioned not only the emerging dominance of the United States in world affairs but an increasing influence of the American Church on the Vatican. With the rapproachment between Catholics and Roosevelt and the establishment of the Myron Taylor Mission, the stage was set for the Vatican finally to fulfill John Ireland's prophecy and to take the American Church seriously because it recognized the United States as a world power. This war was different than the First World War and Pius XII was a different pope than Benedict XV. True, he had love for the German people and, if the report of the German ambassador to the Holy See can be trusted, the Vatican was critical of Roosevelt at the American declaration of war.[1] Yet his direct contacts with the United States government through Taylor or his assistant and the influence on him of the American hierarchy present a portrait of him in subtle shades of gray as he sought to maintain the Holy See's position of neutrality. The role of some of the American bishops in regard to the Roosevelt administration, particularly Spellmann and Mooney, was reminiscent of that played by Ireland with the McKinley and Theodore Roosevelt administrations. Mooney, Stritch, and McNicholas even picked up the theme of religious liberty, but that is a story which belongs to another chapter.

After Italy declared war on the United States on December 10, 1941, Harold H. Tittmann, Taylor's assistant, moved into Vatican City. His move signaled quasi-official diplomatic recognition of the Holy See. On December 13, Cicognani informed Welles that the Italian government might object to Tittmann's residence in the Vatican, unless he were designated "Minister to the Holy See, or at least Chargé d'Affaires".[2] On December 16, Welles wrote Roosevelt noting that

---

[1] Anthony RHODES: *The Vatican in the Age of the Dictators (1922–1945)*, New York 1974, p. 265.
[2] NA, RG 59, DS 121.866 A/204¹/₂, Cicognani to Welles, Washington, Dec. 13, 1941.

Hull supported the suggestion that Tittmann be named Chargé d'Affaires because "it is of very great importance that Tittmann remain in the Vatican City so that we may continue contact through him with the Holy See".[3] Roosevelt scrawled his approval across the top of Welles' letter. Thus, through the exigency of the war, Roosevelt may have fallen, albeit secretly, into the pitfall of granting what in peace he refused – an officially recognized and publicly supported diplomat to the Holy See. Tittmann's new designation caused queries from the Holy See on the status of the mission – the *Osservatore Romano* listed him among accredited diplomats – and postwar consternation in the State Department.[4] Tittmann was to communicate with Washington through the Holy See's diplomatic channels with Switzerland, where, incidentally, Filippo Bernardini was then the nuncio.

On the same day Welles had written to Roosevelt about giving Tittmann an official diplomatic designation, Taylor also wrote the president about the need to keep his assistant in Rome. He had already discussed the situation with the Vatican before his departure from Rome the previous September. Moreover, he said, he had also "conferred with Father Vincent A. McCormick, an American Jesuit, occupying a high position in the Jesuit Church in Rome, and it was agreed with him, and consented to by the Vatican, that he also would remove to Vatican City in case Italy declared war upon the United States". Taylor believed "it would also be useful to have someone, placed as he is in the Catholic world, to be a resident of the Vatican, as being helpful to Mr. Tittmann and in any emergency able to carry on in our relations with the Vatican through the Apostolic Delegate in Washington".[5] McCormick had been Rector of Woodstock College in Maryland until he was named Rector of the Gregorian University in 1934. When Italy declared war on the United States, he resigned his post and moved across the city to the Jesuit curia. During the war years, he maintained a diary in which he recorded frequent meetings with Tittmann and his increasing criticism of the Vatican's neutrality in a war in which he thought such a stance impossible.

2. The Vatican Accepts the Japanese Mission

The Vatican's neutrality very early strained its relations with the United States and the American Church. In February, 1942, the Holy See agreed to accept a dip-

---

[3] FDRL, PPF 1935, Welles to Roosevelt, Washington, Dec. 17, 1941.

[4] NA, RG 59, DS 121.866A/208, Tittmann to Hull, Bern, Jan. 6, 1942; 121.866A/205½, Cicognani to Welles, Washington, Dec. 21, 1941 and Welles to Cicognani, Washington, Dec. 24, 1941 (copy); 121.866A/4–1345, Memorandum on the Personal Representative of the President of the United States to His Holiness Pope Pius XII, Apr. 11, 1945. On the diplomatic significance of a Chargé d'Affaires, see Robert A. GRAHAM: *Vatican Diplomacy*, Princeton 1949, p. 330.

[5] FDRL, OF 76 B, Box 6, Taylor to Roosevelt, New York, Dec. 17, 1941.

lomatic mission from Japan. Maglione confidentially communicated this intelligence to Tittmann and Godolphin D'Arcy Osborne, the British minister, and by the end of the month the news was public. American reaction was immediate. Cicognani cabled Maglione for an explanation noting that Cordell Hull had protested that the Axis propaganda interpreted the Vatican action as recognizing the Japanese occupation of the Far East.[6] Maglione responded on March 2 that the negotiations had first begun in 1922 and had only recently come to maturity. Because of Catholic interests in the Japanese Empire, the Holy See accepted the Japanese government's offer to send a representative.[7]

Ironically, while Cicognani was waiting for his response from Maglione, he left Washington personally to see Archbishops Curley and Beckman and Bishop Noll of Fort Wayne to tell them of the Holy See's desire for them to refrain from criticism of the war and to support the administration. In his absence, Monsignor Egidio Vagnozzi, the auditor of the delegation, conveyed Maglione's response personally to Welles. Immediately upon his return to Washington, Cicognani cabled Welles' reaction to Maglione. The undersecretary, he said, had stated "the information deeply displeased the Government of the United States and will cause in allied countries a 'terrific reaction' against the Holy See". The government, continued the delegate, felt that, if the Holy See had been negotiating with Japan for twenty years, it could have waited until the end of the war to establish diplomatic relations. Then Cicognani gave his own opinion. The Vatican's action, he said, made a "sad impression" on American Catholics and profited "Protestant sects and communist organizations, which were already conducting a subtle propaganda campaign against the Catholic Church in relation to the war". To prevent this the government was helpless.[8] Cicognani's implication that the Vatican's action would arouse American anti-Catholic sentiment was reminiscent of Denis O'Connell and Ireland's warning in the 1890s that a *Kulturkampf* was possible in the United States. But in this instance, the papal representative went a step beyond even what the Americanists had done.

On the evening of March 6, Cicognani met with Welles, told him that he had already sent Rome an account of the undersecretary's conversation with Vagnozzi, and stated his complete agreement with Welles' opinions. Welles then informed Cicognani that he had spoken to Roosevelt about the Holy See's recognition of Japan. Knowing the pope and his policies the president found it "completely incredible that the Vatican at this time could agree to receive an Ambas-

---

[6] Cicognani to Maglione, Washington, Feb. 27, 1942, ADSS, V, 454.

[7] Maglione to Cicognani, Vatican, Mar. 2, 1942, *ibid.*, p. 455.

[8] Cicognani to Maglione, Washington, Mar. 5, 1942, *ibid.*, pp. 462–463.

sador from Japan". Cicognani promised to convey the president's message to Rome and then made a further suggestion. Requesting that his name not be used, he asked "that Mr. Tittmann be instructed to make as forceful and emphatic representations as possible to the Cardinal Secretary of State" and that he also speak with Tardini. Cicognani, Welles recorded, "said he was profoundly disturbed and utterly unable to comprehend any justifiable reason for the step which apparently had been agreed upon by the Vatican".[9]

Tittmann's attitude at this juncture is confusing. On March 2, he met with Tardini and seems to have accepted the official explanation that the Holy See could not refuse a diplomatic initiative from any government. The American argued, however, that the Japanese were clearly trying to influence Catholic sentiment, particularly in Latin America. Nevertheless, he believed that the Holy See was open to the possibility of accepting a Russian envoy under certain conditions, which would provide an "Allied counterbalance". Strangely, he had been kept ignorant by Tardini of Cicognani's original cable demanding an explanation for the Vatican action.[10] But by March 11, he had received new instructions from Welles and had a meeting with Maglione to whom he presented the substance of Welles' comments to Vagnozzi.[11]

Confronted with this American protest, the Vatican now sought to enlist the aid of the American hierarchy in its defense. The day after Maglione saw Tittmann, he cabled new instructions to Cicognani. Beginning with a history of the negotiations with Japan and stating that the Holy See's diplomatic relations with a nation did not imply approval of that nation's actions, Maglione argued that after the publicity given to the Japanese initiative the Holy See could not refuse to accept a diplomat without appearing to side with the Allies. He then outlined for Cicognani two courses of action. First, he was to explain to the United States government the general principles which led to diplomatic relations with Japan. Second, he was to inform the most important of the bishops so that they could enlighten public opinion and establish among themselves a uniform line of conduct in the event of difficulties.[12] The following day, Maglione followed up his cable with additional instructions. Spellman was to see Roosevelt and explain that the Holy See remained neutral and was accepting the Japanese mission out of a desire to safeguard Catholic interests and continue its efforts for charitable works and

---

[9] NA, RG 59, DS 701.9466 A/8½, Memorandum of Conversation by Welles, Mar. 6, 1942, in: FRUS, 1942, V, 781–782.

[10] Tittmann to Secretary of State, Vatican, Mar. 6, 1942, in: FRUS, 1942, V, 783; Tardini's Notes, Mar. 2, 1942, ADSS, V, 455–457.

[11] Tittmann to Maglione, Vatican, Mar. 11, 1942, *ibid.*, pp. 477–478.

[12] Maglione to Cicognani, Vatican, Mar. 12, 1942, *ibid.*, pp. 479–480.

peace. The Holy See, in the meantime, renewed its warm feelings for the United States.[13]

With "profound regret", Ready conveyed Maglione's response to Welles who forwarded it to Roosevelt.[14] Ready and Bishop Hurley had already protested the Vatican action and offered their assistance to the State Department to prevent similar actions in the future. On March 14, Roosevelt wrote Spellman deploring the action and asking why it could not have been deferred. "I shall say nothing officially, in all probability", he wrote, "but my heart is torn because it is bound to get out and there will be definitely a bad reaction to thus [sic] unnecessary move".[15]

Cicognani, in the meantime, had summoned most of the archbishops to meet with him in Washington on March 16. McNicholas was unable to attend, but Cicognani passed over in silence Archbishop Beckman's absence. Cardinal Dougherty was then in Florida, but sent his opinion that the Holy See was free to establish diplomatic relations with any nation it chose and that the bishops should weather the storm of any public protests against it. The other archbishops, save one, basically concurred; the one exception was John J. Mitty of San Francisco, whose diocese harbored strong prejudice against the large Japanese-American population there. The next day Spellman met with Roosevelt to explain the Vatican position and to make a series of proposals which might make the Vatican action more palatable to the American government and people. These proposals, to which the other archbishops agreed, involved first that the Vatican retain a separate apostolic delegate in the Philippines, not subject to the one in Tokyo, and second that it be open to possible diplomatic relations with China and Holland.[16] Tittmann conveyed these suggestions personally to the pope in an audience on April 2. Pius had already agreed to receive a Chinese mission, Tittmann reported to Hull, but the pontiff felt that "religious intolerance" in the Netherlands would prevent the renewal of diplomatic relations.[17]

The American hierarchy had found itself in its traditional dilemma of being both American and Roman Catholic. As it tried to express its loyalty to the nation after the bombing of Pearl Harbor, the Holy See seemed to call that loyalty into question by establishing diplomatic relations with Japan. But the bishops found on this occasion that they had the understanding, if not the outright en-

---

[13] Maglione to Cicognani, Vatican, Mar. 13, 1942, *ibid.*, pp. 481–482.

[14] FDRL, PSF 185, Welles to Roosevelt, Washington, Mar. 14, 1942.

[15] *Ibid.*, Roosevelt to Spellman, n. p., Mar. 14, 1942 (copy).

[16] Cicognani to Maglione, Washington, Mar. 18, 1942, ADSS, V, 491–493.

[17] NA, RG 59, DS 121.866 A/228, Tittmann to Secretary, Bern, Apr. 10, 1942 (cable); Tittmann to Maglione, Vatican, Apr. 2, 1942, ADSS, V, 510. For a summary of this entire issue see *ibid.*, pp. 33–46.

couragement, of the apostolic delegate, to support their loyalty. They therefore drew closer to the administration and attempted to use their efforts to prevent the pope from being used by the Axis nations.

3. Taylor's Visit to Rome, September, 1942: the NCWC's Assistance

In September, Roosevelt decided to send Myron Taylor, with an Italian safe-conduct, on his third visit to Rome. Before departing, he conferred with Cicognani and Spellman. Moreover, he had Mooney, Hurley, and Ready draft a memorandum for him to present to the pope. On September 17, accompanied by Vagnozzi, Taylor arrived in Rome to begin his nine day-stay. Two days later, in the first of his three audiences, he presented two memoranda, his own and the one drafted by Mooney, Hurley, and Ready. In his own, he pointed to the Japanese attack which had made the American entry into the war necessary. Yet it was against the Japanese and the Nazis that the United States was primarily waging war. Toward the Italian people there was no American hatred and there was still time for them to withdraw from the Axis alliance. But an Allied victory was inevitable.[18]

The second memorandum, which Welles had already given to Roosevelt, was more forthright. Drafted by the prelates but presented in Taylor's name only, it spoke of future collaboration between the United States and the Holy See "when the anti-Christian philosophies which have taken the sword shall have perished by the sword...". So similar were papal pronouncements and American objectives, it said, that "we are fighting against the very things which the Popes condemned...". Nor could there be any giving quarter, for "in the conviction that anything less than complete victory would endanger the principles we fight for and our very existence as a nation, the United States of America will prosecute this war until the Axis collapses". The nation was united in the war effort, it continued, and "among the architects of this unity are the foremost Catholic leaders in our country...". Among their most outstanding pronouncements was the "letter of the Catholic hierarchy" to Roosevelt, "pledging the wholehearted cooperation of Catholics in the national war effort". Mooney's letter, to which the Vatican had demanded adherence, had thus officially become a letter of the hierarchy. The memorandum was adamant that the United States would not be misled by any "stop-gap peace", for "our Christian ideas, as well as our national existence, would be in jeopardy if we consented to forego now our manifest advantages". It concluded by pledging "to support the Holy See in resisting" any Axis "proposals

---

[18] Taylor to Pius XII, Vatican, Sept. 19, 1942, ADSS, V, 681–684.

of peace without victory".[19] Here were words of which Ireland and Denis O'Connell would have been proud, but they were placed in the mouth of an American diplomat. There is no evidence that any Vatican official suspected the real origin of the memorandum.

Taylor had two more audiences with the pope, one on September 22 and the other on September 26. He also spoke with Maglione, Tardini, and Montini. He protested the deportation of French Jews and Nazi brutality in other occupied territories and urged that the pope speak out. To this Maglione replied that the pope had already spoken but would speak again when it was opportune.[20] The indirect Vatican support for Roosevelt's extension of Lend-Lease to Russia had been coupled with a plea for increased Soviet religious toleration. On this point Taylor optimistically argued that such toleration would be forthcoming if Russia were admitted to the family of nations, but here Vatican officials were more pessimistic. Taylor also discussed with Montini the Allied bombing of German and Italian cities. To Montini's suggestion that the Allies spare civilian populations, Taylor replied sardonically that he was not aware of any papal interventions on behalf of the German bombing of London, Warsaw, or other cities. To his memorandum, he attached photographs of London after the blitz.[21] To raise the question of Allied bombing, Taylor said, would create the impression that the Vatican was partisan.

Vincent McCormick was requested by Robert Leiber, S.J., Pius XII's confidant, to prepare the pope's English replies to Taylor. He had already met with Taylor on several occasions even when the latter was keeping himself incommunicado from Tardini and Montini prior to his first audience with the pope. He implied that he may have altered the final wording of the pope's official appeal to Taylor to intervene with Roosevelt to spare civilian populations in aerial bombing.[22] By far the most interesting reply, however, was the one to Taylor's first "personal" memorandum. The pope, said the letter, had "never thought in terms of peace by compromise at any cost" and would reject any proposal from any source which would give "free rein to those who would undermine ... the founda-

---

[19] NA, RG 59, DS 212.866A/245B, draft attached to: Welles to Roosevelt, Washington, Sept. 4, 1942 (copy) in: ADSS, V, 684–690.

[20] Carroll's notes of conversation between Taylor and Maglione, Sept. 25, 1942, ADSS, V, 717–722.

[21] Tardini's Notes, Sept. 24, 1942, *ibid.*, pp. 712–713; Taylor to Montini, Vatican, Sept. 27, 1942, *ibid.*, pp. 729–731.

[22] James HENNESEY: *American Jesuit in Wartime Rome: The Diary of Vincent A. McCormick, S.J. (1942–1945)*, in: Mid-America: An Historical Review 56 (1974) 33. See also ADSS, V, 681 n.; Pius XII's letter to Taylor of Sept. 26, 1942, is given *ibid.*, pp. 722–723.

tions of Christianity and persecute religion and the Church".[23] Thus, Pius seemed to imply agreement with the principle of unconditional surrender which Roosevelt and Churchill would enunciate at the Casablanca conference the following February. And the pope had done so, unknowingly, in response to a letter actually written by the leadership of the NCWC. If Gibbons had hoped to get his views across to the Vatican through the British during the First World War, his successors had an even more direct mode of approach through their own government.

It is difficult to determine what Pius XII meant by neutrality. One thing which seems certain is that he did not wish to see the Holy See's influence in world affairs reach the low point it had reached during the pontificate of Benedict XV to which he had personally been a witness. A case in point was the continued American consternation at the Vatican recognition of Japan which Taylor had reported to the pope. The Holy See's official position was that it could not refuse to accept any diplomatic mission. But this might not have prevented some Vatican officials from being more partisan. On December 8, the day after the first anniversary of Pearl Harbor, McCormick recorded that the Irish embassy was hosting a party at which the ambassadors or ministers from Germany, Italy, and Japan would be present. The Irish ambassador had even invited Monsignor Walter Carroll, an American working in the Secretariat of State, who refused when he found out who the other guests were. McCormick was livid that Montini had attended.[24] A history of the American Office of Strategic Services, the forerunner of the Central Intelligence Agency, however, makes the undocumented statement that Montini and the Irish embassy were important links in a chain passing strategic information to Washington from Tokyo, where Paolo Marella was still apostolic delegate.[25]

Whatever may have been the feeling in Vatican circles toward the Allies, Taylor had departed from Rome on September 27. As the leaders of the NCWC had helped him influence Vatican officials, now he assisted the bishops in drafting their pastoral, issued on November 14, to influence American Catholics. The United States, wrote the bishops, was "associated with other powers in a deadly conflict against" other nations which were "united in waging war to bring about a slave world...". Such an essential "conflict of Principles", they maintained, made "compromise impossible". Roosevelt, they said, had assured friendly na-

[23] Pius XII to Taylor, Vatican, Sept. 22, 1942, ADSS, V, 692–694; an appended note indicates that this was given to Taylor only on Sept. 26. See also FLYNN: *Roosevelt and Romanism*, pp. 198–200 and CONWAY: *Taylor's Mission*, p. 92.

[24] HENNESEY: *Diary of McCormick*, p. 36.

[25] R. Harris SMITH: *OSS: The Secret History of America's First Central Intelligence Agency*, Berkeley 1972, pp. 84–85.

tions that "the United States has no designs of permanent conquest or sordid interest", but only sought "to guarantee to countries under temporary occupation as well as to our own the right to live in security and peace". In responding to the NCWC's letter after the declaration of war, the president had said that "in victory we shall seek not vengeance but the establishment of an international order in which the spirit of Christ shall rule the hearts of men and of nations". The bishops then touched upon a series of themes which would dominate their concern after the war. Neither "secularism", nor "exploitation", nor "totalitarianism, whether Nazi, Communist, or Fascist", could "write a real and lasting peace", but only "the Spirit of Christianity".

They turned next to a characteristic theme of the American Church – the compatibility of Christianity and American law as a basis for social reform: "In the epochal revolution through which the world is passing, it is very necessary for us to realize that every man is our brother in Christ. All should be convinced that every man is endowed with the dignity of human personality, and that he is entitled by the laws of nature to the things necessary to sustain life in a way conformable to human dignity. In the postwar world, the profit element of industry and commerce must be made subservient to the common good of communities and nations if we are to have a lasting peace with justice and a sense of true brotherhood for all our neighbors. The inequalities of nations and of individuals can never give to governments or to the leaders of industry or commerce a right to be unjust. They cannot, if they follow the fixed principles of morality, maintain or encourage conditions under which men cannot live according to standards befitting human personality". The bishops had thus moved the issue of social justice onto the international plane and provided the virtual basis for American Catholic support for the United Nations.

In regard to the atrocities of the war, they expressed their "deepest sympathy to our brother bishops in all countries of the world where religion is persecuted, liberty abolished, and the rights of God and of man are violated" and their "deep sense of revulsion against the cruel indignities heaped upon the Jews in conquered countries and upon defenseless peoples not of our faith". They protested "against despotic tyrants who have lost all sense of humanity by condemning thousands of innocent persons to death in subjugated countries as acts of reprisal; by placing other thousands of innocent victims in concentration camps, and by permitting unnumbered persons to die of starvation".

The issue of racism was not limited to Europe; it existed in the United States. The bishops therefore also addressed this problem. "The war has brought to the fore conditions that have long been with us. The full benefits of our free institutions and the rights of our minorities must be openly acknowledged and honestly respected. We ask this acknowledgement and respect particularly for our colored fellow citizens. They should enjoy the full measure of economic opportunities and advantages which will enable them to realize their hope and ambition to join with us in preserving and expanding in changed and changing social conditions our national heritage".[26] McCormick's reaction in Rome was: "Splendid; they have done themselves honor".[27] He, like the American bishops, was coming increasingly to identify the victory of the Allies with the victory of Christianity and to criticize the Holy See's neutrality. But just at this point, the Holy See sought to mobilize the American Church on an issue which made it appear anything but neutral.

4. First Efforts to Declare Rome an Open City

During the fall of 1942, the Allies bombed Genoa and Milan, an event which the Fascist radical Roberto Farinacci blamed on Taylor. Maglione, on the other hand, believed that Taylor and Cicognani were responsible for sparing Rome up to that point. But he reported to Cicognani new rumors that Rome was to be bombed and requested that Spellman see Roosevelt about sparing "the diocese of the Supreme Pontiff and the Capital of Catholicism". He furthermore noted the reports of the archbishops of Milan, Genoa, and Turin that there had been bombing of non-military targets.[28] Cicognani pointed out to Secretary of State Hull that the bombing of Rome would be a moral victory to the Axis. Spellman phoned Roosevelt for an appointment. Taylor had also spoken to both Roosevelt and Hull in an effort to spare Rome. The emotional campaign waged by the Vatican to save the Eternal City, however, fell on deaf ears, as least as far as the British were concerned. They argued that, in addition to being the diocese of the pope, Rome was also the capital of Italy, whose planes had taken part in the bombing of London. The Vatican overture thus fell between the different perspectives on Rome of the United States and Great Britain.[29] Maglione sought to neutralize the British argument and encourage Roosevelt to declare Rome an open city by quoting from the London *Tablet* that the Italian participation in the bombing of London was ineffective.[30] Churchill's reaction to this unusual argument is not recorded.

As Spellman prepared for his meeting with Roosevelt, Ready also consulted with Stritch, McNicholas, and Mooney. They agreed to speak for American

---

[26] HUBER (ed.): *Our Bishops Speak*, pp. 110–115.
[27] HENNESEY: *Diary of McCormick*, p. 39.
[28] Maglione to Cicognani, Vatican, Dec. 1, 1942, ADSS, VII, 123–124.
[29] Cicognani to Maglione, Washington, Dec. 4, 1942, *ibid.*, pp. 127–128.
[30] Maglione to Cicognani, Vatican, Dec. 11, 1942, *ibid.*, pp. 132–133.

Catholics against the bombing of Rome, but could give no publicity to their action. They felt that it would be impossible for the United States to guarantee that the city would never be bombed. With this view Roosevelt concurred when Spellman, in the name of the American hierarchy, saw him on December 7. He himself did not want to bomb Rome, but the military situation might demand it. Nevertheless, he promised to speak with the British.[31] To gain support for having Rome declared an open city, Maglione reported that all military targets in the city would be removed and that he had already so informed both Tittmann and the British minister.[32]

As Rome prepared for the possibility of bombing, McCormick had some poignant reflections: "Italy is filled with fear and terror. The Pope's public appearance at this moment may have unexpected effect. And yet we cannot leave it to George VI & Roosevelt to call for days of prayer. The moral, I was going to say religious leadership of the world is being asserted by non-Catholic countries. Cf. Roosevelt's Thanksgiving Procl[amation]".[33]

As for the endeavours to have Rome declared an open city, he recorded: "Vatican is all agog, moving every power to call off threatened bombing of Italian cities. Alas, I fear, the voice has lost its resonance for its too long silence; and I only pray that not too much harm may come to Church and souls thru policy of H[oly] S[ee]".[34] He had heard a first-hand description of the British bombing of Naples on December 4 in which many civilians were killed. "It sounds bad for English", he thought, but then queried whether the buildings in which the civilians died or neighboring buildings did not house military personnel. He predicted there would be "a howl" if some of the principal churches and seminaries in Rome were bombed, but he pointed out that nearby each of them were German military commands.[35]

In the last days of 1942 and first of 1943, McCormick recorded a growing Italian sentiment for peace. The film "Pastor Angelicus" on Pius XII had a short run in Rome when it was ordered stopped by the government. McCormick gave the reason: "Pope became too popular, it is said: it occasioned shouts for peace". But Italian thought was changing. An article in a Fascist journal, he reported, "challenges Germany's exclusion of religion in New Order, and was printed with explicit imprimatur of Duce". He gave a copy of the article to Tittmann and remarked in his diary that "it shows a very gratifying and healthy Italian independ-

---

[31] Cicognani to Maglione, Washington, Dec. 12, 1942, *ibid.*, pp. 134–135.

[32] Maglione to Cicognani, Vatican, Dec. 15, 1942, *ibid.*, pp. 140–141.

[33] HENNESEY: *Diary of McCormick*, Dec. 4, 1942, p. 35.

[34] *Ibid.*, Dec. 5, p. 35.

[35] *Ibid.*, Dec. 6, p. 35.

ence of Germany, which in turn is an index of Germany's increasing weakness".[36]

While the Vatican was attempting to prevent the bombing of Rome and Italian sentiment began to shift, Spellman received a letter from Enrico Galeazzi outlining a proposal for presentation to Roosevelt. "The American landing in Africa and the British advance in Cyrenaica have been successful in lowering the morale of the people of the Axis", he wrote, but the British air raids over Italy had driven the Italian people to use the Fascist party's "institutions of assistance and protection". The Italians, unlike the Germans, he continued, preserved friendly feelings toward the Americans and British, but "the air attacks on Italy come to destroy, or at least to lessen, an actual advantage of the Anglo-Saxons; in Germany, instead, the air raids find no favorable moral situation to destroy". Moreover, destruction of Italian factories was of far less importance than destruction of German ones, upon which Italy depended for its very defense. In addition, Italy was virtually occupied by the German army and could not break from its government even if it would. While the Holy See could make a plea to spare Rome, the bombing of which would drive the Italian people farther from the Americans and British and would "provoke a harmful reaction in the entire Catholic world", it could not "make special appeals to avoid air attacks against Italian cities because this intervention on the part of the Holy See, in favor of one of the belligerent nations, might be misinterpreted and taken advantage of by other nations".

Galeazzi then made the following suggestion for Spellman to bear to Roosevelt: "Without prejudicing the efficient execution of his political and military plans, the President of the United States should not neglect the opportunity of imposing on the Allied Command a more generous war conduct with regard to the Italian people, who have always nurtured cordial feelings of friendship for the American people, especially because the air attacks as presently directed, do not result in substantially important advantages and perhaps serve only to redirect these trends of friendship and to create in Italy an heroic climate of desperate resistance".[37] Here was a rather shocking proposal from a confidant of Pius XII — to concentrate the Allied offensive on Germany and not on Italy. The pope must surely have known of Galeazzi's letter and have given it at least tacit approval. Such approval, of course, need not have meant so much that his love for the German people was growing less as that he loved his own Italian people more. It is not known, however, whether Spellman actually presented Galeazzi's suggestions to the president, though he was to meet with him at this time precisely about the conduct of the war.

---

[36] *Ibid.*, Jan. 3, 10, 11, pp. 37–38.
[37] AANY, Galeazzi to Spellman, Vatican, Dec. 5, 1942.

B. THE ALLIES TAKE THE INITIATIVE

1. Spellman's Visit to Rome, 1943

In January, 1943, Roosevelt met at Casablanca with Churchill and General de Gaulle. At their meeting, they decided on the invasion of Sicily and announced their policy of accepting none but an unconditional surrender. This policy had already been articulated in the letter drafted by the NCWC and presented by Taylor as his own to the pope in September of 1942. But it now presented the Vatican with a new problem. Did "unconditional surrender" as an official policy mean that the Allies were making war on the people of the Axis nations and not just on their governments? Did it mean the imposition of either democracy or communism on all of Europe?[38] Only an Allied victory would give the answers to these questions.

Spellman, in the meanwhile, had expressed his desire to Roosevelt to visit the troops overseas. The president approved this visit, but asked the archbishop to wait his return until early in February, so they could meet. Their meeting took place on February 4 at which time the president placed at Spellman's disposal all the resources of the armed forces which he would require.[39] Apparently at this meeting Spellman then presented to Roosevelt letters from the archbishops of Naples, Milan, Turin, and Genoa protesting against the indiscriminate bombing of civilians. Taylor, too, continued to urge that Rome be spared, but the government could give no guarantee.[40] Two days after the meeting, Maglione cabled Cicognani requesting that Spellman also come to the Vatican. Spellman gained White House approval of this visit, which would take him through enemy territory; the State Department then instructed the American ambassador to Spain, Carlton J. H. Hayes, to arrange for his safe-conduct from the Italian government.[41]

On February 9, Spellman departed from New York amid rumors that he was taking a secret message from Roosevelt to open negotiations with the Axis, but particularly with Italy. On February 12, he arrived in Madrid after spending a night in Lisbon. He learned from Ambassador Hayes that the Italian government had granted him a safe-conduct. While in Madrid, he also received an invitation to confer with Franco. As he later explained to Roosevelt, he took the opportu-

---

[38] Cf. FLYNN: *Roosevelt and Romanism*, pp. 203–204.

[39] GANNON: *Spellman*, pp. 198–200; FDRL, PPF 4404, Spellman to Roosevelt, New York, Feb. 1 and 8, 1943; Tully to Watson, memo, Feb. 1, 1943.

[40] Cicognani to Maglione, Washington, Feb. 10, 1943, ADSS, VII, 221.

[41] Maglione to Cicognani, Vatican, Feb. 6, 1943, *ibid.*, p. 218; Cicognani to Maglione, Washington, Feb. 7, 1943, *ibid.*, p. 221; GANNON: *Spellman*, p. 200.

nity to explain American intentions in the war. Pro-Axis feeling, he believed, was diminishing in Spain and any such residual feeling was due to fear of communism. This Spellman sought to assuage by noting that Stalin had adhered to the Atlantic Charter and had stated that Russia had no desires "to possess any non-Russian territory or to impose its form of government on any nation".[42] Nothing could have been more useful to Roosevelt than to have a Catholic archbishop to convince the Fascist-leaning Franco to remain neutral.

Rome, in the meantime, was preparing for Spellman's arrival. Only on February 18 did McCormick learn that he was coming the next day. He also discovered that the news was a complete surprise to Tittmann. The Jesuit, by this time, was becoming increasingly critical of the Holy See's policy of neutrality. Early in February he had given Tittmann a copy of the bishops' pastoral of the previous November. A week before Spellman's arrival, he expressed his irritation at the pope's letter of sympathy to Cardinal Luigi Lavitrano, Archbishop of Palermo, which had been bombed by the Allies: "Holy See seems to manifest very keen interest in sufferings of civilian population when this population is Italian. They are fully aware of what cruel sufferings have been inflicted on civil population in Slovenia, Croatia and Greece, and this by Italians—burning of whole towns, murder of innocent hostages in revenge, and no letter of sympathy has been published as sent to Bishops of those parts. I am finding it more and more difficult, really impossible to defend the neutrality of the present-day Vatican. Catholicity is very much compromised. Would that I were miles away from here, in some place where I could forget it all!!"[43] The Jesuit, then, would have been out of sympathy with Galeazzi's proposals to the United States, which may well have comprised part of Spellman's agenda for his conversations with the pope.

The archbishop arrived in Rome on February 20, a day later than expected, and remained until March 3, but neither to his diary nor to his official biographer did he confide whom he saw and what he discussed during his visit.[44] Tittmann held a reception in the archbishop's honor on February 22, Washington's Birthday, attended by prominent clergy and Latin American diplomats. McCormick had two meetings with Spellman, one in which they discussed the situation of the American Jesuits and the other in which the archbishop showed him a letter of introduction from Roosevelt to Chiang Kai-shek.[45] Only one other source of firsthand information is available for Spellman's visit. Prince Erwin Lobkowicz, the

---

[42] FDRL, PSF 185, Spellman to Roosevelt, Seville, Mar. 4, 1943; copy in AANY. See also GANNON: *Spellman*, p. 203.
[43] HENNESEY: *Diary of McCormick*, Feb. 13, 1943, pp. 40–41.
[44] AANY, Spellman Diary, Feb. 20–Mar. 3, 1943; GANNON: *Spellman*, p. 204.
[45] HENNESEY: *Diary of McCormick,* p. 41.

representative of the puppet Croatian state in Rome, met with Spellman on March 2. Spellman expressed his sympathy with the Croatian cause and stated that Roosevelt's intention was to win freedom for all peoples and that included the Croats. While waiting to see Spellman, however, Lobkowicz' companion noticed several visiting cards from highly placed Italian dignitaries, including the President of the Court of Appeals and several senators.[46]

The day after Spellman's departure from Rome, he addressed a lengthy letter to Roosevelt summarizing his trip up to that point. About his conversations with the pope he said only that the pontiff asked about the president and was deeply grateful for Myron Taylor for whom he had the "highest esteem and appreciation". About the Italian political situation, however, he was more effusive. Repeating many of Galeazzi's earlier observations, he said that the Italians continued to regard the Americans with friendship and that the people were actually hoping for an American liberation. "The people are suffering tremendously", he reported, and there was "much hunger and weakness". Food and other commodities were sold at inflationary prices. "The anti-German feeling is very strong and deep", he continued, and "Ninety-nine percent of the Italians, in my opinion, would, if they could, make peace tomorrow, and the only obstacles to peace that I see are Mussolini and the fact that if peace were obtained, then the Germans would retaliate by bombing Rome". But Spellman said nothing about discontinuing the bombing of Italian cities.[47]

Spellman's schedule included visits to North Africa, the Middle East, and the Holy Land and he broke it to go to London to attend the funeral of Cardinal Arthur Hinsley, Archbishop of Westminster, and have lunch with the Churchills. Before leaving the Vatican, Spellman had also received instructions to consult with papal representatives about prisoners of war and civilians being held in various countries.[48] Among his priorities was a visit to Egypt where Italian priests and nuns had been interned at the request of the British. The Regent of the Apostolic Delegation in Cairo, Father Arthur Hughes, W.F., though English-born, was snubbed by both Egyptian and British officials. Spellman, coming with the authorization of Roosevelt and Churchill, created confusion among the diplomats

---

[46] In Carlo FALCONI: *The Silence of Pius XII*, Boston 1970, pp. 371–373. Spellman had already forwarded to Rome early the previous year protests he had received about the treatment of Jews in Croatia from Mrs. Anne O'Hare McCormick, Mrs. Henry Rowland, and Mrs. John Nash McCullough. He received assurances from the Holy See that it was intervening in behalf of Croatian Jews and that those who took refuge in Italian-occupied territory would not be returned to their country. AANY, Maglione to Cicognani, Apr. 21, 1942, printed in ADSS, VIII, 514; AANY, Cicognani to Spellman, Washington, May 12, 1942.

[47] FDRL, PSF 185, Spellman to Roosevelt, Seville, Mar. 4, 1943; copy in AANY.

[48] Notes of Maglione, Mar. 1, 1943, ADSS, IX, 149.

who believed that he came on a political as well as spiritual mission. He used their confusion to his advantage. On May 2, he dined with forty interned priests. At the end of the month he made a second trip to Cairo and reported that he was making some progress in alleviating conditions of the internees and in improving relations between the British and the Holy See. Sometime later he succeeded in having Roosevelt intervene with Churchill to allow the interned priests to leave the country or return to their work.[49]

Spellman was conscious of avoiding any discussion of the military or political situation, although, as will be seen, he may have at some point received instructions from the Holy See to discuss an Italian armistice with American authorities. On May 14, he arrived in Istanbul and was met by Archbishop Angelo Roncalli, the Apostolic Delegate to Turkey and future John XXIII, D. Emanuele Clarizio, a member of the Secretariat of State, and Burton Y. Berry, the American consul. Just before Spellman's arrival, the German and Italian forces had surrendered in North Africa. Journalists linked the two events; Clarizio, they said, had brought a message to Spellman from the Holy See to offer "a compromise settlement in the Mediterranean".[50] Roncalli, however, reported nothing of what may have passed between himself, Clarizio, and Spellman. The archbishop, he said, conducted himself in the presence of journalists with the utmost diplomacy, as they urged on him the universal question of peace. His stay at the delegation enhanced Roncalli's office and the Holy See. Despite the public confusion about his real purpose, Spellman was "extremely reserved about political or military subjects. Above all he maintained silence on the problem of peace and of the Russian danger", which were the Turkish preoccupations.[51]

Spellman's trip took him through Africa and he was then supposed to go to the Far East, where he was to have met with Chiang Kai-shek. But the surrender of Axis troops in North Africa opened the way for the Allied invasion of Sicily. This, in turn, reopened the question of the bombing of Rome. On July 19, Spellman, then in South Africa, recorded in his diary, "Rome bombed!!!!"[52] The Roman basilica of San Lorenzo had been seriously damaged and 1500 people in the neighborhood had been killed, Maglione cabled Cicognani. The pope had personally visited the site and now wished the American Church to demonstrate its "participation in such great grief".[53] On July 23, Spellman received a telegram from an unnamed source telling him to hasten back to New York.[54]

---

[49] GANNON: *Spellman pp. 210–211.*

[50] *Ibid.,* pp. 212–213.

[51] Roncalli to Maglione, Istanbul, May 20, 1943, ADSS, VII, 351–354.

[52] AANY, Spellman Diary, July 19, 1943.

[53] Maglione to Cicognani, Vatican, July 20, 1943, ADSS, VII, 500–502.

[54] AANY, Spellman Diary, July 23, 1943.

2. Bombing of Rome and Fall of Mussolini

The bombing of Rome was a crisis in the Holy See's relations with the United States. On May 19, Pius XII had sent Roosevelt a letter drafted for him by Tardini and McCormick. It was a plea to recognize the sacred character of Rome and to spare civilian populations.[55] In his response on June 16, Roosevelt said that "the sympathetic response of Your Holiness to the many appeals of the Italian people on behalf of their country is understood and appreciated by me". "Americans", he added, "are among those who value most the religious shrines and the historical monuments of Italy", but they were "likewise united in their determination to win the war which has been thrust upon them and for which the present government of Italy must share its full responsibility". Bombing was to be limited as much as possible to military targets, he said, and American airmen had been carefully instructed "as to the location of the Vatican and have been specifically instructed to prevent bombs from falling within the Vatican City". But the president also warned that Axis planes could "bomb Vatican City with the purpose of charging Allied planes with the outrages they themselves committed".[56] On the eve of Roosevelt's letter, Cicognani reported his efforts to have the American hierarchy intervene with Roosevelt. In Spellman's absence, he first turned to Cardinal Dougherty, but his known antagonism for the president did not make him an apt negotiator. He then hoped to have Archbishop Mooney act with the president in the name of the episcopate.[57] Negotiation, however, could not keep pace with military events. On July 10, the combined forces of the United States, Canada, and Great Britain invaded Sicily. On the same day Roosevelt telegraphed the pope informing him of the event. The troops, he said, "have come to rid Italy of Fascism and of its unhappy symbols and to drive out the Nazi oppressors who are infesting her". Then in a passage intended to assuage the fears of the bombing of Rome, the president pledged to respect the neutrality of Vatican City and other papal territories outside the city: "There is no need for me to reaffirm that respect for religious beliefs and for the free exercise of religious worship is fundamental to our ideas. Churches and religious institutions will, to the extent that it is within our power, be spared the devastations of war during the struggle ahead. Throughout the period of operations the neutral status of the Vatican City as well as of the Papal domains throughout Italy will be respected".[58] Roosevelt's recognition of the neutral status of "Papal domains throughout Italy" would later

---

[55] Pius XII to Roosevelt, Vatican, May 19, 1943, ADSS, VII, 500–502. See also HENNESEY: *Diary of McCormick,* p. 45.

[56] Roosevelt to Pius XII, June 16, 1943, in ADSS, VII, 430–431.

[57] Cigognani to Maglione, June 15, 1943, *ibid.*, p. 429.

[58] Roosevelt to Pius XII, Washington, July 10, 1943, *ibid.*, 479–480.

cause tension between the Holy See and the United States, due to the American bombing of the papal and Propaganda villas at Castel Gandolfo.

McCormick discussed Roosevelt's message with Tittmann. Now that the invasion was on, the Jesuit noted the change in the Italian mood. Whereas before the Italian people had looked forward to an Allied invasion, now that it had occurred the prospect of national humiliation made them unsure. "Who would not be", McCormick wrote, "to see one's country invaded, ruined, bankrupt?" On the other hand, "all that should have been thought of in 1940, even in 1935. God's justice could not let so many crimes go unpunished". McCormick was then summoned to assist in drafting the pope's reply to Roosevelt, which he discussed with Tittmann and Sir d'Arcy Osborne, the British minister to the Holy See. They all agreed that Pius' answer would probably omit reference to Roosevelt's statement of the Allied purpose, but McCormick wrote, "the strong Fascist sentiments of so many of the 'smaller monsignori' in Vat[ican] employ will get a shock. They may have reason to tremble", for the Allied purpose of destroying Fascism could alter the status of the Catholic Church in Italy guaranteed by the Lateran pacts concluded between the Vatican and the Fascist government of Mussolini.[59]

On July 17, Allied planes dropped leaflets over Rome calling in the name of Roosevelt and Churchill for Italian resistance against Fascism and Nazism. McCormick discussed this with Osborne who felt the people could do nothing, despite what London believed; they both agreed that "few of them are looking for a martyr's crown at the hands of the Nazis". In the meantime, the Jesuit continued working with Tardini on a reply to Roosevelt's message, the draft of which had to be changed with the bombing of Rome on July 19. Tittmann and his family had witnessed the raid in the company of Montini. McCormick thought the bombing of San Lorenzo was "the greatest American defeat of the war", for the Americans had sacrificed psychological advantage with the Italians. He could understand the bombing of military targets around Rome, "but who ever ordered them to come so near as S. Lorenzo? It might show daring; it showed poor sense. History will tell, guides will tell tourists how American bombs destroyed one of the seven Basilicas and massacred the pious, poor women and children. Quite true, they have a right to bomb Rome, it has been for three years the sanctuary of safety for German military forces, and Italian powers: but fool-hardy to use that right".[60] In the United States, Archbishop Mooney and Bishop Hurley echoed McCormick's sentiments that the United States should not have taken the moral risk involved in bombing Rome.[61]

---

[59] HENNESEY: *Diary of McCormick*, p. 47.
[60] *Ibid.*, p. 48.
[61] ADSS, VII, 637 n.

On July 20, the day after the attack, Tardini summoned McCormick to the Secretariat of State to redraft the pope's reply to Roosevelt. That evening the Jesuit was back with a new draft of the letter, on the thrust of which he and Tardini initially disagreed: "He is not satisfied because I stressed the killing of labourers' families as more horrible than destruction of church! I appeared shocked and remarked that I did not want to give the impression that the Vatican was more interested in the material than in the spiritual, in churches than the church. He showed a bit of resentment; perhaps I had shown a bit of heat. He said: Let us not enter on that discussion, a church has a spiritual value, and its loss may be greater than that of a human life. The fact is that Lon[don] and Wash[ington] have always admitted that loss in civilian pop[ulation] is inevitable; we shall try to keep it as low as possible, but it cannot be avoided. But they defended the thesis staunchly that they could bomb military objectives around Rome without damaging churches and monuments. That thesis has now been disproved. Hence, the point to be made in the letter is that they demonstrated the untenability of their thesis, without suggesting which is more deplorable, to destroy a church or kill women and children. I understand his position fully, and made the changes then and there. It now goes to H[oly] F[ather]".[62]

In the final version of the letter, the pope expressed his dismay at witnessing "the harrowing scene of death leaping from the skies and stalking pitilessly through unsuspecting homes striking down women and children" and at personally visiting "the gaping ruins of that ancient and priceless Papal basilica of St. Lawrence, one of the most treasured and loved sanctuaries of Romans, especially close to the heart of all Supreme Pontiffs, and visited with devotion by pilgrims from all countries of the world". He told how he had "suffered from the first days of the war for the lot of all those cities that have been exposed to aerial bombardments ..., but since divine Providence has placed Us head over the Catholic Church and Bishop of this city so rich in sacred shrines and hallowed, immortal memories, We feel it Our duty to voice a particular prayer and hope that all may recognize that a city, whose every district, in some districts every street has its irreplaceable monuments of faith or art and Christian culture, cannot be attacked without inflicting an incomparable loss on the patrimony of Religion and Civilization". The pope signed the letter on July 26 and it was given to Tittmann the following day.[63]

While drafting the pope's letter, McCormick moved toward a more benign reaction to the bombing. The Axis, he noted, could have prevented it by declaring Rome an open city and the Vatican had failed to "let the world know more clear-

---

[62] HENNESEY: *Diary of McCormick*, p. 48.
[63] Pius XII to Roosevelt, Vatican, July 20, 1943, ADSS, VII, 502–504.

ly, honestly, that the chief offenders are those who have delivered Rome over to the enemy by using it as a military centre! There seems to be no courage for saying anything that might offend and show up Ger[mans] and It[alians] in a bad light. Lord have mercy!" To Cardinal Francesco Marchetti-Salvaggiani, the Vicar of Rome, he even suggested that "after the war Romans will have to erect a monument to Roosevelt and Churchill. How many other nations would have spared their city under the conditions prevailing in it these last three years?"[64]

a. The End of Fascism

But Pius' letter to Roosevelt came at a critical juncture. He may well have delayed signing it because he was aware of the imminent fall of Mussolini, for on July 26, Il Duce submitted his resignation as premier; Fascism had come to an end. The new government of Marshall Pietro Badoglio immediately made overtures to Washington through the Vatican to declare Rome an open city.[65] It also began negotiations for a surrender.

Tittmann had some choice observations on why the bombing of Rome was so crucial to Vatican officials. "It would have been a tremendous tribute to Holy See, to Pope, a feather in their cap for them", he told McCormick, "if war had ended without Rome being bombed, so they are bitterly disappointed, ripping mad".[66] Tittmann, in the meantime, had notified Secretary Hull that, since the pope had given his protest at the bombing to his vicar, he was not protesting formally as pope but as Bishop of Rome. Nevertheless, the American regretted that the pope had not protested against the bombing of German cities.[67] Tittmann may not have been so surprised at the pope's silence had he read Galeazzi's earlier proposal to Spellman that the Allies concentrate their bombing on Germany. Subsequently, however, he reported that even curial officials admitted that the bombing of Rome had precipitated the overthrow of Fascism.[68] Whatever may have been the Vatican's original mentality, with a new Italian government in power, it now made another bid, through the American hierarchy, to the American government – this time not only to cease the bombing of Rome but also possibly to negotiate a separate Italian peace.

On August 1, Spellman had arrived back in Washington from his six-month trip. He was met by Monsignor Ready and a representative of the State Depart-

---

[64] HENNESEY: *Diary of McCormick*, pp. 49–50.

[65] Maglione to Cicognani, Vatican, Aug. 1, 1943, ADSS, VII, 534.

[66] HENNESEY: *Diary of McCormick*, p. 51.

[67] NA, RG 59, DS 740.0011 EW39/30403, Tittmann to Secretary, Vatican, July 28, 1943 (cable).

[68] *Ibid.*, 30824, Tittmann to Secretary, Vatican, Aug. 6, 1943 (cable).

ment who conveyed a message from Roosevelt, then in Quebec, asking him to confer with Hull. This Spellman decided to defer. Instead, he visited Cicognani and began preparing statements for the press, which was speculating on his role in arranging an Italian armistice and even in overthrowing Mussolini.[69] As it turned out, he waited for over a month before conferring with Roosevelt or any other government official.

The situation in Rome had, in the meantime, become desperate. As the government waited for a response to its overture on declaring Rome an open city, Pius issued a public letter to Maglione calling on all the bishops of the world to offer prayers at this moment when "dangers of evil are rushing in upon the Christian family of peoples".[70] McCormick interpreted the letter as "a document published to defend Vatican before Italy against the charge of doing nothing for peace. For Vat[ican] seems to be victim of terror just now lest Rome or Italy be taken over by Germans or anti-clerical Italians. But what an unfortunate document! At a time when Sicilians are jubilant over their liberation, and hundreds of millions of people from Norway to the Medit[erranean] are breathing a sigh of hopeful relief, seeing at last after four years of subjection to tyranny and slavery the light of freedom beginning to spread along the horizon, the H[oly] F[ather] speaks to tell us that the heavens, far from clearing, are becoming blacker than ever, Christianity is threatened. Is that His true feeling about a German defeat, or is it that His horizon is bounded by the Alps and the Sicilian straits? The robbed and starving in Greece, in France, in Belgium, Holland, Austria, in concentration camps – religious, priests, seminarians, the enslaved workers – does their liberation mean nothing to Vat[ican]? Sad, sad."[71] But McCormick with his pro-Allied sympathies had picked up only part of the Vatican's pulse. The pope's advisers were indeed fearful that the Germans might take him off as a prisoner to Munich[72] and that the working class might gravitate more and more toward communism.

In the meanwhile, as the new Italian government waited for the Allied conditions for declaring Rome an open city, American planes again bombed the city on August 13. This time they hit two churches. On August, 14, Maglione instructed the American hierarchy and people to demonstrate their concern for the "center of Catholicism".[73] The next day, the Italian government declared Rome an open city.[74]

---

[69] AANY, Spellman Diary, Aug. 1, 1943; GANNON: *Spellman*, pp. 220–221.

[70] Pius XII to Maglione, Vatican, Aug. 4, 1943, ADSS, VII, 540–541.

[71] HENNESEY: *Diary of McCormick*, pp. 51–52.

[72] Notes of Tardini, Aug. 4, 1943, ADSS, VII, 537–538.

[73] Maglione to Cicognani, Vatican, Aug. 14, 1943, *ibid.*, p. 550.

[74] Maglione to Osborne and Tittmann, Vatican, Aug. 15, 1943, *ibid.*, pp. 555–557.

b. Renewed Vatican Initiative with the American Hierarchy

This declaration paved the way for a three-fold Vatican initiative. First, the pope again wrote to Roosevelt. Second, the Vatican dispatched Enrico Galeazzi to the United States. Third, it mobilized the American hierarchy to intervene with Roosevelt to prevent further bombings.

From August 19 to 30, McCormick was prevented by papal gendarmes from entering the precincts of the Vatican where Tittmann was lodged. The Vatican may have wished to prevent the two Americans discussing the Italian situation at the time when the Jesuit was collaborating with his German colleague, Father Robert Leiber, in drafting Pius' new letter to Roosevelt.[75] In the letter, the pope pointed out that, despite the new government in Italy, she was not "entirely free to follow the policy of her choice ..., but in the presence of formidable forces opposing the actuation or even the official declaration of that desire [for peace] she finds herself shackled and quite without the necessary means of defending herself". If Italy was "to be forced still to bear devastating blows", the pope prayed "that the military leaders will find it possible to spare innocent civil populations and in particular churches and religious institutions the ravages of war". Pius drew hope from Roosevelt's "message of assurance" of July 10, "even in the face of bitter experience, that God's temples and the homes erected by Christian charity for the poor and sick and abandoned members of Christ's flock may survive the terrible onslaught".[76] The letter was to be carried to Washington personally by Enrico Galeazzi.

Toward the middle of August, the pope decided to inform the Allies of Italian conditions by sending Galeazzi to Washington. As a layman, Galeazzi would not draw too much attention. Moreover, he had met Roosevelt during Pacelli's visit to the United States in 1936. While Tardini favored the mission, Maglione opposed it and Galeazzi's departure remained in doubt until he could get the necessary visas. In the event that he could not go, duplicate instructions were drawn up for Monsignor Walter Carroll, who was then in Madrid on his way to the United States.[77]

On August 30, however, Galeazzi set out for the United States. With him he carried the letter from the pope to Roosevelt and a second one from Maglione to Cicognani. The latter repeated the observations the pope made that the Italian people and government desired peace but could do nothing because of the presence of German troops who held a strangle hold on Rome. But an even more

---

[75] HENNESEY: *Diary of McCormick*, p. 52.
[76] Pius XII to Roosevelt, Vatican, Aug. 30, 1943, ADSS, VII, 597–598.
[77] Maglione to Cicognani, Vatican, Aug. 22, 1943, *ibid.*, pp. 576–577.

long-range danger existed, said the cardinal, if the Allies persisted in bombing Italian cities. The sufferings of the long war, the privation of the necessities of life, and the obstacles to obtaining peace were already driving many of the people, and especially the workers, toward communism. This movement, continued Maglione, was only accelerated by "the great destruction and slaughter produced by the recent terroristic bombings of Italian cities, which has excited in the people, previously well disposed toward the Allies and especially the Americans, a lively resentment...". In the cardinal's mind, "skillful agitators" were organizing demonstrations to take advantage of the situation. "Some recent demonstrations, occurring on the occasion of the fall of Fascism", he concluded, "have shown that communism in Italy is already well organized, and is provided with arms and economic support. With this situation, it is easy to foresee how difficult – not to say impossible – the governing of the whole Church would be for the Holy See in the event that Italy should have fallen to the power of communism".[78] Maglione thus articulated what would be the Vatican's abiding concern in the post-war years when it would turn increasingly to the American Church to ward off the peril of communism in Italy.

In the meantime, on August 23, Cicognani informed Spellman, Mooney, and Stritch of Maglione's cable of August 14, requesting that the American hierarchy and laity demonstrate their concern for the bombing of Rome. Reporting their response, Cicognani first included excerpts of a letter from Cardinal Dougherty after the first bombing, stating that any protest against the bombing would arouse anti-Catholic feelings. The three archbishops each responded that the bombings of Rome had been well publicized in both the secular and Catholic press, that they had expressed their consternation at this action, but that any further protest from Catholics would make them appear unpatriotic or at least opposed to Roosevelt's war policy.[79] The issue, as Cicognani saw it, was, while the prelates favored the American government's recognizing Rome as an open city, they were also conscious of the American public's desire that the Italian government guarantee that all military objectives and German troops be removed from Rome.[80]

A few days after Spellman had sent his opinion to Cicognani, he was summoned to the White House. Roosevelt was then conferring with Winston Churchill and seems originally to have planned to meet with the archbishop after the prime minister's departure.[81] But then he changed his plans. He met with Spell-

---

[78] Maglione to Cicognani, Vatican, Aug. 28, 1943, *ibid.*, pp. 592–593.
[79] Cicognani to Maglione, Washington, Sept. 21, 1943, *ibid.*, pp. 636–641.
[80] Cicognani to Maglione, Washington, Sept. 4, 1943, *ibid.*, p. 603.
[81] FDRL, PPF 4404, Tully to Watson, Aug. 30, 1943; Watson to Spellman, Washington, Aug. 31, 1943 (copy).

man and Churchill on the evening of September 2 and with the archbishop alone on the morning of September 3. The bombing of Rome was only one of the topics they discussed. Spellman made a memorandum of their conversation. The president outlined his plans for postwar Europe, including his hope of personally coming to terms with Stalin to keep Russia from expanding too much beyond its borders while allowing communist governments to be established elsewhere. Leaving the White House, Spellman met with Cicognani, who cabled Maglione that, while Roosevelt hoped that further bombing of Rome would be unnecessary, it would depend on military exigencies, for the United States could adopt no policy toward Italy which might favor Germany.[82]

The Allied military advance, however, rapidly changed the status of Rome. Even as Spellman was meeting with Roosevelt, General Montgomery was moving his troops across the Straits of Messina; the Allied invasion of the continent had begun. On September 8, Badoglio and Roosevelt announced the surrender of Italy. German troops immediately occupied Rome. Regardless of the Italian government's declaring Rome an open city, it was now a military target. On September 11, Galeazzi arrived in New York and he and Spellman immediately departed for the apostolic delegation in Washington. The next day, they conferred with Cicognani and Monsignor Carroll. Spellman learned that he had been appointed apostolic visitor to Sicily to investigate the material damage to churches, collaborate with the bishops to reestablish, where necessary, schools and charitable institutions, to initiate the Vatican Information Service between the island and the mainland, and finally to report personally to the pope on the situation.[83] He also arranged an appointment with Roosevelt for himself and Galeazzi only to have to cancel it the next day when Maglione cabled "per ordine superiore" that Galeazzi was to limit his discussions to administrative matters, information about prisoners of war, and the situation of the Church in Sicily, but he was not to treat political matters.[84] With Rome now occupied by the Germans, the Vatican would be placed in a delicate position if its emissary were to speak directly to Roosevelt.

Stritch and Mooney were now summoned to join Spellman in Washington where they were to see the president on September 15, the appointment originally set for Galeazzi. The three archbishops drew up a memorial for Roosevelt. They reminded him of "the grave fears we expressed on the moral risks our Country assumed in bombing Rome" and subsequent information "on the results of that action show how ineffective were the diligently planned precautions to restrict

---

[82] Cicognani to Maglione, Washington, Sept. 4, 1943, ADSS, VII, 602–603. See also GANNON: *Spellman*, pp. 220–224.

[83] AANY, Maglione to Spellman, Vatican, Aug. 29, 1943; in: ADSS, VII, 595–597.

[84] Maglione to Cicognani, Vatican, Sept. 13, 1943, *ibid.*, p. 624; notes of Tardini, June 26, 1944, *ibid.*, pp. 593–594.

precision bombing to military objectives". Civilians were killed and a whole district of Rome, including San Lorenzo, was damaged, they said, with the sole American justification that the Fascist government had not made Rome an open city. Even the Nazis, they noted, had not taken this action in regard to Athens and Cairo. Furthermore, after Badoglio's government had "enlisted the good offices of the Holy See" to ask the Allies for conditions for declaring Rome an open city, the Allies had failed to respond for more than a month. This delay, said the prelates, "not only weakened the position of the Holy See as a strong force for peace but increased our responsibility for the events that followed". During the delay, the second bombing of Rome, they continued, had occurred "with further serious loss of life in the civilian population and further damage to religious establishments". Finally, the Allies had still not stated their conditions for declaring Rome an open city when the Italian armistice was signed. That failure had aggravated "the imperilled position of the Sacred City now occupied by Nazi troops, and makes us even more clearly share the moral responsibility for eventual disastrous consequences of the military occupation".

The archbishops were concerned to remind Roosevelt of his pledge to the pope on July 10 to safeguard the Vatican and papal domains, but "with the City of the Popes in control of forces that hate Christianity and its outstanding spokesman in the world today and would welcome any pretext for wreaking destructions there, the plight of the Holy See and all that it stands for in Rome is, indeed, critical". Nevertheless, they were confident that there was "in the councils of the United Nations the wisdom, the restraint, and the military genius to dislodge the enemy from Italy without making Rome the theater of direct military operations". They were not averse to alluding to the political power "of more than twenty million American Catholics ... [who hoped] that their government will not have to share further responsibility for even more disastrous developments that threaten the Holy See under the conditions" then existing in Rome. Nor should the international political influence of Catholicism be ignored, for "military measures which offend the religious sense of so many citizens in so many nations may have consequences fatally prejudicial to the interests we all have at heart in the making of the peace and to the national and international collaboration necessary to that blessed end".[85]

At the meeting, Roosevelt proposed a free zone of twenty miles around Rome, provided the Germans agreed to respect it. "It will be O.K. if he keeps his promise", Spellman recorded. "I am glad the three of us went".[86]

---

[85] Mooney, Stritch, and Spellman to Roosevelt, Sept. 15, 1943, attached to Cicognani to Maglione, Washington, Sept. 21, 1943, *ibid.*, pp. 648–650.

[86] AANY, Spellman Diary, Sept. 15, 1943; GANNON: *Spellman,* p. 227.

Spellman, and the Holy See for that matter, seemed to ignore the fact that Roosevelt's promise depended on a German agreement to respect Rome as an open city. The Germans and the Allies, however, both abided by the agreement. But certain statements of Roosevelt seemed to jeopardize the Vatican's position. The president had stated in a press conference that some people had called the Allied advance in Italy a "crusade" to liberate Rome and the pope and he acknowledged that the campaign did have many elements of a crusade. He also said that he hoped there would be no more damage to Rome, but that depended on the enemy.[87] The statement may have been intended to win over American Catholics, but it also implied the Allied cause was identical with the Holy See's. Other news stories, moreover, continued to state that Spellman's visit to Rome in February had been to arrange an armistice, which the *Osservatore Romano* and Vatican Radio firmly denied. Maglione warned Spellman "to refrain from any declaration which may serve to render still more difficult the present situation of the Holy See".[88] That situation, however, now became yet more difficult for other reasons.

On November 5, an unidentified plane dropped four bombs on Vatican City. Maglione immediately protested to the American, British, and German representatives to the Holy See; each denied that his respective government was responsible. Then the story appeared that Stalin had telegraphed Churchill congratulating him on bombing the Vatican and that Spellman had telegraphed Roosevelt his grief at the action. Cicognani reported to Maglione that Spellman had neither sent a telegram to Roosevelt nor spoken to him about the bombing and that the British ambassador had denied Stalin had congratulated Churchill. Rumors in Rome placed the blame for the bombing on Roberto Farinacci, a die-hard Fascist, but Monsignor Carroll, then in Algeria, forwarded a report that an American pilot had lost his way and jetisoned his bombs over the Vatican.[89]

The status of Rome placed American Catholics in a dilemma. On the one hand, they recognized the Eternal City as the home of their spiritual leader; on the other, they were sensitive to the delicate *modus vivendi* they had with their fellow citizens and to the outrage they could provoke by protesting the bombing of Rome. On November 8, the administrative board of the NCWC met in Washington and afterwards Spellman, Mooney, and Stritch conferred with Cicognani about what to do for the Holy See. The next day, Spellman lunched with Lord

---

[87] Cicognani to Maglione, Washington, Oct. 2, 1943, *ibid.*, pp. 655–656. The press conference is given in: *New York Times,* Oct. 2, 1943.

[88] AANY, Cicognani to Spellman, Washington, Oct. 7, 1943; see also Cicognani to Spellman, Oct. 8, 1943.

[89] Notes of Tardini, Nov. 5, 1943, ADSS, VII, 688–689; Tittmann to Maglione, Nov. 8, 1943, *ibid.*, p. 693; Osborne to Maglione, Nov. 7, 1943, *ibid.*, pp. 691–692; Maglione to Cicognani, Vatican, Nov. 10, 1943, *ibid.*, p. 696; Cicognani to Maglione, Washington, Nov. 11, 1943, *ibid.*, p. 699; see also *ibid.* pp. 63–64.

Halifax, the British ambassador to the United States, and "told him that diplomatic privileges were denied Holy See in England and other places".[90] On November 11, the bishops held their annual meeting at which they adopted a resolution expressing their filial devotion to the Holy See and pledging that they would continue to inform public opinion and the government to guarantee the safety of the Holy See and the Vatican. But they said nothing explicitly about the bombing.[91]

The Holy See, however, wanted more. On December 5, Maglione requested that Spellman, Mooney, and Stritch again see Roosevelt to have him guarantee the twenty-mile free zone around Rome; they were also to convene the hierarchy so that it might consider the gravity of the Holy See's situation.[92] The three archbishops, however, did not think they should make another joint approach to Roosevelt. Instead, each would ask laymen, highly placed in national or local government, to intervene with Roosevelt. Thus the hierarchy would keep a low profile in whatever emanated from the White House. It was likewise inopportune, reported Cicognani, to reconvene all the bishops due to the difficulty of wartime transportation.[93] Late in December the delegate reported that Secretary of State Hull and the president wished to spare Rome, but this depended on what course of action the Germans took. This too was the basic strategy of the Supreme Allied Command as Taylor reported confidentially to Cicognani. The delegate concluded his report by saying that Spellman would again see Roosevelt.[94]

The issue of bombing Rome strained the relations between the bishops and the Roosevelt administration and these were strained still more by the bombing on four separate occasions, February 1, February 10, May 31, and June 4, 1944, of the papal villa at Castel Gandolfo. After the first bombing, Cicognani sent a letter of protest to the State Department. On February 5, Edward Stettinius, who had succeeded Welles as Under-Secretary of State, responded that Roosevelt's letter of July 10, 1943, promising to respect papal domains remained in force and "Allied forces have instructions to carry out that policy to the extent that is humanly possible under conditions of modern warfare".[95] After the second bombing, Spellman wrote Roosevelt a strong letter stating: "After my several talks with you and my repeated assurances to the Holy Father of our desire to show him every respect, I feel that I must do something to comfort him, and others who reverence him and are pained to see his home at Castel Gandolfo bombed by our airmen,

---

[90] AANY, Spellman Diary, Nov. 8–9, 1943.

[91] Cicognani to Maglione, Washington, Nov. 11, 1943, ADSS, VII, 700.

[92] Maglione to Cicognani, Vatican, Dec. 5, 1943, *ibid.*, pp. 716–717.

[93] Cicognani to Maglione, Washington, Dec. 9, 1943, *ibid.*, pp. 721–722.

[94] Cicognani to Maglione, Washington, Dec. 27, 1943, *ibid.*, pp. 734–735.

[95] Cited in Memorandum on the Vatican Claims, Apostolic Delegation, June 4, 1951, AANY (copy).

the while the Vatican states that 'no German soldier has been admitted within the borders of the neutral Pontifical Villa and that no German military whatsoever are within it at present'. There are only helpless and homeless people refuged there". Spellman felt compelled to make a public statement on the matter, "lest many people think me failing in my duty". He was however open to an alternative suggestion, "if ... you see some other action that can be taken".[96]

The audience for Spellman's public protest was the annual memorial Mass of the Knights of Columbus at St. Patrick's Cathedral on February 22, George Washington's Birthday. In his address, Spellman deplored "the fact that the armed forces of our country have attacked the territory of a neutral state, thereby violating rights which are among those for which America is waging war. We have the word of the Pope, expressed by the Apostolic Delegate to the United States, that no Germans were there or had ever been allowed there. In the winning of the war, let us keep not only the respect of others but also our own self respect. I also hope and pray that, as Britain once spared the Holy City of Mecca, military ingenuity will overcome 'military necessity', which would destroy the Eternal City of Rome, the citadel of civilization".[97]

Mooney, too, wrote Roosevelt about sparing Rome, but he made no mention of the bombing of Castel Gandolfo. The "pressure of considerations advanced in the name of military necessity", he said, in a short time might "lose their extenuating force in view of the accusing finger raised in every pillar that would stand amidst the new made ruins of Rome". He admitted that "these are strong words", but he felt "so deeply that the judgment of plain-thinking men would, on reflection, be against those who even allowed themselves to be trapped by Nazi cunning or provoked by Nazi malice into wreaking destructions on the shrines and monuments of Rome". Such "Nazi provocation", he continued, "would serve only to highlight our lack of cleverness or our failure to rise above Nazi standards of cultural appreciation and religious reverence".[98] The bombing of Castel Gandolfo was a relatively minor event in the war, but the settlement of the Vatican claims for damages would become controversial in the post-war United States.

C. ALLIED ENTRY INTO ROME AND THE END OF THE WAR

The bombing of Rome ceased to be an issue on June 4, 1944, when at last Allied troops entered the city. Roosevelt dispatched Taylor to see the pope. Pius, in

---

[96] FDRL, PPF 4404, Spellman to Roosevelt, New York, Feb. 20, 1944.

[97] AANY, attached to: Spellman to Roosevelt, New York, Feb. 20, 1944 (draft); GANNON: Spellman, pp. 229–230.

[98] AANY, Mooney to Roosevelt, Detroit, Feb. 23, 1944 (copy).

turn, again sent for Spellman, who was already making plans to revisit the American troops. Before Spellman set out for Rome, he won from Roosevelt the pledge that the city would not become a military base but would be used only for recreation by troops stationed outside.[99] In the meantime, just after the fall of Rome, King Victor Emmanuel transferred his power to Crown Prince Humbert and a new government was formed under Ivanhoe Bonomi, an anti-Fascist leader.

By July 28, Spellman had arrived in Rome and had the first of several audiences with Pius XII. He also met with American, Italian, and Vatican officials. He had an hour and a half audience with the pope on July 31 and another one on August 4, during which the pope "wept".[100] On August 14, Spellman left Rome to begin his visit to the troops only to be summoned back five days later. On August 20, he again had a lengthy audience with the pope who was "restless and nervous". "I took a definite stand on two matters different from what others [sic] who had been consulted", Spellman crypticly entered into his diary, nor was the pope "persuaded that I am doing right outside of N.Y." The next day, he met with several Vatican officials and prepared an unspecified "memo for Holy Father on visit and on other matters". The pope was still "nervous", he wrote, and "doesn't want me to go away".[101]

One reason for the pope's nervousness may have been the declining health of his Secretary of State, Maglione, who died on August 22. Again Spellman saw the pope and learned that Churchill was to have an audience the following day.[102] On August 23, the archbishop left Rome to visit the troops in England, France, and North Africa. On September 26, he was back in Rome and learned shortly later that Bishop Richard Cushing had been named to succeed O'Connell as Archbishop of Boston.[103] Of more immediate significance to Spellman and the American Church, however, was an entry in his diary for September 28: "I was asked today about the position of Secretary of State. I said I was indifferent, that I would leave New York, family or anything else if the Holy Father thought I could serve in any place for the Church".[104] He made no further direct reference to his becoming Secretary of State, though he was to have several more meetings with

---

[99] AANY, Spellman Diary, July 4–5, 1944; GANNON: *Spellman,* pp. 230–233; CONWAY: *Taylor's Mission,* p. 98.

[100] AANY, Spellman Diary, July 28, 29, Aug. 3, 4, 1944. During this time, Spellman also met with Taylor, Tittmann, Galeazzi, William Bullitt, Montini, Tardini, Prince Humbert, and Bonomi.

[101] *Ibid.,* Aug. 20, 21, 1944.

[102] *Ibid.,* Aug. 22, 1944.

[103] Spellman had written a memorandum for the pope about Boston on July 24, but it is unclear whether he promoted the appointment of Cushing. When he returned to Rome on September 26, he recorded only that Cushing had not yet responded to the letter of appointment; *ibid.,* July 24, Sept. 26, 29, 1944.

[104] *Ibid.,* Sept. 28, 1944.

the pope. For more than the next year, however, well-substantiated rumors would persist that Pius intended to name him to the post.

Spellman had originally intended to go to China and India, but by early October he was growing uncertain. On September 10, Leo Crowley, then the American Foreign Economic Administrator, had cabled him to return immediately to the United States, but he replied that Mooney, Stritch, McIntyre, and O'Hara could act in his place if there were any important matters. By October 4, he recorded: "Pope still fixed on my return and it looks hopeless now to him though I represented that reason for me going could be attended to by others or by me with a telegram". The next day, Crowley again cabled him to return; Spellman agreed to go, if Roosevelt desired it. Both the pope and the president wanted him back in the United States. On October 10, Spellman had his final audience with Pius and two days later departed for New York.[105]

What had brought Spellman home without completing his visit to the troops in the Far East was the disastrous policy of the Allied Control Commission, the virtual government in Italy. This agency distributed rations to the Italian people who were reduced to about one-fifth of their pre-war consumption. The situation had been known the previous May to the War Relief Services of the NCWC, which began negotiating with the War Department and the State Department to send six people to Italy for relief work. But they found themselves blocked and on August 30, Crowley learned that the opposition came from the War Department. Crowley then requested that Roosevelt send a memorandum to the War Department to give clearance for four priests to go to Italy for relief work. At the same time Crowley sent Spellman the first cable asking his return. At the end of September, Roosevelt found his memorandum had been ignored and sent a second stronger one, which finally brought approval for the priests to leave for Italy.[106]

How much Spellman had to do with expediting this matter is unclear, but on October 18, he met with Leo Crowley and Monsignor Ready, had lunch with Roosevelt, and then saw Harry Hopkins, the president's special assistant. "The President seemed shocked at what I told him about Italy & promised immediate action", Spellman recorded. He then "saw Apostolic Delegate & discussed various Roman & American matters".[107] Yet, Spellman's reaction to the Italian situation is surprising. He may have discussed it in his conversations in Rome with Taylor and Tittmann and Vatican officials, but he recorded nothing of it in his diary. Nor did he seem to think it sufficiently important to return to the United States.

---

[105] *Ibid.*, Sept. 10, Oct. 4, 5, 10, 12, 1944; GANNON: *Spellman,* pp. 242–243.
[106] GANNON: *Spellman,* pp. 243–244.
[107] AANY, Spellman Diary, Oct. 18, 1944.

There were other tensions between the Vatican and the United States. At the Casablanca conference in early 1943 Roosevelt had announced that the Allies would accept nothing short of an "unconditional surrender" of the Axis powers. That the term did not mean a total subjugation of the conquered nation was indicated by the relatively generous surrender conditions negotiated for Italy in the fall of 1943. Yet it still was an emotionally laden term which the Vatican thought would only prolong the war by making the Axis fight all the harder. Allied policy toward Germany took a turn for the worse at the second Quebec conference in September, 1944, just before Spellman returned to the United States. For some time Henry Morgenthau, Secretary of the Treasury, had urged Roosevelt "that Germany should be stripped of all industries and converted into an agricultural country". This conflicted with the opinions of Cordell Hull and the State Department, members of which had been for some time devising a more moderate plan for post-war Germany, but it gained the support of Roosevelt, who said he did not want the Germans "to starve to death, but, as an example, if they need food to keep body and soul together beyond what they have, they should be fed three times a day with soup from Army soup kitchens".[108]

Morgenthau was present at the second Quebec conference, where Churchill, with grave reservations, accepted the proposal, apparently because he saw it as the condition for Britain receiving American financial assistance after the war. The memorandum embodying this policy was dated September 15 and received Roosevelt's approval. But the president's health by this time was beginning to fail and later, according to Hull, "he did not seem to realize the devastating nature of the memorandum of September 15 to which he had put his 'O.K. – F.D.R.'". The policy contributed to Hull's resignation as Secretary of State.[109] From his viewpoint and that of the Vatican, it forced the Germans to fight to the death and in the process cost Allied lives as well. It was also the policy with which the Vatican would have to deal through the American Church after the war.

For the last months of the war there is no available correspondence for the Vatican's involvement with American Church leaders. On April 12, 1945, Roosevelt died after serving only three months of his unprecedented fourth term as president. He was succeeded by Vice-President Harry S. Truman. In June, Germany surrendered to the Allies and on August 7, the United States ushered in a new era in warfare by dropping the first atomic bomb on Hiroshima. The next day, Spellman was approached by Henry Luce, President of Time-Life, Inc., and Joseph Kennedy "to ask if I would ask President Truman for 5 or 6 day truce to

---

[108] HULL: *Memoirs*, II, 1602–1603.
[109] *Ibid.*, pp. 1614–1618.

give Japan 'a chance to surrender'".[110] Whether he sought to do this is unknown. But before Japan could respond to any peace offer, the United States dropped a second atomic bomb on Nagasaki on August 9. Japan sued for terms of surrender. On August 11, Spellman was at the White House. As he recorded the event: "John L. Sullivan accompanied me to President Truman. It was an historical meeting. Secretary of State [James] Byrnes came in with document to be sent to Japan accepting Proviso to retain Emperor & President read it to me. Saw Secretary [James] For[r]estal [Secretary of the Navy] and [Robert] Hannegan [Postmaster General]. James Byrnes very nice to me too and Leo Crowley".[111] The war was at last over and the Vatican had now to deal with the Church in the United States which was the strongest power in the west. Moreover, Spellman's first recorded meeting with Secretary of State James Byrnes, an ex-Catholic, was the beginning of a relationship which was directly concerned with the Vatican's attitude toward the new world power.

With peace, Pius XII finally held his first consistory, which he postponed until after the war "as a sign of mourning".[112] As he was making his preparations to name his first cardinals, Tittmann reported to the State Department that Filippo Bernardini had assured him, on the basis of a conversation with Montini, that the pope would name Spellman Secretary of State. The papal motives were manifold: to manifest the Holy See's gratitude for the friendship of the United States and the material aid given by the American bishops; to facilitate the continuation of the Taylor Mission; to strengthen the hand of the Church against communism; to ensure further cooperation between the Holy See and the United States in the work of rescue and relief of displaced persons, who were "victims of political racial and religious persecution"; to render service to Italy by appointing a national of a country known to be friendly to Italy; to internationalize the curia to meet the new world conditions; and to have a close friend as his principal adviser. Bernardini, according to Tittmann, "said Pope was emphatic that Holy See must 'look to the United States' and that many more non-Italian prelates should be brought to Holy See in important positions". Tittmann believed that the pope was publicizing his pro-American policy not only as a defense against communism but also as a warning to the British who had shown "lack of comprehension" in dealing with the Holy See.[113]

---

[110] AANY, Spellman Diary, Aug. 8, 1945.

[111] *Ibid.*, Aug. 11, 1945. Truman, who had just returned from the Potsdam Conference, made only a passing reference to seeing Spellman that day; see Robert H. FERRELL: *Off the Record: The Private Papers of Harry S. Truman,* New York 1980, p. 62.

[112] GANNON: *Spellman,* p. 283.

[113] NA, RG 59, DS 866 A.404/7–545, Tittmann to Secretary, Vatican, July 5, 1945 (cable).

By November, however, Tittmann reported that Spellmann was no longer considered a candidate for Secretary of State both because of his own disinclination and the pope's desire to keep him in the United States. Montini, he thought, would be the most likely choice.[114] Pius, however, decided not to appoint a new Secretary of State as the State Department was informed in December.[115] On February 18, 1946, he opened the consistory and appointed thirty-two cardinals. His choice of four Americans indicated the growing importance of the American Church, which, with Cardinal Dougherty in Philadelphia, now had five members of the college. Late in 1939, Spellman had been assured that he and Archbishop John Glennon of St. Louis were to be elevated to the purple. These two were now joined by Archbishops Mooney of Detroit and Stritch of Chicago. Glennon had been the Archbishop of St. Louis since 1903, but he remained aloof from most interdiocesan affairs and died on his way back from the consistory. His appointment together with those of Mooney and Stritch indicated the Holy See's growing awareness of the importance of the mid-west. Missing from the archbishops who were influential in American ecclesiastical affairs was McNicholas of Cincinnati, who with his friends in Chicago and Detroit exercised a more powerful influence than Spellman on the domestic affairs of the American Church. Mooney had been chairman of the administrative board of the NCWC from 1936 to 1945, except for 1940 when he was replaced by Stritch, who again held the post in 1946. McNicholas was then elected chairman and continued in office until his death in 1950.

The significance of World War II for the American Church, however, went far beyond the Vatican's now recognizing its importance because of the political and military influence of the United States in world affairs. First, the Holy See fully recognized and not merely tolerated the NCWC as the official voice of the American hierarchy. It thus paved the way for the concept of collegiality which would emerge at the Second Vatican Council and which was part of the American Church's earlier tradition. Second, it realized that, despite ethnic diversity, American Catholics constituted one Church. Regardless of their immigrant backgrounds, American Catholics were by and large loyal to their country and fought for it against the nations of their ancestors. This would prove to be an important point as the Vatican sought American Catholic assistance in the settlement of post-war Europe, particularly of the issues of placing Germany on a peacetime footing and of combatting communism in Italy. Third, American Catholics had proven to the American cultural majority that they were truly American. Their alliance with Roosevelt's New Deal, despite the aberrations of Coughlin and his

---

[114] *Ibid.*, 866 A.404/11–2145, Tittmann to Secretary, Vatican, Nov. 27, 1945 (cable).
[115] *Ibid.*, 866 A.404/12–2145, Gowan to Secretary, Vatican, Dec. 21, 1945 (cable).

supporters, provided a preliminary basis for their acceptance, which was extended still further by their support of the war. The hierarchy, to be sure, protested against the bombing of Rome, but it avoided any overture which might be construed as disloyal to the nation's war efforts.

Still the acceptance was not complete and in the years after the war, there was again an outbreak of some forms of anti-Catholic bigotry. There were already signs of this as early as May of 1945, when the State Department, noting the opposition to the Taylor Mission, suggested its termination as soon as hostilities ended.[116] This bigotry would gradually be cancelled out by Catholic opposition to the new enemy of the United States, communism. Though the Holy See likewise lapsed into its former suspicion of the peculiar American institution of religious liberty, it too was already awakening into a new appreciation of the United States as the strongest bulwark against communism.

---

[116] *Ibid.*, 121.866 A/5 – 845, Joseph Grew to Truman, memo, May 4, 1945. Taylor himself had attempted to resign at the end of 1944, CONWAY: *Taylor's Mission,* p. 99.

CHAPTER XIII

POST-WAR SETTLEMENTS: DIPLOMATIC RELATIONS AND THE
PROBLEM OF COMMUNISM

Between the end of the Second World War and the opening of the Second Vatican Council, a series of changes took place within American society, which were reflected in the Holy See's relations with the American Church. One of these changes was the temporary eclipse of the rapprochement Catholics had established with their fellow citizens during the war. An indication of this was the end of the Myron Taylor Mission and President Truman's failure to have an ambassador to the Holy See appointed in the midst of an outbreak of anti-Catholicism. These changes made the Holy See ambivalent toward the American Church. On the one hand, it continued to use American Catholics to combat communism in Italy; on the other, it grew increasingly suspicious of the American notion of religious liberty because of the apparent second-class status of American Catholics within their own nation. The reconciliation of the Holy See with American religious liberty occurred only at the Second Vatican Council. The establishment of permanent rapprochement between Catholics and their fellow citizens occurred in 1960 with the election of John F. Kennedy as President of the United States. But these events marked the end of a rather tortured trail, trod by a new group of American churchmen.

A. CHANGING COMPOSITION OF THE AMERICAN HIERARCHY

For whatever reason, Pius XII acted as his own Secretary of State after the death of Cardinal Maglione in 1944 and in the appointment of bishops who were to emerge into prominence he seems to have increasingly relied on the advice of powerful American prelates, who in turn enjoyed either his own or the favor of Cicognani, the apostolic delegate. This represented a slight shift away from direct Roman patronage and a gradual step toward the Americanization of the hierarchy. Two of the important prelates who influenced the new generation of bishops were Cardinal Spellman and Edward F. Hoban, Archbishop-Bishop of Cleveland.

Spellman had already written to Pius XII in 1941 to praise his auxiliaries,

James F. McIntyre and John F. O'Hara, C.S.C. In 1946, McIntyre was named Coadjutor Archbishop of New York, but without right of succession. The next year, the Archdiocese of Los Angeles fell vacant with the death of its first archbishop, John J. Cantwell. Spellman succeeded in gaining the appointment to the see of McIntyre, on whom he conferred the pallium on March 19, 1948.[1] It was the only time Spellman managed to cross the "Hindenburg Line", as the bishops of the mid-west called their otherwise successful campaign geographically to contain his sphere of influence.[2] In the east, however, he was dominant. In 1945, O'Hara had been named Bishop of Buffalo and in 1951, at Dougherty's death, he became Archbishop of Philadelphia, where again Spellman had the opportunity to confer a pallium.[3]

Spellman's precise influence in these appointments is unknown, but at times his advice seems to have differed from Cicognani's. In the spring of 1947, Galeazzi counselled him "that whenever you have to make recommendations for appointments, you should write at length to Biltmore [the former address of the apostolic delegation], giving facts and considerations and reasons, and address a letter to H[is]. H[oliness]. telling him what you have proposed to Biltmore, stating the same facts and considerations. Try to do so for Baltimore. It is too important, and whenever you have some specific elements for an appointment your friend here should be supplied with all reasons, and considerations in regard to your proposals, so that he might with full conscience give instructions against possible different advices from Biltmore".[4] Such intrusion into the American Church not only by a foreigner but also by a layman may well have antagonized some American bishops, had they known of it, but Spellman really needed little encouragement. On June 15, he wrote to both Cicognani and Pius about the succession to the Archdiocese of Baltimore, where the truculent successor to Gibbons, Michael Curley, had died, and about the appointment of the first Archbishop of Washington. What he wrote he did not say, but on November 21, 1947, he received word that the new Archbishop of Washington was Monsignor Patrick A. O'Boyle, whom he had appointed his archdiocesan director of Catholic Charities earlier that year.[5] Whether Spellman's recommendations for Baltimore were followed is unknown, but on November 29, 1947, Bishop Francis P. Keough of Providence was transferred to the Archdiocese of Baltimore, where he made no threat to revive the spirit of Gibbons. By 1950, then, Spellman had

[1] AANY, Spellman Diary, Nov. 26, Dec. 30, 1947, Mar. 19, 1948.
[2] Interview with Bishop Clarence Issenmann, Jan. 8, 1981.
[3] Thomas T. McAvoy: *Father O'Hara of Notre Dame: The Cardinal-Archbishop of Philadelphia*, Notre Dame 1967, pp. 196–368.
[4] AANY, Galeazzi to Spellman, n.p., May 15, 1947.
[5] AANY, Spellman Diary, Mar. 14, June 2, Nov. 21, 1947.

friends and former associates as ordinaries in the Archdioceses of Los Angeles, Washington, and Philadelphia and a man in Baltimore, who was at least neutral toward him; unlike Spellman, however, none of them would be national leaders.

Bishop Hoban's influence seems to have derived from his close friendship with Cicognani, who may have been trying to establish a counter-poise to Spellman. Hoban had become Mundelein's auxiliary bishop in 1921, Bishop of Rockford, Illinois, in 1928, Coadjutor Bishop of Cleveland in 1942, and finally Bishop of Cleveland in 1945. From his seminary and chancery staff came some of the leaders of the American hierarchy in the 1960s and 1970s. John F. Dearden taught at St. Mary's Seminary in Cleveland, became Coadjutor Bishop of Pittsburgh in 1948 and Bishop in 1950. In 1958, he succeeded Cardinal Mooney in Detroit. John J. Krol had also taught in the Cleveland seminary, served in the chancery office from 1943 to 1954, became Hoban's auxiliary in 1953, and succeeded O'Hara as Archbishop of Philadelphia in 1961. Floyd L. Begin was appointed vice chancellor of the Diocese of Cleveland in 1930, became Hoban's auxiliary in 1957, and was named Bishop of the newly established Diocese of Oakland, California, in 1962. John P. Treacy was Cleveland's Director of the Society for the Propagation of the Faith from 1931 to 1945, when he was appointed Coadjutor Bishop of LaCrosse, Wisconsin; he succeeded to the See of LaCrosse in 1948. Paul J. Hallinan had been engaged in pastoral work in Cleveland, had done a doctorate in history at Western Reserve University in Cleveland, and was named Bishop of Charleston in 1958; four years later, he was named the first Archbishop of Atlanta. Finally, John F. Whealon had done pastoral work and taught in the seminary before being named Auxiliary Bishop of Cleveland in 1961. He was named Bishop of Erie in 1966 and was transferred to the Archdiocese of Hartford in 1968. These were but a few of the prelates who began their careers during the post-war years and who would remain prominent during and after the Second Vatican Council.

B. VATICAN-AMERICAN DIPLOMACY

1. End of the Taylor Mission

In post-war America, however, the rapport established during the war between Catholics and Protestants suffered some setbacks. One of the first signs of this was the attitude toward the continuation of the Myron Taylor Mission to Pius XII. Early in January, 1946, the weekly journal, *Newsweek,* carried the story that once the peace was established, Taylor would be recalled. Spellman immediately sought information on the matter from Robert Hannegan, the Postmaster General, and gained his intervention with Truman.[6] For the next few months, however, the campaign began to mount against the mission as a violation of the separation of Church and State. Spellman made these attacks the topic of his commencement address at Fordham University on June 12, 1946. They were, he said, the product of "bigotry". Countering the assertions of Protestant leaders that they had been assured that Taylor's mission was only a temporary one to last only to the signing of the peace treaties, the cardinal pointed to the statements of praise of both Presidents Roosevelt and Truman for Taylor's work, which still had significance in post-war Europe. Against those who argued against "the accreditation of an Ambassador to the Holy See" as a violation of the separation of Church and State, he cited the contrary opinion of the presidents as well as of "two men who have been candidates for the Presidency and two others who have held the high office of Secretary of State".[7] Spellman did not at this time disclose the names of the presidential candidates or secretaries of state, but clearly he was paving the way for the effort to establish full diplomatic relations. For the time being, however, the question was moot.

But the Vatican was growing concerned about the precise status of Taylor's mission. In February, 1947, the pope directed the hierarchy in general, and Spellman in particular, to see to it "that the continuation of the personal representation of the President of the United States at the Vatican may be assured, at least in its present status, with personnel of the American diplomatic corps and with the decorum befitting the United States and the Holy See". In particular, the Holy See was concerned with the proposed reduction of personnel of the mission and with the transfer of its office to "a smaller and less fitting location".[8] Cicognani immediately informed both Spellman and McNicholas, who was then chairman of the administrative board of the NCWC. Spellman's initial reaction was that McNicholas should see President Truman, but then he conferred with Justice Frank Murphy and other presidential confidants, who assured him that Truman would continue the mission, that there would be no reduction of personnel but only a replacement of Franklin Gowan, who had succeeded Tittmann, with J. Graham Parsons of the Foreign Service, and that the mission's location would not be changed.[9] To McNicholas, Spellman added that Truman intended to maintain the mission, although the "pressure against the mission is continuous and increasing". He also thought, in response to a query from McNicholas, that

---

[6] AANY, Spellman to Hannegan, New York, Jan. 18, 1946 (copy); Hannegan to Truman, Washington, Feb. 12, 1946 (copy).

[7] GANNON: *Spellman,* pp. 169–171.

[8] AANY, Cicognani to Spellman, Washington, Feb. 8, 1947.

[9] AANY, Spellman to Cicognani, New York, Feb. 11 and 14, 1947 (copies).

if the Republicans were successful in the 1948 campaign, they would not end the mission.[10]

Galeazzi, however, notified Spellman that the replacement of Gowan was really part of Taylor's growing hostility to the position. "The truth is", he wrote, "that the Boss wants to keep on destroying any importance of the office – he has surely a furious hate for the church and its Leader – very sad but true".[11] This was the first indication of what became a growing conviction that Taylor himself wished to see the mission substantially changed or abolished. The replacement of Gowan with Parsons was seen as indicative of this attitude because the latter was originally listed as "First Secretary of the American Embassy", which was unacceptable according to Vatican protocol. At Cicognani's request, Spellman spoke with Truman who agreed to have Parsons' orders changed to make him exclusively part of Taylor's staff. Taylor also spoke with Truman and with George Marshall, the Secretary of State, and assured Cicognani that Parsons was to be "appointed only as his assistant as Personal Representative of the President to the Holy See".[12] On August 6, 1947, Truman wrote Pius XII saying he was sending Taylor back to Rome to facilitate "parallel endeavours for peace and the alleviation of human suffering".[13]

For a while, at least, it seemed that the Taylor mission was safe. On August 21, 1947, Spellman wrote Truman to express his appreciation for "continuing your contact with His Holiness in a joint effort for the alleviation of human misery and for other good and cogent reasons". Though Spellman knew the president would receive numerous letters of opposition, he was convinced "that there are millions who approve and who are grateful to you for continuing this policy and practice initiated by President Roosevelt".[14] The cardinal also suggested to McNicholas that, if he agreed, other bishops should write Truman.[15] The president's response was pleasant, but somewhat non-committal. "I am thoroughly convinced that Mr. Taylor is doing a great and constructive work", wrote Truman. "It is therefore encouraging to know that you believe his mission has such widespread approval".[16]

Just how widespread the approval of the mission was, even among Catholics, is difficult to determine. In September, however, strong disapproval was voiced in a

---

[10] AANY, Spellman to McNicholas, New York, Feb. 15, 1947 (copy).

[11] AANY, Galeazzi to Spellman, Vatican, Feb. 1, 1947.

[12] AANY, Spellman to Cicognani, New York, May 15, 1947 (copy); Cicognani to Spellman, Washington, May 17, 1947.

[13] AANY, Truman to Pius XII, Washington, Aug. 6, 1947 (printed copy).

[14] AANY, Spellman to Truman, New York, Aug. 21, 1947 (copy).

[15] AANY, Spellman to McNicholas, New York, Aug. 19, 1947 (copy).

[16] AANY, Truman to Spellman, Washington, Aug. 25, 1947.

piece of fictional journalism in the Soviet-sponsored *Berlin am Mittag*. In Berlin, Taylor had seen Cardinal Count Conrad von Preysing, Archbishop of Berlin, who had recently visited Spellman. The article creatively linked the Holy See with American capitalism, represented by Taylor, Spellman, and German Catholics and Protestants. This, concluded the article, was all part of "a dark Jesuit intrigue", orginally devised "by the Jesuit Secretary [*sic*] General Ledochowski and carried out by the Jesuit Secretary [*sic*] General Janssens".[17] German Communists may have seen Taylor and the Holy See engineering an anti-communist crusade by his calling on Catholic as well as Protestant leaders, but his action was precisely what caused tension between him and the Vatican.

An early sign of Spellman's growing reservations about Taylor came in early 1948, when the cardinal was mobilizing the Italian-American community to influence the outcome of the Italian elections. The cardinal arranged for a member of the embassy staff in Rome to speak with the pope about the Italian situation. Taylor learned of this only from reading a cabled report from Parsons and felt that his office should have been the vehicle for the discussion.[18] Further difficulty arose when Monsignor James Griffiths reported to Spellman of his attempt to have the Voice of America help influence the outcome of the elections by broadcasting the contributions of the American people to Italy since the establishment of the relief program. "The difficulty anticipated at the moment", wrote Griffiths, "is the attitude of Mr. Taylor who, I am told, quite habitually opposes any proposal from within the organization if it has not originated with him".[19] But the major problem with Taylor related to the nature of the mission and his occupancy of it.

On May 2, 1949, Domenico Tardini, Substitute Secretary for the Extraordinary Affairs of the Church, sent Spellman a lengthy letter containing four points. First, since Taylor was not officially an accredited diplomat, he felt that he could fulfill his mission while remaining in the United States. Second – and this was probably the major objection – whenever Taylor did come to Rome, he was also entrusted with other missions, notably to other religious leaders. In Tardini's mind, "it would seem that these other missions have been purposely assigned to him in order to engender the impression that his visit to the Pope is just one of many missions entrusted to Mr. Taylor during his voyage to Europe and that the Holy Father is thus placed on the same level with other religious leaders who are

---

[17] AANY, *Berlin am Mittag*, Sept. 16, 1947, translation attached to: Taylor to Spellman, New York, Oct. 6, 1947.

[18] AANY, Taylor to Spellman, n.p., Feb. 3, 1948.

[19] AANY, Memo, Griffiths to Spellman, Mar. 4, 1948.

casually interviewed. Hence, this attitude is obviously not well received here in our circles and is regarded as inconsistent with the respect which is due to the Holy See". Third, while Taylor's visits were anticipated with great publicity, "the results have not been even remotely proportionate to the previous hew and cry (as a matter of fact, our experience has shown that Mr. Taylor has in reality obtained little or nothing for the Holy See by his efforts)". Finally, Taylor's concern for the Protestant attacks on him led to "his indecisive, timid and illogical attitude" and to his reduction of the personnel in his Rome office. Tardini hoped that Spellman might be able to bring this situation to Truman's attention and point out that it was "flattering neither to the Holy Father nor to the President of the United States".[20]

Tardini received no reply from his request,[21] and on July 4 he wrote Cicognani with instructions to bring the information to Spellman's attention "with the greatest haste". He repeated many of the observations he had earlier made to Spellman and said that at Taylor's last audience on July 1, the pope spoke openly to Taylor about the mission. The pope began by expressing his dismay at the American Protestant attacks on the mission, "notwithstanding the fact that the United States is reputed to be the land of liberty and tolerance". In view of the "equivocal uncertainty" regarding the mission, the Holy See wanted Truman to give it "an official and stable character". To Taylor's objections that official diplomatic relations would be construed as unconstitutional, Tardini explained to Cicognani that countries such as Brazil, Chile, and France, where there was the separation of Church and State, countries, such as Great Britain, where there was an established church and where Catholics were in the minority, and countries such as Egypt, which was non-Christian, all maintained diplomatic relations. At this point in time, however, Tardini was not urging such relations, which might "stir up a religious war". But the United States was faced with the alternative of continuing relations through the personal representation "in official, stable form, and not vague and subject to continuous equivocation and recrimination", or of discontinuing all such relations altogether. At one point in Taylor's conversation with the pope, he said that the Protestant "attacks would cease if he were at the same time the representative to the various religious groups, a thing which is evidently impossible". Furthermore, concluded Tardini, while Taylor was "so solicitous in regard to his contacts with the heads of non-Catholic churches, the

---

[20] AANY, Tardini to Spellman, Vatican, May 2, 1949. Taylor had been entrusted with visiting non-Catholic religious leaders; see Truman to Taylor, Washington, Aug. 7, 1947, in: Ennio DI NOLFO: *Vaticano e Stati Uniti, 1939–1952 (dalle carte Myron C. Taylor)*, Milan 1978, pp. 530–531.

[21] AANY, Galeazzi to Spellman, Vatican, July 3, 1949.

questions that interest the Holy See remain generally without any positive result".[22]

Cicognani immediately communicated Tardini's letter to Spellman who then tried to make an appointment with Truman before Taylor had a chance to return to the United States. On July 15, he was optimistic that he would see the president within a week. He would then report both to Cicognani and to Galeazzi.[23] To the latter he also sent an article from *America* by Father Wilfrid Parsons, criticizing Taylor's conduct. As soon as possible after seeing Truman, he was then to fly to Rome to report personally to the pope. But this time Spellman was not successful. On July 31, he wrote Truman again asking for a "ten minute appointment", but received the reply from the president's secretary that due to the proximity of Congress' adjournment, the president would have no time to see him.[24] Unfortunately, Spellman's diary, if he then kept one, is not extant to report his reaction to this snub. And it must have been around that time that he had a memorandum drawn up, possibly by Griffiths, detailing the history of the Taylor Mission and, in accordance with Tardini's observations, calling for a more permanent mission.[25]

In view of the public outcry at the continuation of the Taylor Mission and of Truman's coolness toward Spellman, it is difficult to explain why at this point the cardinal began a movement toward establishing official diplomatic relations. Late in the fall of 1949 Taylor paid Spellman a visit and told him that he definitely intended to resign his post and would take his leave of the pope after representing the president at the opening of the Holy Year.[26] Taylor also asked for the names of candidates as his successor, but Spellman was unable to give any. Galeazzi, however, did have some candidates, including Winthrop Aldrich, whom Spellman thought unsuitable because he was a Republican. But the cardinal added a further note in reply to Galeazzi's suggestions. "I think that anytime the representation at the Vatican might be changed into a legation or embassy would be a most acceptable time", he wrote, and "it is my opinion that Mr. Taylor's recommendations are very strong with the President".[27]

---

[22] AANY, Tardini to Cicognani, Vatican, July 4, 1949, translation, enclosed in Cicognani to Spellman, Washington, July 9, 1949.

[23] AANY, Spellman to Cicognani, New York, July 15, 1949 (copy); Spellman to Galeazzi, New York, July 15, 1949 (copy).

[24] AANY, Spellman to Truman, New York, July 31, 1949 (copy); Matthew Connelly to Spellman, Washington, Aug. 3, 1949.

[25] AANY, Spellman Memorandum, n.d., n.p.

[26] AANY, Spellman to Galeazzi, New York, Nov. 7, 1949 (copy).

[27] AANY, Spellman to Galeazzi, New York, Dec. 14, 1949 (copy).

2. Attempts to Establish Diplomatic Relations

a. Spellman's Preliminary Overtures

The occasion for Spellman's new overture for diplomatic relations came with Taylor's resignation as personal representative to the pope on January 18, 1950.[28] Taylor then wrote Spellman that in Washington "the matters which you and I have discussed were completed".[29] In his typical laconic style, Spellman's reply indicated that Taylor had strongly suggested in their conversation that Truman might establish diplomatic relations. "I know nothing more than what you told me before your departure for Rome", the cardinal said. "I do hope that the ideas of President Truman as expressed by you to me will eventuate before very long".[30]

In the meantime, Joseph Kennedy had written Truman on January 31. Truman replied on February 3 in a letter marked "CONFIDENTIAL", but forwarded to Spellman: "It is indeed helpful to have all this background information concerning the origin of the Taylor mission from one who had so large and influential a part in the preliminary negotiations. I am glad to tell you that His Holiness the Pope, Mr. Taylor, the State Department and I are in complete accord as to the next step. The whole question is now under study at the State Department. Because of certain legislation which followed the discontinuance of our representation to the old Papal States, it may be necessary to seek authority from the Congress. Meanwhile, everything is in abeyance until I have a report from the State Department. I appreciate very much your interest and may ask for your counsel as things develop".[31] Spellman then sent Truman's letter to Cicognani with "an extra copy in case you think it will be of interest to the Holy See".[32] It was curious that Truman was considering official diplomatic relations, for when Taylor submitted his resignation to the president, the Vatican received no official notification that the mission was terminated. Instead, the mission's office was simply closed and Franklin Gowan, who had returned to Rome as Taylor's assistant, was reassigned to another foreign service post. In the United States, there was a renewed attack against a successor to Taylor as a personal representative.[33]

In March, 1950, Spellman accompanied a group of pilgrims to Rome. Upon his

---

[28] AANY, Taylor to Truman, Jan 18, 1950; Truman to Taylor, Jan. 18, 1950 (printed copies).

[29] AANY, Taylor to Spellman, New York, Jan. 25, 1950.

[30] AANY, Spellman to Taylor, New York, Feb. 2, 1950 (copy).

[31] AANY, Truman to Kennedy, Washington, Feb. 3, 1950; in: GANNON: Spellman, p. 172.

[32] AANY, Spellman to Cicognani, New York, Feb. 11, 1950 (copy); Cicognani to Spellman, Washington, Feb. 15, 1950.

[33] U.S. News and World Report, Feb. 10, 1950, pp. 24–25.

return, he wrote the pope: "I had the opportunity today to have as guest at luncheon one of President Truman's closest advisers who is a Catholic. I told him quite frankly of the brutal manner in which Mr. Gowan was recalled and of the insult that was offered to the Holy See. I told him further that sooner or later there would be a protest in regard to this situation unless some remedial action was taken. I suggested the possibility of a Chargé d'Affaires to open up a permanent and stable relationship. I do not know what will result from my renewed efforts but nevertheless I wish to keep Your Holiness informed".[34]

By June, the issue was being vented in the press. David Lawrence, a columnist, pointed out that Gowan had been ordered to a new assignment without the Vatican's being given any notice whether the mission would continue. Russia, he asserted, regarded Gowan's transfer as the end of the mission, which would be regrettable in view of the strong anti-Communist blocs comprised of Catholics in western Europe and even in Poland, Hungary, and Czechoslovakia. It was possible, he thought, that Truman was waiting until after the fall congressional elections to make any decision, but Representative John McCormack of Massachusetts, the Democratic majority leader, had already proposed to Truman that he send the nomination of a minister to the Senate for confirmation. Lawrence's column was given wide circulation through the National Catholic News Service.[35] In a subsequent column, Lawrence stated that the State Department report on the matter, to which Truman had alluded in his letter to Kennedy, had recommended another personal representative, but it had been sent back with a notation that the matter should be held in abeyance for a while.[36]

For the rest of the year, the issue continued to be bruited in the press. Gowan reported to Spellman in June that the Holy See wanted an ambassador or chargé d'affaires, but not another personal representative.[37] In September, the *Washington Post* editorialized in favor of an ambassador, noting that the United States had diplomatic relations with nations whose heads of state were also religious and that non-Christian states maintained missions at the Holy See. Thanking the editor for his comments, Spellman pointed out that, according to the Institute of Public Opinion at Princeton, most Americans would approve such an appoint-

---

[34] AANY, Spellman to Pius XII, New York, Mar. 27, 1950 (copy). For a contrary view of the possibility of appointing a Chargé d'Affaires, see *America,* 98 (Mar. 25, 1950), 714, which takes issue with C. L. Sulzberger's dispatch from Rome in the *New York Times,* Feb. 24, 1950, stating the Vatican would accept a chargé. *America* pointed out that such an official is accredited not to the head of state but to the foreign minister and presupposes the existence of a full envoy.

[35] AANY, *New York Herald Tribune,* June 6, 1950; NCWC News Service, June 12, 1950; Spellman to Lawrence, New York, June 14, 1950.

[36] AANY, *New York Herald Tribune,* June 21, 1950.

[37] AANY, Gowan to Spellman, Rome, June 16 and 22, 1950.

ment.[38] How accurate the institute was is difficult to determine, but during the fall there was a strong Protestant movement against the appointment of an ambassador. J. Ralph MaGee, Methodist Resident Bishop of the Chicago Area, for instance, wrote his pastors urging them to organize opposition to the appointment. "We have not believed in a Clerical Party in government as European countries have", he wrote. "We do not believe in the dominance of any one Church or religious group in governmental decision." For him, "the Roman Catholic Hierarchy is political minded. Through the centuries the Popes have attempted to make governmentals [sic] and rulers bow to his will. We want none of it".[39]

Despite increasing anti-Catholic protests which were finding expression in the writings of Paul Blanshard, Cicognani and Spellman soon began an attempt not only to have a replacement appointed for Myron Taylor but also to establish official diplomatic relations. On December 1, 1950, Cicognani had spoken to Taylor, who assured him that Truman intended to appoint "a representative of the United States to the Holy See" and would "propose this matter to the Congress shortly after the first of January". Although Cicognani's expression was ambiguous, his mention that Truman would submit his appointment to Congress indicates that there was serious consideration of diplomatic relations and not merely the appointment of another personal representative. To ward off "objections from certain Protestant circles", the delegate wrote Spellman and Stritch to "be prepared to present the Catholic side", which "would involve a study of the history of Papal representations, the status of the Holy See under the aspect not only of a sovereign state but especially as the head of the Catholic Church, the position of American Catholics and various allied questions". He concluded his request to Spellman by asking for the name of "someone who might be called upon to present the Catholic position in a way that will be understood and appreciated here in America".[40]

Spellman replied immediately with the recommendation that Bishop James H. Griffiths and Father Robert A. Graham, S. J., an expert in Vatican diplomacy, be delegated to draw up the Catholic position on the matter.[41] On December 28, Spellman further informed Cicognani that he had already instructed Griffiths "to lay the ground work for a presentation of our viewpoint" and to consult with Cardinal Stritch. "It is agreed", Spellman wrote, "that the matter should not be permitted to assume the proportions of a religious controversy but realistically this may be ... completely impossible, since the non-Catholic phalanx will un-

---

[38] AANY, Spellman to Editor of *Washington Post,* New York, Sept. 5, 1950 (copy).

[39] AANY, MaGee to "Dear Pastor", Chicago, Sept. 20, 1950 (copy), enclosed in Noll to Spellman, Ft. Wayne, Sept. 26, 1950.

[40] AANY, Cicognani to Spellman, Washington, Dec. 5, 1950 (copy).

[41] AANY, Spellman to Cicognani, New York, Dec. 9, 1950 (copy).

doubtedly leave no stone unturned to emphasize as primary the religious aspects of the question". Graham, he reported, would work with Griffiths in preparing "a memorandum setting forth the issues from the standpoint of history and international law with special attention to the period extending from 1870 to 1929, to demonstrate the persistent international character of the Holy See even before the creation of the State of Vatican City".

Spellman then suggested the formation of a committe of informed laymen, including perhaps Taylor, from various regions of the country to present the arguments for diplomatic relations. But he also recognized that the proposal would provoke "strong opposition from Blanshard and his secularist group as distinct from Protestants as such". This group, he thought, "will very probably endeavour to draw us out to the point of basing the right of passive papal legation on the fact that the Holy Father is not merely the supreme spiritual head of the Catholic Church but also the head of a sovereign state. Then the question of dual allegiance of Catholics in the United States will very likely be raised". Blanshard, he noted, had already raised this point in his book *American Freedom and Catholic Power* where he urged that American Catholic bishops be made subject to the Foreign Agents Registration Law. He assured Cicognani that he would forward the memorandum drawn up by Griffiths and Graham and concluded: "if we can demonstrate a case for an official diplomatic representative to the Holy Father on the grounds that objectively it will contribute to the elaboration, extension and improvement of current United States' foreign policy on which the Department of State is spending so freely, we may be able to achieve a favorable action".[42]

The memorandum in question outlined the position of the Catholic Church as a perfect society with public juridical authority which was recognized in both theory and in fact by civil powers. Because the "Church has personality at public law and the Roman Pontiff who is its personification has *de jure* a legal position in the international order", it followed that "the Holy See possesses the right of active and passive legation". Presenting the history of the Holy See's diplomacy from the early and late middle ages to the modern post-reformation period, the memorandum presented the views and arguments used by various civil governments in establishing diplomatic relations with the Holy See in the twentieth century.[43]

But Spellman was concerned with mustering more than theoretical justification. He now turned toward gaining political support. His first approach in this

---

[42] AANY, Spellman to Cicognani, New York, Dec. 28, 1950 (copy).

[43] AANY, "Pro-Memoria" on diplomatic relations, n.d.

realm was toward James Byrnes, former Senator from South Carolina, Secretary of State, and Supreme Court Justice. Byrnes, an ex-Catholic, was about to be inaugurated as Governor of South Carolina and had invited Spellman. Unable to attend, the cardinal wrote both Byrnes and Leo Crowley. To Byrnes he wrote: "I understand that President Truman is about to make a recommendation that a permanent United States Minister be appointed to the Vatican. As you know Mr. Taylor and the President interpreted the appointment of the Personal Representative as something temporary. This was not the idea of President Roosevelt and I was amazed to find this interpretation made at the time when Mr. Taylor announced his retirement and a conclusion drawn that therefore the office was abolished. I knew there will be a battle on the old argument of separation of Church and State. I would like to make as strong a case as possible for the establishment of this mission on the grounds that in this present world conflict between Communism and Freedom such a mission would be of benefit to our country. I shall send you a memorandum on the subject and if you are convinced of the propriety and the usefulness of such a mission, I would be most grateful if you could either appear or write a letter to the Senate Foreign Relations Committee to that effect. With your prestige as former Justice of the Supreme Court, former Secretary of State and Governor of South Carolina you could help us tremendously with the Southern Senators".[44]

To Crowley, who was to attend the ceremonies, Spellman wrote urging him to use the opportunity of the inauguration to speak with Byrnes about establishing diplomatic relations.[45] Crowley promised his compliance and stated that he would also speak with Senators Walter F. George of Georgia and Alexander Wylie of Wisconsin who were on the Foreign Relations Committee. He further suggested that Spellman have James Farley speak with Senator Thomas Connolly, the chairman of the committee.[46]

Before Spellman could even receive a reply from Byrnes or Crowley, however, he had also written to Cicognani suggesting that the bishops of Ohio seek the support of Senator Robert Taft.[47] Cicognani, in turn, advised that Spellman himself gain the intermediation of Archbishop Karl J. Alter of Cincinnati.[48] In the meantime, Spellman received the encouraging support of Myron Taylor and his former assistant, Harold Tittmann.[49] On January 16, he wrote Alter stating the

---

[44] AANY, Spellman to Byrnes, New York, Jan. 6, 1951 (copy).
[45] AANY, Spellman to Crowley, New York, Jan. 6, 1951 (copy).
[46] AANY, Crowley to Spellman, Chicago, Jan. 8, 1951.
[47] AANY, Spellman to Cicognani, New York, Jan. 9, 1951 (copy).
[48] AANY, Cicognani to Spellman, Washington, Jan. 12, 1951.
[49] AANY, Taylor to Spellman, Palm Beach, Fla., Jan. 15, 1951; Tittmann to Spellman, Lima, Peru, Jan. 13, 1951.

problem and noting that "it would be essential to our success to have the endorsement of Senator Taft or at least not to have his opposition".[50] It was at this point, however, that Spellman met with a reservation, not from a political leader but from a fellow bishop. Alter, who was the chairman of the administrative board of the NCWC, represented a growing consensus of some bishops, notably Mooney and Stritch, that the United States was different from Europe and that what was condemned in the latter may not have real application in the former. The mid-west triangle of Alter, Stritch, and Mooney, gradually came to the support of the Jesuit theologian, John Courtney Murray, who began urging universal Catholic acceptance of religious liberty. In January, 1951, Alter could voice his concern about the state of American Catholicism in terms reminiscent of the Americanists in the 1890s. "It is unfortunate", he wrote Spellman, "that this question of official representation at the Vatican should come before the public at this particular moment when the decree respecting International Rotary has caused so much bewilderment and unfavorable discussion among our fellow citizens. While loyally accepting the direction of the Holy See it is difficult for us here in this country to substantiate the facts concerning any serious religious or moral significance in the rather loose wording of the terms 'service' and 'creed' used at times by Rotarians in their public expressions. In European countries I understand that the use of such terms convey [sic] a much more precise meaning with dogmatic implications or overtones. ... The above ... may seem to be a digression but it does have a bearing upon the question of timing and the successful achievement of the objective".[51] Alter also enclosed for Spellman's reading a draft of a letter he prepared for Senator Taft arguing that the proposed establishment of diplomatic relations be considered on its own merits and not with emotional rancor. Spellman, however, urged the archbishop not to send the letter but to speak with Taft personally.[52] Alter himself later confided that he and other members of the hierarchy were far from enthusiastic about the establishment of diplomatic relations because they felt that, if the Holy See wished to communicate with the American government or vice versa, an American citizen could be used as intermediary.[53]

But Cicognani and Spellman's information that Truman intended to name a minister to the Holy See at this juncture seems to have been precipitate. First, Bishop Griffiths had spoken to a close political associate of the president's who

---

[50] AANY, Spellman to Alter, New York, Jan. 16, 1951 (copy).

[51] AANY, Alter to Spellman, Cincinnati, Jan. 22, 1951.

[52] AANY, Alter to Taft, Cincinnati, Jan. 20, 1951 (draft); Spellman to Alter, New York, Jan. 31, 1951 (copy).

[53] Alter interview with the author, May 26, 1974.

denied that Truman had any intention of naming a minster. Second, the Religious News Service had reported on January 19 that the Senate Foreign Relations Committee had privately advised the president against such an appointment and that the State Department had submitted a study opposing the appointment. Finally, Father Graham had consulted with friends in the State Department, which he learned maintained a "Vatican desk". From his sources he gained the information that the State Department had indeed submitted a study to the White House but had presented "merely the alternatives" to official representation and had not, as the Religious News Service reported, urged against such representation. Griffiths and Graham had then prepared a lengthy report arguing for diplomatic relations should Truman change his mind.[54]

Spellman forwarded Griffiths' report to Cicognani and queried the delegate if he had heard anything further of Truman's intention.[55] In the meantime, in early February, Governor Byrnes responded to Spellman's letter. When he left the Senate, Byrnes wrote, he had decided never to offer that body "unsolicited advice" and had since that time "never appeared before a committee unless invited to appear". On the other hand, he was "anxious to help in the matter to which you refer because I believe Myron Taylor rendered splendid service at the Vatican". Personally he preferred sending another personal representative to the pope for this would avoid the difficulty of obtaining Senate approval. As he noted, "I recall President Roosevelt in referring on one occasion to the valuable service rendered by Mr. Taylor, expressing the opinion that the Congress would not authorize the sending of a representative. President Truman having continued Mr. Taylor at the Vatican would not be establishing a new policy. He would be continuing a policy by sending a Personal Representative to serve as Taylor has served. If the President submits legislation to the Senate and House Committees and it is not favorably acted upon, he would then be precluded from sending a representative. In any event, I hope you will send me the memorandum and I will determine then whether I can be of service. Certainly at the first opportunity, I shall talk to some of my friends on the Senate Foreign Relations Committee to ascertain their views".[56] Byrnes' endorsement of diplomatic relations with the Holy See was less than enthusiastic, but Spellman sent copies of the letter to Cicognani and instructed Griffiths to send copies of his memorandum to Byrnes, Cicognani, and Tardini.[57] In April, Spellman again wrote Byrnes saying that he had heard

---

[54] AANY, Griffiths, "Report to His Eminence", Feb. 1, 1951.
[55] AANY, Spellman to Cicognani, New York, Feb. 8, 1951 (copy).
[56] AANY, Byrnes to Spellman, Columbia, S.C., Feb. 8, 1951.
[57] AANY, Spellman to Cicognani, New York, Feb. 15, 1951 (copy); Spellman to Griffiths, New York, Feb. 15, 1951 (copy).

nothing further of Truman's intent and guessed "that he has abandoned or indefinitely postponed the matter".[58]

b. Nomination of Mark Clark and Futile Negotiations

There the matter rested for several months. But on May 16, a memo in Spellman's papers listed the names of "those who would support us if the President considers an Envoy to the Vatican". The list contained fourteen people: William C. Bullitt, Winthrop Aldrich, Harold Tittmann, Frank Walker, Myron Taylor, Bernard Baruch, James Byrnes, William B. Phillips, Sumner Welles, Eric Johnson, Harold Stassen, Porter Chandler, John W. Davis, and James Farley.[59] Davis had been the Democratic presidential candidate in 1924 and Stassen had made several unsuccessful bids for the office. These were probably the two presidential candidates to whom Spellman had alluded in his Fordham address in 1946. Byrnes, of course, had been Secretary of State and the other men were prominent diplomats or political, economic, or foreign affairs advisers to Roosevelt and Truman.

Meanwhile, Spellman was mustering support for his persuasion of Truman. Late in August he wrote Enrico Galeazzi that he had had two long conversations with Taylor who assured him that Truman intended "to send a nomination for the post of Ambassador to the Vatican to the Senate before Congress adjourns in October". The cardinal gave Taylor the memorandum prepared by Griffiths and Graham, and Taylor in turn gave "it to the President to provide him with motivation for his act". But Spellman admitted that he did "not know what the results will be as this is certainly a most contentious question".[60] On October 20, 1951, Truman nominated General Mark Clark as the first United States Ambassador to the Vatican.[61]

The appointment brought immediate protests from the whole spectrum of American Protestants, ranging from the National Council of Churches to Paul Blanshard. On the other hand, some prestigious newspapers such as the *New York Times* editorialized in favor of the appointment.[62] Spellman himself received encouragement from several influential persons in the diplomatic service, notably Arthur Bliss Lane, former ambassador to Poland, and Stanton Griffis, the ambassador to Spain.[63] Bishop John F. Noll of Fort Wayne reported that *Our*

---

[58] AANY, Spellman to Byrnes, New York, Apr. 10, 1951 (copy).

[59] AANY, Memo, May 16, 1951.

[60] AANY, Spellman to Galeazzi, New York, Aug. 27, 1951 (copy).

[61] *New York Times,* Oct. 21, 1951.

[62] *New York Times,* Oct. 22, 1951.

[63] AANY, Lane to Spellman, New York, Oct. 23, 1951, inclosing Lane to Editor of the *New York Times,* Oct. 22, 1951; Spellman to Griffiths, Oct. 31, 1951 (copy).

Sunday Visitor, published in his diocese, was being flooded with letters and he noted the hostile reaction to the appointment. To temper the rising anti-Catholicism, he made an ironic suggestion to Spellman that "if your Eminence is convinced that no pressure was brought on the President by a committee representing the Catholic Hierarchy, I think that a statement should go out from the NCWC to the secular press, apprising them that this appointment was made by the President without any request from the Catholic Church in the United States".[64] Spellman's reply was ingenuous to say the least. "Certainly such a statement could not but weaken the position of the President", he said, "and would be subject to misinterpretation". It would be better, he thought, to discuss the question at the annual meeting of the hierarchy where "proper conclusions will be taken to support the stand of the President and answer the ill informed and malicious Protestant attacks".[65]

In retrospect, if Truman was intent on establishing diplomatic relations with the Holy See, his nomination of Mark Clark was calculated to defeat that intention. As a general in Italy, Clark had aroused strong opposition in Texas by his use of the Thirty-Sixth Texas Division in the bloody battle of the Rapido River. Senator Thomas Connolly of Texas, the Chairman of the Senate Foreign Relations Committee, would oppose Clark's nomination on those grounds alone.[66] Furthermore, Truman submitted the nomination while Congress was not in session, which may have been an indication that his real intention was to make a nomination to placate what he thought was the Catholic opinion but to assure that the public debate would make the withdrawal of the nomination necessary before the Senate actually reconvened to consider it.[67] Whatever may have been Truman's political motivation, Clark withdrew his nomination on January 13, 1952, and Truman announced he would make a new nomination.[68] Although he never did so, he had asked Robert Butler, former ambassador to Australia and later Cuba, to be prepared to have his name submitted to the Senate.[69]

Spellman seems to have given up any hope of establishing diplomatic relations and reported this to Pius XII during the consistory in January, 1953. Upon his return to the United States, the cardinal wrote Monsignor Giovanni Battista Montini, Substitute Secretary of State for the Ordinary Affairs of the Church, that from a survey made at the time of Clark's nomination only nine out of ninety-six senators said they would ratify the appointment and that the nomination would

---

[64] AANY, Noll to Spellman, Ft. Wayne, Oct. 27, 1951.

[65] AANY, Spellman to Noll, New York, Nov. 3, 1951 (copy).

[66] *New York Times*, Oct. 23, 1951.

[67] Cf. Arthur KROCK in: *ibid.*, Oct. 23, 1951.

[68] *Ibid.*, Jan. 14, 1952.

[69] AANY, Butler to Spellman, n.p., Jan. 8, 1952.

probably not have reached the floor of the Senate because of the opposition of members of both the Foreign Relations and Appropriations Committees.[70] Nothing, he concluded, had happened in the previous two years to change the validity of the survey's conclusions.

Spellman's report to Montini occasioned a heated correspondence between himself and the future Paul VI. The issue of diplomatic relations, moreover, had reoccurred just as Paul Blanshard was escalating his attack on the Catholic Church; for him such relations were but one sign of the Church's demand for a privileged position within American society. Noting that the Secretariat of State was "aware of the obstacles that prevent the establishment of diplomatic relations", Montini enclosed an editorial from the *Osservatore Romano,* which clearly pointed out "that the Holy See has remained indifferent in this matter and that It has never exerted pressure or manifested any particular desire in this regard". Of greater concern to Montini was the discussion during Spellman's recent audience with Pius XII that "the Holy See cannot remain indifferent to the unreasonable and unreasoning attitude of non-Catholics in the United States. In connection with this matter of diplomatic representation and on other occasions in the recent past, there have been repeated, vulgar, bitter and entirely unjustified attacks against the Holy See, with unwarranted deductions and unmerited conclusions that are scarcely compatible with the 'freedom' of which the United States claims to be the champion and the custodian". These had "greatly added to the burden of sorrow that weighs upon" Pius XII. He concluded by saying: "I cannot conceal from Your Eminence that it is felt here that such attacks on the part of non-Catholics did not arouse an adequate reaction on the part of the Catholic community in the United States, that neither orally nor in the press has there been a sufficient response or any particularly authoritative voice raised in defence of the Holy See".[71]

Spellman expressed his "surprise and pain" at Montini's statement that the American Catholic community's reaction to anti-Catholic attacks had been inadequate. With the assistance of Robert Graham, he compiled a dossier of public statements of American Catholic leaders defending the Holy See from the time of Taylor's appointment up to the present. While Spellman himself had frequently sent clippings about these statements to the Holy See, he now sent this package of material "to save your Excellency from any inconvenience in locating them in the Vatican archives". He then made a thinly disguised hint at the role American Catholics had played in preventing a Communist take-over of Italy: "Your Excellency is well aware of the Communist threats to the Church and her institutions

---

[70] AANY, Spellman to Montini, New York, Feb. 7, 1953 (copy).
[71] AANY, Montini to Spellman, Vatican, Mar. 12, 1953.

even in countries where the great majority of the people are Catholic. I would say that the Catholics in the United States are hated in the same way by many fanatical people in this country. Thus far, however, although in the minority, we have been able, despite shrewd, well financed and continued attacks, to retain control of our schools and charitable institutions and own our own church properties without taxation or interference. ... The Hierarchy, the clergy and the faithful of the United States are, I believe, as militant, as practical and as successful as the Hierarchy, the clergy, and the faithful of any other country of the globe".

Spellman then mentioned the Vatican refusal of access to archival material to both Leo Francis Stock, who had compiled a documentary history of Vatican-American relations, and to Graham, whose expenses Spellman had paid to Rome to prepare background information for the Senate hearing on Clark. Then alluding to "the burden of sorrow" which weighed upon the heart of Pius XII, he could not describe the "poignancy of grief" he felt because he knew "that the Hierarchy, the priests, the religious and faithful of the United States are second to the people of no country in the world, I repeat, of no country in the world, in their devotion to the Vicar of Christ...". As evidence of this devotion, he thought that "more precious" than the $200,000,000 in money and supplies distributed during the previous ten years through the Catholic War Relief Services were "the numbers of religious men and women from the United States who are leaving their homeland to bring the Gospel of Christ to the pagan world, and even to countries assumed to be almost entirely Catholic". Spellman concluded by asking Montini for any further suggestions he might have and by thanking him "for writing to me with such frankness, thus inviting me to reply with equal candor".[72]

Spellman never received a direct answer to his letter, which effectively ended any serious discussion of the establishment of formal diplomatic relations. In 1958, Paul Blanshard and the POAU demanded that all presidential candidates declare their position on diplomatic relations with the Holy See. In an interview with *Look* magazine early in 1959, John F. Kennedy declared his opposition to the establishment of such relations because the resulting divisiveness would only weaken any ambassador's position at the Holy See.[73] Thus the movement begun in 1935 by Spellman with the aid of Joseph P. Kennedy was now ended with the opposition of Kennedy's son. Spellman, in turn, seems to have accepted the failure of his long-cherished plan.[74]

---

[72] AANY, Spellman to Montini, New York, Apr. 17, 1953 (copy). In compiling the dossier of material, Spellman had enlisted the aid of Graham through Father John J. McMahon, S.J., the Provincial of the New York Province; see AANY, Graham to Spellman, New York, Apr. 10, 1953.

[73] AANY, Kennedy to Frank Folsom, Washington, Mar. 25, 1959.

[74] AANY, Spellman to Galeazzi, New York, Mar. 30, 1959 (copy).

Montini's criticism of Spellman and the American Catholic community, however, merits closer analysis. From 1950, Montini had supported the efforts of John Courtney Murray to show that the Catholic position of Church-State relations had developed under Leo XIII and that the American system of the separation of Church and State was beneficial to the Church and in accord with Leo's teaching. But there was growing opposition to this within the Roman Curia. Only ten days before Montini wrote Spellman, Alfredo Ottaviani, named a cardinal in the consistory during which Spellman discussed the impossibility of establishing diplomatic relations, had given an address stating that the normative Catholic teaching of Church-State relations was a union of Church and State wherever Catholics were in the majority.[75] At the same time, Domenico Tardini, Montini's counterpart in the Secretariat of State for the Extraordinary Affairs of the Church, was completing negotiations of the Spanish concordat, which embodied Ottaviani's views. Montini and those who thought like him were no longer in the inner circle of the curia. Read in this light, his letter to Spellman actually gives no indication of his own opinion, but merely reports the Vatican attitude toward the American Church. Read between the lines and in light of his encouragement of Murray, his letter might be construed as saying that it was difficult for him to defend American religious liberty when Vatican officials continued to hear of American anti-Catholic bigotry.

Spellman, for his part, was particularly annoyed at Montini's criticism for it was followed shortly after with a Vatican request that the Italian-American community and the American bishops be rallied to urge Italians to vote against the Communists in 1953. The irony was not lost on Spellman, who noted to Galeazzi: "This situation is of particular interest to me since only two weeks ago I wrote to Monsignor Montini defending the Bishops of the United States and myself from the accusation of not supporting the Holy See in the United States, and here now the Holy See asks the Bishops of America to defend the Holy See in Italy!!!!!!!!!!!!"[76]

C. ITALIAN-AMERICAN RELATIONS

1. Treaty of Friendship, Commerce and Navigation: Religious Liberty

The issue of the threat of Communism in Italy and the Vatican realization that the United States was a bulwark against Communism was the other side of the coin to the anti-Catholic protests which flowed from the attempts to establish

---

[75] See below pp. 370–376.
[76] AANY, Spellman to Galeazzi, New York, May 25, 1953.

diplomatic relations. Indeed in the United States, also, the issue of Communism served to mollify anti-Catholicism in the 1950s. Anti-Communism was one issue on which the Vatican and the American people were in agreement from the end of the war. But the United States and the American Church were placed on the defensive because of Vatican opposition to the American proposition of religious liberty.

In October, 1947, the Vatican expressed its concern about the forthcoming treaty of friendship, commerce and navigation between the United States and Italy. The treaty contained an article guaranteeing "freedom of conscience and freedom of worship" of nationals of one country within the territories of the other and enabling citizens of either country, "both individually and collectively or in religious corporations and associations and without interference or molestation of any type whatever, to conduct religious functions not only within their own edifices but also in any other suitable edifice, on condition that their doctrines and practices be not contrary to public morals". Tardini pointed out to Cicognani that the latter clause would give Protestants the power "to open throughout Italy centers of worship in any building and to carry on proselytism in all its forms without any limitation or regulations even on the part of the State". It would also jeopardize the rights of the Catholic Church granted in the Lateran Treaty and the concordat between Italy and the Holy See. The nuncio to Italy had attempted to have the clause omitted, but the American delegation was reported to have insisted on it. Tardini, therefore, requested Cicognani to see if the American hierarchy could not work to have the entire article omitted.[77]

Cicognani immediately forwarded Tardini's letter to both Spellman and Stritch.[78] Spellman sent Stritch a memorandum prepared by Griffiths,[79] which Stritch used in preparing two other memoranda for the State Department and for President Truman. Optimistically the Chicago Cardinal wrote Spellman: "In pressing this matter, without putting it in the memoranda, I stated that you join with me in urging the elimination of the objectionable article. I think that we have the negotiations in safe hands and I am directing them".[80] Spellman forwarded a copy of Stritch's letter to Galeazzi and seems not to have pressed the matter further.[81] The treaty with its clause on religious liberty was signed on February 2, 1948.[82]

---

[77] AANY, Tardini to Cicognani, Vatican, Oct. 4, 1947 (copy).

[78] AANY, Cicognani to Spellman, Washington, Oct. 8, 1947.

[79] AANY, Spellman to Cicognani, New York, Dec. 8, 1947 (copy); Spellman to Stritch, New York, Dec. 8, 1947 (copy).

[80] AANY, Stritch to Spellman, Chicago, Dec. 11, 1947.

[81] AANY, notation on bottom of Spellman to Stritch, New York, Dec. 17, 1947 (copy).

[82] Robert Renbert WILSON: *United States Commercial Treaties and International Law*, New Orleans 1960, pp. 270–271.

The controversial article was an indication of how little the Vatican could understand American religious pluralism where various churches and religions enjoyed full freedom. Such an arrangement in Italy, in Tardini's mind, would be "to the detriment of the religion of practically the entire Italian people with resulting disturbance of religious peace in the country".[83] But the issue of the Italian elections of 1948 presented a different series of problems and here the Vatican took advantage of the ethnic pluralism of the American Church to have Italian-Americans write their relatives in Italy of the dangers of Communism.

2. Italian Elections of 1948

The Italian elections of 1948 were of deep concern to both the Church and the American government. As the elections approached, the State Department indicated that American foreign aid to Italy would be cut off in the event of a Communist victory.[84] In February, moreover, several Italian-American newspapers suggested that Americans of Italian origin write their relatives in Italy. Through the NCWC, Cicognani had the bishops in whose dioceses there were Italians to have their pastors urge the letter-writing campaign. The letter sent to all pastors in the Archdiocese of New York stated that "the fate of Italy depends upon the forthcoming election and the conflict is one between Communism and Christianity, between slavery and freedom". It therefore urged all those "of Italian origin living here and all friends of Italy ... to write to relatives and acquaintances first of all to urge all to exercise their right of the ballot and to warn them of the dangers of a communistic victory". The letters were to be sent by air mail and were to "emphasize the help which has been extended to the Italian people through American generosity...".[85]

In the meantime, Spellman received information from Major General William J. Donovan about the Italian situation and had himself issued a statement which had been broadcast to Italy.[86] Apparently ignorant of the fact that Cicognani had already circulated members of the hierarchy, Spellman also wrote McNicholas, chairman of the administrative board of the NCWC, telling what he had already done in his own archdiocese and bringing "this matter to your Excellency's atten-

---

[83] AANY, Tardini to Cicognani, Vatican, Oct. 4, 1947 (copy).

[84] *New York Times,* Mar. 16, 1948.

[85] AANY, Edward R. Gaffney to "Rev. Dear Father", New York, Mar. 24, 1948; Cicognani to Spellman, Washington, Mar. 28, 1948.

[86] AANY, Spellman to Donovan, New York, Mar. 24, 1948 (copy).

tion in the event that you deem a universal appeal to all the Bishops imperative".[87] Even before Spellman began the New York letter-writing campaign,
however, the United States Post Office reported that mail to Italy had doubled.[88]
Early in April, Myron Taylor had an audience with the pope and it was reported
that they discussed the elections and that the Vatican was optimistic that a large
voter turn-out would result in a defeat for the Communists.[89]

Spellman's Conference with George Marshall: Italy, the Italian Colonies and Palestine

The involvement of the American Church in the letter-writing campaign which
led to the election of Alcide De Gasperi's Christian Democrats was well known in
the United States.[90] But much more occurred behind the scenes. Galeazzi had
spoken with Joseph P. Kennedy and subsequently had written to Spellman about
having the Vatican reimbursed by the United States government for some of its
expenditures in defeating the Communists. On August 26, 1948, Spellman summarized his activities on the matter for Galeazzi: "I am informed that there was
no method by which the United States Government officially could participate in
the Italian election even though this government was vitally interested in the candidacy of Mr. De Gasperi. However, everything that it could legitimately do to
support his candidacy was done like the transfer of ships, the action on Trieste
and the gift of grain which were strong factors in convincing the Italian people of
the interest of America in the welfare and re-establishment of Italy as a nation
friendly to the United States. I am also informed that a great deal of American
money which was blocked in Italy was released for the use of the Italians. To
make reimbursement for funds expended by any other means would require
Congressional action which would be overwhelmingly impossible".[91] Spellman
had obtained his information from George C. Marshall, the Secretary of State,
with whom he met on August 24. The problem of direct aid to the Vatican or to
Church institutions was particularly sensitive in the election year of 1948 in
which opposition to Truman was all too ready to attack his administration for
any misuse of funds. According to the pro-memoria Spellman kept of their con-

---

[87] AANY, Spellman to McNicholas, New York, Mar. 24, 1948 (copy); cf. Spellman to Cicognani, New York, Mar. 24, 1948 (copy).
[88] *New York Times,* Mar. 23, 1948.
[89] *Ibid.,* Apr. 14, 1948.
[90] See GANNON: *Spellman,* p. 347.
[91] AANY, Spellman to Galeazzi, New York, Aug. 26, 1948 (copy).

versation, Marshall preferred that it be unknown that the United States had "released American money to the Vatican, even though indirectly conveyed".[92]

It is unclear whether Spellman sent a copy of his pro-memoria to Galeazzi or any other Vatican official. But at the meeting he discussed two other issues of concern to the Vatican: the return of the former African colonies to Italy and the problem of the attacks on and desecration of Church property in Palestine.

The question of the Italian colonies had been referred by Cicognani to Spellman and Stritch early in August.[93] As on other occasions, however, Spellman took the initiative and alone entered the arena of international affairs. He first of all had Griffiths draw up a memorandum arguing for the return of the former Italian colonies. Griffiths had heard that John Foster Dulles, the American representative to the forthcoming General Assembly of the United Nations, "certainly would do nothing if he thought it would benefit the Church", so in his memorandum he omitted all references to the Church and stressed the issue of international relations. Next Griffiths personally presented a copy of his memorandum to Dulles in New York. Finally, an Italian-American delegation called on Governor Thomas E. Dewey of New York, the Republican candidate for president, who issued a statement favoring Italian administration of the former colonies under a United Nations trusteeship.[94]

Making copies of Griffith's account of the above activities and of his memorandum on the subject, Spellman sent them to both Stritch and Cicognani. Stritch felt strongly that Spellman should see Truman who, he thought, needed "guidance and information" on the subject. He further believed that the principal opponents to returning the colonies would be the Arabs and British.[95] With Dewey's statement as a background, Spellman broached the question with Marshall. The principal argument he used was "Economic and humanitarian": Italian refugees had been expatriated from Africa to the war-torn mother country which

---

[92] AANY, "Pro-Memoria" of Spellman-Marshall conference, Aug. 24, 1948. The only reference to this meeting in NA is a telegram inviting Spellman for lunch (NA, RG 59, DS 111.111, Marshall to Spellman, Washington, Aug. 23, 1948). In the George C. Marshall Papers at the Virginia Military Institute, Lexington, Va., there is only an appointment calendar scheduling the meeting and listing the persons to be present. No other reference could be found to the decision of the United States government to use American money to subsidize Church institutions in the campaign against Communism in Italy. In the recommendations to the National Security Council on Mar. 8, 1948, regarding the forthcoming Italian elections, there is an elipsis in FRUS (1948), III, 775–779. In the photocopies of the original of this document in the Marshall Papers, the same sections were blocked out before the document was copied; see Marshall Papers, 1574–NSC 1/3.

[93] AANY, Spellman to Stritch, New York, Aug. 12, 1948 (copy); Spellman to Cicognani, New York, Aug. 14, 1948 (copy); Stritch to Spellman, Chicago, Aug. 17, 1948.

[94] AANY, Griffiths to Spellman, New York, Aug. 18, 1948; *New York Times,* Aug. 18, 1948.

[95] AANY, Stritch to Spellman, Chicago, Aug. 23, 1948.

had no outlet for its surplus population.[96] In the meantime, Tardini had received a copy of Griffiths' memorandum from Galeazzi and had presented it to Pius XII. He had also been informed both of Dewey's statement and of Dulles' having a copy of the memorandum. The Vatican's interest in the return of the colonies, he wrote Spellman, was two-fold. First, it was to the advantage of the Church to have "the presence in Africa of a Catholic nation such as Italy". Second, many Italian refugees from Africa were then in "the mother country in conditions of particularly great poverty" and sought the pope's intervention to facilitate their return.[97]

Spellman, Stritch, and the Vatican had hoped that the question could be settled at the conference in September of the foreign ministers of the United States, Great Britain, France, and Russia. But when that conference convened, it reached no conclusion. In November, Truman defeated Dewey and later in the month the Vatican again enlisted the aid of Spellman and Stritch to intervene with the American government prior to the convening of the General Assembly of the United Nations in Paris.[98] Spellman remained optimistic "of the personal interest of President Truman who is most understanding in having equitable adjustments made to be just to Italy and to promote the cause of world peace".[99] The General Assembly, however, voted to postpone its decision for a year and only in November, 1949, was the question settled by granting only Somalia as a ten-year trusteeship to Italy.[100]

The final issue which Spellman discussed with Marshall in August, 1948, was that of the continuing damage and desecration of churches within the new state of Israel. This issue had been of concern to the Catholic Near East Welfare Association for some time. On June 5, 1947, it had submitted a statement of concern to the United Nations Special Committee on Palestine, but it had heard nothing for a year. On August 20, 1948, Monsignor Thomas J. McMahon, national secretary of the association, wrote Trygve Lie, Secretary General of the United Nations, decrying the continuing "bloodshed and damage all over Palestine, with great human and material losses for both Jews and Arabs" and requesting a formal inquiry into the reported attacks by Israeli forces on Catholic churches and other buildings.[101]

Spellman presented a copy of this letter to Marshall requesting "the helpful in-

---

[96] AANY, "Pro-Memoria" of Spellman-Marshall conference.
[97] AANY, Tardini to Spellman, Vatican, Sept. 2, 1948.
[98] AANY, Cicognani to Spellman, Washington, Nov. 27, 1948.
[99] AANY, Spellman to Cicognani, New York, Dec. 24, 1948 (copy).
[100] New York Times, Nov. 22, 1949.
[101] AANY, McMahon to Lie, New York, Aug. 20, 1948 (copy).

terest of the American Secretariat of State". He also brought up the topic of Christian minorities in Palestine and concurred with Marshall's sentiment that many "declare that they have been abandoned by the Christian world". This topic was closely related to another one of burning concern – the internationalization of Jerusalem. Spellman noted to Marshall that he personally had worked in favor of the proposal and that the United Nations had formally adopted it, but he confided to his pro-memoria that it would be of assistance "if it were possible to know the mind of the Holy See relative to the internationalization issue".[102] Whether Spellman was responsible for having the Holy See state its mind is unknown, but on October 24, 1948, Pius XII issued his encyclical *In multiplicibus curis* calling for the internationalization of Jerusalem, a plea he reiterated in his Christmas message that year. On March 21, 1949, Thomas McMahon incorporated this plea in another letter to Secretary General Lie together with a statement of concern about the displacement of Arab refugees in Israeli territory.[103] Although Spellman, McMahon, and other American churchmen continued to press this concern on American and United Nations officials, the question still remained unresolved in the 1980s.[104]

The issues of the Italian colonies and of the internationalization of Jerusalem, together with the defeat of Communism in Italy and elsewhere in western Europe, are but a few examples of how the Holy See increasingly relied upon the American Church to influence the American government, the strongest political bulwark against Communism. These issues are also examples of why Spellman was so irate at Montini's accusation in 1953 that the American hierarchy and people had not been sufficiently strong "in defence of the Holy See". As was seen above, Spellman saw the irony of Montini's charge when, within a few weeks, the Vatican called on the American Church to defend the Church in Italy against Communism.

3. The Italian Elections of 1953 and 1958

The involvement of the American Church in the Italian elections of 1953 was more extensive than it had been in 1948. Galeazzi alerted Spellman of the need for action toward the end of May, 1953, and Spellman immediately summoned to a meeting all the Italian pastors of his archdiocese asking them to "publicize the desirability" of having their parishioners write to their friends and relatives in

---

[102] AANY, "Pro-Memoria" of Spellman-Marshall conference, Aug. 24, 1948.
[103] AANY, McMahon to Lie, New York, Mar. 21, 1949 (copy).
[104] For a summary of Spellman's involvement, see GANNON: *Spellman,* pp. 353–358.

Italy. The cardinal also communicated with all the other American bishops to have them use the press and radio "to stress the importance of this election".[105] He followed up his meeting with the Italian pastors with a letter to them asking them to urge their parishioners to write letters as they had so successfully done in 1948.[106] This letter Spellman then enclosed in letters to Senator John O. Pastore of Rhode Island, Senator John F. Kennedy of Massachusetts, and Mayor John B. Hynes of Boston. He was informing these political leaders of his actions, he wrote, because "I felt that you might like to issue a statement or make an address to the people of your State in which there are so many Italians".[107] He then issued a statement to the Associated Press and passed on all this information to Galeazzi.[108]

In the meantime, Archbishop Karl J. Alter of Cincinnati, chairman of the administrative board of the NCWC, mobilized the bishops for the effort and utilized the National Catholic News Service to urge the letter-writing campaign.[109] Whether this American campaign was actually the determining factor in the outcome is unknown, but on June 7 the Christian Democrats were again victorious. Galeazzi thanked Spellman for organizing the campaign in such a short time. He noted further that he "thought that the documentation of this initiative, which is another of your important merits, could interest the Secretariat of State" and he had therefore transmitted to that office all the documents and newspaper clippings which Spellman had sent.[110] By mentioning the Secretariat of State, Galeazzi had in mind Montini from whom Spellman had received the earlier reprimand.

Spellman took the same initiative in regard to the Sicilian elections in 1955[111] and again in the general elections of 1958. In the latter situation, however, American anti-Catholicism was picked up by the Italian anticlerical faction which implied that the American Church was exercising undue financial influence on the Vatican. On April 14, 1958, *Paese Sera* published an account of the revised edition of Paul Blanshard's *American Freedom and Catholic Power* under the headline "Il clero in America insidia la libertà religiosa". Irish dominance of the

---

[105] AANY, Spellman to Galeazzi, New York, May 25, 1953 (copy).

[106] AANY, Spellman to "Rev. Dear Father", New York, May 25, 1953.

[107] AANY, Spellman to Pastore, New York, May 27, 1953 (copy with note that it was also sent to Kennedy and Hynes).

[108] AANY, Spellman to Galeazzi, New York, May 27, 1953 (copy).

[109] AANY, Alter to Spellman, Washington, May 26, 1953, with NC News story attached.

[110] AANY, Galeazzi to Spellman, Vatican, June 15, 1953.

[111] AANY, Cicognani to Spellman, Washington, Apr. 29, 1953; Spellman to Cicognani, New York, May 20, 1955 (copy); Cicognani to Spellman, Washington, May 25, 1955; Tardini to Cicognani, Vatican, June 8, 1955; Cicognani to Spellman, Washington, June 11, 1955.

American Church, charged the article, prevented the development of Catholicism. As an example, it cited the fact that there was only one Italian bishop in the United States, Joseph Pernicone, Auxiliary Bishop of New York, and he was intensely disliked by the majority of the Catholics in his parish. No sooner had the article appeared than Monsignor Angelo Dell'Acqua, who had succeeded Montini as substitute secretary of state, wrote Cicognani suggesting that Spellman find an opportunity to protest to the Italian authorities.[112]

In the meantime, Cicognani met with Pernicone who then gathered all the Italian pastors of the Archdiocese of New York together with representatives of the dioceses of Rockville Center, Brooklyn, and Paterson, for a meeting. They all agreed to encourage their people to write letters to Italy urging their relatives and friends to vote for the Christian Democratic Party, but they decided "that printed letters or cards should not be given to our people since these might bring about the opposite effect if they fell into the hands of the communists". In regard to the article in *Paese Sera,* however, Pernicone forwarded to Spellman a rebuttal prepared by one of his priests, but he thought "that no answer should be given".[113] Spellman then forwarded this information to Cicognani for transmittal to Dell'Acqua.[114] The Christian Democrats were again victorious, but it was even more difficult to determine than in the elections of 1948 and 1953 what effect the Italian-American community and the American Church had on the outcome. Yet the issues raised in the course of the 1958 elections were not without significance for the relations between the American Church and the American republic.

D. COMMUNISM: AMERICAN AND VATICAN ATTITUDES

It was paradoxical that *Paese Sera* chose to cite Paul Blanshard as the elections drew near, for by then his attacks on Catholicism were being blunted in the United States as the mood of the country changed. First of all, the American people during the 1950s witnessed the Communist witch-hunt of Senator Joseph R. McCarthy of Wisconsin. Catholic opinion was seriously divided on McCarthy's crusade. Spellman backed him and Bishop Bernard Sheil, Roosevelt's candidate for first Archbishop of Washington, opposed him. *America,* the national Jesuit weekly, challenged McCarthy's conduct of the senate hearings and brought forth

---

[112] AANY, Dell'Acqua to Cicognani, Vatican, Apr. 14, 1958, enclosing copy of *Paese Sera,* Apr. 14, 1958; Cicognani to Spellman, Washington, Apr. 19, 1958.

[113] AANY, Pernicone to Spellman, New York, May 9, 1958; Cicognani to Spellman, Washington, May 3, 1958.

[114] AANY, Spellman to Cicognani, New York, May 12, 1958 (copy).

upon itself attacks from other Jesuits and the Brooklyn *Tablet*. The American Jesuit superiors allowed the editor to continue his statements with the condition that they act as censors and that he avoid the topic of McCarthy unless the "good of the Church" required it. The General of the Society of Jesus, Father John Baptist Janssens, however, thought otherwise, and ordered its editor to cease writing on the topic.[115]

By December, 1954, McCarthy had become too much for his colleagues in the Senate which overwhelmingly censured him.[116] His career and his crusade were over. But a legacy remained. His career rose and plummeted in an atmosphere of the cold war. He was a Catholic and in spite of the fact that polls indicated that Catholics were as much divided as Protestants in their attitudes toward his tactics, he presented the public image that if nothing else Catholics were not Communists. The new American fear of Communism began to cancel out the old American prejudice against Catholicism.

Castel Gandolfo War Claims: Rapprochement between the United States and the Vatican

A relatively minor, yet significant, indication of the nation's change of mood was in the settlement of the Vatican's war claims for damages to Castel Gandolfo from American raids in 1944. The basis for the Vatican's claims were two-fold. First, according to the Lateran Treaty, the pope was given sovereignty over Castel Gandolfo as an extension of the Vatican. Second, in his letter to Pius XII announcing the invasion of Sicily, Roosevelt had pledged to respect "the neutral status of Vatican City as well as of the Papal domains throughout Italy".[117] Enrico Galeazzi was designated to assess the damages to the papal villa and the neighboring villa belonging to the Congregation of Propaganda; he then submitted this assessment to the War Claims Commission.

Since the amount of damages assessed was close to one million dollars, congressional approval of the appropriations was necessary. Spellman was the principal negotiator with American government officials, but until 1956 no bill was introduced into Congress for fear of increasing anti-Catholic feeling. Moreover,

---

[115] Donald F. CROSBY: *God, Church, and Flag: Senator Joseph R. McCarthy and the Catholic Church, 1950–1957*, Chapel Hill 1978, pp. 179–184; cf. pp. 162–163, 170–173.

[116] *Ibid.*, pp. 193–218.

[117] AANY, Roosevelt to Pius XII, July 11, 1943 (copy) given in: *Wartime Correspondence between President Roosevelt and Pope Pius XII*, with an Introduction and Explanatory Notes by Myron C. TAYLOR, New York 1947, p. 93.

the State Department in June, 1953, denied the bases for the Vatican's claims. First, it stated, "the Papal domains damaged were not territory of a neutral state, but had the status of a neutral diplomatic mission located in the territory of a belligerent...". Second, "the statement in the President's letter was too casually made to have been intended to confer upon the Papal domains the formal status of territory of a neutral state".[118] Even if the government accepted a moral obligation derived from Roosevelt's letter, it seemed impossible to submit any bill to congress without arousing the charge that the government was giving money to the Church.[119]

Even Spellman, always ready to enter a debate, seemed reluctant to push the point any further and at the bishops' meeting in the spring of 1955, he proposed another solution. As he told Galeazzi on April 5: "I put the matter before the Board of Bishops and asked them to come to the assistance of the Holy See in this situation. After considerable discussion and with voiced reluctance the Bishops decided to appropriate one hundred-and-fifty thousand dollars. This was in addition to the half a million dollars which they send annually to the Holy Father for relief purposes. If they had failed to make this appropriation it was my intention to have the allocation made from funds of the Archdiocese of New York. I thought, however, that it would be most pleasing to our Holy Father if the Administrative Board of Bishops all cooperated in this assistance, knowing the bitter anti-Catholic debate that would have taken place in Congress if the matter of an appropriation came up".[120]

Galeazzi's own feeling was "that the thing had been unjustly rejected by the American Government, in spite of the promise uttered by President Roosevelt", but on the other hand he expressed his "*personal* opinion on this matter: should it result [*sic*] impossible to obtain the indemnity from the Government without provoking any bitter reaction by anti-Catholic circles or others, I should not hesitate to drop the matter completely, never trying to ask the Board of American Bishops for anything in the way of any appropriation of money for this purpose, and so much the less I would draw from the Archdiocese of New York". But Galeazzi and Spellman were already working on another way to solve the problem. Joseph Kennedy had written Galeazzi lending his support to the settlement and Galeazzi in reply urged him to seek the advice of Spellman.[121] Kennedy did consult with Spellman who reported to Galeazzi: "He is interested in a way that will not necessitate a Congressional appropriation which would be impossible

---

[118] AANY, State Department memorandum on Vatican claims, June 11, 1953 (copy).
[119] AANY, Griffiths to Spellman, July 8, 1954.
[120] AANY, Spellman to Galeazzi, New York, Apr. 5, 1955 (copy).
[121] AANY, Galeazzi to Spellman, Vatican, Apr. 13, 1955.

and would have many recriminations. Joe is fairly optimistic and I am restrainedly optimistic myself".[122] Kennedy then visited Cicognani to speak about his plan and assured the delegate that he would work under Spellman's guidance.[123]

Precisely what Kennedy's plan at this stage entailed is unknown, but as the story unfolded it could have provided a plot for a spy novel. On September 5, Galeazzi drew up a memorandum outlining the Vatican's claims and the history of the American government's rejection of them. The next day, he presented this to Allen W. Dulles, who was then in Rome and who was the Director of the American Central Intelligence Agency and the brother of John Foster Dulles, the Secretary of State. Galeazzi also gave him copies of the various State Department memoranda on the subject. As Galeazzi recounted the conversation for Kennedy, Dulles "was somehow worried about the stern attitude of the State Department about the necessity of the presentation to the Congress of this matter, as most probably, in his opinion, this will mean a complete failure. He did not think before reading that memorandum that they were so rigid about it. We talked about the opportunity that this matter be concluded once for all, even with a reduced payment of the claim, so that there be no reason for disappointment on the part of the Holy See toward the U.S. Government."

Galeazzi then added what was to be a primary, if hidden, motivation for the final settlement: "Finally we have mutually hoped for the establishment of ever more close connections between the Holy See and the U.S. Government at this stage, as there is such a great need of communion in the efforts to keep Communism back, especially in the social, cultural and spiritual fields. Mr. Dulles had visited Msgr. Dell'Acqua the previous evening; he expressed his sentiments of profound respect for the Holy Father, and had emphasized his strong desire of doing anything in his power to establish the best possible relations in the interest of both parties". Upon his return to the United States, Dulles promised to speak with Kennedy whom Galeazzi urged to "insist with this claim request, overcoming the probable serious difficulties ... and go on convincing Mr. Dulles that the main scope of the U.S. Government should be that of ending this pending question in the best and quickest way possible".[124]

One month after the visit from Dulles, Galeazzi received a visit from Joseph Kennedy's son, Senator John F. Kennedy, whom he informed of the Castel Gandolfo case. The senator, in turn, recommended that Galeazzi meet Congressman

---

[122] AANY, Spellman to Galeazzi, New York, Apr. 27, 1955 (copy).
[123] AANY, Cicognani to Spellman, Washington, May 6, 1955.
[124] AANY, Galeazzi to Kennedy, Vatican, Sept. 7, 1955 (copy), enclosed in Galeazzi to Spellman, Vatican, Sept. 8, 1955.

John F. Rooney, a Catholic from Brooklyn, who was soon coming to Rome. Galeazzi hosted a dinner for the congressman and his party at which Rooney promised his assistance. Galeazzi than passed on this information to both Spellman and Joseph Kennedy. The stage was then set for the final act.[125]

Late in February, 1956, Congressman John W. McCormack from Massachusetts, the Democratic majority leader, and Congressman Joseph Martin from Massachusetts, the Republican minority leader, introduced a bill into the House of Representatives calling for the appropriation of $ 1,523,810.98 for damages to Castel Gandolfo. Clare Booth Luce, the United States Ambassador to Italy, sent it to Spellman with the suggestion that "a word or two to friendly members of the House Appropriations Committe might speed it on its way to passage".[126] The State Department then altered its position. While it upheld its earlier interpretation that Castel Gandolfo was not properly speaking neutral territory, it recommended that a lower sum of $ 964,199.35 be paid to the Vatican as "a matter of grace" in order not to set a precedent. The higher sum, originally suggested by Martin and McCormack, noted the State Department, had taken into consideration the loss of art works which were irreplaceable. Early in June, Congress then approved this lesser appropriation.[127] For this action, Spellman told Galeazzi, credit was due to McCormack, Martin, Joseph Kennedy and his son, John, and Clare Booth Luce.[128] A short time later, Spellman commented on a letter Galeazzi had written to the Vatican Secretariat of State that "I think it is not necessary that any expression be given to me, but I do believe that a special word of appreciation should be communicated to the Ambassador [Luce] and the Apostolic Delegate".[129] Spellman's demur was probably not due to modesty. He may have feared being too publicly identified with the settlement of the claims issue. Perhaps too he wished finally to acknowledge the achievements of Cicognani who had faithfully served the Holy See in the United States since 1933.

The final word in the episode was more symbolic than significant. Spellman was apparently not happy with the State Department's terminology in regard to the appropriations and chose the occasion of the ordination to the priesthood of Avery Dulles, S.J., the convert son of John Foster Dulles, to state his reservations. The Secretary of State wrote the cardinal a week after the ceremony saying: "I must admit that the formal expression, signed by Assistant Secretary [Robert C.] Hill, did not adequately express my own personal hope that we would make

---

[125] AANY, Galeazzi to Spellman, Vatican, Oct. 6, 1955.

[126] AANY, Luce to Spellman, New York, Mar. 21, 1956.

[127] Congressional Record, 102, Pt. 7 (1956), 9570–9571.

[128] AANY, Spellman to Galeazzi, New York, June 4, 1956 (copy).

[129] AANY, Spellman to Galeazzi, New York, June 18, 1956 (copy).

compensation for this damage. This, however, was, I think, more than compensated by the very active personal support which was made manifest not only by Mr. Hill but by Bob Murphy [Deputy Assistant Secretary] and others".[130] Later that summer, Dulles received from Pius XII a reply to his notification that compensation to the Holy See had been authorized. The pope's letter said in part: "In acknowledging this kind communication, We extend Our sincere gratitude to your Government for this considerate action; and We likewise express Our thankfulness to Your Excellency personally and the State Department under your direction for the valued assistance given in promoting and obtaining the passage of the requisite legislation. We offer our warm congratulations to Your Excellency on the happy occasion of the sacerdotal Ordination of your son Avery, to whom we impart our special Apostolic Benediction as a pledge of abiding divine assistance in his priestly ministry...".[131] The common fear of Communism had brought the American people and the American Church closer together. It had made possible the settlement of the war claims which was to the mutual advantage of both the Vatican and the United States in their respective campaigns against Communism.

The end of the Myron Taylor mission and the failure to appoint an American ambassador to the Holy See had been due to anti-Catholic feeling among the American people. This breach in relations made the Vatican revert to reliance on the American hierarchy and, through it, on friendly Catholic and non-Catholic political leaders to influence the American government on issues ranging from the Italian elections to the Palestinian question. The cool relations of the majority of the American people toward the Catholic Church and the Vatican were made colder yet with the attacks of Paul Blanshard and the sometimes Protestant-baiting defense of Spellman. But the relations began to thaw on the issue of Communism. The year 1958, the year in which *Paese Sera* picked up Blanshard's attacks, was a politically crucial one for the United States and American Catholics. In that year, Senator John Kennedy, rebuffed in his bid for the Democratic vice-presidential nomination in 1956, announced his candidacy for the presidency. That same year, Pius XII died to be replaced by John XXIII. The American Church had reached a watershed both politically and ecclesiastically. If the American Church and through it the Vatican had established warm relations with the American government, it had now to establish similar relations with the American people. To do that meant proving to the Vatican that the American principle of religious liberty, somewhat disparaged in Montini's letter to Spellman in 1953, was compatible with Catholic teaching.

---

[130] AANY, Dulles to Spellman, Washington, June 25, 1956.
[131] Pius XII to Dulles, Vatican, Aug. 4, 1956, copy given to this writer by Rev. Avery Dulles, S.J.

CHAPTER XIV

THE RE-EMERGENCE OF THE QUESTION OF RELIGIOUS LIBERTY

The rapprochement of American Catholics and the Vatican with the United States government was one side of a complicated question. The other side was the theological development in the American Church of the notion of religious liberty and the acceptance of that development by the Vatican. The American Church was composed of doers and builders but not thinkers and scholars. Archbishop McNicholas lamented this frequently to Cardinal Giuseppe Pizzardo, then Prefect of the Congregation of Seminaries and Universities. "We have not arrived as yet at the stage of producing outstanding scholars among either priests or laity", he wrote in 1940, "but a great recognition of the need is acknowledged in many quarters".[1] Over seven years later, he made a similar observation in an almost defensive manner: "Considering the whole of the United States, we should be doing more in giving opportunities to laymen to become real scholars. A hundred outstanding lay scholars, whether they were physicians, lawyers, journalists, or scientists, would make a tremendous impression on our country for the Church. We are, of course, a young country, and we have not the traditions of the past, like Europe. We are energetic, resourceful, and practical. It will take time; it will take a few more decades before we can hope for greater results in scholarship, both among our priests and our laity".[2]

Lack of scholarship in the American Church was due not only to the Church's immigrant composition but also to the stifling of intellectual life in its infancy with the condemnation of Americanism followed so closely by the condemnation of Modernism at the beginning of the century.

A. PRELIMINARY DISCUSSION OF CATHOLIC COOPERATION WITH NON-CATHOLICS

One legacy of Americanism, however, remained – the issue of religious liberty, of a Catholic Church existing side by side with other churches in a nation whose

---

[1] AACi, McNicholas to Pizzardo, Cincinnati, Feb. 9, 1940 (copy).

[2] AACi, McNicholas to Pizzardo, Cincinnati, Sept. 18, 1947 (copy).

government accorded none of them special privileges. The issue, of course, was directly related to ecumenism, and for the American Church was expressed in the problems of Catholic cooperation with other denominations, of whether the Church taught that communion with it was necessary for salvation, of the relationship between Church and State, and, finally in a more ecumenical sense, of the relationship between the Church and the churches. With each of these problems the American Church dealt especially in the post-war years against the backdrop of Vatican misunderstanding. The overcoming of that misunderstanding led to the distinctive American intellectual contribution to the Second Vatican Council of the Declaration on Religious Liberty, formulated in part by the Jesuit theologian, suspect during the 1950s, John Courtney Murray.

The problem of the Catholic Church's relation with other churches was raised in the midst of the war in the context of how much Catholics could formally cooperate with non-Catholics on social problems. Here the universal Church seemed to have the mandate of the popes since Leo XIII but particularly of Pius XII who, in his Christmas address in 1941, called for "the collaboration of all Christendom in the religious and moral aspects" of rebuilding society after the war, and imparted his blessing to those who were "not members of the visible body of the Catholic Church...".[3] In September, 1942, John LaFarge, S.J., had traced in *Theological Studies* the plea for Catholic collaboration with other denominations through papal documents up to Pius XII.[4] But the problem was brought to a focus in March, 1943, with a contribution to the same periodical by its editor, John Courtney Murray, S.J.

Murray reported on the pre-war dialogue in Germany between Catholics and Protestants on cooperation on social issues and argued that some form of "intercredal cooperation" was essential to thwart the growing materialism and secularism in the United States. Such cooperation, he felt, rather than leading to indifferentism, as many feared, might actually prevent it.[5] While the nascent Jesuit scholarly review of theology began its discussion of the positive aspects of interfaith cooperation, the principal bishops of the mid-west, McNicholas, Stritch, and Mooney, were concerned with the same issue.

While Spellman was the principal figure in dealing with the government in regard to Catholic affairs, particularly in the realm of diplomacy, the mid-western archbishops were the dominant figures in the NCWC. Mooney had been chair-

---

[3] As quoted in: Wilfried PARSONS: *Intercredal Co-operation in the Papal Documents*, in: Theological Studies 4 (1943) 172–173.

[4] John LAFARGE: *Some Questions as to Interdenominational Cooperation*, in: *ibid.* 3 (1942) 315–322.

[5] John Courtney MURRAY: *Current Theology: Co-operation, Some Further Views*, in: *ibid.* 4 (1943) 100–111.

man of the administrative board from 1936 to 1939 and again from 1941 to 1945. Stritch held the post in 1940 and 1946. When both he and Mooney were named cardinals in 1946, McNicholas became chairman holding the office until his death in 1950. In their early discussions on Catholic cooperation with non-Catholics, they made no reference to the war and the status of the Vatican, which so preoccupied Spellman. Nor, from the evidence examined, did they at any point correspond about cooperation with Spellman or any other leading bishop. The issue seems to have been the exclusive concern of the power bloc within the NCWC.

But why did these three prelates take such a dominant role in the domestic affairs of the American Church? Unfortunately, the archives of the Archdioceses of Chicago and Detroit for this period are not available as of this writing. Mooney, as has been noted, may have achieved his prominence within the NCWC because he had been previously an apostolic delegate and could thus gain the respect of Cicognani. Stritch, moreover, was his classmate at the North American College and the two maintained a close friendship. Mooney, however, frequently had to goad him into action. McNicholas presented a different profile. A Dominican, he had been a bishop since 1918 and was widely regarded as the leading theologian in the hierarchy. Both he and Stritch had reason to resent Spellman's dominance of the hierarchy, the former because he was chafed at being passed over for the Archdiocese of New York in 1939 and the latter because Spellman had challenged his loyalty to Roosevelt in 1940.[6]

Yet another factor may have influenced their cohesion as a group. McNicholas, at least, had a distinctive vision of the Church in the mid-west. As early as 1930, he argued: "there is much more vision and much more courage in the Mid-West than there is in the East. The dioceses and the parishes of the Mid-West are doing far more for religion than those of the East".[7] Finally, just as John Burke envisioned World War I as an opportunity for Catholics to influence American society and was instrumental in forming the War Council, so by 1943 the three mid-western prelates may have seen World War II as providing another opportunity for Catholics to play an important role in restructuring American society after the war. Whatever may have been their motives for excluding Spellman from their counsels, they had Cicognani's support for their course of action which brought them not only to deal with the problem of cooperation but also gradually to accept Murray's position.

Possibly in response to Murray's article, McNicholas discussed the matter with Bishop Gerald O'Hara of Savannah who sent him a copy of Leo XIII's letter to

---

[6] See above, pp. 256, 266.
[7] AACi, McNicholas to Thomas Garde, O.P., Cincinnati, July 29, 1930 (copy).

Satolli in 1895 forbidding interfaith gatherings and calling for Catholics to hold their own meetings.[8] McNicholas forwarded this letter to Stritch, whose own attitude at this point was ambiguous. Apparently ignorant of the original context of the Leonine letter, opposing Catholic participation in such functions as the World Parliament of Religions, he felt the pope was condemning public debates on religion. He saw the danger of Catholics and non-Catholics joining together in "making a plea for charity in a community", for regardless of the safeguards against compromising religious principles, "the effect is to put the Church on the level of sectarianism and Judaism".

There was, however, the "grave danger" of "materialism and atheism" to combat which "we must in some way associate with ourselves ... all believers in God in our communities". He himself tacitly tolerated the presence of priests in the National Conference of Christians and Jews, which was not nearly as dangerous as some alarmists would say. While Stritch had reservations about the organization, he also believed that apart from it "the plain fact is that in our struggle against materialism and atheism we have much potential strength in many non-Catholics which we are not using". A Catholic organization to which non-Catholics would be invited to attend to collaborate as "citizens" would also "not [be] satisfactory", for "in this struggle we really do need the organized strength of the sects and even of the synagogue".

Stritch was, therefore, leaning hesitantly toward the Church's collaboration not only with non-Catholics as individuals but with other churches and even the Jewish community. He still hesitated to embrace that position, but he hoped McNicholas would "find a formula for us which will be theologically sound and practical". He thought, furthermore, "that it is not the mind of the Holy See that we should be quite so tight and narrowminded as some of us have been in the past".[9] Stritch thus took the first step toward ecumenism, but the path to that goal would be long and tortuous.

In June, 1943, two more articles on the subject of intercredal cooperation appeared in *Theological Studies,* the one by Wilfrid Parsons, S.J., professor of politics at the Catholic University, analyzed papal documents and the other by Murray suggested modes of organization.[10] Parsons subsequently published a more popular version of his conclusions in *Columbia,* the magazine of the Knights of Columbus. Arguing for cooperation "with all believers in God in bringing know-

---

[8] AACi, O'Hara to McNicholas, Savannah, June 9, 1943; see also above p. 140.

[9] AACi, Stritch to McNicholas, Chicago, June 23, 1943.

[10] Parsons: *Intercredal Co-operation,* pp. 159–182; John Courtney Murray: *Current Theology: Intercredal Co-operation: Its Theory and Its Organization,* in: Theological Studies 4 (1943) 257–268.

ledge of the natural law back to human society", Parsons stated that in the present spiritual crisis "our first duty is not, as unfortunately many still seem to think, to win the recognition of the spiritual authority of the Church ... but to rouse the torpid world to a sense of the Divine life that exists within it...".[11] The article provoked a harsh rebuttal from the Cincinnati *Catholic Telegraph-Register,* McNicholas' diocesan newspaper.[12]

The appearance of the articles coincided with the bombing of Rome, but Stritch was more preoccupied with his hesitant musings on the subject of cooperation. Murray and Parsons' articles, he thought, had gone beyond the evidence in arguing for a papal call for cooperation with all men of good will. He also queried whether popes prior to Leo XIII had not also made similar appeals; his problem was the inability to recognize historical development. On the other hand, he wondered if Parsons and Murray were correct in limiting "this cooperation to questions affecting the common social good". He had difficulty with the expression "intercredal" – a phrase which Murray himself later regretted having used. Still seeking "the right formula", he confessed "that I do not get satisfaction out of these articles of Father Parsons and Father Murray. Maybe I am too dull". Stritch was well-intentioned, but concerned to show his loyalty to Rome on all matters, great and small. While looking for the "right formula" for interfaith cooperation, he could also ask "whether the skull cap should be kept on or taken off at the singing of the Gospel".[13] Agreeing with the *Catholic Telegraph-Register's* criticism of Parsons, he thought the American Church could make no adaptation of papal teaching and could find only a formula "which limits its cooperation to the civic fields and excludes every sort of formal cooperation with the sects and the synagogue".[14] He thus took a step backward from his earlier ecumenical tendency.

Yet it is difficult to determine at this juncture precisely where Stritch differed from Murray in the form which cooperation should take. Murray had received a copy of the editorial from the *Telegraph-Register* and had replied to Monsignor Edward A. Freking, the editor. First of all, Murray did not like the editorial's broad accusation that "Jesuit theologians", in general, were in error and queried whether such "strictures ... reach my own writings on the subject of co-operation". He therefore enclosed a lengthy comment on the editorial without implying that Freking was the author. He asserted that he did indeed find development in papal teaching on cooperation, but emphatically denied what seemed to lie at

---

[11] PARSONS: *No Lavender, No Old Lace,* in: Columbia (July, 1943) 6, 17.

[12] AACi, *Catholic Telegraph-Register,* July 30, 1943.

[13] AACi, Stritch to McNicholas, Chicago, Aug. 3, 1943.

[14] AACi, Stritch to McNicholas, Chicago, Aug. 17, 1943.

the heart of the fears of the editorial writer and of Stritch that the proposed organization for cooperation "be 'on the basis of different religious *groups'*, as groups. As I have already suggested, the idea is not to bring religious groups together in their corporate entities as religious groups, but to bring religious men together on the basis of the religious and moral principles, pertinent to the social order, which the Pope supposes to be held within all truly religious groups. Cooperation in the papal sense has nothing to do with 'super-churches', or, in general, with the union of faiths or churches".[15] Murray thus seemed to ally himself with Stritch's final conclusions.

McNicholas forwarded Murray's correspondence to Stritch and noted that he had had a visit from Parsons, who had requested the interview as a result of the editorial. The meeting was amicable, but McNicholas was not "sure at all that I convinced him that the position which he takes is not safe and may not be tenable". The archbishop's theological stance clearly coincided with, if it was not the inspiration for, the editorial in his paper. He furthermore wished to impress on Parsons that "the Bishops would welcome the united wisdom of the Society of Jesus", but he "did not like to see any members of his Order taking a position that might not be tenable and which would give wrong impressions to non-Catholics". McNicholas was incapable of envisioning a situation in which Jesuits, much less Catholic theologians in general, might express theological pluralism. He concluded his letter to Stritch by saying that he would be unable to attend the meeting of the NCWC administrative board which Mooney had called in Chicago.[16]

Stritch, as was seen above, had just attended a meeting in Washington with Mooney and Spellman to write a protest to Roosevelt about the bombing of Rome. It is therefore indicative of how much importance he placed on cooperation that on September 18 he made no reference to the bombing but rather prevailed on McNicholas to attend the meeting of the administrative board which would try to work out a "formula of cooperation" to be presented to all the bishops at the annual meeting in November. To prepare for this, he had read Murray's articles and drafted a memorandum. From papal teachings he derived two points: that there should be "some sort of organized action" and "there should be no surrender of Catholic truth and therefore no formal co-operation between the Church and the Sects or the Synagogue". Within this framework, he felt that such cooperation "should not be formally religious but formally social". In his mind, the NCWC already provided the organization for national coopera-

---

[15] AACi, Murray to Freking, Woodstock, Aug. 22, 1943.
[16] AACi, McNicholas to Stritch, Cincinnati, Sept. 16, 1943 (copy). See also Parsons to McNicholas, Keyser Island, Conn., Aug. 24, 1943; McNicholas to Parsons, Cincinnati, Aug. 29, 1943 (copy).

tion with other agencies, both government and religious, in many areas of social action. But Stritch was still leery of any appearance of formal cooperation. Only recently, he said, the NCWC had refused to "join with the [Federal] Council of Churches and the Jewish Group" in issuing a joint statement "on the points of agreement between Catholics, Protestants and Jews on certain fundamental social issues", and instead had proposed "that each of these groups on a given day at a given hour issue the Statement as its own, adding its own preamble".[17]

From Stritch's memorandum, the NCWC board drew up four propositions: that "cooperation with all men of good will in securing the recognition of the sovereignty of God and the supremacy of the moral law in social life is urgently needed"; that "cooperation ... with other *religious* groups should be established through committees which will engage in *joint conference* but in *independent action*"; that "*joint action* with men accepting these principles and who are organized exclusively for social or civic purposes is commended"; and finally that there could be "simultaneous promotion on the part of Catholic committees and other religious committees or joint action under the auspices of civic or social groups...". The board approved these proposals at its meeting in Chicago on September 28–29, 1943. They were subsequently read in November to the annual meeting of the bishops, none of whom voiced any objection.[18]

The proposals, in retrospect, were cautious. They allowed for no formal cooperation with other religious groups, but did provide for Catholics to cooperate with non-Catholic groups under non-religious organizations. It was not cooperation to the extent Stritch seemed to wish, but it was the most he could formulate without seeming to violate Roman decrees. Over the next decade, Stritch and his two mid-western friends moved toward the position that closer and more formal cooperation with other religious groups was needed. But in 1943 there were still some prelates who dissented, in action if not in word, from Stritch's reasonably safe proposals. McNicholas, who at this point was the most conservative of the mid-west triumvirate, quipped to Mooney: "I heard recently that the C.I.O. [Congress of Industrial Organizations], through Mr. [Philip] Murray, requested your friend, my Ordinary of Philadelphia [Dougherty], to have a priest say a prayer at the Convention. The request was refused. One must be very peaceful who can make decisions with certainty and have no anxiety about them".[19]

While the hierarchy searched for some form of practical cooperation with non-Catholics, Murray ran into theological obstacles. In October, 1943, Francis J. Connell, C.Ss. R., professor of moral theology at the Catholic University, pub-

---

[17] AACi, Stritch memorandum enclosed in Stritch to McNicholas, Chicago, Sept. 18, 1943.
[18] AACi, "Principles of Cooperation for Catholics and Other Groups."
[19] AACi, McNicholas to Mooney, Cincinnati, Dec. 20, 1943 (copy).

lished an article, "Pope Leo XIII's Message to America" in the *American Ec-clesiastical Review*. Connell, who together with the *Review's* editor, Joseph C. Fenton, would become arch-enemies of Murray in the years to come, argued that while Pius XII was less restrictive than Leo XIII, there was still danger of indifferentism in cooperation. The source of that danger for Connell was emphasis on religious liberty. This liberty he supported but he held no Catholic could defend it "to the extent of denying that a Catholic government has the right ... to restrict the activities of non-Catholic denominations...".[20]

Here was Americanism revisited. In the years which followed, Connell and Fenton would hurl the charge of the "phantom heresy" at Murray and his supporters. In this they seemed to have the support of Roman statements and attitudes that Catholics, when in the minority, should be given religious liberty, but, when in the majority, the Catholic Church should either be the established church or be given a privileged status. The attitude had been exemplified by the Vatican's attempt to remove the clause on religious liberty for Protestants from the American treaty of commerce, trade, and friendship with Italy. Espoused in the United States by Connell and Fenton, this mentality served to fuel the fires of anti-Catholicism stoked by Blanshard and his supporters in post-war America.

From the available documents, there was little further discussion among the bishops of the problem of interfaith cooperation until 1946. That year the National Conference of Christians and Jews, of which Murray was a member, wished to send him as one of its representatives to Oxford, England, for a symposium on religious liberty. The Conference had been specifically cited by Connell as the type of organization which led to indifferentism.[21] Murray was himself somewhat hesitant to accept the invitation because of the known hostility of Cardinal Spellman to the group, so he asked for but was denied permission to attend by his provincial, Francis McQuade, S.J. "I have no trouble in relinquishing all thought of the Oxford conference of Christians and Jews", Murray wrote his superior, but he said: "In honesty, I should add that, unlike yourself, I have a certain sympathy with the project; moreover, I have no sympathy at all with the unintelligent attitude of the N.Y. Chancery. However, I see the practical difficulties...".[22]

Catholics, then, were to stand apart from corporate endeavours with non-Catholics on social issues and all the more so from the delicate theological problem of religious liberty. But did that stance extend to a priest offering a joint

---

[20] Quoted in: Donald E. PELOTTE: *John Courtney Murray: Theologian in Conflict*, New York 1975, p. 153.

[21] *Ibid.*, p. 14.

[22] Murray to McQuaid, May 8, 1946, quoted in *ibid.*, p. 23, n. 25.

prayer with a Protestant minister on a civic occasion? Bishop Patrick McGovern of Cheyenne, Wyoming, raised this question in his quinquennial report to the Holy See in 1947. He had always forbidden his priests to take part with Protestant ministers in baccalaureate exercises and Thanksgiving Day services, he wrote, because such participation would violate the prohibition of *communicatio in sacris*. He was confused, however, to learn from newspapers that in other dioceses priests took part in such functions. Cardinal Marchetti-Selvaggiani, the Secretary of the Holy Office, asked Cicognani for information and advice on the matter. Cicognani forwarded the letter to McNicholas.[23]

For a priest and minister jointly to offer a prayer on certain civic occasions was a long-standing custom in the United States and one which was frequently misunderstood in Rome. Immediately upon receiving Cicognani's letter, McNicholas forwarded copies of the Holy Office's request to both Stritch and Mooney, who were by that time cardinals. To both he wrote that he felt that priests speaking in public schools gave them an opportunity to explain "Catholic principles". Moreover, the "Chapel Services" of some universities were actually held in buildings which served also as auditoriums used for other purposes.[24]

Both cardinals answered McNicholas immediately. Stritch outlined six points for McNicholas' answer to Cicognani. First, in the United States, where there was religious pluralism, the custom of invoking God at the beginning and end of civil functions implied "no thought of a religious service but of a purely civil recognotion [*sic*] of God". A priest participating with a minister had the "civil effect of keeping God in our life" at a period when "materialism is making such headway" and when there was "now in this country a strong movement to banish religion from our public life". Second, when a priest and minister spoke at public school functions, it gave "the priest a chance to instruct on vital fundamental truths in our civil life"; in these functions there was "no question of a 'participation in sacris'".

Third, the bishops had carefully avoided Catholic participation in strictly religious services in non-Catholic institutions. Fourth, how could Catholics "cooperate with our non-Catholic citizens in emphasizing the need of religion in civil life"? He continued: "with the spread of irreligion and materialism", there was "a necessity" to draw strength from and cooperate with "our fellow citizens who worship God and still hold to some fragments of christian truth". The popes had called for this, he noted, and the bishops had been careful to avoid any danger of indifferentism by issuing their own statements parallel to those issued by Protes-

---

[23] AACi, Cicognani to McNicholas, Washington, Apr. 17, 1947; Marchetti-Selvaggiani to Cicognani, Vatican, Mar. 20, 1947 (copy).

[24] AACi, McNicholas to Stritch and Mooney, Cincinnati, Apr. 30, 1947 (copy).

tant leaders. Fifth, there was no need for the Holy Office to issue new directives. If any bishop had erred, his error had not been interpreted as *"participatio in Sacris"* but as the result of "an earnest desire to stress the need of relugion [*sic*] in our civil life".

Finally, Stritch alluded to the recent *Everson* decision of the United States Supreme Court and to the *McCollum* case, then pending with the court. The court, said the cardinal, had interpreted the Constitution as granting "freedom from religion" rather than "freedom of religion" in civil life. In regard to the pending decision, Stritch granted that the case involved "a plan for teaching religion in a certain public school [which] is not satisfactory because it envisions a course in religion which is not acceptable". He saw the danger, however, that the court might declare it "unconstitutional for public school authorities to permit parents to secure during school hours the instruction of their children in the religion of their choice".[25] The haste with which Stritch replied to McNicholas' letter – the original contains numerous typographical errors – indicates how strongly he felt about the issue of cooperation. He saw the decisions of the Supreme Court affecting both Catholics and Protestants, but as on other occasions, it was impossible for them to issue a joint statement.

Mooney's reply was similar but more succinct. He began by saying that the bishop who wrote to Rome "of course, is the only one who could report in greater detail on the newspaper accounts which gave him concern. Even then it would be pertinent to check his appraisal of the facts". Among the civil ceremonies he would not include "patriotic exercises in memory of deceased soldiers and sailors". On the other hand, he had "quietly" prohibited Catholic participation in Thanksgiving Day "Services" and similar functions when they were advertised as "Interdenominational or Interfaith Services".[26]

McNicholas incorporated Stritch and Mooney's responses in his letter to Cicognani. In a covering letter to the delegate, he said of Bishop McGovern: "I cannot think that the good, sick Bishop is now in close touch with the affairs of the country". To the suggestions from the two cardinals he added his own personal tone. Some cooperation was essential, he said, for "even though Catholics are a strong minority, they are not strong enough to win the battle against materialists, secularists, communists, so-called liberals, and those who profess no religion in public, without some cooperation from our fellow citizens worshipping an omnipotent, personal God, believing in the divinity of Christ and in Revelation". Just as the issue of Communism was bringing the Vatican to accept the United States, so too Communism and secularism were drawing Catholics to-

---

[25] AACi, Stritch to McNicholas, Chicago, May 2, 1947.
[26] AACi, Mooney to McNicholas, Detroit, May 6, 1947.

gether with Protestants and Jews. He noted, too, that "Chapel Services" held in non-Catholic colleges and universities were not properly speaking religious and were "watched very carefully by Newman Clubs and by priests who are directors of Newman Clubs". McNicholas reported that he was designated at the annual meeting of the bishops in 1942 to draw up norms for Catholic cooperation with non-Catholics and that these norms were approved at a meeting of the administrative board of the NCWC presided over by Mooney, who was subsequently named a cardinal.[27] Cicognani commented that he was sure McNicholas' "report will be very valuable to the Holy See in forming a proper appreciation of the problem as it exists in this country".[28]

But the Holy See was slow in appreciating the problem. First, it persisted in seeing a priest and minister sharing the same platform and offering prayers as *communicatio in sacris*. Only gradually would it perceive that this was not religious indifferentism. Second, it still construed the problem in terms of Catholic relations with non-Catholic believers, whereas the problem in the United States had to be seen in terms of the relations of believers, Catholic, Protestant, and Jew, with non-believers. As Stritch remarked of McNicholas' report, "How in a mixed country is it possible to fight secularism if in civic affairs we abstain from saying a prayer simply because there is some Protestant minister who also says a prayer?"[29] McNicholas himself was beginning to see the problem more clearly in an American context. Urging the establishment of a national office for Catholic information, he wrote Howard Carroll, the secretary of the NCWC, that he was no longer worried about attacks on the Church from Protestants, since they retained Christian principles, but from Communists.[30]

But the Holy See was not yet ready to embrace interdenominational cooperation in any form. The American Church therefore had to tread cautiously. Late in 1947, John Wright, then the Auxiliary Bishop of Boston, intervened, at the request of the Philadelphia chancery office, to have Congressman John F. Kennedy cancel a scheduled appearance at a fund-raising dinner in Philadelphia for a chapel to be built in the memory of four chaplains, Catholic, Protestant, and Jewish, killed in the war.[31]

The Holy See's suspicion also prevented the American Church from collaborating with other religious groups on matters of mutual concern. While McNicholas had been corresponding with Stritch and Mooney about Catholic participation

---

[27] AACi, McNicholas to Cicognani, Cincinnati, May 11, 1947 (copy).
[28] AACi, Cicognani to McNicholas, Washington, May 14, 1947.
[29] AACi, Stritch to McNicholas, Chicago, May 17, 1947.
[30] AACi, McNicholas to Carroll, Cincinnati, Sept. 25, 1947 (copy).
[31] AABo, Cletus Benjamin to Wright, Philadelphia, Dec. 9, 1947; Wright to Benjamin, Boston, Dec. 12, 1947 (copy); Benjamin to Wright, Philadelphia, Dec. 28, 1947.

with non-Catholics in civic events, he received a letter from Charles P. Taft, President of the Federal Council of Churches, asking him as chairman of the administrative board of the NCWC to appoint a committee to meet with Protestant and Jewish leaders about religion in public education. McNicholas was benevolently disposed toward Taft, but after a long delay in answering he had to note the difficulties of any formal cooperation.[32] Even on such a pressing issue as religion in public schools, American Catholics were wary of any type of formal cooperation. The issue on which Taft wished McNicholas' cooperation was a case then before the Supreme Court. Stritch, as was seen, had already alluded to the case of *Everson v. Board of Education*. There the court held that a state could provide free bus transportation for parochial school children without violating the constitutional provision for the separation of Church and State. But he was disconcerted by the use in the dissenting justices' opinion of the phrase "wall of separation between Church and State". This phrase had been used by Thomas Jefferson in a private letter, but was not part of the Constitution. In a second case, *McCullum v. Board of Education* in 1948, the court decided that it was unconstitutional for voluntary religious instructions to be given on public school premises. This time the court ruled that such religious activity did constitute a breach in the "wall of separation".

It was not so much the decision as the basis for it which alarmed religious leaders. In a statement issued on June 17, 1948, several prominent Protestant leaders declared that "this development of the conception of separation of Church and State seems to us to be unwarranted by the language of the first amendment and to bring about a situation in which forms of cooperation between Church and State that have been taken for granted by the American people will be endangered".[33] The development of that concept by the court, furthermore, "will greatly accelerate the trend toward the secularization of our culture". Protestant and Catholic concern with the issue, therefore, coincided. Unable formally to cooperate with the Protestant group, however, the administrative board of the NCWC had to be content to quote that statement in the pastoral letter issued on November 21, 1948, and significantly entitled "The Christian in Action".[34]

The wariness of the American bishops in cooperating formally with Protestant groups, even on the growth of secularism, was understandable. On June 5, 1948, the Holy Office issued its *monitum, Cum compertum,* reminding Catholics of the prescriptions of the Code of Canon Law prohibiting them, without the Holy See's

---

[32] AACi, Taft to McNicholas, New York, Apr. 19, 1947 (copy); Taft to McNicholas, New York, June 7, 1947 (copy); McNicholas to Taft, Cincinnati, June 12, 1947 (copy).

[33] AWC, attached to: Carroll to Murray, Washington, Dec. 27, 1957.

[34] HUBER (ed.): *Our Bishops Speak*, p. 151.

prior approval, from holding conferences with non-Catholics on matters of faith or from taking any part in non-Catholic religious rites.[35] Though this did not preclude the type of cooperation with Protestants which some of the bishops sought, it did emphasize their fear of being misunderstood in Rome. Nor was their fear unrealistic. Two years later, Cicognani communicated to the American bishops the Holy Office's application of the *monitum* to Catholic participation in the International Council of Christians and Jews. If Catholics were authorized to attend meetings of the organization, they could do so "only as observers" and they should not be "persons who are prominent in Catholic life and activities".[36] In view of his later reputation for ecumenism, it is interesting to note Archbishop Cushing's response. He had "stopped our identification" with the National Conference of Christians and Jews and another related organization "by eliminating the priest" formerly sent to represent the Church. After that the public meetings ceased. While there was therefore no difficulty in the Archdiocese of Boston, he was nevertheless "delighted" with the Holy Office's conclusions. "For all practical purposes", he said, "this whole thing represents indifferentism, or in common parlance, 'One religion is as good as another'".[37] Cushing's less than ecumenical stance at this time, however, was perhaps conditioned by charges hurled against him by Father Leonard Feeney and his followers.

The Holy Office's admonition had stated nothing new, but its publication coincided with the revival of anti-Catholicism and the American Church's search for a formula for cooperation with other religious groups. If the search were to progress and anti-Catholicism be stifled, the Holy See would have to answer three questions which arose within the Church in the United States. First, did the Catholic Church teach that there was no salvation outside of communion with it? Second, did Catholic doctrine require that, where Catholics were in the majority, they must seek to establish their Church? Finally, if the answer to the first two questions was negative, what was the Catholic teaching on religious liberty?

B. THE FEENEY CASE: IS THERE SALVATION OUTSIDE THE CATHOLIC CHURCH?

The first question arose amid circumstances which created one of the most painful crises the American Church had witnessed. Father Leonard Feeney, S.J., had been assigned by his superiors to St. Benedict's Center in Cambridge, Mas-

---

[35] AACi, *Osservatore Romano*, June 6, 1948 (copy).
[36] AABo, Cicognani to Cushing, Washington, Dec. 6, 1950.
[37] AABo, Cushing to Cicognani, Brighton, Dec. 12, 1950 (copy).

sachusetts. The center was originally under the direction of the local parish, St. Paul's, and was to serve the religious needs of the Catholic students who attended Harvard and Radcliffe Colleges. Feeney had a national reputation as a popular speaker and poet. He was a charismatic man, capable of drawing people to intense personal loyalty to him, but he seems also to have been mentally unstable. As allies he had several lay professors at the Jesuit-run Boston College who began increasingly to charge that there was no salvation outside the Catholic Church. With them he began publishing a journal, *From the Housetops*. He had immense influence on some students at Harvard and Radcliffe and induced several to leave those institutions and enroll in courses at the St. Benedict's Center, which he had accredited by the State of Massachusetts but which was not authorized by either his superiors or the Archdiocese of Boston.

On January 7, 1948, Feeney was summoned to meet with John Wright, the auxiliary bishop. He agreed to accept two conditions for what Wright described as "the important work at St. Benedict's". First, all articles from *From the Housetops,* of which Feeney was editor, were to be submitted to Father Louis Gallagher, S.J., who had been appointed as censor by the Jesuit provincial with the agreement of the archdiocese. Second, no students at Harvard, Radcliffe, or any other institution could withdraw from their courses without prior notification of their parents or parish priests.[38]

But Feeney's attacks became broader. In dealing with Protestants he was virulent in asserting that only in the Catholic Church could one be saved.[39] His followers at Boston College even charged the president of the institution with heresy. He also alienated many of the students who used to frequent St. Benedict's Center, which now became a closed group or "family", totally convinced that it alone represented the truth of Catholicism. The American Church had its own Port Royal. In June, Father John J. McEleney, S.J., then the provincial and later Bishop and Archbishop of Kingston, Jamaica, wrote Cushing about "the development of something akin to a state of hysteria at St. Benedict's Center". He then told the story of a girl who, under Feeney's influence, had left Emmanuel College, a Catholic institution, in order to marry a boy who attended the center. The girl was then estranged from her family. The story was typical, said McEleney, and the whole problem arose from "a distorted and erroneous exposition of the Church's dogma – extra Ecclesiam nulla salus". Not only did this lead to "rash judgments in individual cases", he continued, but "avoidance and even active hatred of non-Catholics by Catholics is advocated as a policy". McEleney was concerned for Feeney's "health", but he wished Cushing's "guidance and di-

---

[38] AABo, Wright to Feeney, Boston, Jan. 8, 1948 (copy).
[39] AABo, Pardon Tillinghast to Cushing, Middlebury, Vt., Apr. 22, 1948.

rection" before taking any further action against the priest.[40] McEleney suggested that he and Cushing discuss this in person.

Perhaps as a result of his discussion with Cushing, that summer McEleney assigned Feeney to Holy Cross College in Worcester, Massachusetts. Feeney, however, ignored his superior's orders and remained working at St. Benedict's Center. At the end of 1948, his faculties for the Archdiocese of Boston expired, but he continued hearing confessions. During Holy Week, Feeney's followers increased their activities. On April 14, Holy Thursday, one member of the group abandoned Feeney and, in a sworn statement, testified that he had been to confession to Feeney after the expiration of his faculties. Feeney had, therefore, automatically incurred the penalty of suspension *a divinis*. Cushing's chancellor immediately ordered McEleney to notify Feeney of his suspension. The latter responded by moving out of his Jesuit community. He was then a *fugitivus* from religion. The next day, Good Friday, Feeney's followers marched outside six churches in Boston distributing booklets proclaiming their position that there was no salvation outside communion with the Catholic Church, charging Feeney's Jesuit superiors and colleagues with heresy, and denying Cushing's authority. In view of this, Cushing placed St. Benedict's Center under interdict. On April 25, he wrote Cardinal Marchetti-Selvaggiani, Secretary of the Holy Office, informing him of his action. He concluded by saying that he did not think it was "necessary to impose censures on the lay people, who are already condemned by both non-Catholics and Catholics; and in regard to Father Feeney, it seems that the censure of suspension is enough for the time...".[41]

The same day Cushing wrote the Holy Office, Walter Furlong, the Boston chancellor, McEleney, and Augustine Hickey, the pastor of St. Paul's Church in Cambridge and the vicar general of the archdiocese, sent a report, under a covering letter from Cushing, to all the American bishops describing the actions of Feeney and his followers and the responses of Jesuit and archdiocesan officials.[42] Cushing also sent copies of the report to the Holy Office and to Cicognani.[43]

In the meantime, Feeney and his followers increased their activities during the spring of 1949. They had appealed directly to the pope for support of their position on salvation outside the Catholic Church and staged "resignations" of students from Catholic colleges in the Boston area in protest against supposed deviations from Catholic doctrine. These students then enrolled in St. Benedict Center,

[40] AABo, McEleney to Cushing, Boston, June 17, 1948.
[41] AABo, Cushing to Marchetti-Selvaggiani, Boston, Apr. 25, 1949 (copy).
[42] AABo, Cushing to "Your Excellency", Brighton, Apr. 25, 1949 (copy), attached to report of McEleney, Furlong, and Hickey.
[43] AABo, Cushing to Cicognani, Brighton, Apr. 25, 1949 (copy).

to which Feeney was at that time trying to attract foreign students for which he needed authorization of the United States Justice Department. Feeney and his group spared no one in their attacks: Harvard, Father Hickey, the Jesuits, the Paulists, members of the archdiocesan curia, and Cushing himself, whom they accused to Cicognani of having engaged in a religious service when he spoke to a gathering sponsored by Jewish women. Cushing reported all of this to Cicognani on May 27, 1949, and concluded that "we can not exclude the possibility of Communist influence on and through two or three of these obscure persons who have recently entered into the leadership of Saint Benedict Center". [44] The same day, Cushing's chancellor, Walter Furlong, wrote the Immigration and Naturalization Service of the Justice Department denying that St. Benedict's Center was a Catholic educational institution under the jurisdiction of the archbishop and stating that in fact Cushing had issued a decree placing the center under "an ecclesiastical ban". [45]

Feeney's group continued to escalate its attacks. On June 11, one of its representatives telegraphed Cicognani: "Because we have had no protection from you in the profession of our Catholic faith against the tyrannies of Bishop Wright we are forced in the interests of self preservation to protest to the governor of the State of Massachusetts the interference of local Church authorities in the affairs of the State of Massachusetts in Bishop Wright's program to revoke the State approval of Saint Benedict Center School." Cicognani forwarded the telegram to Wright who denied that either he or any other chancery official had contacted the civil authorities and stated that he had tried to dissuade irate parents from taking civil action against Feeney to remove their children from the center. The use of civil authority, said Wright, was felt to "be ill-advised as long as there still remains any possibility that the Jesuits may be able to bring Father Feeney to his senses". [46]

Neither Feeney's Jesuit superiors nor the archdiocesan officials, however, could bring him "to his senses". On July 27, 1949, the Congregation of the Holy Office met and drew up a decree which received the approval of the pope the following day. The Holy Office stated: "... that one may obtain eternal salvation, it is not always required that he be incorporated into the Church *actually* as a member, but it is necessary that at least he be united to her by *desire* and *longing*. However, this desire need not always be explicit, as it is in catechumens; but when a person is involved in invincible ignorance, God accepts also an *implicit desire,* so

---

[44] AABo, Cushing to Cicognani, Brighton, May 27, 1949 (copy).

[45] AABo, Furlong to Doyle, Brighton, May 27, 1949 (copy).

[46] AABo, Cicognani to Wright, Washington, June 13, 1949, with telegram of Philip Gammans to Cicognani, Cambridge, June 11, 1949; Wright to Cicognani, Brighton, June 14, 1949 (copy).

called because it is included in that good disposition of soul whereby a person wishes his will to be conformed to the will of God".

Citing Pius XII's encyclical, *Mystici Corporis,* to distinguish between actual membership and membership by desire, the decree moved to a consideration of Feeney and his followers. St. Benedict's Center could not "consistently claim to be a Catholic school and wish to be accounted as such" as long as it refused to conform to canon law and continued "to exist as a source of discord and rebellion against ecclesiastical authority and as a source of the disturbance of many consciences". Father Feeney could not present himself as a "Defender of the Faith" while he did "not hesitate to attack the catechetical instruction proposed by lawful authorities, and has not even feared to incur grave sanctions threatened by the sacred canons because of his serious violations of his duties as a religious, a priest and an ordinary member of the Church". The decree concluded: "Therefore, let them who in grave peril are ranked against the Church seriously bear in mind that after 'Rome has spoken' they cannot be excused even by reason of good faith. Certainly, their bond of duty of obedience toward the Church is much graver than that of those who as yet are related to the Church 'only by an unconscious desire' ... to them apply without any restriction that principle: submission to the Catholic Church and to the Sovereign Pontiff is required as necessary for salvation". Feeney thus found himself in the paradoxical position of being told by Rome that he was even less on the road to salvation than those to whom he gave no hope. The Holy Office's decree was embodied in a letter from Cardinal Marchetti-Selvaggiani to Cushing on August 8, 1949.[47]

Cushing immediately prepared a translation, but decided to publish only a "summary of the letter ... since none of us wish unduly to hurt the misguided individuals who have created this disturbance".[48] In retrospect, this was a mistake, for Feeney's group denied the authenticity of the version of the decree published in the archdiocesan newspaper, *The Pilot.*[49] The same day the Holy Office replied to Cushing, Father John Baptist Janssens, S.J., General of the Society of Jesus, also wrote expressing his "sincere regret that so much dissension and harm has been caused in Your Excellency's Archdiocese because of the actions of a member of the Society of Jesus" and begging the archbishop "to accept my expression of regret on the part of the whole Society, and my promise of incessant prayers for

---

[47] AABo, Marchetti-Selvaggiani to Cushing, Vatican, Aug. 8, 1949, translation; the original was not found.

[48] AABo, Cushing to Cicognani, Brighton, Aug. 26, 1949 (copy).

[49] AABo, "Report to the Catholics of Boston", from the St. Benedict's Center; *New York Times,* Sept. 2, 3, 4, 1949.

the sheep who through ignorance or mistaken zeal have gone astray from their true Shepherd".[50] Cushing replied that "we must believe that this evil will pass...". "On the other hand", he continued, "God has known how to draw grace from this tragic history". He praised "the patience" of the provincial and the New England Province Jesuits in accepting "the contumely so recklessly directed against them by their misled brother-in-religion".[51] On October 28, McEleney transmitted to Feeney the decision of the Congregation of Religious dismissing him from the Society of Jesus.[52]

The Feeney case, however, remained an issue for several more years. In July, 1952, the Holy Office again examined the case and decreed that its letter to Cushing of August 8, 1949, should be published in its entirety, that St. Benedict's be placed under a local interdict, and that Feeney be formally invited to make a submission to the local ordinary and to Rome. Only at that point was the full text of the letter to Cushing published, not in the *Acta Apostolicae Sedis,* but in the *American Ecclesiastical Review.*[53] On October 25, 1952, Cardinal Giuseppe Pizzardo wrote Feeney asking him to come to Rome.[54] But again Feeney refused to make any submission. Only in 1972 were he and some of his followers reconciled to the Catholic Church.

Feeney was a tragic figure, but the answers given in his case were important ones if the American Church was to engage in any further type of cooperation with non-Catholics. The Holy Office, it should be noted, said nothing about salvation coming through other churches, but it did clarify, amid great publicity,[55] that it was not Catholic teaching that one had to be an actual member of the Church in order to be saved. It was probably no accident that the question had to be answered in the United States with its religious pluralism. But it was also tragic that some American Catholics had lost sight of their tradition. In 1786, John Carroll had treated the subject in much the same manner as the Holy Office in 1949.[56] But if, indeed, there was salvation outside formal membership in the Church, was it Catholic teaching that the Church had the right to use civil authority to inculcate its doctrines? This was the second question to which the American Church had to address itself.

---

[50] AABo, Janssens to Cushing, Rome, Aug. 8, 1949.

[51] AABo, Cushing to Janssens, Brighton, Aug. 12, 1949 (copy).

[52] AABo, McEleney to Feeney, Boston, Oct. 28, 1949 (copy).

[53] DS 3866–3873; in: American Ecclesiastical Review, 127 (Oct., 1952) 307–315.

[54] AABo, Pizzardo to Feeney, Vatican, Oct. 25, 1952 (copy); Pizzardo to Cushing, Vatican, Oct. 25, 1952.

[55] See *Time* 53 (Apr. 25, 1949) 81 and (May 2, 1949) 67.

[56] *The John Carroll Papers,* edited by Thomas O'Brien HANLEY, Notre Dame, Ind. 1976, I, 89.

C. BLANSHARD: WILL CATHOLICS SEEK TO IMPOSE THEIR RELIGION?

If Catholics ever became a majority in the United States, would they seek to impose Catholicism on the nation or a least seek special privileges for the Church? This was the charge made in Paul Blanshard's book *American Freedom and Catholic Power*. His attack coincided with Spellman's efforts to have the United States establish diplomatic relations with the Holy See – efforts which, as was seen, added fuel to the fires kindled by Blanshard and his followers, Protestants and Other Americans United for the Separation of Church and State. Early in 1950, the NCWC became concerned with answering Blanshard. Dr. James M. O'Neill, professor of English at Brooklyn College, was then preparing an answer, but it raised several difficulties for the NCWC staff. On March 24, Father William McManus, Monsignor Thomas McCarthy, director of the conference's Bureau of Information, and John Courtney Murray, met with O'Neill. According to McManus' later report, "Father Murray tried to impress upon Dr. O'Neill the importance of great discretion and care in the manner in which he treated the Church's position on academic freedom, and a number of other difficult moral problems. To all of this Dr. O'Neill simply replied that he was not a moralist or a theologian and that therefore he would have to rely upon us for the moral and theological passages of his book. Father Murray told me afterwards that he had no intention of 'ghosting' for Dr. O'Neill". McManus felt that the NCWC should "give Dr. O'Neill such help as he reasonably requests and above all to keep in close contact with him in the hope that we may be able to prevent the book from being as bad as advance reports about it would indicate".[57] It was therefore clear to the NCWC staff that O'Neill did not have the competence properly to answer Blanshard.

Blanshard's attacks were of concern not only to the American Church but also to the Vatican. In May, 1950, Blanshard arrived in Rome as a correspondent for *The Nation*. Through Bishop Martin J. O'Connor, Rector of the North American College, he requested a private audience with Pius XII. While in Rome, he said, he was "writing a book which will discuss the Church's program in the struggle against communism, and certain other aspects of Vatican policy in Europe and the United States". He wished in particular to discuss with the pope "the reported desire of the Vatican for the establishment in Rome of an American Embassy to the Holy See, and the proposed program of action of the Church in fighting communism in the future". He concluded by noting that he had been "critical of Vatican policy", in *The Nation* and in his recent book, but that "perhaps His Holiness will consider this a special and additional reason for seeing me". Blan-

---

[57] ANCWC, McManus to Carroll, Washington, July 31, 1950 (copy).

shard's followers, however, may well have been put off could they have read him subserviently closing his letter by "Asking Your Excellency's Blessing".[58] O'Connor replied that, in view of the pope's activities during the Holy Year, such a private audience "would place an almost impossible burden upon His Holiness". [59] O'Connor had copies of the correspondence sent to the NCWC "for information and indirect use if necessary, but not for direct quotation".[60]

Blanshard's request for an audience may have drawn the Vatican's direct attention to him. On June 7, Cicognani met with Monsignor Howard J. Carroll, General Secretary of the NCWC, to indicate the Holy See's interest in being informed of news comments on Blanshard's book and of "Catholic replies to the objections and statements presented in the book...".[61] Carroll complied by collecting several articles and clippings about Blanshard which Cicognani then forwarded to the Secretariat of State.[62] At the same time, Spellman learned from Archbishop O'Boyle of Washington that Alfredo Ottaviani, then the Assessor of the Holy Office, wanted Blanshard answered. But to do so, Spellman wrote Ottaviani, would require a theological library, so for the time being, he sent a review of Blanshard's book in the Cornell Law Quarterly by Father Francis J. Connell and a further comment by Father James M. Gillis C.S.P.[63] Later that summer, O'Boyle sent a further query to the NCWC about an answer to Blanshard. On July 27, Monsignor McCarthy wrote him noting O'Neill's forthcoming book. But then he made a surprising proposal. Apparently ignoring the conflicting theological viewpoints, he suggested the formation of a committee composed of Murray, Connell, and Walter Farrell, O.P., a Thomistic scholar, to answer Blanshard from the viewpoints of political science, theology, and philosophy. This letter O'Boyle forwarded to Spellman, and across the bottom of it one of the cardinal's advisers wrote: "I have not much confidence in Fr. Courtney Murray's *judgment*. He may be a good scholar but needs watching".[64] Thus, with a scratch of the pen, Spellman's office dismissed as suspect, though "a good scholar", the one man who could competently answer Blanshard.

Blanshard continued to plague the American Church. Could Catholics be loyal Americans if they were also loyal to the pope who was the ruler of Vatican City?

---

58 ANCWC, Blanshard to O'Connor, Rome, May 3, 1950 (copy).
59 ANCWC, O'Connor to Blanshard, Rome, May 5, 1950 (copy).
60 ANCWC, Joseph J. Sullivan to Carroll, n.p., June 17, 1950.
61 ANCWC, Cicognani to Carroll, Washington, June 8, 1950.
62 ANCWC, Carroll to Cicognani, Washington, June 13, 1950 (copy); Cicognani to Carroll, Washington, June 17, 1950.
63 AANY, Spellman to Ottaviani, New York, June 19, 1950 (copy).
64 AANY, McCarthy to O'Boyle, Washington, July 27, 1950; O'Boyle to Spellman, Washington, July 29, 1950.

This would be the charge he would make, Spellman told Cicognani, if the United States established diplomatic relations with the Holy See. In fact, noted the cardinal, Blanshard had already accused the bishops of being agents of a foreign power.[65] Yet Spellman at that point made no personal effort to counter Blanshard's arguments. His attitude would change during the next few years.

The Vatican, in the meanwhile, showed no signs of changing its attitude toward the relationship between Church and State, which fed Blanshard's arguments. It did, however, continue to monitor his writings. In 1951, Blanshard published a second book against the Catholic Church, *Communism, Democracy and Catholic Power*. The Secretariat of State again asked Cicognani for information on Catholic and non-Catholic reactions to the book.[66]

But the Vatican became most concerned with Blanshard early in 1953 and its concern precipitated the harsh exchange of letters between Montini and Spellman. Blanshard began arguing for the removal of American citizenship from Archbishop Gerald O'Hara who was nuncio to Ireland.

Alerted to Blanshard's charge by Allan C. Devaney, Assistant Commissioner of Immigration, the NCWC immediately notified Cicognani. After consultation with the Secretariat of State, the delegate communicated to the NCWC two memoranda. The first concerned O'Hara and argued that diplomats for the Holy See came from various nations whose governments "not only do not create any difficulty but are pleased to have their citizens act" in that capacity. It further stated that, if the United States government opposed O'Hara's appointment, "the Holy See would have to remove from its representations very worthy American ecclesiastics who are presently in charge of important missions". The Vatican here may have intended a veiled threat – if the United States wished to influence the Catholic Church in its opposition to Communism, it would have to see the utility of having American citizens act as diplomats of the Holy See. The second memorandum simply gave general background to the Holy See's diplomatic missions.[67] The NCWC then sent this information to Devaney, who first brought Blanshard's attack to its attention,[68] and to Archbishop Aloisius Muench, the Bishop of Fargo, North Dakota, then the nuncio to Germany. Blanshard had ignored Muench in his attacks on O'Hara and so far Muench had not been attacked in Germany.[69]

---

[65] AANY, Spellman to Cicognani, New York, Dec. 28, 1959 (copy).

[66] ANCWC, Cicognani to Msgr. Paul Tanner, Washington, May 30, 1951; Carroll to Cicognani, Washington, June 26, 1951 (copy).

[67] ANCWC, Cicognani to Tanner, Washington, Feb. 21, 1953, with enclosures.

[68] ANCWC, Mohler to Tanner, memo, Feb. 26, 1953.

[69] ANCWC, Muench to Carroll, Bad Godesberg, Mar. 16, 1953.

In the meantime, Spellman leapt back into the fray either to regain his reputation with Vatican officials after Montini's reprimand or to remind them of the difficulty the American Church faced. Blanshard had published his argument in favor of removing O'Hara's citizenship in *The Christian Century* in May.[70] On May 22, Spellman wrote Montini recalling to him their previous correspondence and enclosing Blanshard's article. "Since Mr. Blanshard makes very specific points", he wrote, "I should like to refute him point by point and would appreciate your assistance".[71] If Spellman had intended any sarcasm in his offer to answer Blanshard, Montini had not forgotten his earlier letter to Spellman. He wrote: "I am authorized to inform Your Eminence that the laudable intention manifested of refuting the statements made in this article is appreciated by His Holiness, Who sees therein a disposition on your part effectively to carry out the tenor of the previous communication, in date of March 12th, from this Office. It is felt, however, in view of the past history and known dispositions of the person in question, that entering into a controversy with a writer of this kind, thereby giving him further importance and publicity, would be of doubtful value at this time; and would in all likelihood bring about a new attack upon the Church, with the rallying again of its adversaries to his support. The remedy will be that of avoiding the nomination of American ecclesiastics as representatives of the Holy See. The matter will continue to be under study and I shall not fail to inform you of eventual relevant developments".[72] Montini may have recognized that Spellman and other members of the hierarchy could do little more to prevent attacks such as Blanshard's or he may have felt that Spellman's propensity for public debate would do little to assuage the situation. Spellman ended the series of letters to Montini by saying "we have had a distinguished layman, Mr. O'Neill", reply to Blanshard in *The Christian Century,* a copy of which he enclosed.[73] Spellman apparently was oblivious to the severe reservations of the NCWC staff about O'Neill's competence. The question raised by the Church-State issue was too theological for Spellman's practical mind. To answer it there was needed not a prelate-politician but a theologian.

---

[70] *The Case of Archbishop O'Hara,* in: The Christian Century 70 (May 6, 1953) 539–541. For Montini's reprimand, see above pp. 329–331.

[71] AANY, Spellman to Montini, New York, May 22, 1953 (copy).

[72] AANY, Montini to Spellman, Vatican, June 8, 1953.

[73] AANY, Spellman to Montini, New York, June 27, 1953 (copy).

CHAPTER XV

AMERICANISMUS REDIVIVUS

A. JOHN COURTNEY MURRAY AND RELIGIOUS LIBERTY

Underlying the issue of Catholic cooperation with non-Catholics, the Feeney case, and Blanshard's attacks was fundamentally the question of the Catholic teaching on religious liberty, achieved in the United States through the First Amendment to the Constitution. To set forth the benefit to the Church of the American system of the separation of Church and State was the achievement of John Courtney Murray – an achievement which was not without pain.

As was seen above, in 1943 Murray was regarded with some suspicion by McNicholas and Stritch on the issue of cooperation with non-Catholics. But the attitude of the mid-western trio who dominated the NCWC began to shift. In April, 1945, Murray prepared for Mooney, then the chairman of the administrative board, a memorandum on the principles of religious liberty. And in 1947 he was invited to collaborate with the NCWC legal and education departments in preparing their arguments on the *Everson* and *McCullum* cases before the Supreme Court. It was perhaps in preparation for the latter of those cases that McNicholas, then the chairman of the administrative board, issued a statement on January 25, 1948, which placed him in the tradition of many bishops of the previous century and allied him with Murray's theological analysis. "No group in America is seeking union of church and state", said the archbishop, "and least of all are Catholics". He emphatically denied "that the Catholic bishops of the United States are seeking a union of church and state by any endeavours whatsoever, either proximate or remote". Then he added: "If tomorrow Catholics constitute a majority in our country, they would not seek a union of church and state. They would then, as now, uphold the Constitution and all its Amendments, recognizing the moral obligations imposed on all Catholics to observe and defend the Constitution and its Amendments".[1] It was a courageous statement for a bishop of his time and would later be challenged both in the United States and in Rome. It is difficult to say, however, whether McNicholas was at this point actually con-

---

[1] Quoted in John Tracy ELLIS: *Church and State – An American Catholic Tradition,* in: Harper's 207 (Nov., 1953) 67.

verted to the position that the American situation of the separation of Church and State was an acceptable thesis and not merely a tolerable hypothesis. It is likewise difficult to determine whether he had developed a theological basis for his position and had reconciled himself to the development of the Church's doctrine on religious liberty. But in the practical order, he was now an ally of Murray's.

Like McNicholas, Mooney, and Stritch, Murray saw that the real enemies of the Church and of western society were not Protestants but "technological secularists". Like those bishops, he also saw that, in order to combat these new enemies, cooperation with non-Catholics was necessary. Prior to undertaking any serious cooperation, however, it was necessary not only to assuage non-Catholic fears, as McNicholas had tried to do, but also to present the American notion of religious liberty as an authentic Catholic doctrine. To do this Murray argued that the Catholic teaching on Church-State relations had developed in the papal encyclicals since Pius IX. Development of doctrine had been the sticking point for Stritch in Murray's presentation in 1943, but he would gradually be converted. It was also the sticking point for Monsignor Joseph Fenton, but he would remain intransigent.

Fenton held that where Catholics were in the majority for a government to fail to establish the Church was nothing short of apostasy. Encyclicals were infallible, he said, and if Murray and others advocated the American system of the separation of Church and State, they were condemned by *Longinqua Oceani* and *Testem Benevolentiae* which tolerated the American exception to the Catholic ideal of the union of Church and State. For Murray to claim to find other interpretations of these encyclicals was to water down doctrine and to fall under the condemnation of Pius XII's *Humani Generis,* issued in 1950.[2]

By 1950, therefore, Murray was in the eyes of his opponents a successor to the Americanists. But unlike Denis O'Connell, who had previously attempted a formulation of the distinctiveness of the American tradition, Murray sought to avoid the pitfalls of the thesis-hypothesis argumentation. Addressing the Catholic Theological Society of America in 1948, he questioned whether that argumentation "supplies irrevocably and for all time the categories in which we must continue to debate the problem of Church and State". In his answer he gave his own position which Fenton was incapable of understanding. "For my own part, I incline to think that the usefulness of this particular distinction is increasingly outweighed by its tendency to mislead, and that its categories are too facile to admit of fruitful theological and political thought. If, for instance, on this basis one says that the thesis obtains in Spain, whereas only the hypothesis is verified in the

---

[2] PELOTTE: *Murray,* pp. 154–160.

United States, one steps off on the wrong foot into a morass of futile controversy, that centers on an irrelevance – whether the particular political form of the Spanish state is in any sense part of some Catholic 'ideal'. It may or may not be ideal for the Spanish people – that is their problem. But to predicate 'Catholic thesis' or 'Catholic ideal' of this particular mode of religio-political organization is, I say, at least misleading".[3] In other words, Murray was saying – to the deaf ears of Fenton and others – that neither the American nor the Spanish situation was best for the whole Church. The ideal or "thesis" for Murray was whatever was conducive to the Church's carrying out its mission with freedom and this could be achieved through a variety of historically conditioned arrangements with the State.

During the summer of 1950, Murray visited Rome where he found powerful support in Giovanni Battista Montini. As Murray later reported to John Tracy Ellis, professor of Church history at the Catholic University, Montini "was personally sympathetic with my 'orientations' and rather wanted his hand to be strengthened – but... [sic, in the original]".[4] Sometime after his visit to Rome, Murray had prepared a memorandum for Montini on the Church-State problem, but by April, 1951, he had heard nothing, except that Montini showed it to the pope and that it had then been given to "experts". "Heaven help it, and me... [sic in original]", Murray remarked to McCormick. "If you should chance to hear any rumors or rumblings about it, I would of course be glad to be informed".[5]

B. Ottaviani's Attack on Murray

But Fenton's accusation that Murray's views were condemned by *Longinqua Oceani* and *Testem Benevolentiae* continued, even though the two of them occasionally exchanged friendly letters.[6] It was ironic that Fenton hurled these two letters against Murray. For, just as the Americanists felt justified by Leo XIII's encyclicals to formulate their program, Murray now turned to a careful theological scrutiny of those encyclicals to prove what he had been saying about the development of doctrine. His first in a series of articles on Leo XIII appeared in *Theological Studies* in March, 1953.[7] The article was already at the printers when a bombshell fell. In January, Pius had held his second consistory at which he

---

[3] "Governmental Repression of Heresy", *Proceedings of the Catholic Theological Society of America* (Chicago 1948), p. 37 quoted in *ibid.*, p. 156.

[4] AWC, Murray to Ellis, Ridgefield, Conn., July 20, 1953 (photocopy).

[5] AWC, Murray to McCormick, Woodstock, Apr. 24, 1951 (copy).

[6] PELOTTE: *Murray*, pp. 35–36, 163–166.

[7] *Leo XIII on Church and State: The General Structure of the Controversy*, in: Theological Studies 14 (Mar., 1953) 1–30.

named Alfredo Ottaviani a cardinal and appointed him Pro-Secretary of the Holy Office. On March 2, the new cardinal gave an address at the Lateran Seminary.

After stating that Italy and Spain presented the ideal relationship between Church and State, Ottaviani readily admitted that he was applying "two criteria, or different norms of action". In a country where Catholics constituted a majority, he supported "the idea of the confessional State with the duty of exclusive protection of the Catholic religion". In a country where Catholics were a minority, he claimed "the right to tolerance or to the outright equality of the sects". He recognized that here was "a truly embarrassing double standard from which Catholics, who take into account the present development of civilization, want to free themselves". He thus acknowledged the same sticking point as Stritch and Fenton – development of doctrine reflecting the "development of civilization". But Ottaviani was neither embarrassed by the double standard nor sympathetic with the development of doctrine, for "two weights and two measures are to be applied: one for truth, the other for error. Men who feel in the secure possession of the truth and of justice do not compromise. They demand the full respect of their rights. On the other hand, how can those who do not feel sure of possessing the truth demand that they alone hold the field without sharing it with him who claims respect for his own rights on the basis of principles?" If Paul Blanshard was listening, he did not need to argue for what Catholics believed – here seemed to be clear evidence. For Ottaviani, error had no rights and Catholics, being in full possession of the truth, had an obligation, where they were in the majority, to seek special status for their Church.

Ottaviani's position was clearly at variance with Murray's and he went to pains, without mentioning Murray's name, to indicate his abhorrence for the "erroneous theories ... being set forth also in America". He specifically cited "the controversy ... in the United States between two authors of opposing tendencies", which "was very well summarized by Dr. Fenton" in the *American Ecclesiastical Review* for June of 1951. The two authors had been Murray and one of his opponents, Father George W. Shea of the Newark archdiocesan seminary. In the cardinal's rendition of Fenton's summary,

"the customary arguments were repeated by the author who sustained the liberalizing thesis:

1. That the State, properly speaking, cannot perform an act of religion. (For him the State is a simple symbol or an ensemble of institutions);
2. That "an immediate illation from the order of ethical and theological truth to the order of Constitutional law, is in principle, inadmissible". With this axiomatic language he tries to sustain the position that the obligation of the State with regard to the worship of God could never enter the constitutional sphere;

3. Finally, that even for a State composed of Catholics, there is no obligation to profess the Catholic religion. As far as the obligation to protect is concerned, this does not become operative except in determined circumstances, and precisely when the liberty of the Church cannot be guaranteed otherwise. In other words: even in a non-confessional State the Church can very well be free, without need for relations and protection on the part of the State as such.

It is also sad to note how this writer takes exception to the teaching set forth in the Manuals of Public Ecclesiastical Law, without taking into account the fact that this teaching is for the most part based on the doctrine set forth in Pontifical documents".[8]

The day following Ottaviani's lecture, the *Osservatore Romano* reported it, but, while quoting segments, omitted all references to the United States.[9] But Father Joseph Sullivan, who served as a Roman correspondent for the National Catholic News Service, immediately cabled the Press Department of the NCWC, paraphrasing the above paragraphs as referring to the controversy between Murray and Shea. His cable read in part: "Ottaviani did not repeat not mention either these names but did explicitly say 'controversy was very well outlined by Professor Fenton editor of the same review...'".[10]

The NCWC staff rushed into action. Frank Hall, the lay director of the Press Department, was in a quandary. So far, he reported to Howard Carroll, the secular press had reported nothing of the address, but that situation could change if the *Osservatore Romano* carried any of it. If the Catholic News Service was not to send out the text, Hall wanted "to have instructions from higher up".[11] Carroll reported this immediately to Archbishop Karl J. Alter, who had succeeded McNicholas as both Archbishop of Cincinnati and chairman of the administrative board.[12] Alter quickly replied by telephone, as Carroll reported to Hall:

"a) In advance of receipt of the full text, the NC News Service is to send out a brief notice of the affair and the subject of the discourse. ...

b) The answer to the question, should the complete text be sent out automatically in the usual manner in which the Papal Documents are sent out, is no.

c) If the complete text appears in Osservatore, then

1) if the seculars play it up – NC should send out the complete text.

2) if the seculars do not, then NC may send out a digest".[13]

Alter was clearly trying to avoid giving publicity to Ottaviani's speech and he

---

[8] ANCWC, Discourse of Ottaviani, Mar. 2, 1953 (translation).
[9] *Osservatore Romano,* Mar. 3, 1953.
[10] ANCWC, Sullivan to Press Department, Rome, n.d.
[11] ANCWC, Hall to Carroll, Washington, Mar. 6, 1953.
[12] ANCWC, Carroll to Alter, Washington, Mar. 7, 1953 (copy).
[13] ANCWC, Carroll to Hall, memo, Mar. 9, 1953 (copy).

especially wished to avoid making explicit the cardinal's implicit references to Murray.[14] Alter had been a friend of Murray's for some years and would later support his views at the Second Vatican Council.

But not all the members of the hierarchy saw the issue so clearly at this time. Stritch was still struggling to find the right formula. On March 10, he wrote Carroll thanking him for the cabled report of Ottaviani's address, from which he concluded, "it is evident that His Eminence, a great theologian and authority, cleared the atmosphere. What the report states that he says is just what Pope Leo XIII said so clearly in his Encyclical Letter, IMMORTALE DEI. Nothing else could have been rightly said on the subject".[15] A more surprising reaction came from Spellman. He had received a copy of the address by the end of March and, writing to Monsignor John Fearns, his canonical adviser, he stated: "Archbishop O'Boyle and myself saw no useful purpose in having it published in The Ecclesiastical Review".[16] Fearns felt that the address basically repeated what Ottaviani had already said in his work *Institutiones Juris Publici Ecclesiastici,* with new applications to Spain and Murray's thesis, but that "it should be filed in the Seminary with the documents on canon law of which it will form a most valuable part".[17] Spellman was beginning to become more interested in the question of religious liberty. Despite Spellman and O'Boyle's animadversions, Fenton procured a copy of Ottaviani's speech from the cardinal himself and published it in the *American Ecclesiastical Review,* but his version omitted any reference to American Catholics or to his article.[18]

In the meantime, Ottaviani's speech continued to cause difficulties for those American Catholics who sought to defend the American system. John Tracy Ellis had learned from a Dominican friend that Father Michael Browne, O.P., Master of the Sacred Palace, had repudiated McNicholas' mild statement on the American Church and State situation in 1948. In view of the attitudes of Ottaviani and Browne, Ellis had withdrawn a manuscript from *Harper's* magazine which presented "an historical survey of the statements of American prelates from Carroll to Cushing on Church and State in the United States, all favoring our present arrangement".[19] At the same time, the NCWC was trying to sit on the story of Ottaviani's address. When the editor of one Catholic newspaper demanded that the Catholic News Service send a full text to all its subscribers, Carroll wrote his

---

[14] Interview with Alter, May 26, 1974.
[15] ANCWC, Stritch to Carroll, Chicago, Mar. 10, 1953.
[16] AANY, Spellman to Fearns, New York, Mar. 31, 1953 (copy).
[17] AANY, Fearns to Spellman, Yonkers, N.Y., Apr. 20, 1953.
[18] *Church and State: Some Problems in the Light of the Teaching of Pope Pius XII,* in: American Ecclesiastical Review 128 (May, 1953) 321–334.
[19] ANCWC, Ellis to Carroll, Washington, Mar. 24, 1953.

bishop. The administrative board had been anxious, he said, that the controversy not carry over "to the public press, and above all that POAU [Protestants and Other Americans United] and other organizations of similar character be not given the opportunity to take out of context statements which will involve the Church in the United States in a very bitter controversy". The National Catholic News Service had, therefore, distributed only the *Osservatore Romano's* account but not the full text. Carroll feared that the editor "might be disposed to start the kind of fireworks that the Administrative Board is anxious to avoid". He concluded that "many of us at the N.C.W.C. and the members of the Board have breathed a sigh of relief that the secular press let the speech go by unnoticed".[20]

Late in April, however, it appeared that the NCWC would be forced from within its own organization to release the text. Sullivan cabled from Rome that the Religious News Service, a Protestant agency, had procured a copy of the address. Hall feared that this might actually have been the result of prodding by a Catholic newspaper editor. Carroll immediately notified Alter, whose response was quick and to the point. He was now exercising censorship for the liberal cause. "I can not help but be somewhat perplexed", he wrote, "by the industry and diligence of Monsignor Sullivan in bringing to the attention of our News Service the continuing story of Cardinal Ottaviani's address. It almost seems to me as if we were being forced into a news release giving the substance of his address on Church and State. I still hold firmly to the conviction that we should not do any more at present than what has been done. The Osservatore's article is adequate defense for our position under present circumstances. If the Religious News Service runs the article, then we may have to reconsider our position; but I think we should be willing to risk any embarrassment which some of our newspaper editors might be willing to create by contrasting the enterprise of the R.N.S. with that of our own".[21] Carroll shared Alter's views and commented about Sullivan: "If we have come out of the situation as yet unscathed, it is almost certainly in spite of him".[22]

But the full text of Ottavian's utterance would break neither through the Religious News Service nor through the NCWC. In Spain, where the final steps for a concordat with the Holy See were being taken, the bishops had argued that Ottaviani's address supported their position forbidding proselytizing by other religious groups. The *New York Times* then requested an official clarification from a Vatican spokesman, who stated that the speech "was not official or semi-offi-

---

[20] ANCWC, Carroll to Bishop Ralph Hayes, Washington, Apr. 1, 1953 (copy).
[21] ANCWC, Alter to Carroll, Cincinnati, Apr. 25, 1953; Hall to Carroll, memo, Apr. 24, 1953; Carroll to Alter, Washington, Apr. 24, 1953 (copy).
[22] ANCWC, Carroll to Alter, Washington, May 1, 1953 (copy).

cial but was nevertheless 'unexceptional'". The *Times* then asked the opinion of Murray, who toned down the authority of Ottaviani's statement still more. The cardinal, Murray said, "was speaking only in his purely personal capacity. His statement was neither an official nor a semi-official utterance. It was just the statement of a private theologian – one of very considerable reputation, of course, speaking on his own authority. It is still entirely possible and legitimate for Catholics to doubt or dispute whether Cardinal Ottaviani's discourse represents the full, adequate and balanced doctrine of the Church".[23] Murray's comment received a favorable reaction from the Protestant journal, *The Christian Century,* which otherwise criticized Ottaviani's "Exceptionable Intolerance".[24] But just how far a Catholic could "doubt or dispute" Murray would soon find out.

Murray had drawn the inspiration for his comment from a letter he received from Father Robert Leiber, S.J., who continued to be an adviser to Pius XII. Ottaviani's address, Leiber wrote, "renders only the Cardinal's private view", to which there was attached "no sort of official or even semi-official character". But he also recommended that Murray write Ottaviani personally to correct what the cardinal had mistakenly characterized as Murray's opinion.[25] This letter from Leiber and information Murray obtained from other sources later provided him with the justification for a direct attack on Ottaviani's position. That summer, however, he spent gaining some knowledge of the history of the American Church. He had read Ellis' two-volume biography of Cardinal Gibbons and Ellis then sent him his manuscript on the history of bishops' statements on Church and State. It was a revelation to Murray. "The curious thing", he said, "is that we no longer seem to have any American Catholic bishops like Carroll, England, Hughes, Ireland, et al. Now they are all Roman Catholic. You will rightly understand what I mean". Urging Ellis to publish his article in *Harper's,* he noted that it presented as an historical fact what he was trying to establish as a valid theological position. The American tradition as presented by Ellis, he thought was "vulnerable to the assertion, 'Spain is "the ideal", – the U.S. Constitution is *pis-aller'*. Present-day thought is still cast in terms of the post-Reformation 'Catholic nation-state'. I do not indeed want the American situation canonized as 'ideal'. It would be enough if it could be defended as legitimate in principle, as standing *aequo jure* with the Spanish situation – each representing an imperfect realization of principle in divergent concrete historical contexts. Are we to suppose that 30,000,000 Catholics must live perpetually in a state of 'hypothesis'?"[26]

---

[23] *New York Times*, July 21, 1953.
[24] The Christian Century, 70 (Aug. 12, 1953) 910; typed copy also in ANCWC.
[25] AWC, Leiber to Murray, Rome, June 12, 1953.
[26] AWC, Murray to Ellis Ridgefield, Conn., July 20, 1953 (photocopy).

Ellis agreed with Murray's assessment of the contemporary hierarchy in contrast with the past. "Something fine and bracing has gone out of the American Church", he wrote, "and it is difficult to see how it can ever be regained". As for Murray's remark of "the '*American* Catholic bishops' of several generations ago", Ellis concluded: "If that be 'Americanism' let them make the most of it!"[27] Unlike the Americanist movement of the late nineteenth century, Murray's new effort to explain the American situation to the universal Church lacked episcopal exponents. But it soon had one, though a hesitant convert.

C. Mooney and Stritch Support Murray

On October 16, Cardinal Stritch gave a speech at the dedication of the new North American College in Rome. He stated: "For us our country above everything else is a land of freemen, conscious of their rights and dignity, collaborating together in a brotherly spirit for the common good of all".[28] The speech was innocuous, but Stritch was worried that he may have offended Ottaviani. On November 16, Mooney invited Murray to join him and Stritch for a lengthy dinner. As Murray recounted it to Vincent McCormick: "Cardinal Mooney of course is my good friend and very sympathetic. His idea, as he put it to me privately, was 'to do a job on' H. E. of Chicago. I've never been quite sure whether Cardinal S. is my friend or not". Stritch's difficulties were twofold: "on freedom of religious propaganda, and on the concept of a 'religion of the state'". Murray explained his own position and Stritch listened sympathetically, finally adding "that, as a member of the magisterium he was obliged to be cautious, but that he was glad someone was attempting to cope, on a broad theological, political, and historical basis with these points, which are a genuine source of difficulty to American Catholics (during the evening Cardinal M. had constantly insisted on this point of 'American difficulties')". Stritch also said that while in Rome he was assured by Montini that Ottaviani's speech was a "purely private utterance", and he confessed to Murray that "the *sensus fidelium* in the U.S. is definitely against the canonical thesis insofar as it asserts governmental and legal favor and protection of Catholicism and denies religious freedom as a civil right".[29] At one point in the dinner, Murray told Ellis, Mooney remarked: "None of us today could go as far as Gibbons went". Murray "was dying to ask: 'Why not?'"[30]

---

[27] AWC, Ellis to Murray, Washington, July 22, 1953.
[28] Quoted in Marie Cecilia Buehrle: *The Cardinal Stritch Story*, Milwaukee 1959, p. 114.
[29] AWC, Murray to McCormick, Woodstock, Nov. 23, 1953, no. 1 (copy).
[30] AWC, Murray to Ellis, Woodstock, Nov. 19, 1953 (copy).

Ellis thought "the question that occurred to your mind to ask your dinner companions is altogether pertinent". Stritch's address, he reported, had produced a favorable Roman reaction and "surely it *was* a fine speech and in the right direction, but again there is a distance which separates them from Gibbons – and McNicholas in 1948 – that must be traversed before unquiet minds will be set at ease".[31]

At this point, however, Stritch was a convert to Murray's interpretation of the Catholic doctrine on Church-State relations. On December 7, he wrote Murray: "Our conversation in Washington was a satisfaction to me of a desire which I have had for a long time. If I was frank in stating my difficulties I assure you that I was just trying to find an answer to them. I have thought and worked on this problem and what I said in Rome was the expression of what I hold to be the teaching of the Church. It is a satisfaction that in the aftermath of my address as far as I can discover many whose judgment I esteem approved of what I said. As was said to you, we must go along prudently and thoughtfully in these studies and seek the advice of competent scholars. It pleases me immensely that you are willing to help me and I want you to send me from time to time your further studies on this important question".[32] Stritch had, in fact, then been worrying about the problem of religious liberty for a full ten years. Whether he had overcome his earlier difficulties with Murray's position through a theoretical acceptance of the development of doctrine or through the practical recognition of the American *sensus fidelium* or through Mooney's personal influence, is unknown. But with his conversion, he stood with Alter, Mooney, and the NCWC staff in favor of Murray's new approach to the old problem of Church-State relations.

Just as Stritch was undergoing his conversion, however, Murray's approach came under attack. On October 31, 1953, Cardinal Enrique Pla y Deniel, Archbishop of Toledo and Primate of Spain, wrote an article in *Ecclesia* defending the newly signed concordat between Spain and the Holy See with its provision for prohibiting public exercise of non-Catholic worship. This, he said, was in accord with the "fully authorized lecture" of Ottaviani, despite what "some misguided United States Catholics" and some journals, especially *America,* claimed.[33]

Other problems were also beginning to surface. Clare Booth Luce, the American ambassador to Italy, had arranged for a group of Texas Pentecostals to come to Rome, where they openly proselytized. Moreover, she had failed to apply for a personal audience with Pius XII. Her sins of commission and omission angered the pope, who complained to Vincent McCormick. In regard to Mrs. Luce's not

---

[31] AWC, Ellis to Murray, Washington, Nov. 23, 1953.

[32] AWC, Stritch to Murray, Chicago, Dec. 7, 1953.

[33] *New York Times,* Nov. 2, 1953.

seeking an audience, McCormick "defended her ... , even expressed surprise that He would have expected a member of the other [diplomatic] corps to come. But He did. I remarked that a Catholic [*sic*] to the Quirinal was in a very awkward position, especially with feeling running so high in USA against official connection with the Vatican. I may have softened His feelings; I doubt it".[34] *America's* opposition to Spain's intolerance, Luce's assistance of Pentecostals, and Murray's position on Church and State all became part of a cryptic *mandatum*, which McCormick had conveyed to Father John McMahon, S.J., Murray's provincial in New York.

On November 21, McMahon quoted McCormick's order to Murray: "Read Can. 2316. If I assist a man to come to Italy for that purpose knowing that is why he is coming do I fall under the penalty? Our highest superior – I was with him last month – thinks so, unless excused by ignorance. *America* might know that. I think the time has come for Fr. Murray to put down in simple, clear statements his full, present position regarding this Church-State question and to send it to me for Father General. Sic mandatum".[35] Murray admitted his confusion. He would happily comply with the request to set forth his position, but he needed time. As he put it, he was not sure if he had a "position" or "a purpose: sc. to inquire whether a place in the sun of Catholic principle can be found for the unique American solution to the problem of religious pluralism, or whether American Catholicism is to be obliged to live forever in the shadow of 'hypothesis' as this term is currently understood". But the rest of McCormick's message Murray found "cryptic, enigmatic, mysterious". It had him "quite stumped" and "its implications could be either encouraging or ominous". His chief concern was "am I *suspectus de haeresi* or simply the object of interest?" He was also worried that McCormick and Janssens, the general, were "suspect because you have lent me a manner of encouragement". In this context, he recounted his dinner with Mooney and Stritch.

In a second letter to McCormick on the same day, Murray finally figured out that the canon cited against proselytizing concerned not himself but Mrs. Luce. He explained that he prepared her statements for the approval of her nomination as ambassador and had told her that, while "she might protest arbitrary acts of violence against American citizens ... , she had no right, either as Ambassador and still less as a Catholic, to interfere with the just application of existent Italian laws". "There was no mention of Canon 2316", he said, "(I carry only a limited number of canons in my head!)". Murray recommended that if Mrs. Luce were to

---

[34] AWC, McCormick to Murray, Rome, Nov. 27, 1953.
[35] McCormick to McMahon, Rome, Nov. 15, 1953, quoted in PELOTTE: *Murray,* p. 39.

be given a reprimand, "it will be given gently, preferably by the 'highest superior' himself".

In a postscript, Murray responded to his final deciphering of McCormick's *mandatum*. In the version which he had received, the word *"America"* had not been underlined. He therefore understood it to mean the country and not the periodical. Realizing that the latter was intended, Murray explained that Robert C. Hartnett, S.J., the editor, had recently consulted him about an editorial to be written in response to *Ecclesia*. Murray personally thought Hartnett was "wasting his time pursuing that tack. Spanish law is not going to be liberalized, at least not until the next revolution". His own writings had referred to Spain, but were "rather more dissection than criticism". He would even grant that the Spanish system was "one way of doing things", but not "the only way, the 'ideal' way".[36]

If Murray sought assurance from Rome, at this point he received it. McCormick responded on November 27 promising that, "whenever there may be real cause for anxiety or more than ordinary caution or even a red light appearing on the horizon, I shall let you know at once and clearly". The general had wanted a statement of Murray's position, "so that in case the matter came up here, we would be duly informed". *"Rome has not expressed* any fear for the orthodoxy of Fr. Murray", he continued, "though not everybody in Rome, I presume, accepts his writings". Murray's surmise, McCormick said, was correct that the canon cited referred to Mrs. Luce and he narrated the pope's reaction. He concluded: "I sent Fr. Prov. the opinion of Fr. Gen. on the AMERICA editorial, and I suppose you have heard it. Now we shall listen for Madrid; but I agree with you, there is no point in saying more about the matter; a running controversy is wholly out of place. AMERICA has vindicated itself clearly and modestly and respectfully. Basta. What about Tracy Ellis' article in Harper's? I am so glad you had that four hour conference in Wash. S[tritch]. is cautious, perhaps too fearful, though he talked out boldly here and all were delighted, who knew anything about the controversy. So calm and peace be your fruits of the Spirit, and may He continue to enlighten the path you are opening up. Work without fear. Fear, worry cripple a man in such work as you have undertaken. I'll keep my ear to the ground".[37] McCormick's letter was encouraging, but it also indicated that there were various Roman views. The curia seems to have been divided on the question of Church-State relations. The pope's utterances seemed to reflect whoever got his ear, men like Ottaviani or men like Montini. For the next few weeks, it appears as if the pope listened more to Montini.

On December 6, 1953, Pius XII delivered his allocution, *Ci riesce,* to Italian

---

[36] AWC, Murray to McCormick, Woodstock, Nov. 23, 1953, no. 2 (copy).
[37] AWC, McCormick to Murray, Rome, Nov. 27, 1953.

jurists, which seemed to temper if not reverse Ottaviani's speech and called for the recognition of religious pluralism not only between states but within them.[38] This seemed to be the papal statement which some of Murray's informants said would be forthcoming. Armed with it, Murray accepted an invitation to speak at the Catholic University of America on March 25, 1954. The papal allocution, he said, paved the way for asserting that political unity might be "the preparation for religious unity" and laid to rest the proposition that Spain represented the "thesis" and the United States only the "hypothesis". There were at least three versions of Murray's speech and it is unclear which of them he actually delivered. In one of them, he formally stated that "*Ci riesce* is the Pope's public correction of impressions left by Ottaviani's construction...".[39] The problem was that even as Murray was preparing his speech there was already controversy over the interpretation of *Ci riesce,* waged between Gustave Weigel, S.J., one of Murray's colleagues at Woodstock College, and Fenton, who reported Murray's attack to Ottaviani.[40]

Ottaviani was quick to respond. On April 1, he wrote Spellman a letter, no longer extant, asking that some action be taken against Murray. Spellman's reply indicated either ignorance or guile. Murray, he wrote, had "never been under my jurisdiction from the time of his ordination as he has been on loan to the Catholic University". Murray, in fact, had never taught at the Catholic University and, as a Jesuit, would not have been subject to Spellman's jurisdiction in any case. But Spellman promised to discuss the matter with the rector of the university, if Ottaviani would "give more details of what Father Murray said in his lecture that was offensive to you and just what quotation he made from any address of His Holiness...".[41] Ottaviani, in the meantime, had learned that Spellman was soon coming to Rome and promised then "to give you all the information which you desire...".[42] There is, however, no extant record of what may have transpired in Spellman's personal meeting with Ottaviani.

D. MURRAY CEASES TO WRITE

What occurred over the next year and a half is obscure. At some point Murray was required to submit all his writings on Church and State to his superiors in

---

[38] Acta Apostolicae Sedis, 45 (1953) 794–802.

[39] Quoted in PELOTTE: *Murray,* pp. 46–47.

[40] *Ibid.,* pp. 45–46.

[41] AANY, Spellman to Ottaviani, New York, Apr. 5, 1953 (copy).

[42] AANY, Ottaviani to Spellman, Vatican, May 6, 1954.

Rome for censorship. But in July, 1955, Murray received negative word, put gently by McCormick. He had submitted two articles for censorship, one of which was the final in his series on the encyclicals of Leo XIII, begun the month of Ottaviani's speech. McCormick commended him for his patience in waiting so long for a response to the censor's report, which, he thought, "will help for the introduction of your cause before the Congregation of Rites. But meantime another Congregation should not be provoked, and just now it is rather on edge". The censors rejected the articles because they had "your interests at heart and they know the scene over here". Quoting one censor, he noted that Murray had been delated to the Holy Office by enemies in both the United States and Rome. McCormick, therefore, advised Murray to give up "that controverted question under present circumstances". The general agreed with this, he added, but then said: "Time will bring change".[43]

Murray responded that "it would have been difficult for anyone to find a nicer and more delicate way of saying 'You're through'!" He was grateful for McCormick's support, "but the whole thing represents a defeat and a failure of the first order".[44] A few days later, Murray received word from McCormick that yet another article was turned down by the censors. "All the books on Church and State and on allied topics", Murray wrote, "have been cleared from my room, in symbol of retirement, which I expect to be permanent".[45] Shortly later, Richard Hartnett retired as editor of *America*, worn out by the attacks not only from the McCarthyites but perhaps also from Spain.[46]

Murray thus joined the company of theologians such as Henri du Lubac and Yves Congar who were told no longer to write. He was not officially silenced, but rather warned that the Holy Office was not yet ready to accept his position. Moreover, he retained the loyal support of his Jesuit superiors, who were more optimistic than he that his "retirement" was not "permanent". The rebuke from Rome came in the aftermath of a shift in the curia. Passed over for the red hat in the consistory of 1953, which made Ottaviani a cardinal, Montini was removed from his post as Substitute for the Ordinary Affairs of the Church and promoted to the archiepiscopal see of Milan late in 1954. In retrospect, it is difficult to determine, until the Vatican archives for the period are opened, whether his appointment was a promotion or a retirement; whether his letters to Spellman in 1953 criticizing American freedom expressed his own ideas or reflected Ottaviani's

---

[43] AWC, McCormick to Murray, Rome, June 9, 1955.
[44] AWC, Murray to McCormick, Woodstock, July 15, 1955 (copy).
[45] AWC, Murray to McCormick, Woodstock, Aug. 3, 1955 (copy); McCormick to Murray, Rome, July 21, 1955.
[46] CROSBY: *God, Church, and Flag*, p. 184.

growing power; or whether Pius XII did indeed promote him to get him out of the center of controversy and preserve him for later battles.[47] All that is known is that it was after he left the Secretariat of State that the tide turned against Murray and those Americans who wished to cease living "forever in the shadow of 'hypothesis'".

Murray sought to cast some light into the shadows in 1958. On July 22, he wrote McCormick saying that he would forward to him an Italian translation of a new article he had written, "Unica Status Religio". He wanted this published in *Civiltà Cattolica* and, "since this cannot be done without prior personal approval of the Holy Father, I want that too". The article argued that, within the American context, Catholics could defend the First Amendment to the Constitution as "good law". The occasion for Murray's request was not a religious one, as such, but a political one. Senator John F. Kennedy of Massachusetts had announced his candidacy for president and his office had requested Murray's assistance in case the senator was "forced by circumstances" to make a statement. In addition, Henry Luce, the husband of the ambassador to Italy and the editor of *Time* and *Life,* had asked his "advice about an article that *Life* intends to run sometime in the fall". Finally, the American bishops were seeking to formulate "a united opinion" and the administrative board of the NCWC had rejected a draft written by Connell.[48]

Thus a political event forced the American bishops to consider addressing the issue of religious liberty and Murray again seemed to be finding encouragement for his position from his old supporters at the NCWC. But again Murray received a veto. On August 5, McCormick wrote him telling him "to be content to stay on the sidelines, unless the hierarchy forces you into play: deepen and clarify your own position, and be ready with your solution approved, when the opportune time comes. That is not coming in the present Roman atmosphere".[49]

The Roman atmosphere, however, changed more rapidly than McCormick and many others expected. On October 8, 1958, Pius XII died and the conclave which followed elected the seventy-six year old Patriarch of Venice, Cardinal Angelo Roncalli.

The change in the Roman atmosphere was not immediate. But the change in the American political atmosphere was more apparent. Unlike 1939 when Roosevelt received some protests for sending Joseph Kennedy to represent him at the coronation of Pius XII, President Eisenhower, as a matter of course, dis-

---

[47] Carlo FALCONI: *The Popes in the Twentieth Century: From Pius X to John XXIII,* translated by Muriel Grindrod, Boston 1967, pp. 107–108, 291, and 307.

[48] AWC, Murray to McCormick, Woodstock, July 22, 1958 (copy).

[49] AWC, McCormick to Murray, Rome, Aug. 5, 1958.

patched representatives for the funeral of Pius XII and the coronation of John XXIII.[50] The change in the political atmosphere due in part to the issue of Communism helped contribute to the election of Kennedy as the first Catholic president in 1960. That political event, in turn, may have helped contribute to the influence of the American bishops in gaining the acceptance of the Declaration on Religious Liberty at the Second Vatican Council. But that acceptance was still several years away and the American Church had little dream in 1958 that the new pope would call a council.

The election of John XXIII signalled structural changes in the American Church, the most obvious of which was that Spellman no longer had a close friend on the throne of St. Peter. In March, 1958, however, before Pius' death Stritch had been called to Rome to become Pro-Prefect of Propaganda, but by May he was dead. He was succeeded as Archbishop of Chicago by Albert Meyer, former Archbishop of Milwaukee and a scripture scholar. On October 25, just three days before the conclave elected John XXIII, Cardinal Mooney died at the North American College in Rome. His successor in Detroit was John Dearden, the Bishop of Pittsburgh. Many of the bishops who had prepared the way for Roman acceptance of religious liberty would thus not be the ones who saw it through the council. In December, 1958, John XXIII held his first consistory at which he named two new American cardinals, Richard Cushing of Boston, for whom the Feeney case may have postponed the honor, and John O'Hara, Archbishop of Philadelphia. Pope John wrought yet more important changes in the consistory, affecting both the American and universal Church. Archbishop Cicognani, who had served as the apostolic delegate since 1933, was also named a cardinal. His successor in the United States was Archbishop Egidio Vagnozzi, who lacked Cicognani's deftness in dealing with the American hierarchy and at times impeded their preparedness for the council. But the most important new cardinal named was Archbishop Montini. In less than a year the American Church had new leaders and the universal Church had a new pope. These new men would witness the practical challenge to the American proposition of religious liberty as John Kennedy's candidacy brought the issue out into the open.

In 1958 POAU had demanded that each of the candidates declare their positions on the diplomatic recognition of the Holy See.[51] In a statement in *Look* magazine early in 1959, Kennedy gave his views. He opposed diplomatic relations with the Holy See because the divisiveness which would result from the nomination of an ambassador would only weaken the ambassador's position at the Vatican. In regard to aid to parochial schools, he said that as a citizen he was

---

[50] *New York Times,* Oct. 14, 31, Nov. 5, 1958.
[51] *New York Times,* Jan. 5, 1958.

bound to obey the Constitution as interpreted by the Supreme Court. Through a prominent layman, Frank Folsom, Spellman sought an explanation from Kennedy, but the senator simply stood by his orginal remarks. Spellman then forwarded a copy of Kennedy's letter to Galeazzi.[52] In some ways, Kennedy's statement, as was seen, ended years of Spellman's efforts, initiated and at times assisted by Kennedy's father, to establish diplomatic relations. It also cleared the air of many of the Protestant fears of what would happen if a Catholic were elected president. But a major fear remained. What was the teaching of the Catholic Church about the relations between Church and State?

It was significant that John XXIII's announcement on January 25, 1959, that he would call a council formed the backdrop for Kennedy's campaign. John appealed to Americans, Catholic and Protestant alike, with his humanity and down-to-earth qualities. Kennedy appealed to voters with his charisma and well-reasoned answers to questions. But the issue of religious liberty still hovered on the horizon. In February, 1960, Francis Connell wrote Vagnozzi about the issue. Episcopal Bishop James Pike, a former Catholic, was due to publish a book in April, A Catholic in the White House. Connell suspected that it would be an expansion of an article Pike had already written in which "he tries to prove that most of the Catholics in the United States, and even the Bishops, are opposed to the official teaching of the Church on State-Church relations". He was also certain that Pike would "present Cardinal Ottaviani and myself as representatives of the Church's official teaching", so Connell had already written to the cardinal. He thought that no bishop should lower himself to answer Pike in a secular magazine, but felt "that a clear explanation of this whole doctrine would be a very appropriate subject for our Bishops' November letter, particularly since the elections will then be ended".[53]

Connell's letter could be interpreted as an attempt to increase the Romanization of the American Church by having Vagnozzi set the agenda for the annual bishops' meeting — something Cicognani would not have done. At this point, however, Vagnozzi sent a photocopy of Connell's letter to Spellman, whose reply simply acknowledged receipt and said in a postscript that Pike would no longer be given free time on radio and television.[54] If Connell was trying to force the hierarchy into making his views its own, as it refused to do in 1958, he would get no support from Spellman.

Late in the spring, however, other views appeared. Compiling a series of arti-

---

[52] AANY, Kennedy to Folsom, Washington, Mar. 25, 1959 (original); Spellman to Galeazzi, New York, Mar. 30, 1959 (copy).

[53] AANY, Connell to Vagnozzi, Washington, Feb. 17, 1960 (photocopy).

[54] AANY, Spellman to Vagnozzi, New York, Mar. 8, 1960 (copy).

cles written earlier, Murray published *We Hold These Truths: Catholic Reflections on the American Proposition*. It sold widely and helped clarify what Catholics believed about American rights and liberties. In September, Theodore Sorensen, one of Kennedy's aides, phoned Murray to read him a speech the senator would deliver to the Houston Ministerial Association. As Murray later stated, it was "unfair" to ask him to comment on a text read over the telephone, but he made a few suggestions. Kennedy's speech was the turning point in his campaign.[55] In November, he was elected the first Catholic President of the United States, although Murray himself may have voted for Richard M. Nixon. For Murray, the campaign in which one candidate happened to be a Catholic simply presented the occasion for him to make clear what he sincerely believed was Catholic doctrine. He would have a chance to argue his position at the council, but only after a further rebuff — a rebuff which indicated how ill prepared the American Church was for holding a council.

The road to Roman acceptance of religious liberty was a long and tortuous one for the American hierarchy. It had weathered the domestic storms of the Feeney case and of Blanshard's attacks. But these were the negative aspects of the question. The positive teaching on religious liberty and on its corollaries; interfaith cooperation and ecumenism, had yet to be accepted. Support for that teaching came from the NCWC and the most prominent bishops within it: Mooney, Stritch, McNicholas, and later Alter. But they were not dynamic, courageous leaders like Gibbons, Ireland, and O'Connell had been in the previous century. Rather they were products of the Romanization of the American Church who wished to see adaptation made but were incapable of seeing how to do it without appearing disloyal to the Holy See. For men like Stritch, the sticking point was the development of doctrine. Only when they became convinced that adaptation should be made did they see that it could be made by accepting Murray's position on development. Yet, before the council, except for Alter, all had passed on the mantle of leadership to a new generation of bishops. None of these were willing to risk Roman censure by asking Murray to attend the council as a *peritus*. Paradoxically, it was through none of Murray's earlier supporters that he eventually received an invitation to the council, but through the power politician *par excellence* in the American Church, the bishop who had remained aloof from all the preliminary discussions — Francis Cardinal Spellman.

---

[55] PELOTTE: *Murray*, p. 76.

CHAPTER XVI

THE SECOND VATICAN COUNCIL:
OUT FROM UNDER THE SHADOW OF HYPOTHESIS

A. PREPARATION FOR THE COUNCIL

The election of John Kennedy had resolved one part of the dilemma of American Catholics – they were accepted as Americans and their fellow citizens acknowledged their loyalty to the American Republic. But the other part of the dilemma remained – would Rome accept the American tradition of religious liberty as Catholic doctrine? The political resolution of the dilemma may well have given the American bishops at the Second Vatican Council an advantage their predecessors did not have, for they could show that their nation with its religious pluralism gave Catholics not only toleration but full liberty.

Perhaps no hierarchy, however, was as ill-prepared for the coming council as the American. The long process of Romanization had taken its toll. In some ways, the American bishops who attended the First Vatican Council would have been more at home if they could have changed places with their successors who attended the second one. Though there was a national episcopal conference, which Rome recognized as the voice of the hierarchy in the Second World War, the bishops had lost sight of the American tradition of collegiality as such. They would have to learn the concept anew from European mentors. The American Church was still a Church of doers rather than thinkers. For the 226 bishops who went to Rome, the council would be a learning experience. For some of the European theologians and prelates, the American episcopate – the third largest in the world – was the theologically illiterate representative of the vast, wealthy, military power of the west. Many would recall as typical Cardinal Cushing's departure from the second session because he could not understand Latin.[1] But such an evaluation would be mistaken, for one characteristic which many American bishops shared with their predecessors was pastoral concern, an approach which many Europeans considered to be simply pragmatic. The pastoral approach of the Americans would become manifest particularly in regard to ecumenism and religious liberty.

---

[1] Xavier RYNNE: *Vatican Council II*, New York 1968, p. 206.

On the eve of the council, the American bishops received conflicting signals from the Vatican. On the one hand, John XXIII gave further recognition to the American Church by naming Albert Meyer of Chicago and Aloisius Muench, former nuncio to Germany, cardinals in 1959. Two years later, he raised Joseph Ritter of St. Louis to the cardinalate. There were thus five cardinals in the United States and a sixth American, Muench, resident in Rome. New prelates were also taking the places of the old ones who had presided over the American Church during and after the war. In August, 1960, Cardinal O'Hara died and was replaced by John Krol, former Auxiliary Bishop of Cleveland. In July, 1961, Lawrence Shehan, former Bishop of Bridgeport, was named coadjutor to Archbishop Keough and succeeded to the See of Baltimore in December. In February, 1965, he became the second cardinal to occupy the nation's oldest see. New leaders were therefore going to have to see the American Church through the council.

While the Vatican was bestowing increasing honors on the American Church, it also hampered its preparation for the council. Egidio Vagnozzi had previously served in the apostolic delegation in Washington from 1932 to 1942. As delegate, he sought to retain a Roman hold on the hierarchy. He intruded into the internal affairs of the episcopate on a variety of issues. He had, as was seen, forwarded to Spellman Connell's suggestion that the bishops issue their pastoral letter on Church-State relations in 1960. He also warned the bishops about the use of the vernacular by Oriental-rite priests, lest, "in so doing, they offer to the promotors of the abandonment of the Latin language in the Sacred Liturgy an opportunity to cite as an example and a precedent that which Oriental priests are doing in their midst".[2] Paradoxically, however, his presence may actually have propelled the American Church toward the council, for he antagonized the senior cardinal in the American Church, Francis Spellman. The tension between the cardinal and delegate went back to the early days of their careers when the former was an Auxiliary Bishop of Boston and the latter was auditor of the delegation.

Only slowly did the American Church prepare for the council in those areas where it had the greatest practical experience: ecumenism and religious liberty. Formal participation in the ecumenical movement was gradual. In 1954, the World Council of Churches met in Evanston, Illinois, but the Holy Office on June 17, 1953, forbade Catholics to attend the meeting even as observers.[3] Gustave Weigel, S.J., professor of ecclesiology at Woodstock College who was to become a pioneer in ecumenism, felt at this point that no Catholic could participate in such an organization which at Evanston made an act of contrition for "the sinning Church". For him, the Church was holy and "a holy church by definition

---

[2] AABo, Vagnozzi to Cushing, Washington, Dec. 5, 1959.
[3] AABo, Cicognani to "Your Excellency", Washington, Aug. 7, 1953.

does not sin ...".[4] In August, 1957, however, Dr. Samuel McCrea Cavert, Executive Secretary of the World Council in the United States, through his friend John Wright, then Bishop of Worcester, requested that there be informal Catholic observers at the North American Faith and Order Study Conference to be held in Oberlin, Ohio. Weigel and John Sheerin, C.S.P., editor of the *Catholic World,* were appointed to participate in some of the formal discussions on doctrinal consensus and conflicts held from September 3 to 10, 1958. Afterwards, they submitted a report on the conference to John Krol, Auxiliary Bishop of Cleveland, the diocese in which Oberlin was located.[5] It was a meager beginning of formal ecumenical dialogue, but both priests were positive in their assessment that Catholics should continue to participate in such meetings not only to prevent possible anti-Catholic statements but also to show their common witness to faith in Christ.

In 1960, Weigel, who was to be named an interpreter for the Protestant observers at the council, co-authored a book with a leading Protestant theologian, Robert McAfee Brown. Entitled *American Dialogue: A Protestant Looks at Catholicism and a Catholic Looks at Protestantism,* it was published with the approval of Weigel's superiors and of the Archbishop of Baltimore, but without an *imprimatur.*[6] Formal Catholic-Protestant dialogue in the United States was still tentative and such joint efforts had little canonical precedent. The ecumenical movement in the United States would have to wait for the council to receive the necessary boost.

Prior to the council, however, one of the most interesting ecumenical events was a meeting in Istanbul on Christmas Day, 1959, between Spellman and Patriarch Athenagoras, who had previously been the Metropolitan of the Orthodox Church in New York. Earlier in December, Athenagoras had issued a statement in Jerusalem expressing optimism for the reunion of the Catholic and Orthodox Churches. On December 17, Bishop Griffiths forwarded the statement to Spellman, but he was somewhat reserved about Athenagoras' successor in New York, Archbishop Iakovos. The metropolitan had invited Spellman to his enthronement, which the cardinal could not attend because it would constitute *communicatio in sacris.* This, Griffiths believed, Iakovos knew and had therefore not invited the cardinal to the banquet afterwards which he could have attended. Moreover, while Iakovos had visited both Cardinal Cushing in Boston and Cardinal Emile-Paul Léger in Montreal, he had not visited Spellman. Finally, the me-

---

[4] In: Patrick W. COLLINS: *Gustave Weigel: Ecclesiologist and Ecumenist,* unpublished Ph.D. dissertation, Department of Theology, Fordham University 1972, p. 372.

[5] *Ibid.,* pp. 378–386.

[6] *Ibid.,* p. 397.

tropolitan had formally stated that the Orthodox would not attend the forthcoming council, unless the Protestants were also invited.[7]

Once in Istanbul, Spellman, who was then visiting American troops in Turkey, received an invitation to visit Athenagoras. He and Archbishop Francesco Lardone, the Apostolic Delegate to Turkey and former professor of Roman law at the Catholic University, immediately called on him. After the visit, Spellman cabled the pope for an audience on January 5, 1960, and flew to Rome to present the patriarch's "views to His Holiness and see if some reunion were possible".[8]

Spellman found John XXIII most open to the nascent ecumenical overture, but Cardinal Domenico Tardini, the Secretary of State, less enthusiastic. On January 16, 1960, Tardini wrote the cardinal expressing the pope's appreciation for the patriarch's message and his praise and encouragement of his good intentions Athenagoras, Tardini stated, would have to give his clear opinion that "all dogmatic definitions – ancient and recent – represent one truth which cannot be renounced and which cannot be modified". Finally, the Holy Father was praying "that the Divine Spirit illumine the mind and direct the will toward the auspicious reunion ...".[9]

Spellman's reply was a bit blunt. He thought that in view of the importance of the letter Tardini envisioned being sent to the patriarch, "I would prefer to have you read it before it is sent". He also had no objection in having the letter sent directly from Rome.[10] This Tardini rejected and, after making some alterations, he returned the letter to Spellman.[11] On February 2, the cardinal dispatched the letter to the patriarch. He began by thanking him for "being received by Your Beatitude at such short notice and at such a late hour". He then told of his visit to the pope and of the prayers which the pontiff offered for "the hoped for realization of the prayer of Our Lord that there be one flock and one Shepherd". Before those prayers could "be answered and reunion effected", however, it would be necessary that "the primacy of jurisdiction of the successor of St. Peter ... be believed and admitted ...". He concluded: "I realize, of course, that great difficulties must be encountered and surmounted and that those who lead the journey back to reunion will be greatly criticized and even ostracized; but I do believe that the wounds of many years of separation can be healed and devoted followers of Christ united through the heroic leadership of a great soul like Your Beatitude".[12]

---

[7] AANY, Griffiths to Spellman, New York, Dec. 17, 1959.
[8] AANY, Spellman to "Dear Friends", n.p., "Christmas Night", but probably Dec. 27, 1959.
[9] AANY, Tardini to Spellman, Vatican, Jan. 16, 1960.
[10] AANY, Spellman to Tardini, New York, Jan. 22, 1960 (copy).
[11] AANY, Tardini to Spellman, Vatican, Jan. 30, 1960.
[12] AANY, Spellman to Athenagoras, New York, Feb. 2, 1960 (copy).

Spellman's letter indicated that he and the Holy See, or at least Tardini, at this point envisioned ecumenism in terms of return to Rome rather than of dialogue leading to reunion. More importantly, it may also indicate that the American cardinal was the initial conctact with the patriarch which eventually led to Paul VI's historic meeting with Athenagoras in Jerusalem in January, 1964. Shortly after that meeting, Spellman recounted his earlier role to Vagnozzi. Tardini, he wrote, had deleted "a few sentences from my letter". As a result, "I must say the letter as expurgated was not as cordial as I would like and was not conclusive".[13] During the council, Spellman, like many of the other American bishops, was theologically conservative, but pastorally more progressive than many of his liberally oriented colleagues.

B. Religious Liberty: The American Schema

As preparations for the council got under way in 1959, the first American bishop requested that it deal with religious liberty. The request came, significantly, from Murray's old defender, Karl Alter, the Archbishop of Cincinnati. The next year, Spellman added his voice to what became a growing American demand that the council accept religious liberty as Catholic teaching.[14] Spellman's support would become crucial as the council's debates progressed. Yet, religious liberty underwent a slow evolution.

In June, 1962, the Theological Commission, presided over by Ottaviani, submitted to the Central Preparatory Commission a preliminary schema on the Church which contained a chapter on Church-State relations. In general, it presented the now familiar argument that the Catholic "thesis" was union of Church and State when Catholics were in the majority and "toleration" for any other "hypothesis". At the same time, the newly formed Secretariat for Promoting Christian Unity, under Cardinal Augustin Bea, S.J., a scripture scholar, presented a text on religious liberty as part of its schema on ecumenism. The topic would ultimately be referred exclusively to the Secretariat for further development.[15]

During the summer of 1962, Joseph Fenton prepared to go to the council as a theologian for Ottaviani. Murray prepared to remain at home, "disinvited", as he put it, at the request of the Holy Office and Vagnozzi.[16] Though none of the

---

[13] AANY, Spellman to Vagnozzi, New York, Feb. 26, 1964 (copy).

[14] Vincent A. YZERMANS (ed.): *American Participation in the Second Vatican Council*, New York 1967, pp. 623, 629.

[15] Richard J. REGAN, S.J.: *Conflict and Consensus: Religious Freedom and the Second Vatican Council*, New York 1967, pp. 13–31.

[16] PELOTTE: *Murray*, p. 77.

American bishops risked inviting him as their personal theologian, Archbishop Shehan did consult him on the preliminary schema on the Church. Murray argued that, if the council avoided the Church-State issue, "Ottaviani's 'two standard' theory (what I have called the disjunctive theory) will remain on the books, untouched, as the essential and pure Catholic doctrine ...". He wanted, therefore, to assert that "the whole disjunction, thesis-hypothesis, is invalid in sound and pure Catholic principles, and ought to be discarded. Like its supported concept, the 'Catholic State', it is a time-conditioned disjunction, involved in the relativities of history".[17] Shehan at this point was not about to pick up the banner carried by his predecessor, Gibbons. Nor was Murray for his part about to be defeated by the curial conservatives.

When the first session of the council opened on October 11, 1962, Spellman was appointed to the presidency. But the bishops did not discuss the question of religious liberty. The delay in broaching the all-important question for Americans, however, may have been providential. On April 4, 1963, Spellman gained Murray's appointment as a council *peritus*. Whatever may have been Ottaviani's role up to that point in dominating the discussion of Church-State relations, his principal opponent now had the support of the leading American prelate. As Murray later put it, "it was my Eminent friend of New York who pried me in. He said (and meant it, I think) that the Jesuits had got too slim a deal about *periti*, and that it was 'no more than right' that I in particular should be there".[18] Spellman's assertion that it was "right" for Murray "in particular" to be at the council may have been a veiled hint at his growing opposition to Ottaviani and Vagnozzi. Still, the delegate wielded great influence. Shortly after Murray's appointment, Vagnozzi, through the rector, William J. McDonald, prevented him, Weigel, Hans Küng, and Godfrey Diekmann, another American *peritus*, from speaking at the Catholic University.[19]

Religious liberty according to the American model, in the meantime, received support from a new quarter. On April 11, only a few days after Murray was named a *peritus*, John XXIII issued his encyclical *Pacem in Terris*. He not only spoke of the right of the human person "to honor God according to the sincere dictates of his own conscience, and therefore the right to practice his religion privately and publicly",[20] but he also stated that the primary concern of governments was "to safeguard the inviolable rights of the human person ...".[21] He was

---

[17] AWC, Murray to Shehan, Woodstock, Aug., 1962, in: *ibid.,* pp. 79–80.
[18] Murray to Leo Ward, Woodstock, June 20, 1963, in: *ibid.,* p. 82.
[19] *Ibid.,* p. 81.
[20] JOHN XXIII: *Pacem in Terris,* United States Catholic Conference 1963, p. 6, no. 14.
[21] *Ibid.,* p. 16, no. 60.

reflecting in his thought the rise of the twentieth-century constitutional state, typified by the United States and so different from the nineteenth-century liberal republic which Leo XIII had opposed. The "tendencies" of his day, John wrote, "clearly show that the men of our time are becoming increasingly conscious of their dignity as human persons. This awareness prompts them to claim a share in the public administration of their country, while it also accounts for the demand that their own inalienable and inviolable rights be protected by law. It also requires, that government officials be chosen in conformity with constitutional procedures, and perform their specific functions within the limits of law".[22] Nothing could have been a clearer papal affirmation of what Denis O'Connell had tried to tell his audience at Fribourg in 1897. Now, it provided the needed impetus for Murray and the Americans to assert the advantages of their constitutional system in guaranteeing not only freedom for the Church but also freedom of the person from external coercion in matters of religion.

In early June, 1963, Pope John died. Five American cardinals – the largest number of Americans to take part in a conclave – returned to Rome to elect Cardinal Giovanni Battista Montini as Paul VI. It was a dramatic return from exile of Pius XII's Substitute Secretary of State. He had already played a major role in the first session of the council. Moreover, while he and Spellman had exchanged a sharp series of letters ten years earlier on the precise issue of American religious liberty, he had also supported Murray and may have opposed Ottaviani, at least in the sense of encouraging Stritch that the Roman cardinal's 1953 speech on Church-State relations was not the official Church position.

When the second session opened, Meyer joined Spellman in the council's presidency. The American bishops were beginning to become more of a cohesive group. They had observed other national hierarchies doing what had been regarded as suspicious for Americans – meeting together collegially. No sooner had the session begun than they had to bring this new-found collegial tradition to bear upon promoting religious liberty. Learning that Cardinal Cicognani, the Secretary of State and President of the Coordinating Commission of the Council, had withdrawn religious liberty from the agenda, they assembled at the North American College to discuss their course of action. Murray drafted for them a memorandum demanding that the issue be treated and outlining the content of the proposed document. They unanimously approved the memorandum, drafted a letter which Spellman signed in the name of the hierarchy, and presented their petition to Cicognani, the presidency of the council, and the four moderators. Spellman reportedly also presented the petition personally to the pope who demanded that the Theological Commission consider Chapter V on religious liberty

---

[22] *Ibid.*, p. 20, no. 79.

drafted by the Secretariat in its schema on ecumenism. Had it not been for the united stance of the American bishops, Murray thought, the council might not have considered the issue.[23] The turning point had been reached.

On November 11, 1963, the Theological Commission met. Murray was asked to explain the chapter in the presence of both Ottaviani and Fenton, his arch-opponents. The commission voted eighteen to five to approve the document. A few days later, Murray prevailed on Spellman, once the debate had begun, to "make an intervention in defense of the American Constitutional system and its guarantee of the free exercise of religion". Arguing from the teaching of Pius XI, Pius XII, and John XXIII, he wanted the cardinal to show that not only did the American system have "practical value" but also rested "on sound moral and political doctrine". He wished to demonstrate that "the Catholic Church in America does not 'tolerate' the U.S. constitutional system (this would be nonsense). The American bishops and the American faithful positively approve and support the First Amendment and its provision for the free exercise of religion. They believe that it conforms to the judgment of their civic conscience and of their religious conscience too. They do not consider it to be 'hypothesis' as opposed to 'thesis'. In a word, the American people (here, both Catholic and non-Catholic) believe that there is harmony between their constitutional principles and the doctrine of *Pacem in Terris,* as stated in Chapter V and explained in the *Relatio* of Bishop De Smedt".[24]

On November 19, 1963, De Smedt introduced Chapter V to the council. His *relatio,* substantially the work of Murray, placed the document within the context of the development of papal teachings on religious liberty up to *Pacem in Terris.*[25] After several days of discussion, however, the council voted to accept the first three chapters of the schema on ecumenism but to postpone voting on Chapter V. Even the Secretariat for Promoting Christian Unity saw the advantage of postponing the discussion, for it would now have more time to develop the document.[26]

Though the council would not formally discuss religious liberty during its second session, Cardinals Meyer and Ritter both worked the topic into their interventions in favor of the remaining chapters on ecumenism.[27] The council fathers also heard an example of the American pastoral approach to ecumenism from Stephen Leven, Auxiliary Bishop of San Antonio. There was need, he said, for "a

---

[23] PELOTTE: *Murray,* p. 82.

[24] Murray to Spellman, Rome, Nov. 18, 1963, in: *ibid.,* pp. 83–84.

[25] AWC, Murray to Maher, Rome, Nov. 22, 1963. For a summary of De Smedt's *relatio,* see REGAN: *Conflict and Consensus,* pp. 36–46.

[26] PELOTTE: *Murray,* p. 84; REGAN: *Conflict and Consensus,* pp.46–50.

[27] YZERMANS: *American Participation,* pp. 305–306.

dialogue not only with Protestants, but also among us bishops". So many opponents to collegiality and ecumenism, he continued, "preach to us and chastise us as if we were against Peter and his successors or as if we desired to steal away the faith of our flocks and promote indifferentism. They speak as if our Holy Father, John XXIII, had never cited in our day the expression of St. Augustine: 'They are our brothers; they will not cease to be our brothers until they cease saying Our Father'. They speak as if the whole doctrine of the freedom of conscience due every man, so clearly stated in *Pacem in Terris,* were offensive to pious ears. Again and again in this aula they continue to chastise us as if the prelate who feels compelled by clear evidence to acknowledge the gifts of the Holy Spirit in persons of other ecclesiastical bodies were denying the faith and giving grave scandal to the innocent. They prefer to blame non-Catholics whom, perhaps, they have never seen rather than to instruct children in their parishes. Otherwise, why are they so afraid the effects of ecumenism would not be good? Why are their people not better instructed? Why are their people not visited in their homes? Why is there not an active and working Confraternity of Christian Doctrine in their parishes? It seems the dangers arising from ecumenism may be exaggerated. The prelates who seek a sincere and fruitful dialogue with non-Catholics are not the ones who show disaffection and disloyalty to the Holy Father. It is not our people who miss Mass on Sunday, refuse the sacraments and vote the Communist ticket. ... Our Catholics are good Catholics, loyal to us bishops, to holy Mother Church and to the Holy Father. We have not lost the working class. They are the foundation and the support of the Church".[28] The speech was worthy of one of the American bishops of the previous century. Excerpts of it were given in the *New York Times* as the "Quote of the Day".[29]

As the Secretariat used the period between the second and third sessions to strengthen its document, the forces opposed to it were also mustering their support. Shortly before the close of the second session, Murray had written an article for *America* calling religious liberty "*the* American issue at the Council". He praised the American hierarchy's support for it, but criticized those who tried "to block discussion".[30] This brought forth an admonition from Vagnozzi in the form of a letter to Murray's provincial in New York, John J. McGinty, S.J. The delegate cited norms governing the activities of the *periti* adopted at a meeting of the Coordinating Committee on December 28, 1963. These forbade the *periti* "to organize currents of opinions or ideas, to hold interviews or to defend publicly their personal ideas about the Council". Nor were they to "criticize the Council"

---

[28] In: *ibid.,* pp. 310–311.
[29] *New York Times,* Nov. 27, 1963.
[30] In: PELOTTE: *Murray,* p. 85.

or "communicate to outsiders news about the activities of the Commissions"; they were rather to observe "the decree of the Holy Father about the secret to be observed concerning conciliar matters".[31]

Murray was at that time recovering from a cardiac arrest, so, on February 26, 1964, McGinty wrote him in care of his rector at Woodstock. Only on May 16 did Murray respond. He had received the norms governing the activities of the *periti*, he wrote, but was not yet sure of their precise meaning. The article he had written was the original English version of a press conference he had given to the German-speaking press at the request of the German episcopate. He granted that the new norms might "represent a tightening up", but in the case in point he had done nothing more than the other theologians at the council. More germane to the admonition, however, was "what business is this of the Apostolic Delegate", who was "in no sense an official of the Council" and had "no jurisdiction whatever over the activities of the periti?" In Murray's mind, "the Apostolic Delegate has elected to be my personal enemy and he has made statements about me throughout the country which are libelous". But he remained optimistic, for "if there should be any trouble in my own case, which is hardly likely, I am sure that his Eminence of New York will stand behind me. He is one of the few American bishops who can be counted on to talk back to the Delegate. And he has – bless his heart – elected to be my patron. He mentioned to me in Rome that he had read the article in AMERICA and liked it".[32]

Murray then wrote Vagnozzi a letter, which is unfortunately lost. The delegate responded that he had written the provincial "at the direction of the Holy See" and would forward Murray's letter to Rome.[33] It was somewhat ironic that Spellman who had looked with such disfavor on Murray's earlier involvement in the National Conference of Christians and Jews could now be counted on for support against the apostolic delegate.

While the proponents of religious liberty continued to battle the curial opposition, the American opponents lost a powerful spokesman as Monsignor Fenton resigned as editor of the *American Ecclesiastical Review* and retired to a parish after the second session.[34] Yet the problem remained, as Murray told his rector in November, 1963, of the "enigmatic figure of Paul VI".[35] The new pope would continue to be an enigma during the third session.

On September 21, 1964, Murray addressed the American bishops on the new

---

[31] In: AWC, McGinty to Murray, New York, Feb. 26, 1964.
[32] AWC, Murray to McGinty, Woodstock, May 16, 1964.
[33] AWC, Vagnozzi to Murray, Washington, May 21, 1964.
[34] PELOTTE: *Murray*, p. 87.
[35] AWC, Murray to Maher, Rome, Nov. 22, 1963.

text of religious liberty, now a totally separate document from the schema on ecumenism. Despite the objections of Murray's old antagonists, Connell and Shea, the bishops unanimously agreed to accept the text as a point of departure for further discussion and to have at least eight of their number speak on the issue. Two days later, De Smedt formally introduced the new text. In the debate which followed, Cardinals Cushing, Ritter, Meyer, Archbishop Alter, Bishops Ernest Primeau of Manchester and John Wright of Pittsburgh, and Father Joseph Buckley, S.M., Superior General of the Marists, all spoke in favor of the declaration.[36] On September 25, the council fathers overwhelmingly voted to end debate and to have the Secretariat revise the text.

De Smedt designated Murray as the "first scribe" to begin drafting a new text. Collaborating with him was Monsignor Pietro Pavan of the Lateran University, whose ideas coincided with Murray's. They were assisted by Bishop Jan Willebrands, Father Jerome Hamer, O.P., and De Smedt himself. Their work was proceeding smoothly until October 9, when Cardinal Bea announced to the Secretariat a new obstructionist tactic. Archbishop Pericle Felici, the Secretary General of the Council, had written him that Paul VI wished a mixed-commission to examine and revise the document. The commission was to be composed of Cardinal Michael Browne, O.P., Aniceto Fernandez, O.P., Master General of the Dominicans, Archbishop Marcel Lefebvre, Superior General of the Order of the Holy Spirit, and Bishop Carlo Colombo. The first three were arch-opponents of the declaration.[37] Religious liberty, in fact, was but one in a series of issues which subsequently led Lefebvre to oppose all the council's reforms and to be suspended from exercising his faculties.

Felici's action was a violation of the rules of the council, which provided for a mixed commission to be nominated by both the Theological Commission and the Secretariat. On October 10, ten cardinals met at the residence of Cardinal Josef Frings, Archbishop of Cologne, and drafted a letter to the pope protesting the violation of the council's rules and the removal of the schema from the Secretariat. Among the signers were two Americans, Meyer and Ritter. Subsequently eight more cardinals signed the letter which was presented to the pope on October 12. The next day, Frings had a long audience with Paul VI, who assured him that the schema would remain under the direction of the Secretariat, but would be examined by a joint commission drawn from the Secretariat and the Theological Commission. Bea and Ottaviani accordingly submitted ten names each to the pope who chose five from each list to compose a new mixed-commis-

---

[36] RYNNE: *Vatican Council II*, pp. 296–303. Texts of the interventions are given in: YZERMANS: *American Participation*, pp. 643–656.

[37] REGAN: *Conflict and Consensus*, pp. 95–97.

sion. Of the original names proposed by Felici only Cardinal Browne and Bishop Colombo remained. The cardinals' protest had safeguarded the council's rules and had prevented the desperate efforts of the minority to sabotage the discussion of religious liberty.[38]

In the meantime, the Secretariat had proceeded in revising its text. Though De Smedt continued to oppose Murray and Pavan's legal and juridical emphasis, the Secretariat unanimously approved the new draft on October 24. The joint commission then examined it and only one representative of the Theological Commission rejected it. Murray and Hamer then wrote an introduction to answer the objections to the principle of religious liberty. On November 17, the text was distributed to the bishops. The vote on it was scheduled for two days later.

Murray himself admitted that the text presented to the third session was the least desirable of the various drafts through which it had gone as the Secretariat sought to appease the minority.[39] Nevertheless, he and the majority of the bishops thought that it was imperative that the council formally vote on the prepared text. The bishops were to vote on November 19 after completing their discussion of the declaration on Christian education. Shortly after 11 o'clock, Archbishop Dino Staffa, Secretary of the Congregation of Seminaries and Universities and a known opponent to religious liberty, approached Cardinal Eugene Tisserant, seated at the middle of the presidents' table. The cardinal immediately conferred with the presidents near him and then rose to make an announcement: "Several fathers are of the opinion that not enough time has been allowed for an examination of the text on Religious Liberty, which appears to be an essentially new document. Therefore it has seemed best to the Council presidents, in conformity with the rules, not to proceed to a vote as announced. After the *relatio* on the declaration of Bishop De Smedt, there will be no vote. The Fathers can then examine the document at their leisure and send their observations to the Secretariat by January 31, 1965".[40]

It was a bombshell, but one which the schema's proponents should have expected. Cardinal Meyer, who was sitting at the end of the presidents' table, rose and went around to the front of the table to confront Tisserant. As one of the presidents, he said, he had not been consulted, but Tisserant refused to reverse the decision. As Meyer muttered "this man is hopeless", De Smedt began reading the introduction to what was indeed a new schema. Deprived of their chance to vote on religious liberty, the bishops showed their approval by frequently interrupting De Smedt with applause. On the council floor, pandemonium had broken out.

---

[38] *Ibid.*, pp. 97–98.
[39] PELOTTE: *Murray*, pp. 95–96. See RYNNE: *Vatican Council II*, pp. 416–417.
[40] In: RYNNE: *Vatican Council II*, p. 418.

Meyer joined a rapidly growing circle of bishops and *periti,* who drafted a petition to the pope that a vote be taken on religious liberty before the end of the session. Their rapidly circulated petition had over a thousand signatures by the afternoon. But despite this and a personal visit to Paul VI by Cardinals Meyer, Ritter, and Léger, the pope refused to alter Tisserant's decision but guaranteed that religious liberty would be the first item on the agenda for the fourth session.[41]

It was initially a bleak day for the Americans and other supporters of the schema – they dubbed it "Black Thursday". Shortly after returning from the third session, however, Murray was regaining his composure and predicted that the obstructionist tactics of the minority would actually contribute to a stronger document. In an article for *America,* he noted that factors other than curial opposition had postponed the discussion. First, there was the opposition of those who simply could not accept the development of doctrine. Second, there was disagreement over methodology. He and the English-speaking and Italian proponents took a legal and political situation as the starting point and then supported it with theological and ethical principles. The French-speaking theorists, on the other hand, began with the theological and ethical principles from which they derived a juridical notion of religious liberty. Third, there were some who feared that acceptance of religious liberty would introduce liberty within the Church. Finally, since discussion of religious liberty had been repressed in the Church, it was difficult for the council to find the proper vocabulary to arrive at a consensus on what was basically a new theological topic.[42] To gain a consensus, it would ultimately be necessary to reconcile the two conflicting methodologies. By May, 1965, the Secretariat had distributed a new schema for discussion at the fourth session.

During the summer, Murray was in correspondence with Guy de Broglie, S.J., the principal spokesman for the French theological approach. Soon the American "pragmatic" approach gained the French support of Joseph Sauvage, Bishop of Annecy, and Yves Congar, O.P. On September 15, 1965, the day after the fourth session opened, the bishops turned to the first item on the agenda, the Declaration on Religious Liberty. Following De Smedt's introduction, the debate began. Missing from the supporters of religious liberty was Cardinal Meyer who had died shortly before and who was replaced as Archbishop of Chicago by John Cody, former Archbishop of New Orleans. Spellman led the Americans in favor of the declaration followed by Cushing, Ritter, Shehan, Archbishop Paul Halli-

---

[41] *Ibid.,* pp. 418–420; YZERMANS: *American Participation,* pp. 619–620. For an analysis of De-Smedt's *relatio,* see REGAN: *Conflict and Consensus,* pp. 100–114.

[42] John Courtney MURRAY: *This Matter of Religious Freedom,* in: America 112 (Jan. 9, 1965) 40–43, cited in: PELOTTE: *Murray,* p. 96.

nan of Atlanta, and Bishop Charles Maloney, Auxiliary Bishop of Louisville. On September 21, the historic vote was taken to close debate on the schema with 1,997 voting in favor and 224 against.

The text was then returned to the Secretariat for final revision. Murray was, unfortunately, hospitalized with a collapsed lung. The revision was the work of Bishops De Smedt, Willebrands, Alfred Ancel, and Carlo Colombo, with theological assistance from Pavan, Hamer, Congar, and Pierre Benoit, O.P. On October 25, the council overwhelmingly approved this text with some minor revisions. On December 7, the final vote took place. 2,308 bishops voted in favor, 70 against, and 8 cast invalid ballots.[43] At long last, the peculiar tradition of the American Church was Catholic teaching. American democracy and ideas of freedom were no longer construed in terms of nineteenth-century European liberalism, but in terms of British and American Common Law, which underlay the twentieth-century constitutional forms of government. The American Church no longer lived in "the shadow of a hypothesis".

C. AFTERMATH OF THE COUNCIL

A full study of the American participation in the Second Vatican Council lies beyond the scope of this work. The Declaration on Religious Liberty, however, was the American contribution to the council. It was the one issue in which the American Church had had a long practical experience, though it had so often been misunderstood in Rome. To other conciliar documents the American bishops made less of a contribution. They had lost sight, for example, of their predecessors' tradition of collegiality. In Spellman's intervention on the Bishops' Pastoral Office, he cited the theology he had learned in school that "the authority of the Supreme Pontiff is supreme and full in itself. It is not necessary that he share it with others, even if they are bishops whose collaboration in governing the universal Church can be asked for by the Supreme Pontiff himself, but is neither necessary nor essential". It was likewise not for the bishops, he continued, either "to judge" or "to reform" the Roman Curia.[44] Paradoxically, Spellman made his intervention on November 11, 1963, at the very time that he was leading the American protest to have religious liberty restored to the council's agenda. He was unable to see the logical connection between his practice and his theoretical stance against collegiality.

On the formation of episcopal conferences, one of which had been in existence

---

[43] PELOTTE: *Murray*, pp. 99–100.
[44] In: YZERMANS: *American Participation*, p. 382.

in the United States since 1919, the Americans also displayed a wide spectrum of views. McIntyre objected to the introduction of any juridical element into the decisions of a conference which would bind local bishops – reminiscent of McDonnell's position in 1919. Ritter, on the other hand, wished to see conferences vested with juridical authority, so that they could each speak with an unanimous voice in their nations, represent the needs of their churches to the Holy See, and thus better assist the pope in the exercise of his authority over each of the churches. Meyer took the middle ground, finally adopted by the council, by calling for conference presidents to be elected by secret ballot and for decisions to be juridically binding only in those areas which were part of the common law of the Church or were mandated by the pope.[45]

In conformity with the council's decrees, the NCWC was transformed into the National Conference of Catholic Bishops (NCCB) with a standing secretariat, the United States Catholic Conference (USCC). Only gradually in the years after the council, however, did the American bishops begin to see what their nineteenth-century predecessors had seen: that true loyalty to the Holy See might mean a respectful representation based on pastoral experience.[46]

The Americans made more of a contribution to the decree on ecumenism, but they were not the leaders. Only after the council did the American Church move to the forefront of the ecumenical movement with the establishment of theological commissions to promote the dialogue with each of the other major denominations. The American initiative was made possible partly by the increase in the number of biblical scholars, many of whom had studied in the same universities as their Protestant counterparts in the years after the Second World War. In this area, the American Church might well have an advantage over European Churches, for, while there was strong anti-Catholic prejudice, there was not the intellectual and historical baggage of *cuius regio eius religio*.

In relationship with the government, issues which formerly aroused anti-Catholicism have died out. Here the election of John Kennedy was the watershed and since 1960 several Catholics have made their bid for the presidency without the religious question being raised. On a less significant level, President Richard M. Nixon restored the post of personal representative to the pope by appointing Henry Cabot Lodge during the summer of 1970. Presidents Gerald Ford, Jimmy Carter and Ronald Reagan then continued the office. While there had been almost no criticism of these presidential actions, there was also little indication that the United States and the Holy See would establish formal diplomatic relations.

---

[45] *Ibid.*, pp. 370–372, 381–386.
[46] See Gerald P. FOGARTY: *Independence: The 'Anomaly' of the American Church,* in: America 130 (June 1, 1974) 430–432; and Donald R. CAMPION: *Of Many Things,* in: *ibid.* (June 22, 1974).

In 1977, Senator Richard Stone of Florida attached an amendment to an appropriations bill from the House of Representatives to repeal legislation from 1867 cutting off funds for an American representative to the Holy See. Passed in the Senate, the amendment lost in a Senate-House conference. In June, 1983, however, Congressman Clement J. Zablocki of Wisconsin introduced a similar amendment to the house appropriations bill, which passed with only a voice vote. In September, Senator Richard Lugar of Indiana sponsored a similar amendment, which passed by a voice vote, with no recorded dissenters. In November, shortly after a visit from Cardinal Agostino Casaroli, the Secretary of State, President Reagan signed the legislation. Almost none of these activities, including Casaroli's visit, attracted publicity from the secular press.[47]

On January 10, 1984, the Holy See announced that it was establishing full diplomatic relations with the United States. Several hours later, the White House made a similar announcement and Reagan nominated William Wilson, then his personal representative, as the first ambassador. On March 7, the Senate confirmed Wilson by a vote of 81 to 13 — a stark contrast to the situation Spellman had reported in 1953.[48] Archbishop Pio Laghi, the apostolic delegate, then became the pro-nuncio, the first papal diplomat accredited to the United States government. While there have been some protests against diplomatic relations with the Holy See, these have been largely pro-forma, with none of the anti-Catholicism which accompanied the Myron Taylor appointment or the Mark Clark nomination. On a more popular level, however, other issues continue to arouse anti-Catholic feelings, notably the Church's campaign for public aid to parochial schools and against abortion.

Though Catholics have now established rapport with their fellow Americans, areas of potential tension remain between the American Church and the Vatican. The Declaration on Religious Liberty signalled the Vatican's acceptance of a cherished American Catholic principle, but the philosophy of law underlying that principle is still a source of misunderstanding. The criticism of the American "pragmatic" approach to religious liberty at the council could be reduced to a criticism of the type of legal system within which American Catholics live – the British and American Common Law. To discuss this legal system with its inalienable rights and its laws which are not codified still arouses in the European mind the fear that the discussion is about introducing democracy into the Church.

---

[47] The passage in the Senate of the repeal of the legislation of 1867, for example was reported in *The International Herald-Tribune* on Sept. 24, 1983, but was not reported in that paper's owners, *The New York Times, The Washington Post,* or *The Los Angeles Times.* Casaroli's visit also went unreported in those papers.

[48] *New York Times,* Mar. 8, 1984.

Short of democratizing the Church, however, the issue of freedom within the Church remains. Commenting on the Declaration on Religious Liberty, John Courtney Murray predicted that from the declaration a "great argument will be set afoot – now on the theological meaning of Christian freedom. The children of God, who received this freedom as a gift from their Father through Christ in the Holy Spirit, assert it within the Church as well as within the world, always for the sake of the world and the Church. The issues are many – the dignity of the Christian, the foundations of Christian freedom, its object or content, its limits and their criterion, the measure of its responsible use, its relation to the legitimate reaches of authority and to the saving counsels of prudence, the perils that lurk in it, and the forms of corruption to which it is prone. All these issues must be considered in a spirit of sober and informed reflection".[49] Murray would have found himself at home with those Americanists at the end of the last century who saw the compatibility of the Common Law with the dignity conferred on the human person in Baptism.

Murray had not explicitly mentioned the Common Law, but the advantages of the latter formed part of the thrust of the address of Stephan Kuttner on the occasion of the fiftieth anniversary of the promulgation of the Code of Canon Law. Noting that the Church had accommodated itself to known secular legal systems in adopting the Roman Law, he pointed out that few contemporary nations continued to be governed by that form of law. He had only to cite the Slavic World, the East, Mid East, India, and Africa, where legal systems had developed independently from Roman jurisprudence. Moreover, he continued, "there exists a legal culture which is much closer to us and a part of Western civilization, yet neither Roman nor Romanesque: that of the Common Law – the law which not only governs the nations joined in the British Commonwealth but also forms the basis of the legal order of the United States of America. Its history is part of the medieval and modern tradition of Christian society. Medieval canon law has contributed not a little to its historical development. Nevertheless, the Common Law is even today largely ignored or badly understood by the civil lawyers and canonists of continental Europe. Since it is not a codified law ..., some writers even today would classify it as mere custom – a concept for which the *Codex juris canonici* has maintained the same diffidence as that displayed by Byzantine law. This inadequate classification of a legal order which embodies a highly developed juridical culture is as absurd as if one were to define the Atlantic Ocean as a lake. Perhaps it is not an exaggeration to say that ignorance of the systems of law

---

[49] In: Walter M. ABBOTT, and Joseph GALLAGHER (eds.): *The Documents of Vatican II*, New York 1966, p. 674.

which are not in the Roman pandectistic tradition is one of the most keenly felt limitations of our present Code of Canon Law".[50]

These different approaches to and philosophies of law are, therefore, almost certainly bound to lead to further tensions – and developments. Americans and others who live under the Common Law enact laws only when fundamental rights are believed to be in conflict. They accept personal freedom as a given but also as limited by the correlative responsibility to acknowledge the rights of others. American speech about "freedom", therefore, frequently sounds to the European like a plea for that type of democracy reminiscent of the French Revolution – the exaltation of human reason above all authority. There is, in other words, a communication gap. The American and European Churches still have much to learn from one another.

The Common Law not only provides the basis for American religious liberty; it also created the conditions which led to the strong sense of collegiality among nineteenth-century American bishops.[51] This legal tradition has, moreover, helped shape a milieu from which is derived a non-European approach to pastoral problems. This, too, can lead to misunderstanding. In 1899, the Americanists were accused of watering down doctrine in an effort to win converts, when in fact they were trying to build upon the Christian truth already held by Protestants. In 1980, at the fifth Synod of Bishops, Archbishop John R. Quinn of San Francisco received strong criticism for his intervention recognizing that many Catholic men and women together with many pastors and theologians do not accept the "intrinsic evil of each and every use of contraception". Dissent, he said, was therefore a fact in the pastoral life of the Church. Noting that the Church "has always recognized the principle and fact of development" he proposed that the Church place its teaching in a context geared to reach the people, encourage theologians and the Holy See to dialogue on the meaning of this dissent, and take care in the writing and communication of its magisterial pronouncements. To his European critics the archbishop seemed to be advocating a change in the Church's teaching, whereas in fact, while noting "doctrinal development", he was concerned with a pastoral (practical) problem, not a theological (theoretical) issue.[52]

Despite the tensions which have existed and will probably continue to exist between the Vatican and the American Church, the latter has become a thriving branch of the Church universal. It continues to grow and to manifest its ethnic

---

[50] Stephan G. KUTTNER: *The Code of Canon Law in Historical Perspective*, in: The Jurist 28 (1968) 146–147.

[51] Cf. FOGARTY: *Church Councils*, p. 104.

[52] Richard A. MCCORMICK: *Notes on Moral Theology: 1980*, in: Theological Studies 42 (Mar., 1981) 112.

pluralism. The development from 1870 to 1981 had been dramatic. From 46 dioceses in 1870, the Church grew to 33 archdioceses and 138 dioceses in 1981. Among these were 8 dioceses for Oriental-rite Catholics: the Byzantine Archeparchy of Philadelphia for Ukrainians with suffragan sees in Stamford, Connecticut, and St. Nicholas of Chicago; the Byzantine Archeparchy of Pittsburgh for Ruthenians with suffragan sees in Parma, Ohio, and Passaic, New Jersey; the Maronite Exarchate of St. Maron in Brooklyn; and the Melkite Exarchate of Newton, Massachusetts. There were 10 cardinals, including 4 who were retired and 1 serving in the Roman Curia; another cardinal was in Puerto Rico. There were altogether 40 archbishops and 311 bishops. Catholics numbered 50,449,842 out of a total population of 223,066,798 or 22.6% of the American people.[53] Over the century covered in this study, the American Church has evolved from being a Church in a missionary country to a Church which sends missionaries to foreign countries, from a Church existing in a little known republic to a Church expressing Catholicism in the nation which holds the balance of power in the western world. History alone will attest to the contribution which its size and power will make to future developments of the Catholic Church.

---

[53] Statistics derived from *The Official Catholic Directory, 1981,* New York 1981.

BIBLIOGRAPHY AND SOURCES

A. ARCHIVES AND MANUSCRIPT COLLECTIONS:

Archives of the Archdiocese of Baltimore, 320 Cathedral Street, Baltimore, Maryland 21201.

Archives of the Archdiocese of Boston, 2121 Commonwealth Avenue, Brighton, Massachusetts 02135.

Archives of the Archdiocese of Chicago, St. Mary of the Lake Seminary, Mundelein, Illinois 60060.

Archives of the Archdiocese of Cincinnati, Mt. St. Mary's Seminary of the West, 5440 Moeller Avenue, Norwood, Ohio 45212.

Archives of the Archdiocese of Detroit, 1234 Washington Boulevard, Detroit, Michigan 48226.

Archives of the Archdiocese of Indianapolis, microfilm, University of Notre Dame, Notre Dame, Indiana 46556.

Archives of the Archdiocese of Los Angeles, 1531 West 9th St., Los Angeles, California 90015.

Archives of the Archdiocese of New York, St. Joseph's Seminary, Dunwoodie, Yonkers, New York 10704.

Archives of the Archdiocese of Philadelphia, 222 North Seventeenth St., Philadelphia, Pennsylvania 19103.

Archives of the Archdiocese of San Francisco, P.O. Box 1799, Colma, California 94014.

Archives of the Archdiocese of St. Paul, St. Paul Seminary, 2200 Grand Avenue, St. Paul, Minnesota 55101.

Archives of the Abbey of St. Paul's Outside the Walls, Rome. Microfilm, University of Notre Dame, Notre Dame, Indiana 46556.

Archives of Civiltà Cattolica, Via di Porta Pinciana 1, Rome 00187, Italy.

Archives of the Congregation of St. Paul the Apostle, 415 West 59th St., New York, New York 10019.

Archives of the Catholic University of America, Washington, D.C. 20064.

Archives of the Diocese of Cleveland, 1027 Superior Avenue, Cleveland, Ohio 44114.

Archives of the Diocese of Richmond, 800 Cathedral Place, Richmond, Virginia 23203.

Archives of the Diocese of Rochester, St. Bernard's Seminary, 2260 Lake Avenue, Rochester, New York 14612.

Archives of Georgetown University, Lauinger Library, Georgetown University, Washington, D.C. 20057.

Archives of the Josephite Fathers, 1130 North Calvert St., Baltimore, Maryland 21202.

Archives of the Maryland Province of the Society of Jesus, Lauinger Library, Georgetown University, Washington, D.C. 20057.

Archives of the National Catholic Welfare Conference, 1312 Massachusetts Avenue, N.W., Washington, D.C. 20005.

Archives of the Pontifical German-Hungarian College, Via S. Nicola da Tolentino 13, Rome 00187, Italy.

Archives of the Roman Curia of the Society of Jesus, Borgo Santo Spirito 5, Rome 00193, Italy.

Archives of the Sacred Congregation de Propaganda Fide, Piazza di Spagna 48, Rome 00187, Italy.

Archives of St. Mary's Seminary, 5400 Roland Avenue, Baltimore, Maryland 21210.

Archives of the University of Notre Dame, Notre Dame, Indiana 46556.
Archives of Woodstock College, Lauinger Library, Georgetown University, Washington, D.C. 20057.
Archivio Segreto Vaticano, Vatican City State.
Franklin D. Roosevelt Library, Hyde Park, New York 12538.
George C. Marshall Papers, Virginia Military Institute, Lexington, Virginia 24450.
National Archives of the United States of America, Washington, D.C. 20408.

B. Printed Sources:

Acta et Decreta Concilii Plenarii Baltimorensis Tertii. Baltimore 1886.
Acta et Decreta Concilii Plenarii Baltimorensis Tertii in ecclesia Metropolitana Baltimorensi habita a die IX. Novembris usque ad diem VII. Decembris, A.D. MDCCCLXXXIV. Baltimore 1884.
BLET, Pierre, MARTINI, Angelo, GRAHAM, Robert, and SCHNEIDER, Burkhart (eds.): *Actes et documents du Saint Siège relatifs à La Seconde Guerre Mondiale,* 8 vols. Vatican 1965–1980.
BLET, Pierre, MARTINI, Angelo, and SCHNEIDER, Burkhart (eds.): *The Holy See and the War in Europe: March 1939–August 1940.* Translated by Gerard Noel. Washington 1965.
Concilii Plenarii Baltimorensis II., in Ecclesia Metropolitana Baltimorensi, a die VII., ad diem XII. Octobris, A.D. MDCCCLXVI., habiti, et a Sede Apostolica recogniti, Decreta. Baltimore 1866.
FERRELL, Robert H. (ed.): *Off the Record: The Private Papers of Harry S. Truman.* New York 1980.
Foreign Relations of the United States: Diplomatic Papers. Washington: United States Government Printing Office.
GIBBONS, James Cardinal: *A Retrospect of Fifty Years,* 2 vols. Baltimore 1916.
GILSON, Etienne (ed.): *The Church Speaks to the Modern World: Social Teachings of Leo XIII.* New York 1954.
HOUTIN, Albert: *L'Américanisme.* Paris 1904.
HUBER, Raphael M. (ed.): *Our Bishops Speak: National Pastorals and Annual Statements of the Hierarchy of the United States, 1919–1951.* Milwaukee 1952.
HULL, Cordell: *The Memoirs of Cordell Hull,* 2 vols. New York 1948.
ICKES, Harold L.: *The Secret Diary of Harold L. Ickes,* 2 vols. New York 1954.
IRELAND, John: *The Church and Modern Society,* 2 vols. St. Paul 1905.
KLEIN, Felix: *Americanism: A Phantom Heresy.* Atchison, Ka. 1951.
MAIGNEN, Charles: *Father Hecker: Is he a Saint?* Rome 1898.
NOLAN, Hugh J. (ed.): *Pastoral Letters of the American Hierarchy, 1792–1970.* Huntington, Ind. 1971.
O'CONNELL, William Cardinal: *Recollections of Seventy Years.* New York 1934.
SATOLLI, Francesco: *Loyalty to Church and State.* Edited by John R. SLATTERY. Baltimore 1895.
Wartime Correspondence between President Roosevelt and Pope Pius XII. With an Introduction and Explanatory Notes by Myron C. TAYLOR. New York 1947.

C. Books:

ABELL, Aaron I.: *American Catholicism and Social Action.* Notre Dame, Ind. 1963.
AHERN, Patrick H.: *The Catholic University of America, 1887–1896: The Rectorship of John J. Keane.* Washington 1948.
AHERN, Patrick H.: *The Life of John J. Keane, Educator and Archbishop.* Milwaukee 1955.
AUBERT, Roger: *Le Pontificat de Pie IX (1846–1878),* vol. 21 of *Histoire de l'église depuis les origines jusquà nos jours,* edited by Augustin FLICHE and Victor MARTIN. Paris 1952.

BARRY, Colman J.: *The Catholic Church and German-Americans*. Milwaukee 1953.

BARRY, Colman J.: *The Catholic University of America: 1903–1909: The Rectorship of Denis J. O'Connell*. Washington 1950.

BARRY, Colman J.: *Upon These Rocks: Catholics in the Bahamas*. Collegeville, Minn. 1973.

BRESLIN, Thomas A.: *China, American Catholicism, and the Missionary*. University Park, Pa. 1980.

BRODERICK, Francis L.: *Right Reverend New Dealer: John A. Ryan*. New York 1963.

BROWNE, Henry J.: *The Catholic Church and the Knights of Labor*. Washington 1949.

BUEHRLE, Marie Cecilia: *The Cardinal Stritch Story*. Milwaukee 1959.

CALLAHAN, Nelson J.: *A Case for Due Process In the Church: Father Eugene O'Callaghan, American Pioneer of Dissent*. Staten Island, N.Y. 1971.

COLLINS, Patrick: *Gustave Weigel: Ecclesiologist and Ecumenist*. Unpublished Ph.D. dissertation, Fordham University, N.Y. 1972.

CONNELLY, James P. (ed.): *The History of the Archdiocese of Philadelphia*. Philadelphia 1976.

CONNELLY, James P.: *The Visit of Archbishop Gaetano Bedini to the United States of America (June, 1853–February, 1854)*, Vol. 109 of Analecta Gregoriana. Roma 1960.

CROSBY, Donald F.: *God, Church, and Flag: Senator Joseph R. McCarthy and the Catholic Church*. Chapel Hill 1978.

CROSS, Robert D.: *The Emergence of Liberal Catholicism in America*. Cambridge, Mass. 1958.

CURRAN, Robert Emmett: *Michael Augustine Corrigan and the Shaping of Conservative Catholicism in America, 1878–1902*. New York 1978.

DEVITO, Michael J.: *Principles of Ecclesiastical Reform According to the New York Review*. New York 1977.

ELLIS, John Tracy: *The Life of James Cardinal Gibbons: Archbishop of Baltimore, 1834–1921*, 2 vols. Milwaukee 1952.

FALCONI, Carlo: *The Popes in the Twentieth Century: From Pius X to John XXIII*. Translated by Muriel Grindrod. Boston 1967.

FALCONI, Carlo: *The Silence of Pius XII*. Translated by Bernard Wall. Boston 1970.

FLYNN, George Q.: *American Catholics and the Roosevelt Presidency, 1932–1936*. Lexington, Ky. 1968.

FLYNN, George Q.: *Roosevelt and Romanism: Catholics and American Diplomacy, 1937–1945*. Westport, Conn. 1976.

FOGARTY, Gerald P.: *The Vatican and the Americanist Crisis: Denis J. O'Connell, American Agent in Rome*, vol. 36 of *Miscellanea Historiae Pontificiae*. Roma 1974.

GAFFEY, James P.: *Citizen of No Mean City: Archbishop Patrick Riordan of San Francisco (1841–1914)*. Wilmington 1976.

GAFFEY, James P.: *Francis Clement Kelley & the American Catholic Dream*, 2 vols. Bensenville, Ill. 1980.

GANNON, Robert I.: *The Cardinal Spellman Story*. Garden City, N.Y. 1962.

GLEASON, Philip: *The Conservative Reformers: German-American Catholics and the Social Order*. Notre Dame 1968.

GUILDAY, Peter: *The Life and Times of John England, First Bishop of Charleston: 1786–1842*, 2 vols. New York 1927.

HENNESEY, James J.: *American Catholics: A History of the Roman Catholic Community in the United States*. New York 1981.

HENNESEY, James J.: *The First Council of the Vatican: The American Experience*. New York 1963.

HIGHAM, John: *Strangers in the Land: Patterns of American Nativism*. New York 1965.

HOGAN, Peter E.: *The Catholic University of America: 1896–1903: The Rectorship of Thomas J. Conaty*. Washington 1949.

HOLDEN, Vincent F.: *The Yankee Paul: Isaac Thomas Hecker.* Milwaukee 1958.

KUZNIEWSKI, Anthony J.: *Faith and Fatherland: The Polish Church War in Wisconsin.* Notre Dame 1980.

LECANUET, Edouard: *Les premières années du pontificat de Leon XIII, 1878–1894.* Paris 1931.

LESLIE, Shane: *Henry Edward Manning: His Life and Letters.* London 1921.

McAVOY, Thomas T.: *Father O'Hara of Notre Dame: The Cardinal-Archbishop of Philadelphia.* Notre Dame 1967.

McAVOY, Thomas T.: *The Great Crisis in American Catholic History: 1895–1900.* Chicago 1957.

McNAMARA, Robert F.: *The American College in Rome, 1855–1955.* Rochester 1956.

MARCUS, Sheldon: *Father Coughlin: The Tumultuous Life of the Priest of the Little Flower.* Boston 1973.

MEYER, Jean A.: *The Cristero Rebellion: The Mexican People between Church and State, 1926–1929.* Translated by Richard Southern. Cambridge 1976.

MOYNIHAN, James: *The Life of Archbishop John Ireland.* New York 1953.

O'SHEA, J.J.: *The Two Archbishops Kenrick.* Philadelphia 1904.

PARSONS, Wilfrid: *Mexican Martyrdom.* New York 1936.

PELLEGRINO CONFESSORE, Ornella: *Conservatorismo politico e riformismo: La Rassegna nazionale dal 1898 al 1908.* Bologna 1971.

PELOTTE, Donald E.: *John Courtney Murray: Theologian in Conflict.* New York 1975.

POULAT, Emile: *Intégrisme et catholicisme intégral: un réseau secret international antimoderniste: La "Sapinière" (1909–1921).* Tournai 1969.

QUIRK, Robert E.: *The Mexican Revolution and the Catholic Church: 1910–1929.* Bloomington, Ind. 1973.

REGAN, Richard J.: *Conflict and Consensus: Religious Freedom and the Second Vatican Council.* New York 1967.

REHER, Margaret M.: *The Church and the Kingdom of God in America: The Ecclesiology of the Americanists.* Unpublished Ph.D. dissertation, Fordham University, N.Y. 1972.

REILLY, Daniel F.: *The School Controversy, 1891–1893.* Washington 1943.

REUTER, Frank T.: *Catholic Influence on American Colonial Policies: 1898–1904.* Austin, Tex. 1967.

RHODES, Anthony: *The Vatican in the Age of the Dictators (1922–1945).* New York 1974.

RICE, Sr. M. Elizabeth Ann: *The Diplomatic Relations between the United States and Mexico, as Affected by the Struggle for Religious Liberty in Mexico, 1925–1929.* Washington 1959.

RYNNE, Xavier: *Vatican Council II.* New York 1968.

SCHMIDLIN, Josef: *Papstgeschichte der neuesten Zeit,* Bd. II: *Papsttum und Päpste gegenüber den modernen Strömungen: Pius IX. und Leo XIII. (1846–1903).* Munich 1934.

SHAUGHNESSY, Gerald: *Has the Immigrant Kept the Faith?: A Study of Immigration and Catholic Growth in the United States, 1790–1920.* New York 1925.

SHEERIN, John B.: *Never Look Back: The Career and Concerns of John J. Burke.* New York 1975.

SMITH, R. Harris: *OSS: The Secret History of America's First Central Intelligence Agency.* Berkeley 1972.

SWEENEY, David Francis: *The Life of John Lancaster Spalding: First Bishop of Peoria, 1840–1916.* New York 1965.

TANNENBAUM, Frank: *Mexico, The Struggle for Peace and Bread.* New York 1950.

TULL, Charles J.: *Father Coughlin and the New Deal.* Syracuse 1965.

VON SCHLÖZER, Leopold: *Kurd von Schlözer: Letzte römische Briefe 1882–1894.* Stuttgart–Berlin–Leipzig 1924.

WALLACE, Lillian Parker: *Leo XIII and the Rise of Socialism.* Durham, N.C. 1966.

WAYMAN, Dorothy G.: *Cardinal O'Connell of Boston: A Biography of William Henry O'Connell, 1859–1944.* New York 1955.

WEBER, Ralph: *Notre Dame's John Zahm: American Catholic Apologist and Educator.* Notre Dame 1961.

WILLS, Allen Sinclair: *Life of Cardinal Gibbons, Archbishop of Baltimore.* New York 1922.

WILSON, Robert Renbert: *United States Commercial Treaties and International Law.* New Orleans 1960.

WISTER, Robert James: *The Establishment of the Apostolic Delegation in the United States of America: The Satolli Mission, 1892–1896.* Unpublished D.E.H. dissertation, Roma: Università Gregoriana 1980.

YZERMANS, Vincent A. (ed.): *American Participation in the Second Vatican Council.* New York 1967.

ŽIVOJINOVIĆ, Dragan R.: *The United States and the Vatican Policies: 1914–1918.* Boulder, Colo. 1978.

ZWIERLEIN, Frederick J.: *The Life and Letters of Bishop McQuaid,* 3 vols. Rochester, N.Y. 1926.

D. ARTICLES AND CONTRIBUTIONS TO BOOKS:

ADRIÁNYI, Gabriel: *Friedrich Graf Revertera, Erinnerungen (1888–1901).* In: Archivum Historiae Pontificiae 10 (1972) 241–339.

AUBERT, Roger: *Monseigneur Dupanloup et Le Syllabus.* In: Revue d'histoire ecclésiastique 51 (1956) 79–142.

BLANSHARD, Paul: *The Case of Archbishop O'Hara.* In: The Christian Century 70 (1953) 539–541.

BURRUS, E.J.: *Father Joseph Havens Richards' Notes On Georgetown and the Catholic University.* In: Woodstock Letters 83 (1954) 77–101.

CARBONNEAU, Robert: *The Passionists in China, 1921–1929. An Essay in Mission Experience.* In: Catholic Historical Review 66 (1980) 392–416.

CLEARY, James F.: *Catholic Participation in the World's Parliament of Religions, Chicago, 1893.* In: Catholic Historical Review 55 (1970) 585–609.

CONWAY, John S.: *Myron C. Taylor's Mission to the Vatican 1940–1950.* In: Church History 44 (1975) 85–99.

CUDDY, Edward: *Pro-Germanism and American Catholicism, 1914–1917.* In: Catholic Historical Review 44 (1968) 427–454.

ELLIS, John Tracy: *Church and State – An American Catholic Tradition.* In: Harper's 207 (Nov., 1953) 63–67.

FARRELL, John T.: *Background of the 1902 Taft Mission to Rome.* In: Catholic Historical Review 36 (1950) 1–22.

FOGARTY, Gerald P.: *American Conciliar Legislation, Hierarchical Structure and Priest-Bishop Tension.* In: The Jurist 32 (1972) 400–409.

FOGARTY, Gerald P.: *The American Hierarchy and Oriental Rite Catholics, 1890–1907.* In: Records of the American Catholic Historical Society of Philadelphia 85 (1974) 17–28.

FOGARTY, Gerald P.: *Archbishop Peter Kenrick's Submission to Papal Infallibility.* In: Archivum Historiae Pontificiae 16 (1978) 205–222.

FOGARTY, Gerald P.: *Church Councils in the United States and American Legal Institutions.* In: Annuarium Historiae Conciliorum 4 (1972) 83–105.

FOGARTY, Gerald P.: *The Bishops versus Religious Orders: The Suppressed Decrees of the Third Plenary Council of Baltimore.* In: The Jurist 33 (1973) 384–398.

GAFFEY, James P.: *The Changing of the Guard: The Rise of Cardinal O'Connell of Boston.* In: Catholic Historical Review 59 (1973) 225–244.

GAFFEY, James P.: *Patterns of Ecclesiastical Authority: The Problem of the Chicago Succession, 1865–1881.* In: Church History 42 (1973) 257–270.

GALUSH, William: *The Polish National Church: A Survey of Its Origins, Development and Missions.* In: Records of the American Catholic Historical Society of Philadelphia 83 (1972) 131–149.

GANNON, Michael V.: *Before and After Modernism: The Intellectual Isolation of the American Priest.* In: John Tracy ELLIS (ed.): The Catholic Priest in the United States: Historical Investigations. Collegeville, Minn. 1971.

HACHEY, Thomas E.: *British War Propaganda and American Catholics, 1918.* In: Catholic Historical Review 61 (1975) 48–66.

HENNESEY, James: *American Jesuit in Wartime Rome: The Diary of Vincent A. McCormick, S.J. (1942–1945).* In: Mid-America: An Historical Review 56 (1974) 32–55.

HENNESEY, James: *Papacy and Episcopacy in Eighteenth and Nineteenth Century America.* In: Records of the American Catholic Historical Society of Philadelphia 77 (1966) 175–189.

HUSSEY, M. Edmund: *The 1878 Financial Failure of Archbishop Purcell.* In: The Cincinnati Historical Society Bulletin 36 (1978) 7–41.

KUTTNER, Stephan G.: *The Code of Canon Law in Historical Perspective.* In: The Jurist 28 (1968) 129–148.

LAFARGE, John: *Some Questions as to Interdenominational Cooperation.* In: Theological Studies 3 (1942) 315–322.

LEONARD, Henry B.: *Ethnic Conflict and Episcopal Power: The Diocese of Cleveland, 1847–1870.* In: Catholic Historical Review 62 (1976) 388–407.

LIENHARD, Joseph T.: *The New York Review and Modernism in America.* In: Records of the American Catholic Historical Society of Philadelphia 82 (1971) 67–82.

McAVOY, Thomas T.: *Public Schools vs. Catholic Schools and James McMaster.* In: Review of Politics 28 (1966) 22–36.

McCORMICK, Richard A.: *Notes on Moral Theology: 1980.* In: Theological Studies 42 (1981) 74–121.

McKEOWN, Elizabeth: *Apologia for an American Catholicism: The Petition and Report of the National Catholic Welfare Council to Pius XI, April 25, 1922.* In: Church History 43 (1974) 514–528.

McKEOWN, Elizabeth: *The National Bishops' Conference: An Analysis of Its Origins.* In: Catholic Historical Review 66 (1980) 565–583.

MILLER, Samuel J.: *Peter Richard Kenrick, Bishop and Archbishop of St. Louis: 1806–1896.* In: Records of the American Catholic Historical Society of Philadelphia 84 (1973) 3–163.

MURRAY, John Courtney: *Current Theology: Co-operation, Some Further Views.* In: Theological Studies 4 (1943) 100–111.

MURRAY, John Courtney: *Current Theology: Intercredal Co-operation: Its Theory and Its Organization.* In: Theological Studies 4 (1943) 257–268.

MURRAY, John Courtney: *Leo XIII on Church and State: The General Structure of the Controversy.* In: Theological Studies 14 (1953) 1–30.

PARSONS, Wilfrid: *Intercredal Co-operation in the Papal Documents.* In: Theological Studies 4 (1943) 159–182.

PROCKO, Bohdan P.: *Soter Ortynsky: First Ruthenian Bishop in the United States, 1907–1916.* In: Catholic Historical Review 58 (1973) 513–533.

REHER, Margaret M.: *Leo XIII and "Americanism"*. In: Theological Studies 34 (1973) 679–689.

RUSSIN, Keith S.: *Father Alexis G. Toth and the Wilkes-Barre Litigations*. In: St. Vladimir's Theological Quarterly 16 (1972) 128–149.

THOMAS, Samuel J.: *The American Periodical Press and the Apostolic Letter Testem Benevolentiae*. In: Catholic Historical Review 62 (1976) 408–423.

TRISCO, Robert: *Bishops and Their Priests in the United States*. In: John Tracy ELLIS (ed.): The Catholic Priest in the United States: Historical Investigations. Collegeville, Minn. 1971.

WANGLER, Thomas E.: *John Ireland and the Origins of Liberal Catholicism in the United States*. In: Catholic Historical Review 56 (1971) 617–629.

INDEX